A Guide to Defense Contracting

Principles and Practices

Second Edition

Dan Lindner

LANHAM • BOULDER • NEW YORK • LONDON

Published by Bernan Press
An imprint of The Rowman & Littlefield Publishing Group, Inc.
4501 Forbes Boulevard, Suite 200, Lanham, Maryland 20706
www.rowman.com

86-90 Paul Street, London EC2A 4NE

British Library Cataloguing in Publication Information available

Library of Congress Cataloging-in-Publication Data
Names: Lindner, Dan, 1955- author.
Title: A guide to defense contracting : principles and practices / Dan Lindner.
Description: Second edition. | Lanham : Bernan Press, 2024. | Includes bibliographical references and index.
Identifiers: LCCN 2024021960 (print) | LCCN 2024021961 (ebook) | ISBN 9798892050043 (paperback) | ISBN 9798892050050 (epub)
Subjects: LCSH: Defense contracts—United States. | United States—Armed Forces—Procurement. | Letting of contracts—United States.
Classification: LCC KF855 .L56 2024 (print) | LCC KF855 (ebook) | DDC 346.7302/3—dc23
LC record available at https://lccn.loc.gov/2024021960
LC ebook record available at https://lccn.loc.gov/2024021961

♾™ The paper used in this publication meets the minimum requirements of American National Standard for Information Sciences—Permanence of Paper for Printed Library Materials, ANSI/NISO Z39.48-1992.

Contents

Introduction

The Federal Government is the largest buyer of goods and services in the world, spending hundreds of billions of dollars per year, employing hundreds of thousands of people as civil servants or contractors. The Department of Defense is the largest buying organization within the Government, comprising about 70 percent of total contracting dollars. That's roughly $400 billion out of a total of about $640 billion. The Department of Defense is the proverbial "800-pound gorilla in the room." Yet no textbook is commercially available to discuss how Defense contracting is done. Current treatments of the subject are often written by lawyers and rely on case law to support policies, which is excellent for legal counsel but often obtuse and detached from the practitioner's point of view. Other books delve in depth into certain facets of acquisition, but do not cover a number of other issues and may be too detailed for the classroom student or on-the-job practitioner. This publication was first published in 2019 in order to fill this void—to demystify the multitude of regulations and policies and provide in one volume a succinct yet thorough treatment of Defense contracting requirements and regulations. Subsequent to publication, there have been a number of substantive differences to regulations and topics of interest; hence the need for a second edition.

As with my earlier edition on Federal contracting, my approach is based on what I call the "five P's" of Defense contracting. We begin by reviewing basic contracting legal Principles which apply in both the public and private sectors. These legal principles are critical to understanding the theory of contracting, and how a private firm's dealings with the Department of Defense will differ from those with commercial concerns. Next come the Planning needs of Defense acquisition, demonstrating the extensive scope and variety of considerations that go into setting up a procurement action, as well as the impact of Federal legislation and initiatives. Third is the Placement of awards, concerning the processes used to solicit and evaluate offers, and the variety of methods that the parties use to come to an agreement. A discussion on Pricing follows, which addresses the methods used to develop the contractor's proposal and record contract costs, pricing strategy and analysis, and considerations in the negotiation process. The fifth chapter discusses the plethora of Postaward actions that occur during contract performance, reflecting the scope and complexity of Defense contracts.

The book is organized using a sequential numbering scheme with each level of subdivision separated by a period, since this is the method used in Federal regulations. Each section of text begins with a title and any applicable commercial or regulatory reference, before discussing the concept. Additional regulatory or policy guidance is included throughout a given section. Many sections end with a list of appropriate procurement provisions or clauses and their prescriptive language. Although many Defense services and agencies have their own supplemental guidance, this book tries to be general in approach and refrains whenever possible from delving into service or agency specifics.

To reflect developments in Defense contracting since the first edition of this book was published, the sections on Intellectual Property, Marketing and Research, Using Government Sources, Major Systems Acquisition, Research and Development, Cloud Computing, Cybersecurity, Supply Chain Management, Multiyear Contracting, International Contracting, Statements of Work, Simplified Acquisition Procedures, Competitive Negotiations, Suspension, Evaluation of Offers, Cost Proposals, Cost Analysis Techniques, Profit, Property, and Final Indirect Cost Rates have been revised and enhanced in this second edition. Subsections have been added on Services Requirements Review Boards, Pilot/Mentor Protégé Program, and Work Breakdown Structure. Discussion has been added to cover the new Adaptive Acquisition Framework. Solicitation Provisions and Contract Clauses have been revised to reflect regulatory changes. The Bibliography has also been revised and updated.

This book grows out of a course I taught to prepare professionals to take the Certified Professional Contract Managers examination for a certification issued by the National Contract Management Association, the professional society for contracting personnel (both Government and contractors). Terms of art are identified in italics in the section of the book where they are most important, not necessarily the first time they are used. This is consistent with the concept of a reference book, since most readers will turn to a specific area of interest rather than read the book from front to back. Acronyms are kept to a minimum, including only those frequently used in the profession, and spelled out at the point of first major usage (not necessarily where first used). References to a personal position, such as (s)he, are used to avoid any bias.

The term (sub)contractor is used whenever a concept applies equally to both prime and subcontractor.

Many people have contributed to my success through my years of experience as a Defense contracting officer and project manager. Within the Defense contracting profession, I have been blessed to work with countless professionals who provided their guidance and wisdom, especially Marie Flynn, Dave Brickley, John Dunegan, Graham Wright, Frank Ford, Grey Cammack, and Elliott Branch of the Department of the Navy. Similarly, I am grateful to Hugh Hosford, Ed Traccarella, Paul Robert, and Norm Brown for their legal counsel, B. J. Koehler for knowledge of socioeconomic programs, Bob Lynch for accounting insight, and Bob Long for contract administration experience—all first-rate civil servants. Within the contractor community, I am especially pleased to have known and worked with Jim Sharpe at Northrop Grumman and Norm Steeves at Raytheon, plus a number of consultants—Chuck Schefer, Todd Coen, and Christine and Mark Podracky. The experiences I obtained with the National Contract Management Association and Defense Acquisition Regulatory Council were invaluable in learning much and meeting many. On a personal note, my greatest thanks goes to my wife Jennie for her patience and support.

Chapter 1

Contract Principles

1.1 CONTRACTS AND THE LAW

Our legal system is based on two separate paths of thought.[1] *Civil Law* is based on legislative codes and statutes, drawn on the Greek and Roman systems and current legal principles. To put it simply, civil laws may change but legal principles do not. Judges apply legal principles to the facts without creating law.

By contrast, *Common Law* (also known as *case law*, or *law by decision*) was developed in early England as a body of law common to the entire population. Because this was an environment without a standing legislature, judges made law by hearing the facts in the case. These decisions become a precedent or original rule of law. This concept is also known as *stare decisis*—to stand by decided cases unless their basis of fact has changed. Its deep roots in England led to common law being a forerunner for the legal system in Colonial America.

A major difference between these schools of thought involves the treatment of equity. The common law judge had limited authority to grant relief—only the King could grant monetary damages or property restoration. As a result, separate courts of equity arose over time due to requests for relief (e.g., forfeiture, injunction, rescission, and specific performance). *Rescission* is unmaking a contract, whereas *termination* ends a contract prematurely. Rescission can be either unilateral or bilateral, based on either the need for equity or legal sufficiency, or on the presence of fraud, impossibility, or mutual mistake. In contrast, civil law is adjudicated by standing courts authorized to decide such cases based on statutes, and to grant relief to petitioners.

Because of this sea of confusion, the *Statute of Frauds* was adopted in England in 1677, and after our independence was instituted in American law.[2] It requires that certain contracts be in writing, that they identify the parties, set forth applicable terms and conditions, and be signed by the obligated party. These precautions preclude any argument during an action for breach that the agreement never existed. Here we see a blending of both case and common law.

As our national economy expanded after World War II, the plethora of rules that varied among different states demanded a code of rules to foster consistency throughout the nation of the law governing commercial transactions. Hence, the American Law Institute worked in conjunction with the National Conference of Commissions of Uniform State Laws to develop the *Uniform Commercial Code* (UCC).[3] Formally adopted by 1972 for each state (in whole or in part), it is also used in Washington, D.C., and Puerto Rico. The UCC clarifies and simplifies laws for commercial transactions and unifies state laws. The UCC also applies to personal property transactions, but has little effect on real property. The UCC consists of ten sections or articles:[4]

- Sales;
- Leases;
- Negotiable Instruments;
- Bank Deposits and Collections;
- Funds Transfers;
- Letters of Credit;
- Bulk Sales;
- Documents of Title;
- Investment Securities; and
- Secured Transactions.

The UCC does not address intangible goods or licenses. To fill this gap, the Uniform Computer Information Transactions Act (UCITA) was created to cover software licensing and online transactions. Drafted by the National Conference of Commissioners on Uniform State Laws, UCITA addresses warranties for data accuracy and noninfringement. The intent is to protect the validity of licenses as long as consumers have the right of return if they object to the license's terms. However, UCITA has raised objections from consumer groups and state attorneys general out of concern that it weakens consumer protection and provides terms which are favorable to software producers. As such, the American Law Institute has withdrawn support for UCITA, and only two states have adopted it.[5] The Institute later adopted the Principles of the Law of Software Contracts, but it also raised the same objections and was never adopted.

Federal contracts are not subject to the UCC, but rather are governed by a separate set of regulations to be discussed throughout this book. Nonetheless, the legal underpinnings of Federal contract law are based on the legal principles covered by the UCC.

1.2 COMMERCIAL CONTRACTING

1.2.1 Terms

A *contract* formally defines an agreement between parties to perform an act or fulfill a promise. The basic elements of a contract are:

- two or more competent parties;
- consent;
- consideration;
- proper subject matter; and
- mutual obligation.

These terms need to be defined. Multiple parties are necessary because one cannot make a legal contract with oneself (New Year's resolutions are not legally enforceable!). But the parties must be *competent*, meaning they are capable of understanding what they are agreeing to. This is why children and mental patients are not deemed competent to enter into contracts.

Consent is demonstrated through offer and acceptance, which we will discuss at length in the next section. *Consideration* is something of value which induces the contract. Inevitably, this is either a benefit or a loss to either or both parties, typically either an act or a promise. The concept of *proper subject matter* is all about legality—the contract cannot require illegal activity such as price fixing, unlicensed labor, or a noncompetitive agreement. Finally, the contract must impose *mutual obligation* on all parties, whereby one commits to a specific promise or act in exchange for the other party agreeing to a specific promise or act.

There are several different types of contracts based on the circumstances creating them:

- *express contract*—terms are oral or written;
- *implied in fact*—existence and terms are manifested by conduct of the parties rather than by any written formal agreement;
- *implied in law*—an obligation is imposed on a party by law or court decree to prevent *unjust enrichment*, where one party benefits at the expense of another;
- *quasi-contract*—a contract that should have been formed but was not, again invoked by the court to avoid unjust enrichment;

- *unilateral*—promise for an act (or failure to act). This often is reflected in *performance*, an act of consideration in exchange for the promise to pay or otherwise benefit. The offeree may or may not act as expected, but performance is nonetheless recognized by the court, because no promise was made; and
- *bilateral*—promise for a promise, where each promise constitutes consideration for the other promise.

Other than small purchases, the Federal Government insists on express, bilateral agreements, either by accepting a signed proposal or by both parties signing a document. Normally, this means the Government will pay a set amount once the contractor performs a service or delivers a product. Of course, there are a number of variations in how and when payment is actually derived, but this is the general notion.

A contract cannot be implied if it leads to harm or inequity to either or both parties, but can be implied if doubt prevails in the minds of the parties and the court. This concept ensures fairness to the other party regardless of the amount of money involved, again despite the lack of any written formal agreement. Known in Federal contracting circles as an *informal commitment*, assent of the parties is not required. Moreover, if a contract expires and the parties continue to behave according to its terms, then a new contract is inferred with the same provisions as the prior one. Here again, the Federal Government insists on express bilateral agreements to avoid such confusion.

Contracts are considered to be either formal or informal in nature. *Formal contracts* are written and either under seal or on record. When recording the rights and obligations of the parties, including the terms of agreement, the parties have created an express contract. Federal contracts are express and formal in nature. In contrast, *informal contracts* (also known as *parol* or *simple contracts)* are neither under seal nor of record. They may be written or oral. It can be hard to prove the existence of parol contracts because dissatisfaction or misunderstanding (or even fraud) may be present. Moreover, witnesses may disagree on terms of the agreement since memory is not as reliable as written evidence. Hence, we have more justification for reducing agreements to writing.

We can also categorize contracts in another way. At least six adjectival descriptions of contracts are observed in the legal profession. Some are easily understood. A contract is *executed* when the object of the contract is fully performed. A contract is *executory* if not yet fully executed by either or both parties. But other descriptions are more complicated.

An *unenforceable* contract simply cannot be legally enforced. Usually this is because the subject matter is invalid or one party took unfair advantage of the other. Examples include not putting the agreement into writing when required or if a statute of limitations has expired. Again, Federal contracts are written to contain current clauses and signed to avoid this problem.

A *void* contract cannot be enforced by either party, often due to fraud. *Fraud* is any form of unethical conduct in the creation of the contract, such as a lack of apparent authority, capacity, fair dealing, honesty, legality, or promise. In effect, a void contract is a noncontract.

A *voidable* contract is either void or valid at one party's option. A voidable contract is legally enforceable but may be considered to be nonbinding if one party bears a legal disability or was a victim of fraud at the time of execution. This would occur to a party who is a minor, mentally incapacitated or intoxicated at the time of contract formation. The contract is void only if the disadvantaged party chooses to treat it as void, probably by refusing any enforcement. On the other hand, such a contract may be ratified by the same disadvantaged party, either as an express or implied contract. Even with ratification however, there must still be intent and complete knowledge of all material facts and circumstances.

Finally, an *unconscionable* contract contains unreasonable terms favoring one party, leaving no meaningful choice for the other party, such as one-sided warranties or "take-it-or-take-it" situations. No reasonable person or government would enter into such a bargain, though a desperate, poor or uneducated consumer might. Hence the court needs to step in and ensure the integrity of the free enterprise system. The Federal Government should not experience any of these last four situations.

Any party to a contract is expected to behave as a reasonable party. Each must exercise *due diligence* by providing useful information to the other party to assist in their assessment of the product or service as well as contract terms and pricing. Each must also deal in *good faith* of honesty and observe both care and reasonable commercial standards of fair dealing. These obligations may not be negated by agreement. However, the parties may agree on any reasonable standards to measure the performance of these obligations. This is why the Federal Government has an elaborate process for conducting procurements fairly and impartially.

Commercial contracts for sale of goods are governed by Article 2 of the UCC, which is rather liberal in its treatment of contract enforcement. As long as the parties can show agreement and acceptance of goods tendered, the course of performance demonstrates that a contract is in force. In the event of a conflict between UCC and a state law, the law governs.[6] Any party needing remedy must be put into as good a position as if the other party had fully performed. However, any damages must be specifically provided in the UCC or by rule of law. We shall see that Federal contracts are governed by laws and regulations which are much stricter than the UCC.

1.2.2 Offer and Acceptance

A valid contract requires intent by both parties to be bound by the terms of the contract. *Intent* reflects planning and commitment to carry out a future act. Proving intent requires an objective test to determine mutual assent. To do this, one must examine the parties' acts and words. Moreover, there must be an apparent meeting of the minds.

Such a meeting is usually manifested by an *offer and acceptance*. An offer is usually in the form of a proposal to enter into a contract. It is made by an *offeror* to an *offeree*, and can be in the form of words or action. A mere price quotation or estimate is *not* a binding proposal. Rather, a proposal must define performance by describing subject matter, place, and time. Price is usually but not always included.

Duration of the offer is a function of the parties' behavior. An offer is valid until rejected or counter-offered by the offeree. An offer will lapse if not accepted within its prescribed time period (commercially, this is three months and in the Federal Government it is normally two months, unless specified otherwise in the solicitation). An offer is automatically revoked if the subject matter becomes impossible to perform (e.g., death, illegality, or insanity); however an offer accepted before the incapacity of either party is still binding.

An offer may be revoked by the offeror at any time before acceptance, except for an option or after substantial partial performance has occurred. This is because an option is a right obtained by one party to retain for a specified time under specified price and terms. So to avoid unjust enrichment by either party, the option has become binding and cannot subsequently be revoked.

Acceptance is communicated by the offeree's words or actions to accept the terms of the offer. Hence, the offeree/acceptor must know of the offer. Signing a contract indicates knowledge and acceptance to all terms, which is why the Government always signs its formal contracts. Even if the offeree states additional contract terms, the acceptance is still valid as of the transmittal date. Acceptance by silence does not occur in bilateral contracts unless the offeree accepts or uses the shipment or promise to ship, completes performance, or is bound to act by previous dealings between the parties.

The offeree must show acceptance by the method that is requested or authorized by the offeror. Often the offeror will require acceptance in writing. Under the *postal rule,* a written acceptance is binding as soon as the acceptor places it in the mailbox. The post office becomes in effect an agent of the offeree, and the offeror bears the risk of loss or late acceptance. Since the acceptance of a unilateral contract requires an act rather than a promise, notice of intended performance is unnecessary unless requested by the offeror. If the offeror feels uncomfortable with this arrangement, the contracting officer can always require written acceptance before beginning performance (an e-mail usually suffices). Because of this technological advance, written acceptance does not often become an issue today.

Alternatively, for a bilateral contract where both parties must sign the agreement, the offer is effective only when the offeree receives it. Acceptance of a bilateral contract must be properly addressed and postage prepaid. Negotiated Federal contracts are always bilateral, whereas unilateral awards based on formal offers are accompanied by formal notice to the successful offeror (often with a congratulatory phone call or e-mail!).

An offer may be accepted only by the offeree or his/her authorized agent. However, acceptance of an option may be assigned or transferred without consent of the offeror. Silence by itself is generally insufficient to constitute acceptance; so is an illegal act such as coercion.

Rejection of the offer or revocation of conditional acceptance is a more restrictive situation. Here, rejection is effective only upon receipt by the other party. The postal rule does not come into play for a rejection. Also, a late or defective acceptance is considered a counteroffer, which must then be accepted by the offeror to become effective. If an offer is rejected, the offeror is no longer liable for it, and the offeree may not later accept it.

We have already seen that consideration is something of value to induce the contract that either benefits one party or is a loss to the other. Consideration can be an act, forbearance from conducting an act, a promise, or a change in a legal relationship. An illusory offer ("all you want for a certain price") is neither binding nor enforceable. In fact, consideration must be mutually binding (known as *mutuality of obligation*), such as a promise or act in exchange for another promise or act.

There is no legal or UCC guidance to determine what is deemed *adequate* consideration—that is normally a matter for the parties to agree to without judicial review. The parties usually agree on adequacy of the consideration in terms of equivalent goods, services or money. However, adequacy cannot be a past consideration or something a party is legally bound to do. A moral obligation usually cannot be consideration unless it is based on a pre-existing legal duty or benefits due to the offeror. Ultimately, adequacy means that both parties benefit to some degree, hopefully in an equivalent amount.

Needless to say, courts frequently must step in when the parties are unable to agree on what they think they agreed to (or not agreed to). To overcome this confusion, the court will use the concept of *promissory estoppel* to enforce a promise (by word or conduct) that could be expected to induce action or forbearance by the other party. This concept assumes that the promisee relied on the promise and suffered as a result. In such a case, promissory estoppel provides a legal substitute for consideration. The Federal Government rarely falls into this trap, but does have a method to deal with it, as we shall see.

Courts may sometimes need to decide if a mistake by either or both parties truly resulted in a binding contract. Subjective intent is what the court will investigate to answer this dilemma, and whether such intent significantly changed the subject matter of the contract. The court may then decide to void the contract. Acceptable grounds for voiding include:

- blackmail or *duress*, where one party acts or threatens the other party to perform an involuntary act, such as signing an undesirable contract or bringing suit on an unrelated matter. There is no meeting of the minds and therefore no binding contract;
- fraud, because it involves deceit and precludes a meeting of the minds;
- substitution of another contract for that bargained for, although the court may instead insist on rewriting the contract;
- *undue influence*, where one party controls the other to substitute its will and preclude free choice, usually due to psychological weakness or financial power; or
- willful misrepresentation or concealment of a material fact, once again because there is no real meeting of the minds.

Courts tend to be wary when both parties ask to void a contract. Illiteracy is not a viable reason for voidance, because the party can always ask for an interpretation. Nor is a unilateral mistake, which is most likely to occur in an erroneous bid. Other common scenarios that courts may reject as grounds for avoiding a contract include a party misinterpreting the law or failing to read a contract before signature. Typographical or mathematical errors can be easily corrected and are not grounds for avoidance.

The Federal Government adheres to the concept of offer and acceptance by soliciting for binding offers which the offerors sign. The Government then accepts the offer of its choice by signature. Consideration is accomplished by payment of a specified sum(s) of money in exchange for performance, a mutually binding arrangement.

1.2.3 Performance

The duty of performance is often conditional upon the occurrence of a specified act or promise (but not merely a lapse of time). A *condition* is a qualification placed upon a promise or duty, which keeps it from being absolute. Conditions are ever-present in contracts and can be any of three types:

- a *condition precedent* exists before the promisor incurs any liability, such as a disaster under an insurance contract;
- a *condition concurrent*, by contrast, exists when both parties must perform simultaneously, often a payment for sale of goods or land; and
- a *condition subsequent* ends the obligation for performance or payment, such as a final payment.

Unfortunately, conditions are not always specified in the contract, or even obvious to both parties. To address this concern, the concept of an *implied condition* is introduced, to include a contract provision which the parties should have reasonably expected to be in the contract. Hence, even if only one party strictly complied with the contract terms, the other party might still recover in court if it also substantially performed its obligation. This doctrine ensures fairness and prevents needless forfeit of investment. Nevertheless, recovery may be offset by any damages caused by failure to render complete performance. So if the deviation from the contract was merely accidental or trivial, the plaintiff will receive only nominal damages.

Although contractual duties are normally discharged by act of the parties in fulfillment of the contract terms, other outcomes are possible. A *novation* substitutes a new obligation or party to extinguish the old contract or discharge an original party. This process happens in Government contracts when a contractor merges with another firm or goes bankrupt. Alternatively, a new contract may be created with the new party using the same terms as the original. Or, the parties may agree to voluntarily discharge contract duties.

Impossibility of performance can also discharge the duty, either subjectively or objectively. *Subjective impossibility* results from an extreme event such as natural disaster or war which makes performance abnormally expensive. Similarly, *impracticability* results from unreasonable difficulty or expense, or a major loss which renders performance impossible. The event must occur after contract formation and the parties did not expect it to occur, such as flood damage to a work site just before contract performance is set to begin. By contrast, *objective impossibility* means that nobody can perform, such as destruction of subject matter, events occurring after the contract formation which preclude performance (such as destruction of the work site) or the promisor's inability to perform (such as illness or death). So for example, if a popular singer cancels a live concert due to suffering from laryngitis, it is a case of subjective impossibility because the entertainer decided not to perform a substandard concert and thus disappoint fans who paid good money for tickets. On the other hand, if the concert must be canceled because the arena burns down and no substitute venue is available, we have encountered objective impossibility. The Federal Government can accommodate all such scenarios through contract termination.

1.2.4 Contract Interpretation

Disputes over contract terms and requirements do occur often, unfortunately. Contract interpretation then comes into play to determine what the parties actually agreed to. The contractor performing the services has the responsibility to seek clarification from the other party before going to court.

Once in judicial review, the court will read and interpret the contract as a whole and in light of all circumstances to determine the intent of the parties. Any ambiguous language is interpreted with its everyday meaning and construed most strictly against the author, a concept known as *contra preferentum*. If there are multiple possible interpretations, then the court will give meaning to the words that work against the author of the disputed language. So, the writing party has the burden of proof as to intent of the words (except for *patent ambiguities*, which are apparent within the terms of the contract itself). Express or specific terms within the contract take priority over general terms, though the court will supply a missing term if the intent is evident or otherwise provided by law.

The Government writes a detailed solicitation of offers so that, following the concept of contra preferentum, most if not all of the document will be construed against the Government in court. However, any terms written by the contractor and accepted by the Government will be construed against the offeror. Similarly, any special provisions written into the contract take precedence over standard clauses.

Resolving such disagreements is not easy. Acts of parties after contract execution but before the controversy may reveal their real intent. The court will also follow the *parol evidence rule*, which permits the court to hear evidence other than the written contract such as all prior oral and written agreements, and any contemporaneous oral agreements. The effect is to integrate this evidence into the contract, though it cannot modify the written terms of an ambiguous contract. If the parties agree to the meaning of the ambiguity, then a contract has been formed; otherwise there is no meeting of the minds. If only one party knew of the ambiguity, then whatever meaning is given by the other party will govern. However, there are numerous approaches that courts can explore before implementing this rule, both in common law and under the UCC, including:

- consideration not received by either party;
- course of performance between parties;
- condition precedent that did not occur to make the contract valid;[7]
- customary usage of trade;
- important terms missing from the contract;
- mistake or illegal act;

- oral changes or additions to an executed contract; or
- prior course of dealing between parties.

UCC § 1-303

Several patterns of behavior listed above must be discussed a bit further. A *course of performance* is a sequence of conduct between the parties after the contract is executed. For example, one party repeats its previous performance, and the other party either accepts the performance or declines to formally object. A *prior course of dealing* is a bit different—a sequence of previous behaviors *before* the agreement is signed. These behaviors then create a common basis of understanding between the parties. So, a party can demonstrate that a clause that was not enforced in the past should not be enforced in the current contract. The court can then use the course of performance or dealing to interpret the parties' conduct and any ambiguous language. In contrast, a *usage of trade* is a regular practice or method of multiple firms dealing in a specific trade or location. This regularity is not restricted to the parties of the current contract but does lead one to expect that it will be observed for the given transaction.

Terms of an agreement are construed by the court to be consistent with each other. If such an approach is unreasonable, then the court follows this priority of interpretation:

- express terms;
- course of performance;
- course of dealing; then
- usage of trade.

UCC § 2-209

A party that has waived a portion of a contract may later retract the waiver. (S)he merely needs to notify the other party that strict performance will again be required. However, care must be taken to ensure that no material change of position occurred if one party relied on the waiver. If so, the retraction may be ruled to be unjust, or may require some compensation to the other party. This is why it is usually a dangerous idea to retract a waiver.

UCC § 2-302

A court which finds the contract or any of its terms to have been unconscionable at the time it was made may refuse to enforce the contract. On the other hand, the court could limit application of a term to avoid creating an unconscionable result, or else choose to enforce the rest of the contract without the unconscionable term.

Ironically, the parties may conclude a contract even if the price is not settled. In such a case, the price should be that in effect at the time for delivery, or else will be fixed either at a market standard or by a third person or agency, such as an arbitrator or court. Of course, this problem won't arise if the price is established upfront, or by an agreed-to formula, as the Government does.

1.2.5 Bailment

A *bailment* is a transfer of personal (as opposed to real) property for a specific purpose without transfer of title. *Real property* is land or anything attached to it by act of man or nature, while *personal property* is any other tangible item that is movable. So your house is real property, but your furniture is personal property.

The *bailor* delivers the property to the *bailee*, who accepts it for a temporary period of time for a specific purpose. Ultimate possession of the property reverts to the bailor, who may then keep it or transfer it to another party. The bailment terminates upon completion of contract performance. A bailment can terminate early if the property becomes unfit for use, including destruction by a third party or act of God, or by subsequent agreement of the parties. There is no sale of property, no lease or license of goods, and no pawning of goods.

The contract or local custom will dictate the amount of care and liability by the bailee toward the property. Generally, the bailee does not gain the right to use the property. Hence, renting an apartment is not a bailment, even though the renter stays for a time and returns the apartment to the landlord upon moving. This is also why self-parking garages often print on their ticket that they have not entered into a bailment to protect your car from damage (and why they post "Park at Your Own Risk" signs), because the garage has assumed no right to possess your car. However, leaving your car with a valet in a parking garage does constitute a bailment, since you give the valet the right to drive your car to and from a parking space.

A prime example of a bailment in Federal contracting is providing a unique part to a firm which is being developed as a second source for a production item. The part is loaned to the firm and returned at a later date. The Government retains title to the part for the duration of the bailment.

1.2.6 Agency

Agency is a fiduciary relationship in which a person or firm handles a principal's affairs (especially money and property) to deal with a third party. The principal expressly authorizes the agent to act on the principal's behalf. This decision binds the principal to a relationship with this third party. An agent can be an employee or another contractor. The Federal Government uses specially trained contracting officers (who will be discussed in depth later in this book) to perform this mission.

The issue of authority can be confusing when dealing with an agent. *Authority* means the principal is responsible for the agent's actions. The principal is also *estopped* (prevented by law) from denying the agent's authority in court; this is a legal doctrine designed to avoid unjust enrichment. There are several different variants of authority, which adds to the confusion. Authority can be *express* (oral or written), *implied* (inferred from the principal's words or conduct), or *apparent* (the principal allows a third party to believe the agent has the authority to act).

Apparent authority occurs when the third party reasonably believes from the other party's actions that it really has the authority to act as an agent. In extreme cases, it could also be created by operation of law due to the principal's neglect or act of God to ensure equity between the parties.

The principal may ratify the agent's actions if and only if the principal could have acted for him/herself at the time of the action. So long as the agency is disclosed to the third party, the agent is not liable for his/her actions to that party. However, if the agency is merely apparent, the agent may be liable to the principal for damages or loss. Again, this confusion can be avoided through written express authority and verifying the other party's apparent authority.

An agent's duties include:

- act only as authorized;
- care and diligence;
- good conduct;
- loyalty and candor to provide information to the principal without any conflict of interest;
- maintain money and property accounts; and
- obey directions of the principal.

Duties of a principal include:

- compensate the agent for services;
- good conduct;
- indemnify the agent for any loss or damage that is not his/her fault;
- inform the agent of risks of harm or loss;
- maintain money and property accounts;
- not to interfere with the agent's work; and
- perform in accordance with the contract.

Agency can be terminated by:

- bankruptcy;
- change in business conditions;
- death or insanity;
- impossibility of performance;
- mutual agreement;
- option of either party;
- renunciation by agent;
- revocation of authority by expiration date; or
- war.

Once again, the common way to avoid any confusion is a written document of authority. Government contracting officers have warrants that list any restrictions on their authority. Contractors who have agents or authorized employees should do the same.

1.2.7 Warranty and Liability

UCC § 2-312 through 317

A *warranty* is a promise by the seller as to quality, quantity, or title. It provides assurance to the other party that specific facts that have been promised are in fact true or will occur. Legal remedy is available if the promise is not true or is not complied with.

The warranty may be either express or implied. An *express warranty* is either written into the contract or manifested by the seller's conduct. Any statement of fact or promise about the goods (including a description or model) which is set forth in the contract creates an express warranty that the goods shall conform to that fact or promise. Similarly, any promise of remediation or repair made by the seller creates an obligation to fulfill that promise. The Federal Government prefers express warranties in its supply contracts, either its own clause or the contractor's standard commercial warranty.

In contrast, an *implied warranty* occurs by operation of law, and any disclaimers or exclusions are construed against the seller. Implied warranties include merchantability and fitness for purpose. *Merchantability* provides that an item should fulfill its intended use (i.e., at least average quality compared to items that will sell without objection in the trade or market). An implied warranty of merchantability applies to any regular merchant of the goods. Merchantable goods must

- be of consistent kind, quality, and quantity within each unit;
- be within specifications for the trade or contract;
- conform to any promises or statements of fact made on the container or label; and
- be adequately contained, packaged, and labeled.

An implied warranty of fitness for purpose arises where the buyer relies on the seller's skill or judgment to select or furnish suitable goods. *Fitness for purpose* addresses the need for which the customer will use the items, as long as this is consistent with the intended purpose of the manufacturer or service provider. This is the only instance where an implied warranty can displace an express warranty.

These two concepts are similar but not identical. Say that you wish to buy a cleanser to remove a stubborn stain on your clothing. If you buy a product that really does eliminate stains, it is merchantable because it works as advertised. But if it does not eliminate the specific stain on your clothing because of its chemical composition, it is not fit for purpose. Moreover, the seller need not be a regular merchant to meet the fitness test, merely that (s)he be an expert on whose knowledge you relied to buy the cleanser.

Implied warranties cannot include expressions like "as is" that would alert the buyer to the lack of an express warranty. An implied warranty may also be excluded or modified by course of dealing or performance, or by usage of trade.

Once failure to comply with a warranty is demonstrated, liability comes into play. *Liability* extends the warranty to users other than the buyer. Liability addresses negligence in preparation or manufacture, misrepresentation of character or quality of goods, or providing contaminated products. For instance, this concept requires dangerous products to bear a warning label. In addition, a manufacturer is responsible for injury caused by subcontracted parts. Further, *pecuniary liability* arises when one firm or individual is responsible to another for loss or improper application of funds or property. Government contracts include standard clauses addressing warranties and subsequent liability.

1.2.8 Assignment

An *assignment of contract* transfers the rights of performance from one party to another. The assignment must be written, can be total or partial, and does not require consideration (e.g., it can be a gift). The assignee takes on all rights and obligations of the assignor, although the assignor is still liable as a surety to the promisee.

Common law may not have allowed assignment in its early days, but today most contracts are assignable. The practice is becoming more common as firms increasingly undergo merger and acquisition. Federal contracting does so by using a novation technique.

Nevertheless, assignments are not always permitted, such as contracts for personal services or which expressly forbid assignment (although they can still assign money due, including judgments). Transfer of title is prohibited if it would materially impact the other party (such as a change in a contractual duty, increased risk, or impairing the chance of return performance).

UCC § 2-210

Either party may assign any or all rights without materially changing the duty or risk of the other party. Likewise, either party may perform its duties through a delegate unless prohibited in the contract, or if the other party has a substantial interest in requiring the original party to continue to perform or control performance (such as a recording artist). An assignee who accepts a delegation creates a promise to perform those duties, which is enforceable by either party.

1.2.9 Delivery

UCC § 2-308

The place for delivery is normally stated in the contract; if not, it is by default the seller's place of business. Unless otherwise agreed, specifications of *assortment of goods*—the relationship in terms of features (e.g., color, measure, model, or type)— are at the buyer's option, and shipment arrangements are at the seller's option. *Tender* (formal presentation) of goods entitles the seller to both acceptance and payment.

UCC § 2-501 through 508

The seller holds goods at the buyer's instructions and gives the buyer notification to take delivery. The contract dictates the manner, time, and place for their tender.[8] The seller retains an interest in the goods so long as it retains title. Upon delivery, the buyer obtains an insurable and property interest in the goods, even if they are nonconforming and even if (s)he has an option to return or reject them. This interest can be identified at any time and in any manner agreed to by the parties.

If shipment is required to a destination, the seller must provide the goods to a carrier, promptly notify the buyer of the shipment, and furnish any document necessary for the buyer to obtain possession of the goods.

If tender or delivery is rejected as nonconforming and the time for performance has not yet expired, the seller may notify the buyer of their intention to cure the problem and then make a conforming delivery. Also, the buyer may provide the seller with more time to tender conforming goods.

UCC § 2-311

Either party may be excused for delay in performance if it is materially affected by a specification or a delay in the other party's cooperation. The affected party may continue to perform, or treat the failure as a breach and refuse to deliver or accept the goods. We shall see that the Government has remedies available to it should a contractor delay performance, and likewise can provide day-for-day extensions should it be responsible for contractor delay.

There are so many different ways in which goods may be shipped that the Government has developed clauses of many flavors to specify what is to be done. This subject will need to be covered in much more depth later in this book.

1.2.10 Risk of Loss

UCC § 2-503 through 510

The seller retains risk of loss (and risk of any failure by a bailee to properly perform or issue a proper title) until the buyer has had a reasonable time to review the document or directions. If tender or delivery fails to conform to the contract, the risk of loss remains on the seller until cure or acceptance occurs. On the other hand, if the buyer repudiates or is in breach, then (s)he bears the risk of loss.

In the case of bailment, the risk of loss passes to the bailee when the goods are delivered to the carrier. However, if the seller must ship the goods to a destination specified in the contract, risk of loss passes once the goods are delivered to the final destination. If the goods are held by a bailee for delivery without being moved (known as *shipment in place*), risk of loss passes to the buyer upon receipt of a correct document of title or other written direction, such as the bailee's acknowledgment of the buyer's right to possession of the goods. Clearly, a merchant fulfills this requirement once it furnishes the goods.

1.2.11 Inspection

UCC § 2-511 through 515

Either party may notify the other that it chooses to inspect, test, and sample the goods. The parties may agree to a third-party inspection or survey to determine the conformity or condition of the goods, and may agree that the findings will be binding upon them in any subsequent litigation or adjustment. The buyer bears the cost of inspection, but may recover from the seller if the goods do not conform and are rejected. Since it is best to spell out these issues upfront, the Federal Government always includes an Inspection clause in its contracts and usually retains inspection authority for itself.

1.2.12 Documents of Title

A *document of title* is written proof that its owner is entitled to receive, hold, and dispose of both the written instrument itself and the goods that it covers. Common examples are a bill of lading or warehouse receipt. The document is deemed *negotiable* if it requires that the goods be delivered to the bearer or upon order of a specifically named person.

1.2.12.1 Warehouse Receipts

UCC § 7-202 through 210

A warehouse receipt must provide for each of the following to avoid liability for damages due to omission:

- date of issue of the receipt;
- description of the goods or the packages containing them;
- identification code of the receipt;
- identity of the party to whom the goods will be delivered;
- location of the warehouse facility where the goods are stored;
- note that the receipt is issued for goods that the warehouse owns;
- payment amounts made and/or liabilities incurred for which the warehouse claims a lien or security interest;[9]
- rate of storage and handling charges; and
- signature of the warehouse or its agent.

A warehouse segregates goods covered by each receipt to permit their identification and delivery. Different lots of goods may be commingled, but the warehouse is liable to each owner for his/her share of loss or damage to goods if it fails to take due care.

A storage facility has very specific and significant rights. The warehouse has a lien against the bailor on any goods covered by a warehouse receipt or storage agreement, or on the proceeds thereof. It can recover damages from the issuer due to nonreceipt or incorrect description, unless stated otherwise. However, the warehouse loses its lien on any goods that it voluntarily delivers without authority or unjustifiably refuses to deliver.

The warehouse may notify the owner of the goods or the party who claims an interest in them to pay any charges and remove the goods once the agreed-to storage period expires, or else at least 30 days after giving notice. If the goods are not removed by that date, the warehouse may sell them. The warehouse may specify in the notice a shorter time period to remove any perishable goods, or else sell them at public sale at least one week thereafter.

1.2.12.2 Bills of Lading

UCC § 7-301 through 308

A *bill of lading* is a document issued by a carrier to acknowledge that the listed goods have in fact been received for transport to the specified place and consignee. The document serves as a formal contract of carriage, and may set forth all terms of agreement or refer to an existing contract. The carrier signs it to confirm that the goods match the contract description and are in good condition at time of receipt. A bill of lading contains at a minimum the following:

- description of goods;
- freight rate;
- gross, net or tare weight;
- name of the shipping company; and
- nationality of the carrier.

The carrier is responsible for any loss during shipment because it guaranteed the accuracy of the information it furnished to the issuer at the time of shipment. The carrier will indemnify the issuer against damage caused by any inaccuracies. This obligation is discharged by delivery. The only instances where a common carrier is not liable for the goods are by act of an enemy or God, inherent defect of goods, or shipper fault or fraud.

If permitted by the bill of lading and so directed by the holder of a negotiable bill, a carrier may deliver the goods to a person or destination other than that stated in the bill, or may otherwise dispose of the goods. The consignor who provides a product to be sold on its behalf by another party (a *consignee*) may not recover for misdelivery in these circumstances.

Just like the warehouse with stored items, a carrier has a lien on the goods or on the proceeds for charges after their date of receipt. The lien may be enforced by public or private sale of the goods at a reasonable time, place or terms, after notifying all persons known to claim an interest in the goods. Before the sale, any claimant may pay the amount necessary to satisfy the lien and any associated expenses. And again as with a warehouse, the carrier loses its lien on any goods that it voluntarily delivers or unjustifiably refuses to deliver.

1.2.13 Termination

Contracts can be legally terminated by acts of the parties, impossibility of performance, operation of law, or performance. *Termination by Acts of Parties* results from either or both parties performing a specific event, such as:

- *accord and satisfaction*, where the parties agree that performance was acceptable and to discharge the obligation;
- *account stated*: a new agreement between the parties as to final balance due, in order to discharge obligations under the prior contract;
- mutual release by returning property or money paid;
- novation; or
- one party waives or prevents the other from performing.

Termination by Impossibility of Performance occurs if the parties did not know of the impossibility, or due to death or disability of a key contract performer. This is known in Federal contracting as *key personnel* and will be discussed later. Acts of God, nature or an enemy do not excuse performance unless they make it impossible, or if the contract so permits. Strikes and accidents do not normally excuse performance. In all these cases however, if the party seeking relief is guilty of contributory fault, it cannot collect damages.

Termination by Operation of Law results from a law or court decree that serves to forbid performance, such as expiration of the statute of limitations covering the time period in which to file charges or a lawsuit. Bankruptcy does not preclude the obligation to fulfill the contract. Insolvency can terminate a contract, but the buyer can still recover goods from an insolvent seller if (s)he paid all or part of the purchase price.

Termination by Performance indicates that final payment has been made or the period of performance has expired. This means contract completion as originally intended by the parties. It is the only type of termination that does not require one party to furnish written notification to the other party.

Of course, the Government anticipates all of these scenarios by including prescribed clauses into its contracts, as we shall see later.

1.2.14 Breach

An unjustifiable failure to perform all contractual duties results in *breach* of contract. If one party hinders or prevents the performance of the other party, breach is the result. Breach also occurs if the goods did not conform to the contract requirements once leaving the seller's control. A variant of breach is *anticipatory repudiation*, where the promisor tells the promisee that (s)he cannot or will not perform the contractual duties.

UCC § 2-601 through 615

If the goods fail in any way to conform to the contract, the buyer may accept all or some of the shipment, or reject it entirely. Rejection must be within a reasonable time after their delivery or tender, and requires the buyer to notify the seller. Upon rejection, the buyer forfeits the right to ownership of the goods. If the buyer takes physical possession of the goods before rejecting them, such as a drop shipment, (s)he must hold them until the seller removes them.

Acceptance occurs when the buyer notifies the seller that the goods are conformant, or else will take or retain them in spite of their nonconformity. If the buyer does not make a rejection within a reasonable time or as specified in the contract, acceptance is assumed and cannot later be revoked. Acceptance of any part of any indivisible commercial unit (such as a machine) is deemed to be acceptance of that entire unit. However, if the buyer fails to notify the seller of a defect which could be found by inspection, then the buyer cannot rely on the defect to claim rejection or breach. In any event, upon rejection the seller may request a final written statement of all defects.

There are circumstances where the buyer may revoke acceptance of a lot or commercial unit if its nonconformity substantially impairs its value. The buyer may have assumed that its nonconformity would be cured, but cure has yet to occur. Perhaps the buyer had not discovered the nonconformity due to difficulty of discovery before acceptance (such as a latent defect), or due to seller assurances. In any event, acceptance must be revoked within a reasonable time after discovery of the nonconformity and before any substantial change in condition of the goods. Revocation is not effective until the buyer notifies the seller.

A buyer may not use the goods after rejection or revocation of acceptance, unless the seller concurs. The buyer may be obligated to pay the seller for the value of such usage.

Either party may demand in writing adequate assurance of due performance, and may suspend any related performance until its receipt. Failure to provide such assurance within 30 days is grounds for repudiation of the contract.

When delivery is made in separate lots to be separately inspected (known as an *installment contract*), the buyer may reject any installment if the nonconformity substantially impairs the lot's value and cannot be cured, or if associated documentation is defective. This rejection may cause breach of the entire contract if the defect impairs future performance. However, if the buyer accepts a nonconforming installment without notifying the seller of cancellation, then performance is deemed acceptable. On the other hand, if the seller gives adequate assurance that it will cure the defect(s), the buyer must accept that installment, but may still demand proper performance as to future installments.

Delay in delivery or nondelivery in whole or in part may not be a breach of contract if performance has become impracticable due to an unforeseen contingency or by good faith compliance with a government regulation or order. The seller must notify the buyer that there will be delay or nondelivery, and has the right to withhold or stop delivery unless the buyer provides a resolution.

Clearly, breach is a very complicated contractual situation which shows that things have not gone according to plan. This situation is mitigated greatly in Federal contracting by clearly spelling out the parties' responsibilities in delivery and inspection contract clauses.

1.2.15 Remedies

1.2.15.1 Equitable Relief

There are several means to obtain equitable relief by an injured party. Common forms of remedy include damages, reformation, rescission, restitution, and specific performance. Some are available only to one party, while others are available to both parties.

Damages are money that is paid for injury caused by breach. If a party fails to perform, the amount of damages is whatever is necessary to compensate the injured party to return to the position (s)he would have occupied if performance had been completed. This tenet is known as the *benefit of the bargain.* Damages due to failure which is already known to occur in the future (anticipatory repudiation) are assessed as of the scheduled performance dates.

Similarly, if one party has only provided partial performance, then damages will cover only the expense of completion. This amount may or may not cover the balance of the contract price, but no more, to prevent unjust enrichment. However, the value of materials lost through breach can be recovered.

Damages for defective performance reflect the difference in value between what is actually tendered and what is required. If a defect can be remedied by repairs, then the damages reflect the price of the repairs performed. However, there are several other types of damages that a court can award:

- *compensatory damages* place the plaintiff in as good a position as if the defendant had performed the contract. The compensation covers losses that are a direct, immediate and natural result of the act. The injured party cannot recover attorney's fees;

- *consequential damages* include any loss of which the buyer, at the time of contracting, had reason to know but could not be prevented. This includes injury to person or property resulting from breach of warranty;
- *construction contract damages* are the reasonable cost of reconstruction and completion per contract terms. At the least, this is the difference in value between full and defective performance. The injured party may recover rental cost during delayed performance (usually per a liquidated damages clause) and loss of profit. Interest can be charged as of date of breach;
- *foreseeable damages* are injuries contemplated by the parties at the time the contract was made;
- *incidental damages* include commissions and expenses incurred by the seller to stop delivery and to transport and care for the goods. These expenses include inspection, receipt, transportation, and care and custody of goods which were rightfully rejected;
- *liquidated damages* are payments in lieu of default where the amount cannot be easily calculated. The injured party has a duty to mitigate damages; and
- *punitive damages* are charges to punish the party for reasons beyond mere breach of contract and to discourage others from similar behavior in the future.

Monetary damages are not the sole remedy available to the courts. *Reformation* is a technique to rewrite the contract if it does not reflect the bargain struck by the parties. This is usually due to either fraud or mutual mistake in drafting the contract. Relief for the reasonable value of services rendered is possible in this situation. On the other hand, *rescission* is unmaking a contract (as opposed to *termination*, which ends a contract prematurely). Rescission can be either unilateral or bilateral, based on the need for legal sufficiency or equity, or on the presence of fraud, mutual mistake, or impossibility. It will terminate the contract and restore the parties to their original state as if they never entered into the contract. Usually, the party seeking rescission surrenders all benefits received under the contract.

Another remedy known as *restitution* allows the court to order payment or return of property and money paid.[10] The injured party has a *reliance interest* to be compensated for its detriment suffered or expenses incurred by relying on the other party. However, unlike rescission the contract might not be vacated by the court.

The remedy known as *specific performance* requires one party to perform as promised because monetary damages cannot compensate for the breach (e.g., a sale of land). The court will also enforce a negative covenant which prohibits a key person from working for anyone else during the contract term. However, a personal-services contract is not usually enforced for a variety of reasons (impaired performance, fear of continuing an already strained relationship, and arguably, even a sense of slavery, which is prohibited by the 13th Amendment to the Constitution). Nonetheless, contractual prohibition of an act may be enforced.

Under the Equal Access to Justice Act,[11] small businesses and individuals are entitled to recover legal fees if they prevail in certain actions against the Government. These expenses are usually used to cover fees of attorneys and expert witnesses.

UCC § 2-725

Action for breach of a warranty accrues when the seller has made delivery or completed installation or assembly of the goods, or when the aggrieved party discovers or should have discovered the breach. For breach of a remedial promise, a right of action accrues as soon as the promise is not performed when due. An action for breach of sale must be filed either within four years after the right of action has accrued or one year after the breach was or should have been discovered, whichever is later.

1.2.15.2 Seller Remedies

UCC § 2-703 through 710

Breach of contract by the buyer includes a wrongful rejection, attempt to revoke acceptance of goods, or failure to perform on time. The seller has numerous courses of action to choose from:

- cancel the contract;
- obtain specific performance;
- reclaim the goods;
- recover damages for nonacceptance or repudiation (including liquidated damages);
- recover the price;
- require payment directly from the buyer;
- resell the goods; or
- stop delivery of the goods.

If the seller resells the goods due to breach, (s)he may also recover the difference between the resale price and contract price, together with any incidental damages. However the seller must subtract expenses saved due to the breach. The net proceeds of any resale must be credited to the buyer and any goods not resold are titled to the buyer. The seller might be entitled to consequential or incidental damages.

1.2.15.3 Buyer Remedies

UCC § 2-711 through 717

A breach of contract by the seller includes wrongful failure to deliver or perform a contractual obligation, making a nonconforming delivery or performance, and repudiation. Again, the buyer may choose from a number of options:

- cancel the contract;
- cover incidental damages to all affected goods, including pain and suffering, whether or not identified to the contract;
- deduct or recover damages for accepted goods or a remedial promise, including nondelivery or repudiation;
- obtain specific performance;
- obtain the goods by court order (known as *replevin*); or
- recover the amount paid or liquidated damages.

Upon rightful rejection or revocation of acceptance, a buyer has a security interest in any goods in his/her possession or control to the extent of any payments made for their receipt, inspection, custody, and transportation. The buyer may hold such goods and resell them.

If the seller fails to deliver or repudiates performance, or the buyer rightfully rejects or revokes acceptance, then the buyer may purchase substitute goods. Here again, the buyer may then recover from the seller the difference between the cost of repurchase and the contract price, together with any consequential or incidental damages, but must deduct expenses saved in consequence of the seller's breach.

A buyer who accepted nonconforming goods and properly notified the seller may recover the loss caused by the seller's breach. The measure of damages for breach of warranty is the difference at the time and place of acceptance between the value of the goods accepted and the value they would have had if conformant.

Any incidental and consequential damages may also be recovered. Incidental damages resulting from the seller's breach are the same as for buyer's breach. Consequential damages are also the same as for buyer's breach, plus injury to person or property resulting from any breach of warranty.

1.2.16 Illegal Contracts

UCC § 2-201

Four circumstances are recognized to bar consent:

- duress;
- fraud;
- mistake; or
- undue influence.

Duress means creating fear in the other party through a crime or tort to compel assent. The affected party loses freedom of choice and believes that it had no alternative but to perform in such a manner to avoid harm. To constitute duress, the victim must suffer irreparable loss without recovery from the wrongdoer, and the other party must have no right to perform the act. Such a contract is thereby void.

Fraud is a false representation of a material fact made with knowledge of its falsity or ignorance of the truth. The deceiving party intended some action by the party deceived, which relied and acted upon this false representation, and as a result was injured. Fraud is very difficult to prove because intent must be demonstrated. Within Federal contracting, fraud means acts or attempts to defraud the Government or to corrupt its agents, create a cause for debarment or suspension, or violate the False Claims Act[12] or Anti-Kickback Act[13].

This definition of fraud includes hidden defects and half-truths. A *defect* is a condition where something is missing or the product is incomplete or has a structural weakness. The defect is deemed *patent* if it is easily discovered or one party otherwise knew about it. If the seller is aware of a defect and tries to conceal the defect and misleads the buyer, the latter has recourse to pursue fraud. Regardless, the old commandment of "caveat emptor" ("let the buyer beware") is still good advice.

The defect is *latent* if it existed at the time of acceptance but was not readily discoverable. This occasionally happens in construction where the ground is different than expected (e.g., buried skeletons, caves, higher or lower water tables). If the wronged party cannot show foreknowledge or willful ignorance, any claim will not be sustained in court. This is why Government contracts include defect and warranty clauses.

A *mistake* relates to a material fact or identity, often because the subject matter or something essential to performance ceases to exist before the agreement is consummated. However, unilateral mistake is not a basis for contract rescission, nor is a mutual mistake a basis for price adjustment. The concept of mutual mistake is critical to Government contractors, for it is their only recognized method to obtain relief if the facts vary from the parties' beliefs at the time of contract.

Undue influence means illegally controlling another person's will or judgment. It differs from duress by not including any physical threat or extortion. Instead, undue influence includes deception, flattery, insinuations, and misrepresentation. Courts are naturally suspicious when a party makes this claim, out of concern that the motivation might be solely to avoid unfavorable contract terms. Nevertheless, when a court does intervene in this instance, it is often to order restitution rather than rescinding the contract.

There are several grounds for declaring *illegal contracts*:

- acts against public interest (e.g., corruption);
- discrimination;
- failure to obtain a license to practice a trade;
- relieving a party of negligence;
- unreasonable and excessive restrictions on the seller to avoid future competition; or
- violations of law.

The most famous example of illegal contracts results from Federal law. *Antitrust* actions frustrate the normal competitive forces of the marketplace and restrain trade, leading to reduced economic growth, individual initiative, and market values. Public objections to such actions in America date back to the 19th century.

Antitrust practices can manifest in several ways. A *reciprocal purchase agreement* requires a supplier to buy from its customer, which impacts competition and economic efficiency. It could be ethical if it is not coercive and covers actual needs; however it could lead to restraint of trade due to forced purchase or reduced competition. A variation of this practice is a *tying agreement* which requires a customer to buy another product in order to purchase the originally desired product.

Retail-price maintenance has also come into question for propriety. This involves a manufacturer and a wholesaler or retailer agreeing to fix the consumer price in all outlets, known as a *vertical price agreement*. The consumer benefits to some extent because competition shifts from price to quality, even though price competition is not present. The manufacturer bears the burden of enforcement.

Additionally, contracts can be found to be illegal for violating any of several Federal restraint-of-trade laws. The *Sherman Anti-Trust Act*[14] prohibits contracts and activities that unreasonably restrain trade and commerce. It forbids *price fixing*, or conspiring to set prices among competing firms, even without a formal agreement. The Supreme Court responded to challenges of this Act by introducing the *rule of reason*, saying that only unreasonable restraints of trade were within scope of the Act and therefore illegal.[15] Market control alone does not show the presence of monopoly.

The *Clayton Anti-Trust Act*[16] prohibits price discrimination and restrictions on future contracts. This includes mergers, interlocked corporate management and compulsory contracting with a firm to obtain its business. The Clayton Act excludes organized labor as a commodity, so a labor union can organize anywhere without fear of any allegation of monopolizing the labor supply.

The *Robinson-Patman Act*[17] expanded the Clayton Act by prohibiting price discrimination to buyers or customers with the intent to injure, or to prevent competition with anyone who grants or receives discrimination.

If the Federal Trade Commission brings an antitrust suit against a potential contractor, a contracting officer would be interested in the:

- affected product lines and division;
- impact of nondelivery;
- nature of complaints;
- possible impact on prices and deliveries;
- search for an alternate supplier; and
- timing.

Unusual payments (e.g., bribes and kickbacks) to corporate officials from foreign sources are illegal under the Foreign Corrupt Practices Act,[18] even though the practice might be widely recognized and accepted overseas. Contactors must therefore have an effective system of internal accounting controls and maintain financial accounts, books and records that are accurate, current, and complete in all respects.

1.3 LEASES

UCC § 1-203

Leases are similar to contracts yet different, and therefore require separate discussion. A *lease* is a contract which grants one party the sole right to take possession of someone else's property.[19] The owner of the property is the *lessor* and the user is the *lessee*. When the lease concerns a building, the terminology is unique: the owner is the *landlord*, the user is a *tenant*, the contract is a *tenancy*, the right to possession by the tenant is a *leasehold interest,* and the payment in consideration for the lease is *rent*. A lease for land permits the tenant to rent and use the land, but the lessor owns the buildings and other permanent objects upon it.

A lease is not the same as a license because it does not entitle a lessee to use property subject to termination at the property owner's will. Instead, a lease creates a security interest in personal property or fixtures by securing payment or performing an obligation. Common elements of a lease include:

- conditions for renewal or nonrenewal;
- identification of the property or item leased;
- names of the parties;
- provisions for a security deposit and its return;
- specific consideration (usually a lump sum or periodic payments) for granting use;
- starting date and duration; and
- unique conditions and remedies (e.g., insurance, usage restrictions, maintenance).

The formal requirements for a real property lease are determined by the law and custom of the jurisdiction where the real property is located. However, for personal property, formal requirements are dictated by where the rental agreement is made.

Regardless of geography, any tenancy that covers more than one year must be in writing. A shorter-term lease does not have to be written, but should be. In either case, a *periodic tenancy* exists for a period of time determined by the terms of the rent payment (e.g., weekly, monthly or annually). It may be renewed automatically without further action by either party, or may be terminated at any time by giving notice to the other party. The notice must state the effective date of termination, which often is the last day of the last payment period.

A prime example of a lease in Federal contracting is providing excess equipment and personal property to contractors or even private organizations for a payment, which avoids storage and disposition costs by bringing in an income stream. Another example (in the opposite direction) is when DoD pays rent for commercial space to establish an office or recruiting center.

1.3.1 Formation

UCC § 2A-201 through 221

Similar to a contract, a written offer by a merchant to lease goods cannot be revoked for lack of consideration during the time it is valid (usually three months, unless specified otherwise in the offer). Acceptance can be made in any reasonable manner. However, an agreement modifying a lease needs no additional consideration to be binding.

As with a contract, any written fact or promise, or any description of goods, model or sample made by the lessor to the lessee creates an express warranty of conformance. Further, the lease warrants that nobody else holds a claim to or interest in the goods due to any act or omission by the lessor which interferes with the lessee's performance. These warranties give the lessee confidence that no legal issues will impede performance. In the spirit of contra preferentum, if the lessee furnishes specifications to a lessor or supplier, then the lessor is absolved against any claim for infringement arising out of its compliance.

Leases normally contain no implied warranty with regard to patent defects. The recipient is responsible for inspection for any defects. However, any exclusion or modification of a warranty against interference or infringement must be in writing. This is why contractors carefully examine any property furnished by the Government to ensure that it is in working order.

All warranties must be consistent with each other; if not, the intention of the parties determines which warranty is dominant. Preference is always given to exact or technical specifications, a sample from an existing bulk quantity, any express warranty, or else any implied warranty of fitness for purpose.

As with contracts, risk of loss is retained by the lessor until shipment. The risk of loss passes to the lessee when the goods are delivered to the carrier. However, if the destination is specified in the lease, then risk of loss passes to the lessee only after final delivery.

If the goods are damaged without fault of either party, the lease is terminated if the loss is total. If the loss is partial however, the lessee may demand inspection and has the option to accept the goods with no further right against the lessor.

1.3.2 Performance

UCC § 2A-401 through 407

As in contracts, a lease imposes an obligation on each party not to impair the other party's expectation of receiving due performance. Either party may demand in writing some assurance of due performance from the other party. Until a response arrives, the insecure party may suspend its performance. If the response does not arrive within 30 days after receipt of the written demand, the lease is repudiated. Moreover, acceptance of any nonconforming delivery or payment does not prevent the insecure party's right to demand adequate assurance of future performance.

Another similarity with contracts involves delivery. Delay in delivery or nondelivery by a lessor or supplier is not considered a default if performance has become impracticable by an unexpected contingency. Nor does compliance in good faith with a government regulation or order constitute default.

The lessee may notify the lessor in writing to terminate the lease, or to modify it by accepting a different number of deliverable items than expected, with adjustment for payable rent. If the lessee fails to modify the lease within 30 days, then the lease lapses with respect to those deliveries.

1.3.3 Default

UCC § 2A-108

If the court finds a lease or clause unconscionable at the time it was made, it may:

- award reasonable attorney's fees to the lessee;
- grant appropriate relief;
- limit the application of the unconscionable clause;
- recognize the remainder of the lease contract without the unconscionable clause; and/or
- refuse to enforce the lease contract.

UCC § 2A-502 through 506

No party in default under a lease is entitled to notice of default. Nevertheless, the agreement may include specific rights and remedies for default, and may limit or alter the measure of damages recoverable. Either party can bring an action for indemnity or default when the act or omission is, or should have been, discovered. Such a cause for action can also occur if the actual default occurs later. Nevertheless, an action for default, including breach of warranty or indemnity, must be initiated within four years after the cause of action. However, the parties may agree in the lease to reduce the period of limitation to as little as one year. Federal contracts are open-ended on this issue, requiring only timely written notification from the contractor.

1.3.3.1 Default by Lessor

UCC § 2A-508 through 522

The burden is on the lessee to establish a default by the lessor. Lessee remedies include cancellation, recovery of paid rent and security, or damages for all goods affected or undelivered.

If the goods or their delivery fail in any respect to conform to the lease, the lessee may reject or accept all, some or none of the goods. Rejection of goods requires the lessee to notify the lessor within a reasonable time after tender. The lessee must hold and care for any rejected, nonperishable goods in its care for disposition by the lessor or supplier. Generally, a lessee's failure to state a defect precludes default, rejection, or remedy.

Acceptance occurs after the lessee has a reasonable opportunity to inspect the goods. This signifies to the lessor or supplier that the goods are conforming or else will be retained in spite of their nonconformity. A lessee may revoke acceptance within a reasonable time if the default or nonconformity substantially impairs the value of the deliverable(s), or an expected cure has not occurred. The lessee can also collect damages due to the default.

1.3.3.2 Default by Lessee

UCC § 2A-523 through 532

If a lessee wrongfully rejects or revokes acceptance, fails to make a payment when due or repudiates with respect to a part or the whole, then the value of the whole lease is substantially impaired. Therefore, the lessee is in default of the lease and the lessor is free to cancel the lease or proceed regarding goods not covered by the lease.

A lessor may stop delivery of goods in the possession of a carrier or other bailee upon discovering the lessee to be insolvent. The lessor could also repudiate delivery or refuse to make a payment due before delivery. After the lessee defaults, the lessor may take possession of the goods and dispose of them and any undelivered balance by lease or sale. The lessor may also recover any accrued and unpaid rent, the present value of the rent for the remaining term of the lease, and any incidental damages, less expenses saved due to the default.

A subsequent party who buys or leases from the lessor through the disposition of goods takes the goods free of the original lease and of any rights of the original lessee. The lessor need not pay the lessee for any profit made on any disposition.

If a third party causes injury to a party to the lease, the lessor has a right of action against the third party. By contrast, the lessee has a right of action against the third party only if it has a security or insurable interest in the goods or bears the risk of loss.

1.4 FEDERAL CONTRACTING ENVIRONMENT

1.4.1 Background

A Federal *contractor* is any individual or legal entity that directly (or indirectly through an affiliate) submits offers or receives awards for a Government contract or a subcontract under a Government contract. It includes any entity that conducts business with the Government as agent or representative of another contractor.

Federal Government contracts include many features that differ from those described above for commercial contracts:

- administrative disputes and claims process rather than binding arbitration, followed by direct appeal to court;
- Congressional notification of awards;
- Government liability somewhat limited because it is a sovereign, but equitable estoppel may sometimes be invoked;
- irrevocable sealed bids used in a rigid bidding process;[20]
- no recognition of apparent authority. Express authority is required of the parties' representatives to bind their employer. The Government is not usually held responsible for unauthorized acts of its employees, but may ratify these actions if in the Government's best interest;
- pre-printed boilerplate provisions not subject to negotiations;
- protests over award;
- socioeconomic objectives prescribed by law; and
- unilateral change authority over contractor performance without requiring contractor concurrence.

The issue of boilerplate clauses is pivotal to Federal contracting and therefore protected by judicial review. The *Christian Doctrine* requires parties to read required clauses into Federal contracts that were inadvertently omitted. This position derives from the legal case of *G.L. Christian and Associates vs. U.S.*[21] The Christian Doctrine says that Government regulations have the force and effect of law and must be read into the contract as if written into it, even if the contracting officer omits any FAR-prescribed clauses. Government contractors are presumed by the courts to be familiar with FAR and therefore should know what clauses are required in the contract.

Acceptance is also a different concept for Federal contractors. Government acceptance is performed to specification and is final, whereas commercial firms accept by act of ownership. Government express warranties preserve remedies after acceptance, whereas the UCC protects only for merchantability and fitness for purpose. It is true, however, that patent defects do permit recovery of damages in both commercial and Government sectors.

1.4.2 Federal Statutes and Executive Orders

There are several levels of meaning given to the documentation used to operate federal acquisition. Though people often use these terms interchangeably, they are in fact of different levels of impact and applicability.

Laws (also called *statutes*) are mandates enacted by Congress and must be complied with unless they allow for a waiver or deviation. Our Constitution gives Congress the authority to enact laws to implement Federal powers, which includes acquisition from the private sector when necessary.[22] These *open-market* purchases of supplies or services from private commercial sources can be used if no mandatory sources exist for the requirement, or if the open market can fulfill the requirement at reduced expense to the Government. There are numerous Federal statutes that impact procurement in some fashion. They are introduced and discussed throughout the text with their respective subject areas.

Executive orders are issued by the President without Congressional involvement, but have the same force and effect as laws. Executive Orders are issued by the Office of the President and provide operational direction to agencies. Their authority rests in the Constitution, which requires the President to "take care that the laws are faithfully executed."[23] They are similarly introduced and discussed in their subject areas.

Standards include mandatory actions, rules or regulations which the Government is bound to follow, as well as best practices of the industry which are not always mandatory on the Federal Government. An *industry standard* is a uniform identification of design, performance, quality, quantity, or service. *Policies* are high-level requirements set by the President or the Department or agency head. Policies set the tone for operations, but do not drive a particular solution or technology. *Guidelines* are general statements which implement specified operations, whereas *p*rocedures are step-by-step specifics of implementing guidelines and standards.

1.4.3 Federal Regulations

Regulations are developed by various bodies throughout the Executive Branch of the Federal Government and have the same force and effect as laws. Regulations are the result of the Executive Branch implementing a statute or Executive Order or policy. They are considered quasi-legislative in nature by Federal courts, which give them similar respect without substituting their judgment as to content.[24] It is also a fact that regulations are far more voluminous than statutes, often because details of implementation must be determined and then codified.

Regulations are developed by panels of civil servants who are subject matter experts. These panels tend to be standing committees with members who perform these regulation-creating duties on a regular basis. This approach frees agency heads from these mundane deliberations to focus on broader issues.

FAR 1.1 thru 1.5

Authorized by the Federal Property and Administrative Services Act of 1949,[25] the *Federal Acquisition Regulations System* writes and maintains standard acquisition policies and procedures for all executive departments and agencies. An *agency* is any department, military service, or entity within the executive branch. This system comprises the *Federal Acquisition Regulation* (FAR) and any supplementary agency acquisition regulations. FAR is issued under the authority of the Office of Federal Procurement Policy Act of 1974,[26] as amended at 41 U.S.C. 410. It is maintained under the statutory authorities of GSA, DoD, and NASA.[27]

The FAR is updated periodically as regulations are approved for inclusion. Updates are made through Federal Acquisition Circulars (FACs). They are numbered sequentially after identifying the year of the current FAR edition. This book is current through FAC 2023-04, through the end of May 2023. In this citation, the number 2023 represents the fiscal year in which the FAC was issued and the second number represents the serial number of the latest revision to the FAR. This book is current (due to its publication deadline) to the fourth update of that year.

The Federal Acquisition System strives to obtain the best value product or service for the Government, maintain public trust and fulfill public policy goals. The system envisions such objectives as:

- achieving public policy goals;
- acquisition team members working together with authority to make decisions within their area of responsibility;
- competition whenever practicable;
- contractors with a proven record of success;
- cost reductions;
- fair and open business dealing to maintain public integrity;
- maximum use of commercial off-the-shelf (COTS) products and services; and
- satisfied customers.

The FAR uses the same numbering system as this book. Discussion is broken down into part, subpart, section, and subsection. These are divided by periods except for use of a hyphen between subpart and section. Subdivisions at a lower level are designated by parenthetical letters and numbers, logically distinguished by alternating capital and small letters with Arabic or Roman numerals. Hence the most complicated citation would look something like: 1.2-3.4(E)(6)(g)(viii).

The *Office of Federal Procurement Policy* (OFPP) is an office within the Office of Management and Budget (OMB) to assist in FAR development and develop overarching acquisition policy for the entire Federal Government.[28] OFPP has issued reports about best procurement practices, contracting statistics and trends, workforce development, and contracting out governmental functions. However, OFPP may not always practice a proactive approach, to carefully avoid organizational battles with executive agencies and departments with their own defined jurisdictions and their own tried-and-true methods. For example, Department of Labor exercises sole authority to issue labor policies, not OFPP. As a result, OFPP has achieved few policy accomplishments of note.

The FAR is managed by the FAR Secretariat within the GSA and consists of two councils. First, the Civilian Agency Acquisition Council (CAAC) reports to the Administrator of GSA. The CAAC members are full-time representatives of the

- GSA (chair);
- each Department except Defense, Justice and Housing and Urban Development;[29]
- Environmental Protection Agency;
- Social Security Administration; and
- Small Business Administration.

CAAC members must agree on any FAR revisions and submit to the FAR Secretariat all proposed actions for publication and a public comment period (usually 60 days). They must then consider all comments received, arrange public meetings if necessary, and prepare a final revision. They will then submit final rules to the FAR Secretariat for publication.

Individual agencies are free to develop and implement their own regulations to supplement FAR. Prominent among these supplements are the DoD FAR Supplement (DFARS) and NASA's Procurement Regulation. DoD's supplement is in fact even larger than the FAR due to the myriad of defense-unique legislation and peculiar requirements of military weaponry.[30] As with the FAR, all proposed changes to DFARS must go through the public comment process. This book is current through DFARS Change of May 2023.

Because a large amount of contract dollars are spent by the Department of Defense (DoD), it draws special interest from Congress, along with numerous statutory requirements unique to itself. Hence, DoD has created a second council, the Defense Acquisition Regulations Council (DAR Council), reporting to the USD(AT&L) Director of Defense Procurement and Acquisition Policy (OUSD(AT&L)(DPAP). Members of the DAR Council represent the

- Undersecretary of Defense (chair);
- Department of the Army;
- Department of the Navy (including Marine Corps);
- Department of the Air Force (including the Space Force);
- Defense Contract Management Agency;
- Defense Logistics Agency; and
- National Aeronautics and Space Administration.[31]

There are some significant differences in the numbering scheme between FAR and DFARS. While FAR sequentially numbers its Parts between 1 and 53, DFARS uses the number sequence 201 through 253. Also, the second level of numbering in FAR begins with the number 1, whereas DFARS will begin with 500. Hence a citation such as 1.5 in FAR would be 201.500 in DFARS. Finally, any citation down to the third breakdown level in DFARS will append a supplemental number in parenthesis, beginning with 70. So FAR 1.2-3(d)(5) would read in DFARS 201.502-3(d)(5)(S-70). Whereas FAR solicitation and clauses begin at number 1 with a prefix reflecting the section where it is prescribed, DFARS provisions or clauses use a four-digit sequential number in the 7000 series, e.g., -7000, -7001, -7002. Individual service or agency supplemental provisions or clauses use four-digit sequential numbers in the 9000 series.

Agency regulations are not run through the FAR Secretariat for review and comment, but rather are managed by the Department or agency itself. However, they must still go through public comment if they impact contractors in terms of cost or administrative burden. They must therefore be submitted through the FAR Council for publication in the *Federal Register*. Public comment periods are normally 60 days (30 for urgency). Due consideration is given to all responses, and the proposed rule may be altered to enter a final state. Final rules are also submitted to the FAR Council for publication in the *Federal Register.*

All proposed regulations are also subject to two specific statutes. The Paperwork Reduction Act mandates that any regulation requiring the public (including a contractor) to provide information or complete a form must explain to an office within OMB why it needs the information and how much time and money the public will spend in its completion and submission.[32] Second, the Regulatory Flexibility Act requires the agency to examine the impact of its proposed regulation and information collection on small businesses and consider flexible alternatives to mitigate this burden.[33]

The FAR Council adjusts all statutory acquisition-related dollar thresholds in the FAR for inflation every five years (the next revision is anticipated in 2025) based on the Consumer Price Index.

A department or agency may seek a *deviation* to use (or not use) a policy or provision as required in FAR, including modifications thereto, or to change a prescribed financial limitation. This may be perfectly acceptable to recognize a unique agency circumstance, or as an improved method of doing business. The agency head can approve any individual deviation that pertains to only one contract action, but a deviation applying to a class of contract actions must be reviewed by the FAR Secretariat, DAR Council or NASA Assistant Administrator for Procurement, before agency head approval. Deviations to comply with a treaty or executive agreement are automatically granted if they are not inconsistent with statute-based FAR coverage.

USD(AT&L)DPAP is the approval authority for any DoD class deviation. However, the senior procurement executives for each service and the Directors of the Defense Commissary Agency, the Defense Contract Management Agency, and the Defense Logistics Agency, may approve any class deviation that does not impact their internal operating procedures, cost or administration of contractors or offerors, preference given small business concerns, or conflict with statutes or regulations of other agencies.

PGI 201.301

Departments and agencies may develop *local clauses* for contracts and solicitations they issue, but must first obtain approval by the senior procurement executive. A local clause is considered a significant revision and must therefore be published for public comment in the Federal Register if it

- contains a new certification requirement for contractors or offerors;
- creates a cost or administrative impact on contractors or offerors;
- deviates from any of the following areas:
    - applicability of contract cost principles;
    - contract financing (except payment clauses);
    - contracts with commercial organizations;
    - cost accounting standards administration;
    - procurement integrity; and
    - rights in copyrights and data;
- impose a new requirement to collect information from at least ten members of the public; or
- will be used on a repetitive basis.

Other DoD directives bear heavily on the contracting process. One is the Defense Acquisition Guidebook (DAG), which addresses many procedures used by Government acquisition personnel as a "how-to" manual.

There are 12 (soon to be 13) guidebooks published to cover specific arenas of defense acquisition.[34] Similarly, Procedures, Guidance and Information (PGI) provides guidance on procedures as well as useful background information.

DoD Directive 5000.01

The Defense Acquisition System is designed to acquire products and services to meet user needs in a measurable and timely manner, thereby harnessing technological innovation and performance to provide a military advantage to US forces. The key policies to meet these goals include

- begin life-cycle management planning for operations and support at program inception, and balance supportability requirements with other requirements that impact program cost, performance, and schedule;
- collaborate among DoD components;
- comply with statutes and international agreements;
- conduct data-driven analysis;
- decentralize responsibility for acquisition of systems to the maximum extent practicable, empower program managers and hold them accountable for results;
- develop a culture of innovation through creativity and critical thinking;
- employ performance-based strategies to emphasize results rather than work methodology;
- follow approved program baseline parameters as control objectives;
- identify operational concepts and gaps to develop system capabilities that improve the warfighters' capabilities;
- identify, evaluate, and integrate infrastructure and security requirements throughout the life cycle of a system, service, or critical technology;
- implement corrosion prevention and control procedures early in the program life cycle to prevent impact on the availability, cost, and safety of military equipment;
- implement fundamentals of design, manufacturing and management resulting in reliable and maintainable systems early in the acquisition process and improved over the system's service life;
- include the best use of public and private sector capabilities (e.g., artificial intelligence, deep or machine learning, etc.) through government and industry partnering initiatives to facilitate affordable and lasting support and sustainment;
- incorporate a modular and open design to enable technology refreshes, upgrades, and future re-competes throughout the life cycle;

- integrate advanced technology into developmental prototypes and production systems, and deploy to the operational community as soon as possible;
- integrate test and evaluation throughout the defense acquisition process, to optimize total system performance and total ownership costs, while ensuring that the system is designed, operated, and maintained consistent with mission requirements;
- maintain transparent data in native form with minimal formatting and manipulation;
- manage environment, occupational health and safety requirements and risks to minimize the injury to or loss of Service members, degradation of their equipment, and impact on the environment;
- manage records effectively;
- obtain appropriate data rights;
- plan for coalition partners to enhance US military capability, collaboration opportunities, potential partnerships, and international acquisition and exportability features and limitations in the early design and development phase;
- prepare realistic program life cycle cost estimates;
- promote competition:
- recruit, develop and maintain a fully proficient military and civilian acquisition workforce that is highly skilled across a broad range of business, management, and technical disciplines;
- simplify acquisition policy;
- tailor acquisition approaches to use an adaptive acquisition framework;
- use joint concepts, standardization, and integrated architectures to the maximum extent possible for the exchange of data, information, materiel, and services to and from platforms and systems to assure all systems effectively and securely interoperate with other US forces and coalition partner systems; and
- verify that the item is producible by conducting assessments to ensure there is sufficient industrial base capability and capacity.

The critical directives that bear on DoD contracting are DoDI 5000.01, The Acquisition System, and DoDI 5000.02, Operation of the Defense Acquisition System.[35] The first document provides overarching policy, while the second document implements the new Adaptive Acquisition Framework (AAF) approach of DoD to furnish timely acquisition support to the end user by authorizing decision-makers to plan and manage their programs using sound business practices. The previous version of this instruction has been renumbered 5000.02T and will be phased out over time as additional instructions are issued. The replacement policies which have been issued as of this publication will be referenced where applicable.

1.5 DEFENSE CONTRACT FORMATION

1.5.1 Acquisition Organization

The acquisition office is the focal point for the acquisition team to handle each procurement action. This office hosts the contracting officer, negotiator, legal counsel, and small business specialist. The requiring activity or program will provide the program manager (PM) and technical representative, and its cognizant finance office will furnish the financial analyst both to certify availability of funds and to provide the accounting data against which the contractor will be paid. Other specialists such as logisticians and security specialists are furnished by agencies as required. Each acquisition team member uses personal initiative and sound business judgment to provide best value service to meet customer needs. Teamwork is truly the key to success of the acquisition.

A purchasing organization, both Government and corporate, strives to develop reliable multiple sources of supply to ensure competitive pricing and uninterrupted flow of materials, while minimizing inventory investment. It must maintain good vendor relations to keep up this flow. The organization must also integrate with other organization functions to do so.

Written purchasing policies and a procedures manual are necessary to communicate and clarify goals of the contracting office. Policies can be furnished to both employees and vendors to disseminate procedural changes, facilitate consistent buying practices, illustrate organizational responsibility and authority, and set any limits and prohibitions. These policies and procedures can be issued by the department, higher command and/or local office.

Some organizations use a centralized purchasing office to perform all operations. There are some advantages to this arrangement because it permits:

- economic ordering;
- formal and on-the-job training;
- long-range planning;
- negotiating strength;
- operating multi-site operations; and
- procurement research.

Centralized procurement can challenge local vendor selection or responsiveness to local customer concerns, however, and could result in longer lead times. Hence, many agencies also use decentralized field contracting offices to support a local facility in a wide range of requirements. Examples of such local facilities include a military base or station. Local buying has the advantage of obtaining services from local operators, thereby improving community relations. It can also buy smaller quantities of materials and simple specialized items. This leads to reduced transportation costs and shorter lead times.

Purchasing and production departments/program offices have a common goal of efficient and productive operations. Their philosophies differ however—production wants all they need of the best materials, while procurement wants a reasonable quantity of acceptable quality. Yet these departments must effectively communicate with each other regarding requirements and priorities, such as urgent need versus lead time. They must also cooperate in developing standards and specifications.

In the private sector, corporate decisions may have ramifications for the corporate procurement office which places subcontracts. A firm may undergo vertical integration to gain control of additional shares of production and marketing, which means the purchasing department may need to expand. Or a firm can horizontally expand to buy a competitor, which promotes opportunities to buy in larger quantities. Finally, a firm that diversifies may introduce opportunities to buy into other product lines. Consolidations or mergers also have implications for the corporate procurement office. Issues to deal with include establishing a common purchasing policy, consolidating orders to achieve economies of scale, and buying exclusively from other divisions.

Many contracting offices use a checklist to review incoming purchase requests to ensure that all necessary documents are present, and to help the contract specialist notify the requestor what else is needed. These checklists will then serve as a to-do list for the contract specialist as a visual cue of what remains to be done, and a record of dates when individual steps in the procurement process have been accomplished.

Contracting offices may be subject to *contract management review* by higher-level headquarters units. Such a review is designed to assess their interpretation and application of contracting policies, general performance, use of good business sense, and operational issues such as staffing talent and shortages.

Some programs may participate in a *fast track program,* an acquisition with tight time constraints which compresses or overlaps design, development, production, testing, and other support processes. These programs are designed to quickly deliver a capability which is urgently needed, though at the risk of reduced or inadequate oversight. However, fast track contracting may be controversial because it introduces a chance of taking shortcuts and limiting managerial oversight.

The performance of a contracting office must be measured to validate its success as an organizational asset. Performance measurement criteria include management effort and profitability, as well as purchasing effectiveness, efficiency and proficiency. A common metric is *procurement administrative lead time*, the period between receipt of a valid purchase request and award (some firms extend this time to include receipt of goods ordered). Also, review and approval by upper management is required for specified contracting actions. These normally include acquisition plans, negotiated deals (to ensure consistency with pre-negotiation position and good business sense), and legal actions. The firm or agency may have an average length of time for the given transaction type to use as a barometer for performance. Similarly, standards assess each procurement employee to measure quality by number of errors and timeliness for completing each action.

The procurement request must be workable before this lead time may commence, since the contract specialist cannot begin procurement work until the package is adequate. Lead time is thus a valid metric to assess the effectiveness of the contracting office. Typically, each specialist will need to submit an exception report explaining why actions have been on hand for an excessive period of time, as defined by office management. As a rule of thumb, excessive time could be 30 days for simplified actions and six months for major acquisitions. Factors which impact lead time include

- advanced planning;
- completion of procurement package;
- level of competition;
- procurement complexity; and
- requirements definition.

PGI 202.1

Major DoD and Service contracting activities are:

Department of Defense:

- Defense Advanced Research Projects Agency
- Defense Commissary Agency
- Defense Contract Management Agency
- Defense Counterintelligence and Security Agency
- Defense Finance and Accounting Service
- Defense Health Agency
- Defense Human Resources Activity
- Defense Information Security Agency

- Defense Intelligence Agency
- Department of Defense Education Activity
- Defense Logistics Agency
- Defense Media Activity
- Defense Microelectronics Activity
- Defense Threat Reduction Agency
- Missile Defense Agency
- National Geospatial-Intelligence Agency
- National Security Agency
- Space Development Agency
- United States Special Operations Command
- United States Transportation Command
- University Services University of the Health Sciences
- Washington Headquarters Services

Department of the Air Force:

- Air Force Materiel Command
- Air Combat Command
- Air Education and Training Command
- Air Force District of Washington
- Air Force Global Strike Command
- Air Force Life Cycle Management Center
- Air Force Operational Test and Evaluation Center
- Air Force Reserve Command
- Air Force Space Command
- Air Force Special Operations Command
- Air Mobility Command
- Pacific Air Forces
- Space and Missile Systems Center
- United States Air Force Academy
- United States Air Forces in Europe—Air Forces in Africa

United States Space Force:[36]

- Space Operations Command
- Space Operations Command West
- Space Systems Command
- Space Training and Readiness Command
- Space Rapid Capabilities Office
- Space Development Agency
- Space Warfighting Analysis Center

Department of the Army:

- U.S. Army Contracting Command
- U.S. Army Medical Command
- U.S. Army Corps of Engineers
- National Guard Bureau

Department of the Navy:

- Marine Corps Installations and Logistics
- Marine Corps Systems Command
- Military Sealift Command
- Naval Air Systems Command
- Naval Facilities Engineering Command
- Naval Sea Systems Command
- Naval Supply Systems Command
- Office of Naval Research
- Space and Naval Warfare Systems Command
- Strategic Systems Program

1.5.2 Contracting Officer

FAR 1.6

The *contracting officer* is a Federal employee or military officer who is authorized to award and administer contracts on behalf of the United States. This official receives a warrant (suitable for framing) from the agency head which sets forth any limitations on authority, such as dollar threshold of obligation. The contracting officer bears great latitude to exercise business judgment and maintain fairness and integrity of the acquisition process, and has the authority to determine the application of regulations and policies to a specific contract. Contracting officers are selected based on their experience in Government or commercial contracting and administration, education (e.g., accounting, business administration, law, or engineering), and training in acquisition courses. Some military personnel also hold warrants as part of their work duties. Warrants are terminated for departure or reassignment, or for unsatisfactory performance, but cannot be terminated retroactively.

Contracting officers often have assistants (often called *procurement analysts* or similar nomenclature) who develop documentation and solicitations, analyze cost and pricing data, assist in negotiations, and source selection activities, and handle a myriad of other tasks. These are usually civil servants or contract employees and provide an environment to develop future contracting officers.

FAR Part 4

Only contracting officers sign contracts on behalf of the United States, normally after signature by the contractor, ensuring that the signer(s) have authority to bind the contractor. Contracting offices distribute copies of contracts or modifications within 10 working days after final signature to the contractor, procuring contracting officer, paying office, administrative contracting officer, and accounting office(s). Electronic commerce and transmission of documents is encouraged for all parties. Contractors who must submit any paper documents are encouraged to print double-sided on recycled paper, although there is no penalty for not doing so.

Contracting officers work closely with legal counsel to select appropriate solicitation provisions and contract clauses. *Provisions* are used in solicitations, while *clauses* are included in contracts, though many citations are used for both purposes. Provisions and clauses are listed in their topical section throughout this book, including their FAR or DFARS citation.

The authority to make decisions and be accountable for same is delegated to the lowest level within the agency that is permitted by law or regulation. Agencies can also issue a *delegation of procurement authority* to another agency to take advantage of a contracting vehicle already in place, or to consolidate requirements for greater purchasing power.

The contracting officer is part of an interdisciplinary *Integrated Project Team* created from multiple stakeholders to successfully execute an acquisition. Government team members must be empowered to make acquisition decisions within their areas of responsibility, including selection, negotiation and administration of contracts and determining the application of rules, regulations and policies on a specific contract. The contracting officer uses the warrant to commit the Government, leads the negotiation team and serves as business manager for the acquisition. Yet the contracting officer reports along a separate, business-oriented chain of command, rather than through the program office.

All acquisition officials, especially contracting officers, must meet education and training standards established by the department or agency.[37] DoD has taken the lead in establishing such standards to comply with the Defense Acquisition Workforce Improvement Act.[38] In compliance with this Act, to obtain a warrant to award contract actions above the simplified acquisition threshold, a person must have earned a baccalaureate degree from an accredited educational institution, including at least 24 semester credit hours of study in business courses. Examples of business courses include accounting, business law, contracting or purchasing, economics, finance, industrial management, management and organization, marketing, and quantitative methods. A contracting officer must also have at least two years contracting experience and complete all contracting courses required for the specific grade.[39] The warrant may be restricted by dollar value and complexity of the contracts to be handled.

Undergoing extensive training for the position, the contracting officer must have the personality and experience to work with technical personnel. Key traits for the contracting officer are:

- ability to perceive and exploit power;
- analytical capability of contractor:
  - accounting systems;
  - costs and prices;
  - decision-making process; and
  - purchasing system;
- communicating effectively as Government spokesman;
- knowledge of acquisition laws and regulations;
- knowledge of economic and market conditions, and the industry and product/service;
- mathematical analytic techniques (e.g., learning curves, regression, and correlation);
- performance measurability;
- planning ability; and
- sound judgment and common sense.

1.5.3 Central Contractor Registration

FAR 4.11

Prospective contractors must register in the System for Award Management (SAM),[40] which consolidates a number of previous databases, such as the Central Contractor Registry and the Online Representations and Certifications Application database, in order to receive a contract or agreement. This registration involves answering questions concerning the firm's background and identification. The firm must also describe its ownership and report its Electronic Funds Transfer address and Taxpayer Identification Number issued by the Internal Revenue Service. The only awards allowed for unregistered contractors are:

- classified contracts;
- contracts under $30,000 with foreign firms;
- deployed or contingency contracting;
- micro-purchases (currently limited to $3,500) paid on a Government purchase card; and
- public urgency.

The firm must complete a questionnaire of several pages affirming compliance with Federal laws, then submit these *representations and certifications* to SAM for use across all Federal contracting offices. This process replaces the need to complete this questionnaire for each solicitation and every contracting office. The contractor should update SAM data entries annually to ensure currency and accuracy, especially if its size status changes for different categories of supply or service.

The contracting officer twice verifies the contractor's enrollment in SAM: once when establishing a competitive range, and again before issuing an award. If not listed, the contractor is provided a specified number of days to enroll or else lose the award.

Once enrolled in SAM, a prospective contractor receives a Commercial and Government Entity (CAGE) code unique to its location, and its basic identification information is stored in the database. A firm with multiple locations will have multiple CAGE codes. CAGE codes are assigned by the Defense Logistics Agency for firms operating within the United States and its possessions, or by a NATO agency or member nation if outside this geographic area.[41]

The contractor must also have a Data Universal Numbering System (DUNS) number for database entry. This is a unique nine-digit number assigned by Dun & Bradstreet to register the firm to obtain solicitations, submit offers and issue shipping notices and invoices. A unique number is assigned to each division, location, and subsidiary of the firm. It is a necessity to conduct electronic commerce as a trading partner, which serves to expedite the procurement process and expedite cross-industry and international transactions. Issuing unique numbers eliminates any confusion that might result when multiple firms have similar names, and its electronic nature permits cross-reference to delivery and performance information and other members of the same corporate family.[42]

Solicitation Provisions

FAR 52.204-3, Taxpayer Identification.

FAR 52.204-6, Data Universal Numbering System (DUNS) Number, if expecting to notify FPDS.

FAR 52.204-7, Central Contractor Registration, in which case do not include the following representations and certifications:

- 52.203-2, Certificate of Independent Price Determination.
- 52.203-11, Certification and Disclosure Regarding Payments to Influence Certain Federal Transactions.
- 52.203-18, Prohibition on Contracting with Entities that Require Certain Internal Confidentiality Agreements or Statements-Representation.
- 52.204-3, Taxpayer Identification.
- 52.204-5, Women-Owned Business (Other Than Small Business).

- 52.209-2, Prohibition on Contracting with Inverted Domestic Corporations—Representation.
- 52.209-5, Certification Regarding Responsibility Matters.
- 52.204-17, Ownership or Control of Offeror.
- 52.204-20, Predecessor of Offeror.
- 52.204-26, Covered Telecommunications Equipment or Services—Representation.
- 52.209-2, Prohibition on Contracting with Inverted Domestic Corporations—Representation.
- 52.209-5, Certification Regarding Responsibility Matters.
- 52.209-11, Representation by Corporations Regarding Delinquent Tax Liability or a Felony Conviction under any Federal Law.
- 52.214-14, Place of Performance—Sealed Bidding.
- 52.215-6, Place of Performance.
- 52.219-1, Small Business Program Representations (Basic & Alternate I).
- 52.219-2, Equal Low Bids.
- 52.222-18, Certification Regarding Knowledge of Child Labor for Listed End Products.
- 52.222-22, Previous Contracts and Compliance Reports.
- 52.222-25, Affirmative Action Compliance.
- 52.222-38, Compliance with Veterans' Employment Reporting Requirements.
- 52.222-48, Exemption from Application of the Service Contract Act to Contracts for Maintenance, Calibration, or Repair of Certain Equipment Certification.
- 52.222-52, Exemption from Application of the Service Contract Act to Contracts for Certain Services—Certification.
- 52.223-1, Biobased Product Certification.
- 52.223-4, Recovered Material Certification.
- 52.223-9, Estimate of Percentage of Recovered Material Content for EPA-Designated Items (Alternate I only).
- 52.223-22, Public Disclosure of Greenhouse Gas Emissions and Reduction Goals-Representation.
- 52.225-2, Buy American Act Certificate.
- 52.225-4, Buy American Act—Free Trade Agreements—Israeli Trade Act Certificate (Basic, Alternate I & II).
- 52.225-6, Trade Agreements Certificate.
- 52.225-20, Prohibition on Conducting Restricted Business Operations in Sudan—Certification.
- 52.225-25, Prohibition on Contracting with Entities Engaging in Certain Activities or Transactions Relating to Iran-Representation and Certifications.

- 52.226-2, Historically Black College or University and Minority Institution Representation.
- 52.227-6, Royalty Information (Basic & Alternate I).
- 52.227-15, Representation of Limited Rights Data and Restricted Computer Software.

Include Alternate I if awarding without competition or for urgency.

If the -7 clause is used, do not include the following DFARS clauses:

- 252.204-7007, Alternate A, Annual Representations and Certifications;
- 252.209-7002, Disclosure of Ownership or Control by a Foreign Government;
- 252.216-7008, Economic Price Adjustment—Wage Rates or Material Prices Controlled by a Foreign Government—Representation;
- 252.225-7000, Buy American—Balance of Payments Program Certificate;
- 252.225-7020, Trade Agreements Certificate;
- 252.225-7031, Secondary Arab Boycott of Israel;
- 252.225-7035, Buy American—Free Trade Agreements—Balance of Payments Program Certificate;
- 252.225-7042, Authorization to Perform;
- 252.225-7049, Prohibition on Acquisition of Commercial Satellite Services from Certain Foreign Entities—Representations;
- 252.225-7050, Disclosure of Ownership or Control by the Government of a Country that is a State Sponsor of Terrorism;
- 252.229-7012, Tax Exemptions (Italy)—Representation;
- 252.229-7013, Tax Exemptions (Spain)—Representation; and
- 252.247-7022, Representation of Extent of Transportation by Sea.

FAR 52.204-8, Annual Representations and Certifications, except for commercial item solicitations.

FAR 52.204-16, Commercial and Government Entity Reporting.

FAR 52.203-17, Ownership and Control by Offeror.

FAR 52.204-18, Commercial and Government Entity Maintenance.

FAR 52.204-20, Predecessor of Offeror.

FAR 52.209-13, Violation of Arms-Control Treaties or Agreements—Certification.

FAR 52.212-1, Instructions to Offerors—Commercial Items.

DFARS 252.204-7007, Alternate A, Annual Representations and Certifications.

Contract Clauses

FAR 52.204-1, Approval of Contract.

FAR 52.204-4, Printed or Copied Double-Sided on Recycled Paper, if over the simplified acquisition threshold.

FAR 52.204-12, Unique Entity Identifier Maintenance.

FAR 52.204-13, System for Award Management Maintenance.

FAR 52.204-19, Incorporation by Reference of Representations and Certifications.

FAR 52.209-9, Updates of Publicly Available Information regarding Responsibility Matters.

1.5.4 Contract Reporting

FAR 4.6

The Federal Procurement Data System (FPDS) is a web-based means for agencies to report contracts, orders and modifications. Data is reported to Congress, Government Accountability Office (GAO), and OMB to assess the effectiveness of socioeconomic programs and public policy initiatives, and to publicize Federal award data. The contracting officer submits a *contract action report* for each procurement action and must confirm its content for accuracy before award. FPDS also runs an *ezSearch* function for users to locate Federal contracts and procurement data.[43] All actions are reported to FPDS except:

- any nonappropriated fund obligations, even if mixed with appropriated funding;
- contract actions in which the required data would constitute classified information;
- grants and entitlement actions;
- interagency agreements;
- lease and supplemental lease agreements for real property;
- letters of obligation used for A-76 studies;
- orders from GSA stock and the GSA Global Supply Program;
- resale activity (i.e., commissaries, exchanges or GSA or AbilityOne service stores);
- revenue-generating arrangements (i.e., concessions);
- training expenditures not issued as contracts or orders; and
- transactions at or below the micro-purchase threshold, including imprest fund and Government purchase card charges.

1.5.5 Government Contract Files

FAR 4.8

Contracting offices maintain complete contract files for each solicitation and each award. Contracts generally result in three different files—contracting office, contract administration office and paying office. The contracting office file (sometimes called a *jacket*) includes many documents, which should be tabbed for easy location upon file review. These documents should be stored in roughly the following order, as applicable:

- purchase request;
- acquisition planning information;
- Justifications and Approvals;
- Determinations and Findings (e.g., contract type and deviations from regulations);
- documentation of availability of funds;
- non-disclosure and conflict of interest statements;
- synopsis of proposed solicitation;
- list of sources solicited;
- list of sources denied with reasons;
- set-aside decision;
- Government cost estimate;
- draft solicitation and all comments and responses thereto;
- solicitation and all amendments thereto;
- security requirements and evidence of required clearances;
- complete copy of each offer or quotation with date received;
- abstract of bids or proposals;
- determinations of late offers or quotations (unsuccessful offers may be stored separately with a cross-reference in the contract folder);
- contractor's representations and certifications;
- preaward survey reports;
- source selection documentation;
- determination of contractor responsibility;
- past performance information from CPARS and research;
- competitive range decision documentation and SSEB and SSAC reports;
- Small Business Administration Certificate of Competency;
- records of contractor compliance with labor and equal employment opportunity policies;
- Certificates of Current Cost or Pricing Data;
- packaging and transportation data;
- cost or price analysis;
- audit reports or reasons for waiver;
- record of negotiation;
- correspondence with offerors that occurred during source selection;
- required approvals of award and legal review;
- notice of award;
- original signed contract and modifications;

- synopsis of award;
- notice to unsuccessful offerors and record of debriefing;
- acquisition management reports;
- bond documents and notices to sureties;
- report of postaward conference;
- notice to proceed;
- stop-work orders;
- overtime premium approvals granted at the time of award;
- documents requesting and authorizing modification of contract administration functions and responsibility;
- requirements justification/validation;
- (dis)approvals of requests for waivers or deviations from contract requirements;
- rejected engineering change proposals;
- royalty, invention, and copyright reports;
- contract completion documents;
- documentation of termination actions;
- cross-references to pertinent documents that are filed elsewhere;
- documents that reflect other pertinent contracting office actions; and
- chronological list identifying and dating the awarding and successor contracting officers.

The contract administration file includes:

- copy of the contract and all modifications;
- authorized modification of contract administration functions and responsibility;
- security requirements;
- cost or pricing data and certificates of currency;
- cost or price analysis;
- preaward surveys;
- purchasing system information;
- consent to subcontract or purchase;
- bonds and surety information;
- postaward conference records;
- delivery and task orders;
- notice to proceed and stop-work orders;
- insurance policies or certificates;
- advance or progress payments documentation;
- expediting and production surveillance records;
- quality assurance records;
- property administration records;

- termination actions;
- cross-references to pertinent documents filed elsewhere;
- administrative actions; and
- contract completion documents.

The paying office contract file contains:

- the contract and any modifications;
- invoices, vouchers, and acceptance documents; and
- record of payments or receipts.

A contract or agreement is considered physically complete and no longer active when delivery or services are complete and accepted, all options have expired, or termination has been issued by the contracting officer. Agreements for rental or storage are physically complete upon termination or when the contract period expires.

All contract files are closed out to minimize storage needs once the contracting officer completes the following actions:

- receive notification of physical completion;
- resolve remaining administrative issues:
  - appeals, litigations, or terminations;
  - classified material disposition;
  - final patent and royalty reports;
  - plant or property clearance reports; and
  - value engineering change proposals;
- finalize price:
  - contract audit;
  - interim or disallowed costs;
  - prior year indirect cost rates; and
  - subcontract settlements;
- ensure the contractor completes a closing statement and final invoice;
- deobligate any excess funds;
- issue a contract completion statement; and
- issue a final invoice.

The paying office closes its contract files when issuing the final payment voucher. Files for simplified acquisitions are generally closed upon receipt of property and final payment. Files for higher-value firm-fixed-price contracts are due for closeout within six months after the contracting officer receives evidence of physical completion. Files for other contract types requiring settlement of indirect cost rates are closed within 36 months of when the contracting officer receives evidence of physical completion, or longer if rates remain unsettled. Any other contract is normally closed within 20 months of physical completion.

FAR 4.7

Closed-out contracts are sent to off-site storage and retained for possible litigation or inquiry. Various contract-related documents have differing retention periods, as shown in table 1.1.

DFARS 204.804

A reconciliation audit is not required if certain timeframes have elapsed. If the contract(s) is for military construction and at least ten years old, no

Table 1.1 Document Retention Periods

Document	*Retention Period*
Simplified acquisition files (non-construction)	3 years after final payment
Contract files exceeding the simplified acquisition threshold* (non-construction)	6 years and 3 months after final payment
Construction contracts: $2,000 or less	3 years after final payment
Construction contracts: Over $2,000	6 years and 3 months after final payment
Construction contractor's payrolls and related data	3 years after contract completion
Unsuccessful offers within the simplified acquisition threshold	1 year after date of award or until final payment, whichever is later
Unsuccessful offers above the simplified acquisition threshold	Same as contract file (if filed separately, until contract completion)
Data submitted to FPDS	5 years after submittal
Files for canceled solicitations	5 years after cancellation
Records pertaining to Contract Disputes Act actions	1 year after final action or decision
Investigations, protests or cases pending or in litigation	Until final clearance or settlement, or specified retention period, whichever is later
Contractor and subcontractor records of contract negotiation and administration	3 years after final payment
Financial and payment records	4 years after final payment
Timesheets and payroll disbursements	2 years
Supply and service requisitions	2 years
Maintenance and property records, purchase orders, and quality and inspection records	4 years after final payment
Contractor paper copies of key records	1 year to validate accuracy of the imaging system

* Currently $150,000.

reconciliation audit is required. Any other contracts more than seven years old may be closed out if performance has been completed for at least four years, payment records are lost or destroyed, the amount due to the Federal Government is insignificant, and a written determination of same has been approved at a level above the contracting officer.

PGI 204.201

The procuring contracting officer retains the original signed contract and modifications. However, the office that issues orders under basic ordering and provisioning agreements keeps the original orders for its contract file.

Contracts and modifications are distributed electronically in PDF format via the Global Exchange system to the Electronic Document Access website via the Procurement Integrated Enterprise Environment (PIEE at https://piee.eb.mil/xhtml/unauth/home/login.xhtml). Copies are sent via either American National Standards Institute X.12 Electronic Data Interchange standard transaction sets 850 and 860 or Procurement Data Standard Extensible Markup Language (XML) format (https://www.acq.osd.mil/asda/dpc/ce/index.html) to the following:

- accounting office;
- consignee;
- contract administration office, along with a distribution list;
- military interdepartmental purchase request requiring activity, if any;
- payment office; and
- receiving activity.

Electronic notice of award will be sent via Electronic Document Access (EDA) to the cognizant Defense Contract Audit Agency (DCAA) office if the procurement action is other than firm-fixed-price (with or without an economic price adjustment clause). Notice is also sent to any contract administration offices which will support the procuring office but are not assigned administration cognizance, especially if the contract contains a Cost Accounting Standards clause. The cognizant Defense Security Service office will also be notified when the contract includes DFARS 252.223-7007, Safeguarding Sensitive Conventional Arms, Ammunition, and Explosives.

PGI 204.270

Document loading through EDA is not required for classified or sensitive documentation (such as health or secured data or personally identifiable information), or bulk items such as drawings or models.

Contracting officers maintain an account in Invoicing, Receipt, Acceptance, and Property Transfer (iRAPT), formerly known as Wide Area

WorkFlow. This is an eBusiness application which also accesses EDA to validate and verify data and documents to process contract deficiency reports and payments.[44] The deficiency report must be reviewed by the contracting officer and either accepted, returned for revision, or rejected.

PGI 204.804

When a contract is ready for closeout, a DD Form 1594, Contract Completion Statement, is electronically transmitted throughout DoD. This process can be done automatically if the contract is firm-fixed priced, does not exceed $500,000 in value (including exercised options), and does not contain clauses pertaining to:

- government property;
- liquidated damages;
- patent rights;
- royalties;
- special payment arrangements; or
- value engineering.

Solicitation Provision and Contract Clause

DFARS 252.204-7022, Expediting Contract Closeout, for any contract up to $1,000 when expedited contract closeout is mutually agreed to by both parties.

1.6 STANDARDS OF CONDUCT

1.6.1 Ethics

Ethics address professional actions in terms of behavior, character, conduct, and morality. Executive Order 12674, "Principles of ethical conduct for Government officers and employees," as modified by Executive Order 12731 (same title), requires all public servants to:

- act without preferential treatment to any private organization or individual;
- avoid any actions creating the appearance of violating the law or ethical standards;[45]
- avoid financial transactions using Government information for private interest;
- comply with all laws and regulations that provide equal opportunity for all Americans;

- disclose waste, fraud, abuse, and corruption to appropriate authorities;
- make no unauthorized commitments alleging to bind the Government;
- place loyalty to the Constitution, law and ethics above private gain;
- protect and conserve Federal property;
- refrain from any financial interests or outside employment or activities that conflict with duty; and
- solicit or accept no gift or item of monetary value from any contractor or its employee.

Each agency head develops annual agency ethics training plans which include mandatory annual briefings on ethics and standards of conduct for all designated employees, including contracting officers and procurement officials. Members of the Senior Executive Service and military flag officers must file financial reports annually and face limits on outside income. All Federal employees have current and post-employment restrictions on their financial interests and activities, which are subject to civil sanctions.

Military officers also face ethics rules. Per 18 U.S.C. 281, retired regular military officers cannot ever sell anything to their former Department, or else they will face a $10,000 fine and two years in prison. The 37 U.S.C. 801 prohibits the same officers from selling to anyone in DoD for the first three years of retirement. Since avoiding even the appearance of a conflict of interest is paramount, retired officers must complete a DD Form 1357 annually to address their activities. There is no criminal penalty for failure to furnish; however it does contain an acknowledgment of the Privacy Act to avoid privacy concerns. Since this requirement is stated for all officers before they sign on, it is not considered to be discriminatory or a conflict of interest. This restriction does not apply to reserve officers to avoid concern over civilian job instability and insecurity, nor to active or reserve enlisted personnel.

Contractor employees undergo training each year to ensure that neither they nor their immediate family members have any financial interest or simultaneous employment with a subcontractor. Nor can they have any offer of prospective employment with another firm that might benefit from the knowledge they obtain during contract performance. Some contractors will go so far as to forbid their employees any financial benefit gained from any firm which does business with the Federal Government.

1.6.2 Conflict of Interest

FAR 3.11 and 9.5

A *conflict of interest* occurs if a person or entity has a personal or financial interest that conflicts or appears to conflict with his or her official responsibility. An *organizational conflict of interest* arises when the nature of the work to be performed on a contract creates an actual or potential conflict of interest for the entity on the current or a future contract. This would more likely occur when providing consulting or management support services, engineering effort with follow-on development or production, or technical evaluations of other contractor proposals. Such services could lead to an unfair competitive advantage or impair objectivity or unbiased judgment in contract performance. There are statutes on both the Federal and state levels to address these conflicts, and most firms impose similar restrictions on their employees to ensure corporate responsibility. There are several scenarios which could lead to such conflicts, each of which will need to be fully discussed below.

No company may use proprietary or sole-source information obtained from a Government official for personal gain—namely, obtaining a contract. *Proprietary information* is not publicly available and may only be used with the owner's permission. The contracting officer alerts the company in writing of the issue and why it is a perceived conflict, and requests a response. Then the Government decides whether to establish a conflict on record, withdraw the concern or pursue a waiver. The agency head or designee may waive any conflict of interest upon written determination that enforcing the rule would not be in the Government's interest.

To avoid making decisions favoring its own capabilities, any contractor that provides systems engineering or technical direction cannot become responsible for follow-up development or production effort, and must agree not to receive a supply (sub)contract for the system. This restriction requires some explanation. A *system* organizes hardware, software, data, facilities, material, personnel, and services to perform a specific operational function with desired results. *Systems engineering* applies scientific and engineering efforts to convert this operational need into a description in terms of system design, written specifications, test requirements and data evaluation, and interfaces resolution. Systems engineering also strives to integrate with other disciplines and specialties, thereby assuring compatibility of program interfaces. Ultimately, a successful systems engineering program will optimize total system definition and design while achieving technical parameters.

Key to success of systems engineering is the *technical direction* from the Government program office needed to write work statements and performance parameters, direct other contractors' performance and address technical controversies. This process will ultimately lead to approved approaches, designs, and solutions of the final system.

DFARS 209.571

Associated with systems engineering is the concept of *technical assistance*, which includes analyses and support for acquisitions and programs. It is generally more practical to separate systems engineering and technical assistance-type effort from design- and development-type work to avoid an organizational conflict of interest. However, these two concepts can be combined to:

- conduct risk assessment;
- create acquisition strategies and cost estimates;
- derive requirements, specifications and statements of work;
- develop test requirements and evaluate test data;
- direct operations of other contractors (but not their own subcontractors);
- evaluate contractor performance and conduct independent verification and validation; and
- perform technology assessments.

This definition does not cover design and development work, nor effort to prepare statements of work by contractors serving as industry representatives under the supervision and control of Government representatives.

To promote competition and access to the experience and expertise of qualified contractors, contracting officers use organizational conflict of interest approaches to increase the number of potential offerors. Further, contracting activities do not restrict the use of specific resolution methods.

A Government-approved Organizational Conflict of Interest Mitigation Plan is incorporated into the contract to reflect the contractor's actions to address a conflict. If the contracting officer determines that the otherwise successful offeror cannot effectively mitigate an organizational conflict of interest, both instant and long-term, the contracting officer must either use another approach to resolve the organizational conflict of interest, select another offeror, or request a waiver. If an acquisition exceeds $1 billion, the contracting officer must brief the senior procurement executive before rejecting an offeror's mitigation plan.

When evaluating organizational conflicts of interest, contracting officers consider if the contractor simultaneously owns a business unit competing (or potentially competing) to perform as both the prime contractor for the same major defense acquisition program and supplies a major subsystem or component for the same program. They also consider the impact of a proposed award of a major subsystem subcontract to business units or other affiliates of the same parent corporate entity, particularly for software integration or development of a proprietary software system architecture, and the performance or assistance by contractors in technical evaluation.

A contract for systems engineering and technical assistance for a major or pre-major defense acquisition program must prohibit the contractor or any affiliate from participating as a (sub)contractor to develop or produce a weapon system under such program. However, this does not apply if the head of the contracting activity determines that an exception is necessary because DoD needs the domain experience and expertise of the highly qualified, apparently successful offeror to provide objective and unbiased advice, without a limitation on future participation in development and production.

FAR 3.11 and 9.5

Another scenario concerns a *nondevelopmental item*, either a commercial product or one that was developed under a previous contract. These items require no research, development, test, or evaluation (with or without minor modification) to make the product suitable for Government needs. They may or may not already be in Government inventory. However, any contractor who develops specifications for a nondevelopmental item which will be competitively acquired cannot furnish the item as either a prime or subcontractor for a reasonable period of time (at least for the initial production contract). Again, this prevents the contractor from biasing specifications to favor its own product or production capabilities. Of course, this is not a problem if the contractor is the sole source of supply, or one of several contractors involved in developing the statement of work. Moreover, this rule does not apply where the contractor furnishes information for a product it already supplies or serves as an industry representative to help the Government develop specifications while under Government supervision. These exceptions occur because such a contractor has often done an extensive amount of development in the field and can apply its knowledge to the Government's advantage. If so, the Government would not be wise to impose a conflict resolution, even if competition suffers.

A contractor who evaluates products or services from another vendor cannot evaluate its own products or services. It must perform under Government-imposed safeguards to ensure objectivity and avoid any feedback which favors its own offerings.

Any contractor who obtains proprietary information from other firms during contract performance could gain an unfair competitive advantage in future work. The contractor must therefore sign a *nondisclosure agreement* with these other firms to protect their information from unauthorized use or disclosure and promise not to use it for any purpose other than that for which it was furnished. Similarly, any marketing consultant engaged by the contractor must sign such an agreement, since the consultant might have access to proprietary information which could give the contractor an unfair advantage in future competition. The contracting officer retains signed copies of all these agreements.

Where contractor employees perform acquisition functions close to inherently Government functions, they may gain access to nonpublic information. To protect its interests, the Government can obtain from each such employee a disclosure of financial interests of the employee and family and household members. This disclosure must be updated by the employee whenever a financial circumstance changes, rather than merely updating on an annual basis. The employee must also sign a nondisclosure agreement. Any conflicts must be reported by the contractor to the contracting officer for review and resolution. This issue does not apply to a self-employed individual contracting with the Government.

Under any of these scenarios, should the contracting officer decide that an acquisition presents a potential organizational conflict of interest, (s)he must submit to the chief of the contracting office before solicitation an analysis and recommendation of action, with a proposed solicitation provision and contract clause. The provision alerts potential offerors to the nature of the potential conflict, proposed restraint on their future activities, and whether these terms are subject to negotiation. The head of the agency can waive the requirement if determining this is in the Government's best interest.

Solicitation Provisions and Contract Clauses

FAR 52.203-16, Preventing Personal Conflicts of Interest, if over the simplified acquisition threshold and for acquisition functions which are similar to inherently Government functions.

DFARS 252.209-7008, Notice of Prohibition Relating to Organizational Conflict of Interest—Major Defense Acquisition Program, for systems engineering and technical assistance for major or pre-major defense acquisition programs.

DFARS 252.209-7009, Organizational Conflict of Interest—Major Defense Acquisition Program, for systems engineering and technical assistance for major or pre-major defense acquisition programs.

1.6.3 Procurement Integrity

FAR 3.104

Restrictions on individual behavior ensure integrity of the procurement process. Some restrictions are absolute in nature. Bribes and gratuities are strictly forbidden. Procurement-sensitive information and contractor-specific information cannot be released outside appropriate channels. An employee cannot use nonpublic information to advance one's own interest or a financial transaction. Also, no proposal or source-selection information may be disclosed before award by a Government official (past or present) or advisor who had access to such information. Similarly, anyone who receives such information and does not report it is subject to criminal sanctions.

In accordance with the Procurement Integrity Act (41 U.S.C. 423), Government employees cannot seek employment with potential offerors or contractors on a task where they are personally and substantially involved. The term *participating personally and substantially* means to:

- develop or approve a solicitation, specification, or statement of work;
- evaluate offers;
- negotiate price or terms and conditions;
- recommend, review, or approve an award; or
- supervise an employee who performs any of these duties.

This definition excludes:

- certain general advisors;
- clerical support;
- members of boards or advisory committees who evaluate and recommend technologies or methods to achieve agency objectives; or
- participation in A-76 management studies.

Any Government official engaged in a procurement action above the simplified acquisition threshold who is contacted by an offeror regarding possible employment must report the contact to a supervisor. The official must either reject the possibility of employment or else be disqualified from further involvement in the procurement action.

A one-year compensation ban applies to certain Federal officials if the award value exceeded $10 million. These officials include:

- contracting officer;
- evaluator for either source selection or for financial or technical reasons;
- payment approver;
- program manager;
- rate determination official; or
- source selection authority.

However, this prohibition applies only to the division of the contractor performing under the given contract—the official is free to accept employment from the same corporation in a separate division or affiliate unrelated to this contract. Any violation of these laws could result in contract termination and contractor suspension or debarment. Damages are also possible.

All evaluators of proposals must be free of conflict of interest and *bias*, the intent and act of favoring or disfavoring a particular offeror. The Government takes great care in educating its evaluators and protecting against conflicts and biases. Unless it can prove that the agency maliciously intended and in fact did cause it injury, an offeror will have great difficulty gaining relief from the courts or GAO.

DFARS 203.171

Limitations apply to activities for any DoD official who leaves Government service and participated personally and substantially in an acquisition over $10 million. This applies to anyone who served as a:

- contracting officer;
- evaluation board member;
- flag officer;
- member of the Senior Executive Service;
- program manager or deputy; or
- source selection authority.

Such an official may not receive compensation from a DoD contractor for the first two years after leaving DoD service, unless first requesting a written opinion from a DoD ethics counselor regarding the applicability of post-employment restrictions. Nor can a DoD contractor knowingly provide compensation to such a covered DoD official within two years after leaving DoD service unless determining that the official has received or requested the post-employment ethics opinion at least 30 days beforehand. Failure to do so could lead to solicitation cancellation or contract termination, or even suspension or debarment.

Solicitation Provision

DFARS 252.203-7005, Representation Relating to Compensation of Former DoD Officials.

Solicitation Provisions and Contract Clauses

DFARS 252.203-7000, Requirements Relating to Compensation of Former DoD Officials.

DFARS 252.203-7001, Prohibition on Persons Convicted of Fraud or Other Defense-Contract-Related Felonies, if exceeding the simplified acquisition threshold, except for commercial items.

1.6.4 Other Improper Practices

FAR 3.103

Any firm-fixed-priced offeror above the simplified acquisition threshold certifies that it has not engaged in price *collusion*, or any agreement or understanding with another offeror. This includes any effort to induce another party not to submit an offer, as well as disclosing an offer price before public announcement of award. This restriction does not apply for two-step bids or utility services where prices are regulated. The contracting officer rejects any offer that is improperly certified, unless the offeror encloses a signed statement describing why he disclosed prices, in which case the contracting officer investigates whether collusion has in fact occurred. The contracting officer reports any positive findings to the Attorney General for investigation and prosecution.

FAR 3.3 through 3.10

The contracting officer reports any positive findings to the Attorney General for investigation and prosecution. Potential antitrust violations are reported to the Attorney General because they could indicate agreements between competitors to restrict open market behavior. Examples of possible antitrust behavior include:

- an industry price list used by multiple companies;
- bidding low on some geographical areas or products and high on others;
- comments by employees (past or present) or competitors that such an agreement exists;
- identical calculation or spelling errors in two or more offers;
- joint bids without proper agreements of a teaming or pool arrangement;
- rotation of offers to allow competitors to take turns as low bidder; or
- simultaneous price increases.

Contractor employees undergo training each year to ensure that neither they nor their immediate family members have any financial interest or simultaneous employment with a subcontractor. Nor can they have any offer of prospective employment with another firm that might benefit from the knowledge they obtain during contract performance. Some contractors will go so far as to forbid their employees any financial benefit gained from any firm which does business with the Federal Government.

Although contractors often have standing arrangements to pay contingent fees or commissions to marketing firms or consultants to solicit or obtain contracts, the potential of improper influence is evident. Therefore, a provision is included in all negotiated contracts above the simplified acquisition threshold (except for commercial items) to prohibit contingency fees other than standing arrangements with commercial agencies, at the risk of contract denial or price reduction by the amount of fee paid.

The Government policy of paying fair and reasonable prices means that an offer below anticipated costs is suspicious because the contractor could be planning to increase the contract price later through change orders, or else establish a noncompetitive future where prices will be greatly increased to recover initial losses. The Government can try to avoid these problems through multiyear contracting by pricing out the entire quantity to ensure the same unit pricing each year, or by using fixed-priced options to avoid future unexpected price adjustments.

The Anti-Kickback Act of 1986 (41 U.S.C. 51-58) specifically bars subcontractors from paying prime contractors to improperly obtain or reward favorable treatment regarding a contract award, or including the amount of a kickback in the contract price. Criminal and civil penalties may be imposed. The GAO and the Inspector General of the contracting agency have the right to inspect the contractor's facilities and books, and the contracting officer can withhold the dollar amount of the kickback from payment. This restriction does not apply below the simplified acquisition threshold or for commercial items.

To avoid any conflict of interest or appearance of favoritism, no contractor owned or controlled by a Government employee may receive an award. This does not apply to special Government employees (as defined in 18 U.S.C. 202) who serve as consultants or on advisory committees. However, the contract cannot arise directly out of the individual's activity as a special Government employee, nor can award be influenced by the special employee. And of course, gratuities are strictly restricted by contract clause.

Where a contractor or its official has been convicted (or pled guilty) and sentenced for the crimes listed next, or fails to disclose violation of same, the agency head or designee may rescind contracts and recover payments and property, and can begin suspension or debarment action:

- antitrust violations;
- bribery;
- embezzlement;
- falsification or destruction of records;
- forgery;
- fraud;
- making false statements, such as using a "Made in America" label on a foreign-made item;
- receiving stolen property;

- tax evasion;
- theft; or
- violating Federal criminal tax laws.

Every contractor must certify that neither it nor any employee has influenced a member or employee of Congress. Contractors may participate in general business discussions with agency personnel concerning their product or service offerings in conjunction with agency needs. Contractors may also engage in technical discussions regarding an unsolicited proposal submitted on its own initiative without a formal Government solicitation. Contractors are also free to hire employees or consultants to assist in bid and proposal preparation.

Any contractor employee can file a complaint with the Inspector General of the agency that awarded the contract claiming illegal demotion, discrimination or dismissal. The head of the agency can order the contractor to take affirmative action or reinstate the employee with backpay and compensation for legal fees. Failure of the contractor to comply with this order will result in referral to the Attorney General for injunctive relief and compensatory and exemplary damages. Similarly, the contractor cannot fire, demote or discriminate against an employee who discloses to a Government authority any information concerning abuse of authority, danger to public health or welfare, mismanagement of contract funds, or violation of any law or regulation.

A contractor who fails to disclose a violation of Federal law involving fraud, conflict of interest, bribery, or gratuity faces up to three years of suspension and debarment. A *gratuity* is any item of monetary value given to an individual in expectation of receiving preferential treatment, and a *bribe* is a gratuity of money. Similarly, failure to refund an overpayment could lead to suspension or debarment.

Several other similar restrictions are also in force. Unless a contractor furnishes only commercial items or performs entirely outside the United States, it must display a poster provided by the Government identifying the Inspector General's Fraud Hotline existence and telephone number in accordance with agency direction. DoD contractors performing outside the United States may instead publicize by a means other than public display if there are security concerns (e.g., oral briefing or written instruction).[46] DoD has the authority to reduce or suspend contract payments for up to six months based on evidence of fraud without any formal conviction. DoD also has a Voluntary Disclosure Program for contractors to disclose their potential civil or criminal fraud violations and conduct their own internal investigation, which freezes any Government administrative action until the investigation is verified. Finally, insider trading of securities or property or assets is illegal if based on nonpublic information obtained from a consultancy.

DFARS 203.903 and 906

(Sub)contractors cannot discriminate (including demotion or discharge) against an employee as a reprisal for disclosing information believed to be evidence of gross mismanagement under a DoD contract.[47] This includes abuse of authority, danger to public health or safety, violation of law or contracting regulation, or waste of funds. However, this prohibition does not apply to the intelligence community if related to an element of the community. Nor can a DoD contractor require employees to sign a confidentiality statement banning any report of waste, fraud or abuse related to performance under a DoD contract.

Any complaint received from a contractor employee or contracting officer will be investigated by the DoD Inspector General's office within 30 days of the complaint. Any positive findings are submitted to the head of the agency, who can order the contractor to mitigate the reprisal and reinstate the person with compensatory damages (backpay and benefits), perhaps including attorneys' fees and expert witnesses' fees incurred for bringing forth the complaint. Failure of the contractor to comply could lead to court action for enforcement of the order. The complainant can also bring suit in court against the contractor.

Solicitation Provisions and Contract Clauses

FAR 52.203-2, Certificate of Independent Price Determination.

FAR 52.203-3, Gratuities.

FAR 52.203-5, Remedies to the Government for Contingent Fees.

FAR 52.203-7, Anti-Kickback Procedures.

FAR 52.203-8, Cancellation, Rescission, and Recovery of Funds for Illegal or Improper Activity.

FAR 52.203-10, Price or Fee Adjustment for Illegal or Improper Activity.

FAR 52.203-11, Certification and Disclosure Regarding Payments to Influence Certain Federal Transactions.

FAR 52.203-12, Limitation on Payments to Influence Certain Federal Transactions.

FAR 52.203-13, Contractor Code of Business Ethics and Conduct, if expected to exceed $5.5 million and a performance period of at least 120 days.

FAR 52.203-14, Display of Hotline Poster(s).

FAR 52.203-15, Whistleblower Protections Under the American Recovery and Reinvestment Act of 2009 (Public Law 111-5), in contracts funded by the Act.

FAR 52.203-17, Contractor Employee Whistleblower Rights and Requirement to Inform Employees of Whistleblower Rights.

FAR 52.203-19, Prohibition on Requiring Certain Internal Confidentiality Agreements or Statements.

DFARS 252.203-7002, Requirement to Inform Employees of Whistleblower Rights.

DFARS 252.203-7003, Agency Office of the Inspector General.

DFARS 252.203-7004, Display of Hotline Posters, if over $5.5 million, unless the contract is for the acquisition of a commercial item.

DFARS 252.216-7009, Allowability of Legal Costs Incurred in Connection with a Whistleblower Proceeding.

1.7 FEDERAL OPERATIONS

1.7.1 Inherently Governmental Functions

FAR 7.503

Contractors cannot perform *inherently governmental functions*. Agencies decide what tasks are entailed in this term, subject to OMB approval. Examples of these functions include effort to:

- administer public trusts;
- approve agency responses to Freedom of Information Act requests;
- approve contractual documents;
- approve Federal licenses and inspections;
- ascertain agency or foreign policy and application of regulations;
- award and administer contracts;
- collect, control, and disburse public funds (unless authorized by statute);[48]
- command military forces;
- conduct administrative hearings to determine eligibility for a security clearance or participation in Government programs;
- conduct criminal investigations;
- control Treasury accounts;
- decide budget policy, guidance, and strategy;
- decide Government property disposition;
- decide whether contract costs are reasonable, allocable, and allowable;
- determine Federal program priorities for budget requests;
- determine what supplies or services are to be acquired by the Government;
- direct and control Federal employees;
- direct intelligence and counterintelligence operations;
- draft testimony and correspondence responses to Congress or a Federal auditor;
- interview and select individuals for Federal Government employment;

- perform prosecutions and adjudications;
- ratify position descriptions and performance standards for Federal employees;
- terminate contracts; and
- vote on any source selection boards or performance evaluation boards.

Examples of functions that are not generally considered to be inherently governmental functions, but which might come close to crossing the line, include:

- acquisition planning;
- arbitration or providing alternative methods of dispute resolution;
- budget preparation;
- construction secured from electronic eavesdropping;
- developing regulations or statements of work;
- evaluating another contractor's performance;
- feasibility studies and strategy options to develop policy;
- gaining access to confidential business information;
- inspection services;
- legal advice and interpretations of regulations and statutes;
- policy interpretation (e.g., attending conferences on an agency's behalf or conducting agency training courses or community relations campaigns);
- preparing responses to Freedom of Information Act requests;
- prisoner detention or transport and national security details;
- reorganization and planning activities; and
- technical evaluation of contract proposals and advising a source selection board.

Several precautions are in place to address these gray areas. A designated agency official provides with the statement of work a written determination that no functions to be performed are inherently governmental. This assessment includes discretionary authority, decision-making responsibility and accountability of Government officials using contractor services or work products. Also, consulting services should be temporary or intermittent in duration and cannot be used to bypass personnel ceilings or pay limitations. Finally, preference for award cannot be given to former Government personnel.

DFARS 207.153

Although procurement activities are deemed inherently governmental in nature, they can be contracted out if no DoD personnel are available to perform or oversee such performance. However, any potential organizational conflict of interest must be addressed first.

1.7.2 Federal Budget

A *budget* lists all planned expenses and revenues for a firm or a given program. A budget can be thought of as a model of how the firm or program might perform financially if certain plans are fully implemented. Management will then measure financial performance against the budgeted forecast to assess performance. Budgets usually cover an entire 12-month period, known as a *fiscal year*, which may or may not coincide with the calendar year (the Federal Government's fiscal year begins October 1 and expires September 30). All governments at all levels prepare budgets. Nearly all states are required to have balanced budgets, where revenues equal expenditures, but the Federal Government is allowed to run deficits.

The budgeting process in the Federal Government is unique and follows a series of individually named steps which are followed one at a time. First, the annual United States Government budget is prepared by the Office of Management and Budget, which conducts data calls through all Federal departments and agencies and compiles the results. The budget includes a spending plan that shows the state of the Treasury at three different points of time:

- end of last fiscal year (September 30);
- end of current fiscal year; and
- end of upcoming fiscal year.

The President then signs the budget and submits to Congress by the first Monday of February. Related documents such as the Economic Report of the President are included, along with a description of proposed spending priorities and justifications. This submission is necessary because Federal budget authority to enter into financial obligations derives from the Constitution which says, "No money shall be drawn from the Treasury, but in Consequence of Appropriations made by Law."[49] At this point, Congress enters the budgeting process.

Both the House of Representatives and the Senate have Committees on the Budget which draft budget resolutions, usually before the Easter break. These resolutions are then submitted to their respective chambers for consideration and adoption. The two chambers then select members to serve on a conference committee to resolve differences between the two versions, after which the chambers will vote on the conference version. This resolution may bind Congress, but not the nation, so it does not require Presidential approval. Rather, it is a blueprint for the upcoming appropriation process.

Next, Congressional committees and staff members hold public hearings and mark-up sessions, and inevitably make numerous substantial changes. Some changes result from legitimate disagreements with the Administration over spending priorities and program needs, while others are Congressional initiatives resulting from political desires to spend Federal dollars on a specific project or initiative.[50] The end result will be a process to authorize and appropriate funds to operate the Federal Government. Congressional committees concerned with defense oversight consist of:

- The Committee on Appropriations of the Senate and its Subcommittee on Defense;
- The Committee on Armed Services of the Senate;
- The Committee on Appropriations of the House of Representatives and its Subcommittee on Defense; and
- The Committee on Armed Services of the House of Representatives.

Unfortunately, these are two separate processes with two separate sets of players. *Authorization* by Congress permits agencies to run programs, but funding is not included. This is because funding for Federal programs must first be authorized by an oversight committee for the department or agency concerned. Their deliberations lead to an Authorization Act for the department. These committees have the authority to decide what programs and policies to allow. This also means that the authorization phase comes before the appropriation phase.

Appropriation is the process by which Congress approves funds for specifically authorized programs. Appropriations are set aside by Congress for specific purposes, such as operations and maintenance, procurement, and research and development. However, the Appropriations Committee for both the House and Senate are responsible for "seeing the big picture" of Federal operations and is free to make changes to the Authorization Committee decisions. So despite the directions set down in the various authorization acts, the Appropriations Committee of each chamber sets the funding levels, which may not be consistent with the authorization bill. All appropriations must go only to authorized programs, but not all authorized programs may be funded. To add to the confusion, authorizations for some programs may lapse yet still be funded, while other authorized programs may receive no funds at all. Appropriation bills may also contain policy direction, which may or may not coincide with the authorization committee's wishes. It is not unheard of to be a program manager with no money and hence no program to manage.

There are currently 12 appropriation bills enacted each fiscal year, corresponding to the jurisdiction of the respective House and Senate appropriation subcommittees:

- Agriculture;
- Commerce, Justice, and Science;
- Defense;
- Energy and Water;
- Financial Services;
- Homeland Security;
- Interior and Environment;
- Labor, Health and Education;
- Legislative Branch;
- Military Construction and Veterans Affairs;
- State and Foreign Operations; and
- Transportation, Housing and Urban Development.

Notice that DoD is unique among all departments in that it has two separate appropriation bills—one for construction and housing and one for everything else. This raises the interesting circumstance where one part of DoD is funded on time and the other is delayed. This has happened several times in the past. Generally, military construction is not a controversial subject because Americans want their service members to have decent housing; however the procurement programs contained in the Defense Authorization bill may be more controversial and hence delayed in enactment.

Once both chambers of Congress agree on an appropriations bill, it must be signed by the President to become law. The President is free to veto the bill within 10 days of arrival, outlining in writing his reasons for veto. Congress may override the veto by a two-thirds margin in each chamber, in which case the bill automatically becomes law without further action. Otherwise, Congress must act to revise the bill to meet the President's objections, propose an alternate approach, and then resubmit the bill to the President.

If Congress cannot enact a bill by the end of the fiscal year, a *continuing resolution* may be adopted to continue Government operations at the same spending rate as the prior year. If such a resolution is not adopted and signed by the President, the Government is theoretically out of business and Federal agencies must shut down. This is because the *Anti-Deficiency Act* (31 U.S.C. 1341) prevents the contracting officer from making any commitments without sufficient appropriated funding. Contractors must cease performing against their contracts or else face the prospect of not being reimbursed for their effort (known in contracting circles as *working at risk*). Alternatively, the Department may be allowed to spend the funds provided by the continuing resolution at the same pace as in the prior year, or in compliance with additional Congressional direction. This process is most often used at the beginning of the fiscal year (October 1).

As if more bewilderment were necessary, some appropriations bills may be enacted, but not others. It is therefore conceivable that come October 1, some departments may be fully funded and operating as usual, while others are either under a continuing resolution or else shut down (or maybe partly closed and partly open). The legislative process is truly a series of multiple power centers, repetitive processes, and endless compromises.

Each budget item can be classified as either discretionary or direct spending. *Discretionary spending* is an appropriation for a fixed period of time, usually concurrent with the fiscal year. Since these funds must be obligated by September 30, federal contracting offices are under pressure to obligate them by the end of the fiscal year before they expire (hence the term *expiring funds*). This is why the Federal Government awards so many contracts and obligates so many dollars each September.

In an alternative vein, *multiyear funding* is specifically granted by Congress for programs they designate. Congress will make multiyear appropriations for purposes of housing, research and development, and some military systems. This approach reduces administrative burden, broadens the competitive base through higher quantities, lowers costs, and permits continuity of performance or phase-out costs. Alternatively, *no-year funds* assure timely liquidation for acquisition and availability of adequate funds at time of award but are not required to be funded in any specific year.

By contrast to discretionary spending, *direct spending* is enacted by law but not dependent on an annual appropriation bill. This includes most entitlement programs such as Food Stamps, Medicare, Medicaid, and Social Security. It is not normally used to fund Federal contracts.

Once money has been fully appropriated, the Executive agencies proceed through several steps to ensure the money goes where intended. *Apportionment* is how OMB provides appropriated funds to the departments and agencies. *Allotment* is how a department divides apportioned funds among its operating divisions. Each division then follows their Department guidance to provide funds to the individual program office.

Once funds have been provided to the appropriate office, they must go through yet another lengthy process to get on contract. *Commitment* is the administrative reservation of funds against a future contract, and is done before the procurement package reaches the contracting officer. *Obligations* are funds reserved for payment by the authorized administrative component (e.g., Comptroller or accounting authority). *Expenditures* or *outlays* are funds actually disbursed to a contractor for work completed. This will not match the budget authority for the fiscal year because some of the funds can be disbursed in future years, just so they are obligated in the current fiscal year. The program office and contracting officer must take care to ensure that funds are used only for their intended purpose (known colloquially as the *color of money*) to ensure that the directions of Congress are correctly implemented.

The biggest difference between public and private sector accounting is fiscal accountability. A Government agency must demonstrate compliance with law and budgetary directives for managing resources. By contrast, the private sector uses budgeting as a planning tool, not as a compliance (and sometimes, not even as a management) tool. Another difference is that the Government recognizes revenue when the money is available, not when earned to liquidate liabilities. Similarly, the Government records expenses when charged to revenue rather than when incurred.

1.7.3 Delegation of Authority

Authority to make decisions within the acquisition community is generally delegated to the lowest level, consistent with law. The contracting officer has the authority to determine the application of rules, regulations and policies on a given contract.

FAR 1-602.3 and 50.103-2

As prescribed by Public Law 85-804,[51] under rare circumstances the Government can amend a contract without consideration to ensure fairness and the national interest, such as when a loss under one contract will impair the contractor's ability to perform on a separate, essential contract. The loss must be more than just lost profit—it must go to the heart of the contractor's ability to perform. If the Government caused the action which led to the contractor's distress, fairness would dictate such an adjustment.

Mistakes can be corrected as well by the contracting officer, such as ambiguity in contract wording as to the meaning of the parties, obvious mistakes that the parties did not see during contract formation, or mutual mistake of a material fact. But mistakes in authority are more serious.

Unauthorized (or informal) commitments occur when a firm responds to a Government official's written or oral instructions and delivers supplies or services in anticipation of compensation without a formal contract. The official must have the apparent authority to issue the instruction but lack real authority (which should be a rare occurrence, since somebody has overstepped their authority to create the situation). Again, fairness would dictate the contractor be paid a reasonable amount for expended effort. Only the head of the contracting activity can ratify an unauthorized commitment. However, if the value of the action exceeds $70,000, ratification must be furnished by the Secretary of the Department. The resulting contract must still fulfill all requirements for properness, including a fair and reasonable price and available funding at the time of the occurrence. The firm must submit its request for payment within six months of the incident which gave rise to the informal commitment.

Contract Clause

FAR 52.250-1, Indemnification Under Public Law 85-804, for indemnification against hazardous or nuclear risks. Add Alternate I for cost-reimbursement contracts.

1.7.4 Personal Identity Verification

FAR 4.13

If a contractor will have routine physical access to a Federally controlled facility and/or information system during performance, the contract will contain provisions to comply with Federal Information Processing Standards Publication (FIPS PUB) Number 201, "Personal Identity Verification of Federal Employees and Contractors," and Office of Management and Budget (OMB) Guidance M-05-24, "Implementation of Homeland Security Presidential Directive (HSPD) 12-Policy for a Common Identification Standard for Federal Employees and Contractors."[52] Agency procedures often require that the contractor account for all Government Personal identity cards or badges issued to its employees, and return them upon contract completion or employee departure. If the contractor fails to do so, final payment may be withheld.

Contract Clause

FAR 52.204-9, Personal Identity Verification of Contractor Personnel.

1.7.5 Protection of Individual Privacy

Personally Identifiable Identification (PII) is data about an individual that identifies or relates to him or her (e.g., a social security number, age, home or office phone numbers, marital status, military rank or civilian grade, race, or salary). This includes any biometric, demographic, financial, medical, and personnel information.

FAR 24.1

The Privacy Act of 1974[53] mandates agencies follow certain procedures and safeguards to collect, store and disseminate personally identifiable information. PII is defined in NIST SP 800-122 as "any information about an individual maintained by an agency, including (1) any information that can be used to distinguish or trace an individual's identity, such as name, social security number, date and place of birth, mother's maiden name, or biometric records; and (2) any other information that is linked or linkable to an individual, such as medical, educational, financial, and employment information."

Protecting such information is essential to engender public trust in data collection and prevent identity theft. Agencies prescribe their own procedures for protecting such information, such as applying protective markings, encrypting internal e-mail, keeping data off Internet pages or share drives, and locking up hardcopy. These procedures will warn the individual against unauthorized information loss or sharing, browsing without authority or leaving a workstation without protection. Any Government employee who willfully discloses or obtains such information could be fined up to $5,000, and any contractor could be responsible for paying costs for replacement, theft protection and possibly attorney's fees. Both Government and contract employees must undergo annual training regarding both personal identification information and safekeeping records.

Within the context of privacy, a *record* is any item or collection of information about an individual that is maintained by an agency (e.g., criminal or employment history, education, financial transactions, and medical history). A record contains the individual's name and identifying number or symbol (including a fingerprint, photograph, or voiceprint). When an agency contracts to design, develop, maintain, or operate a *system of records* (a group of records from which information is retrieved by the individual's name or identifying number or symbol) on individuals on behalf of the agency, then the contractors and their employees are considered employees of the agency in terms of Privacy Act criminal penalties. The system of records is deemed to be maintained (or collected, used or disseminated) by the agency and is subject to the Privacy Act. Agencies which fail to require that such contractor operations conform to the Act may be civilly liable to individuals who claim injury under the Act. The contract work statement specifically identifies the system of records on individuals and the design, development or operational work to be performed. The solicitation will also make available any agency rules and regulations implementing the Act.

Contract Clauses

FAR 52.224-1, Privacy Act Notification.

FAR 52.224-2, Privacy Act.

FAR 52.224-3, Privacy Training.

1.7.6 Freedom of Information Act

Most countries have laws which promote an individual to obtain information pertaining to the local and national government and its actions. This is intended to open up government operations to public scrutiny, and to better understand and evaluate decisions which affect the lives of citizens. The United States is no different and has a plethora of legal decisions addressing this subject.

FAR 24.2

A proposal submitted in response to a competitive solicitation is not provided to any person unless incorporated by reference in a contract. Agencies do not disclose any information that is exempt from disclosure by the Freedom of Information Act[54] due to:

- agency personnel practices;
- classified information;
- confidential commercial or financial information;
- interagency or intra-agency memoranda;
- law enforcement;
- personal and medical information pertaining to an individual; and
- trade secrets.

Releasable information is provided through the Federal Register, a requestor visit to the archives with copy privileges, or mailing a copy to the requestor.

1.8 INTELLECTUAL PROPERTY

Unlike tangible items, *intellectual property* pertains to creations resulting from mental labor and original thought. These creations are intended to improve competitiveness, employment, productivity, public services, or standard of living. They give rise to intangible yet legal monopoly rights for the creator or owner, which are then codified in paper or software. For example, someone who buys this book owns the physical or electronic copy purchased; however the publisher retains the intellectual rights to the content (through a copyright). There are several different types of intellectual property to be discussed here.

1.8.1 Patents

FAR 27.2

A *patent* is a set of rights granted by a government to an inventor which lasts for a predetermined number of years (usually 20), in exchange for the inventor publicly disclosing details of the invention. One can patent a product, process or composition, including an improvement thereto, but not an abstract idea or a law of nature or physics.

Patent rights originated in common law. A patent prevents another party from making, using or selling the item or process without the inventor's permission. However, it does not in and of itself grant the inventor the right of use or practice, but rather just a property right. An employer owns the patent for an invention developed by its employee; in all other instances, the individual owns the patent rights.

The Government may authorize and consent to the use of inventions to perform contracts, even if covered by existing US patents. Moreover, the Government encourages practical commercial use of any inventions made under its contracts. In fact, the potential of patent infringement is not usually a bar to award. Permitting the contractor to retain patent rights (with licensing to the Government for contract performance only) motivates commercial development of inventions, promotes competition, and minimizes the costs and rights of Government usage.

The rule for indemnification depends on the nature of the product. Contractors providing commercial items indemnify the Government against liability for patent infringement. But if the product is specifically manufactured for the Government, the contractor will usually be indemnified by the Government for patent infringement.

The Government requires notice and assistance from its contractors regarding any claims for patent or copyright infringement. However, a third party can neither enjoin the Government nor sue a contractor for infringement. The only remedy for patent or copyright infringement in Government contracting is for monetary damages in the Court of Federal Claims (injunctive relief will not be granted). This court has exclusive jurisdiction to hear claims for monetary damages due to Federal laws, regulations, and contracts. The statute of limitations calls for filing a claim within six years from first accrual of the claim.

Section 6 of Executive Order 12889, "Implementation of the North American Free Trade Act," waives the need for a Federal contractor to obtain advance authorization to use or manufacture an invention. However, the patent owner must be notified in advance (or in cases of urgency, as soon as possible) whenever the agency or its contractor knows or should know that a patented invention is or will be used or manufactured without a license. This notification does not constitute admission of patent infringement.

Solicitation Provisions and Contract Clauses

FAR 52.227-1, Authorization and Consent, whenever patents are involved. This clause is optional in simplified acquisitions and prohibited when complete performance and delivery are outside the United States. Use the clause with its Alternate I for research and development, but not for standard construction and architect-engineer effort. Use the clause with its Alternate II for communication services with a common carrier which are not regulated by a tariff schedule approved by a regulatory agency.

FAR 52.227-2, Notice and Assistance Regarding Patent and Copyright Infringement, if using the Authorization and Consent clause.

FAR 52.227-3, Patent Indemnity, for delivery of commercial items. Do not use this clause for simplified acquisition procedures, performance, and delivery outside the United States, or when inconsistent with commercial practice. Use the clause with either its Alternate I (to identify excluded items) or II (to identify included items) if performance also requires delivery of non-commercial items. Use the clause with its Alternate III for a common carrier whose communication services and facilities are not regulated by a tariff schedule from a regulatory body.

FAR 52.227-4, Patent Indemnity—Construction Contracts, for construction or fixed-price contracts to dismantle, demolish or remove improvements. Do not use for architect-engineer services. Use the clause and Alternate I for patent indemnification to use nonstandard or noncommercial structures, products, processes, or methods.

FAR 52.227-5, Waiver of Indemnity, in addition to the appropriate patent indemnity clause. List the invention which is granted indemnification for contract performance.

FAR 52.227-10, Filing of Patent Applications—Classified Subject Matter, where the classified nature of the work might result in a patent application containing classified subject matter.

The clauses set forth next are examples which may be used in patent release and settlement agreements, and license agreements, to cover the subject matter, or if the contract provides for payment of a running royalty.

DFARS 252.227-7006, License Grant, for practice of the invention by or for the signatory Department(s).

DFARS 252.227-7007, License Term-Running Royalty, for expressing the license term.

DFARS 252.227-7008, Computation of Royalties, depending upon the nature of the royalty bearing article, the volume of procurement, and the type of contract pursuant to which the procurement is to be accomplished.

DFARS 252.227-7009, Reporting and Payment of Royalties, for expressing the process of reporting and payment of royalties' requirements. Where more than one department or agency is licensed and there is a ceiling on the royalties payable in any reporting period, the licensing departments or agencies coordinate to set the pro rata share of royalties to be paid by each.

DFARS 252.227-7010, License to Other Government Agencies, when it is intended that a license on the same terms and conditions be available to other departments and agencies of the Government.

DFARS 252.227-7011, Assignments, when assigning patent rights to the Government. To facilitate proof of contracts of assignments, the acknowledgment of the contractor should be executed before a notary public or other officer authorized to administer oaths.

DFARS 252.227-7012, Patent License and Release Contract, appropriately modified where necessary, for contracts of release, license, or assignment.

1.8.2 Inventions

FAR 27.3

An *invention* is a discovery that is or may be patentable.[55] Recall that the Government uses the patent system to promote the use of inventions arising from federally supported research or development to boost free enterprise and commercialization. This approach ensures that the Government obtains sufficient rights in federally supported inventions to meet its needs and protect the public against their nonuse or unreasonable use.

The contractor must notify the Government of an invention created or made under contract performance (known as a *subject invention*) within two months after notification by the inventor. *Made* means the conception or first actual reduction to practice of the invention. Generally, each contractor may, after required disclosure to the Government, elect to retain title to any invention made in the performance of work under a Government contract.

The contractor will then issue a license to cover its technical data, knowledge, or related assistance. The license can be exclusive, partially exclusive, or nonexclusive. The license is *exclusive* if it allows production or sales within a given territory without competition. A partially exclusive license has limits on the field of use, geographic area or number of licenses, while a nonexclusive license has no such restrictions.

The Government may examine records and laboratory notebooks up to three years after completion of performance to discover any unreported instances or to verify compliance with disclosure procedures. A negative finding could lead to the contracting officer withholding five percent of the contract price (up to $50,000, or $100,000 for major weapon systems).

The Government reserves a license to practice, or have practiced for it, any subject invention with the following five rights, at a minimum:

- *irrevocable*—cannot be terminated by the licensor during the contract period of performance (the only remedy is for monetary damages);
- *nonexclusive*—more than one party has the right to practice, which reflects the Government's desire to promote use of the invention;
- *nontransferable*—ownership of the invention remains with the original owner and is not transferred to either the Government or a third party;
- *paid-up*—all royalties are included within the contract price; and
- *worldwide*—no restriction on the geographic territory for the right to practice.

Regardless of the type of license, the Government reserves the rights to continue prosecution of a patent application and to require periodic reporting on how any subject invention is being used by the contractor or its licensees or assignees. Contractors mark their utilization report with a confidential or proprietary legend. The Federal Government can also receive and retain title to an invention in which the contractor has failed to disclose or file a patent application in time. Of course, the Government can retain additional rights to comply with treaties or other international agreements.

A special problem results for inventions which are not created as part of contract performance. This would occur if the contractor employs on its contract a *background invention* that was created before contract award or at private expense and is licensed or owned by the contractor. Any background inventions used during contract performance will be subject to negotiated rights and restrictions between the parties. Generally, a commercial item or one developed without Government financial support (either internally or with support of an external, non-Government entity) will yield only the contractor's standard commercial license.

The Government has the right to revoke or modify the contractor's license. However, the contracting officer must first furnish the contractor with a written notice of intention to do so, and allow the contractor 30 days to show cause as to why the license should not be revoked or modified. The contractor has the right to appeal the contracting officer's decision.

The contracting officer will (dis)approve, in writing, any contractor request to transfer its licenses to an outside party. If the Government wishes a third party be licensed for performance but the patent holder does not concur, the Government has avenues open to it.

Agencies have *march-in rights* that require the contractor (or its assignee or licensee) to grant a license to responsible applicants for any invention conceived or first reduced to practice under a Government contract. This must be a functional and workable invention (rather than one which is simulated or contemplated but still nonexistent). This requirement exists because the Government may object to paying a royalty for an item not yet workable. Moreover, the Government wants to ensure that the research it has funded reaches the general public. Here the parties must negotiate a contract clause to protect their respective rights. March-in rights are rarely invoked but are available if the contractor fails to grant a license when required.[56] The Government can also exercise march-in rights if the contractor or assignee has not satisfied health or public use requirements.

Even if the contractor refuses to grant such a license, the agency can grant the license itself if it shows that the contractor is not achieving practical application of the subject invention. *Practical application* means to manufacture a composition or product, practice a method or process, or operate a machine or system. Before a license is granted however, the contractor or assignee has an opportunity to establish that the invention is being utilized and that its benefits are available to the public on reasonable terms.

No contractor or assignee titled to any invention may grant anybody the exclusive right to use or sell the invention in the United States unless that person or entity also manufactures domestically any products which include the subject invention. This is a manifestation of the Buy American preference endemic to Government contracting. However, the agency can waive this requirement if the contractor or assignee has tried without success to grant licenses to potential domestic manufacturers, or if domestic manufacture is not commercially feasible.

If the contractor elects not to retain title to an invention, the Government may grant the inventor retention of rights. However, if a Government employee is a co-inventor under a contract with a small business or nonprofit organization, the employee's agency may license or assign its rights in the invention from its employee to the contractor.

Alternatively, the Government may choose to acquire title to a subject invention. In this case, the contractor is normally granted a worldwide, revocable, nonexclusive, paid-up license which extends throughout the corporate structure to all divisions and subsidiaries. Such a license includes the right to grant sublicenses if legally required.

Other special situations may lead to Government titling. The Government may require a foreign contractor to assign to it the title to an invention. Perhaps a Government authority in foreign intelligence or counterintelligence activities determines to restrict or eliminate the contractor's right to retain title in an invention in order to promote Federal patent policy or national security, or in accordance with agency regulations. This may also apply to managing naval nuclear propulsion or weapons facilities. However, even when the Government has the right to acquire title, the contractor may still request greater rights to a subject invention. These additional rights are subject to negotiation.

The contracting officer may require the contractor to:

- furnish a copy of each subcontract containing a patent rights clause;
- provide the filing and issue dates, serial and patent numbers, and title for any patent application filed on any subject invention in any country;
- submit interim and final invention reports and notification of all subcontracts awarded for experimental, developmental or research work; and
- submit periodic reports on the utilization of a subject invention.

A small business or nonprofit contractor may assign title to the Government for national security. Such a contractor may also elect to own an unclassified invention with unlimited dissemination within six months of its report to the agency.

Generally, a contractor obtains patent rights for its employees' creations. This is in practice a *shop right*, a common law right of an employer to use an invention patented by one or more employees without liability for infringement. The employer receives a royalty-free license to use a patented invention of the employee(s) developed on the employer's time or facilities.

When the Government acquires the entire right, title, and interest in an invention by contract, the chain of title from the inventor to the Government is clearly established by an assignment. The path of assignment is either from the inventor through the contractor to the Government, or from the inventor directly to the Government with the consent of the contractor.

A contract with a small business or nonprofit firm precludes the Government from requiring a license of any contractor-owned invention to third parties. However, the agency head may approve a written justification that use by others is necessary to achieve practical application of subject invention. The contractor may appeal this determination within 60 days after the notification.

Contracting activities establish appropriate procedures to detect and correct failures by the contractor to comply with its obligations under the patent rights clauses. These efforts focus on research and development, high dollar value projects and any firm that may not be complying with its contractual obligation. An agency official may check the Official Gazette of the United States Patent and Trademark Office for other patents issued to the contractor. The agency will observe the work on site, interview contractor technical personnel and inspect contractor laboratory notebooks and technical reports.

Use of patent rights clauses is controversial because contractors have invested great sums of money in developing these methods or inventions, and understand that venture capitalists view them with suspicion as additional risk creators. As a result, some commercial firms may refuse to participate in Federal research and development contracts, and private lenders and venture capitalists may consider this right to be too risky for investment. Yet the Government wants to fully utilize inventions paid for under contract to benefit the public. Hence, the contracting officer must carefully choose a proper patent rights clause from the selection provided next. Often, the contracting officer will consult a patent attorney who specializes in patent law. If one Government agency requests another to award a contract on its behalf, the request either specifies the patent rights clause to be used or else directs the awarding agency to use its own clause. In any case, there is no patent rights clause required for construction work or architect-engineer services that use only previously developed equipment, methods, and processes. Also, variations in aesthetics or artistry alone are insufficient grounds to include a patent rights clause.

Contract Clauses

FAR 52.227-11, Patent Rights—Ownership by the Contractor. The contracting officer may modify to require contractor invention listings and filing information and to furnish the Government an irrevocable power to inspect and copy the patent application file if a Government employee is a co-inventor. Use alternate versions as follows:

- Alternate I to grant a foreign government a sublicense per treaty or executive agreement;
- Alternate II to allow for impact of future treaties or agreements;
- Alternate III for a nonprofit organization to operate a Government-owned facility;
- Alternate IV to operate a Government-owned facility; and/or
- Alternate V to reserve the right to inspect data at the contractor's facility.

FAR 52.227-13, Patent Rights—Ownership by the Government, if:

- the contractor is not located in the United States or is subject to the control of a foreign government;
- the agency head determines that restriction or elimination of the right to retain title to any subject invention will better promote the Government's policy and objectives;
- a Government authority in foreign intelligence or counterintelligence activities determines that restriction or elimination of the right to retain any subject invention is necessary to protect national security; or
- the contract includes the operation of a Government-owned, contractor-operated facility of the Department of Energy primarily dedicated to naval nuclear propulsion or weapons-related programs.

Use the clause with its Alternate I if the Government must grant a foreign government a sublicense in subject inventions pursuant to a treaty or executive agreement, or the agency head determines at time of award that it would be in the national interest to sublicense foreign governments or international organizations pursuant to any existing or future treaty or agreement. Use the clause with its Alternate II to reference such a treaty or agreement.

1.8.3 Rights in Data

The data rights definitions and policies in FAR and the DFARS differ from one another, so DoD personnel follow the DFARS implementation.

1.8.3.1 Technical Data

Data is recorded information, regardless of form or the media on which it is recorded. Within the context of data rights, the term includes technical data and computer software, but not administrative, cost or pricing, financial, or management information.

Across the Federal Government, agencies require data to obtain competition and ensure logistics support. They disseminate and publish the results of their activities and release technical information to promote subsequent technological developments. But because contractors may have proprietary interests in their data, the Government must protect proprietary data from unauthorized use and disclosure while encouraging contractors to participate in and apply innovative concepts to Government programs.

The Government obtains rights in technical data by means of an irrevocable license granted by the contractor or else obtained from a third party by the contractor. The contractor or licensor retains all rights in the data not granted to the Government. The scope of the license is generally determined by the source of funds used to either develop the item or process or else create the data.

DoDI 5000.87, 3.2.e

The program manager must develop an Intellectual Property Strategy to address data and software deliverables, license rights and patented technologies. This document shows how (s)he will manage the data needs that will affect the program's cost, schedule, and performance. The strategy includes available data and its rights and licenses, and what data is needed when to support production, operations, cybersecurity, and sustainment. The strategy must address Government rights to the source code (e.g., open-source vs. Government-sponsored software), and any third-party components within the software, in order to permit compilation and debugging. For example, this could include automation scripts, build procedures, databases and sets, executables, firmware, libraries, source code, test results, tools, and training materials. These materials are necessary to integrate, test and evaluate, debug, deploy, and operate the software application in all relevant environments (e.g., development, staging, and production). The IP strategy should address collaboration with other potential software developers and users whenever the Government will be taking delivery of, and potentially modifying, the source code to reduce unnecessary duplication. The strategy should also address when and how the program will either accept or improve software component source code from other agencies or to an open-source project managed outside DoD, especially when developed at government expense; and a list of all third-party software components included in the software. Creating program-specific versions of software components should be avoided if possible. The IP strategy should also identify technological areas where IP may result from Government investment and how to treat them appropriately. Finally, the strategy should address the risks and opportunities associated with non-availability of data and its cost impact on both the existing contract and total life-cycle cost.[57]

The PM must approve the use of any commercial or proprietary software not previously identified in the IP strategy before its insertion into the software developed for the government. The software licensing agreement must be compared against the IP strategy to ensure that any government-unique IP rights are negotiated and included in the contract license agreement.

Any commercial or proprietary software used in or interoperable with software developed for the Government must have documented open interfaces. This will permit technology insertion and the use of modular open systems approaches.

The PM should require delivery of all the source code for software developed at the Government expense. This includes all software capability descriptions and as-built architecture and design products and interface definitions (including those to proprietary software elements). Delivery timelines should plan for any transition to a different contractor or the Government. The PM will need to define the software transition in a lifecycle support plan and identify the point of transition in the product roadmap.

DFARS 227.71

Data needs must be established by first considering the contractor's economic interests in data pertaining to items or processes developed at private expense. On the other hand, the Government's costs to acquire, protect, retrieve, and store the data must also be considered. Needs for maintenance and overhaul operations, including repair and spare parts, as well as reprocurement expenses, are contributing factors. These rights also pertain to *form, fit and function data* that provide a technical description of the product, which will enable physical and functional interchangeability of items or processes. This approach covers such product features as configuration, functional characteristics and performance capabilities and requirements.

DFARS 227.7203

Data requirements personnel will address in the procurement planning and requirements documents the acquisition of all computer software and related recorded information and license rights necessary to reproduce or recompile the software from its source code and required software libraries; conduct required software testing and evaluation; integrate and deploy computer programs on relevant hardware; and sustain and support the software over its life cycle.

The assessment of life-cycle needs should consider alternatives to the delivery of source code and related software design details for privately developed computer software, such as access to software and technical data sufficient to implement a modular open systems approach, including access agreements for cloud-based or subscription-based software products or services, software support and maintenance provided directly from the contractor, or other contracting or licensing mechanisms. Such mechanisms could include priced options, direct licensing between contractors for qualifying second sources, data escrow agreements, deferred delivery solutions, and subscription agreements.

Data rights clauses do not specify the type, quality or quantity of data to be delivered, but only the respective rights of the contractor and government regarding the data's disclosure, reproduction, or use. Hence, the contract must specify the data to be delivered. This means that DoD cannot assume it has any usable rights in data delivered; they must be explicitly granted by the contractor.

There are five basic levels of rights to "use, modify, reproduce, perform, display, release, or disclose" data that can be applied to noncommercial items and any negotiable intellectual property:

- *Unlimited Rights*—the Government may give the data to anyone or use it for any purpose.
- *Government Purpose Rights*—the Government may use the data internally or release or disclose it to a party outside the Government if the recipient uses the data for government purposes only.
- *Limited Rights*—The Government may use the data only internally, though it may release to another party for emergency repair and overhaul.
- *Restricted Rights*—The Government may use the software on one computer, processing unit or terminal at a time within the Government and

make any necessary archival copies, but cannot reverse-engineer the software. It may release the data outside the Government only for emergency repair and overhaul, or to respond to urgent tactical situations. The Government may release the data to a service contractor to diagnose and correct software deficiencies or to adapt or merge it with other computer programs.

- *Specifically Negotiated Rights*—The Government and the contractor may modify these predetermined levels of rights so long as the Government receives no less than limited rights in technical data related to noncommercial items and restricted rights in noncommercial computer software.

Some commercial items come with pre-existing rights, which are not normally negotiable. When obtaining licenses in technical data pertaining to commercial items, DoD may use technical data only within the Government. The data may not be used to manufacture additional quantities of the commercial items, except for emergency repair or overhaul, and for *covered contractors* that process, store or transmit Government information. Moreover, the data may not be disclosed to or used by third parties without the contractor's written permission.

For commercial computer software licenses, DoD may use the software and documentation only in accordance with the terms of the license customarily provided to the public. If that license is inconsistent with Federal law or does not otherwise satisfy user needs, the Government must first negotiate with the contractor to determine if acceptable terms can be reached. The terms of any license for commercial computer software are specified in the contract or in an addendum thereto.

From the previous lists, the standard license rights that a licensor grants to the Government are either unlimited, government purpose or limited rights. If these standard rights do not satisfy the Government's needs or the Government is willing to accept lesser rights in data in return for other consideration, a special license may be negotiated. The licensor is not obligated to provide the Government greater rights and the contracting officer is not required to accept lesser rights than those provided in the standard grant of license.

The Government generally obtains unlimited rights in technical data that are:

- analyses, studies, or test data specified to be produced in the performance of a contract;
- changes or corrections to technical data furnished to the contractor by the Government;
- created exclusively with Government funds under a contract that does not require the development or production of items or processes;

- form, fit and function data;
- furnished to the Government with Government purpose license rights where either the limited rights with restrictive condition(s) or the contractor's exclusive right to use such data for commercial purposes has expired;
- necessary for installation, maintenance, operation, or training (other than detailed manufacturing or process data);
- pertaining to an item or process which has been or will be developed exclusively with Government funds;
- publicly available or already released by the (sub)contractor without restrictions on further use or release. However, rights can be restricted if resulting from the assignment, sale, or transfer to another party of interest in the software or in a business entity or its assets; or
- where the Government has obtained unlimited rights under another contract by negotiation.

Technical data may be created during the performance of a contract for a conceptual design that does not require development or production of items or processes. The Government generally obtains unlimited rights in such data created exclusively with Government funds, government purpose rights when the data were created with mixed funding, and limited rights when the data were created exclusively at private expense.

When an item or process is developed with mixed funding, the Government may use, display, modify, reproduce, or release the data pertaining to such items or processes within the Government without restriction, but may only release or disclose the data outside the Government for official government purposes. This is the government purpose level of rights previously introduced. This creates a DoD-unique hybrid that exists within both limited and unlimited rights to use the data for its own purposes, including reprocurement, while allowing the contractor to retain unlimited rights for commercial use. These rights normally transition to an unlimited status after five years unless the parties agree otherwise. Changes to the government purpose rights period may be made at any time prior to delivery of the technical data without further consideration from either party. Longer periods should be negotiated when a five-year period does not provide sufficient time to apply the data for commercial purposes, for life-cycle needs of the product or system under contract, or when necessary to recognize subcontractors' interests in the data.

The government purpose rights period commences upon execution of the (sub)contract, modification or option exercise that required the development. Upon expiration of the government rights period, the Government gains unlimited rights in the data and may authorize others to use the data for commercial purposes. During this period, the Government may not use, or authorize other persons to use, technical data marked with government purpose rights legends for commercial purposes. Nor may the Government release or disclose data in which it has government purpose rights to any person, or authorize others to do so, unless the intended recipient is either subject to the use and nondisclosure agreement prior to release or disclosure, or else is a Government contractor receiving access to the data for performance of a Government contract.

Public announcements must provide notice of the use and nondisclosure requirements. Class use and nondisclosure agreements (e.g., agreements covering all solicitations received by the company within a reasonable period) are authorized and may be obtained at any time prior to release or disclosure of the government purpose rights data. Documents transmitting government purpose rights data to persons under class agreements will identify both the class agreement and the technical data subject to government purpose rights.

The Government usually obtains limited rights in technical data that pertain to items or processes developed exclusively at private expense. The exceptions are when the Government is entitled to unlimited rights, or the data was created exclusively at private expense under a contract that does not require the development or production of items or processes. Data in which the Government has limited rights normally may not be used or released outside the Government without the permission of the contractor asserting the restriction. However, there are exceptions: emergency repair and overhaul, to a covered Government support contractor, or to a foreign government (other than detailed manufacturing or process data) when in the interest of the United States and required for evaluation or information.

The party asserting limited rights must be immediately notified of the Government's intent to release, disclose, or authorize others to use such data prior to its release or disclosure except for emergency repair or overhaul. This party must complete a use and nondisclosure agreement or receive the data for performance of a Government contract prior to release or disclosure of the limited rights data.

Specific licenses are negotiated when the parties agree to modify the standard license rights granted to the Government or when the Government wants to obtain rights in data in which it does not currently have any rights. The Government may accept lesser rights when it has unlimited or government purpose rights in data but may not accept less than limited rights in such data. The negotiated license rights must stipulate what rights the Government must release or disclose the data to other persons or to authorize others to use the data. Negotiated rights are codified in a license agreement made part of the contract.

When the Government needs additional rights in data acquired with government purpose or limited rights, the contracting officer must negotiate with the contractor to determine whether there are acceptable terms for transferring such rights. Generally, such negotiations should be conducted only when there is a need to disclose the data outside the Government or if the additional rights are required for competitive reprocurement and the anticipated savings are estimated to exceed the acquisition cost of the additional rights. One alternative approach includes using performance specifications and form, fit and function data to acquire or develop functionally equivalent items or processes. Another approach is to obtain a contractor's commitment to qualify additional sources and maintain adequate competition among them. Or the Government can provide items from Government inventories to contractors to facilitate the development of equivalent items through reverse engineering.

Nonetheless, although DoD policy is to acquire only the technical data customarily provided to the public with a commercial item or process, it will insist on any form, fit or function data necessary to install, maintain or repair commercial items or processes, or to describe any modifications made at Government expense.

This data may not be used to manufacture additional quantities of the commercial items. Except for emergency repair or overhaul and for covered Government support contractors, the data may not be released or disclosed to, or used by, third parties without the contractor's written permission. If additional rights are needed, contracting activities must negotiate with the contractor to determine if there are acceptable terms to transfer such rights and then document them in a license agreement made part of the contract.

Solicitations and contracts establish separate contract line items for technical data to identify the type and quantity of data to be delivered under the contract and the format and media in which the data will be delivered. These line items must include delivery schedules, destinations, and acceptance criteria. The solicitation should require offerors to separately price each deliverable data item and identify technical data to be furnished with restrictions on the Government's rights prior to delivery.

Offerors are not required to furnish the Government any rights in technical data related to items or processes developed at private expense, except for specified data. However, they may furnish or offer items or processes developed at private expense but restrict the Government's rights to use, modify, release, reproduce, perform, display, or disclose the data. Contractors must obtain permission from copyright owners before including their copyrighted works in data deliveries.

In fact, per 10 U.S.C. 2305, solicitations for major systems development may not permit the Government to competitively acquire items identical to those developed at private expense. This restriction can be overcome if a determination is made at a level above the contracting officer that the offeror will not otherwise be able to satisfy program schedule or delivery requirements or meet mobilization needs.

A contractor must provide any technical data in which the Government has previously obtained rights unless the parties have agreed otherwise or restrictions on the Government's rights have expired. When restrictions are still applicable, the contractor may mark the data with the appropriate restrictive legend for which the data qualified.

Offerors must identify any technical data specified in the solicitation as deliverable data items that are the same or substantially the same as items already delivered or obligated to deliver as a (sub)contractor, under any other federal agency contract. In addition, offerors must identify in an attachment to the offer any technical data that it asserts should be provided to the Government with restrictions on disclosure, modification, reproduction, or use. This requirement is in addition to copyright protection. Failure to do so under sealed bidding is deemed a minor informality. The Government has the right to review, verify, challenge, and validate restrictive markings.

For a noncommercial acquisition, the offeror develops and provides the contracting officer with a data assertions list of any data where the government will not receive unlimited rights, such as a copyright. The Government will have unlimited rights to any technical data pertaining to noncommercial items or computer software not on that list. However, an SBIR contract does not need to include assertions for data rights in technical data or computer software developed under that contract.

The contractor may submit change proposals to add more data onto the program. It must specify whether it wishes to provide the Government less than unlimited rights. If the Government agrees with any restrictions, the contracting officer would add the data to the data accession list in the contract.

DoDI 5010.44

The PM and contracting officer must consider the types of IP deliverables and level of associated license rights into source selection evaluation factors, and as negotiation objectives in sole-source awards. They must ensure there is sufficient clarity when contractors identify and assert restrictions on IP rights so they can assess how those assertions may affect DoD interests over the life cycle. This requires the program manager to avoid requirements and strategies that limit DoD options to access vital technology and commercial solutions available from industry. This can also be done by requiring contractors to align assertions to specific IP deliverables, to particular system components or processes, or specific funding types.

Upfront planning by the program office is also key to IP strategy. For instance, it may consider how contractor and government changes impact delivered IP and data reuse and life-cycle support. Another idea is to communicate clearly with industry on IP matters early in the program life cycle regarding expectations, objectives and plans for system sustainment and upgrade. IP needs should be included in industry days, draft solicitations, one-on-one meetings with potential offerors, and presolicitation notices. The IP strategy will describe how program management will assess long-term program requirements, and total ownership costs of IP deliverables and associated license rights necessary for competitive and affordable operation, maintenance, modernization, and sustainment over the entire product life cycle. It should also reflect IP-related matters necessary to support the program's use of modular open systems approaches. It must discuss how solicitations and contracts will identify and require all major systems interfaces to be based on widely supported and consensus-based standards, preferably non-proprietary. IP strategies to obtain appropriate rights should be customized based on the common and unique characteristics of the system and its components, its architecture and interfaces, the product support strategy, the agency's industrial base strategy, commercial availability, and whether the standard commercial licensing terms meet DoD needs. Finally, IP strategies must consider the use of specially negotiated licenses and rights to acquire customized IP data and software appropriate for the product support strategy.

Solicitation Provisions

DFARS 252.227-7017, Identification and Assertion of Use, Release, or Disclosure Restrictions, in all solicitations that include DFARS 252.227-7013, Rights in Technical Data–Noncommercial Items.

DFARS 252.227-7028, Technical Data or Computer Software Previously Delivered to the Government, when the resulting contract will require the contractor to deliver technical data.

Solicitation Provisions and Contract Clauses

DFARS 252.227-7013, Rights in Technical Data–Noncommercial Items, when the successful offeror(s) will be required to deliver to the Government technical data pertaining to noncommercial items or commercial items for which the Government will have paid for any portion of the development costs. In the latter case, this clause will govern the technical data pertaining to any portion of a commercial item that was developed in any part at Government expense, and DFARS 252.227-7015 will govern the technical data pertaining to any portion of a commercial item that was developed exclusively at private expense. The clause is not used when the only deliverable items are computer software or its documentation, commercial items developed exclusively at private expense, existing works, or special works. Nor is the clause used in most architect-engineer and construction contracts or when contracting under the Small Business Innovation Research Program. Use the clause with its Alternate I in research solicitations and contracts when the contracting officer determines that public dissemination by the contractor would be in the interest of the Government and facilitated by the Government relinquishing its right to publish the work for sale, or to have others publish the work for sale on behalf of the Government. Use the clause with its Alternate II in solicitations and contracts that are for the development or delivery of a vessel design or any useful article embodying a vessel design. When using this clause or provision, use the following clauses:

- DFARS 252.227-7016, Rights in Bid or Proposal Information;
- DFARS 252.227-7030, Technical Data—Withholding of Payment; and
- DFARS 252.227-7037, Validation of Restrictive Markings on Technical Data (paragraph (e) of the clause contains information that must be included in a challenge).

DFARS 252.227-7015, Technical Data—Commercial Items, when the contractor will be required to deliver technical data pertaining to commercial items, components, or processes. Use the clause with its Alternate I in solicitations and contracts for the development or delivery of a vessel design or any useful article embodying a vessel design.

DFARS 252.227-7022, Government Rights (Unlimited), for architect-engineer services and for construction involving architect-engineer services.

DFARS 252.227-7023, Drawings and Other Data to Become Property of Government, for architect-engineer services, or for construction involving architect-engineer services, to obtain a unique architectural design of a building, a monument, or construction of similar nature, which for aesthetic, artistic or other special reasons the Government does not want duplicated. The Government may acquire exclusive control of the data pertaining to the design.

DFARS 252.227-7024, Notice and Approval of Restricted Designs, may be included in architect-engineer contracts to permit the Government to make informed decisions concerning noncompetitive aspects of the design.

DFARS 252.227-7025, Limitations on the Use or Disclosure of Government-Furnished Information Marked with Restrictive Legends, when it is anticipated that the Government will provide the contractor (other than a litigation support contractor), for performance of its contract, technical data marked with another contractor's restrictive legend(s).

DFARS 252.227-7033, Rights in Shop Drawings, when the Government obtains unlimited rights in shop drawings for construction.

Contract Clause

FAR 52.227-19, Commercial Computer Software License.

1.8.3.2 Deferred Delivery and Ordering

DFARS 227.7103-8

The Government may opt to defer the delivery of technical data for up to two years after acceptance of all other items under the contract (or contract termination). The obligation of subcontractors or suppliers to deliver such technical data expires two years after the date the prime contractor accepts the last item from the subcontractor or supplier for use in the performance of the contract. The contract must specify which technical data is subject to deferred delivery and the desired delivery date.

Sometimes a firm requirement for a specific data item(s) has not been established prior to contract award but there is a potential need for the data. In this case, the contracting officer may order any data that has been generated in the performance of the (sub)contract at any time until three years after acceptance of all other items under the contract or contract termination, whichever is later. When the data are ordered, the delivery dates must be negotiated and the contractor compensated only for converting the data into the prescribed form, plus delivery and reproduction costs.

DFARS 227.7103-14

10 U.S.C. 2320 permits remedies to be applied to technical data found to be incomplete or inadequate, or which do not satisfy the requirements of the contract. Agency heads may withhold payments (or exercise such other remedies they consider appropriate) during any period if the contractor does not meet the requirements for the delivery of technical data.

The contracting officer may choose to either withhold up to 10 percent of the contract price pending correction or replacement of the nonconforming technical data, or else negotiate an equitable reduction in contract price. The amount subject to withhold may be expressed as a fixed dollar amount or as a percentage of the contract price, but it should consider the relative value and importance of the data. When the sole purpose of a contract is to produce the data, the relative value of that data may be much higher than if produced under a contract where the production of the data is a secondary objective. Also, repair and maintenance data may have a higher relative value than merely describing the item or providing performance characteristics. Exceptions to this policy are for nonconforming restrictive markings, correction or replacement of nonconforming data, or an equitable reduction in contract price when other approaches are not practicable or in the Government's interests.

The intended use of the technical data and any cost to obtain the warranty should be considered before deciding to obtain a data warranty. For example, a data warranty should be considered if the Government intends to repair or maintain an item and defective repair or maintenance data would either impair the Government's effective use of the item or result in increased costs to the Government.

Solicitation Provision and Contract Clause

DFARS 252.227-7013, Rights in Technical Data—Noncommercial Items.

Contract Clauses

DFARS 252.227-7026, Deferred Delivery of Technical Data or Computer Software, if a delivery date can be established at time of award.

DFARS 252.227-7027, Deferred Ordering of Technical Data or Computer Software, if a delivery date cannot be established at time of award.

DFARS 252.227-7030, Technical Data—Withholding of Payment.

DFARS 252.246-7001, Warranty of Data, and its alternates, or a substantially similar clause when the Government needs a specific warranty of technical data.

1.8.3.3 Rights of Third Parties

DFARS 227.7103-15

10 U.S.C. 2320 provides subcontractors at any tier the same protection for their rights in data as is provided to prime contractors. Further, 10 U.S.C. 2321 permits a subcontractor to transact directly with the Government any matters relating to the validation of its asserted restrictions on the Government's rights to use or disclose technical data. This direct transaction does not establish or imply privity of contract.

The Government cannot require contractors to have their subcontractors or suppliers at any tier relinquish rights in technical data (beyond those obtained by the Government) to the contractor, a higher tier subcontractor, or to the Government itself, as a condition for award of any (sub)contract.

Prime contractors whose contracts include the following clauses must include them without modification (except for appropriate identification of the parties) in subcontracts at all tiers to furnish technical data for noncommercial items:

- DFARS 252.227-7013, Rights in Technical Data—Noncommercial Items;
- DFARS 252.227-7025, Limitations on the Use or Disclosure of Government-Furnished Information Marked with Restrictive Legends;

- DFARS 252.227-7028, Technical Data or Computer Software Previously Delivered to the Government; and
- DFARS 252.227-7037, Validation of Restrictive Markings on Technical Data.

DFARS 227.7103-16

Technical data may be released or disclosed to foreign contractors, governments, or organizations only if permitted by Federal export controls and other national security laws or regulations. Subject to such laws and regulations, DoD may release or disclose technical data in which it has obtained unlimited rights to foreign entities or authorize the use of such data by those entities. It may not release or disclose to foreign entities any technical data for which restrictions have been asserted, or authorize their use of the data, unless the intended recipient is subject to the same provisions as in the use and nondisclosure agreement. Also, the requirements governing disclosure, display, modification, performance, reproduction, release, or use of such data must be satisfied.

For foreign and Canadian contractors, the Government should obtain rights in the technical data that are not less than the rights it would have obtained under the data rights clause(s) for a comparable procurement performed within the United States or its outlying areas.

Contract Clause

DFARS 252.227-7032, Rights in Technical Data and Computer Software (Foreign), may be used in contracts with foreign contractors to be performed overseas, except Canadian purchases, in lieu of DFARS 252.227-7013, Rights in Technical Data—Noncommercial Items, when the Government requires the unrestricted right to use, modify, reproduce, perform, display, release or disclose all technical data to be delivered under the contract. Do not use in contracts for existing or special works. When the Government does not require unlimited rights, the clause may be modified to accommodate the needs of a specific overseas procurement situation.

1.8.3.4 Contractor Data Repositories

DFARS 227.7108

Contractor data repositories may be established when permitted by agency procedures. The contractual instrument establishing the data repository must require the data repository management contractor to:

- deliver data to the Government on paper or in other specified media;
- indemnify the Government from any liability to data owners or licensors resulting from release or disclosure of technical data made by the data repository contractor or its employees or representatives;
- maintain the currency of data delivered directly by Government (sub)contractors to the repository;
- obtain use and nondisclosure agreements from all persons to whom government purpose rights data is released or disclosed; and
- protect technical data delivered to or stored at the repository from unauthorized release or disclosure.

The contractor's data management and distribution responsibilities must be identified in the contract, or else the contract must reference the agreement between the Government and the contractor that establishes those responsibilities. If a third party will be the data repository manager, the (sub)contractor cannot deliver technical data marked with limited rights legends to the data repository unless the (sub)contractor who has asserted limited rights agrees to release the data to the repository or has authorized in writing the Government to do so.

Repository procedures may provide for the acceptance, delivery and subsequent distribution of technical data in storage media other than paper, including direct electronic exchange of data between two computers. The procedures must provide for the identification of any portions of the data provided with restrictive legends. The acceptance criteria must be consistent with the authorized delivery format.

1.8.3.5 Use and Nondisclosure Agreements

DFARS 227.7103-7

Technical data or computer software delivered to the Government with restrictions on its disclosure, display, modification, performance, reproduction, release, or use may not be provided to third parties unless the intended recipient completes and signs the use and nondisclosure agreement prior to release or disclosure of the data.[58] The specific conditions for third-party use must be stipulated in an attachment to the use and nondisclosure agreement. If the release is subject to special license rights, they must be included in the agreement. However, no such agreement applies to Government contractors who require access to a third party's data or software if the contract contains DFARS 252.227-7025, Limitations on the Use or Disclosure of Government-Furnished Information Marked with Restrictive Legends.

DFARS 209.505-4

Contractors may be required to enter into nondisclosure agreements directly with the third party that asserts commercial restrictions or limited rights on technical data or computer software. The contracting officer is not required to obtain copies of these agreements or to ensure that they are properly executed. However, litigation support contractors are not required to enter into nondisclosure agreements directly with any third party asserting restrictions on any litigation information.

1.8.3.6 Contracts under the Small Business Innovation Research Program

DFARS 227.7104

The Government obtains Small Business Innovation Research (SBIR) data rights in technical data and computer software generated under the contract and marked with the SBIR data rights legend. In this way, the Government obtains limited rights in such technical data and restricted rights in such computer software during the data protection period beginning at contract award and ending five years after completion of the project under which the data were generated. Upon expiration of the five-year restrictive license, the Government has unlimited rights in the SBIR technical data and computer software. During the SBIR data protection period, the Government may not release or disclose SBIR technical data or computer software to any person unless authorized for limited rights technical data or restricted rights computer software, respectively.

Solicitation Provision and Contract Clause

DFARS 252.227-7018, Rights in Noncommercial Technical Data and Computer Software—Small Business Innovation Research (SBIR) Program, when technical data or computer software will be generated during performance of contracts under the SBIR program. Use the following provisions and clauses in SBIR solicitations and contracts that include this clause:

- DFARS 252.227-7016, Rights in Bid or Proposal Information;
- DFARS 252.227-7017, Identification and Assertion of Use, Release, or Disclosure Restrictions;
- DFARS 252.227-7019, Validation of Asserted Restrictions—Computer Software;
- DFARS 252.227-7025, Limitations on the Use or Disclosure of Government-Furnished Information Marked with Restrictive Legends;

- DFARS 252.227-7028, Technical Data or Computer Software Previously Delivered to the Government;
- DFARS 252.227-7030, Technical Data—Withholding of Payment;
- DFARS 252.227-7037, Validation of Restrictive Markings on Technical Data (paragraph (e) of the clause contains information that must be included in a challenge). Use the clause with its Alternate I in research contracts when the contracting officer determines that public dissemination by the contractor would be in the interest of the Government and facilitated by the Government relinquishing its right to publish the work for sale, or to have others publish the work for sale on its behalf.

1.8.4 Computer Software

Organizations use many different variations and combinations of software development methods, but they generally fall into three major categories: Waterfall, Incremental, and Agile. These development methods are also used for other types of project implementation plans other than software development.

The *Waterfall* method is a traditional software development method where tasks are arranged sequentially. One phase is completed before the next phase is started and several software builds are completed before deployment. Programs best use this method where the requirements are very well understood at the onset and functionality to be delivered is mature and static. Because all functionality is delivered at once, it has easy delivery schedule management. Ideally, the finished product is not delivered until all tasks are completed. For large and complex projects however, this can mean that the underlying technology is obsolete before delivery. It also assumes an often-unrealistic view that organizations are static, and the product's requirements remain the same throughout the life of the project. It is difficult to incorporate user feedback, and any experimental code or prototypes are discarded after use. If one task is not completed on time, the entire project can be halted. This method provides the greatest risk to user satisfaction (though it also typically provides the lowest risk to meeting contractual requirements). Because of these concerns, the Waterfall method is no longer used very often in DoD.

The *Incremental* method corrects some of the problems associated with the Waterfall method. Note that "Spiral" and "Evolutionary Acquisition" are sometimes used synonymously; however "Incremental" is the official term of use. The idea is to deliver additional improved capability in block increments over time so that it can be developed and delivered concurrently and earlier. Often, some 60–80% of the product requirements will be delivered early and the remaining capabilities delivered incrementally later. This is usually accommodated through manageable releases (i.e., Increment 1, Release 1.1,

Release 1.2, etc.) of smaller "chunks" of capability, thereby getting functionality into users' hands more quickly. Users can provide feedback earlier and developers have opportunity to identify potential problems earlier. Although scheduling concurrent tasks is difficult to manage, the project can be delivered earlier.

For the *Agile* method, a group of software developers have created a set of best practices for developing software earlier, with greater customer satisfaction and higher quality, known as the Agile Manifesto:[59]

- customer collaboration during contract negotiation;
- individuals interacting over processes and tools;
- responses to change following a plan; and
- working software prioritized over comprehensive documentation.

The idea is that end user(s) should sit with developers to make decisions on user functionality. High-level requirements are initially prioritized and developed quickly by small teams to get a working product quickly to the customer. Agile methods are typically used for small, low-risk projects. However, some large programs have recently begun to incorporate agile principles to some degree of success, such as using Scrum Sprints as part of their normal software development practices.

DFARS 227.72

Commercial computer software or documentation is normally acquired competitively on a firm-fixed-price basis under the same licenses provided to the public so long as they are consistent with Federal procurement law and satisfy user needs. Offerors and contractors will furnish nontraditional technical information regarding commercial software or documentation only to document the specific modifications made at Government expense to meet the requirements. Except for a transfer of rights that are mutually agreed upon, they need not relinquish to or provide the Government rights to disclose, display, modify, perform, reproduce, release, or use commercial software or related documentation. The specific rights granted to the Government must be specified in the contract license agreement or addendum.

DoD policy is to acquire only the software and documentation, and the rights thereto, necessary to satisfy agency needs. To fulfill this aim, solicitations and contracts must include a list of software or documentation to be delivered under a contract, along with acceptance criteria and delivery schedules. Any offeror or contractor must identify any software or documentation furnished with restrictions on the Government's rights. Separate contract line items are established for the software or documentation to be delivered and require offerors and contractors to price separately each deliverable data item. This requirement may be satisfied by an exhibit to the contract.

Contracting officers should set forth any requirements for multiple users at one site or for multiple site licenses when desired, as well as the format and media in which the software or documentation will be delivered. Prices must be established for each separately priced deliverable item of computer software or documentation under a fixed-price type contract.

License rights for computer software are similar to those for technical data. An irrevocable license is provided by the contractor while retaining all rights in the software or documentation unless granted to the Government or held by a separate licensor. Contractors or licensors may, with some exceptions, restrict the Government's rights to disclose, display, modify, perform, reproduce, release, or use computer software developed exclusively or partially at private expense. However, they may not, without the Government's agreement, restrict the Government's rights in software developed exclusively with Government funds or in computer software documentation required to be delivered under a contract. A contract attachment must identify the software or documentation, the asserted rights category, the basis for the assertion, and the name of the person asserting the restrictions prescribed by the clause.

The determination of the source of funds used to develop computer software should be made at the lowest possible identifiable portion of the software or documentation (e.g., a software sub-routine that performs a specific function). Contractors may assert restricted rights in a segregable portion of software which otherwise qualifies for restricted rights.

Contractors are not required to provide the Government additional rights in computer software delivered or otherwise provided to the Government with restricted rights. When the Government has a need for additional rights, it must negotiate with the contractor to transfer such rights and list them in a license agreement made part of the contract. Once agreement is reached and the contract is executed, the Government has rights in any computer software, documentation, or portions thereof that the contractor subsequently uses to prepare derivative software or includes in other software or documentation. The Government retains the rights it obtained under the development contract in the unmodified portions of the derivative software or documentation.

Computer software that is a component of a weapon (sub)system should be warranted as part of the weapon system warranty. Approval of the chief of the contracting office must be obtained to use a computer software warranty other than a weapon system warranty. Once obtained, DFARS 252.246-7001, Warranty of Data, and its alternates, may be appropriately modified for use with computer software, or else a procurement-specific clause may be developed.

Just like technical data, software or documentation may be released or disclosed to foreign contractors, governments, or organizations only if release or disclosure is otherwise permitted both by Federal export controls and other national security laws or regulations. DoD may release or disclose software or documentation in which it has obtained unlimited rights to such foreign entities. But it cannot authorize the use or release of such software or documentation for which restrictions have been asserted by the contractor unless the intended recipient is subject to the same provisions as included in the use and nondisclosure agreement.

There is no specific contract clause governing the Government's rights in commercial software or documentation (there are clauses for noncommercial software, however) because the circumstances are specific to the situation. This is why a license agreement is essential.

DFARS 227.7203

A contractor cannot incorporate a third party's copyrighted software into a deliverable software item unless the contractor has obtained an appropriate license for the Government and any others acting on the Government's behalf, or else has obtained the contracting officer's written approval to do so. Approval to use third-party copyrighted software without a copyright license can only be granted when the Government's requirements cannot be satisfied without the third-party material or when the use of the material will result in cost savings to the Government which outweigh the lack of a copyright license.

A contractor who desires to restrict the Government's rights in computer software or documentation will place restrictive markings on the software or documentation, or else provide instructions to place restrictive markings. Software or related documentation delivered without restrictive markings is presumed to have been delivered with unlimited rights and may be released or disclosed without restriction. When it is anticipated that the software will or may be used in combat or situations which simulate combat conditions, contractors may not insert instructions into computer programs that interfere with or delay operation of the software to display a restrictive rights legend or other license notice.

An offeror's or contractor's assertion(s) of restrictions on the Government's rights to disclose, display, modify, perform, reproduce, release, or use software or documentation do not, by themselves, determine the extent of the Government's rights. The Government may require an offeror or contractor to submit sufficient information to permit evaluation of an asserted restriction and may challenge its validity. However, a need for additional license rights is not, by itself, a sufficient basis for requesting information concerning an asserted restriction.

As with data rights, the Government may transact matters directly with a subcontractor or supplier at any tier, without creating or implying privity of contract. It will permit a subcontractor or supplier to transact challenge and validation matters directly whenever a subcontractor's or supplier's business interests in its technical data would be compromised if the data were disclosed to a higher-tier contractor. The Government will also consider a direct challenge if the contractor will not respond in a timely manner to a challenge and an untimely response would jeopardize a subcontractor's or supplier's right to assert restrictions, or whenever requested to do so by a subcontractor or supplier.

To avoid delaying competitive procurements, the contracting officer will avoid challenging asserted restrictions prior to a competitive contract award unless resolution of the assertion is essential for successful completion of the procurement.

Asserted restrictions should be reviewed before acceptance of the computer software deliverable under a contract. The Government's right to challenge an assertion expires three years after final payment under the contract or three years after delivery of the software, whichever is later. Those limitations on the Government's challenge rights do not apply to software that is publicly available, or has been furnished to the Government without restrictions.

Contracting officers must have reasonable grounds to challenge the current validity of an asserted restriction. They may request the person asserting a restriction to furnish a written explanation of the facts and supporting documentation for the assertion in sufficient detail to demonstrate the validity of the assertion. Additional supporting documentation may be requested when the explanation provided by that person does not, in the contracting officer's opinion, establish the validity of the assertion. Challenges must be in writing and issued to the person asserting the restriction. The contracting officer may extend the time for response contained in a challenge if the contractor requests and justifies an extension.

Contracting officers must promptly issue a final decision denying or sustaining the validity of each challenged assertion unless the parties have agreed on the disposition of the assertion. When a final decision denying the validity of an asserted restriction is made following a timely response to a challenge, the Government is obligated to continue to respect the asserted restrictions through final disposition of any appeal unless the agency head notifies the person asserting the restriction that urgent or compelling circumstances do not permit the Government to continue to respect the asserted restriction. A contracting officer's final decision, or actions of an agency Board of Contract Appeals or a Federal court, is necessary to sustain the validity of an asserted restriction.

When more than one contracting officer challenges an asserted restriction, the contracting officer who made the earliest challenge is responsible for coordinating the Government challenges. That contracting officer will consult with all other contracting officers making challenges, verify that all challenges apply to the same asserted restriction and, after consulting with the (sub)contractor or supplier asserting the restriction, issue a schedule that provides that person a reasonable opportunity to respond to each challenge.

DFARS 227.7103

The contracting officer may require the delivery of data identified as "deferred delivery" data or computer software at any time until two years after acceptance by the Government of all items (other than technical data or computer software) under the contract or contract termination, whichever is later. The obligation of subcontractors or suppliers to deliver such data expires two years after the date the prime contractor accepts the last item from the subcontractor or supplier for use in the performance of the contract. The contract must specify the computer software or documentation that is subject to deferred delivery. The contracting officer must notify the contractor sufficiently in advance of the desired delivery date for such software or documentation to permit timely delivery.

If no firm requirement for computer software or documentation has been established at time of contract award, yet is nonetheless possible and to be determined at a later date, the contracting officer may order any software or documentation generated in the performance of the (sub)contract thereunder at any time until three years after acceptance of all items (other than technical data or computer software) under the contract or contract termination, whichever is later. When the software or documentation are ordered, the delivery dates must be negotiated and the contractor compensated only for converting the software or documentation into the prescribed form and delivery and reproduction costs.

Solicitation Provisions

DFARS 252.227-7017, Identification and Assertion of Use, Release, or Disclosure Restrictions, if including DFARS 252.227-7014, Rights in Noncommercial Computer Software and Noncommercial Computer Software Documentation. Offerors must identify any software or documentation for which restrictions (other than copyright) are asserted and to attach the identification and assertion to the offer. The contractor, under certain conditions, may make additional assertions of restrictions.

DFARS 252.227-7028, Technical Data or Computer Software Previously Delivered to the Government, when the resulting contract will require the contractor to deliver computer software or computer software documentation. The provision requires offerors to identify any software or documentation specified in the solicitation as deliverable items that are the same or substantially the same as software or documentation which the offeror has delivered or is obligated to deliver, either as a contractor or subcontractor, under any other Federal contract.

Solicitation Provisions and Contract Clauses

DFARS 252.204-7014, Limitations on the Use or Disclosure of Information by Litigation Support Contractors, for litigation support contractors accessing litigation information.

DFARS 252.227-7013, Rights in Technical Data—Noncommercial Items.

DFARS 252.227-7014, Rights in Noncommercial Computer Software and Noncommercial Computer Software Documentation, when the successful offeror(s) will be required to deliver computer software or related documentation. Do not use the clause when the only deliverable items are technical data (other than computer software documentation), or commercial computer software or commercial computer software documentation. Do not use the clause in architect-engineer and construction contracts unless for construction supplies or related experimental, developmental, or research work, or test and evaluation studies of structures, equipment, processes, or materials. Use the clause with its Alternate I in research contracts when the contracting officer determines, in consultation with counsel, that public dissemination by the contractor would be in the interest of the Government and facilitated by the Government relinquishing its right to publish the work for sale, or to have others publish the work for sale on behalf of the Government.

DFARS 252.227-7016, Rights in Bid or Proposal Information.

DFARS 252.227-7019, Validation of Asserted Restrictions—Computer Software, for the validation of asserted restrictions on the Government's rights to use, release, or disclose computer software.

DFARS 252.227-7025, Limitations on the Use or Disclosure of Government-Furnished Information Marked with Restrictive Legends, when it is anticipated that the Government will provide the contractor (other than a litigation support contractor), for performance of its contract, computer software or computer software documentation marked with another contractor's restrictive legend(s).

DFARS 252.227-7026, Deferred Delivery of Technical Data or Computer Software, when it is in the Government's interests to defer the delivery of computer software or documentation.

DFARS 252.227-7027, Deferred Ordering of Technical Data or Computer Software, when a firm requirement for software or documentation has not been established prior to contract award but there is a potential need for computer software or documentation.

DFARS 252.227-7037, Validation of Restrictive Markings on Technical Data, when the contractor will be required to deliver noncommercial computer software documentation (technical data). Paragraph (e) of the clause contains information that must be included in a formal challenge.

Prime contractors should include the following clauses, without modification except for appropriate identification of the parties, in contracts with subcontractors or suppliers who will be furnishing computer software:

- DFARS 252.227-7014, Rights in Noncommercial Computer Software and Noncommercial Computer Software Documentation;
- DFARS 252.227-7019, Validation of Asserted Restrictions—Computer Software;
- DFARS 252.227-7025, Limitations on the Use or Disclosure of Government Furnished Information Marked with Restrictive Legends; and
- DFARS 252.227-7028, Technical Data or Computer Software Previously Delivered to the Government.

DFARS 252.227-7038, Patent Rights—Ownership by the Contractor (Large Business), instead of FAR 52.227-11, for experimental, developmental, or research work if the contractor is not a small business concern or nonprofit organization and no alternative patent rights clause is used. Use the clause with its Alternate I if the acquisition of patent rights for the benefit of a foreign government is required under a treaty or executive agreement, the agency head determines at the time of award that it would be in the national interest to acquire the right to sublicense foreign governments or international organizations pursuant to any existing or future treaty or agreement, or other rights are necessary to effect a treaty or agreement, in which case Alternate I may be appropriately modified. Use the clause with its Alternate II in long-term contracts if necessary to effect treaty or agreements to be entered into.

DFARS 252.227-7039, Patents—Reporting of Subject Inventions, when containing the clause at FAR 52.227-11, Patent Rights—Ownership by the Contractor.

Contract Clauses

DFARS 252.227-7025, Limitations on the Use or Disclosure of Government-Furnished Information Marked with Restrictive Legends, for contractors accessing third-party proprietary technical data or computer software.

DFARS 252.227-7000, Non-Estoppel.

DFARS 252.227-7001, Release of Past Infringement, may be modified or omitted as appropriate for particular circumstances, but only upon the advice of cognizant patent or legal counsel.

DFARS 252.227-7002, Readjustment of Payments, for payment of a running royalty.

DFARS 252.227-7003, Termination, for the payment of a running royalty. This clause may be modified or omitted as appropriate for particular circumstances, but only upon the advice of cognizant patent or legal counsel.

DFARS 252.227-7004, License Grant, for use in patent release and settlement agreements, and license agreements not providing for payment by the Government of a running royalty

DFARS 252.227-7005, License Term, Alternate I or Alternate II, as appropriate, for use in patent release and settlement agreements, and license agreements not providing for payment by the Government of a running royalty.

1.8.5 Markings

FAR 27.404-5

The Government has the right to return data containing unauthorized markings, or to cancel or ignore the markings. If marking adjustments are necessary to comply with the Freedom of Information Act, the Government must notify the contractor in writing and allow 60 days to respond substantiating the validity of the markings. If the final decision is negative, the markings will be canceled or ignored and the data released from disclosure prohibitions, unless the contractor files suit within 90 days.

Data delivered without a limited rights or restricted rights notice or copyright notice is presumed to have been delivered with unlimited rights as to disclosure, reproduction or use. A *copyright* protects an author from another party copying or using his/her creative works without permission. This prohibition includes modifying content into a derivative work or distributing copies of the work without permission. A copyright is valid for the life of the author plus 70 years. However, within six months the contractor may request permission to place the omitted notice on qualifying data at its own expense. The contracting officer may permit adding a notice if the contractor identifies the data affected, demonstrates that its omission was inadvertent, and establishes that use of the proposed notice if authorized. The contracting officer may permit correction, at the contractor's expense, of incorrect notices.

Contracting officers may obtain the right to inspect data at the contractor's facility to verify a contractor's assertion regarding the limited rights or restricted rights status of the data, or for evaluating work performance under the contract. This right may be exercised up to three years after acceptance of all items to be delivered under the contract.

DFARS 227.7103-13

If a contractor delivers any data it wishes to be proprietary, it must mark it with a legend indicating the level of rights it believes the Government should have. If the contracting officer notifies the contractor that restrictive markings are not in the format or language authorized by the contract, the contractor has 60 days to remove or correct the markings. Other format inconsistencies noted by the contracting officer may include restrictive markings that do not conform to the marking instructions of the data rights clauses, are applied to technical data related to a noncommercial item or computer software or documentation, or are inconsistent with the contractor's data rights assertions. If the contractor fails to act, the Government can correct, ignore, or remove the marking(s).

Under 10 U.S.C. 2321, the Government has the right to challenge asserted restrictions when there are reasonable grounds to question the validity of the assertion and continued adherence would make it impractical to later procure competitively the item. This includes restrictive markings that are in the appropriate format but not justified (i.e., restrictive markings that purport to provide lesser rights than the government is entitled to under the contract). Since the challenge could significantly delay awards, they are not typical prior to a competitive award unless resolution of the assertion is essential for successful completion of the procurement. Nor does the contracting officer challenge a contractor's assertion that a commercial item was developed exclusively at private expense unless the Government financially contributed to development of that item.

Contracting officers normally presume that a commercial item was developed exclusively at private expense regardless of whether a (sub)contractor submits a justification when challenged. A (sub)contractor's failure to respond to the challenge notice cannot be the sole basis for denying the validity of an asserted restriction.

A contracting officer may challenge an asserted restriction on technical data for a major weapon (sub)system or component thereof on the basis that the technology was not developed exclusively at private expense. The presumption applies to a commercial subsystem or component of a major weapon system that was acquired as a commercial item and any other component that is a commercially available off-the-shelf item (including modifications thereto). Information provided by the (sub)contractor must demonstrate that the item was developed exclusively at private expense in order to overcome the challenge.

Asserted restrictions are reviewed before acceptance of technical data deliverable under the contract. Assertions must be challenged within three years after final payment under the contract or three years after delivery of the data, whichever is later. However, restrictive markings may be challenged at any time if the technical data are publicly available without restrictions, unless they result from a release or disclosure due to the sale or transfer of either its assets or interest in the technical data to another party or business entity.

The contracting officer may request the person asserting a restriction to explain in writing the facts and supporting documentation for the assertion. If the person asserting the restriction fails to respond to the contracting officer's request for information or additional supporting documentation, or if the information submitted does not justify the asserted restriction, a challenge will be considered.

The Government may transact these matters directly with a subcontractor at any tier without creating privity of contract concerns. Contracting officers should permit a subcontractor or supplier to transact challenge and validation matters directly with the Government upon request or when a subcontractor's or supplier's business interests in its technical data would be compromised if the data were disclosed to a higher-tier contractor. Likewise, a direct challenge is permitted when there is reason to believe that the contractor will not respond in a timely manner to a challenge and an untimely response would jeopardize a subcontractor's or supplier's right to assert restrictions.

Challenge notices must be in writing and issued to the contractor or the person asserting the restriction. The contracting officer may extend the time for response contained in a challenge notice if the contractor submits a timely written request showing the need for additional time to prepare a response.

Contracting officers must issue a final decision for each challenged assertion, whether or not justified, within 60 days of the challenge, or any extension to that time granted by the contracting officer. If the approved restriction was asserted after submission of the contractor's offer, (s)he adds the asserted restriction to the contract attachment. A contracting officer who determines that the validity of an asserted restriction has not been justified will issue a contracting officer's final decision. However, the Government must abide by the marking if within 90 days the contractor provides notice that it will appeal the final decision to the Armed Services Board of Contract Appeals, or files suit in the Court of Federal Claims within 12 months. If an appeal or suit is filed in an appropriate court, the Government must still abide by the marking until final disposition by the Board or Court. The Government will only be excused from abiding by the markings if the agency head notifies the person asserting the restriction that urgent or compelling circumstances do not permit the Government to continue to respect the asserted restriction.

As with assertions of limited rights in computer software or documentation, when more than one contracting officer challenges an asserted marking restriction, the contracting officer who made the earliest challenge is responsible for coordinating the Government challenges. That contracting officer shall consult with all other contracting officers making challenges, verify that all challenges apply to the same asserted restriction and, after consulting with the (sub)contractor or supplier asserting the restriction, issue a schedule that provides that person a reasonable opportunity to respond to each challenge.

DFARS 227.7103-10

Technical data delivered or otherwise provided under a contract without restrictive markings is presumed to have been delivered with unlimited rights and may be released or disclosed without restriction. If a contractor has requested permission to correct an inadvertent omission of markings, the Government cannot release or disclose the technical data pending evaluation of the request. A contractor may request permission to have appropriate legends placed on unmarked technical data at its expense. The request must be received by the contracting officer within six months following the furnishing or delivery of such data, or any extension of that time approved by the contracting officer. The requestor must identify the technical data that should have been marked, demonstrate that the omission of the marking was inadvertent, justify that the proposed marking conforms with the requirements for the marking of technical data, and acknowledge that the Government has no liability for any disclosure, reproduction or use of the technical data made prior to the correction of the marking. Contracting officers should grant permission to mark only if the technical data were not distributed outside the Government or were distributed with restrictions on further use or disclosure.

The contracting officer should return technical data bearing nonconforming markings to the person who has placed the markings to provide an opportunity to correct or strike the marking at that person's expense. If that person fails to correct the nonconformity and return the corrected data within 60 days after receipt of the data, the contracting officer may correct or strike the nonconformity at that person's expense. When it is impracticable to return technical data for correction, contracting officers may unilaterally correct any nonconforming markings at Government expense. Prior to correction, the data may be used in accordance with the proper restrictive marking.

An authorized marking is nonetheless deemed unjustified if it does not accurately depict restrictions applicable to the Government's rights to disclose, display, modify, perform, reproduce, release, or use the marked technical data. A common example is a limited rights legend placed on technical data pertaining to items or processes that were developed under a Government contract, with some or all effort funded by the Government, where the Government obtains unlimited or government purpose rights.

At any time during performance of a contract and notwithstanding existence of a challenge, the contracting officer and the person who has asserted a restrictive marking may agree that the restrictive marking is not justified. Upon such agreement, the contracting officer may strike or correct the unjustified marking at that person's expense or else return the technical data to the person asserting the restriction for correction at that person's expense. The same time limit as in nonconforming markings applies.

DFARS 227.7203-11

A (sub)contractor that will deliver software or related documentation with other than unlimited rights will establish and follow written procedures to assure that restrictive markings are used only when authorized. They must maintain records sufficient to justify the validity of markings that assert restrictions to disclose, display, modify, perform, release, reproduce, or use.

Solicitation Provision and Contract Clause

DFARS 252.227-7037, Validation of Restrictive Markings on Technical Data, when using FAR Part 12 procedures to acquire commercial items that include either DFARS 252.227-7015 or 252.227-7013.

Contract Clauses

DFARS 252.227-7017, Identification and Assertion of Use, Release, or Disclosure Restrictions.

DFARS 252.227-7037, Validation of Restrictive Markings on Technical Data.

1.8.6 Special and Existing Works

FAR 27.405-1

The contract may specify the purposes and conditions (including time limitations) under which data for special works may be used, released or reproduced for noncontract performance. *Special works* include:

- agency histories;
- data whose release could prejudice follow-on acquisitions or agency enforcement or regulatory activities;
- development of computer software programs that may give a commercial advantage or are agency-mission sensitive;
- investigatory reports;

- motion pictures or television recordings and scripts;
- musical compositions and sound tracks;
- personally identifiable information whose disclosure would violate the right of privacy;
- reports and books not involving research, development or experimental work;
- surveys of Government establishments; and
- works instructing Government officers and employees about their official duties.

As a rule, the contractor must indemnify the Government against any liability incurred as the result of any violation of copyrights, libel, right of privacy or publicity, or trade secrets due to any data production or compilation performed for Government use. However, this position is subject to negotiation or modification. For instance, the contracting officer may delete Government copyright assignment of data that was produced under the contract. When special works are produced for a public purpose rather than the Government use, agencies may modify the clause with other data rights provisions that meet mission needs yet still protect freedom of speech and expression, and the creator's artistic license.

Commercial computer software and documentation is acquired under licenses customarily provided to the public consistent with Federal law and needs. However, a vendor's standard commercial lease, license or purchase agreement may be directed to commercial sales and therefore may not be appropriate for Government contracts. Hence, the contract terms take precedence over the vendor's standard commercial agreement.

DFARS 227.7105

A contractor may not incorporate into a special work any content copyrighted by others without the contracting officer's permission to do so, provided it obtains for the Government the same license as for existing works, and to permit others to do so for Government purposes. Permission may be granted only when the Government's requirements cannot be satisfied unless the third-party work is included in the deliverable work. Special works can include collections of data containing information pertaining to individuals that, if disclosed, would violate the right of privacy or publicity of the individuals to whom the information relates.

Existing works are media recordings that were not first created, developed, generated, originated, prepared, or produced under a Government contract. Therefore, the Government must obtain a license in the work if it intends to reproduce it, distribute copies, prepare derivative works, or perform or display it publicly. When the Government is not responsible for the content of an existing work, it should require the copyright owner to indemnify the Government for liabilities that may arise out of the content, disclosure performance, or use of such data. Examples of existing works include:

- audiovisual works;
- choreographic works and pantomimes;
- motion pictures;
- musical, dramatic, and literary works;
- pictorial and graphic works;
- sculptures;
- sound recordings; and
- television and video recordings.

The Government, and others acting on its behalf, receive a paid-up, nonexclusive, irrevocable, worldwide license to reproduce, prepare derivative works and publicly perform or display the works called for by a contract and to authorize others to do so for Government purposes. No clause is required to acquire existing works such as books, magazines and periodicals, in any storage or retrieval medium, provided the Government will not reproduce them or prepare derivative works.

The contract may specify the purposes and conditions (including time limitations) under which the data may be used, released, or reproduced by the contractor for other than contract performance. Contracts for production of audiovisual works and sound recordings may include limitations in talent releases and music licenses. The contractor retains use and disclosure rights in that work. If the Government needs to restrict a contractor's rights to use or disclose a special work, it must also negotiate a special license which specifically restricts the contractor's use or disclosure rights.

DFARS 227.7203-16

The rules for overseas contracts with foreign sources and for special works are the same as for technical data. The Government should obtain rights to the computer software and/or documentation that are not less than the rights the Government would have obtained under the software rights clause(s) for a comparable procurement performed within the United States or its outlying areas.

Solicitation Provisions and Contract Clauses

FAR 52.227-17, Rights in Data—Special Works, if primarily to produce or compile data (other than limited rights data or restricted computer software) for the Government's internal use, when there is a specific need to limit data distribution and use, or to obtain indemnity for liabilities that may arise out of the data content, disclosure, or performance. Use the clause if existing works are to be edited, modified, or translated.

FAR 52.227-18, Rights in Data—Existing Works, if exclusively for existing audiovisual and similar works without any modification. The contract may need to address any reproduction rights to be acquired.

DFARS 252.227-7020, Rights in Special Works, for modified existing works in lieu of DFARS 252.227-7021, Rights in Data—Existing Works. Use where the Government has a specific need to control the distribution of works first created or generated in the performance of a contract and required to be delivered under that contract. This includes controlling distribution by obtaining an assignment of copyright, or a specific need to obtain indemnity for liabilities that may arise out of the disclosure, display, modification, performance, reproduction, release, or use of such works. Use the clause in lieu of DFARS 252.227-7013, Rights in Technical Data—Noncommercial Items, when the Government must own or control copyright in all works first produced, created, or generated and required to be delivered under a contract. Use in addition to DFARS 252.227-7013, Rights in Technical Data—Noncommercial Items, when the Government must own or control copyright in a portion of a work first produced, created, or generated and required to be delivered under a contract. The specific portion in which the Government owns or controls copyright must be identified in a special contract requirement.

DFARS 252.227-7021, Rights in Data—Existing Works, in lieu of DFARS 252.227-7013, Rights in Technical Data—Noncommercial Items, when exclusively for existing works which the Government will acquire without modification; requires the right to reproduce, prepare derivative works, or publicly perform or display the existing works; or has a specific need to obtain indemnity for liabilities that may arise out of the content, performance, use, or disclosure of such data.

Contract Clause

DFARS 252.227-7032, Rights in Technical Data and Computer Software (Foreign), may be used in contracts with foreign contractors to be performed overseas, except Canadian purchases, in lieu of DFARS 252.227-7014, Rights in Noncommercial Computer Software and Noncommercial Computer Software Documentation, when the Government requires the unrestricted right to use, modify, reproduce, release, perform, display, or disclose all computer software or computer software documentation to be delivered under the contract. Do not use the clause in contracts for special works.

1.8.7 Data Acquisition

FAR 27.406

Data deliverables may include drawings, manuals, and reports. Data activities such as cataloging, maintenance and updating, preparation, reformatting, and storage are expensive for both the Government and the contractor. Hence, contract data requirements must be minimized, and may even be assessed by a data requirements review board prior to solicitation to ensure their necessity and propriety. The contract must specify the data to be delivered because data rights clauses address only the respective rights of the Government and contractor regarding the data use, disclosure, or reproduction. To accomplish this, the contracting officer specifies in separate contract line items all known data requirements, including the place and time for delivery and any restrictions for data handling. These items are spelled out in a *contract data requirements list* that is attached to the contract, and includes specifications for writing the data and delivery instructions. Typically, this list is DD Form 1423. Specifications may be written in local format or entered on a DD Form 1664. The contract may identify and specify which data is to be delivered with unrestricted rights and which with limited rights. As a rule, listed data may be ordered any time up to three years after final acceptance. The contractor is entitled to reimbursement for converting data into the prescribed format.

Form, fit and function data may be solicited with unlimited rights (instead of the usual limited or restricted rights) for the offeror to price out. To minimize storage costs for data retention, the contracting officer may relieve the contractor of retention requirements. The contracting officer may also permit the contractor to identify any data which is not necessary to meet the Government's requirements and therefore should not be ordered. The Government will then review such identification to determine its necessity.

If the Government wishes to acquire unlimited rights to technical data contained in a winning proposal, the offeror may specifically identify proposal pages containing technical data to be excluded from the grant of unlimited rights. Any excluded commercial, financial or technical information in the proposal will be used for evaluation purposes only.

The contracting officer reviews any delivered technical data included on a contract data requirements list, and the contractor's declaration that the data are complete, accurate and compliant with contract requirements. If (s)he finds to the contrary, the contracting officer requests the contractor to correct the deficiencies, and may withhold payment until the data delivery requirements have been met.

A number of contracts will not utilize standard data acquisition rights. Cosponsored research and development effort may include a clause providing for less than unlimited rights if authorized. Contracts for existing data or commercial software and production of special works have their own unique contract clauses. Contracts for small business innovation research grant the Government limited rights for four years after final acceptance, then unlimited rights under a paid-up license thereafter. Agencies are free to develop their own clauses for architect-engineer services or construction, or for contract performance outside the United States (neither circumstance has a prescribed clause). Similarly, no standard clause is required (but can be developed) to design, construct, manage, or operate a Government-owned facility to perform research, development, or production work.

Some contracts involve co-sponsored research and development where the contractor contributes funds (by cost-sharing or repayment of nonrecurring costs) but cannot segregate Government contributions to any item or process developed or produced under the contract. In such cases, the contracting officer may limit the acquisition of, or acquire limited rights to, any data developed and delivered under the contract. These lesser rights must still assure that the data is used for agreed-to Governmental purposes (and perhaps also reprocurement rights), and must address any disclosure limitations or restrictions imposed on the data. The contractor could be required to directly license others to meet the contract objectives. On the other hand, if the contractor's contributions are identified in the contract and can be segregated by performance requirements and contract funding, then any resulting data may be treated as limited rights data or restricted computer software.

Solicitation Provisions and Contract Clauses

FAR 52.227-14, Rights in Data—General, in solicitations and contracts where data will be produced or acquired, except for the special cases outlined above. Use the clause with its Alternate I if an agency determines to adopt the alternate definition of "Limited Rights Data." Use the clause with its Alternate II if a contracting officer determines to obtain limited rights data and specify any purposes for which limited rights data are to be disclosed outside the Government. Use the clause with its Alternate III if a contracting officer determines it is necessary to obtain restricted computer software, specifying any greater or lesser rights regarding the use, reproduction, or disclosure of restricted computer software than those set forth in the Restricted Rights Notice. Use the clause with its Alternate IV in contracts for basic or applied research (other than for the management or operation of Government facilities or programs being conducted at those facilities, or where international agreements require otherwise) to be performed solely by universities and colleges (the contract may exclude items or categories of data from the permission granted). Use the clause with its Alternate V if the Government needs the right to inspect certain data at a contractor's facility.

FAR 52.227-15, Representation of Limited Rights Data and Restricted Computer Software, in any solicitation containing the clause at 52.227-14, Rights in Data—General, if the contracting officer desires to have an offeror state in response to a solicitation whether limited rights data or restricted computer software are likely to be used in meeting the data delivery requirements set forth in the solicitation.

FAR 52.227-16, Additional Data Requirements, for experimental, developmental, research, or demonstration work. Do not use for basic or applied research to be performed solely by a university or college. The contract amount must be $500,000 or less, unless all the requirements for data are believed to be known at the time of contracting and specified in the contract.

FAR 52.227-23, Rights to Proposal Data (Technical), if a contracting officer desires to acquire unlimited rights in technical data contained in a successful proposal upon which a contract award is based.

Contract Clauses

FAR 52.227-20, Rights in Data—SBIR Program, in all Phase I, II and III contracts awarded under the Small Business Innovation Research Program.

FAR 52.227-21, Technical Data Declaration, Revision, and Withholding of Payment—Major Systems, for major systems acquisitions or their support. This includes detailed design, development or production of a major system or any individual component, part, (sub)assembly, subsystem, or spare part integral to the major system.[60] The subject technical data is specified in the contract.

1.8.8 Royalties

FAR 27.202

A *royalty* is a right delegated to an individual or corporation by the Government (hence the name, since it is a sovereign entity) to share in the profit or product reserved by the grantor. A royalty is a payment to the holder of a copyright, patent, or trademark for its use under a Federal contract. This would include payments made to an author or composer for a sold work or to an inventor for each sold patented item.

In contrast, a *trademark* is a distinctive indicator, such as a design or logo, used by an individual or firm to identify its products or services to consumers, and to distinguish them from competitors. The owner of a registered trademark may sue for infringement to prevent unauthorized use, but registration is not required if it is used only in a certain geographical area. If not used over a five-year period, the owner loses his/her legal standing.

If the proposal includes a charge for royalties, the contracting officer forwards the information to the cognizant patent office for advice. The contracting officer must take care to avoid paying royalties to which the Government has a royalty-free license, or at a rate greater than which the Government is licensed, or if they are improperly charged. Hence, the contracting officer may request a copy of the license, and the contractor may need to redact any confidential information before furnishing a copy.

When the Government is obligated to pay a royalty on a patent because of an existing license agreement and the contracting officer believes that the licensed patent applies to a prospective contract, the solicitation includes notice of the license, patent number and royalty rate cited in the license. The solicitation requires an offeror to state if it is the patent owner or licensee. The Government may either evaluate an offeror's price by adding an amount equal to the royalty, or else negotiate a price reduction with an offeror who is licensed under the same patent at a lower royalty rate.

Agencies provide necessary policy and procedures regarding foreign technical assistance agreements and license agreements involving intellectual property, including avoiding unnecessary royalty charges.

Solicitation Provisions

FAR 52.227-6, Royalty Information, in a negotiated solicitation for which royalty information is desired and cost or pricing data are obtained. It can be used in sealed bid solicitations only if the need for such information is approved at a level above the contracting officer to properly protect the Government's interests. Use the provision with its Alternate I if the solicitation is for communication services and facilities by a common carrier.

FAR 52.227-7, Patents—Notice of Government Licensee, if the Government is obligated to pay a royalty on a patent involved in the prospective contract. Otherwise, the contracting officer may require offerors to provide information sufficient to provide this notice to the other offerors.

Solicitation Provision and Contract Clause

FAR 52.227-9, Refund of Royalties, in negotiated fixed-price solicitations and contracts when royalties may be paid. The clause may be used in cost-reimbursement contracts with agency approval of royalties to protect the Government's interests.

1.9 CONTRACTOR TAX LIABILITY

FAR 29.4

Generally, Federal contractors need not pay direct taxes for contract performance. However, a Federal contractor performing overseas or directly for a foreign government may need to bear tax payments if so required by the host nation. Specific contract clause coverage will be necessary.

The Federal Government is not exempt from Federal excise taxes imposed on purchasing:

- ammunition and firearms;
- coal;
- fishing equipment;
- heating and motor fuels; and
- motor vehicle tires.

In these cases, prices are solicited on a tax-exclusive basis, or else justified on a tax-inclusive basis. However, excise taxes are not imposed for:

- a nonprofit educational institution;
- emergency vehicles;
- export to a foreign country or distant U.S. possession within six months;
- resale or further manufacture (however, tires or inner tubes are still subject to excise tax);
- the exclusive use of a state or territory (or the District of Columbia); or
- use as fuel or stores onboard a war vessel (including aircraft and guided missiles bought on a tax-exclusive basis).

The Federal Government is exempt from a communications usage tax, and from the federal highway vehicle users tax if the vehicle is owned or leased by the Federal Government.

Federal purchases and leases are generally exempt from state or local taxes, although exemption forms may need to be filled out and filed. However, the law of agency does not apply to contractors, so subcontractors may be subject to state or local taxation. Also, because equipment rental contracts involve contractor-owned equipment, the possibility of property and usage taxes occurs.

The state of North Carolina has a unique law that authorizes local governments to be reimbursed by the state government for sales and use taxes paid on equipment and materials included in any building construction, alteration, or repair. The Federal Government is entitled to such a refund but must formally request it through a contractor-certified statement for property purchase and withdrawal.

The New Mexico Gross Receipts and Compensating Tax applies to cost-reimbursement contracts for services performed in whole or in part within the state. If the contractor acquires personal property as a direct cost and passes title to the U.S. Government, then the tax payment is an allowable cost.

Contract Clauses

FAR 52.229-1, State and Local Taxes, for leased equipment under a fixed-price indefinite-delivery contract, within the United States or its outlying areas, but unspecified at time of award.

FAR 52.229-2, North Carolina State and Local Sales and Use Tax, for construction to be performed in North Carolina. Use Alternate I for vessel repair.

FAR 52.229-3, Federal, State, and Local Taxes, for fixed-price contracts exceeding the simplified acquisition threshold and performed within the United States or its outlying areas.

FAR 52.229-4, Federal, State, and Local Taxes (State and Local Adjustments), instead of FAR 52.229-3, for noncompetitive contracts to avoid contingency pricing for postaward changes in state or local taxes.

FAR 52.229-6, Taxes—Foreign Fixed-Price Contracts, for fixed-price contracts exceeding the simplified acquisition threshold to be performed in a foreign country by a commercial firm.

FAR 52.229-7, Taxes—Fixed-Price Contracts with Foreign Governments, for fixed-price contracts that exceed the simplified acquisition threshold issued directly to a foreign government.

FAR 52.229-8, Taxes—Foreign Cost-Reimbursement Contracts, for cost-reimbursement contracts to be performed in a foreign country, unless contracting directly with a foreign government.

FAR 52.229-9, Taxes—Cost-Reimbursement Contracts with Foreign Governments.

FAR 52.229-10, State of New Mexico Gross Receipts and Compensating Tax.

NOTES

1. A *system* is defined in this book as a combination of elements that interact to achieve a specific purpose.

2. The official name is "An Act for Prevention of Frauds and Perjuries." It can be found at http://www.british-history.ac.uk/statutes-realm/vol5/pp839-842, Institute of Historical Research, London, United Kingdom. The original publication is *Statutes*

of the Realm: Volume 5, 1628–80, Great Britain Record Commission, South London, United Kingdom, 1819.

3. The American Law Institute and the National Conference of Commissioners on Uniform State Laws, *Uniform Commercial Code*, Thomson West, Eagan, MN, 2014. A readily available location to access the UCC is https://www.law.cornell.edu/ucc.

4. References to sections in UCC will be designated by the section symbol §.

5. These states are Maryland and Virginia. Further information can be found at http://www.ucitaonline.com. However, since it has no bearing on Federal contracting, UCITA will not be discussed further in this book.

6. UCC § 1-302 and 305.

7. A condition precedent can also be a specific event that must occur in order for a party's right to become enforceable.

8. In a court of law, to make tender in a timely manner is said to be *seasonable*; however this term is not used in Federal contracting.

9. If the precise amount of advance payments or liabilities is unknown at the time of the issue of the receipt, then a statement that they have been incurred and their purpose suffices.

10. This approach is stated in *Russell v. Farley*, 105 US 433 (1881): "[w]here no bond or undertaking has been required . . . the court has no power to award damages sustained by either party in consequence of the litigation, except by making such a decree in reference to the costs of the suit as it may deem equitable and just." All legal citations are from Government Printing Office, *United States Reports*, Washington, D.C. In this particular citation, the decision was handed down in year 105 of our nation and the case begins on page 433 of that volume.

11. 28 U.S.C. 2412.

12. 31 U.S.C. 3729.

13. 42 U.S.C. 1320.

14. 15 U.S.C. 1.

15. *Addyston Pipe and Steel Co. v. U.S.*, 175 U.S. 211 (1899).

16. 15 U.S.C. 12.

17. 15 U.S.C. 13.

18. 15 U.S.C. 78.

19. The official term in the UCC is *lease contract*; however, the common term will be used in this book.

20. As used in this book, *process* means a group of tasks that are sequential and logically related to provide a product or service, either to a customer or to another organization of the firm.

21. 375 US 954.

22. U.S. Constitution, Article I, Section 8, paragraph 18.

23. U.S. Constitution, Article II, Section 3, Clause 4.

24. *Skidmore v. Swift & Co.*, 65 S.Ct. 161, and *American Telephone and Telegraph Co, v, United States*, 57 S.Ct. 170.

25. 41 U.S.C. 251, *et seq.*

26. 31 U.S.C. 1352, as amended at 41 U.S.C. 410.

27. FAR is printed in the Code of Federal Regulations, Title 48, Chapter 1, and available online at www.acquisition.gov/?q=browsefar and in print from the Government Printing Office. The current edition was published in 2020. This regulation will be cited throughout this book.

28. OMB is responsible for developing and issuing Government-wise guidance on management processes, such as procurement, and to recommend and monitor funding levels.

29. Both Justice and Housing have lower levels of contract awards than other Cabinet Departments (in part because they issue many grants to local agencies), and therefore do not pursue acquisition regulatory matters as vigorously.

30. DFARS is available at http://www.acq.osd.mil/asda/dpc/pcf/index.html. Additional citations are https://www.acquisition.gov/dfars is the DAU website. https://www.acq.osd.mil/DPAP/dars/dfarspgi/current/index.html is the Defense Dept. site.

31. The legislation that created NASA provided it with authority to write its own procurement regulation. NASA procurement policies follows DoD regulations very closely. So when it came time for NASA to select which Council to sit on, it found more in common with the DAR Council, and thereby gained a seat at its table. Nonetheless, DoD in no way controls NASA's procurement procedures.

32. 44 U.S.C. 3501, *et seq.*

33. 5 U.S.C. 601, *et seq.*

34. See https://aaf.dau.edu/guidebooks.

35. DoDI 5000.02, Operation of the Defense Acquisition System, is available at https://www.dau.mil/guidebooks/Shared%20Documents%20HTML/DoDI%205000.02.aspx. DFARS and PGI are available at https://www.acq.osd.mil/dpap/dars/dfarspgi/current/index.html. DAG, Directive 5000.02 and PGI will be cited recurringly in this book.

36. At the time of this publication, the United States Space Force remains part of the Department of the Air Force, without its own departmental structure.

37. For further information, see DoD Instruction 5000.72, DoD Standard for Contracting Officer's Representative (COR) Certification.

38. 10 UCC 87. See also 10 U.S.C. 1724.

39. The college education requirement does not apply in a contingency contracting environment or for a three-year developmental position.

40. https://www.acquisition.gov

41. Certain entities do not have CAGE codes, so they receive a unique entity identifier. These are usually foreign entities who never perform within the US Foreign Service, or else are an individual student or dependent of a foreign service or military member.There is no allowance for a whistleblower to obtain part of any penalty imposed by a court, as would be the case in a *qui tam* action, where the claimant sues on behalf of both the Government and self to assert a right or demand.

42. Due to the confusion between both CAGE codes and DUNS numbers, the SAM process now permits companies with a CAGE code to bypass the DUNS process. However, the time and heavy demand involved with getting a CAGE code have made this process very confusing for small businesses. Time will sort out this problem.

43. https://www.fpds.gov.

44. Contract deficiencies are listed at http://www.acq.osd.mil/dpap/pdi/eb/procurement_data_standard.html.

45. There is no allowance for a whistleblower to obtain part of any penalty imposed by a court, as would be the case in a *qui tam* action, where the claimant sues on behalf of both the Government and self to assert a right or demand.

46. DFARS 203.1003.

47. 10 USC 2409.

48. Exceptions are concession sales or examining vouchers and invoices, which are not considered to be inherently Governmental in nature..

49. Article I, section 9, clause 7.

50. This is also known as *earmarking* or, more colloquially, *pork barrel politics*. The rise of several political movements could challenge the future of this political tradition.

51. 15 U.S.C. 1431.

52. Federal Information Processing Standards Publication (FIPS PUB) Number 201, "Personal Identity Verification of Federal Employees and Contractors", National Institute of Standards and Technology, Gaithersburg, MD, 2013. See also Office of Management and Budget (OMB) Guidance M-05-24, "Implementation of Homeland Security Presidential Directive (HSPD) 12-Policy for a Common Identification Standard for Federal Employees and Contractors," OMB, Washington, DC, August 5, 2005.

53. 5 U.S.C. 552a.

54. 5 U.S.C. 552.

55. This includes any variety of plant that is or may be protectable under the Plant Variety Protection Act (7 U.S.C. 2321, *et seq.*). A plant variety is made when it has been reproduced with recognized characteristics. Yes, a person really can patent a plant!

56. At the time of this writing, this topic is being quietly discussed in Congress for use by the National Institute of Health to control drug prices, but not yet introduced as legislation.

57. An excellent research paper on this subject is "Development of an Intellectual Property Strategy: Research Notes to Support Department of Defense Programs" from the Software Engineering Institute.

58. The agreement is posted at DFARS 227.7103-7(c).

59. See http://agilemanifesto.org for further details.

60. An *assembly* or *assemblage* is a collection of items designed to accomplish a general function and both identified and issued as a single item.

Chapter 2

Planning

2.1 MARKETING AND RESEARCH

2.1.1 Strategizing

Marketing is the process by which a firm decides what products or services are of interest and value to current and potential customers, and then induces demand to buy those products or services. Marketing identifies a customer base and its needs and wants. In this way, a firm decides what steps are necessary to satisfy and retain a prospective customer, and how to do so better than its competitors. This effort is absolutely necessary for its growth and survival.

The firm must review the findings from its marketing efforts to develop a target customer base. It will then develop a *marketing strategy* to enable it to focus resources on the most likely sales targets and obtain a competitive advantage within the marketplace. For example, creating the Department of Homeland Security led to many Federal contractors identifying it as a new market target and revenue source. The birth of the Space Force has created another wave of marketing effort. This strategy is the basis for a *marketing plan* of specific actions and tactics to reach these goals.

Marketing strategies may differ with each firm's needs, but most firms choose from several common schemes. *Market domination* is intended to obtain a significant amount of market share. Such a firm may adopt a position as a cost or technological leader, challenger, follower, or product differentiator. Any of these roles provide the firm with an approach to establish a dominant position in the marketplace. Second, a firm may be an *innovator* through product development. It will exploit the cutting edge of technology, either as pioneer or follower. Alternatively, a firm with an established product or service may commit to a *growth strategy* through diversified or intensified product choice. Or it can integrate, either horizontally or vertically.

Horizontal integration emphasizes specialized and integrated employee skills to promote economies of scale, while *vertical integration* requires the firm to broaden its product line and bring associated work in-house to control its supply chain of components.

When developing its marketing strategy, a contractor must also consider its customer type. Examples include consumer marketing (*Business to Consumer—B2C*), industrial marketing (*Business to Business—B2B*) and Federal marketing (*Business to Government—B2G*). B2C is a one-to-many relationship with unidentified customers in distant relationships (often through retailers and mass-marketing) for low-value items (with high-value exceptions such as houses or cars). Within defense contracting, this marketing type is primarily involved with standard commercial items.

Both B2B and B2G marketing involve a known seller building a face-to-face relationship with prospective customers. These transactions may involve complex deals for high-valued items, requiring many meetings between trained professionals and multiple decision-makers. A firm may also pursue *horizontal marketing*, the process of selling goods and services between entities. This effort manifests itself when firms pursue subcontracting opportunities with Federal contractors.

Integral to both B2B and B2G is the process of *solution selling* (or *technical selling*). This process involves making an appointment with the customer, understanding his/her needs, and then developing a solution. Such a mission requires identifying program managers and procurement offices which are, or could be enticed to enter, the market of the firm's goods or services. This process can also be pursued in a broader sense by setting up a table at trade shows, with mobile signboards, colorful trifold brochures, and lots of business cards and free handouts!

In a more personal and directed vein, some companies dispatch or train consultants already under contract to become *thought leaders* to advocate initiatives that reflect their areas of expertise.[1] They often speak at professional and public meetings, and will also call on program managers for more intimate and focused meetings. This is fine as long as everybody understands the hidden agenda here. Their employer is in business to make money and is promoting a service in their specialized area of expertise and is therefore ripe for contract coverage. Thought leadership is all about creating a demand for the company's ideas. The Government audience should indeed pay attention to their advocacy and incorporate it into their knowledge base and planning, but should not fall into the trap of blindly adopting the company behind the message without searching for alternative approaches.

Regardless of the method, care must be taken not to "sell the solution" before understanding the customer's requirements. The idea is to create a marketing program around the customer's requirements and the firm's proposed solution, rather than trying to sell an established product or service without modification or customer input.

As another process to use when developing a marketing strategy, *market segmentation* begins by searching for classes of buyers who differ in product interest or tendencies. This process emphasizes an understanding of a class of customer needs, wants and behaviors. Segmentation can be based on demographic or geographic criteria, such as Federal Government only or East Coast only. In any event, these segments must be measurable and substantial. In this process, the firm must consider its competitors and how it differentiates its offering from theirs. A firm must also consider market demand, especially whether it is expected to be durable or merely short-term. Finally, a firm must consider costs involved in new market entry, including advertising and product refinement to adapt to market demands.

A firm can use an *environmental scanning* technique to gather and analyze factual or subjective information on its business operating environment. Scanning can be done on an ad-hoc short-term basis (usually in a crisis mode), on a regularly scheduled basis, or continuously in response to current threats to take advantage of opportunities before their competitors.

Laws can also be the subject of scanning, covering areas such as:

- anti-monopoly,
- business investment,
- copyright and patent,
- environmental protection,
- minimum wage,
- municipal licenses,
- union, and
- worker safety.

A more specific area of investigation covers industrial productivity. Such an effort would cover such topics as competitor products and services, customer buying decisions, manufacturing processes, and technology.

As a result of developing its strategy, a firm performs *positioning* when it creates a brand or image in the minds of the market and potential customers. Once the firm defines the target market, it collects data from customers to learn how they perceive the product and its attributes, and to measure its own level of market dominance. The firm will then assess how well the product or service fits within the target market. Common inputs to conduct this assessment include customer benefits, problem solution, public perception and image, and stimulation of customer senses and cognition.

Another approach is *narrowcasting*, an effort intended for a specific, clearly defined audience interested in a specific product, service, or topic.

Sample techniques include infomercials and web-based productions, word-of-mouth and targeted advertising in trade journals. These publications do get read by professionals and decision-makers at customer entities and are an excellent means for a firm to broadcast its capabilities.

Once positioning is determined, the firm is ready to enter the desired marketplace. *Market entry* is the strategy to deliver product to the marketplace. A firm could choose to enter one market at a time, such as a specific department or agency, or several markets with similar requirements at once. This decision would entail considering such options as in-house production, importing, licensing, or teaming.

Despite all this, there are significant differences between B2B and B2G other than for standard commercial items. Government-unique products have no commercial sales base, and many other products developed for the Government have limited commercial sales opportunities. Moreover, the Government sets rules on marketing based on the public interest, which do not apply in the private sector. Of course, Government source selection and pricing are restrictive procedures compared to the more flexible corporate buying processes. Finally, business decisions are made to achieve long-term Government goals, sometimes at the expense of the short-term.

Moreover, the Government is not a homogeneous market. It is differentiated by the type of product purchased, contract policies and types, and geography. In contrast, a commercial firm can have a complex network of wholesalers, brokers, and retailers to move products efficiently from manufacturer to distributor.[2] Hence, a firm wishing to enter the Government marketplace must consider:

- administrative burden;
- areas of possible commercial expansion;
- competitors' activities;
- performing a cost-benefit analysis;
- socioeconomic requirements; and
- unique aspects of government contracting.

From the seller's viewpoint, one could say that there are 4Ps of the marketing mix that are critical to marketing success:

- Product,
- Promotion,
- Price, and
- Place.

From the customer's viewpoint however, different labels can be applied to each factor above:

- Product = Solution,
- Promotion = Information,
- Price = Value, and
- Place = Access.

The Price component is the subject of Part 4 of our study. However, the other three are also critical to a firm's Federal marketing success and will now be examined in turn.

2.1.2 Product Planning

Central to any corporate R&D program, *new product development* (*NPD*) is a process which emphasizes external interaction to reduce product cost and time-to-market. This idea is geared toward increasing innovation and profitability. For instance, some firms may wish to transfer design responsibility upstream to their suppliers. A firm can use techniques to speed up cycle time such as concurrent engineering and product simplicity. They may also employ integrated teams for design, development, manufacturing, marketing, and research. This development process also considers such areas as quality, reliability, responsiveness, robustness, service, and technology. Ideas are generated to analyze such items as:

- brainstorming,
- competitors and their responses,
- corporate spies,
- customer benefits,
- employee preferences,
- focus groups,
- growth potential,
- industry and market trends,
- market and consumer trends,
- profitability,
- sales ability,
- technical feasibility, and
- trade shows.

Next, the firm enters into development to identify the target market and decision makers. It will assess consumer reaction to key product features and benefits. It must also consider production techniques and feasibility, which may require investigating patent and intellectual property issues.

The firm may sample possible customers for their input, a technique known as *choice modeling*. Next, the firm will conduct a business analysis to estimate sales volume, selling price and profitability, and hence a breakeven level. This is the point in time where the firm makes a commitment to go in a certain direction and begins to incur significant development costs. Once this commitment is made, the firm will produce and test a prototype unit (including packaging). It will then produce an initial production run and sell to a test market group. Or it may obtain customer feedback through focus groups or trade fairs. The firm will then adjust the offering as necessary before going to market.

The *implementation phase* to invoke the chosen path requires the firm to plan engineering operations and logistics, as well as schedule production and procurements. During this phase, the firm must initiate program review and monitoring functions while finalizing the quality management process. It will then need to publish availability and product data sheets.

The commercial step in the lifecycle consists of product launch, advertising, and shipment. The firm strives to eliminate steps or run them concurrently to reduce time-to-market and proactively seize emerging market opportunities. Cross-functional teams are used to combine engineering and marketing personnel to plan commercialization. The more technically complex the product, the more expensive the research and development process will be and the shorter the product life cycle will be, so interaction between departments becomes critical.

There are several common approaches to developing a new product or service. First, a firm can design and build a new product or service on its own initiative. A new business venture may use this approach based on its own perception and desire, perhaps without customer commitment to buy. Alternatively, if the firm understands customer needs, it can develop a product or service (perhaps resembling what it now sells to minimize start-up cost), or else develop the product or service over time.

A more structured, market-based approach is to utilize formal business development or planning. *Business development* involves upfront examination of opportunities to provide products and services to multiple customers to generate more revenue. This approach is market-driven to identify new or unexpected markets. By contrast, *business planning* can be product-driven and focus on a target market. Both development and planning can have a variety of selection criteria (e.g., competitors, laws or regulations, sales and profit targets, and technical feasibility). Such a structured approach could better understand target markets and needs, while making operations more efficient. Moreover, it could build credibility with potential customers and interest among potential investors.

Another key aspect of Product Planning is *demand management*. This approach entails market discovery and associated product or service planning to fulfill customer demands by name recognition in the minds of customers. Useful areas of investigation include:

- customer experience,
- demand creation,
- inventory and supply channel management,
- pricing structure,
- source selection, and
- transportation.

This process involves developing industry *demand forecasts* to help make decisions involving product inventory, mix, revenue projections, and services. Point-of-sale data is integrated with internal data and partner firms' input to forecast demand and develop operational plans. The firm can develop software in a bottoms-up analytical approach by using software programs, historical sales data (including stock-outs), test market data, and old-fashioned educated guesses. Demand modeling techniques consider market size and dynamics, competitors, impact over time on the firm, and promotional events. These techniques can be qualitative or quantitative in nature.

Care must be taken to avoid the *bullwhip effect*, where each entity up the supply chain wishes to carry their own safety stock. The effect grows with each link of the supply chain and leads to unnecessary inventory on hand. This effect can also be caused by anticipated shortages, forecasting errors, lost synchronization between lot sizes and ordering, misperceptions, panic ordering, replenishment lead time, and revised inventory parameters.

There are numerous qualitative and quantitative methods used for demand forecasting. Qualitative methods include:

- *conjoint analysis*, which determines statistically how customers value different features of a product or service, then assesses which attributes are most influential in the customers' mindset;
- *Delphi technique*, using a panel of experts to answer questionnaires that are summarized, then the participants go through one or more rounds of revisions to their answers, as the group converges onto a consensus position;
- expert opinion;
- *game theory*, using strategies to identify people's rational behavior by seeking equilibrium in an industry where each firm adopts a steady strategy which could overlap with that of other firms; and
- *prediction markets* such as PredictIt, which create assets of cash value derived from the occurrence or probability of a particular event; in effect, a betting exchange without a bookmaker. Like the stock market, winners are those who buy low and sell high.

Quantitative methods of demand forecasting include:

- analogies;
- causal models that use cause-and-effect logic to decide market behavior;
- data mining to help analyze behavioral observations of unknown interrelationships (also known as *collinearity*);[3]
- discrete event simulation which represents system operation as a chronological series of events which occur instantaneously and change the state of the market;
- extrapolation of new amounts based on projecting off known data points;
- rule-based forecasting; and
- simulating specific events.

2.1.3 Promotion

Once a firm decides to market to the desired customer base, it uses the *promotion* process to transmit information about itself and its offering. Promotion includes advertising displays and prints, direct mail campaigns and personal sales calls. More subtle and less-targeted methods of public relations, such as sponsoring a youth sports team or participating in trade shows and conventions, can also be useful means of promotion. In defense contracting, promotion can include business development initiatives such as visiting program managers and agency decision-makers to learn about their needs and exchange general information about product or service offerings.

A defense contractor can use *account-based marketing* as a more targeted approach to sell as many products or services to the chosen customer at a time. This serves to expand business within existing customer accounts. Buyers are often satisfied with this approach because their existing suppliers keep them up-to-date with relevant proposals, while contractors enjoy the ease of maintaining their current customer base. This also obviates the need for a shotgun approach to potential customers with an unknown level of interest. This approach is especially useful for firms that sell information technology and consulting services. These services may include data acquisition, analysis, display, management, manipulation, storage, switching, or transmission. Associated hardware includes computers, peripherals, and storage devices.

Firms must focus on key accounts to make this approach workable. They will look at customer preferences, profitability, revenue history, and the desire for a long-term relationship with a client having similar interests. The firm will then argue that the client cannot find this kind of service anywhere else, in an effort to secure the sale.

2.1.4 Placement

To ensure that the marketing program actually reaches its objectives in a cost-effective manner, marketing managers must measure progress against predetermined objectives. These objectives are derived from the corporate mission (or more bluntly, its reason for operating), identifying customers and their needs, and technology needed to meet those needs. Typical methods include sales forecasts and incentives, customer relationship initiatives and return on investment. The marketing manager then establishes individual evaluation criteria to indicate success or failure such as sales revenue, profit and return on investment. The manager uses data, comparisons, and projections to derive standards and measure individual criteria performance.

This data can be useful in positioning the firm to its greatest advantage. The *law of competitive advantage* holds that a firm can produce a good or service at a lower opportunity cost than a competitor can, probably by leveraging off greater efficiency of production. In this way, two parties can trade with each other for mutual benefit, which is the basis for international trade.[4] By contrast, the *law of absolute advantage* prescribes that a firm can make a product at lower production cost than another firm, or else produce more product using the same amount of labor input.[5]

Some firms will succeed while others will fail under this theory; however free trade will allow different nations to specialize in their strong supplies or services, and therefore everyone will benefit through mutually beneficial exchanges.

Economists also speak of *conjectural variation*, which addresses interdependence between firms by assessing how much one firm responds to other firms' strategic variables (e.g., price, quantity, location, and advertising). If marginal costs are constant, then competitive behaviors will be constant. However, if marginal costs are rising in the market, then competitive behavior will adjust to meet the firm's best interest or desired outcome.

Of course, the Government marketplace is hardly a perfect world of supply-and-demand interaction. Federal contracting procedures provide for full coverage of legitimate costs plus *return on investment* (income or profit divided by costs incurred to obtain the income or profit), both of which may well be below the return of the commercial marketplace. Government sales centers may show only 1/3 the return of commercial profit centers, measured either as net profit/total assets, or income/owner's equity. Numerous costs that are legitimate in the commercial sector are disallowed on Federal contracts (e.g., charitable contributions, entertainment, and interest). DoD contractors must also deal with the weighted guidelines method of profit calculation, which tends to reduce contractor profits.

The Profit '76 study of Federal contracting showed that the rate of return on sales is low due to lower net profit after taxes and strict profit guidelines and limits.[6] On the other hand, the rate of return on invested capital is high due to the availability of Government property, equipment, and special tooling. These two phenomena combine to make Federal contractors less motivated to invest than private sector firms. To encourage such investment requires a firm to:

- accept less profit,
- add production capacity,
- diversify to reduce risk,
- expand distribution facilities,
- improve product quality,
- insure its position in the industry, and
- replace obsolete equipment or methods.

Since goods are supplied in a free enterprise system through the interaction of supply and demand, the best way to meet price competition and maximize profit is to minimize cost by making operations more efficient. Cost is therefore often more important in a competition than in a sole-source situation.

Each operating division must be measured against its own environment rather than against each other. For a truly diversified firm however, it is hard to compare measurements of supply and services divisions. Corporate decision rules to measure divisional performance should therefore include a variety of factors such as advertising expenses, facilities expansion and research and development expenditure. Interdepartmental buying and new product introduction may also play roles in divisional assessment. Ultimately, profitability and return on investment will be the yardsticks of measurement.

Federal procurement gives rise to several areas of risk for the firm. *Consumer risk* is an uncertainty surrounding a procurement caused by lack of past experience with the product or vendor, uncertainty of future needs, or the presence of a new product or vendor. It can be inherent in the procurement function, dictated by the market, or assumed by the buyer. *Producer risk* is an uncertainty surrounding the production functions due to physical destruction or deterioration, theft, credit extensions or market conditions. Finally, *change in law risk* is the probability that proposed or required legislation will be enacted, or not.

2.1.5 Government Market Research

By the same token, agencies conduct *market research* to collect and analyze information about the marketplace to develop the best strategy to acquire and support supplies and services. The procurement office will seek sources and solutions before developing new requirements documents or soliciting offers exceeding the simplified acquisition threshold (or less if adequate information is not on hand to decide strategy). Market research is necessary to determine:

- ability of the industrial base to produce a quality product or service. The *industrial base* reflects the national capacity and capability to produce goods sufficient to meet commercial and military needs;
- availability of items that contain recovered materials;
- commercial or nondevelopmental items, including electronic and information technology, which are available or can be modified to meet agency needs;
- competitiveness of a planned procurement, including price sensitivity;
- ease of entry and exit to/from the market;
- emerging technologies;
- if bundling or consolidation is necessary and justified;
- information for economic and technical evaluations;
- market trends (supply/demand) and how to leverage the trend;
- past purchasing experience and suppliers, including how other activities acquire similar services or supplies;
- potential small businesses and set-asides;
- practices of firms that produce, distribute, and support commercial items, e.g.:
    - buyer financing,
    - contract type,
    - discounts,
    - maintenance,
    - marking and packaging, and
    - warranty terms;
- rapid delivery capability;
- reasonableness of the requirement and specifications against industry capabilities, manufacturing processes and market demand; and
- whether the Government can fill the requirement in-house at a lower price.

In assessing a specific prospective source's overall market position, some specific areas which are important for the contracting officer to consider include:

- business strategy;
- company organization;
- competitors;
- core products and new products;
- financial health;[7]
- identity of major suppliers;
- investments for the future, both in capital and research and development; and
- risks tied to potential incentives/strategies it is willing and capable of handling.

41 USC 253, Competition in Contracting Act of 1984, requires the use of advance procurement planning and market research for all major procurements, as well as commercial products wherever practicable. Research is not necessary for awards expressly authorized by statute or using simplified acquisition procedures (but sole-source acquisitions of commercial items are subject to market research).

Research is also required for contract modifications and priced options evaluated as part of the initial competition and within the scope of an existing contract. Orders placed under a requirements or definite-quantity contract which was awarded after market research need not be researched. However, orders placed under indefinite-quantity contracts would only escape research if all responsible sources were permitted to compete for the requirements.

In assessing a prospective source's overall market position, some specific areas which are important for the contracting officer to consider include:

- business strategy;
- company organization;
- competitors;
- core products and new products;
- financial health (the company's own annual (10K) and quarterly (10Q) reports are a good place to start);
- identity of major suppliers;
- investments for the future, both in capital and research and development; and
- risks tied to potential incentives/strategies it is willing and capable of handling.

Defense companies are generally focused on the long term—to earn profits that exceed the cost of capital, attract investors by demonstrating profitability, and recruit and retain world-class employees. The company's financial pipeline is kept afloat by sales, cash flow and profit. Business development personnel work the corporate strategy into a five-year operating plan to identify program priorities based on market intelligence and capture plans.

FAR 10.002

Contracting officers document the results of market research in a manner appropriate to the size and complexity of the acquisition. The contracting officer may use market research conducted within the past 18 months, since the rule of thumb is that after that length of time, the information is too outdated to be reliable. Techniques for conducting market research may include any or all of the following:

- hold presolicitation conferences to involve potential offerors early in the acquisition process;
- obtain market research and source lists of similar items from other contracting activities;[8]
- participate in interactive online communication among acquisition professionals and industry personnel regarding market capabilities to meet requirements;
- publish formal requests for information in technical or scientific journals or business publications;
- query the Government-wide database of contracts and procurement instruments available at www.contractdirectory.gov; and
- review catalogs and other generally available product literature published by dealers, distributors, and manufacturers.

PGI 212.102

The contracting officer must determine if a commercial product or service can meet agency needs. The starting point for this research is the DoD Commercial Item database.[9] The contracting officer is looking to determine that the product or service is customarily used by the general public or nongovernment entities. Within 30 days of award, the determination must be uploaded to the DoD commercial item database. A prior decision of commerciality may be used unless already overturned.

Meaningful communications with Industry should begin early during the development of the contract requirements and the acquisition strategy and continue up to release of RFP.[10] The intent is to remove unnecessary communication barriers with Industry. This helps ensure the Government has realistic requirements and is aware of industry best practices, new technologies, innovative alternatives, and potential capabilities while building specifications, statements of work. This approach may include one-on-one meetings with individual firms. An excellent technique to collect information and feedback is the use of Industry Days (e.g., pre-solicitation conferences, pre-proposal conferences).

A draft solicitation (or even multiple solicitations for a complex acquisition) is an important tool to seek input from Industry on the Department requirement and ensure greater understanding on both sides of the acquisition. The specific content of a draft solicitation ultimately will be determined by the PM and PCO and should be coordinated with Legal Counsel prior to release to Industry. This tool will benefit the level of competition, volume of offerors' questions, number of amendments, and quality of the solicitation, proposals, and resultant contract.

A pre-proposal conference can prevent future delays by explaining the content of the solicitation, ensuring offerors understand the requirements and resulting in better-quality proposals. In these meetings, the bulk of attention is usually given to proposal preparation instructions, evaluation criteria and selection methodologies. Further questions are often raised by inexperienced or small-business offerors, and when changes have been made to the solicitation since the issuance of a draft. This is also an opportunity to announce any expected rules of engagement during discussions—such as the use of change pages, recording of conversations (and which party will be responsible for doing that recording), anticipated timeframes, etc.—to give the offerors ample opportunity to prepare. When reviewing evaluation criteria, the PCO should define terms, adjectival ratings, documentation of evaluations (including use of any templates), use of standardized evaluation language and any outside resources. Appointing a Records Custodian for the source selection process is a good idea to ensure propriety and fairness.

Through market research, or in consultation with subject matter experts, teams may uncover minimum standards such as critical qualifications, certifications, facility clearances, or required experience. These findings can be used to establish the criteria for a gate or phased selection process. The Instructions to Offerors should clearly discuss the process to evaluate proposals under this approach. How an offeror can meet the gate criteria to move to the second phase should be specified in the evaluation criteria. Offerors not meeting the established criteria would then be excluded from further evaluation. Using a gated/phased approach can help teams narrow the competition to the most highly qualified vendors and reduce overall source selection timelines. Teams must identify objective (pass/fail or go/no go) criteria that can achieve this objective.

DoDI 5000.02T, ENCLOSURE 2: 8

An additional area of research within DoD is the *defense industrial base*, the collection of assets used to produce equipment and supplies to the nation's armed forces. Market research must consider the availability of assets and the desire to support economic and stable development and production rates. The research will look for industrial risks such as single points of failure and unreliable suppliers, committing to sole-source suppliers, and the inevitable procurement surges and contractions.

Program management must consider industrial base aspects such as capacity and capability in developing its acquisition strategy and identify such problems as access to raw materials, export controls, mitigation strategies, and production abilities that could impact the DoD both near- and long-term. This information is combined with other sources of information to inform Service- and Department-level industrial base decisions.

Solicitation Provision and Contract Clause

FAR 52.210-1, Market Research, for noncommercial item contracts over $5.5 million.

2.1.6 Announcing Proposed Actions

FAR 5.2 and 10.0

Per the Small Business Act and the Office of Federal Procurement Policy Act, contracting officers release information on proposed contract actions to increase competition, broaden industry participation and assist small socioeconomic concerns to obtain (sub)contracts.[11] This process is done electronically for any proposed contract action expected to exceed $25,000. For proposed contract actions between $10,000 and $25,000 that are not orally solicited, the notice can still be done by electronic means; otherwise, it must be displayed in a public place by the solicitation date for at least 10 days until quotations have been opened. The contracting officer may also advise local trade associations, issue handouts or place announcements in newspapers or trade magazines without cost to the Government. Actions estimated below $10,000 need not be announced.

Electronic solicitation is the standard method of solicitation, especially for actions over $25,000. The contracting office sends an announcement to Federal Business Opportunities (better known as the System for Award Management, SAM).[12] This is a *Government Point of Entry* (*GPE*), a public-facing website sponsored by the GSA. However, the contracting officer has many common-sense exceptions to preclude submitting the notice, such as if the proposed procurement is:

- accepting a proposal under the Small Business Innovation Development Act of 1982, or that demonstrates a unique and innovative concept, and

publication of a notice would disclose either proprietary information or the originality of research or thought;
- for brand name-only commercial items for authorized resale;
- for perishable subsistence supplies;
- for the services of an expert to support the Federal Government in any current or anticipated litigation or dispute;
- for utility (not telecommunications) services and only one source is available;
- of a file size or format incapable of loading on CD-ROM or electronic mail and therefore is not cost-effective to submit through the GPE;[13]
- ordered under a previously solicited indefinite delivery contract;
- reserved for minority firms or the severely handicapped or blind organizations;
- is so urgent that the Government cannot allow 15 days for responses;
- soliciting only local sources to perform services outside the United States and its outlying areas for a Defense agency;
- treaty which restricts solicitation to specified source(s);
- such that one cannot phrase the announcement without compromising national security;
- to a directed source(s) by a foreign government reimbursing the Federal Government for the procurement; or
- will not exceed the simplified acquisition threshold and permits electronic proposals.

The notice must be published at least 15 days before issuance of a solicitation, which is usually the day after submission to SAM. To acquire commercial items, the contracting officer may establish a shorter period to issue a solicitation, or else combine the synopsis and solicitation.

The contracting officer provides enough response time, normally at least 30 days from the date of issuance, although the contracting officer can allow less time for commercial items or purchases below the simplified acquisition threshold. However, agencies will allow at least 45 days for research and development actions exceeding the simplified acquisition threshold. For acquisitions under the World Trade Organization Government Procurement Agreement or a Free Trade Agreement, the period of time is at least 40 days (though it can be reduced to 10 days if the acquisition falls within the Agreement's annual forecast).

The contracting office may transmit a notice to SAM to seek competition for subcontracts or to increase participation by qualified socioeconomic entities, such as for a total or partial small business set-aside or local area set-aside. A prime contractor receiving an award exceeding $100,000 that is likely to result in the award of any subcontracts is free to use SAM too, as well as any subcontractor with a $100,000 award who anticipates a subcontracting opportunity exceeding $10,000.

2.1.7 Synopses of Contract Awards

FAR 5.3

Contracting officers synopsize nearly all awards exceeding $25,000 to SAM. A lower-amount award may be submitted if likely to result in the award of any subcontracts. A notice is not required if the award is:

- an order under an indefinite delivery contract (because the contract award itself was already announced);
- due to acceptance of an unsolicited research proposal that demonstrates a unique and innovative research concept (to avoid revealing that information to the competition);
- for the services of an expert to support the Federal Government in any current or anticipated litigation or dispute (to avoid prejudicing an upcoming legal action);
- for utility (not telecommunications) services and only one source is available (obvious who is getting the award);
- from a proposal submitted under the Small Business Innovation Development Act (another innovation award whose secrets must be withheld from the competition);
- made for perishable subsistence supplies (no time to wait for responses to the solicitation);
- such that disclosure of agency needs would compromise the national security (protected by national security); or
- to a foreign firm and performance is outside the United States and its outlying areas (limited number of qualified contractors).

Regardless of dollar value, unless the award is competitive fixed-price, an award notice includes the rationale for contract type and/or lack of competition.

The agency head or designee may release long-range acquisition estimates to help industry plan to meet the acquisition requirements, without indicating the existing or potential mobilization of the industry as a whole. Hopefully, unknown or unexpected companies will show interest and answer the call to submit offers, and actually broaden the marketplace.

Advance written authorization is not required to place advertisements in media other than newspapers. Orders may be placed directly with the media or through an advertising agency via basic ordering agreements. The services of advertising agencies often can be obtained at no cost to the Government (other than space cost) because many media give advertising agencies a commission or discount on the space cost that is not given to the Government. Paid advertisements are used only as a last resort and require written approval by a designated official.

2.2 COMPETITION

2.2.1 Full and Open Competition

FAR 6.1

10 U.S.C. 2304 and 41 U.S.C. 253 require, with certain limited exceptions, that contracting officers promote full and open competition in soliciting offers and awarding contracts. *Competition* is defined as an environment where the buyer relies on the marketplace for sellers to independently contend for award. Seeking competition harnesses the motive to send the buyer's business elsewhere. It tends to lower prices and boost quality while encouraging adequate sources of supply. Competition also applies to basic and applied research if award results from a broad agency announcement identifying areas of interest and a peer or scientific review. Use of multiple award schedules is also a competitive procedure.

Seeking competition is often an ideal method to:

- enhance the industrial base for mobilization and surge capacity;
- improve delivery schedules, efficiency, quality, and reliability;
- increase the program manager's leverage over contractor activity;
- motivate contractors to suggest design changes, leading to efficient production techniques and long-term planning; and
- reduce overhead cost.

Another advantage of competition is the desire to obtain standard commercial items where practicable. These *commercial off-the-shelf* (*COTS*) supplies are sold, leased, or licensed to the general public. They include items that evolved from other commercial items due to technological advances. Prices are established when parties are free to bargain with each other based on competition or independent sourcing. Items that are not offered to the general public may still qualify as nondevelopmental items if they were developed exclusively at private expense and sold in substantial quantities competitively to multiple government agencies (state and local included). Such items are termed *Government off-the-shelf* (*GOTS*) but are treated as if they were COTS.

Agencies prescribe procedures to promote full and open competition, encouraging offerors to supply commercial or nondevelopmental items.

Nondevelopmental items are either commercial in nature or else were developed for a prior acquisition. This definition also includes commercial off-the-shelf items that reduce R&D costs and speed up the acquisition process. These items require no research, development, test, or evaluation (with or without minor modification) to make the product suitable for Government needs. They may or may not already be in Government inventory.

Commercial services would be those that are offered to the general public. Such services are sold competitively in substantial quantities commercially based on established catalog or market prices for specific tasks. Basic and applied research is bought competitively if award results from a broad agency announcement identifying areas of interest and a peer or scientific review.

Care must be taken to avoid fallacies in assumptions regarding the attractiveness of competition. Cost savings projections are not always accurate due to the dynamic and nonlinear nature of the corporate world. Moreover, investment costs for a new contractor must also be considered, such as drawing development and validation, facility development and setup, licenses or royalties, technical data rights, and tooling and test equipment.

The procurement is said to be *unrestricted competition* if all firms are eligible to compete regardless of any preference program. However, if a socioeconomic preference program limits the number of firms which can be considered, it creates an instance of *restricted competition*. These socioeconomic programs will be discussed in great depth later in this book.

2.2.2 Other Than Full and Open Competition

FAR 6.3

10 U.S.C. 2304(c) authorizes for DoD, NASA, and Coast Guard, under certain conditions, contracting without providing for full and open competition. Each contract awarded without providing for full and open competition refers to the specific authority under which it was awarded. A lack of advance planning or funding by the requiring activity is not a basis for avoiding full and open competition. When not providing for full and open competition, the contracting officer still solicits offers from as many potential sources as is practicable under the circumstances. However, the contracting officer must justify in writing why full competition is not sought. The following seven exceptions are the only authorized conditions which allow less than full and open competition.

1. Only One Responsible Source and No Other Supplies or Services Will Satisfy Agency Requirements.

There are many instances when this exception, commonly called *sole source*, may come into play. A firm may receive a contract without competition if the

Government accepts its unsolicited research proposal. The firm must demonstrate a unique and innovative concept or capability not available to the Government and not resembling a pending competitive acquisition. This exception also covers a follow-on contract to continue development or production of a major system or highly specialized equipment. However, the contracting officer must explain how award to any other source would either substantially duplicate cost that will not be recovered through competition, or else would create unacceptable delays in fulfilling the requirements. Within DoD, the office must also post a request for information or sources sought notice and report any results.

Highly specialized provisioning services may be deemed to be available only from the original source when award to any other source would result in the same concerns. Other situations which could prevent competition include:

- agency minimum needs can only be met by unique supplies or services available from only one source;
- construction of a part of a utility system and the utility company itself is the only source available to work on the system or provide the service;
- control of basic raw material;
- existence of limited rights in copyrights, data, patent rights, or secret processes; or
- the agency head determines that only specified equipment and parts meet agency needs, and only one source is available.

An acquisition using a brand name description or part number peculiar to one manufacturer does not provide for full and open competition, regardless of the number of sources solicited. Hence, the justification in these cases indicates that the use of such descriptions is essential to the Government's requirements, thereby precluding consideration of a product manufactured by another company.

Although the discussion above covers a multitude of situations, this exception is not very popular with outside reviewers because it is very broad and could be abused to cover a multitude of situations where competition might have been obtainable, such as poor planning or desire to award to a specific firm. Hence, this authority is used in preference only to exception 7—exceptions 2 through 6 always take priority over exception 1.

DFARS 206.302-1

Defense Appropriations Acts usually prohibit DoD from contracting after receiving an unsolicited proposal for consulting services or analyses or studies unless the chief of the contracting office or departmental senior procurement executive determines otherwise. Such a determination must show that the proposal offers original thinking or significant scientific or technological promise that benefits the national defense through a unique and significant industrial accomplishment (or by ensuring financial support to a new product or idea). Alternatively, an unsolicited proposal pertaining to improvement of equipment that is in development or production can be accepted without competition. In addition, the DoD Foreign Comparative Testing Program allows procurement of test articles and associated support services from a designated foreign source.

2. Unusual and Compelling Urgency

This exception applies when delay in award would result in serious injury (usually financial) to the Government. Examples include construction to prevent damage to a structure or its contents, disaster relief, or operational needs of a mission or deployment. Offers must still be solicited from as many potential sources as practicable.

For a simplified acquisition, the total period of performance of a contract awarded using this authority may not exceed the time necessary to meet the unusual and compelling requirements and for the agency to then enter into another contract for the necessary goods and services. For an acquisition exceeding the simplified threshold, this time period may not exceed one year unless the head of the agency determines that exceptional circumstances apply. Any time extension which would result in performance exceeding one year (excluding option years) will require a separate justification.

3. Industrial Mobilization; Engineering, Developmental, or Research Capability; or Expert Services

Examples of this exception include the need to:

- continue any contractors who manufacture critical items to avoid a break in production;
- create or maintain domestic capability to produce critical supplies by limiting competition to items manufactured in the United States, its outlying areas or Canada;
- develop a second source to enhance the mobilization base and foster competition;[14]
- divide current production requirements among multiple contractors to maintain the industrial mobilization base;
- establish or maintain an essential capability for engineering or developmental work;
- establish experiments, exploratory studies, or theoretical analyses in science or technology, including effort at an educational or nonprofit institution or federally funded research and development center;

- increase or maintain competition to obtain reduced overall costs;
- limit competition for selected supplies or services approved under (or agreed to enter) the DoD Industrial Preparedness Program;
- maintain a facility, manufacturer, or supplier in case of a national emergency or to achieve industrial mobilization;
- prevent the loss of a supplier's ability and employees' skills;
- provide experts (e.g., evaluators, factfinders, mediators arbitrators, or witnesses) in a hearing, proceeding or trial (whether or not the expert is expected to testify);
- satisfy a critical need for emergency, medical or safety supplies; or
- satisfy projected needs based on a history of high demand.

PGI 206.202

Any written justification for development of an alternative source for supplies or services must address:

- acquisition history, including award dates, prices, quantities, and sources;
- current and projected annual requirement;
- if the basis for the justification is reduced cost, then the likelihood of future competition and lower costs (e.g., economic orders, facility startup and life cycle);
- if the current source must be completely or partially excluded, and the potential effect of exclusion on the current supplier;
- in case of national emergency or industrial mobilization, then both current and future mobilization needs compared to current production capacity, risks of relying on the current source only, and estimated time until a new source can attain production capacity and facilities to meet mobilization needs; and
- reasons for the lack of alternative sources, such as technical complexity and criticality.

4. International Agreement

An international agreement or treaty between the United States and a foreign government or entity, or the written directions of a foreign government that reimburses the agency for the cost of supplies or services, may restrict competition to one or a limited group of sources. Place of performance can be within either the United States or the foreign country.

DFARS 206.302-4

A written justification is not required if the head of the contracting activity documents an agreement, treaty, or written directions (e.g., a Letter of Offer and Acceptance) that require the use of noncompetitive procedures for the acquisition.

5. Authorized or Required by Statute

A statute may require acquisition through another agency or from a specified source, such as:

- 8(a) Program awards;
- Federal Prison Industries (UNICOR);
- Government printing and binding;
- HUBZone awards;
- qualified nonprofit agencies for the Blind or other Severely Disabled; or
- veterans' preference awards.

Likewise, this exception could also cover a brand name commercial item for authorized resale, such as a commissary or GSA supply store.

DFARS 206.302-5

A military exchange located outside the United States may receive a contract under $100,000 from another DoD element to provide supplies (except for domestically produced soft drinks) and services within its normal operations and stores for use by military personnel stationed overseas. Overseas bases may contract with local governments for community services such as airfield, fire or police operations.

Per 10 U.S.C. 2361, DoD may not contract noncompetitively with a college for research or development, or construction of research facilities, unless mandated by law which specifically supersedes the statute and specifies the college to receive the award. Award cannot occur within 180 days of enactment, and the Secretary of Defense must notify Congress in writing of intent to award before its execution.

6. National Security

If disclosure of the agency's needs would compromise the national security, the agency may limit the number of sources solicited. However, it is not sufficient to say that the contractor will need access to classified material to perform the contract. Nonetheless, classified acquisitions often require this exception. A maximum number of sources must still be solicited.

7. Public Interest

This exception is used as a last resort when no other options apply. The Secretary of Defense must make such a determination and notify Congress within 30 days. This exception is not encouraged and is rarely used.

2.2.3 Justifications

FAR 6.303

A *justification and approval* (J&A) is a written document specifically supporting the need to restrict competition. It is drafted by the contracting officer and must be executed before negotiations or award unless it would unreasonably delay award, in which case it must be executed as soon as possible thereafter. The J&A provides in a prescribed format a written argument to justify the use of an exception, certifies the accuracy and completeness of the justification, and documents the approval by an authorized official. J&A's may be done on a class basis or for individual acquisitions. Each justification contains facts and rationale to justify the use of the specific authority cited, including in order:

- name of the agency and contracting activity;
- the action planned;
- the supplies or services and estimated value;
- the statutory authority permitting other than full and open competition;
- how the proposed contractor's unique qualifications (or the nature of the acquisition) requires use of the authority;
- efforts to ensure that offers are solicited from as many sources as possible, and whether a notice was/will be publicized;
- how the anticipated cost will be fair and reasonable;
- market research results or rationale why research was not done;
- why technical data packages, specifications or statements of work are not available for full and open competition;
- for exception 1, an estimate of the cost to the Government that would be duplicated if competed and how the estimate was derived;
- for exception 2, identification of data or estimated cost of harm to the Government;
- names of any sources that expressed in writing an interest in the acquisition;
- possible actions to remove barriers to competition before the acquisition; and
- contracting officer certification that the justification is accurate and complete to the best of his/her knowledge and belief.

Technical and requirements personnel certify their technical input as being accurate and complete. Legal counsel concurrence for sufficiency is required. The J&A must be approved in writing per the following thresholds (class J&A's are assessed by total value of all covered acquisitions), including option values:

- if under $750,000, the contracting officer is sufficient unless agency procedures require a higher approving level;
- between $750,000 and $15 million, the competition advocate for the procuring activity;
- between $15 and $100 million, the head of the procuring activity, or a designated flag officer or member of the Senior Executive Service; and
- if above $100 million, the senior procurement executive of the agency. This would be either an Assistant Secretary of Defense or else a flag officer or ranking civil servant.

J&A's are published on SAM and the agency website within 14 days of execution (30 days after award for exception 2). Contracting officers delete any classified, FOIA-exempted or proprietary information from the J&A before submission to the website.[15]

Each procurement office has access to a designated employee to become a key player in developing competition plans. The *competition advocate* for the agency and each procuring activity is a senior staff aide with specialists on call to promote full and open competition, as well as acquisition of commercial items. This includes the ability to challenge restrictive statements of work, specifications, or contract clauses. The advocate will identify and report to the agency senior procurement executive and the chief acquisition officer any goals and plans to increase competition for the current and upcoming fiscal year, and all actions taken to accomplish them. This official will also recommend recognition and awards to motivate program managers and contracting officers to promote competition.

There is another document sometimes written to justify contracting actions, which should not be confused with a J&A. In a variety of instances, the contracting officer needs to write a *determination and findings* (D&F) to request formal approval to take a specified action. A D&F follows an agency-prescribed format to set forth the facts and circumstances in the form of findings to support the specific determination made. Necessary supporting documentation must first be obtained from appropriate requirements and technical personnel. Several instances which require a D&F will be mentioned throughout this book.

In terms of noncompetitive justifications, contracting officers may set aside solicitations to restrict competition to socioeconomic concerns or local firms during a major disaster or emergency without a separate justification or D&F. However, several types of awards under Exception 5 do need a D&F:

Government printing, HUBZone, UNICOR, or veterans' preference. Also, when using exception 7, the D&F may take the place of a J&A.

DFARS 206.303

No J&A is required for an 8(a) sole-source contract valued under $100 million. If over $100 million, the head of the procuring activity must approve the J&A, unless delegated to a flag officer or member of the SES.

2.3 USING GOVERNMENT SOURCES

FAR 8.002

Because there are often multiple sources to fulfill Government needs, a prioritization order for obtaining supplies must be established. This order is:

- agency inventories;
- excess from other agencies;
- Federal Prison Industries, Inc.;
- supplies on the Procurement List maintained by the Committee for Purchase From People Who Are Blind or Severely Disabled;
- wholesale supply sources (e.g., stock programs of GSA, the Defense Logistics Agency, the Department of Veterans Affairs, and military inventory control points);
- mandatory Federal Supply Schedules;
- optional use Federal Supply Schedules; and
- commercial sources (including educational and nonprofit institutions).

The priority order for obtaining services is:

- the Procurement List maintained by the Committee for Purchase From People Who Are Blind or Severely Disabled (including subcontracts);
- mandatory Federal Supply Schedules;
- optional use Federal Supply Schedules;
- Federal Prison Industries, Inc.; and
- commercial sources (including educational and nonprofit institutions).

Information regarding the availability of excess personal property can be obtained through GSA property catalogs, bulletins and reports, personal contacts, and requirements submissions.

2.3.1 Federal Prison Industries, Inc.

FAR 8.6

Federal Prison Industries, Inc., also referred to as UNICOR, is a self-supporting, wholly owned Government corporation under the Department of Justice established per 18 U.S.C. 4121-4128. It is designed to train and employ federal prisoners by creating and providing supplies and services to Government agencies. Its offerings are listed in the UNICOR Schedule at www.unicor.gov. Examples of UNICOR's range of offerings include:

- awards and plaques;
- cable and wire harnesses;
- call center operations;
- clothing;
- computer-aided design;
- distribution and warehousing;
- electronics recycling;
- eyewear and safety glasses;
- facilities management;
- HVAC filters and steam trap services;
- laundry and dry cleaning services;
- lighting and power distribution;
- office furniture;
- printing and binding services;
- signage (both internal and external);
- tableware; and
- vehicle upgrades and customization.

Ordering procedures for UNICOR are found at the UNICOR website.[16] Before purchasing an item on the UNICOR Schedule, the contracting officer conducts market research to determine whether the UNICOR item is comparable to supplies available from the private sector in terms of price, quality, and time of delivery. This is because the contracting officer is still responsible for protecting public funds and must pursue the lowest price whenever possible. If the products are not comparable, the contracting officer's written determination authorizes soliciting the private sector without a waiver. Other reasons to publicly solicit rather than going to UNICOR include:

- acquiring services;
- estimated value below the micro-purchase threshold;
- item classified by UNICOR as non-mandatory;
- public exigency;
- surplus item availability; and
- use outside the United States.

UNICOR is treated as any other small business. Contractors are never required to use UNICOR as a subcontractor but may voluntarily do so.

Needless to say, care must be taken to ensure that prisoners working on these contracts do not access classified, financial, or personal data, or any utility infrastructure or pipeline or water data.

DFARS 208.602-70

If UNICOR has a market share greater than five percent for a given item, the item must be procured competitively (including fair opportunity procedures if ordered under a competitive delivery-order contract).[17] UNICOR will be solicited and is free to submit an offer, but it will not be given its usual preferred status.

2.3.2 Agencies for the Blind or Disabled

FAR 8.7

The Committee for Purchase from People Who Are Blind or Severely Disabled was established under the Javits-Wagner-O'Day Act as an independent Government activity that determines the supplies and services to be purchased by Government agencies and their contractors from designated nonprofit agencies.[18] The Committee establishes prices and regulations for their purchase through an entity known as *AbilityOne*.[19] Examples of their offerings include supplies for aircraft and electrical equipment, bedding, clothing, food processing and distribution, janitorial supplies, medical and dental supplies, office furnishings and supplies, paints, textiles, and writing instruments.

AbilityOne participating nonprofit agencies employ people who are blind or have other severe disabilities approved by the Committee to furnish a commodity or a service to the Government. The Committee runs the program through two *central nonprofit agencies*: National Industries for the Blind (NIB) and National Institute for the Severely Handicapped (NISH, now known commercially as SourceAmerica).

NIB provides employment opportunities for veterans who are blind. Their products and services are set forth at www.nib.org and include:

- batteries;
- belts and holsters;
- carrying cases;
- cleaning and janitorial supplies;
- clothing design and cutting;
- computer media and accessories;
- contact centers;
- contract closeout services;
- cybersecurity;

- document management;
- door and cabinet hardware;
- embroidered clothing;
- food service supplies;
- hand trucks;
- helmet bands and covers;
- hydration systems;
- kitting;
- lawn and garden tools;
- lighting;
- location markers;
- machining and fabrication;
- mail management and office support;
- office products;
- packaging and assembly, including liquid and aerosol products;
- paints and related supplies;
- paper cutting, binding, and converting;
- personal care products;
- plastics injection and blow molding;
- safety apparel and supplies;
- Section 508 compliance; and
- supply chain services.

NISH creates workplace technology for people with a variety of disabilities. Its offerings are found at www.sourceamerica.org and include:

- administrative services,
- contact center and information technology services,
- document management,
- electronics recycling,
- environmental services,
- facilities management,
- food products and distribution,
- hardware,
- healthcare services,
- laundry services,
- medical supplies,
- office supplies,
- packaging,
- personal protective equipment, and
- supply chain management.

NIB and SourceAmerica set a standard delivery or performance lead time for orders. The ordering office grants when possible any request by a central nonprofit agency or AbilityOne participating nonprofit agency to revise the delivery or completion schedule. If not, it contacts the central nonprofit agency to request either reallocating the order or granting a purchase exception to allow commercial sources to fill the requirement. Similarly, if the ordering office decides to cancel an order, it notifies the central nonprofit agency for reallocation of the order. In such a case, the central nonprofit agency could grant a purchase exception permitting use of commercial sources, but it must get Committee approval if the value of the purchase exception is $25,000 or more. Exceptions can also be granted if the quantity cannot be produced or provided economically by the participating nonprofit agencies.

The Committee sets supplies prices semiannually and services prices annually. All prices exclude delivery charges because the final destination is not predictable until actual orders arrive. The Committee has the authority to establish prices without prior coordination with the responsible contracting office.

Sometimes an AbilityOne participating nonprofit agency produces items identical to those available through UNICOR. UNICOR may then grant a waiver to permit the Government to purchase a portion of its requirement from the AbilityOne nonprofit agency. Otherwise, UNICOR takes priority for identical supplies, and AbilityOne takes priority to provide services.

Contract Clause

FAR 52.208-9, Contractor Use of Mandatory Sources of Supply and Services.

2.3.3 Other Mandated Sources of Supply

FAR 8.8

Government printing (including printing and binding) must be procured through the Government Printing Office. However, this effort can be contracted out if this office cannot provide the service, the agency uses its own printing service, or if directed by statute.

FAR 8.11

GSA is responsible for furnishing motor vehicles for official Government business. Any motor vehicle leased commercially must comply with Federal and state Motor Vehicle Safety regulations. This does not apply to motor vehicles leased outside the United States and outlying areas.

When leasing a motor vehicle by contract, the requiring activity must certify that required leased motor vehicles are fuel efficient and small enough to meet the need (the Government does not want to pay for a full-size car if it only needs a compact). Any car larger than a compact must be justified by the agency head or designee of the requiring activity.[20] Also, GSA must state that it cannot furnish the vehicles. Current-year production models are also frowned upon unless they are more economical than prior-year models. The contractor must comply with all marking, safety and tagging standards. The contract must specify which party is required to maintain its vehicle, including providing gasoline, oil, and antifreeze.

DFARS 212.271

10 U.S.C. 2253(a)(2) limits purchase of any right-hand drive passenger sedans to a cost of $40,000 or less per vehicle.

DFARS 212.272

Certain services must be bought as commercial services when exceeding the simplified acquisition threshold, namely:

- facilities;
- knowledge-based, other than engineering;
- medical; and
- transportation.

Any exception to this rule requires a written determination by the contracting officer. If over $10 million, the combatant or USD(A&S) approval is necessary.

Contract Clauses

FAR 52.208-4, Vehicle Lease Payments.

FAR 52.208-5, Condition of Leased Vehicles.

FAR 52.208-6, Marking of Leased Vehicles.

FAR 52.208-7, Tagging of Leased Vehicles, for vehicles leased over 60 days.

Do not use the following clauses:

- 52.211-16, Variation in Quantity;
- 52.232-1, Payments;
- 52.222-20, Walsh-Healey Public Contracts Act; and
- 52.246-16, Responsibility for Supplies.

2.4 FEDERAL SUPPLY SCHEDULES

FAR 8.4

Title III of the Federal Property and Administrative Services Act established the Federal Supply Schedule program to provide Federal agencies with a simplified process to acquire commercial supplies and services and obtain volume discounts.[21] Also called the GSA Schedules Program and the Multiple Award Schedule Program, it is run by GSA to award indefinite delivery contracts using competitive procedures. The contracted firms provide supplies and services at stated prices for given periods of time. There are four different types of schedules:

- single award,
- multiple award,
- new item introductory, and
- international.

Each schedule identifies agencies that are required to use the contracts as primary sources of supply when UNICOR and AbilityOne cannot fulfill the requirement. GSA schedule contractors publish an "Authorized Federal Supply Schedule Pricelist" of all covered supplies and services, along with pricing and the terms and conditions for each *Special Item Number,* a group of generically similar supplies or services that serve the same general purpose.

GSA delegates responsibility for certain commodities to specific agencies (e.g., the Department of Veterans Affairs to procure medical supplies). DoD manages a similar system of schedule contracting for military items, but it is not a part of the Federal Supply Schedule program. Architect-engineer services are not bought under Federal Supply Schedules, due to their unique source selection process.

A schedule may include special ordering procedures that take precedence over normal procedures.[22] GSA also manages an online shopping service named "GSA Advantage!" to electronically place orders.[23] GSA provides search features (i.e., national stock number, part number and common name), delivery options, ordering, and payment using the Government-wide commercial purchase card. GSA has a solicitation tool called "eBuy" to post requirements, obtain quotes and issue orders electronically.[24] Contractors may publish pricelists on this site, though this is not required and is by no means a comprehensive process.

Orders placed against a schedule are considered to be issued using full and open competition; hence ordering activities do not seek competition outside of the Federal Supply Schedules and do not synopsize the requirement (because award of the supply schedule itself has already been synopsized). However, the contracting officer may still need an acquisition plan and information technology acquisition strategy, must determine in writing that use of such a schedule is the best procurement approach, and may need to take steps to avoid contract bundling. Moreover, any restriction falling into one of the seven exceptions to competition still requires a J&A.

Ordering activities may place orders below the micro-purchase threshold with any Federal Supply Schedule contractor, but try to distribute orders among several contractors, preferably small businesses. Above the micro-purchase threshold however, the ordering officer surveys at least three schedule contractors either through GSA Advantage or else by reviewing vendor catalogs or pricelists. Of course, socioeconomic considerations are still in play, and the contracting officer is free to limit competition to small businesses only. In addition to price, non-price evaluation factors may include:

- delivery terms;
- environmental and energy efficiency;
- maintenance availability;
- past performance;
- probable lifespan of the item selected;
- special performance features;
- trade-in considerations; and
- warranty terms.

Each schedule contract has a maximum order threshold for each item number. Schedule prices are fixed. Services are priced either at hourly rates or for an entire task (usually for installation, maintenance, and repair). GSA has already determined the prices to be fair and reasonable. Although an ordering officer must still do a price evaluation, the ordering officer need not assess price for reasonableness, yet is free to pursue additional discounts with the contractor before placing an order. The contractor is under no obligation to reduce price however, and the ordering activity may then place an order at the contract price. Any contractor decision whether or not to reduce price presents a dilemma; on the one hand, lowering prices for one customer will lead to demands to lower prices for all, but on the other hand the loss of the sale is never an attractive possibility.

For services above the micro-purchase threshold priced at hourly rates in the schedule, the ordering activity must provide a Request for Quotation (RFQ) to include the statement of work and evaluation criteria (e.g., experience and past performance), to three or more schedule contractors and any other schedule contractor who requests a copy. The activity is free to post the requirement to eBuy. Statements of work include description, location, period of performance or deliverable schedule, performance standards, security clearances, and travel needs. The ordering activity evaluates all responses received using the evaluation criteria provided to the schedule contractors. The ordering activity documents the:

- description of the service purchased;
- evaluation methodology;
- price reasonableness determination and amount paid;
- rationale for any tradeoffs during selection;
- rationale if not using a firm-fixed price order or performance-based order; and
- schedule contracts considered and the awardee.

For proposed orders between $25,000 and the simplified acquisition threshold, any circumstances which restrict consideration must be submitted to eBuy. For proposed orders exceeding the simplified acquisition threshold, the J&A itself must be furnished. The posting requirement does not apply when disclosure would compromise the national security (e.g., would reveal classified information) or create other security risks. The fact that access to classified matter may be necessary to submit a proposal or perform the contract does not, in itself, preclude use of these schedules. Also, posting is not required if the file size or format does not make it cost-effective or practicable to provide access through eBuy, or the agency's senior procurement executive determines in writing that access through eBuy is not in the Government's interest.

2.5 ACQUISITION PLAN

2.5.1 Strategic Planning

FAR 7.1

The *acquisition strategy* is the business and technical management approach to achieve program objectives within resource constraints. The strategy is a coordinated overall plan to satisfy the mission need in the most economical, effective, and timely manner. In short, it is a plan to support successful delivery of the capability at an affordable life-cycle price on a realistic schedule.

The strategy should be tailored to program objectives and flexible enough to allow innovation and modification as the program evolves. The strategy should balance cost and effectiveness by developing technological options, exploring design concepts, and planning and conducting the acquisition. The strategy should be structured to achieve program stability by minimizing technical, schedule and cost risks by promoting common sense, policy compliance and sound business practices. It serves as a decision aid to evaluate and select issue alternatives, identify opportunities and times for critical decisions, and prioritize and integrate diverse functional requirements.

The process of acquisition planning begins when the agency need is identified, prior to the fiscal year in which award is required. A team is formed of contracting, fiscal, legal, logistics, and technical personnel. The program manager will then develop and execute the acquisition strategy. This leads to a comprehensive and integrated baseline which will identify the acquisition approach and key assumptions, and describe the strategies (business, support and technical) that the program manager plans to use to manage risks and meet program objectives. The strategy evolves over time as the program status changes. The *system acquisition process* encompasses requirements definition in terms of capabilities, priorities, and resources, and ends when the system enters operational use.

A credible acquisition strategy must have several characteristics. It must include *realism*, since program objectives must be attainable, and can be measured by ranking, probability or statistical methods. The strategy must promote *stability* in terms of funding, industry risk, policy, requirements, and changes in organization and personnel. To mitigate these threats to stability requires knowing the direction in which the program should head, advocating targets for program changes and gaining commitment through signed agreement or contract. The strategy must promote *balanced resources* by using time, people, facilities, and money to achieve program goals. The degree of balance can be measured either directly or in terms to overcome barriers to meet program objectives. The program manager must recognize that the user wants a top-performing system quickly, financial officers want to lower cost, and contractors want to lower risk. Consequently, the program manager must try to overcome these parochial interests, promote understanding of mission requirements and priorities, and allocate resources to achieve required capability with acceptable risk. *Flexibility* of accommodating changes and failures without consuming needless resources can be analyzed through "what-if" drills and identifying areas of probable change or failure.

DoD uses a Service Acquisition Mall, a guide for contracting officers through the acquisition process.[25] It is hosted by a website at Defense Acquisition University. This process comprises seven distinct steps:

- Form the team.
- Review strategy.
- Research marketplace.

- Define requirements.
- Develop acquisition strategy.
- Execute strategy.
- Manage performance.

The website includes a toolkit, known as Acquisition Requirements Roadmap Tool, to help build the documents used in the acquisition process.

DoDI 5000.02 ENCLOSURE E2: 6.a.

The *program manager* will develop and execute the acquisition strategy. This comprehensive and integrated baseline will identify the acquisition approach and key assumptions, and describe the strategies (business, support and technical) that the program manager plans to use to manage risks and meet program objectives. The strategy evolves over time as the program status changes. The strategy must consider many issues:

- business environment;
- contract awards and incentive structure;
- costs;
- foreign concerns (disclosure, exportability, security, and technology transfer);
- operational deployment objectives;
- opportunities in both the domestic and international markets;
- production lot or delivery quantities;
- risks and risk mitigation approach;
- small business strategy;
- technical alternatives; and
- test activities.

Minor changes to the plan due to changed circumstances or increased knowledge are common and do not require higher approval. However, major changes such as contract type or basic program structure do require approval prior to implementation. All changes should be noted and reflected in an update at the next program decision point or milestone.

The acquisition strategy serves as an agreement between the contracting officer and program manager. The program manager is responsible for the design and development of the product or service and associated operations and logistics support to accomplish program objectives to develop, produce and sustain a capability that satisfies validated user requirements. This includes managing acquisition, business, and technical aspects of the program as well as executive leadership. Ultimate responsibility for meeting cost, schedule, and technical goals rests with the program manager. The contracting officer serves as business advisor to the program manager and handles procurement operations.

DFARS 207.103

The acquisition strategy of development, production and operation must be coordinated with the cognizant small business specialist if the estimated contract or order value, including options, is at least $10 million for development and $25 million for production or services. No plan is required for a one-time buy or a buy-out.

DoDI 5000.85.2.2

The acquisition strategy document contains sufficient detail to allow senior leadership and the Milestone Decision Authority (MDA) to assess whether the strategy makes good business sense, effectively implements laws and policies, and reflects management's priorities. The strategy could evolve over time and should always reflect the status and desired mission outcome. The following are key areas of review by the MDA of the acquisition strategy:

- balancing of priorities and resources;
- competition;
- contract type;
- performance incentive approach;
- planning documents;
- requirements creep;
- small business participation;
- source selection approach; and
- tradeoffs among cost, performance, schedule, and technical feasibility.

For service acquisitions, the program manager should create decision points ("on- and off-ramps") for longer periods of performance and multiple award contracts to ensure the Government has a qualified pool of contractors who can provide continuous service throughout the life of the contract.

For each of these broad topics, other program documents provide the foundation for the positions summarized in the strategy. Hence, the goal of the acquisition strategy is not to provide all the basic information, but rather to reflect the data with references to prove the validity of the approach and the acquisition planning.

DAG: A Guide to DoD Program Management Business Processes, p. 36

The acquisition strategy should be tailored to program objectives and be flexible to allow innovation and modification as the program evolves. The program manager can adjust the management approach to fulfill regulatory requirements and acquisition procedures to more efficiently and effectively achieve program objectives. However, tailoring must consider program risk and operational urgency and complexity, while promoting streamlining processes, documents and work efforts and reviews. Tailoring is not just a one-time event, but rather a continuous review of the program's maturity and its costs, risks and technical progress.

DAG: A Guide to DoD Program Management Business Processes, pp. 39-40.

Unfortunately, all interested parties have their own priorities. The program manager must recognize that the user wants a top-performing system quickly, financial officers want to lower cost, and contractors want to lower risk. The program manager faces a "triple constraint" of three independent factors—time, cost, and performance—competing with or against each other as the program evolves. In addition, the program manager is affected by risk, scope, and customer satisfaction. Consequently, the program manager must try to consolidate these parochial interests, promote the understanding of mission priorities and requirements, and allocate resources to achieve the needed capability with acceptable risk. One way to do this, without consuming too many resources, is to analyze through "what-if" drills and identifying areas of probable change or failure.

The program manager reports to a *Program Executive Officer* (PEO), a senior acquisition manager who is typically responsible for cost, schedule, and performance for either a specific program or a portfolio of similar programs. The PEO normally only reports to, and receives guidance and direction from, the service or agency Acquisition Executive. PEOs are responsible for program management responsibilities such as interoperability, logistics support, quality, readiness, risk, standardization, sustainability, and technical capabilities. PEOs are also responsible for programmatic processes and the planning and budgeting required to oversee their assigned program(s) through the decision points and milestones. This provides the necessary direction and integration of assigned programs and assures effective interface with other services, combat system developers and supporting activities.

PEOs are responsible for, but not limited to the following:

- assess program and organizational health and the workforce's abilities to execute assigned authorities and responsibilities;

- communicate effectively with DoD Component level senior leaders, staff and Congress to support the programs;
- encourage innovation and competition, including capability and science/ technology priorities;
- enforce value added programmatic processes and procedures across the portfolio of programs to and ensure baselines are established and maintained throughout the lifecycle of the program;
- ensure organizations under their leadership have appropriate resources, including knowledge and skills, to execute their assigned tasks;
- establish and execute portfolio level activities, processes and tradeoffs that allow program and project monitoring, often using a dashboard approach;
- project current and future workforce, skills and practices necessary to sustain the PMO and matrix personnel; and
- provide executive review for all program strategies.

Risk management is another aspect of acquisition planning. This process identifies uncertainties that threaten cost, schedule, and performance objectives, while developing and implementing actions to deal with them. Exposure to these uncertainties constitutes *acquisition risk.* Risks can originate either outside of or within the program. External risks include:

- audit recommendations;
- changing threats;
- contractor financial difficulties;
- funding cuts;
- labor strikes; and
- management directives.

Internal risks include:

- accuracy of cost and schedule estimating process and assumptions;
- achieving reliability, availability, and maintainability requirements;
- contractor ability to perform;
- immature technology;
- inadequate performance standards;
- incorrect or changing requirements; and
- translating technological capabilities into reliable configurations.

The individual agencies establish criteria and thresholds to add detail in the planning process as an acquisition becomes more complex and costly. The agencies will decide when written plans are required and standard acquisition plan formats. Moreover, the department or agency must establish criteria and thresholds to use two prominent cost management techniques. The *design-to-cost* approach is where cost becomes a design constraint during product conception throughout the design and development phase and a management concern during operations. Secondly, *life-cycle cost* covers the total cost to the Government to acquire, operate, support, and dispose of items acquired techniques, as well as to ensure Government control over contract performance.

2.5.2 Acquisition Plan

FAR 7.1

A written *acquisition plan* is a document designed to achieve agreement between program manager and approving official. It documents the ground rules and assumptions of program and show program progress to provide a documented audit trail. It serves as the basis of consensus that the developed approach is optimal.

Creating an acquisition plan begins when the agency need is identified, prior to the fiscal year in which award is required. A team is formed of contracting, fiscal, legal, logistics, and technical personnel to develop the plan. At key milestone dates (or at least annually), the program manager reviews the plan and revises if necessary.

The written acquisition plan serves as a signed agreement between program manager and approving official that the developed approach is optimal. It identifies decision milestones and business, management and technical considerations that will control the acquisition(s). An acquisition plan can cover either one or multiple contracts; however every procurement action over $9 million must be addressed within an acquisition plan. Acquisition plans for service contracts discuss strategies for performance-based acquisition methods or a rationale for not using those methods.

FAR 7.1 and PGI 207.105

The written plan will have two major parts: one for background and objectives, and the other for a plan of action. The acquisition background and objectives section of the plan discusses:

- *Statement of need* – feasible acquisition alternatives, impact of prior acquisitions on each alternative, and related in-house effort;
  - acquisition decision document or a milestone decision or service review;
  - approval date for operational use or waiver and;
  - acquisition milestone chart (including acquisition plan updates, Defense Acquisition Board reviews and phase transitions).

- *Applicable conditions*—compatibility with existing or future systems or programs, and constraints on cost, schedule, and capability;
- *Cost*—including life-cycle cost, design-to-cost, and should-cost;
- *Capability or performance*—standards and how they are related to the need;
- *Delivery or performance-period requirements*—reasons for any urgency;
- *Trade-offs*—among the various cost, capability, performance, and schedule goals;
- *Risks*—technical, cost and schedule risks, risk reduction efforts, consequences of failure to achieve goals, and concurrency of development and production; and
- *Acquisition streamlining*—effort that results in more efficient and effective use of resources to design and develop or produce quality systems (e.g., draft solicitation or bidders conference), and using cost-effective requirements where appropriate.

The plan of action section discusses:

- *Sources*—including socioeconomic firms, bundling concerns and market research;
- *Competition*—how to obtain competition (or the basis for noncompetition) at both prime and subcontract levels, component breakout plans, spare and repair parts, key logistical milestones, and technical data needs;
- *Contract type(s)*—including the strategy to transition to firm-fixed-price contracts to the maximum extent practicable, including awarding some line items on a firm-fixed-price basis (either in the current contract or option items or follow-on contracts);
- *Source-selection procedures*—schedule for proposal submission and evaluation, evaluation factors and use of earned value management and integrated baseline review (e.g., whether offerors will be directly compensated for the costs of participating in a preaward review);
- *Acquisition considerations*—e.g.:
    - equipment lease or purchase,
    - FAR deviations,
    - if ordered under a non-DoD contract, how it will comply with DoD requirements,
    - solicitation method,
    - special clauses or provisions,
    - use of multiyear contracting or options,
    - use of performance-based acquisition or the rationale why not, and
    - for acquiring information and communications technology, the applicable accessibility standards in terms of help desks/call centers, plans, self-service technical support specifications, and training;[26]

- *Use of Internet Protocol when acquiring information technology*—the requirements documents must include the USGv6 Profile and the corresponding declarations of conformance defined in the USGv6 Test Program.[27] Usage of Internet Protocol version 6 to agency applications, infrastructure, and networks specific to individual acquisitions must comply with the agency's Enterprise Architecture.[28] The plan must also address the means to achieve capital planning and investment control;
- *Budgeting and funding*—budget estimates, basis of derivation, budget line items and program elements, estimated production unit cost, and the total cost for remaining production, and funding schedule;
- *Product or service descriptions*—including performance-based acquisition descriptions, and for development acquisitions, the market research to identify commercial or nondevelopmental items;
- *Priorities, allocations, and allotments*;
- *Contractor versus Government performance*—applicability of OMB Circular No. A-76;
- *Inherently governmental functions*;
- *Management information requirements*—methodology to analyze and use the earned value data to assess and monitor contract performance (if applicable); verification for compliance with the American National Standards Institute/Electronics Industries Alliance (ANSI/EIA) Standard-748, Earned Value Management Systems; and the timing and conduct of integrated baseline reviews (whether prior to or postaward);[29]
- *Make or buy*;
- *Test and evaluation*—of both the contractor and the Government for each phase of a major system acquisition, including any concurrent testing before production release. *Test and evaluation* is the process of gaining knowledge of both capabilities and limitations of the (sub)system and its components, materiel, and software. It assesses design and technological maturity, production and operational readiness, and acceptability. This effort will be structured to provide essential information to decision makers, assess attainment of technical performance parameters, and determine whether systems are operationally effective, suitable, survivable, and safe for intended use;
- *Logistics considerations*—
  - contractor data (e.g., cost, rights, and usage),
  - contractor or agency maintenance and service,
  - equipment standardization for future purchases,
  - extent of implementing Computer-Aided Acquisition and Logistics Support;[30]
  - integrated logistics support planning, including total life cycle system management and performance-based logistics;
  - quality assurance,

    - reliability and maintainability (e.g., plan, corrective action and feedback, design reviews and trade-off studies, failure analysis, parts and material qualification, predictions, prevention, and mitigation plans of corrosion, qualified parts lists, redundancy, and vendor requirements); and
    - warranties,
- *Government-furnished property*;
- *Government-furnished information*—any added controls to monitor access and distribution;
- *Environmental and energy conservation objectives*—applicability of environmental assessment or impact statement, and proposed resolution of environmental issues, elimination, or authorization to use Class I ozone-depleting chemicals and substances, and compliance with pollution prevention measures;
- *Security considerations*—
    - agency requirements for personal identity verification of contractors,
    - contractor physical access to a Federally controlled facility and/or information system,
    - monitoring,
    - technical requirements, and
    - security establishment and maintenance;
- *Contract administration*—e.g., inspection and acceptance;
- *Other considerations*—
    - defense production,
    - foreign sales implications,
    - higher-level quality standards,
    - industrial readiness,
    - performance in a designated operational area or supporting a diplomatic or consular mission;
    - SAFETY Act,[31]
    - standardization,
    - workplace safety;
    - compliance with national technology and industrial base in terms of:
        - ability to develop, produce, maintain, and support system performance requirements (e.g., components, composite materials, production tooling and test equipment raw materials, and special alloys);
        - availability of alternatives outside the current industrial base and impact of their acquisition on both the domestic industry base and military vulnerability;
        - uninterrupted maintenance, operation, and repair of the systems;
    - requirements for efficient manufacture during system design and production;
    - use of advanced manufacturing processes, subsystems, and technology;

- acquiring modern technology and production equipment, and systems to improve productivity and reduce life-cycle costs;
- methods to encourage investment by domestic sources in advanced manufacturing technology production equipment and processes by:
  - emphasizing source selection to promote efficient production; and
  - recognizing contractor investment in advanced manufacturing technology production equipment, processes and organization of work systems, and work force skill development;
- elimination of barriers to, and facilitation of, integrated manufacture of both commercial and military items;
- expanded use of commercial items and manufacturing processes, along with any modifications or nondevelopmental items;
- industrial capacity strategy for surge and mobilization, or rationale for not having a plan, including impact by logistics support plans;
- workforce mix per DoD Instruction 1100.22, Policy and Procedures for Determining Workforce Mix;
- crisis performance, including probability of occurrence and operational plans and resources;
- any contractor written plan for continuity of essential services and the criteria for assessing the sufficiency of the plan;
- operational plans resulting from combatant commander planning (e.g., theater entry, country clearance, use of weapons, living on-base);
- confirmation that inherently Governmental functions are not included in the contract requirements;
- any need for the contractor to train military personnel if the combatant commander's contingency plan requires military members to replace contractor employees during a crisis or contingency;
- contract compliance if delivery or performance occurs in whole or in part in a foreign country;
- contract administration planning in support of contingency operations:
  - resourcing contract administration and oversight personnel, including administrative contracting officers, quality assurance specialists, contract administrators, property administrators, and contracting officers' representative;
  - need for logistics support of contract administration and oversight personnel;
  - combatant or joint force commander requirements and considerations for contract administration;
  - plan for reachback support of contract closeouts;
  - requirements and resources necessary for both the Government and contractor to keep the Synchronized Predeployment and Operational Tracker current for contractor personnel;[32] and

        - requirements and resources necessary for both the Government and contractor to implement and maintain compliance with Federal and DoD trafficking in persons requirements.
    - if services will be delivered to or performed on a DoD installation or ship, compliance with DoD Instruction 2000.16, DoD Antiterrorism Standards, by considering:
        - past performance as an evaluation factor for award and as a performance metric under the resultant contract;
        - incorporation of security considerations into the contracting process, including suggestions for specific security measures that should be employed;
        - risk assessment results when developing alternative solutions to contract requirements that will mitigate security risks, including the impact of local security measures on contract performance and outcomes that could improve or leverage local security measures;
        - antiterrorism procedures, random schedules, access, search requirements, frequent changes in the local threat level, and their impact of these practices when developing performance work statements and special contracting requirements, especially those related to site access controls;
        - need for contractor personnel screening requirements to be met prior to commencing work under the contract;
        - the conduct of periodic inspections to ensure adherence to access control procedures; and
    - software and its maintenance;
- *Milestones for the acquisition cycle—*
    - acquisition plan approval;
    - statement of work;
    - specifications;
    - data requirements;
    - completion of acquisition package;
    - receipt of purchase request;
    - J&A and/or any D&F approval;
    - issuance of synopsis;
    - issuance of solicitation;
    - evaluation of proposals, audits and field reports;
    - start and completion of negotiations;
    - contract preparation and review; and
    - contract award; and
- *Identification of participants in acquisition plan preparation*—with contact information.

DFARS 207.106

- *For major weapon (sub)systems*—assessment of long-term technical data and computer software needs and a plan to obtain technical data deliverables and license rights needed to sustain those (sub)systems over their life cycle (either through competition or in-house maintenance). These assessments must be prepared before the solicitation and address:
  - merits of including a priced contract option for the future delivery of technical data and computer software, and associated license rights, that were not acquired upon initial award;
  - potential for changes in the sustainment plan over the life cycle of the weapon subsystem; and
  - support by performance-based logistics arrangements both to this and other (sub)systems that are to be supported by other sustainment approaches.

DFARS 207.106(S-72)

- *For all major systems*—measures to ensure competition at both the prime and subcontract levels, such as:
  - acquiring complete technical data packages;
  - build-to-print approaches to promote multiple production sources;
  - competitive prototyping;
  - competitiveness of source-to-repair decisions;
  - dual-sourcing;
  - encouraging use of incentive fees and penalties, including reliability and maintainability in the performance metrics;
  - funding next-generation prototype (sub)systems;
  - licensing multiple suppliers;
  - make-or-buy decisions by the prime contractor(s);
  - modular open architectures to promote competition for upgrades;
  - periodic system or program reviews to assess long-term competitive effects of program decisions; and
  - unbundling contracts; and
- *Preparation and storage of special tooling*—tools needed through the end of service life, including any necessary special contact clauses, facilities or funding.

2.6 MAJOR SYSTEMS ACQUISITIONS

FAR 34

A *major system* is a combination of elements that will function together to produce the capabilities necessary to fulfill a mission need. The definition of a major system is up to the individual agency (the default threshold is $2 million). It sets forth management objectives and structure, as well as key decision points. However, Congress may give input before committing resources and establishing objectives. An agency can establish alternate approaches through competing development contracts, so that industry can propose a variety of technical solutions with cost tradeoffs. Mission budgeting and funding processes allow comparative analysis of agency programs and prioritized alternatives.

The process of managing major systems over their life cycle is known as *systems engineering*. This complicated process consists of many phases and steps, such as these examples (in somewhat chronological order):

- *Concept exploration design:*
  - needs and requirements identification and analysis of alternatives,
  - feasibility analysis,
  - system design specifications, and
  - conceptual design review.
- *Demonstration and validation:*
  - functional analysis,
  - requirements review,
  - detailed trade-off studies,
  - development phase specifications,
  - operational support planning,
  - acquisition strategy development and documentation, and
  - preliminary design review.
- *Full-scale development:*
  - detailed product and facilities design,
  - integration of logistical, maintenance and support requirements,
  - development of engineering and prototype models,
  - product, process and material specifications,
  - funding profile,
  - critical design review, and
  - production decision.
- *Production stage:*
  - production of system components,
  - acceptance testing, and
  - system distribution.
- *Deployment:*
  - system operation in user environment,
  - validated maintenance plans,
  - ensuring adequate funding and integrated logistics support,

  - change management, and
  - assessment to correct deficiencies and adapt for continued improvement.
- *Phase-out and disposal:*
  - feasibility of system phase-out versus continued maintenance, and
  - system retirement.

2.6.1 Exploration and Development Phases

Contracts may be awarded for concept exploration for relatively short periods. These contracts refine the proposed concept and reduce technical uncertainties. The scope of work must be consistent with the Government's planned budget for this phase. Follow-on contracts for tasks in the exploration phase may be awarded as long as the concept approach remains promising, the contractor's progress is acceptable, and performance is economically practicable.

Contracts for the demonstration phase may be awarded to provide for contractors to submit, by the end of the phase, priced proposals for full-scale development. The contracting officer provides contractors with operational test conditions, performance criteria, life-cycle cost factors (development, procurement, operation, maintenance, and disposal), and selection criteria for the contractors to prepare their proposals.

Full-scale development contracts provide for the contractors to submit priced proposals for production that are based on logistics, quantity and schedule requirements that will be used in making the production decision. The agency head reaffirms the mission need and program objectives, and grants approval to proceed with production.

Proposals for major system design may include items available within the Federal Supply Service, commercially available from more than one source, and available competitively during the service life of the system. Proposals may also discuss the right to use technical data deliverables for competitive future acquisitions (with acquisition and usage costs), and qualification or development of multiple sources of supply for competitive future acquisitions.

The Government will normally pay for any testing and qualification required to use or incorporate the industrial resources manufactured or developed with assistance provided under Title III of the Defense Production Act of 1950.[33] Firms receiving requests from a Title III project contractor to test and qualify a Title III industrial resource refer such requests to the contracting officer. The contracting officer evaluates the request in accordance with agency procedures to determine whether the resource is or may be used to develop or manufacture a major system or supply and whether remaining quantities to be acquired are sufficient to justify incurring test and qualification costs. If the determination is affirmative, the contracting officer modifies the contract to require the contractor to test the Title III industrial resource for qualification.

To obtain initial program approval, the program manager estimates operational and technical characteristics, schedule, and acquisition cost. An estimating relationship will be used as a planning factor to compute the amount and type of effort or resources necessary to develop, produce, and/or operate the system. The program manager will also use a statistical *process capability analysis* during both development and production to analyze the variability of a process relative to product specifications. A basis of analysis is the *procedural support data* used by the contractor during the development phase for assembly, operation or maintenance tasks pertaining to production, test or inspection.

An advance procurement plan is developed to describe the procurement method, timetable and expected price. Advance notification of the acquisition should be given the widest practicable dissemination, including publicizing through www.sam.gov. Distribution should occur to as many potential sources as practicable, including smaller firms, Government laboratories, FFRDCs, educational institutions, nonprofit organizations, and foreign sources. The Government can also encourage industry participation by using draft solicitations and presolicitation conferences with prospective offerors for comment and solicitation revision.

2.6.2 Production Design

Once the engineering design effort is completed and a decision is made to enter production, the firm enters a new phase of management considerations. In this regard, the *production design* team tries to optimize the fabrication process. The team uses engineering and production talents to improve maintenance, plant layout, quality control, and work methods. It also strives to improve labor performance through such techniques as wage incentives and zero defects programs. The team may also use communication methods such as employee goal setting, plantwide recognition, problem identification, and suggestions.

Early in the production design process, the program manager will develop a flow chart (formally known as a *process chart*) that uses symbols to graphically depict inputs, sequential production activities and outputs to the customer. Boxes in the flow chart depict activities, and their connecting arrows show the data flow between the boxes. Managers can analyze these graphic depictions as decision aids.

A commonly used design technique to investigate design options involves tearing down a process or item to discover its underlying content. Known as *reverse engineering*, this process is designed to discover the technological principles of a product or system by analyzing its function, operations, and structure. The product is usually taken apart or decomposed to analyze its workings or makeup. *Value engineering* is a similar activity also used by firms to find opportunities for cost cutting. Sometimes the intent is to reproduce the item without using any original parts, but more often it is used for design decisions. This process is especially useful for computer-aided design to create a virtual three-dimensional model of a component or system.

Software is likewise subject to detailed examination by using reverse engineering to learn code or to replace unavailable documentation. After representing the system at a high level of abstraction, the computer-aided design process can trace the *source code* created by the programmer backward to its development phase without modifying it. Care must be taken to avoid modifying the product itself, since this would constitute re-engineering. The firm can then examine the *source data* (unprocessed raw data) that was originally recorded in the media. To record data transfer between electronic systems and verify its integrity, an audit log of all transactions is maintained in most database management systems. A firm may also use black-box testing to look for software bugs or undocumented features.

Reverse engineering is legal for an item protected by trade secrets. It is not necessary for a patented item because the public disclosure provides sufficient notice. As such, a firm may reverse-engineer a competitor's product to assess whether its own patent has in fact been abridged.

The contracting officer sends the final production solicitation to all prospective offerors to:

- describe the required mission capabilities without reference to any specific systems;
- include selection requirements;
- indicate and explain the schedule, capability, cost objectives, and known constraints;
- provide or indicate how to access all Government data related to the acquisition;
- require the use of an Earned Value Management System that complies with the guidelines of ANSI/EIA Standard-748-D; and
- state that each offeror is free to propose its own technical approach, design features, subsystems, and alternatives to capability, cost and schedule goals.

2.6.3 Production Control

It is now time to move on to manage and control the production process. *Production management* strives to produce the desired product at the desired rate at a minimum cost. The key elements of production management are performance and volume. Performance is a function of efficiency, equipment, facilities, quality, and schedule. Volume is a function of inventory level, production rate and work force. Because these objectives are often in conflict, the firm must strive to obtain an optimal balance, given their cost and schedule constraints. This approach may require *satisficing* (selecting a course of action to meet the minimum requirements to achieve the goal) among possible outcomes. The firm must also ensure producibility within its current manufacturing labor capabilities and a reliable supply of components.

Production control is concerned with inventory control, production planning and scheduling. Serving both staff departments and line organizations, this type of control entails measuring, evaluating, and adjusting system performance to meet system goals. The five phases of control are to:

- gather data from accounting statements, control charts, observation, or timecards;
- compare operating data with predetermined standards of performance. Statistical process control can monitor process variations over time to identify any nonrandom issues;
- detect causes of malfunction from customers, design engineers, output reports, and profit-and-loss statements;
- select one or more corrective actions from a set of alternatives; and
- implement the action.

There are several cautionary notes about the production control process. Care must be taken to exclude irrelevant and outdated data, and to focus on error detection and trouble-shooting. The firm may need to use sequential analysis or group brainstorming to break down a problem area into component parts to discover cause-and-effect or cause-and-solution relationships. Feedback about status or output could also affect input and therefore performance, since any delay in the feedback loop could lead to system instability (e.g., stockouts). The Government usually takes a hands-off approach to avoid micromanaging the production process (after all, the contractor is paid to resolve production problems), although program office engineers may be available to provide advice to the contractor.

Production control ultimately leads to quality control. *Quality* is a function of grade and fitness for use, or perhaps consistency in characteristics. Quality tends to become more important as price becomes more competitive. *Quality control* determines how well a product is being made. Quality control may be achieved by sampling (using operating characteristics and control charts), or by variables (using upper and lower control limits). However, higher quality may require higher-priced labor, more specialized or higher-tolerance equipment, and longer production time. One can perform a series of tradeoffs between quality conformance and cost, and plot the results on a graph to derive an optimal point where total cost is minimized. The Government is most interested in these tradeoff results to see if higher quality is worth a higher cost.

A firm may choose to either centralize or decentralize production, based on its analysis of the relative strengths and weaknesses of each approach. *Centralized production control* places all planning and control activities in one location. It allows close coordination and control with other functions such as engineering, finance, purchasing, and sales. *Decentralized production control* is common with larger firms, where individual departments handle some or all of the planning and control activities. Decentralized control tends to promote innovation, solve problems by those most familiar with them, and still allow for effective monitoring.

Several programs may be used to implement production control. *Manufacturing resource planning* is a method using an automated system to check capacity requirements, forecast production demands, purchase or redirect materials, and schedule production jobs. These are usually modularized computer programs that include bill of materials, control programs and scheduling for cost, design, inventory, and quality.

DoD runs a program to encourage contractors to upgrade their production equipment. The *Industrial Modernization Improvement Program* motivates contractors by awarding additional profit dollars to invest in facility improvements, including equipment, processes and software. This effort should reduce acquisition costs over the long run and improve productivity, while providing the participating contractor some insurance in case of program termination. The process includes analysis of the factory line or other production capability, validating engineering applications of new technology through a capital investment proposal, and purchase and installation of capital equipment.

Contractors may also have a formal *manufacturing technology* program to improve production equipment, processes, or techniques. This program would also include effort to assure production availability, increase efficiency and reliability, and reduce lead time and costs. The program emphasizes rapid transition from development to production, best manufacturing practices, and customization through smaller production lots.[34]

The program may use a risk-reduction method known as *low-rate initial production* to restrict the number of units built upon leaving full-rate production to reduce the Government's exposure to retrofit issues and costs. The contractor still produces enough units for final development and operational testing prior to a full production decision. Synonyms for this approach are *limited production* and *pilot production*. The solicitation does not reference or mandate Government specifications or standards unless the agency is mandating a subsystem or other component as approved under agency procedures.

The role of production control becomes strained compared with other aspects of the firm when things do not go according to design or plan, since it has broad influence over the production process and readiness. The production department may view the activities of designers as infringing on their responsibility or as intrusive by other departments involved in systems or procedures. However, the production department typically has autonomy, as long as it does not affect the operating budgets of other departments. Other common problems of production control may include:

- complex assembly processes;
- delayed planning;
- equipment and worker downtime;
- inaccurate forecasts;
- inadequate capacity, materials or tooling;
- long scheduling cycles;
- repair times and priorities; and
- work-in-process backlogs.

Solicitation Provisions and Contract Clauses

FAR 52.234-1, Industrial Resources Developed under Title III, Defense Production Act.

DFARS 252.209-7006, Limitations on Contractors Acting as Lead System Integrators.

DFARS 252.209-7007, Prohibited Financial Interests for Lead System Integrators.

DFARS 252.234-7003, Notice of Cost and Software Data Reporting System, in any solicitation that includes the basic or the alternate of DFARS 252.234-7004, Cost and Software Data Reporting. Use the basic provision when the solicitation includes DFARS 252.234-7004, Cost and Software Data Reporting without its Alternate I. Use Alternate I when the solicitation includes DFARS 252.234-7004, Cost and Software Data Reporting and its Alternate I.

DFARS 252.234-7004, Cost and Software Data Reporting System, for major defense acquisition programs or major automated information system programs. Use the basic clause in solicitations and contracts for major defense acquisition programs or major automated information system programs that exceed $50 million. Use Alternate I in solicitations and contracts for major defense acquisition programs or major automated information system programs with a value equal between $20 million and $50 million, when so directed by the program manager with the approval of the OSD Deputy Director, Cost Assessment.

2.6.4 Productivity

Productivity is the ratio of output to input of a production process, measured by comparing actual performance with historical figures or changes in ratios. This approach studies production processes and techniques to measure quantity of output per unit of resource (e.g., labor, money or time). By contrast, *efficiency* is a ratio of units of output to cost of input. These two concepts may or may not work together. Hence, a labor-saving approach could boost output without improving efficiency, while using lower-priced labor could improve efficiency without aiding productivity.

A special engineering discipline has grown around this subject. *Industrial engineering* provides guidance on optimal task performance. Time standards can be established for a variety of labor types. These standards assume average time for an average worker under average conditions. The standards can easily apply to manual and repetitive operations with collectible data, but are harder to develop for jobs that require thinking or planning. Use of standards may help to measure performance, but could stifle effectiveness at the expense of efficiency.

The most common tool to assess labor productivity over time is the learning curve. A *learning curve* is a mathematical analysis of efficiency or cost reduction based on the number of units produced. Using historical data, it projects efficiencies in labor, purchasing, production processes, and tools. Used for manual and repetitive tasks, it predicts the cost of future production or estimates hours to produce a unit. It assumes the amount of time to complete a task diminishes with each successive undertaking (reflected in a learning percentage). The learning percentage can be derived by arithmetic or logarithmic calculation of actual history and can be projected into the future for same or similar products.

Nonetheless, there are some concerns about learning curves. Early preproduction units may have very high learning, distorting projections for follow-on production. Managers may use learning curves as a goal and self-fulfilling prophecy, thereby avoiding further learning opportunities. Changes in indirect labor and supervision, organizational structure and procurement methods could impact direct labor in the future by changing conditions from those incurred in the recent past. Project phaseout could lead to personnel transfers and eliminate equipment maintenance, thereby impacting performance in the latter stages of production.

Results of the productivity assessments will lead to several ramifications for the firm. Staffing decisions can be made through job design or by specifying individual or group work activities. These decisions are complicated because the worker and transformation process have inherently conflicting needs and goals, different people respond differently in a given task, and employees may question traditional work behaviors and work approaches. To minimize these differences, the firm may employ a *Best Current Practice*), a procedure proven during operations to be the most logical way to perform a function or operation. Though not a mandate or standard, it can be changed whenever the state of the art changes or a better method is devised. Jobs can also be enlarged to interest the employee, though impact on output, quality and the worker must be considered. Social group and cultural impacts are also at issue. Task boundaries must be established in terms of what, when and where, to avoid overlooking environmental factors. A particular job should have:

- a pattern that draws together a variety of tasks into a set of meaningful overall tasks;
- contribution to product utility;
- feedback of results;
- quality of production;
- reasonable length of work cycle; and
- respect in the professional and cultural community (care, skill or knowledge).

Productivity in the plant can also be increased by:

- automated factories;
- cross-training and job rotation;
- investment incentives;
- job enrichment and flexible work hours;
- material handling equipment;
- numerically controlled machine tools; and
- recovery of precious metals.

Challenges to productivity growth include:

- aging capital equipment;
- changing market conditions and structure;
- cost constraints;
- evolving technology;
- international competition; and
- reduced labor base of skilled craftsmen.

Two recent advances in office management are also becoming widely employed. *Ergonomics* is a process which analyzes user interface with equipment and furniture to enhance worker productivity and avoid physical discomfort and disability. This approach optimizes human well-being and job performance. Another approach involves accommodations for physically-challenged employees to comply with the Americans with Disabilities Act.[35] These changes include removing architectural barriers and allowing for service animals and special telecommunications equipment.

As another technological advance to improve working conditions, a *virtual office* uses live remote communications for users to reduce office costs while preserving business professionalism. They are not the same as office business centers because they do not require a lease. They may include:

- call centers to receive telephone requests;
- conference room space on demand (perhaps including a kitchenette and waiting lobby);
- mailing address to provide 24/7 access to individual locked mailboxes;
- office equipment (e.g., conference and video calling, copier, facsimile machine, Internet, and printer);
- professional address to avoid personal security concerns of a home-based business;
- receptionist to receive and sign for incoming packages and provide document drop-off/pick-up services; and
- voicemail to store voice messages electronically.

2.6.5 Program Manager Considerations

In addition to the systems engineering life cycle already discussed, there is a *program management life cycle* which the program manager and associates follow. A typical program consists of five phases:

- Initiate:
  - compile a project charter and
  - develop a project scope statement in a preliminary (if not final) version;
- Plan:
  - create a project management structure,
  - develop program scope,
  - develop a work breakdown structure,
  - establish communications,
  - estimate activity resources and duration:
    - define and sequence activities,
    - develop a schedule,
    - estimate and budget costs, and
    - plan quality and human resources;
  - identify and assess risk and plan responses, and[36]
  - numerate contracting needs;

- Execute:
  - acquire and develop a project team,
  - direct program execution,
  - distribute information,
  - implement quality assurance, and
  - solicit and select contractors;
- Control:
  - administer contracts,
  - control cost, schedule and scope,
  - integrate change control,
  - maintain quality control,
  - manage project team,
  - manage stakeholders,
  - monitor and control risk,
  - monitor project work, and
  - report performance;
- Close project and contracts.

To obtain initial program approval, the program manager estimates operational and technical characteristics, schedule, and acquisition cost. An estimating relationship is used as a factor to compute the amount and type of effort or resources necessary to acquire, develop, produce, and/or operate the system. The program manager may also use a statistical process capability analysis during both development and production phases to analyze process variability based on product specifications. Also analyzed is the procedural support data used by the contractor during the development phase for assembly, operation or maintenance tasks pertaining to production, test or inspection.

This management approach places authority and responsibility for the project under one individual to whom all resources report, unless they are matrixed in from other functional areas. The *matrix concept* is a small project office with functional specialists loaned by other areas and using a dual reporting chain of command. This approach eliminates shared responsibility and can focus resources on a line basis. However, the program manager still has challenges within this framework. Support from the functional managers, competition for resources with other program managers, and turnover and workload challenges are common. Even an inability may occur to shift resources or obtain the right skills and inefficiencies due to changing skill set needs.

2.6.5.1 Cost Control

Cost control is a critical facet of program management. *Earned value management* is a commonly used technique to objectively measure program progress. This is frequently implemented by using a DoD methodology, *Cost Schedule Control Systems Criteria*, which evaluates the contractor's internal system for soundness and effectiveness on an ongoing basis during the life of the contract.[37] This process examines specified criteria to assess a program's management control systems. The firm chooses what management procedures to use, provided they comply with the characteristics and capabilities of such a system. There are no reporting requirements to the Government; however it can and will monitor results of criteria usage. There are 32 specific criteria grouped into five broad categories:

- organization—the WBS is integrated with the firm's organizational structure to assign responsibility for individual work tasks. Full integration is also required for planning, scheduling, budgeting, work authorization and cost accumulation systems;
- planning and budgeting—requires a performance measurement baseline;
- accounting—the *cost performance report* flows from the cost management system in a prescribed format to the program manager;
- analysis—compare actual versus planned performance against pre-established thresholds for variance analysis; and
- revisions and access to data—changes authorized by the customer or due to internal replanning without changing the baseline or available funding.

There are several calculations which are used to track cost performance to budget:

- the planned value or *budgeted cost of work scheduled* (BCWS) adds the budgets for all work packages scheduled to be accomplished, whether or not started yet;
- the earned value or *budgeted cost of work performed* (BCWP) adds the budgets for all completed work packages and any completed portions of open packages;
- *Actual cost of work performed* (ACWP); and
- *Estimate at completion* (EAC) is the sum of actual direct cost, allocable indirect costs, and estimated direct and indirect costs for all remaining work.

The first three values are plotted on a graph over time to compare data points for a given month and derive trends. The fourth metric is static at a given point of time.

Comparing BCWP with BCWS leads to a schedule variance, while comparing BCWP with ACWP yields a cost variance. The two budgeted values are calculated at the cost account level by summing the values of all lower-level work package budgets. However, ACWP may be collected either at cost account level or at the lower work package level. In either event, cost variances are investigated to determine cause and develop a resolution. Similarly, schedule variance is investigated to cross-check the validity of both BCWP and cost variances.

Program managers can identify specific roles and responsibilities of project personnel by listing activities and then identifying for each which individual is responsible, accountable, consulted, and informed. This is known as a *RACI Model* and looks like the example in table 2.1. The letters in the table reflect the roles of each individual. The *responsible* person(s) carries out the task. The *accountable* person is responsible for success or failure of the task and has decision-making responsibility. Hence, only one person can be accountable for any given task. *Consulted* persons are conferred with in two-way communications, while *informed* persons are subject to one-way communications without need for response. However, care should be taken to ensure that responsibility is not obscured by re-delegation, that individual agendas do not interfere with the firm's goals, and that any shared responsibilities are considered.

Strategic planning requires analysis of *strengths, weaknesses, opportunities, and threats* (*SWOT*) of any project. This involves first defining the objective of the project, then identifying any internal or external factors that support or challenge achievement of the objective. The four components of this analysis are:

- strengths—internal attributes that help reach the objective,
- weaknesses—internal attributes that harm reaching the objective,
- opportunities—external conditions that help reach the objective, and
- threats—external conditions that could damage the objective.

Strengths and weaknesses are internal to a firm, while opportunities and threats are external. Both strengths and opportunities help a firm to reach an objective, while weaknesses and threats could prevent the firm from reaching an objective. One can try to match strengths to opportunities to finds competitive advantages, or else convert weaknesses or threats into strengths or opportunities (or else try to minimize or avoid them).

Table 2.1 RACI Model

Activity	*Adam*	*Brianna*	*Carlos*	*Denise*
Develop Request	R/A	C	C	x
Approve Request	I	R/A	I	x
Implement Change	R/A	x	x	C
Test Change	R	R	R/A	I
Approve Change	I	I	I	R/A

Internal factors may include personnel, finance, and manufacturing. External factors include changes in technology, legislation, socio-cultural issues, and market or competitive posture. Lists or matrices are compiled to compare and assess these factors, a gap analysis may be performed, and develop compensating strategies are then developed. Critical success factors will be needed to implement strategies. Then the results must be monitored for any corrective actions.

As another key aspect of program management, *knowledge management* comprises a range of strategies and practices for a firm's employees to identify, record and distribute knowledge on organizational areas of interest (e.g., performance, winning proposals, innovation, lessons learned, eliminating redundant work, and continuous improvement). Knowledge management is especially useful to train new employees and record intellectual capital of current employees to guard against "brain drain" upon their departure. Many strategies are used to implement knowledge management, such as:

- collaborative technologies such as groupware,
- cross-project learning,
- encoding knowledge into a shared knowledge repository for networking and sharing,
- individuals requesting input of an in-house expert on an ad hoc basis,
- knowledge mapping of repositories for employee access (such as communities of practice or discussion boards),
- mentor-mentee relationship,
- rewarding participants, and
- systematic evaluation of employee competencies.

The Government will normally pay for any testing and qualification required to use or incorporate the industrial resources manufactured or developed with assistance provided under Title III of the Defense Production Act of 1950 (50 U.S.C. Appendix 2170). This program is designed to determine affordable and viable production capabilities for items which are deemed essential to the national defense. Firms receiving requests from a Title III project contractor to test and qualify a Title III industrial resource refer such requests to the contracting officer. The contracting officer evaluates the request in accordance with agency procedures to determine whether the resource is or may be used to develop or manufacture a major system or supply, and whether remaining quantities to be acquired are sufficient to justify incurring test and qualification costs. If the determination is affirmative, the contracting officer modifies the contract to require the contractor to test the Title III industrial resource for qualification.

2.6.5.2 Scheduling

A scheduling system is intended to arrange and optimize resources, typically using common automated processes. It helps determine how to commit resources to produce extra units for stock storage during slack periods, reduce demand during peak production and maintain multiple suppliers.

There are numerous scheduling techniques. A *unit* (one-by-one) method may use charts (bar, Gantt, and milestone events). *Gantt charts* are used for load control, drawings and specifications control for processing manufacturing and variations of serialized batch control or block order control. Gantt charts are actually bar charts that show planned and actual performance for the resource to be controlled. *Milestone charts* are similar to Gantt charts but use a different method of displaying project status. The organization could use job shop scheduling, treating each order as a separate project to be separately routed and tracked. Another option assigns work to specific machines to minimize either cost or production time.

A *batch* method can be employed to schedule a few units at a time. It usually establishes lot sizes to balance machine setup costs and inventory holding costs, or else allocates work units by machine capacity or limitation. The process determines for each item when scheduled production plus inventory on hand meets item demands. It then schedules performance, beginning with the item having the shortest turnout time. By contrast, a *mass* process involves many units at once. It derives operator task time to achieve the desired output rate, then coordinates materials flow throughout the departments or assembly line.

Another frequently used method is the *line-of-balance* technique to identify lagging steps upfront to minimize delivery delay. This process employs an objective delivery schedule, production plan, progress chart, and comparison of process to the objective delivery schedule (the line of balance) to show the quantities needed at each control point to remain in line with the objective.

Critical path scheduling consists of graphical techniques to plan and control projects in terms of time, cost, and resources. The best-known techniques are Critical Path Method (CPM) and Program Evaluation and Review Technique (PERT). CPM uses a network approach to provide well-coordinated schedules to shorten project time and reduce cost. This method uses flow diagrams of the network, critical time paths, schedule leeway and time-cost functions. It then analyzes program uncertainties by highlighting activities that are most essential to successful project completion.

PERT breaks down work into manageable packages integrated into a network that outlines the most efficient manner to complete a program. This process measures actual vs. planned progress and costs on a project rather than functional basis, all to determine whether the project is on schedule and to analyze sources of delay and overrun. PERT schedules activities in a development program based on a network concept and identifies the critical path to treat schedule uncertainties.

Both methods utilize optimistic time, most likely time and pessimistic time, and probabilistic theory. However, there are differences in their applicability. CPM is generally limited to routine plant operations. By contrast, PERT treats probability in time estimates as well as cost estimates, therefore it can be used in advanced development projects of some uncertainty which require developing experimental hardware for operational or technical testing before deciding whether to design or engineer the items for future use. Time-cost models which strive to minimize cost scheduling favor CPM networks. Budgetary control models tend toward PERT because they define activity direct costs to expedite activities (e.g., overtime and hiring costs) and project indirect costs and try to find the project duration that minimizes their sum (an optimum point in a time-cost tradeoff).

Regardless of which method is chosen, several guidelines help to schedule production operations. The factory should schedule only items it can make, and only after all materials, components and tools are available. It should sequence orders by the latest requirements rather than original required dates. Using a short scheduling cycle such as daily or weekly is often best, especially at keeping backlogs off the shop floor. Of course, it may be necessary to accept some amount of worker inactivity, but even this may be cost-beneficial instead of a plant shutdown.

2.6.5.3 *Decision Analysis*

The process by which choices are made is known as *decision analysis*. This process uses diagrams and decision trees to assess alternatives and their uncertainty and probability of achieving desired outcomes. The process emphasizes logic rather than intuition, so the manager should consider its results as only one source of input rather than the sole means of decision-making. Common methods of decision analysis are:

- *linear programming* to mathematically allocate limited resources over competing activities optimally (e.g., product mix, resource allocation, plant and machine scheduling, and work scheduling);
- *mathematical programming methods* (e.g., nonlinear or dynamic programming, network analysis, game theory, and integer programming);
- *probabilistic models* (e.g., stochastic processes, queuing theory and Markov decision process);
- *regression analysis* to forecast the expected value of a dependent variable;

- *simulation and modeling* using predictable behavior elements for probability distribution of each possible system state and input. Random numbers can generate simulated events over time in accordance with the appropriate probability distribution to create operational simulation or sampling experiments on a system model; and
- other *statistical methods* (probability theory, exponential smoothing, statistical sampling, and hypothesis testing).

2.6.5.4 Change Management

Change management is a means to migrate from the "as-is" state to a desired "to-be" state by empowering employees to embrace change in the business environment. Successful change management requires both marketing and understanding leadership styles, group dynamics and communications to design strategies to achieve desired changes. Personal counseling of employees may also be necessary. In this vein is the expanding role of social responsibility in the business sector. *Social responsibility* is the theory that a firm is obligated to benefit society by acting to advance social goals and not acting to harm society. Examples include corporate philanthropy, compliance with laws and regulations to minimize liability, and maintaining a quality of life for employees. This concept is becoming a strategic movement by corporations on a global scale to attract and retain talent and avoid government interference with daily operations.

Organization Development is a systematic approach for a firm or office to respond to change (e.g., technology or marketing opportunities) to enhance its effectiveness and viability in terms of attitudes, values, and structures. It stresses the concept of achieving goals to enhance effectiveness. A change agent (usually either a trained employee or outside consultant) is introduced to use behavioral science to help the office improve performance by identifying and solving its own problems, with support from higher management. The change agent focuses on the total organization and processes rather than a single department or product structure. The agent also looks at group behaviors and influences rather than personalities or individual work groups. The contracting officer will use the scientific method to collect data (e.g., interviews, questionnaires and meetings) and feed it back to the office for analysis and planning. The change agent focuses on:

- conflict,
- coping with organizational problems and conflict,
- decision processes,
- entity norms,
- feedback,

- group processes and communications,
- knowledge and skills, and
- leadership styles.

The change agent will seek an environment which encourages learning and change, especially through sharing feelings and feedback. The office can then adopt a *systems approach* to operations by emphasizing openness and feedback in relationships rather than individuals' perspectives, studying systems holistically and humanely.

The change agent may assess data using quantitative methods such as multiple regression, time-series analysis, and analysis of variance. *Regression* tries to derive a relationship between variables by estimating parameters from the collected data by using linear functions. Usually, this means expressing the mean of one variable as a function of the value of another variable. Using a table of predictive values of one variable, a formula can be derived to predict the value of the other variable, then both values can be plotted on a graph. A succession of data points can be identified in this manner, leading to a plotted curve to predict the value of the second variable for any given value of the first.

Next, a *time series*, a sequence of data points measured at different times, can be analyzed to derive statistics and data characteristics. A model can be constructed to forecast future events based on the past, including future data points. They must be ordered temporally using a one-way order of time. Observations near in time to each other are more closely related than those far apart in time. *Analysis of variance* collects statistical models and splits their variance based on different causes to test statistically whether several groups (generally at least three) have the same mean value.

2.6.5.5 Cost-Benefit Analysis

Cost-benefit analysis is a process used to assess the economic wisdom for a project or program, or for policy initiative.[38] The process compares the total expected costs against the total expected benefits of one or more actions to choose the best or most profitable option. Benefits and costs are often expressed in monetary terms. Flows which could occur at different points in time are expressed in their *present value* on a given date of a future payment or series of future payments, discounted to reflect both the time value of money and investment risk.

Cost-benefit analysis is often used by government agencies to evaluate the cost effectiveness of different alternatives to see whether the benefits outweigh the costs. These costs and benefits are evaluated in terms of the public's willingness to either pay for them (benefits) or to avoid them (costs).

Inputs are measured in terms of the value in their best alternative use (known as *opportunity costs*). First described by the English economist John Stuart Mill, opportunity cost is the expense of the next-best choice available to ensure that scarce resources are used efficiently.[39] These costs can be expressed in terms of money or time.

Deriving expected costs and benefits of specific actions is often very difficult, usually through surveys or inferences from market behavior. A discount rate is used to compute all relevant future costs and benefits in present-value terms, usually an interest rate from a bank or financial market. This can be very misleading however, since a high discount rate implies a low value in future generations, thereby reducing the desirability of any initiative.[40] Monetary values may also be assigned to other factors such as loss of reputation, market share or the firm's teaming arrangements.

Principal cost-benefit indicators include:

- NPV (net present value),
- PVB (present value of benefits),
- PVC (present value of costs),
- BCR (benefit-cost ratio = PVB / PVC), and
- Net benefit (= PVB – PVC).

Inaccurate cost-benefit analyses introduce an element of risk in the planning because they may rely on past projects which differ in size and skill levels of participants, as well as crude heuristics to estimate the cost of intangible elements. Arbitrariness and inexperience may be present in decisions by the current project's members of which cost drivers should be included in an analysis. Moreover, there are humanistic aspects to consider, since unconscious biases of team members may reflect a hidden interest in advocating a decision or direction to go.

2.6.6 Program Approvals

Decision reviews by higher authority carefully assess a program's readiness to proceed to the next acquisition phase and to make a sound investment decision of financial resources. These reviews focus on data and issues to allow the decision authority to judge whether the program is ready to proceed.

2.6.6.1 Overview

DoDI 5000.02T, 5.b

The "ABCs" of program management are acquisition, budgeting, and capabilities. These three components are related and must operate simultaneously in close coordination. Adjustments may have to be made throughout the system life cycle to keep the three processes aligned. Capability requirements may have to be adjusted to conform to technical and fiscal reality, such as changing requirements and funding availability. Budgeted funds might be adjusted to make programs executable or to adapt to evolving requirements and priorities. Acquisition programs may need to adjust to these changing requirements and funding availability. Hence, the responsible parties at both the DoD and Component levels must work closely together to adapt to changing circumstances as needed, and to identify and resolve issues as early as possible.

PGI 201.170

The Office of Defense Pricing and Contracting team of USD(A) will facilitate preaward peer reviews for procurements with an estimated value of $1 billion or more under major defense acquisition programs for which USD(A&S) is the milestone decision authority or which USD(A&S) designates as requiring a peer review regardless of value. DoD components may request DPC-led peer reviews for acquisitions valued below the $1 billion threshold. This includes new contracts, modifications to existing contracts, requests for equitable adjustment, claims, etc. IDIQ (indefinite delivery/indefinite quantity) contracts that will not establish pricing terms in the basic contract are not subject to peer review, but individual orders that exceed the threshold are subject to peer review. They will review solicitations, pre-negotiation positions and proposed awards. Their input is normally advisory in nature; however any significant findings not followed by the contracting activity must first be reported to the senior procurement official of the activity.

DoDI 5000.02T, 4.a

The Defense Acquisition Executive (DAE) is the Under Secretary of Defense for Acquisition, Technology, and Logistics (USD(AT&L)).[41] The DAE serves as the Major Decision Authority (MDA) for Major Defense Acquisition Programs (MDAPs) and Major Automated Information System (MAIS) programs. A *Major Defense Acquisition Program* is estimated to exceed $300 million (in Fiscal Year 1990 terms) for research and engineering effort (including test and evaluation) or $1.8 billion dollars for procurement.[42] A *Major Automated Information System* (MAIS) will use computer hardware, software, data, or telecommunications to perform information collection, display, processing, storage, or transmission. They are usually either part of a weapon system or have classified or sensitive application. The DAE may delegate the MDA role to the head of a DoD Component, who may further delegate the authority to the Component Acquisition Executive (CAE). The DAE may also delegate MDA authority to another official within the Office of the Secretary of Defense.

DAG: A Guide to Program Management Business Processes, pp. 2-4

The DoD decision support systems for major systems consists of three separate but interrelated systems: the Joint Capabilities Integration and Development System (JCIDS) to establish requirements; Planning, Programming, Budgeting, and Execution (PPBE) to address resources; and the Defense Acquisition System to acquire supplies and services.[43] These three systems are aligned to operate simultaneously to provide an integrated approach to strategic planning and execution. Collectively they are known as the "Big A."

JCIDS is a systematic method to support the Joint Requirements Oversight Council (JROC) and Chairman of the Joint Chiefs of Staff responsibilities to identify, assess, validate, and prioritize joint capability requirements.[44] JCIDS uses a variety of approaches to determine capability requirements, establish quantifiable attributes and metrics, and trace these requirements to the missions, threats, standards, strategic guidance, and tasks and conditions.[45] JCIDS analysis compares these capability requirements to current and programmed capabilities to determine if any capability gaps present an unacceptable level of risk and warrant development of capability solutions.

The JCIDS process gives birth to several documents, in sequence: the Initial Capabilities Document, Materiel Development Decision, Analysis of Alternatives, DoD Capabilities Requirements, Joint Emergent Operational Need (JEON), and Joint Urgent Operational Need (JUON), Capabilities Development Document, and Capabilities Production Document.[46]

DAG CH 6-3.5

The PPBE process is designed to properly allocate resources across the Federal Government.[47] The process creates both a five-year plan and budget projections for the upcoming year. The Secretary of Defense establishes goals, policies and strategy for DoD, which are subsequently used to guide resource allocation decisions that balance the guidance with fiscal constraints. The PPBE process consists of four distinct but overlapping phases: Planning, Programming, Budgeting, and Execution Review.

The Planning portion reviews the National Security Strategy from the National Security Council, the SECDEF's Defense Strategy Guidance and the National Military Strategy from the Joint Chiefs of Staff. These documents examine potential threats, strategy, force structure, readiness posture, modernization programs, infrastructure, and information operations and intelligence. The end-result of this review is the Defense Planning Guidance to serve as an investment objective for the next five fiscal years for DoD a long-term view of the security environment to help shape the investment blueprint for the five fiscal years to be developed by the Military Departments and Defense Agencies.

The Programming Phase allocates resources (primarily funds and people) to support the roles and missions of the various DoD departments and agencies by pricing out various scenarios over the next five years and developing the Program Objectives Memorandum to record the resultant decisions. This document is a detailed description of the proposed programs, including a time-phased allocation of resources (forces, funding and manpower) by program projected five years into the future.

In the third phase, USD(C) budget analysts (along with OMB budget examiners) focus on using proper funding policy for each appropriation category, proper pricing of the effort, phasing of the work efforts for acquisition programs, and efficiency of budget execution in the current year as well as projected executability in the budget year. Components then update their budget figures to reflect those final decisions and to prepare budget justification materials that will be provided to OMB for incorporation into the President's Budget, and the FYDP is updated again.

The final phase evaluates how well current appropriations are being obligated and expended by measuring their percentage versus OSD goals. It also compares what DoD said it would accomplish with its appropriations and what it actually accomplished (i.e., outcomes achieved). The execution review may lead to recommendations to adjust resources and/or restructure programs to achieve desired performance goals. This analysis then enables DoD to prepare its Annual Performance Report. Note that, while the acquisition process is "event driven," the PPBE process is "calendar driven."

DAG: A Guide to Program Management Business Processes, p. 4

DoD has instituted a new methodology to acquire products, services, and systems of major value, known as the Adaptive Acquisition Framework (AAF). It contains several acquisition pathways which provide opportunities for decision authorities and program managers to develop tailored acquisition strategies that match the characteristics of the capability being acquired. The framework has six (6) distinct acquisition pathways:[48]

1. Urgent Capability Acquisition;
2. Middle Tier of Acquisition;
3. Major Capability Acquisition;
4. Software Acquisition;
5. Defense Business System; and
6. Acquisition of Services.

Each pathway is governed by the following directives, in order:

- DoDI 5000.74, Defense Acquisition of Services
- DoDI 5000.75, Business Systems Requirements and Acquisition
- DoDI 5000.80, Middle Tier of Acquisition
- DoDI 5000.81, Urgent Capability Acquisition
- DoDI 5000.85, Major Capability Acquisition
- DoDI 5000.87, Software Acquisition

DoDI 5000.81

DoD strives to provide warfighters in conflict or contingency operations with the capabilities urgently needed to overcome unforeseen threats, achieve mission success, and reduce risk of casualties. To accomplish this mission, special rules apply for *Urgent Capability Acquisition* programs that can be fielded within two years and are below the cost thresholds of ACAT I and IA programs (the highest-level ACAT programs are not subject to these accelerated processes).[49] The maximum dollar amount is currently $525 million. USD(A&S) determines which programs are covered by these special procedures and serves as the acquisition executive for them. These programs often combine pre-development, development, production, deployment, and operational phases at the same time.

DAG: Engineering of Defense Systems Guidebook, 3.3

The Middle Tier of Acquisition pathway allows mature capabilities to be rapidly prototyped or fielded within five years. This approach is often used for available or emerging commercial technology, maturing technology from government labs, Independent Research and Development (IR&D) efforts, and Small Business Innovation Research (SBIR) solutions.

The Major Capability Acquisition Pathway has several phases, each ending in Authority to Proceed decision points. The first phase selects the general system concept and begins translating validated capability gaps into system-specific requirements. It then includes a preliminary design review and multiple competitive sources which investigate new technologies, risk reduction and any potential impacts to cost, performance, and schedule. Next come engineering and manufacturing development, including a critical design review and test to assess readiness for pre-production prototype hardware fabrication or software coding. This leads to low rate initial production, personnel training, initial operational test and evaluation, and the full-rate production or full-deployment decision. Then come operations, sustainment and disposal. The PM works with system users to document objective measures and outcomes, performance and sustainment requirements, resource commitments, and stakeholder responsibilities. These inevitably lead to system modifications to improve performance and reduce ownership costs, as well as the use of digital technology to enable continuous evaluation of software changes and cyber threats over the system life cycle. The details of milestone approvals will be discussed later in this section.

The Software Acquisition pathway requires active collaboration with end users to ensure software deliverables address their needs, maximize mission impact, and undergo regular assessment of performance and risk. Leveraging existing enterprise services is preferable to creating unique software services, and encourages modified hardware and cloud computing platforms, and improvements to software embedded in military-unique hardware and weapon systems. This approach will require government and contractor software teams to use modern software development methodologies (e.g., agile or lean), modern tools and techniques, and human-centered design processes.[50] These modern approaches will also promote automated critical monitoring functions related to software health, operational effectiveness and security, as well as to continually assess and measure cybersecurity preparedness and responsiveness, identify and address risks and execute mitigation actions.

The Defense Business System pathway covers such data areas as financial, human resources management, installations management, logistics, planning, procurement, readiness, and training. Although commercial best practices are emphasized, development and test activities are still needed. Once again, there are several major phases on this pathway, separated by Authority to Proceed decision points. The first phase establishes understanding of required business capabilities to develop requirements and attributes, with associated threshold and objective values to measure them. The next phase determines the high-level business processes supporting the future capabilities to maximize use of existing business solutions and minimize unique requirements. The third phase establishes the acquisition strategy and capability support approach required to meet the functional requirements. Next come contract award, vendor management, delivery of the business system, and risk management. The final phase supports business capability, continued cybersecurity readiness and appropriate upgrades to the business system. At this point, the functional sponsor accepts full deployment of the system and approves transition to capability.

DAG CH 1-3.2.3 and DoDI 5000.85, with Change 1, November 4, 2021

DoD uses acquisition categories (ACATs) defined by definitions and dollar thresholds. DoDI 5000.02 (Encl. 1, Table 1) identifies the cognizant MDA for each ACAT level, as designated by the CAE. The categories determine the level of review procedures and decision authority. Thus, we see a tiered designation scheme based on statutory requirements of increasing dollar value and management oversight and reporting. Acquisition programs are divided into these categories to facilitate decentralized decision-making, execution and compliance with statutory requirements.

ACAT I programs are of a specific dollar size. The program must be estimated to cost a total of over $525 million (as measured in Fiscal Year 2020 constant dollars) in Research, Development, Test, and Evaluation expenditures or else all planned increments of over $3.065 billion (FY 2020 constant dollars).[51] Alternatively, a program can be designated by the MDA as ACAT I based on a "special interest" designation due to achievement of critical capabilities, Congressional interest, heavy use of resources, a Joint program, as part of a system-of-systems, or technology complexity. Programs that already meet the MDAP and MAIS thresholds cannot be designated as Special Interest.

A MAIS becomes an ACAT IA program when it is either so designated by the MDA or by statute when it is estimated to exceed:

- $200 million (FY 2020 constant dollars) for all expenditures for all increments related to system definition, design, development, and deployment; or
- $940 million (FY 2020 constant dollars) for all expenditures for all increments directly related to the above functions plus operation and maintenance.

Once again, these programs can also be designated by the MDA as ACAT I programs based on a "Special Interest" designation. However, the MAIS designation does not cover purchases of standalone hardware or software, nor those that are integral parts of a weapon or weapon system or used for highly sensitive or classified programs.

Some programs which do not meet the criteria for an ACAT I program but do meet the criteria for a major system may be designated as ACAT II programs. These programs are estimated by the DoD Component head to require total expenditure for Research, Development, Test, and Evaluation Appropriations (RDT&E) of more than $185 million in FY 2014 constant dollars, or for procurement of more than $835 million in FY 2014 constant dollars. They can also be so designated by the DoD Component head to be ACAT II. The MDA for ACAT II programs is the DoD Component Acquisition Executive.

All ACAT I and II programs have their own dedicated program manager. ACAT I programs will also have dedicated personnel serving as Deputy Program Manager, engineer(s), logistician(s), and tester(s), plus a Business and Financial Manager.

Those acquisition programs that do not meet the criteria for ACAT II are deemed ACAT III. This includes MAISs that are not deemed ACAT I, since they cannot be designated as ACAT II because they do not have any limited production runs.

Programs in the Navy and Marine Corps not otherwise designated as ACAT III are designated ACAT IV. These tend to be testing or monitoring programs. Neither the Army nor the Air Force use this designation.

DoDI 5000.02T, 5.a.-b.

MDAs will tailor program strategies and oversight to satisfy validated capability requirements. This tailoring can cover acquisition phase content and the timing and scope of decision reviews and decision levels. When there is a strong threat-based or operational need to field a capability solution quickly, MDAs may implement streamlined procedures to accelerate responsiveness. Statutory requirements must still be complied with, unless waived in accordance with relevant provisions. In fact, the Secretary of Defense may waive acquisition law or regulation to acquire a capability that would not otherwise be available to the DoD Components.[52] This waiver authority may not be delegated.

The Major Capability Acquisition Pathway is the only pathway which still utilizes the old Milestone A/B/C approval process. This process creates numerous documents to record analyses and decisions. The reams of paper and electrons so generated has created a plethora of program analysts and support contract personnel who draft all these records. A comprehensive listing of these documents is well beyond the scope of this book; however those which bear some significance to the contracting process will be mentioned. Hence, we now return our attention to this Pathway.

The Defense Acquisition System to acquire supplies and services contains five phases, three milestone decisions, and five decision points, listed in chronological order:

  - Materiel Development Decision Point;
- Materiel Solution Analysis (MSA) phase;
  - Milestone A;
- Technology Maturation and Risk Reduction (TMRR) phase;
  - Requirements Decision Point (Capability Development Document-Validation);
  - Development Request For Proposal (RFP) Release Decision Point;
  - Milestone B;
- Engineering and Manufacturing Development (EMD) phase;
  - Milestone C;

- Production and Deployment (P&D) phase;
  - Low Rate Initial Production Decision Point or (for IT) Limited Deployment Decision Point;
  - Full Rate Production Decision (Point), authorizing Full Rate Production or Deployment (for IT); and
- Operations and Support Phase.

2.6.6.2 Milestone A

The Materiel Development Decision is based on a validated initial requirements document such as an Initial Capabilities Document and completion of preliminary study guidance and plan. This decision directs execution of the Analysis of Alternatives and authorizes the DoD Component to conduct the Materiel Solution Analysis Phase.[53] This analysis provides life-cycle cost estimates for every alternative under consideration such as research, development, operations, support, and disposal. Operating expenses include logistics, maintenance, and manpower. Fully burdened fuel costs and unit acquisition costs must be derived. Investment costs can vary between alternatives, such as learning, reuse of current equipment, specific support or training equipment, and military construction. The analysis may also need to include common, social, sunk, and support costs. Contractor prototypes may be useful to reduce initial production costs. Different alternatives may have different economic lives, which may require the analysis to create or even truncate economic lives.

Here the program office begins translating validated capability gaps into system-specific requirements, including the Key Performance Parameters and Key System Attributes. Other activities required before Milestone A include planning to support a decision on the acquisition strategy, tradeoffs among cost, schedule, and performance, affordability, and risk analyses, and planning for risk mitigation.

DoDI 5000.02T, 5.d.(3)

The Milestone A decision approves program entry into the Technology Maturation and Risk Reduction (TMRR) Phase. The DoD Component may decide to perform technology maturation and risk reduction work in-house and/or award contracts. Competitive prototypes are usually part of this phase. Key considerations are:

- adequacy of the plans and programmed funding to mitigate risks;
- affordability, feasibility, and justification of the planned materiel solution;
- efficiency and effectiveness of the proposed acquisition strategy;
- projected threat and its impact on the materiel solution;
- scope of the capability requirements and understanding of priorities; and
- understanding technical, cost and schedule risks of acquiring the materiel solution.

At the Milestone A Review, the program manager presents the business approach to acquire the preferred materiel solution. This approach is based on an acquisition strategy, affordability analysis and goals and should-cost management targets to support the proposed long-term capital investments at specific capability levels. The review will also require an assessment of program risk, including how specific technology development and risk mitigation activities will reduce the risk to acceptable levels.

Upon Milestone A approval, the MDA will make a written determination in an Acquisition Decision Memorandum (ADM). This document will direct the materiel solution, plan for the TMRR Phase, release the final RFP, and specify exit criteria to complete TMRR and enter the Engineering and Manufacturing Phase (EMD). Any substantive changes to the plan resulting from the source selection process will require the DoD Component to notify the MDA, who may choose to conduct an additional review prior to any contract awards.

DAG: Engineering of Defense Systems Guidebook, 3.2.1.3.1.-2

The TMRR phase will determine the appropriate set of technologies to integrate into a full system. Technologies and their associated representation in digital models will mature, including demonstrating and assessing them. As a result of prototyping of the system and/or system elements, the program office will perform trade studies, refine requirements and revise designs, including functional and allocated baselines, interface control drawings/documents, specifications, and system architectures and models. It will then develop a digital engineering ecosystem to transfer into the program of record.

The key technical objectives in this phase are initial system development to derive a preliminary design and technical risk reduction. This phase ensures that the expertise necessary to operate and maintain the product is consistent with the force structure. Technology development is an iterative process of maturing technologies and refining user performance parameters via requirements tradeoffs to accommodate any technologies that do not sufficiently mature. The program office will evaluate prototyped solutions against cost, performance and schedule constraints to finalize the system performance specification. This phase also provides the opportunity to establish the technical planning and digital engineering ecosystem needed during the design and development phase.

Developed during this phase is a system model or architecture that captures operational context and envisioned concepts, describes the system boundaries and interfaces, and addresses operational and functional requirements. Additional artifacts created include the program's digital engineering ecosystem, preliminary system performance specification of the preferred materiel solution, and advice to the PM regarding what components of the system should be prototyped, including how and why.

Any system requirements that map directly to software requirements should be identified at this stage to conduct trade-off studies in terms of life cycle costs and risks. The program should consider software and system alternatives and interface specifications to refine the system concept and permit vendor selection, including technical data rights. As the MDA selects preferred solutions, the resulting requirements form the basis for the system performance specification placed on contract, and also risk mitigation plans. The requirements manager prepares a concept of operations (CONOPS) consistent with the approved capability requirements document. The CONOPS includes the operational tasks, events, durations, frequency, operating conditions and environment in which the recommended materiel solution is to perform each mission and each phase of a mission.

DoDI 5000.88, Section 3.4

The systems engineering plan is a tool to manage technology in systems development.[54] It is included in the solicitation and will include:

- contract deliverables, design artifacts and technical data, and frequency of reporting;
- description of technical baselines and their management process;
- description of the program's integrated master plan and schedule process, including audits, baseline control, and integration between program-level and contractor detailed schedules;
- development and operations strategy for integration and testing to validate mission effectiveness throughout development;
- digital engineering implementation plan including model elements and block definitions, as well as activity, relationship and use case diagrams;
- engineering management approach to address baseline, configuration, opportunities, requirements traceability, risk, and technical tradeoffs and evaluation;
- engineering trade-off analyses to assess system affordability and technical feasibility;
- interdependencies with other programs and components, interfaces, and schedule;
- planning assumptions, frequency, and methods to assess health, risk and schedule;
- program technical issues, opportunities, planning and mitigation activities, and risks;

- reliability growth curves with assumptions, planning factors and assessment tools and methods;
- software development approach including architecture design, metrics tracking and reporting, obsolescence and risks, resources, security, and system safety;
- specialty engineering and architecture;
- technical approach for system design and development by balancing system performance, life-cycle cost, risks, and schedule, including a modular open systems approach to the maximum extent practicable;
- technical data to be provided digitally, frequency of the availability and management of data rights;
- technical performance metrics and system engineering leading indicators to assess technical maturation, including assumptions and strategy, and reporting methodology for each metric traceable to system requirements and mission capability;
- the CONOPS including mission scenarios and operational functions of the system; and
- timing, conduct, and entry and exit criteria for technical reviews.

DoDI 5000.91, Section 4

Product support planning and development begins prior to program initiation is re-evaluated and updated throughout the program's life cycle.[55] The PM conducts early risk identification, mitigation, and product support analyses to provide best value solutions. Product support management includes numerous support elements to accomplish materiel and system readiness:

- design interface;
- facilities and infrastructure;
- information systems support;
- maintenance planning and management;
- manpower and personnel;
- packaging, storage, and transportation;
- product support management;
- supply support;
- sustaining engineering;
- technical data; and
- training.

The program manager will submit an updated Acquisition Strategy to describe the approach to acquiring the capability including the business strategy, funding, risks, and schedule. The business strategy will describe the rationale for the contracting approach and how competition will be maintained throughout the program life cycle, and detail how contract incentives will be employed to support the Department's goals.

2.6.6.3 Milestone B

This decision to commit resources to develop a product for manufacturing and fielding leads to the *Engineering and Manufacturing Development* (EMD) phase. It follows completion of any needed technology maturation and risk reduction, including cost, engineering, integration, manufacturing, sustainment, and technology risks.

DAG: Engineering of Defense Systems Guidebook, 3.2.1.3.3

The primary objective of the EMD phase is to develop the initial product baseline, verify it meets the functional and allocated baselines, and transform the preliminary design into a producible design, all within the schedule and cost constraints of the program. Systems engineering activities during this phase develop the detailed design, verify that requirements are met, reduce risk, and assess readiness to begin production or deployment. It does this by completing the detailed build-to design of the system, establishing the initial product baseline, conducting the integration and tests of system elements and the entire system, and demonstrating system maturity and readiness to begin production for operational test and/or deployment and sustainment. Programs should use digital artifacts such as models or simulations to support decisions throughout a program's life cycle. Using a digital system model can help ensure consistency and integration among analytical and engineering tools and can help assess potential design changes or system upgrades throughout the life cycle. The EMD phase includes technical assessment and control efforts to effectively manage risks and increase confidence in meeting system cost, performance, and schedule goals. Upon assessing system maturity and the effectiveness of risk reduction strategies, the program will put the product baseline under formal configuration control.

DoDI 5000.02T, 5.c

The Milestone B decision point commits the organization's resources to a specific product, budget profile, choice of suppliers, contract terms, schedule, and sequence of events leading to production and fielding. In practice however, most of these decisions must be made prior to the release of the RFP to give potential offerors time to work on their proposals. Hence, the

Development RFP Release Decision Point is critical for reviewing plans to ensure all risks are understood and under control, and that the program will be affordable and executable. The Development RFP Release Decision Point authorizes solicitation for Engineering and Manufacturing Development and often for Low-Rate Initial Production (LRIP) or Limited Deployment options.

The component combat developer will prepare a document which combines the CONOPS, Operational Mode Summary and Mission Profile that includes the operational events and tasks, durations, frequency, and the operating conditions and environment for the recommended materiel solution to perform each mission and each phase thereof. This documentation will in turn lead to further documentation for the next phase such as acquisition strategy, capability requirements tradeoffs and test planning. It will be provided to industry as an attachment for the next acquisition phase RFP.

Next comes the actual Acquisition effort to pursue the development effort. Then comes the Materiel Solution Analysis effort to choose the concept for the product that will be acquired, begin translating validated capability gaps into system-specific requirements and plan to support a decision on the acquisition strategy for the product. Highlights of this effort include analysis of alternatives, affordability, market research, risk mitigation, systems engineering, threat projections, and tradeoffs among cost/schedule/performance.

DFARS 234

The MDA selects, with the advice of the contracting officer, the contract type for a development program at the time of Milestone B approval. The basis for the contract type selection shall be documented in the acquisition strategy with an explanation of the level of program risk and the steps taken to reduce program risk and the reasons for proceeding with Milestone B approval. If a cost-reimbursement type contract is selected, the contract file will include the MDA's written determination that the program is so complex and technically challenging that it would not be practicable to reduce program risk to a level that would permit the use of a fixed-price type contract. In any event, the contract must include criteria to measure reliability and maintainability.

Cost-reimbursement line items cannot be used to acquire production of major defense acquisition programs, unless USD(AT&L) submits to the congressional defense committees a written certification that the cost-reimbursement line items are needed to provide a required capability in a timely and cost-effective manner and an explanation of the steps taken to ensure that cost-reimbursement line items are used only when necessary.

A contract that is initially awarded from the competitive selection of a proposal may contain a contract line item or option for advanced component development, prototype or initial production of technology or the delivery of initial or additional items if created as the result of work performed under the contract. These circumstances would occur if the contract line item or option is not more than 12 months in length or is limited to the minimal amount of initial or additional items or prototypes that will allow for timely competitive solicitation and award of a follow-on development or production contract. The dollar value of the work to be performed should not exceed three times the dollar value of the work previously performed under the contract (not to exceed $20 million).

DoDI 5000.02T, 5.d.(8) and (9)

Milestone B also commits the required investment resources to the program. Most requirements for this milestone should be satisfied at the Development RFP Release Decision Point. Milestone B requires final demonstration that all sources of risk have been adequately mitigated to support a commitment to design for production. This includes affordability (through an independent cost estimate), engineering, integration, manufacturing, sustainment, and technology risks. Validated capability requirements, full funding in the FYDP, and compliance with goals for production and sustainment are required.

Milestone B is normally the formal initiation of an acquisition program with the MDA's approval of the Acquisition Program Baseline (APB). The APB is the agreement between the MDA and the program manager and his or her acquisition chain of command to track and report for the life of the program. The APB will include the affordability caps for unit production and sustainment costs.

The EMD phase completes all needed hardware and software detailed design, retires any open risks, builds, and tests prototypes or first articles to verify compliance with capability requirements, and prepares for production or deployment. It includes the establishment of the initial product baseline for all configuration items.

Now we enter the formal development effort. Developmental Testing and Evaluation (DT&E) provides feedback to the Program Manager on both design progress and product compliance with contractual requirements. DT&E activities also evaluate the ability of the system to provide effective combat capability by meeting its validated and derived capability requirements. They also show that initial system production, deployment and operational test and evaluation (OT&E) can be supported. OT&E supports the evaluation of the operational performance of units equipped with systems operated under realistic operational conditions in an operationally representative threat environment (Initial Operational Capability, plus ten years), including joint combat operations and system-of-systems concept of employment. Operational testing provides data required to enable credible evaluation of operational effectiveness, suitability and survivability.

Independent operational assessments, conducted by the component's operational test organization, will normally also occur during EMD. This could be an independent evaluation of developmental test results or of separate dedicated test events.

Early in the EMD Phase, the initial product support performance requirements will be refined based on the results of engineering reviews. Later in this phase, programs will test product support performance to ensure the system will meet the sustainment requirements within the affordability caps established at Milestone B.

The EMD Phase will end when the:

- capability requirements are validated by developmental and initial operational testing;
- design is stable;
- industrial production capabilities are available;
- manufacturing processes have been demonstrated and are under control;
- software sustainment processes are functional; and
- system meets or exceeds all EMD Phase exit criteria and Milestone C entrance criteria.

EMD will often continue past the initial production or fielding decision until all EMD activities have been completed and all requirements have been tested and verified.

In most programs for hardware intensive products, there will be some degree of concurrency between initial production and the completion of developmental testing. Such concurrency can reduce the lead time to field a system, but it also can increase the risk of design changes and costly retrofits after production has started. In general, there should be a reasonable expectation that the design is stable and will not be subject to significant changes following the decision to enter production. At Milestone B, the specific technical event-based criteria for initiating production or fielding at Milestone C will be determined and included in the Milestone B ADM.

If the strategy and associated business arrangements planned and approved at Milestone B have been changed due to EMD phase results, or if the validated capability requirements have changed, an updated Acquisition Strategy will be submitted for MDA review and approval prior to the release of the RFP for competitive source selection or the initiation of sole-source negotiations.

The MDA may authorize procurement of long lead items at any point during EMD or at the Development RFP Release Decision or Milestone B, subject to the availability of funds. These items are procured in advance of a Milestone C production decision to provide for a more efficient transition to production. Long lead authorization will be documented in an ADM.

2.6.6.4 Milestone C

DoDI 5000.02T, 5.d.(10)

Milestone C and the Limited Deployment Decision are the points at which a program or increment of capability is reviewed for entrance into the Production and Deployment Phase or for Limited Deployment. Approval depends on specific criteria included in the Milestone B ADM. The following criteria will normally be applied:

- a stable production/deployment design that will meet stated and derived requirements based on acceptable performance in developmental test events;
- a validated Capability Production Document or equivalent requirements document;
- an operational assessment;
- costs within affordability caps;
- demonstrated interoperability;
- demonstrated operational supportability;
- deployment support;
- full funding in the FYDP;
- mature software capability consistent with the software development schedule;
- no significant manufacturing risks; and
- properly phased production ramp up.

The MDA will consider any new validated threats that were not included in the Capabilities Production Document and might affect operational effectiveness. The MDA will also consult with the requirements validation authority as part of the production decision making process to ensure that capability requirements are current. MDA decisions will be documented in an ADM following the review.

Some programs, notably ships and spacecraft, will not produce prototypes during EMD because of the very high cost of each article. In this case, the first articles produced will be tested and then fielded as operational assets. These programs may be tailored by combining development and initial production commitments. If so, then a combined Milestone B and C will be conducted.

DoDI 5000.02T, 5.d.(11)

In the Production and Deployment Phase, the product is produced and fielded for use by operational units. The phase encompasses LRIP, Limited Deployment, OT&E, and the Full-Rate Production or Deployment Decision followed by full-rate production or deployment. All system sustainment and support activities are initiated. The operational authority will declare Initial Operating Capability when the defined operational organization has been equipped and trained and is deemed capable of conducting mission operations. Should cost management will be used continuously to control and reduce cost.

LRIP establishes the initial production base for the system or capability increment, provides the OT&E test articles and an efficient ramp up to full-rate production, and maintains continuity in production pending OT&E completion. While this portion of the phase should be of limited duration so that efficient production rates can be accomplished as soon and as economically as possible, it should be long enough to permit identification and resolution of any deficiencies prior to full-rate production. Limited Deployment for software developments is principally intended to support OT&E and can be used to provide tested early operational capability to the user prior to full deployment.

The appropriate operational test organization will conduct operational testing in a realistic threat environment. For its cognizant systems, the DOT&E will provide to the MDA a report providing its opinion as to whether the program is operationally effective, suitable and survivable.

Manufacturing development should be complete at Milestone C, but improvements or redesigns may require additional manufacturing process development and testing.

DoDI 5000.02T, 5.d.(12)

For the Full-Rate Production Decision or Full Deployment Decision, the MDA will assess the results of initial OT&E and manufacturing and limited deployment to determine whether to approve proceeding to Full-Rate Production or Full Deployment. Continuing into a Full-Rate mode requires demonstrated control of the manufacturing process, acceptable performance and reliability, and the establishment of adequate sustainment and support systems.

In making the Full-Rate Production Decision or the Full Deployment Decision, the MDA will consider any new validated threat environments that might affect operational effectiveness and may consult with the requirements validation authority as part of the decision-making process to ensure that capability. Critical deficiencies identified in testing will be resolved prior to proceeding beyond LRIP or limited deployment. Remedial action will be verified in follow-on test and evaluation. Once again, the decision to proceed into full-rate production or full deployment will be documented in an ADM.

DoDI 5000.02T, 5.d.(14)

The purpose of the Operations and Support Phase is to execute the product support strategy, satisfy materiel readiness and operational support performance requirements, and sustain the system over its life cycle (to include disposal).

During this phase, the program manager will deploy the product support package and monitor its performance according to the Life Cycle Sustainment Plan. The Plan may include time-phased transitions between commercial, organic and partnered product support providers. The program manager will ensure resources are programmed and necessary intellectual property deliverables and associated license rights, as well as equipment and facilities, are acquired to support each of the levels of maintenance that will provide product support. The program manager will also establish necessary organic depot maintenance capability in compliance with statute and the Plan.

Over the system life cycle, operational needs, technology advances, evolving threats, process improvements, fiscal constraints, plans for follow-on systems, or a combination of these influences and others may warrant revisions to the Life Cycle Sustainment Plan. When revising the Plan, the program manager will revalidate the supportability analyses and review the most current product support requirements, senior leader guidance and fiscal assumptions to evaluate product support changes or alternatives and determine best value.

At the end of its useful life, a system will be demilitarized and disposed in accordance with all legal and regulatory requirements and policy relating to safety, security, and the environment.

A program uses a defined block change or follow-on increment to deliver new or evolved capability, maintenance, safety, or urgent upgrades to the field in a controlled manner.[56] Procedures for updating and maintaining software on fielded systems often require individual user action and may require specific training. Procedures should be in place to facilitate and ensure effective configuration management and control.

DoD component heads and program managers will tailor and streamline program strategies and oversight. This includes program information, acquisition activity, delegation of authority, and the timing and scope of decision reviews. Streamlined strategizing is encouraged to expedite production and deployment of a solution. This often results in parallel rather than sequential processes to expeditiously identify and refine capability requirements, identify resources, and execute acquisitions. Acquisition decision-making will be tailored to expedite acquisition, perhaps by limiting development and authorizing production at the same time development is approved. An assessment approach and (where appropriate) live-fire testing are still required. A Course of Action Analysis is necessary in lieu of an Analysis of Alternatives for approval by the Milestone Decision Authority. A formal TEMP is not usually required.

2.7 SOCIOECONOMIC PROGRAMS

The Federal Government has instituted a number of programs to benefit designated groups of individuals and their firms by promoting diversity and accessibility to contracts and financial support. These are collectively known as *socioeconomic programs* and result in a number of source selection preferences and additional contract-related benefits to such firms. These entities include small businesses, firms owned by service-disabled veterans, companies located in HUBZones, and those owned by socially disadvantaged persons or women.

The objectives of these programs are not seemingly related to procurement goals. Rather, they are intended to promote fair wages and working conditions, domestic economy, employment within small and minority business firms, and the environment. In addition, these practices also promote multicultural diversity within a firm through equitable status for employees without regard to their ethnic, gender, physical, or religious status.

All federal contractors are encouraged to consider socioeconomic issues in choosing suppliers. However, it can be challenging to measure results of these programs on society. They certainly impose more paperwork requirements on firms and may increase procurement prices, and therefore public spending.

2.7.1 Small Business Policies

FAR Part 19

The small business policy applies only to contracts performed in the United States or its outlying areas, except as noted.

Small businesses make up roughly 99.7 percent of all American firms, and nearly half of all private sector employees.[57] They provide significant levels of competition and innovation. Yet they often lack the resources to handle large and complex projects, may not always be able to follow up on production issues, cannot spread costs over a wide base (and thereby may not be price competitive with large businesses), and may find it difficult to deal with the Federal Government. Hence the need for preference programs to promote awards to small businesses. The result is a Federal program of set-asides to maximize opportunities in its acquisitions for socioeconomic concerns as prime and subcontractors.

For a firm to be considered a small business, it must be:

- a for-profit entity;
- independently owned and operated;
- located and operating primarily within the U.S.;
- not nationally dominant in its field; and
- paying taxes or using American labor, materials, or products.

Implementation of socioeconomic programs requires a team of specialists to assist the contracting officer, who also plays a leading role in the program's success. The specific policies and procedures are discussed in the following sections.

2.7.1.1 Size Standards

FAR 19.102

The Department of Commerce manages the North American Industry Classification System (NAICS) and annually determines small procurement mechanisms and size percentages by NAICS Industry Subsector and region.[58] These percentage determinations affect all solicitations that are issued on or after its effective date. These procurement mechanisms are used as a price evaluation adjustment (sub)factor to reflect the level of participation of small concerns. They could include monetary subcontracting incentive clauses for large concerns.

The Small Business Administration (SBA) establishes small business size standards by industry category of supplies and services.[59] Size standards tend to be expressed in terms of annual revenue for suppliers and number of employees for service contractors, though there are exceptions. Some service categories are based on annual corporate income and different categories have different income levels. For these categories, the number of employees is irrelevant when categorizing service providers.

The appropriate size standard is placed in the solicitation for offerors to represent their status as small or large. If multiple size standards apply to the various deliverables of a given solicitation, the standard which comprises the greatest percentage of the contract price governs.

A firm that offers to furnish an end product it did not manufacture (i.e., a *nonmanufacturer*) is considered a small business if it has no more than 500 employees (150 employees if a value-added reseller of information technology) and furnishes the product of another small business manufacturer or producer. A firm which buys items and packages them into a kit is considered a nonmanufacturer small business if it meets the size qualifications for the acquisition and if at least 50 percent of the total value of the kit and its contents are manufactured by small business.

On the other hand, a firm which proposes a product manufactured by a large business does not qualify as a small business. Hence, a small business which is a dealer for a large business will not gain consideration as a small business. This rule does not apply however to a small business set-aside not over $25,000 in value if the offer is an end product that is manufactured or produced in the United States.

If a multiple-award contract is contemplated which includes multiple line items reflecting different size standards, then a firm must qualify under each standard for which it chooses to propose. For a joint venture, each member party must qualify as a small business or else be a protégé under an SBA member-protégé program.

2.7.1.2 Encouraging Small Business Participation

FAR 19.202-1l

Heads of contracting activities must implement the small business programs within their activities. They have annual goals for total dollars awarded to small businesses, further broken down into the various types of socioeconomic categories. Performance of contracting office management is in part assessed on their ability to meet or exceed these goals.

To achieve program goals, contracting office management must ensure that their contracting and technical personnel maintain knowledge of small business program requirements and take all reasonable actions to increase participation in contracting. They do this through in-house training, written procedures, and reviews of pending procurement actions. Moreover, each procurement office has annual socioeconomic goals to achieve, usually expressed in terms of percentage of total awards or dollars awarded to small businesses. The management techniques discussed below are designed to help achieve these goals.

Whenever more than one small business concern is capable of performing the work, the contracting officer may divide proposed acquisitions of supplies and services (except construction) into small lots (at least the size of economic production runs) to encourage more offers. Delivery schedules should be realistic enough to encourage small business participation and motivate prime contractors to subcontract with small business concerns.

The contracting office must maintain an open and professional relationship with the small business community. To any requesting small business concern, the contracting officer provides at Government expense a copy of the solicitation and specifications, contact information of a person to answer questions, and citations to applicable Federal laws or agency rules.

Each prospective contractor represents if it qualifies in one or more socio-economic categories. Each agency measures the level of participation of these firms by total value of contracts placed during each fiscal year and reports the data to the SBA.

SBA maintains the *Procurement Automated Source System* as a centralized inventory and referral system that contains the names and capabilities of small businesses interested in Government (sub)contracts. Purchasing offices can query the database to obtain potential sources. The database is not available to contractors or the general public, and hence is not present on the World Wide Web.

In the event of equal low bids, awards are made first to small business labor surplus area concerns, and second to small business concerns which are not also labor surplus area concerns.

2.7.1.3 Cooperation with the SBA

FAR 19.4

Each agency with contracting authority has an Office of Small and Disadvantaged Business Utilization (known within DoD as the Office of Small Business Programs). The SBA may assign one or more *SBA procurement center representatives* to any contracting activity or contract administration office to carry out SBA policies and programs. They will review proposed acquisition packages and recommend firms for inclusion on a bidders' mailing list. They may also recommend any alternate contracting method that could increase small business prime contracting opportunities, such as newly certified firms and component breakout for separate competitive acquisitions. Such components then become Government Furnished Equipment to the systems manufacturer. The recommendation is due to the contracting officer within 15 days after receipt of the package. The representative will appeal to the chief of the contracting office any contracting officer's determination not to solicit any small business recommended by the SBA. On an ongoing basis, the representative will also conduct periodic reviews of the contracting activity to assess compliance with small business policies, and sponsor and participate in conferences and training to increase small business participation in the contracting office.

The SBA will also assign a *breakout procurement center representative* to any procurement office it designates as purchasing substantial amounts of non-commercial items. This representative advocates the use of full and open competition and item breakout, while still maintaining the integrity of the system which uses these items. Each breakout representative is aided by at least two co-located small business technical advisors. The breakout representative is authorized to attend evaluation sessions discussing acquisition strategy and make recommendations, and to appeal any failure by the procurement center to act favorably on any recommendation. They will review any unsolicited engineering proposal, conduct a value analysis to determine any cost reduction within acquisition objectives, and forward the results to procurement center reviewers. Breakout experts will also review the validity of past competitive restrictions and technical data rights to help prepare a competitive solicitation package for a supply or service previously acquired noncompetitively. On an ongoing basis, the representative formally briefs contracting officers and other procurement office personnel about the representative's duties and objectives, and the methods designed to promote item breakout for competitive procurement, and annually reports on past and planned activities to the head of the procurement office.

The contracting officer strives to respond in writing within 30 days to any written request from a small business firm regarding a contract administration matter, or else advise when a response will be forthcoming. This policy does not apply to matters under the Disputes clause.

DFARS 219.402

The procurement center representative is not required to review acquisitions for foreign military sales (including an agreement with a foreign nation where United States forces are deployed), in support of humanitarian and civic assistance or an emergency operation, or awarded and performed outside the United States and its outlying areas.

PGI 207.171

Breakout reviews include the following issues:[60]

- administrative and operational factors;
- advance acquisition funds available to provide the new source additional lead time;
- alternative sources capable of supplying the component;
- availability of a suitable data package with rights to use it for Government acquisition;
- complicating production scheduling or preventing identification of responsibility for end item failure due to a defective component;
- development of quality assurance, specifications, and testing requirements, and whether the Government or another contractor has the resources (facilities, manpower, technical competence, etc.) to provide such support;
- estimated acquisition savings less any offsetting costs;
- financial risks and other responsibilities assumed by the Government after breakout;
- jeopardizing standardization of components;

- need for the end item contractor to do further design or engineering effort on the component;
- potential risks to the end item due to delayed delivery and reduced reliability;
- quality control and reliability problems of the component without requiring effort by the end item contractor; and
- whether the component will be acquired directly by the Government as a support item in the supply system or as Government-furnished equipment in other end items.

2.7.1.4 Set-Asides for Small Business

FAR 19.5

A *small business set-aside* is an acquisition or class of acquisitions reserved for only small business concerns to compete. A small business set-aside may be either total or partial, but must still be awarded at a fair and reasonable price. The contracting officer reviews acquisitions to determine if they can be set aside for small business, and documents if and why a set-aside is inappropriate. The SBA procurement center representative may review all proposed acquisitions that are not unilaterally set aside for small business. However, the set-aside requirement does not apply to micro-purchases, acquisitions for contingency or emergency recovery valued at $20,000 or less, or purchases from NIB, SourceAmerica or Federal Supply Schedule contracts.

Each acquisition of supplies or services exceeding the micro-purchase threshold but not over the simplified acquisition threshold is automatically reserved exclusively for small business concerns. However, if the contracting officer determines there is not a reasonable expectation of obtaining competitive offers from at least two responsible small business concerns, (s)he may be able to convince the procurement center representative to forego a set-aside. If the contracting officer receives only one acceptable offer from a responsible small business under a set-aside, award can still be made to that firm. But if no acceptable offers from responsible small business concerns are received, the set-aside is withdrawn and the requirement is resolicited on an unrestricted basis.

The offeror for a supplies contract must provide goods manufactured by either itself or another small business within the United States. This means that the firm could itself transform raw materials, parts, or other components into the final end product. If multiple vendors are involved, whichever one transforms raw material or purchased parts into the final product must be a small business. At least 50 percent of the contract amount must be performed either in-house or by other firms which meet the same size standard for a small business (known as a *similarly situated entity*). For construction contracts, this percentage increases to 85 percent (75 percent for special trade contractors).

If an action exceeding the simplified acquisition threshold does not lend itself to a total set-aside, the contracting officer may still create a *partial set-aside* of a portion of the acquisition for exclusive small business participation. This is possible if the requirement is severable into two or more economic production runs or lots.[61] The contracting officer must first be certain that one or more small business concerns have the technical competence and productive capacity to satisfy the set-aside portion at a fair market price. Both portions of the procurement must have comparable terms and delivery schedule.

Offers received from large business concerns are considered only for the non-set-aside portion. After all awards have been made on that portion, the contracting officer then addresses those small businesses who offered on both the non-set-aside and set-aside portions, in the order of priority indicated in the solicitation. Moreover, if equal low offers are received, the non-set-aside awardee has first priority to negotiate for the set-aside amount. So, a small business is at a disadvantage if it elects to only offer on the set-aside portion of the solicitation.

A contracting officer rejecting a recommendation of the SBA procurement center representative must respond in writing and permit the SBA procurement center representative to appeal the rejection to the chief of the contracting office. Since this process can take up to seven weeks, the contracting officer suspends action on the acquisition, unless determining in writing that the public interest requires performance. If the head of the contracting activity agrees with the contracting officer, the SBA procurement center representative may then appeal. This requires a request to the contracting officer to continue to suspend action on the acquisition until the SBA Administrator appeals to the agency head for a final decision (this process can take up to nine more weeks). By this time, the issue has become both lengthy and political in nature. So the contracting officer must carefully consider any challenge to an SBA recommendation, and whether the procurement can be delayed for such a length of time (it often cannot). This is also our first (but not last) indication of the political power of the SBA and the small business community.

DFARS 219.201

Small business specialists within the DoD contracting office review and make recommendations for all acquisitions (including orders placed against Federal Supply Schedule contracts) over the micro-purchase threshold before solicitation, except those under the simplified acquisition threshold that are totally set aside for small business concerns. They also conduct annual reviews to assess how much consolidation of contract requirements has occurred and their impact on the availability of small business concerns to participate as (sub)contractors. However, funding actions or modifications that do not increase the scope of the contract generally should not be reviewed because it would add little or no value.

DFARS 219.502-1

Set-asides do not occur for supplies developed and financed in whole or in part by Canadian sources under the U.S.-Canadian Defense Development Sharing Program. Set-asides are customary for construction, including maintenance and repairs, under $2.5 million, dredging under $1.5 million, and architect-engineer services for military construction or family housing projects under $1 million.

DFARS 213.7001

Procurement of religious services to be performed on a military installation must be competitive in nature, allowing nonprofit organizations to compete.

Solicitation Provision

DFARS 252.219-7000, Advancing Small Business Growth, when the estimated annual value is expected to exceed the small business size standard or $70 million where the small business size standard is expressed as number of employees for the NAICS code.

DFARS 252.219-7012, Competition for Religious-Related Services.

Solicitation Provisions and Contract Clauses

FAR 52.219-6, Notice of Total Small Business Set-Aside. Use the clause with Alternate I for a product in a class for which the SBA has found no small business manufacturer. Use the clause with its Alternate II when including Federal Prison Industries (UNICOR) in the competition.

FAR 52.219-7, Notice of Partial Small Business Set-Aside. Use the clause with its Alternate I for a product in a class for which the SBA has found no small business manufacturer. Use the clause with its Alternate II when including UNICOR in the competition.

FAR 52.219-13, Notice of Set-Aside of Orders, applied to an individual order under an indefinite delivery contract.

FAR 52.219-14, Limitations on Subcontracting, in solicitations and contracts expected to exceed $100,000 if any portion of the requirement is to be set aside for small business.

FAR 52.219-31, Notice of Small Business Reserve.

FAR 52.219-32, Orders Issued Directly Under Small Business Reserves.
FAR 52.219-33, Nonmanufacturer Rule.

2.7.1.5 Determination of Small Business Status

FAR 19.3

To be eligible for award as a small business, an offeror must represent that it meets the definition of a small business concern applicable to the solicitation, and that it has not been determined by the SBA to be other than a small business. The contracting officer accepts in good faith this representation unless another offeror or interested party (or the contracting officer him/herself) challenges the concern's representation. The offeror's representation is not binding on the SBA however, and if challenged, the SBA will evaluate the status and issue a final determination to the contracting officer. If the finding is negative, the concern cannot become eligible for a set-aside award; if positive, the offeror is eligible for award. Since the contracting officer lacks the expertise of the SBA in the field of size determination, (s)he has no avenue of appeal.

Although a size determination is normally valid for the life of the contract, there are several exceptions. A contractor must re-represent its size status for the NAICS code in the contract within 30 days after execution of a novation agreement or associated contract modification, or after a merger or acquisition. For contracts more than five years in length, it must re-represent its size status within 120 days before the end of the fifth year of the contract or the date for exercising any subsequent option. However, for competitive 8(a) contracts, only the contracting officer may challenge the firm's status. The protest goes to the SBA Government Contracting Area Office for the geographical area covering the principal office of the challenged concern.

As stated above, another offeror may challenge the size status of a firm representing itself as a small business. In order to affect a specific solicitation however, such a protest must be timely. This means it must be received by the contracting officer by closing time of the fifth business day after bid opening (in sealed bid acquisitions) or receipt of the contracting officer's notification that identifies the apparently successful offeror (in negotiated acquisitions). A protest may be made orally if it is confirmed in writing and postmarked or hand-delivered to the contracting officer by the next business day, or within the five-day period. On the other hand, a contracting officer's protest is always considered timely, whether filed before or after award. Any protest under a Multiple Award Schedule is timely if received by SBA prior to the expiration of the contract period.

After receiving such a protest, the contracting officer cannot award the contract until either the SBA has made a size determination or 15 business days have expired since SBA's receipt of the protest. Again, early award is permitted only to protect the public interest. The SBA Government Contracting Area Director or designee determines the small business status of the questioned firm and notifies both the contracting officer and firm of the determination. Award may be made (or denied) on the basis of that determination. If award was made before the contracting officer received notice of the appeal, the contract is considered valid.

Any potential offeror may appeal a contracting officer's NAICS code designation and the applicable size standard. Such an appeal must be filed within 10 calendar days after the issuance of the solicitation. Since SBA selects the standard to be used in the solicitation, they must handle the protest. SBA's Office of Hearings and Appeals (OHA) will dismiss summarily an untimely NAICS code appeal. If OHA's decision arrives to the contracting officer before the offer is due, the decision is final and (if necessary) the solicitation is amended to reflect the decision. An OHA decision received after the due date of the initial offers does not apply to the pending solicitation, but will apply to future solicitations of the same products or services.

Although other socioeconomic programs will be discussed later in their separate sections, we will include here their rules for size protests. This provides the reader with a more centralized location to access protest policies and procedures.

To be eligible for consideration on its disadvantaged status, a concern must either be certified as a small disadvantaged business (SDB) at the time of its offer or have a completed SDB application pending at the SBA or a Private Certifier (there are private companies who are authorized to certify a firm's socioeconomic eligibility). The contracting officer may accept an offeror's representation that it is an SDB concern for statistical purposes, and may then confirm it by accessing SBA's PRO-Net database or by contacting the SBA's Office of Small Disadvantaged Business Certification and Eligibility.[62]

No offeror determined to be non-responsive, outside the competitive range, or previously found by the SBA to be ineligible for the requirement, may protest the apparently successful offeror's representation of disadvantaged status. This is because such a firm is not in line for the award even if successful in its protest, and is therefore not considered to be an interested party. Any other offeror may submit a written protest to the contracting officer after bid opening or notification of intended award. In addition, the contracting officer or the SBA may protest in writing a firm's representation of its disadvantaged status at any time after bid opening or notification of intended award, even if award has already been made. In all cases however, SBA normally will not consider a postaward protest, unless the contracting officer agrees to terminate the contract if the protest is sustained.

When the contracting officer makes a written determination that award must be made to protect the public interest, award can occur notwithstanding the protest. Otherwise, the contracting officer will forward the protest to the SBA, and the Assistant Administrator for Small Disadvantaged Business Certification and Eligibility will notify the protestor and the contracting officer whether the protest will be processed or dismissed for lack of timeliness or specificity. Within 15 working days after receipt of a timely and specific protest, the SBA will determine the disadvantaged status of the challenged offeror and notify all parties. Failure to respond within 15 days is grounds for the contracting officer to presume that the challenged offeror is disadvantaged and award may proceed (unless the contracting officer has granted SBA an extension). Any SBA determination may be appealed by any of the three parties (awardee, protestor, or contracting officer) to the SBA Administrator's designee within five working days after receipt of the determination.

The same three parties may protest an apparently successful offeror claiming HUBZone small business status. The deadlines for timely protest are the same as for SDB protests. Again, SBA determines the HUBZone status of the protested concern within 15 business days after receipt of a protest; otherwise the contracting officer may award the contract (unless the contracting officer grants SBA an extension). Here again, the contracting officer may determine in writing to award the contract if necessary to protect the public interest. Unlike the disadvantaged business however, the SBA decision regarding HUBZone status is final and not protestable by any party.

The same protest process applies to service-disabled veteran-owned and woman-owned small business set-asides. SBA's Associate Administrator for Government Contracting makes the final decision in these cases, which also is not protestable.

Solicitation Provision

FAR 52.219-1, Small Business Program Representations, with its Alternate I if exceeding the micro-purchase threshold and the contract will be performed in the United States or its outlying areas.

FAR 52.219-2, Equal Low Bids, in sealed bid solicitations if performance will be in the United States or its outlying areas.

FAR 52.219-28, Postaward Small Business Program Representation, if exceeding the micro-purchase threshold and the contract will be performed in the United States or its outlying areas.

2.7.1.6 Certificate of Competency

FAR 19.6

A Certificate of Competency (COC) can be issued by the SBA to affirm a small business's responsibility regarding:

- capability;
- capacity;
- competency;
- credit;
- integrity;
- perseverance and tenacity; and
- subcontracting limitations.

The COC program applies to all Government acquisitions, including those performed outside the United States (the only socioeconomic requirement that does).

If a contracting officer determines an apparent successful small business offeror to be nonresponsible, even if the next acceptable offer is also from a small business, (s)he withholds contract award and refers the matter to the cognizant SBA Government Contracting Area Office of the offeror's headquarters.

Contract award is withheld by the contracting officer for up to 15 business days (or longer if agreed to by the SBA and the contracting officer) after the SBA Office receives all required documentation, and the small business concern applies for a COC. The SBA may elect to visit the applicant's facility with industrial and financial experts to review its responsibility. If the SBA rules against the concern, or does not issue a COC within 15 business days after receiving the referral, the contracting officer assumes that no COC will be granted and may award as intended. If the decision favors granting a COC, the contracting officer will then award the contract to the concern because a COC conclusively determines responsibility (and is not subject to further appeal). A COC will not be granted to a firm which is suspended or debarred.

PGI 219.6

An offeror receiving an unfavorable decision has no avenue of appeal. However, if the contracting officer believes the agency should appeal, (s)he must immediately inform the departmental or agency director of the SBA Office of Small Business Programs via the contracting activity's small business specialist and send a formal request for appeal, summarizing the issues in the contracting activity's position in writing, timed to arrive within five working days after receipt of the SBA written position. The departmental director will determine whether the agency will appeal and will notify the SBA of the agency's intent. The SBA Associate Administrator for Government Contracting will make a final written determination, which is not subject to further appeal.

2.7.1.7 Small Business Subcontracting

FAR 19.702 and .704

Any contract above the simplified acquisition threshold requires maximizing contracting opportunities for socioeconomic concerns. Therefore, each solicitation expected to exceed $750,000 ($1,500,000 for construction) with subcontracting possibilities requires the apparently successful offeror to submit a subcontracting plan covering the entire contract period (including options), with goals based on the offeror's planned subcontracting support. When a contract modification is large enough to merit its own plan, then its goals are added to those in the existing subcontracting plan. Subcontracting plans are not required from small business prime contractors, for personal services or for contracts performed entirely outside of the United States and its outlying areas.

The plan must be acceptable to the contracting officer and is subject to negotiation. Any (sub)contractor failing to comply in good faith with the requirements of the subcontracting plan is in material breach of contract and subject to liquidated damages.

A contractor must confirm that a subcontractor representing itself as a small disadvantaged business concern is listed in SBA's database (PRO-Net) or else contact the SBA's Office of Small Disadvantaged Business Certification and Eligibility. Likewise, the contractor must confirm a HUBZone certification by accessing the SAM database or by contacting the SBA. The contractor, the contracting officer or any other interested party can challenge a subcontractor's size or disadvantaged status prior to completion of performance by the intended subcontractor.

Subcontracts awarded to an Alaskan Native Corporation (ANC) or Indian tribe count towards the subcontracting goals for small business and SDB concerns, regardless of the size or SBA certification status of the ANC or Indian tribe. A contractor may rely on the written representation of status as an ANC or Indian tribe unless an interested party or the contracting officer challenges its status.

Each subcontracting plan must include:

- assurances that the offeror will:
  - cooperate in any studies or surveys;

- for construction contracts, that it will make a good faith effort to contract with the small businesses included in its proposal or provide the contracting officer a written explanation to the contrary; and
- not prohibit a subcontractor from discussing with the contracting officer any matter dealing with payment or utilization;
- provide its prime contract number, DUNS number and email address of the Government or contractor official responsible for acknowledging or rejecting the reports, to all first-tier subcontractors with their own subcontracting plans so they can enter this information into their eSRS reports;
- require that each subcontractor with a subcontracting plan provide the same information for its subcontracting plans; and
- submit periodic reports for the Government to determine compliance with the subcontracting plan;

- a description of the efforts to ensure that socioeconomic concerns have an equitable opportunity to compete for subcontracts;
- a description of the procedures to comply with plan goals and requirements, including establishing source lists and efforts to locate and award to socioeconomic concerns;[63]
- if the offeror included indirect costs in establishing subcontracting goals, how it determined the proportionate share of indirect costs for socioeconomic concerns;
- methods used to develop the subcontracting goals and identify potential sources;
- percentage goals for using socioeconomic concerns as subcontractors, with separate goals for each category (e.g., small, disadvantaged, etc.);
- planned subcontract amounts, both in total dollars and to socioeconomic firms;
- the name of the subcontracting program administrator and a description of duties;
- types of supplies and services to be subcontracted, both in total and to socioeconomic firms; and
- whether a *master subcontracting plan* is developed on a plant or division-wide basis without goals. Master plans are effective for three years after approval, but must be maintained and updated by the contractor. Upon approval by the contracting officer, they may be incorporated into individual contract plans.

A contractor with subcontracting opportunities must submit the Individual Subcontract Report and the Summary Subcontract Report using the Electronic Subcontracting Reporting System (eSRS), the Government-wide web-based system for small business subcontracting program reports.[64] The Individual

Subcontract Report is submitted semi-annually for the performance periods ending March 31 and September 30. A report is also required for each contract within 30 days of contract completion. A Summary Subcontract Report is also due semi-annually.

An offeror of commercial products or services may also use its *commercial plan*, a subcontracting plan with goals that covers the offeror's fiscal year and applies to commercial items sold by the entire company or a portion thereof. The Government does not require another subcontracting plan from the same contractor while this commercial plan remains in effect and the product or service continues to qualify as a commercial item.

PGI 215.304

Small business subcontracting plans must be evaluated by the contracting officer in terms of the extent to which all socioeconomic programs are implemented, unless award is made to the lowest price technically acceptable offeror. The solicitation may require proposals to discuss the extent of small business performance for evaluation purposes, but subcontracting plans must be in a separate document. Evaluation factors may include the extent of:

- commitment to use such firms (e.g., enforceable commitments are to be weighted more heavily than non-enforceable ones);
- complexity and variety of the work small firms are to perform;
- participation of such firms in terms of the value of the total acquisition;
- past performance of the offerors in complying with requirements for small business subcontracting and utilization;
- realism of the proposal; and
- which such firms are specifically identified in proposals.

When information technology is acquired under a Federal Supply Schedule, an evaluation factor for supply chain risk must be employed. Evaluating supply chain risk requires review of the supply chain, namely all proposed information technology subcontractors and suppliers, and may involve the use of all-source intelligence information obtainable by the requiring activity.

2.7.1.8 *Contracting Officer Responsibilities under Subcontracting Assistance*

FAR 19.705

The contracting officer determines whether subcontracting possibilities exist by considering whether firms which furnish the required types of items customarily perform all work in-house or else contract-out part of the work to qualified vendors. This review draws on previous involvement of small business concerns as prime contractors or subcontractors in similar acquisitions, and the relative success of methods to meet the goals and requirements of the plan. If a plan under a sealed bid does not cover each required element, the contracting officer requests submission of a revised plan by a specific date, or else the bidder is ineligible for award. If the plan demonstrates no intent to comply with its obligations under the Utilization of Small Business Concerns clause, the contracting officer may find the bidder to be nonresponsible.

In negotiated acquisitions, the contracting officer ensures that the offeror has not submitted unreasonably low goals to avoid the administrative burden of good faith efforts.[65] Goals may be negotiated upward unless they would greatly increase cost. The contracting officer may encourage the offeror (except for SDBs) to increase subcontracting opportunities by providing monetary incentives for exceeding goals. Subcontracting can also be a factor in determining the award fee in a cost-plus-award-fee contract. When establishing goals, the contracting officer evaluates:

- achievability of goals based on available subcontractors and opportunities;
- capacity to provide specialized products or services through subcontracting;
- consistency with the offeror's cost or pricing data, and make-or-buy policy or program;
- known availability of socioeconomic concerns in the geographical area where the work will be performed;
- past performance of the offeror in fulfilling subcontracting plans;
- performance of other contractors on similar efforts; and
- the offeror's long-standing contractual relationship with its suppliers.

To demonstrate good faith effort in managing subcontracts with small businesses, a firm should conduct market research to identify potential small business subcontractors (e.g., searching SAM, posting notices or solicitations on SBA's SUBNet, participating in business matchmaking events, and attending preproposal conferences). Utilizing the available services of small business associations and assistance offices is always a wise idea. It must solicit small business concerns early in the acquisition process and providing adequate and timely information about plans and requirements (including breaking out work into economically feasible amounts) to encourage submission of a timely offer. It should assist small businesses to obtain bonding, credit, insurance, services, and supplies when necessary, referring them to SBA when necessary for more assistance.

Participating in a formal mentor-protégé program is always a positive sign because it provides developmental assistance with one or more small business protégés. A *mentor* firm is a large business with at least $100 million in DoD contracts and otherwise in good standing. A *protégé* firm is a small business unrelated to the mentor firm and of under half the applicable NAICS size standard. It must meet one of the SBA socioeconomic categories or else provide DoD-critical goods or services. Fulfilling all of the requirements of the subcontracting plan, including exceeding the subcontracting goal in one socioeconomic category if missing another goal, is also attractive to contracting officer approval.

The contracting officer may advise the offeror of available sources of information on potential socioeconomic concerns, or specific concerns known by name, and recommendations from the SBA procurement center representative and the agency small business specialist. The contracting officer will then evaluate the plan as outlined above, perhaps with the help of the SBA procurement center representative. If a firm replies that it has no subcontracting opportunities when a plan is required, this position must be approved at a level above the contracting officer.

Liquidated damages are authorized when a contractor's *failure to make a good faith effort* to comply with the subcontracting plan reflects intentional failure to perform or frustrate the plan. The fact that the contractor failed to meet its subcontracting goals does not, by itself, constitute a failure to make a good faith effort. Instead, indicators of such a failure include lack of:

- company policies, procedures or records that support the objectives of the plan;
- designating a company official to administer the subcontracting program and monitor and enforce compliance with the plan;
- effort to identify, contact, solicit, or consider any socioeconomic concern for award;
- Individual or Summary Subcontract Reports submitted to eSRS; or
- timely payments to small business subcontractors.

If the contracting officer finds that the contractor failed to make a good faith effort to comply with its subcontracting plan, (s)he issues a final decision to the contractor and requires payment of liquidated damages. These damages will equal the actual dollar amount by which the contractor failed to achieve each subcontracting goal. This decision is subject to appeal under the Disputes clause.

DFARS 219.702

A DoD test program permits selected contractors selected by the contracting office to negotiate plant, division, or company-wide comprehensive subcontracting plans instead of individual contract subcontracting plans for DoD contracts. These plans are negotiated on an annual basis by the designated contracting activities, incorporated by the contractor's cognizant contract administration activity into all active DoD contracts that require a plan, and accepted for use by contractors at both the prime or subcontract level. DCMA selects the contractors for this program (multiple DoD contracts totaling at least $100 million) and assesses their actual awards against planned awards to determine whether a good-faith effort has been made. The contractor must report every six months each subcontract, which ones are small businesses, and costs incurred and avoided by using a comprehensive plan. Liquidated damages are authorized if the contactor fails to make a good-faith effort to comply.

Solicitation Provisions and Contract Clauses

FAR 52.219-8, Utilization of Small Business Concerns, if the contract amount is expected to exceed the simplified acquisition threshold. Do not use for personal services or performance outside of the United States and its outlying areas.

FAR 52.219-9, Small Business Subcontracting Plan, when subcontracting possibilities are expected to exceed $700,000 ($1,500,000 for construction of any public facility), and the Utilization of Small Business Concerns clause is included. Do not use if the acquisition is set aside or is to be accomplished under the 8(a) program. Use the clause with Alternate I when contracting by sealed bidding. Use the clause with its Alternate II when contracting by negotiation, and subcontracting plans are required with initial proposals.

FAR 52.219-10, Incentive Subcontracting Program, when a monetary incentive is necessary to increase socioeconomic subcontracting opportunities. Do not use if the test program is invoked for the contractor.

FAR 52.219-16, Liquidated Damages —Subcontracting Plan, when including the Small Business Subcontracting Plan clause.

DFARS 252.219-7003, Small Business Subcontracting Plan (DoD Contracts), if including FAR 52.219-9, Small Business Subcontracting Plan. Use Alternate I when using Alternate III of FAR 52.219-9. However, DoD Class Deviation 2018-00007, Small Business Subcontract Reporting, issued December 13, 2017, is used in lieu of FAR 52.219-9, Alternate IV, and DFARS 252.219-7003.[66] Use Alternate II for a demonstration project.

DFARS 252.219-7004, Small Business Subcontracting Plan (Test Program), instead of DFARS 252.219-7003, Small Business Subcontracting Plan (DoD Contracts), and FAR 52.219-9, Small Business Subcontracting Plan, when contractors have comprehensive subcontracting plans approved under the test program. This clause requires flowdown to subcontractors of FAR 52.219-9, Small Business Subcontracting Plan, and DFARS 252.219-7003, Small Business Subcontracting Plan (DoD Contracts). However, if the contract will not be reported in FPDS, use FAR 52.219-9, Small Business Subcontracting Plan with its Alternate III and DFARS 252.219-7003, Small Business Subcontracting Plan (DoD Contracts), with its Alternate I. If the contractor has comprehensive subcontracting plans approved under the test program, do not use FAR 52.219-16, Liquidated Damages—Subcontracting Plan. Do not use FAR 52.219-10, Incentive Subcontracting Program, in contracts with contractors that have comprehensive subcontracting plans approved under the test program. Include in subcontracts with such firms if over $700,000 ($1.5 million for construction).

2.7.2 Small Disadvantaged Business Firms

For Federal contracting purposes, *disadvantage* is a long-term, chronic, and substantial condition based on color, gender, national origin, or physical handicap. The cause of the disadvantage must arise from one of the above detriments within American society, not from a foreign nation. This detriment must then result in difficulty in gaining access to working capital, such as failure to obtain a loan from a lending institution. If all these conditions apply, then the firm can qualify under one or more of the disadvantaged categories.

FAR 19.8

Section 8(a) of the Small Business Act authorizes the SBA to enter into contracts with other agencies and then subcontract to firms eligible for program participation, referred to as *8(a) contractors*.[67] The SBA selects firms in which at least 51 percent of the ownership is held by socially and economically disadvantaged entrepreneurs. These firms typically spend four years in a developmental stage (often in a mentor-protégé relationship with an established firm) and then up to five years building the company to transition into self-sufficiency and graduate from the 8(a) program.

The SBA serves as prime contractor to the agency and subcontracts the effort to an 8(a) contractor. These subcontracts may be awarded on either a sole-source or competitive basis. The size of an 8(a) contract cannot exceed $25 million, including all options. The SBA and agency cooperate, usually with the assistance of the SBA procurement center representative, to match the agency's requirements with the capabilities of 8(a) participants. The SBA issues a search letter of an 8(a) firm's capabilities and asks the contracting agency to identify acquisitions to support the firm's business plans. The SBA can also identify a specific requirement for a particular 8(a) firm(s), and agencies may review planned acquisitions to identify requirements to offer to the SBA. The SBA then submits a letter to the agency which includes the

8(a) firm's technical capability and capacity to perform (including bonding capability for a construction contractor), as well as any contracting assistance or equipment and real property needed for both the present and future. A sole-source procurement must include the rationale for selecting this specific firm (such as past performance) and its eligibility in terms of size status and business activity. A competitive request must provide the above information for two or more 8(a) participants. This letter is formally sent to DoD's Office of Small Business Programs.

The procurement office can also review its requirements and offer to set-aside an individual action(s) for an 8(a) procurement. This notification also addresses monthly production rates or construction site, if applicable, impact of delivery delay, prior small business set-asides for the requirement, and any problems in prior acquisitions.

Alternatively, the procurement office can send an offering letter to the SBA for consideration for 8(a) contracting, either on a sole-source or competitive basis. For each planned procurement action, the letter should address:

- contract type;
- description of work or deliverables;
- estimated dollar amount, including options;
- geographic restrictions on work performance;
- level of competition;
- NAICS code;
- period of performance;
- potential 8(a) awardees (e.g., based on past performance or direct contact or request by an 8(a) firm);
- procurement history in the past two years;
- requirements for bonding;
- SBA field offices showing interest in the acquisition;
- special capabilities needed for performance; and
- statement that no solicitation has been made under any type of socioeconomic set-aside.

The SBA will determine whether to accept the requirement for the 8(a) program within 10 working days of receipt (two days if the contract is at or below the simplified acquisition threshold). If the acquisition is accepted as a sole source, the SBA advises the contracting activity of the 8(a) firm selected for negotiation, which is often the contracting activity's recommended source. However, sometimes the SBA will wish to rotate the award to another firm that needs the business to survive and grow. In fact, for any 8(a) contract exceeding five years in length, the contracting officer must confirm within 120 days of the end of the fifth year that the firm is still enrolled in the 8(a) program before extending the contract. SBA also can negotiate on behalf of the 8(a) firm or else authorize the procurement office to negotiate directly with the firm. Repetitive acquisitions awarded through the 8(a) program require separate offers and acceptances so that the SBA may determine competitiveness, a nominated firm's eligibility, and the effect of contract award on the equitable distribution of 8(a) contracts. Separate offers and acceptances are not made for individual orders under multiple awards or multi-agency contracts. In fact, a firm which graduates from the 8(a) program may still receive orders under an indefinite delivery contract it received under the 8(a) program.

An 8(a) acquisition can be awarded based on a competition limited to eligible 8(a) firms if there is a reasonable expectation that at least two responsible 8(a) firms will submit offers and that award can be made at a fair market price. To establish a competitive acquisition, the anticipated total value of the contract, including options, must exceed $7 million for acquisitions with manufacturing NAICS codes and $4 million for all other requirements. An acquisition exceeding these thresholds can still be accepted as sole source if competition is not expected or if it is performed by an Indian tribe or ANC. An agency request for a competitive 8(a) award below the thresholds will be approved only where technical competitions are appropriate or if many responsible 8(a) firms are available for competition.

The negotiated contract price and the estimated fair market price are subject to the concurrence of the SBA. To determine a fair market price, the contracting officer may compare the pricing to commercial prices for similar products and services, or any prior purchase history by the office or other agencies. If this is not available, then the contracting officer will perform cost or price analysis, including data submitted by the SBA or the 8(a) contractor, and any in-house cost estimates.

The estimated price is then adjusted for differences in packaging and packing, performance periods, quantities, specifications, transportation, and other terms and conditions. Price indices may be used as guides for revised labor and material costs.

The SBA Administrator may appeal to the agency head if the SBA and the contracting officer fail to agree on making a particular acquisition available for award under the 8(a) Program, or for rejecting a specific 8(a) firm for award after SBA's acceptance of the requirement for the 8(a) Program. An appeal can also occur if they fail to agree on pricing or terms and conditions of a proposed 8(a) contract. Notification of a proposed appeal must be received by the contracting officer within five working days after the SBA is formally notified of the contracting officer's decision. The contracting officer suspends action on the acquisition until the agency head makes a decision, unless (s)he determines in writing that urgent and compelling circumstances will not permit waiting. SBA's response is due within 15 days thereafter.

Moreover, an 8(a) contract is normally terminated for convenience if the firm transfers ownership or control to another firm.

DFARS 219.8

The SBA has signed a Partnership Agreement which delegates to the USD(AT&L) its authority to sign 8(a) prime contracts and award the performance of those contracts to eligible 8(a) Program participants. An SBA signature on the contract is not required. For acquisitions that exceed the competitive threshold, the SBA also may accept the requirement for a sole-source 8(a) award on behalf of a small business concern owned by a Native Hawaiian Organization, a not-for-profit organization chartered by the State of Hawaii and controlled by Native Hawaiians whose business activities will principally benefit Native Hawaiians. SBA concurrence in the negotiated price is not required. However, when exceeding the simplified acquisition threshold, the contracting officer must notify the SBA prior to withdrawing a requirement from the 8(a) program due to failure to agree on price or other terms and conditions.

PGI 219.804 and .805

For requirements processed under the Partnership Agreement, the notification to the SBA must confirm the use of the Agreement. SBA acceptance or rejection of the offering is required within five working days of receipt of the offering. For sole-source requirements, an SBA acceptance must include a size verification and a determination of the 8(a) firm's program eligibility. Upon acceptance, the contracting officer will solicit a proposal, conduct source selection and make award directly to the 8(a) firm. No separate agency offer or SBA acceptance is needed for requirements that are issued under purchase orders that do not exceed the simplified acquisition threshold. Upon notification of award, SBA has two working days to notify the contractor and contracting officer that the 8(a) contractor is ineligible for award. For negotiated acquisitions, the contracting officer may submit a request for an eligibility determination on all firms in the competitive range if discussions are to be conducted, or on all firms with a realistic chance of award if no discussions are to be conducted.

DFARS 226.72

A demonstration project can be used to provide contracts to firms specifically to employ severely disabled persons. These persons must make up at least 20 percent of the firm's workforce on a full-time basis paid at least the minimum wage.[68] Written justification is required due to the resultant limitation on competition. The contracting officer must decide the appropriate percentage of employment reserved for such persons.

Solicitation Provisions and Contract Clauses

FAR 52.219-14, Limitations on Subcontracting.

FAR 52.219-17, Section 8(a) Award, in competitive solicitations and awards.

FAR 52.219-18, Notification of Competition Limited to Eligible 8(a) Concerns, in competitive solicitations and awards. Use the clause with its Alternate I when competition is to be limited to 8(a) concerns within one or more specific SBA districts. Use the clause its Alternate II when the acquisition is for a product in a class for which the SBA has waived the non-manufacturer rule.

DFARS 252.226-7002, Representation for Demonstration Project for Contractors Employing Persons with Disabilities.

Contract Clauses

FAR 52.219-11, Special 8(a) Contract Conditions, in sole-source contracts.

FAR 52.219-12, Special 8(a) Subcontract Conditions, in competitive contracts.

DFARS 252.219-7003, Small Business Subcontracting Plan. Use Alternate II for a demonstration program.

DFARS 252.219-7009, Section 8(a) Direct Award, instead of the clauses at FAR 52.219-11, Special 8(a) Contract Conditions, FAR 52.219-12, Special 8(a) Subcontract Conditions, and FAR 52.219-17, Section 8(a) Award, in solicitations and contracts issued under the Partnership Agreement.

DFARS 252.219-7010, Notification of Competition Limited to Eligible 8(a) Participants—Partnership Agreement, in lieu of the clause at FAR 52.219-18, Notification of Competition Limited to Eligible 8(a) Concerns, in competitive solicitations and contracts when the acquisition is accomplished issued under the Partnership Agreement.

DFARS 252.219-7011, Notification to Delay Performance, in solicitations and purchase orders.

2.7.3 Price Evaluation Adjustment for Small Disadvantaged Business Concerns

FAR 19.11 and 19.12

At times, discussion has arisen over how to favor SDBs who submitted offers in an unrestricted competition. At one time, Congress directed DoD and certain agencies to introduce an adjustment factor in price determinations by adding an amount to the evaluated price of non-SDBs. However, per the U.S.

Court of Appeals, DoD contracting activities may not use such a price evaluation adjustment for SDBs in its procurements.[69]

2.7.4 Labor Surplus Area Set-Asides

Labor surplus areas (LSAs) are communities and counties that have experienced severe unemployment, based on a yearly survey by the Department of Labor. An area receives an LSA designation when its average unemployment rate rises at least 20 percent above the national average over a two-year period. This implies that an area has more labor available than needed, so an employer will find it easier and more economical to staff a contract. Executive Order 12073, Federal Procurement in Labor Surplus Areas, and Executive Order 10582, Implementing the Buy American Act, create procurement preferences for employers located in LSAs. As a result, LSAs are another source of socioeconomic preference and may come into play as a tie breaker if evaluation results in a tie for low bidder. Currently however, the program is just voluntary.

2.7.5 Service-Disabled Veteran-Owned Small Business Procurement Program

FAR 19.14

The Veterans Benefit Act of 2003 created the Service-Disabled Veteran-Owned Small Business Program to provide Federal contracting assistance to service-disabled veteran-owned small business concerns.[70] A joint venture may qualify if at least one member of the joint venture is a service-disabled veteran-owned small business concern and the other concerns are small businesses under the NAICS code for the procurement. The Veterans' benefit does not apply to procurements below the micro-purchase threshold or otherwise awarded under other socioeconomic programs. Nor does it apply to orders under indefinite-delivery contracts or Federal Supply Schedules, since these contracts have already been awarded. The contracting officer must have a reasonable expectation of receiving offers from at least two service-disabled veteran-owned small business concerns, and awarding at a fair market price. Receiving only one offer at a fair price can still constitute award; however the lack of any such offers will lead to cancellation of the solicitation and reversion to a small business set-aside. A sole-source solicitation can be made if only one service-disabled veteran-owned small business concern can satisfy the requirement and the anticipated award price of the contract (including options) does not exceed $3 million ($5.5 million for manufacturing).

Contract Clause

FAR 52.219-27, Notice of Total Service-Disabled Veteran-Owned Small Business Set-Aside.

2.7.6 Indian Incentive Program

FAR 26.1

25 U.S.C. 1544 provides an incentive to prime contractors that use Indian-owned organizations and economic enterprises as subcontractors.[71] *Indian organizations* are any community, economic enterprise, group, pueblo, or village of natives recognized by the Federal Government as eligible for services from the Bureau of Indian Affairs (BIA) in the Department of the Interior. An *Indian* is a member of any tribe or community recognized as eligible for services from the BIA, and any "native" as defined in the Alaska Native Claims Settlement Act.[72] An *Alaska Native Corporation* (ANC) is a regional, urban or village corporation which is organized under the laws of the State of Alaska and is deemed a minority and economically disadvantaged concern. The Indian Incentive Program allows an incentive payment equal to five percent of the amount paid to an Indian organization or Indian-owned economic enterprise subcontractor.

Contracting officers and prime contractors may rely on the representation of an Indian organization or Indian-owned economic enterprise as to its eligibility, unless another potential offeror challenges its status prior to (sub) contract award or the contracting officer has independent reason to question that status. The contracting officer then refers the matter to the BIA, to determine the eligibility and notify the contracting officer. This process can take up to seven weeks. The prime contractor withholds award of the subcontract pending the determination by BIA, unless the prime contractor and contracting officer determine that award must be made in order to permit timely performance of the prime contract. Challenges received after award of the subcontract are referred to BIA, but its determination has prospective application only. If the BIA determination is not received within the prescribed time period, the contracting officer and the prime contractor may rely on the representation of the subcontractor.

Solicitation Provisions and Contract Clauses

FAR 52.226-1, Utilization of Indian Organizations and Indian-Owned Economic Enterprises, if subcontracting possibilities exist for Indian organizations or Indian-owned economic enterprises, and funds are available for any incentive payment.

DFARS 252.226-7001, Utilization of Indian Organizations, Indian-Owned Economic Enterprises, and Native Hawaiian Small Business Concerns, for supplies or services exceeding $500,000 in value.

2.7.7 Disaster or Emergency Assistance

FAR 26.2

The Robert T. Stafford Disaster Relief and Emergency Assistance Act provides a preference for local firms, individuals and organizations when contracting for major disaster or emergency assistance activities.[73] Agencies performing response, relief and reconstruction activities must transition to local firms any work performed under contracts in effect on the date on which the President declares a major disaster or emergency, unless the head of such agency determines in writing that it is not feasible or practicable.

Preference may be given through a local area set-aside or an evaluation preference. The contracting officer may set aside solicitations to allow only local firms within a specific geographic area to compete, but must define the specific geographic area for the local set-aside. This geographic area may or may not include all the counties in the declared disaster/emergency area(s), but cannot go outside the area(s). The contracting officer also determines whether a local area set-aside should be further restricted to small business concerns in the set-aside area. Any decision against a set-aside requires written justification.

A list of prospective vendors voluntarily participating in the Disaster Response Registry can be retrieved using the SAM Search tool. Contractors must register with SAM to gain access to the Disaster Response Registry.

Solicitation Provision and Contract Clauses

FAR 52.226-3, Disaster or Emergency Area Representation.

FAR 52.226-4, Notice of Disaster or Emergency Area Set-aside.

FAR 52.226-5, Restrictions on Subcontracting Outside Disaster or Emergency Area.

2.7.8 Historically Black Colleges and Universities and Minority Institutions

FAR 26.3

Executive Order 12928 of September 16, 1994, promotes procurements to Historically Black Colleges and Universities and Minority Institutions.[74]

There are no set-aside provisions to these entities, but they are included in an agency's goal of awards to SDBs (usually, at least five percent of total contract dollars).

Solicitation Provision

FAR 52.226-2, Historically Black College or University and Minority Institution Representation, in solicitations exceeding the micro-purchase threshold, for research, studies, supplies, or services of the type normally acquired from higher educational institutions.

2.7.9 Food Donations to Nonprofit Organizations

FAR 26.4

The Federal Food Donation Act of 2008 encourages executive agencies and their contractors to donate excess food that would otherwise be discarded to nonprofit organizations that provide assistance to needy people in the United States.[75] The food must meet all labeling and quality standards imposed by Federal, State and local laws and regulations. The Government will not reimburse any costs incurred by the contractor for donation of Federal excess foods.

Solicitation Provision and Contract Clause

FAR 52.226-6, Promoting Excess food Donation to Nonprofit Organizations, if greater than $30,000 to provide, service, or sell food in the United States.

2.7.10 Historically Underutilized Business Zone (HUBZone) Program

FAR 19.13

The Historically Underutilized Business Zone (HUBZone) Act of 1997 created the HUBZone Program ("HUBZone Empowerment Contracting Program") to provide Federal contracting assistance for qualified small business concerns located in economically disadvantaged geographic zones and owned in majority by American citizens or native Americans.[76] The program is designed to increase economic development, employment and investment in those areas. The company must have its principal office in the HUBZone and at least 35 percent of its employees must live in any HUBZone (not necessarily the same zone as the office or of other employees).[77]

If the SBA determines that a firm (including a joint venture) qualifies, it issues a certification and adds the concern to the List of Qualified HUBZone Small Business Concerns on its Internet website.[78] A listed firm is eligible for HUBZone program preferences without regard to place of performance.

HUBZone preference does not apply to requirements:

- for commissary or exchange resale items;
- ordered against Federal Supply Schedules or indefinite delivery contracts;
- that can be satisfied through award to UNICOR or Javits-Wagner-O'Day Act nonprofit agencies for the blind or severely disabled;
- that SBA has accepted for performance under the authority of the 8(a) Program, unless SBA releases the requirements; or
- within the micro-purchase threshold.

To set aside an acquisition for competition restricted to HUBZone small business concerns, the contracting officer must reasonably expect that offers will be received from two or more HUBZone small business firms, and award will be made at a fair market price. Any HUBZone small business concern proposing a product that it did not itself manufacture must furnish the product of another HUBZone small business concern manufacturer to receive the benefit. The HUBZone concern must perform at least half of the work in-house (for construction contracts, it must perform 15 percent in-house, or 25 percent for special trades). For a joint venture, each member party must qualify as a small business or else be a protégé under an SBA member-protégé program, and must perform at least 40 percent of the work (excluding administrative effort) in-house.

As with other set-aside methods, if the contracting officer receives only one acceptable offer from a qualified HUBZone small business concern in response to a set aside, award to that concern may proceed. If the contracting officer receives no acceptable offers from HUBZone small business concerns, the set-aside is withdrawn and the requirement is set aside for small business concerns.

A contracting officer may award contracts to HUBZone small business concerns on a sole-source basis without considering small business set-asides if:

- award can be made at a fair and reasonable price;
- only one HUBZone small business concern can satisfy the requirement, and has been determined to be a responsible contractor;
- the anticipated price of the contract, including options, will not exceed $5.5 million for a manufacturing requirement or $3.5 million otherwise; and
- the requirement is not currently performed by a non-HUBZone small business concern.

The SBA has the right to appeal the contracting officer's decision not to make a HUBZone sole-source award. The cognizant SBA official will decide within five business days, and the decision is final on all parties without appeal.

The contracting officer gives preference to offers from HUBZone small business by adding a 10 percent factor to all other offers except those from HUBZone small business concerns that have not waived the evaluation preference, and from otherwise successful offers from small business concerns. The factor is applied on a line item basis or to any group of line items. Other evaluation factors, such as transportation costs or rent-free use of Government property, are added to the offer price before adding the factor of 10 percent. The price evaluation preference for HUBZone small business concerns is used in full and open competition that exceeds the simplified acquisition threshold, where price is not a selection factor (e.g., architect/engineer acquisitions), or where all fair and reasonable offers are accepted (e.g., the award of multiple award schedule contracts).

A concern that is both a HUBZone small business concern and a small disadvantaged business concern will receive the benefit of both the HUBZone and the small disadvantaged business evaluation adjustments. Each price adjustment is calculated independently against an offeror's base offer, then added to the base offer to arrive at the total evaluated price.

Solicitation Provisions and Contract Clauses

FAR 52.219-3, Notice of Total HUBZone Set-Aside, for acquisitions that are set aside for HUBZone small business concerns. Use the clause with Alternate I if HUBZone firms cannot meet the 50 percent in-house rule.

FAR 52.219-4, Notice of Price Evaluation Preference for HUBZone Small Business Concerns, if exceeding the simplified acquisition threshold and using full and open competition. Use the clause with Alternate I if HUBZone firms cannot meet the 50 percent in-house rule.

2.7.11 Woman-Owned Businesses

FAR 19.15

Another size preference program covers firms where at least 51 percent is owned and controlled by one or more women who perform daily business management functions. The SBA will determine those NAICS codes where such firms are underrepresented in Federal contracting. The firm must be designated in SAM as a woman-owned small business to be eligible and may be further designated as an *economically designated woman owned small business*. Such firms must be certified by an SBA-approved third-party certifier; however self-certification is acceptable if proper documentation has already been submitted but the SBA has not yet completed its review and no protest is filed. Again, a protest process through SBA exists which allows 15 days after receipt to respond to any protest. The contracting officer does have an appeal right and can maintain an award based on a written D&F to any adverse decision. However, no options or further orders may be placed.

Both sole-source and competitive awards are possible under this program. Competition is required for set-aside procurements of $6.5 million for manufacturing or $4 million for services. The set-aside may be further restricted to economically disadvantaged woman-owned businesses if sufficient competition is expected.

A sole-source award to a woman-owned business is permitted if the procurement is not reserved for 8(a), Unicor or AbilityOne award. However, it must bear a NAICS code which SBA determines to be underrepresented by woman-owned businesses in Federal procurement, and it must be determined that competition among woman-owned businesses is unlikely.

Solicitation Provisions and Contract Clauses

FAR 52.219-29, Notice of Set-Aside for, or Sole-Source Award to, Economically Disadvantaged Women-Owned Small Business Concerns.

FAR 52.219-30, Notice of Set-Aside for, or Sole-Source Award to, Women-Owned Small Business Concerns Eligible Under the Women-Owned Small Business Program.

2.7.12 Disabilities

Although no preference programs exist for commercial concerns run by non-service-disabled persons, all firms must comply with Section 508 of the Americans with Disabilities Act.[79] A critical player in this program is the United States Access Board, an independent Federal agency which provides guidance on accessibility standards for people with physical disabilities. These include design criteria for buildings, classroom acoustics, computer systems, public transportation vehicles, and telecommunications equipment. The Board provides technical assistance and training on these guidelines to firms and enforces standards on federally-funded construction projects. There are no FAR clauses for this program as of yet.

2.8 RESEARCH AND DEVELOPMENT

2.8.1 Policy

FAR Part 35

Government *research and development* (R&D) programs advance and apply scientific and technical knowledge to achieve agency and national goals. Unlike contracts for supplies and services, most R&D contracts have objectives for which the work or methods cannot be precisely described in advance. These contracts bear a risk to both parties because they may offer little or no assurance of full success.

Research and development consists of four stages:

- basic research;
- applied research;
- design; and
- development.

Basic research investigates a physical phenomenon in an effort to collect and analyze knowledge of a particular issue or topic of interest. Research on Federal contracts often focuses on product improvement, including highlighting mathematical results, or else new initiatives with social benefits. Research effort is driven to achieve specified objectives rather than predetermined end results written in a work statement. To pursue this focus, technical and contracting personnel must consider:

- area of exploration and objectives;
- background information for the objective (e.g., known phenomena, methodology, techniques, or results of related work);
- contract type;
- design-to-cost requirements;
- for level-of-effort work statements, an estimate of applicable professional and technical effort involved;
- information on environment, interfaces and personnel that may constrain the results; and
- reporting requirements or deliverables due at specific intervals as the work progresses.

Applied research normally follows basic research, but may not always be severable into a separate contract. Designed to identify possible application of the knowledge, it attempts to determine and exploit the potential of scientific discoveries or improvements in devices, materials, methods, processes, techniques, or technology. The basic intent, of course, is to advance the state of the art.

Design uses creativity and problem-solving skills to explore possibilities and constraints to create a new or revised product or service. The firm will investigate external trends and revise current specifications, then test and modify them to ultimately reach full-scale operability at an acceptable cost. Sometimes, the firm may also prototype possible solutions.

Development first reduces the potential application to a model, prototype or specification(s) of the selected design to demonstrate physical capability or operational feasibility. The firm then systematically uses the scientific and technical knowledge gained in the research phases to further design, test and evaluate the target product or service to meet the performance requirements or objectives. This phase does not include any subcontracted technical effort which would be designed solely to develop an additional source for an existing product. A program is said to reach *full-scale development* when the items have been fully designed, fabricated, tested, and evaluated. The designed production process should by now mimic full-scale production. Documented test results provide confidence that the final product will meet the requirements.

Note that the four stages of these programs do not necessarily mean four segregable phases or even four separate contracts. There is often a significant level of overlap, such as uncovering an unexpected problem during full-scale development which requires a return to basic research to find an answer.

Corporate research and development activities may have a different objective than the Government, as they are intended to enhance the firm's competitive posture. Corporate research entails discovering and expanding product and technological knowledge, including knowledge of competitors' products. Research can also lead to processes that reduce capital and operating costs, and to improve performance of existing products and processes. Corporate development projects can find and create not only new products, but also new uses for existing products. The results can also provide technical expertise to the firm's other functional departments.

A firm often allocates a set percentage of projected revenue (say, three percent) to such effort, since such an investment is essential in this era of quickly evolving technology. The firm's management must decide on how to evaluate potential research and development projects. It may consider analysis of cost, intrinsic worth, literature and patent search, and usability within the firm's capabilities. Project selection methods are either qualitative (using checklists of evaluation factors) or quantitative (e.g., determining rate of return and present value using an index of relative worth or project value). Projects may also be selected to leverage off existing processes, software or technology. Decisions could also be driven by customer need or competitors' development projects.

There are several ways in which a firm can decide to pursue development. It can be done sequentially using one approach at a time and then discarding it for another approach if it proves unworkable. Alternatively, development effort may be performed in parallel using multiple approaches. This *parallel development* method involves concurrent work on different products which may go into production at different times. Sometimes customizations can be done simultaneously to products that are otherwise unrelated to each other. Dependencies sometimes result where two teams implement components which are related to each other. This parallel approach avoids the need to choose a best solution up front; however management must eventually decide when to focus on only one approach and drop the others. Further, the project must still set goals and furnish progress reports, evaluation and corrective actions, and follow-up activities. Liaison among departments is essential to smoothly transfer approaches into production and convert lab language into shop talk.

Engineering design is critical so that high quality and lower cost can be achieved. The *Pareto Rule* can be applied to this discipline—80 percent of the manufacturing costs are determined during the first 20 percent of the design process. A product parameter design can be used to find those design factors that can be adjusted to open up tolerances to achieve high quality at low cost, and to understand materials and functional performance. This process can also be used to choose the best idea among several alternatives.

Engineering design is also needed to provide deliverables from vendors. This requires development of sources to provide needed supplies. *Supplier development* is a process whereby a buyer tries to improve a supplier's performance and/or capabilities to meet supply needs. This is critical because perhaps half or more of a manufactured product consists of purchased inputs. Suppliers impact cost, quality, technology, and time to market, and thereby profitability. Both buyer and seller must commit facilities, financial capital and personnel to the work. They must also share sensitive information in a timely manner and create a means of measuring performance. The process requires the prime contractor to identify the critical components, suppliers and commodities to be outsourced to each supplier. Key performance indicators with weighted factors can be used to select and evaluate the performance of the suppliers, which is not an easy task.

Before entering production, the program office and Government may schedule a *production readiness review*. This is a formal program examination to assess design readiness, resolution of production engineering issues, and production planning. The review determines whether cost, schedule and performance criteria can be attained with acceptable risk. Officials determine if the system implements all requirements correctly and completely.

An *Integrated Process* (or *Product*) *Team* may be established to review manufacturing process readiness and quality management. It will also look at production planning in terms of facilities, inventory management, personnel qualifications and certifications, process documentation, and tooling and test equipment. Approval at this stage leads to either low-rate or full-rate initial production.

PGI 216.1

The absence of precise specifications and difficulties in estimating costs with accuracy normally precludes using fixed-price contracting for R&D. The nature of research and exploratory development usually leads to a cost-reimbursement type of contract, though it is often too early in the product life cycle to incentivize contractor performance. However, if the Government and the contractor can identify and agree upon the level of contractor effort required, they may use a firm-fixed-price level-of-effort contract. On the other hand, an incentive-type contract may be appropriate if the parties agree and can evaluate performance after completion of work.

For advanced development effort, a cost-plus-fixed-fee completion type contract is customary. However, incentive contracts can be used if the targets are measurable and realistic. In such a case, technical incentives will be necessary if there will be many technical changes or circumstances beyond the contractor's control may impact cost.

Engineering and operational systems development effort is usually cost-reimbursable because the contractor is often unable to provide accurate cost estimates and may overlap other stages of effort. Often the contractor needs technical direction by the Government and requires some level of Government configuration control. In later stages of effort when firm pricing can be derived, fixed-price contracting may be appropriate.

R&D projects with future production requirements normally move from cost-reimbursement to fixed-price contracts as designs become more firmly established and risks are reduced. Adopting a fixed-price contract will occur as production equipment, processes and tooling are developed and proven.

Some people would argue against contracting out too much research capability to the private sector. Proponents of this argument could posit that a proper mix to meet national interest would be necessary based on:

- agency responsiveness,
- cost,
- facilities and equipment investment,
- national priorities for science and technology,
- project risk,
- training, and
- urgency of need.

2.8.2 Solicitations

FAR 35.007

Contracting officers solicit only sources that are technically qualified to perform research or development in the specific field of science or technology.

They rely on technical personnel to recommend potential sources that appear qualified based on their ability to acquire and retain the professional and technical capability and facilities to perform the work. This review also looks at past and present performance of similar work. Technical personnel will also consider a firm's professional stature and reputation, as well as its relative position in the field of study.

Solicitations require offerors to describe their technical and management approach, identify and propose resolution of any uncertainties, and include any planned subcontracting of scientific or technical work. They contain evaluation factors to determine the most technically competent offeror, such as novel ideas in the specific branch of science and technology involved and the approach proposed to accomplish the scientific and technical objectives, or the merit of the ideas or concepts proposed. The agency will always evaluate the offeror's past experience and understanding of the scope of the work. Usually, it will also assess the availability and competence of experienced engineering, scientific or technical personnel and necessary laboratory, research, shop, or testing facilities.

The contracting officer also considers management capability (including cost management techniques), past performance and subcontracting practices. Generally, an R&D contract is awarded to the firm that proposes the best ideas and has the highest competence in the specific field of science or technology. Although cost or price is not normally the controlling factor in selecting a contractor to perform R&D, it is nonetheless considered for source selection.

R&D contracts require contractors to furnish scientific and technical reports as a permanent record of the work accomplished under the contract. Agencies provide R&D contract results to other Government activities and the National Technical Information Service, as well as the private sector. This agency within the Department of Commerce emphasizes new ways to use data in solving problems. It is the largest data repository of Federally sponsored research, dating back to World War II, and promotes new ways to collect, store and analyze data.[80]

Contracting officers follow agency regulations regarding data protection, national security and new-technology dissemination. As stated before, R&D contracts must specify the technical data to be delivered under the contract, since the FAR data clauses do not require delivery of any such data.

In planning a developmental program when subsequent production contracts are contemplated, program offices consider the need and time required to obtain a technical package (drawings, plans and specifications) to achieve competition for production. Sometimes, the developmental contractor may be in the best position to produce such a technical package.

If the contractor obtains the contracting officer's advance approval, it automatically acquires and retains title to any item of equipment costing less than

$5,000 (or a lesser amount established by agency regulations). For a larger dollar value, title may vest in the contractor, either upon acquisition without further obligation to the Government, or subject to the Government's right to directly transfer title to the Government or to a third party within 12 months after contract completion or termination. If title to equipment is vested in the contractor, no charges for amortization, depreciation or use are allowable under any existing or future Government (sub)contract. If the contract is performed at a Government installation and there is a continuing need for the equipment after contract completion, the Government may choose to retain title.

An educational institution or other nonprofit organization performing R&D work bears primary responsibility for the research if it is not defined precisely, and the contract states only a period during which work is conducted. The contractor must obtain contracting officer approval to change the phenomenon under study, or the stated research objectives or methodology. The contractor also provides the name of the principal investigator or project leader who is continuously responsible for the conduct of the work, estimates the amount of time that individual will devote to the work, and advises the contracting officer if this person will, or plans to, either leave the contract or devote substantially less effort to the work than anticipated.

An advance procurement plan is developed to describe the procurement method, timetable and expected price. Advance notification of the acquisition should be given the widest practicable dissemination by publicizing through the GPE and distribution to educational institutions, FFRDCs, foreign sources, Government laboratories, nonprofit organizations, and small businesses. The Government can also encourage industry participation by using draft solicitations and presolicitation conferences with prospective offerors for comment and solicitation revision.

The contracting officer sends the final solicitation to all prospective offerors to:

- describe the required mission capabilities without reference to any specific systems;
- include selection requirements;
- indicate and explain the capability, cost objectives, known constraints, and schedule;
- provide or indicate how to access all Government data related to the acquisition;
- reflect (if required) the use of an Earned Value Management System; and
- state that each offeror is free to propose its own design features, subsystems, technical approach, and alternatives to capability, cost and schedule goals.

The solicitation does not reference or mandate Government specifications or standards, unless the agency is mandating a subsystem or other component as approved under agency procedures. Proposals should include a discussion of the right to use technical data deliverables for competitive future acquisitions (including acquisition and usage costs), and development or qualification of multiple sources of supply for competitive future acquisitions.

DFARS 235.006

Contracting officers for major defense acquisition programs must notify the USD(AT&L) of an intent not to exercise a fixed-price production option on a development contract well before expiration of the option exercise period. For other than major defense acquisition programs, DoD does not award a fixed-price type contract for a development program effort unless realistic pricing is obtainable and use of a fixed-price type contract permits an equitable and sensible allocation of program risk between the Government and the contractor. A written determination must be executed by the USD(AT&L) if the contract is over $25 million and is for research and development for a non-major system or development of a major (sub)system (e.g., program risk does not permit realistic pricing), or else by the contracting officer for any other circumstance.

The contracting officer must obtain USD(AT&L) approval of both the prenegotiation position and the negotiated agreement before execution for any action that is an increase or repricing of more than $250 million, or a reduction of at least $100 million, in the price or ceiling price of a fixed-price development contract, or a fixed-price contract for the lead ship of a class.

2.8.3 Broad Agency Announcement

FAR 35.016

A *broad agency announcement* (*BAA*) may be used by agencies for scientific study and experimentation directed toward advancing the state of the art, or increasing knowledge rather than focusing on a specific system or hardware solution. The emphasis is on seeking new and innovative approaches and ideas to solve a specific problem. The BAA technique is only used when meaningful proposals with varying technical or scientific approaches can be reasonably anticipated. The BAA describes the agency's research interest, either for an individual program requirement or for broad areas of interest. Like any written solicitation, a BAA contains instructions for the preparation and submission of proposals, and describes the criteria for selecting proposals, their relative importance, and the method of evaluation. It also specifies the time period during which proposals will be accepted.

Availability of the BAA must be publicized through the GPE and may also be published in scientific, technical, or engineering periodicals at least annually. Proposals are evaluated in accordance with the evaluation criteria through a peer or scientific review process. Written evaluation reports on each proposal are necessary, but proposals need not be evaluated against each other since they are not submitted in accordance with a common work statement. The primary bases for selecting proposals for acceptance are technical ability, importance to agency programs and available funding. Cost realism and reasonableness are considered if appropriate. Synopsis of any awards is not required.

2.8.4 Grants and Cooperative Agreements

Per the Federal Grant and Cooperative Agreement Act of 1977, the Federal Government may not directly procure for a non-Federal entity, but rather must use an instrument of assistance such as a grant or cooperative agreement.[81] *Grants* are awards of funding by the Government to a nonprofit entity, educational institution, firm or individual. In order to receive a grant, an application or proposal is usually required. Often, a project office will fund multiple proposals through grants based solely on technical compliance, so price competition may not be present. Most grants fund a specific project and require some level of compliance and reporting. Grants have several unique features.

A *parent company guarantee* is used if the customer requires an awardee to provide a guarantee of its performance from its parent company. This document is drafted by the parent company and says that its liability only arises if its subsidiary commits a breach of contract and fails to rectify it. The parent's liability is limited to that of the subsidiary.

Grants may have a *long stop date* which sets a point in time where performance must end, regardless of where research stands or how promising it could be. Continuation of effort would require a new solicitation and consideration of other sources.

A *cooperative agreement* is similar to a grant in that a Government agency provides financial assistance to a commercial firm. However, the agency also provides management support of the project collaboratively, often on a cost-sharing basis with the firm. In contrast, grants have little or no Federal involvement in their management.

Independent research and development consists of projects involving basic research, applied research, development, and systems or concept formulation studies. This effort is not directly reimbursed under a contract or grant (but may be to some extent allowable as an indirect expense), nor does it include development of technical data to support bid or proposal preparation. Some major contractors enter into agreement with a Federal agency to be reimbursed a certain amount per year to cover IR&D expenses for projects of interest to that department.

2.8.5 Small Business Innovative Research

The *Small Business Innovation Research* (SBIR) program is coordinated by the SBA to reserve for small business 2.8 percent of any federal agency's extramural research budget in excess of $100 million.[82] The program funds early-stage innovation ideas that are too risky for private investors or venture capital firms. Recipient firms must have fewer than 500 employees to be eligible. Similarly, the *Small Business Technology Transfer Program* expands partnerships between small businesses and nonprofit U.S. research institutions. This type of effort is funded at 0.3 percent of the same agency's extramural research budgets.[83]

There are three phases in the SBIR Program. Phase I is intended to establish the technical merit, feasibility, and commercial potential of the proposed R&D efforts, as well as the quality of performance of the firm itself. SBIR Phase I awards are generally limited to $150,000 and six months of effort. Phase II continues the R&D efforts from Phase I; only Phase I awardees are eligible for a Phase II award. Funding is based on the scientific and technical merit and commercial potential results achieved in Phase I. SBIR Phase II are usually limited to $1,000,000 and two years of effort. A Phase III award allows the small business to pursue commercialization based on the results from earlier phases. The SBIR program does not fund Phase III; however some Federal agencies may provide their own funding for processes, products or services intended for Government use.

2.8.6 Federally Funded Research and Development Centers

FAR 35.017

The Federal Government provides funding support for a number (currently 41 and growing) of licensed nonprofit organizations to conduct effort in specific initiatives of interest. Known as *Federally Funded Research and Development Centers* (FFRDCs), these entities furnish state-of-the-art research and education, and seek discoveries, knowledge, and technological innovation in such areas as astronomy, cybersecurity, defense, health, nanoscience and nanoengineering, and safety. FFRDCs are operated and managed by a university or consortium thereof, other nonprofit organization, or an industrial firm, as an autonomous or identifiable separate operating unit of the parent organization.[84] Primary sponsors will provide information on each FFRDC, including funding data, mission statements, sponsoring agreements, and type of R&D being performed, to the Foundation upon its request.

An FFRDC meets a special long-term research or development need which is not achievable by existing in-house or contractor resources. FFRDCs allow agencies to use another set of private sector resources to accomplish tasks that are critical to their mission and operations. An FFRDC has access beyond what is common to the normal contractor to Government and supplier data (including proprietary and sensitive data), employees, installation equipment, and real property. Recall that real property includes land and rights in land, buildings and other structures, ground improvements, and utility distribution systems. It does not include foundations and other work necessary to install plant equipment or special tooling or test equipment. Therefore, the FFRDC is responsible to operate in the public interest independently and objectively, remain free from organizational conflicts of interest, and fully disclose its affairs to the sponsoring agency. It is not intended to use these special benefits to compete with the private sector.

Long-term relationships between the Government and FFRDCs provide the continuity that will attract high-quality personnel. This encourages the FFRDC to maintain currency in its field(s) of expertise, familiarity with the needs of its sponsor(s), and a quick response capability.

A written agreement of sponsorship is created with the Government when the FFRDC is established. A sponsor is the executive agency which administers, funds, and monitors the overall use of an FFRDC. Multiple agency sponsorship is possible as long as one agency agrees to act as the *primary sponsor* or lead agency under a multiple sponsorship agreement. The following requirements are addressed in either a sponsoring agreement or sponsoring agency's policies and procedures:

- a purpose and mission of the FFRDC;
- considerations which will affect negotiation of any fees;
- cost elements which require advance agreement for cost-type contracts;
- identification of retained earnings and a plan for their use and disposition;
- orderly termination or nonrenewal of the agreement, including disposal of assets and settlement of liabilities;
- prohibition against the FFRDC competing with any non-FFRDC concern in response to a Federal solicitation, though any parent organization or other subsidiary is free to compete; and
- whether or not the FFRDC may accept work from other than the sponsor(s), and if so, the procedures and limits to the nonsponsors from which work can be accepted.

The term of the agreement will not exceed five years, but can be renewed, as a result of periodic review, in increments not to exceed five years.

To establish an FFRDC, or change its basic purpose and mission, the sponsor will:

- confirm that sufficient Government expertise is available to objectively evaluate the work to be performed by the FFRDC;
- determine that existing alternative sources cannot effectively meet the special research or development needs;
- ensure that all work placed with the FFRDC is within the purpose, mission, general scope, or special competency of the FFRDC;
- ensure that the FFRDC refrain from quantity production or manufacturing unless authorized by legislation;
- establish controls to ensure that the costs of the services are reasonable;
- maintain continuity in the level of support to the FFRDC, consistent with the agency's need for the FFRDC and the terms of the sponsoring agreement;
- notify the Executive Office of the President, Office of Science and Technology Policy;
- operate in the public interest, free from organizational conflict of interest;
- place notices required for publication;
- receive approval from the head of the sponsoring agency; and
- state the basic purpose and mission of the FFRDC to differentiate from work which should be performed by non-FFRDCs.

The head of the sponsoring agency, prior to extending the contract or agreement with an FFRDC, conducts a comprehensive review of the use and need for the FFRDC. The review is coordinated with any co-sponsors and may be performed in conjunction with the budget process. A negative decision requires the sponsor to allow other agencies which use the FFRDC to assume sponsorship, or else phase out operation. An FFRDC review should examine the:

- adequacy of the FFRDC management to ensure a cost-effective operation;
- alternative sources to meet the sponsor's needs;
- criteria for establishing the FFRDC;
- efficiency and effectiveness of the FFRDC in meeting the sponsor's needs;
- FFRDC's ability to maintain currency in its field(s) of expertise, familiarity with the sponsor's needs, independence, objectivity, and quick response capability; and
- sponsor's technical needs and mission requirements that are performed by the FFRDC to determine if and at what level they continue to exist.

DFARS 235.017

No DoD funds may be used to finance activities of a DoD FFRDC if a member of its board of directors or trustees simultaneously serves on the board of directors or trustees of a profit-making company under contract to DoD, unless the FFRDC has a DoD-approved conflict of interest policy for its members.

DFARS 235.015-70

If an educational institution is unable to provide the capital for new laboratories or expanded facilities needed to conduct scientific research for defense contracts, DoD may employ a *special use allowance.* This is a negotiated amount to construct or acquire buildings, real property (other than land) and structures. The head of a contracting activity may approve special use allowances only if the:

- existing facilities, either Government or nongovernment, cannot meet program requirements practically or effectively, and providing Government-owned facilities is undesirable or impractical;
- proposed agreement for special use allowances is a sound business arrangement; and
- proposed use of the research facility is to conduct essential Government research which requires the new or expanded facilities.

In negotiating a special use allowance, consideration must include a comparison of DoD and the institution for the research facility to determine the amount of the special use allowance, as well as rental costs for similar space in the area where the research facility is or will be located. Cost calculations do not consider the cost of land, interest charges on capital, and operational costs such as maintenance or utilities. The period of allowance generally will be at least ten years or less if the total amount to be allowed is less than the construction or acquisition cost for the research facility. The special use allowance is allocated equitably among the Government contracts using the research facility. These allowances apply only in the years in which the Government has contracts in effect with the institution. However, if in any given year the level of Government research effort is reduced to the point that the allowance becomes excessive compared to the Government research funding, then a separate special use allowance may be negotiated for that year. Special use allowances may be adjusted for the period before construction is complete if the facility is partially occupied and used for Government research during that period.

A special use allowance may be based on either total or partial cost of construction or acquisition of the research facility. When based on total cost, neither the normal use allowance nor depreciation will apply during the special use allowance period and after the educational institution has recovered the total construction or acquisition cost from the Government or other users. When based on partial cost, normal use allowance and depreciation apply to the balance of costs during the special use allowance period to the extent negotiated in the special use allowance agreement. They do not apply after the special use allowance period, except for normal use allowance applied to the balance.

During the special use allowance period, the research facility will be available for Government research use on a priority basis over nongovernment use and cannot be put to any significant use other than that which justified the special use allowance, unless the head of the contracting activity who approved the special use allowance consents.

The Government will pay only an allocable share of the special use allowance when the institution makes any substantial use of the research facility for parties other than the Government during the period when the special use allowance is in effect. The Government will not pay the institution more than the acquisition costs.

2.9 SERVICE CONTRACTS

A *service* delivers value to customers by using the firm's employees to obtain or facilitate desired outcomes. A customer will contract out for services when it does not want to own the costs and risks of performance, or else lacks the needed knowledge or technological expertise in-house. Moreover, the supplier of the service can spread its costs among multiple customers, which not only lowers prices but also allows each customer to focus on its specific needs. By definition, services are intangible and perishable if not delivered.

To deliver value to its customers, a firm must use its own service assets, which are normally a capability or a resource. Examples of assets include:

- capital;
- information;
- infrastructure;
- knowledge;
- management;
- organization;
- people;
- processes; and
- software applications.

Services must have utility to support customer performance and remove some constraints. Services must also have the functionality to meet a need. To ensure the functionality and utility of a service, the firm should strive to reduce variation between predicted and actual value of services, thereby minimizing unpredictable impact on customer operations. This in turn should enable the customer to integrate the service into its business processes with confidence, thereby setting customer expectations on performance and use of results.

Many service contracts (especially those in support of information systems) use *service level agreements* to define service targets and responsibilities of both parties, in an effort to enhance service performance. Tailored to the specific needs of the operation, service level agreements document customer needs and provider responses. Each service level requirement is based on a business objective and a target level of support. These requirements can be geared toward the customer or the service, or both.

Integral to proper operation of these agreements is the process of *continual service improvement*. This concept is intended to boost quality of services delivered, as well as both the return and value of the firm's investment to deliver these services. Continual service improvement examples include efforts to:

- assess and recommend areas for improvement;
- conduct customer satisfaction surveys;
- conduct internal audits to verify process compliance;
- furnish a benefit that exceeds the amount expended for its achievement;
- increase value of non-monetary or long-term outcomes;
- increase a desirable metric or reduce an undesirable metric; and
- review management information and trends.

Any improvements must be both objective and measurable, and must meet the firm's business strategy. Once the improvement is implemented, the firm must then measure its achievements, validate the action as being correct, and provide any necessary change in direction. These metrics can address improved process efficiency and effectiveness, technology, or just achievement of a goal.

2.9.1 Federal Service Contracting

FAR 37.1

A *service contract* directly engages the time and effort of a contractor to perform an identifiable task rather than to furnish an end item of supply. A service contract can cover services performed by either professional or nonprofessional personnel on an individual or organizational basis. Some areas in which service contracts are found include:

- advice and assistance;
- architect-engineering;
- communications;
- housekeeping and base support;
- modernization, modification, overhaul, rehabilitation, repair, salvage, or servicing of equipment, supplies, or systems;
- operation of Government-owned equipment, real property, and systems;
- recurring maintenance of real property;
- research and development; and
- transportation.

Note that these services are commercial in nature, rather than being peculiarly Governmental.

As a special type of service, a *personal services contract* is characterized by the employer-employee relationship it creates between the customer and the contractor's personnel. Such a relationship occurs under a service contract when, as a result of contract terms or the manner of administration during performance, contractor personnel are subject to the relatively continuous supervision and control of a customer officer or employee.

The very nature of a personal services contract is inherently a real problem in Federal contracting. The Government is required to obtain its employees by direct hire. Obtaining personal services by contract circumvents those laws unless Congress has specifically authorized acquisition of these services through contracting. Hence, agencies do not award personal services contracts unless specifically authorized by statute. However, giving an order for a specific item or service, with the right to reject the finished product or result, is an acceptable action. When comparable services that meet similar needs performed in the same or similar agencies using civil service personnel, or the services are integral to the mission of the agency, the situation raises the specter of personal services. Likewise suspicious is when the nature of the service or its performance requires Government direction or supervision of contractor employees to retain Government control of the function. Concern that services are approaching personal in nature may also arise when the Government furnishes equipment or tools to perform the service.

On-site performance is another especially tricky situation. Government personnel must respect the need for distance between themselves and contractor employees. Even though many service contracts require on-site performance (especially where access to classified information is regularly required), it still presents an easy opportunity for Government personnel to "cross the line" and provide personal direction contrary to the arm's-length distance they are required to obey. This problem can best be avoided through constant vigilance by supervisors and the contracting officer.

Per DFARS 211.106, purchase descriptions for service contracts and resulting statements of work must require a clear distinction between Government and contractor employees. Contractor employees must identify themselves as contractor personnel by introduction as contractor personnel and displaying distinguishing visible identification for meetings with Government personnel. Contractor personnel must also identify themselves as contractor employees in telephone conversations and in (in)formal written correspondence.

For service contracts funded by annual appropriations, the period of performance does not normally extend beyond the end of the fiscal year of the appropriation except when authorized by law. Nevertheless, a defense agency may enter into a contract, exercise an option, or place an order for severable services for a period that begins in one fiscal year and ends in the next fiscal year if the total period of the contract, option or order does not exceed 12 months. Funds made available for the current fiscal year may be obligated for the total amount of such an action.

Award of contracts for recurring and continuing service requirements are sometimes delayed due to circumstances beyond the control of contracting offices. The contracting officer may need to issue a short-term bridge contract to the incumbent contractor to buy time and continue services until the contract is awarded. This is not a desirable situation, especially if the incumbent contractor is one of several offerors, and should be avoided if possible, but does happen.

To avoid recurring short contract extensions, the contracting officer may include an option clause to require continued performance of services within the limits and at the rates specified in the contract. However, these rates may be adjusted only as a result of revisions to prevailing labor rates provided by the Secretary of Labor. The option provision may be exercised more than once, but the total extension of performance may not exceed six months.

Contracting officers may enter into contracts with temporary help service firms for the brief use of private sector temporaries. These services are not regarded as personal services, but cannot be used in lieu of recruitment under civil service laws or to displace a Federal employee.

An agency head may waive the cost allowability limitations on severance payments to foreign nationals before awarding a contract performed in whole or in part outside the United States that provides significant support services for members of the armed forces or Federal employees stationed outside the United States. However, contracts are prohibited with organizations that offer quasi-military armed forces for hire, or with their employees. However, guard or protective services are not considered to be armed forces and may be covered by contract.

Any time the Government requires the contractor to provide advice, analyses, ideas, opinions, recommendations, or reports raises a concern that the services could influence the accountability, authority and responsibilities of Government officials. Hence, agencies must again ensure that qualified Government employees oversee contractor activities, especially to support Government policy or decision making. All contract personnel who attend meetings and answer Government telephones, and whose contractor status is not obvious to third parties, must identify themselves as contractors to avoid creating an impression that they are Government officials, unless the agency decides that no harm can come if they fail to identify themselves. The Government will also ensure that all documents or reports produced by contractors are marked as contractor products.

A very controversial subject concerns the use of *uncompensated overtime*. In this situation, contract employees are working more than 40 hours per week with little or no pay or premium for their extra time. An *overtime premium* is the difference between the regular rate of pay and the higher payment rate for the overtime period. It is not a *shift premium*, which is paid merely for working unusual hours such as nights or weekends. This results in free labor to the Government, which is cost effective but contrary to public labor policy. To address this two-sided problem, the Government has adopted the position that uncompensated overtime is neither encouraged nor prohibited. When professional or technical services are acquired by number of hours rather than task, the solicitation requires offerors to identify uncompensated overtime hours and the overtime rate for proposed personnel, including subcontractors. A weighted average including both regular and uncompensated labor costs will be derived for evaluation purposes. The use of uncompensated overtime cannot degrade the level of technical expertise required to meet Government requirements. Contracting officers conduct a risk assessment and look for unrealistically low labor rates and unbalanced distribution of uncompensated overtime.

The solicitation may afford potential offerors the right to visit the site where services will be performed (known as a *site visit*). This permission is at the discretion of the Government. If such an opportunity is available, then the contractor cannot come back later and claim that it was not aware of any obvious issues which would impact performance. And of course, for services performed on a Government facility, the contractor must take reasonable care to protect Government property and pay restitution in case of damages.

If an incumbent contractor loses the opportunity to perform in the follow-on contract, it may still be required by contract clause to provide training to the follow-on contractor's management and personnel to effect an orderly transition. It must also provide personnel records to the follow-on contractor. This phase-in period could last up to 90 days. Of course, the incumbent contractor will be paid for time spent in this transition effort.

Severance payments to foreign nationals employed under a service contract performed outside the United States are restricted. However, the agency grants a waiver to ensure the continuation of an activity that provides significant support services for Federal employees or military personnel. Nonetheless, the contractor must minimize the amount and number of incidents of such payments. This situation would normally occur in those countries where a significant number of businesses make such payments as a matter of routine, or else where a collective bargaining agreement requires such a practice.

DFARS 204.72

Contractor personnel who must access a Federal facility or military installation must complete Level I antiterrorism training within 30 days of requiring access and annually thereafter.

FAR 4.17

All service contractors are required to submit an annual report both the total dollars and direct labor hours charged to each of its Government contracts. First-tier subcontractors must report the same information to their prime contractors, unless their only contracts are fixed-price and below $500,000.

DFARS 204.17

A contractor must report to SAM every subcontract or order over $3 million in value, including options, for certain services (i.e., electronics and communications equipment or knowledge-based or logistics management).

Solicitation Provision

FAR 52.237-1, Site Visit, for services performed on Government installations, except for construction.

FAR 52.237-8, Restriction on Severance Payments to Foreign Nationals, where the cost accounting standard for such payments has been waived. However, the clause is still required for military banking contracts or for certain work performed in the Philippines.

FAR 52.237-10, Identification of Uncompensated Overtime, if above the simplified acquisition threshold, for professional or technical services to be acquired based on the number of hours.

Solicitation Provisions and Contract Clauses

FAR 52.237-2, Protection of Government Buildings, Equipment, and Vegetation, for services to be performed on Government installations, except for construction.

FAR 52.237-3, Continuity of Services, for services vital to the Government that must continue without interruption and which, upon contract expiration, can be continued by either the Government or another contractor. It can also be used when the Government anticipates difficulties during the transition from one contractor to another or to the Government (e.g., services in remote locations or requiring personnel with special security clearances).

FAR 52.237-9, Waiver of Limitation on Severance Payments to Foreign Nationals, when the head of an agency has granted a waiver.

DFARS 252.204-7023, Reporting Requirements for Contracted Services, for services specified above. Use Alternate I in orders agreements for same.

DFARS 252.211-7002, Availability for Examination of Specifications, Standards, Plans, Drawings, Data Item Descriptions, and Other Pertinent Documents, if contract performance requires use of specifications, standards and data item descriptions that are not listed in the ASSIST database.

DFARS 252.204-7004, DoD Antiterrorism Awareness Training for Contractors.

Contract Clauses

FAR 52.204-14, Service Contract Reporting Requirements.

FAR 52.204-15, Service Contract Reporting Requirements for Indefinite-Delivery Contracts.

2.9.2 Service Contract Act of 1965

FAR 22.10

Service employees are those persons performing in service contracts who are not administrators, executives, or professionals. Contracts over $2,500 for services performed within the United States or its possessions require determination of equivalent Federal employee classifications and wage rates (or minimum wages if no Federal classifications apply) and fringe benefits for service employees, plus safe and sanitary working conditions.[85] The firm must notify employees of same by posting notices addressing these requirements. Contracts for service employees may not exceed five years in length.

If a predecessor contractor had a collective bargaining agreement for substantially the same services performed in the same locality, the successor contractor must pay wages and fringe benefits (including accrued wages and benefits and prospective increases) at least equal to those contained in the agreement. If no predecessor contractor's collective bargaining agreement applies, then the Department of Labor may issue a wage determination to determine minimum wages and fringe benefits, based on employment of class(es) of service employees in the given locality. The contractor must then pay employees the amount set forth in the wage determination; otherwise, the minimum wage set forth in the Fair Labor Standards Act applies, based on a 40-hour workweek.

Examples of services which are covered by the Service Contract Act include:

- aerial spraying and reconnaissance for fire detection;
- custodial and housekeeping services;
- data analysis, collection, and processing;
- drafting, illustrating and graphic arts;
- electronic equipment maintenance and operation;
- engineering support;
- food service and lodging;
- grounds maintenance and landscaping;
- laundry, dry-cleaning, linen-supply, and clothing alteration and repair;
- maintenance and repair of equipment such as aircraft, construction equipment, electrical motors, electronic office equipment, engines, and vehicles;
- mortuary services;
- operation, maintenance or logistics support of a Federal facility;
- packing, crating and storage;
- repair of equipment other than remanufacturing or major overhaul;
- security guard services;
- snow and trash removal;
- stenographic reporting; and
- vehicle services such as ambulance, motor pool operation, parking, and taxi services.

The Service Contract Act does not apply to a contract for:

- agricultural, nursery and livestock products, and related work subject to 41 USC 65;
- calibration, maintenance, or repair of the following types of equipment if used for nongovernment purposes and sold in substantial quantities to the general public:[86]
  - automated data processing and information/word processing systems;
  - office or business machines serviced by the manufacturer or supplier; or

  - scientific and medical equipment using micro-electronic circuitry or similar sophisticated technology;
- construction of public buildings or works;
- direct services to a Federal agency by an individual(s);
- hotel/motel services for conferences, including lodging and/or meals;
- issuance and servicing of financial cards (credit, debit, purchase, and smart cards);
- operating postal contract stations or mail delivery service for the U.S. Postal Service;
- public utility services;
- radio, telegraph, telephone, or cable services;
- real estate and property appraisal services;
- transportation of persons or freight by common carrier (air, marine vessel, motor vehicle, or rail) or pipeline under published tariff rates; or
- vehicle maintenance services (unless to operate a Government motor pool).

The real estate and property appraisal services listed above must be related to housing or disposal of real property to be excluded from the Service Contract Act. This includes relocation services of real estate brokers and appraisers to assist Federal employees or military personnel in buying and selling homes. However, actual moving or storage of household goods and related services are subject to wage determinations.

Executive Order 13658, Establishing a Minimum Wage for Contractors, of February 12, 2014, may also apply to certain individuals who will be subject to minimum wage standards.[87] These wage rates are set forth in an Executive Order. The hourly minimum rate is adjusted either by law or annually based on the Consumer Price Index, rounded off to the nearest nickel. These amounts may exceed a collective bargaining agreement wage level or a minimum wage determination issued by the Department of Labor, in which cases this higher amount takes precedence. If the minimum wage rate is increased during performance, the contractor may be entitled to a price increase. There is no decrease if the minimum wage should go down, since the Government does not want to encourage wage cuts to individual contract employees. The Department of Labor will investigate any claims of below-minimum-rate payments, and may instruct the contracting officer to withhold payments.

To obtain the applicable wage determination from the Department of Labor, the contracting officer determines certain information concerning the service employees expected to be employed by the (sub)contractor. This information includes the classes of service employees to be used in performing the contract and locality(ies) where the services will be performed. The contracting officer must also discover whether a predecessor contract is covered by the Act and if the incumbent (sub)contractor(s) and employees have a collective bargaining agreement. The Department of Labor will assess the wage rate that would be paid each class if employed by the agency, which forms the basis for its wage determination.

If service employees of the incumbent (sub)contractor are represented by a collective bargaining agent, the contracting officer must receive a copy of the agreement (usually from the administrative contracting officer). The contracting officer then provides both the incumbent contractor and its employees' collective bargaining agent with written notification of the upcoming successor contract or modification and critical acquisition dates (e.g., issuance of solicitation, bid opening, negotiations, contract award, start of performance, and contract anniversary date) at least 30 days before the acquisition or anniversary date.

The wage determination will be posted on the SAM website. The contracting officer must monitor the website to learn of any revisions to wage determinations and incorporate them into the acquisition. Any revision at least 10 days before sealed bid opening or 30 days after award of a negotiated contract must be incorporated, with equitable adjustment if necessary.

Upon award, the contracting officer furnishes the contractor with a copy of Department of Labor Publication WH-1313, Notice to Employees Working on Government Contracts, for posting at the workplace in an accessible location. This poster addresses employee rights regarding minimum wages, attaching a copy of any wage determination which dictates a higher pay rate. It must also discuss overtime pay (time-and-a-half for all effort in excess of 40 hours in a week) and fringe benefits required by the wage determination. It will include a prohibition on child labor, since employees on a federal contract must be at least 16 years of age, and highlight safety and health considerations, namely that work conditions must be sanitary and not hazardous or dangerous for employees. Finally, it will discuss enforcement and include email addresses and phone numbers for Department of Labor and Occupational Safety and Health Administration.

If a contract is performed at a Federal facility where employees may be hired or retained by a succeeding contractor, the incumbent prime contractor furnishes a certified list of all service employees on the payroll and anniversary dates of employment to the contracting officer at least 10 days before contract completion. At the beginning of the succeeding contract, the contracting officer provides the list to the successor contractor to determine employee eligibility for vacation or other fringe benefits based upon length of service with predecessor contractors.

Any violations of the Service Contract Act render the contractor liable for the amount of any deductions, rebates, refunds, underpayments, or nonpayment of compensation due to contract employees. The contracting officer withholds (either on his/her own initiative or upon written request of the

Department of Labor) the amount needed to pay such employees from accrued payments due to the contractor on any contract (whether subject to the Service Contract Act or not). Any contractor failure to comply with the requirements of the Service Contract Act contract clause may be grounds for termination for default.

A list of persons or firms found to be in violation of the Act is contained in the Excluded Parties List System. No Government (sub)contract may be awarded to any violator or entity in which the violator has a substantial interest, without the approval of the Secretary of Labor.

DFARS 237.1

10 U.S.C. 2463 requires contracting officers to notify in writing any incumbent contractors of Government in-sourcing determinations within 20 business days of receiving a decision from the component in-sourcing program official that the service is being in-sourced. No formal hiring or contract-related actions may be initiated prior to such notification, except for preliminary internal hiring actions or contract modification.[88]

DoD has special requirements for personal service contracts. A D&F is required to acquire the personal services of experts and consultants. The D&F usually authorizes one contract at a time; however, an authorizing official may issue a blanket D&F for classes of contracts. The determination must indicate that:

- a nonpersonal services contract is not practicable;
- acquisition of the services is advantageous to the national defense;
- DoD personnel with necessary skills are not available;
- excepted appointment cannot be obtained;
- statute-mandated determination has been made;
- statutory authority applies; and
- the duties are temporary or intermittent.

Personal services contracts for health care may be used to acquire services from individuals provided within or outside medical treatment facilities (e.g., medical screening examinations at entrance processing stations) or counsellors (e.g., family or victim advocates, social workers, psychologists, and psychiatrists). The request for contract must be approved by the commander of the medical/dental treatment facility where the services will be performed.

The contracting officer must provide advance notice of contracting opportunities to individuals residing in the area of the facility through at least one local publication. The notice must include the qualification criteria against which individuals responding will be evaluated and fulfills the standard posting and synopsis requirements.

The contracting officer provides the qualifications of individuals responding to the notice to the commander of the facility for evaluation and ranking with rationale. Upon receipt of the ranked listing, the contracting officer will negotiate with the highest ranked applicant. If a mutually satisfactory contract cannot be negotiated, the contracting officer terminates negotiations with the highest ranked applicant and begins negotiations with the next highest. Alternatively, (s)he can enter negotiations with all qualified applicants and select based on qualifications and rates, fees or other costs.

Per 10 U.S.C. 129b(d), a personal services contract is permitted for individuals outside the United States if they support the mission of a defense intelligence component or counter-intelligence organization or special operations command. Moreover, the head of the contracting activity must determine in writing the above condition exists and that the services to be procured are urgent or unique and cannot be obtained such services by other means.

Personal service contracts for expert or consultant services cannot exceed one year or not cumulatively more than 130 days in one year. Payment to each expert or consultant for personal services cannot exceed the highest rate for grade GS-15.

Per 10 U.S.C. 2330, for acquisitions of services that are not performance-based at or below $93 million, the contracting officer must obtain the approval of the official designated by the department or agency. Acquisitions above $93 million require the approval of the senior procurement executive.

If contractor personnel must interact with detainees, they must receive Government-provided training regarding the international obligations and laws of the United States applicable to the detention of personnel (including the Geneva Conventions) and receive a training receipt.

Solicitation Provision

FAR 52.222-48, Exemption from Application of the Service Contract Act to Contracts for Maintenance, Calibration, or Repair of Certain Equipment—Certification, if applicability of the Service Contract Act of 1965 clause is unclear due to the exception for calibration, maintenance or repair of equipment.

FAR 52.222-52, Exemption from Application of the Service Contract Act to Contracts for Certain Services—Certification, if applicability of the Service Contract Act of 1965 clause is unclear due to the presence of another exception.

Solicitation Provisions and Contract Clauses

FAR 52.222-41, Service Contract Act of 1965, for services over $2,500, unless the solicitation includes either FAR 52.222-48 or FAR 52.222-52.

FAR 52.222-42, Statement of Equivalent Rates for Federal Hires, if expected to be over $2,500 and the Service Contract Act is applicable.

FAR 52.222-43, Fair Labor Standards Act and Service Contract Act—Price Adjustment (Multiple Year and Option Contracts), if fixed-price containing the Service Contract Act of 1965 clause, exceeds the simplified acquisition threshold and could run longer than one year (including options). This clause may be modified in overseas contracts when laws, regulations or international agreements require contractors to pay higher wage rates. The contract may include an economic price adjustment clause if potential fluctuations are not included in cost contingencies.

FAR 52.222-44, Fair Labor Standards Act and Service Contract Act—Price Adjustment, if fixed-price containing the Service Contract Act of 1965 clause, exceeds the simplified acquisition threshold and is not expected to run longer than one year.

FAR 52.222-49, Service Contract Act—Place of Performance Unknown.

FAR 52.222-51, Exemption from Application of the Service Contract Act to Contracts for Maintenance, Calibration, or Repair of Certain Equipment—Requirements (or FAR 52.222-53), if FAR 52.222-48 applies.

FAR 52.222-53, Exemption from Application of the Service Contract Act to Contracts for Certain Services—Requirements, if FAR 52.222-52 applies.

FAR 52.222-55, Minimum Wages under Executive Order 13658.

DFARS 252.237-7019, Training for Contractor Personnel Interacting with Detainees, if DFARS 252.225-7040, Contractor Personnel Supporting U.S. Armed Force(s) Deployed Outside the United States, is included in the solicitation or contract or the services will be performed at a facility holding detainees, and contractor personnel in the course of their duties may be expected to interact with the detainees.

2.9.3 Advisory and Assistance Services

FAR 37.2

Agencies may contract for *advisory and assistance services* to obtain:

- advice regarding developments in foundation, industry or university research;
- operational support and improvement of an organization or its hardware or managerial systems;

- opinions, skills or special knowledge of noted experts;
- outside points of view to avoid too-limited judgment on critical issues; or
- understanding of, and developing alternative solutions to, complex issues.

Advisory and assistance services are not awarded for:

- architectural and engineering services;
- awards on a preferential basis to former Government employees;
- basic research of biological, medical, physical, psychological, or social phenomena;
- bypassing personnel ceilings, pay limitations or competitive employment procedures;
- decision-making, managerial or policy effort which is a direct responsibility of agency officials;
- influencing or enacting legislation;
- obtaining professional or technical advice which is readily available within the agency or another Federal agency;
- research on theoretical mathematics; or
- routine information technology services, unless integral to acquire advisory and assistance services.

Contractors (other than FFRDCs) may not be paid for services to evaluate a proposal submitted for an initial award unless no civil service or military personnel with adequate training and capabilities are readily available, including from other agencies. However, FFRDCs may evaluate proposals because they are not in direct competition with the offerors.

Contracts for health care providers require the contractor to indemnify the Government for any act or omission committed by itself, its employees or agents occurring during contract performance. Although the Government may evaluate the quality of professional and administrative services provided, it cannot retain control over their professional judgments or diagnosis for specific medical treatment. The contractor must maintain medical liability insurance, at least in the amount in the locally prevailing community.

Solicitation Provision and Contract Clause

FAR 52.237-7, Indemnification and Medical Liability Insurance.

2.9.4 Utility Services

FAR Part 41

Utility services include furnishing chilled or hot water, electricity, natural or manufactured gas, sewage, steam, or thermal energy. Generally, utility services are provided by a publicly regulated source. Other services such as rubbish or snow removal may be appropriate when the acquisition is not subject to the Service Contract Act of 1965. Utility services provisions do not apply to:

- cable television and telecommunications services;
- construction or maintenance of Government-owned equipment and real property;
- natural or manufactured gas when purchased as a commodity;
- rights in public utility facilities, real property and on-site equipment needed for the facility's own distribution system;
- third-party financed shared-savings projects;[89]
- utility services in foreign countries; or
- utility services obtained by purchase or exchange by a Federal power or water marketing agency's distribution program, or provided by another Federal agency under interagency agreements.

The GSA prescribes policies and methods governing the acquisition and supply of utility services for Federal agencies. This includes managing public utility services and representing Federal agencies in proceedings before Federal and state regulatory bodies. GSA contracts for utility services for periods not exceeding ten years. Requests for delegations of contracting authority from GSA must include a certification from the acquiring agency's Senior Procurement Executive that the agency has an established acquisition program, personnel technically qualified to deal with specialized utilities problems, and the ability to accomplish its own preaward contract review.

Purchase of electricity must be consistent with state or local law governing the provision of electric utility service. This includes state utility commission rulings and electric utility franchises or service territories established pursuant to state or local regulation or statute, or territorial agreement. The contracting officer conducts a market survey of other qualified sources who can meet the Government's requirements, or consults with state or local officials before acquiring electric utility services on a competitive basis. If competition for an entire utility service (e.g., energy, sewage, transportation, water, standby or back-up service, transmission and/or distribution service) or associated services (e.g., billing, metering, operation and maintenance, quality assurance, or system reliability) is not available, the market survey may be used to determine the availability of competitive sources for certain portions of the requirement.

GSA enters into an area-wide contract with a utility service supplier to cover needs of Federal (but not defense) agencies within the supplier's franchise territory. A *franchise territory* is a geographical area that a utility supplier has a right to serve based upon either a franchise or a certificate of public convenience and necessity. Each area-wide contract includes an authorization form to request service, (dis)connection or change in service within the franchise territory or service area. Rates must be approved and/or established by a regulatory body and published in a tariff or rate schedule. Agencies are free to negotiate other rates and terms and conditions of service with the supplier, but may require the approval of the regulatory body to change them. Though these contracts normally run for just one year, they can last up to ten years if the provider insists or can offer lower rates or charges. GSA will require at least four months to provide these services. The service request to GSA includes:

- accounting data for contractor payment;
- connection charges to be paid by the Government;
- date of service initiation;
- demand and consumption estimates (both initial and maximum, along with time frame to ramp up to maximum);
- meter and facility locations (including meter placement with regard to the transformer);
- necessary new connection facilities;
- termination liability; and
- twelve-month actuals for demand and cost.

Agencies review utility service invoices on a monthly basis, and all utility accounts with annual values exceeding the simplified acquisition threshold on an annual basis. This ensures that the utility supplier is furnishing services under the most economical applicable rate, and permits examining competitive markets for more advantageous service offerings. The annual review is based upon the facility's usage, conditions values and characteristics of service at each delivery point are collected for the most recent 12 months. If a more advantageous rate is appropriate, the Federal agency requests the supplier to change the rate immediately.

Any rate change by a regulatory body is added to the contract by unilateral modification or otherwise documented in accordance with agency procedures. The contractor need not sign the modification because it has been decreed by the applicable Government agency. The approved rate is effective on the date determined by the regulatory body. No other regulatory change by a state or local authority is binding on the Government if it violates any Federal law or regulation.

DFARS 241.103

DoD is authorized to acquire utility services for military facilities. The contracting officer may enter into a utility service contract related to the conveyance of a utility system for a period not to exceed 50 years and an energy savings contract for a period not to exceed 25 years. Contracts for energy commodities such as electricity and natural gas purchased as supplies may not exceed five years for facilities and installations or four years for military housing.

DFARS 241.2

DoD tries to comply with current decisions, practices and regulations of independent regulatory bodies. However, purchases of utility services outside the United States may use formats and provisions consistent with local practice rather than American custom, as well as dual language forms and contracts. Rates established by an independent regulatory body are considered "prices set by law or regulation," thereby negating the need to obtain certified cost or pricing data and providing a valid basis on which prices can be determined fair and reasonable.

Utility service contracts usually contain one or two unique charges. A *connection charge* covers all nonrecurring costs, whether refundable or not, to be paid by the Government to the utility supplier for the required connecting facilities (including usage meters) which are installed, owned, operated, and maintained by the utility supplier. The *termination liability* is a contingent Government obligation to pay a utility supplier the unamortized portion of a connection charge and nonrefundable service charge if the Government terminates the contract before the utility supplier has recovered the cost of the connection facilities.

The Government may pay a connection charge when required to cover the cost of the connecting facilities based on the estimated labor cost of installing and removing the facility (excluding salvage cost). The order of precedence for contractual treatment of connection and service charges is:

- no connection charge;
- termination liability. The obligation must not exceed the agreed connection charge, less any net salvage material costs. Use of a termination liability requires the approval of the service power procurement officer or designee.
- connection charge is refundable when the supplier refuses to provide the facilities due to lack of capital or published rules which prohibit providing up-front funding. The contract should provide for refund of the connection charge within five years unless a longer period or omission of the refund requirement is authorized by the service power procurement officer or designee.
- connection and service charges are nonrefundable when the Government pays certain nonrefundable, nonrecurring charges which include service

initiation, construction assistance membership fees, and charges required by the supplier's rules and regulations to be paid by the customer. The Government can share with nongovernment users the use and costs for facilities when large nonrefundable charges are required.

PGI 241.2

Unless authorized by legislation, DoD does not use the connection charge provisions to install Government-owned distribution lines and facilities, nor new facilities related to the supplier's production and general "backbone" system. Construction labor standards ordinarily do not apply to construction accomplished for connection charges but may apply if installation includes construction of a public building or public work.

Requests for proposals state the anticipated service period in terms of months or years. If the period extends beyond the current fiscal year, the contracting officer will evaluate offers of incentives for a definite term contract of between one and ten years. If the expected service period is less than the current fiscal year, the solicitation will be based on an indefinite term contract. An indefinite term utility service contract is also appropriate when considered to be in the Government's best interest to have the right to terminate on a 30-day (or longer, up to one year) notice, or to grant the supplier the right to terminate the contract if beneficial to the Government in the form of lower rates, larger discounts or more favorable terms and conditions.

Solicitation Provision

FAR 52.241-1, Electric Service Territory Compliance Representation, for utility services when proposals from alternative electric suppliers are sought.

Solicitation Provisions and Contract Clauses

FAR 52.241-2, Order of Precedence-Utilities.

FAR 52.241-3, Scope and Duration of Contract.

FAR 52.241-4, Change in Class of Service.

FAR 52.241-5, Contractor's Facilities.

FAR 52.241-6, Service Provisions.

FAR 52.241-7, Change in Rates or Terms and Conditions of Service for Regulated Services, when the utility services are subject to a regulatory body.

FAR 52.241-8, Change in Rates or Terms and Conditions of Service for Unregulated Services, when the utility services are not subject to a regulatory body.

FAR 52.241-9, Connection Charge, when the Government must pay a refundable connection charge to compensate the contractor for furnishing additional facilities necessary to supply service. Use Alternate I to the clause if a nonrefundable charge is to be paid.

FAR 52.241-10, Termination Liability, when the contractor will be paid upon termination of service, either with or in lieu of a connection charge upon completion of the facilities.

FAR 52.241-11, Multiple Service Locations, if possible alternative service locations or delivery points are considered, except under area-wide contracts.

FAR 52.241-12, Nonrefundable, Nonrecurring Service Charge, when the Government pays a nonrefundable and nonrecurring membership fee, a charge for service initiation, or a contribution for the cost of facilities construction. The Government may include this amount or fee in the connection charge, the initial payment for services, or as periodic payments to fulfill the Government's obligation.

FAR 52.241-13, Capital Credits, when the Federal Government is a member of a cooperative and is entitled to capital credits, consistent with the bylaws and governing documents of the cooperative.

DFARS 252.241-7000, Superseding Contract, if the Government must execute a superseding contract and capital credits, connection charge credits or termination liability exist.

DFARS 252.241-7001, Government Access, when FAR 52.241-5, Contractor's Facilities, is used.

2.9.5 Commercial Studies

It is clear from the previous discussion that the Federal Government relies on the private sector for commercial services. OMB has issued Circular A-76, Performance of Commercial Activities, of May 29, 2003, to govern how this process is executed. Each agency identifies all activities performed by government personnel as either commercial or inherently governmental, retaining the latter for government personnel. The agency then conducts studies to determine if government personnel should perform the former or if contractor performance is more cost-effective. The agency develops a cost estimate in accordance with Circular A-76 rather than traditional agency methods, and then compares the estimate to competitive commercial offers to decide whether to retain the effort in-house or contract out. A-76 cost comparisons are very controversial within Congress because they could result in eliminating Government billets and thereby drive civil servants (i.e., voters) out of work. Hence, there is always a risk that this program could be suspended by legislation.

A competition is not required for continued private sector performance of a commercial activity, a new requirement, or expansion to an existing commercial activity performed by government personnel.

FAR 7.306

For sealed bidding, the contracting officer opens and records commercial bids, then opens the sealed cost estimate of Government performance. After entering the price of the apparent low bidder on the cost comparison form, the contracting officer announces the result, subject to further evaluation and protest. Both the bid abstract and cost comparison form are available for public inspection, along with detailed data supporting the cost estimate for Government performance. The contracting officer determines responsibility of the apparent low bidder, while the preparer of the cost estimate completes a comparison with the apparent low bidder. The responsible agency official makes a final written determination for performance by the Government or contractor, and the contracting officer either awards a contract or cancels the solicitation.

For negotiated procedures, the contracting officer conducts negotiations as necessary and selects the most advantageous proposal. Before public announcement however, the contracting officer opens the sealed estimate in the presence of the preparer, enters the amount of the most advantageous proposal on the cost comparison form, and returns the form to the preparer for completion. If the result of the cost comparison favors performance under contract and the responsible agency official approves the result, the contracting officer awards a contract and notifies the offerors of the cost comparison result and the winning offeror's name. The contracting officer then makes the cost comparison data available for review and awaits the public review period (15–30 working days) and any appeals. Should the result of the cost comparison favor Government performance, the contracting officer either notifies the incumbent contractor to stop work, or else cancels either performance or the solicitation.

Each agency establishes an appeals procedure for informal review of the initial cost comparison by an official at a higher level than the official who approved that result. This protects the rights of affected parties and ensures that final agency determinations are fair and equitable, and in accordance with established policy. Appeals address only questions concerning the calculation of the cost comparison, not the selection of one contractor over another (those questions are still treated under the Protests clause).

FAR 7.305

Displaced Government employees have the right of first refusal for employment with the new contractor. The contracting officer will provide a list of their names to the contractor within 10 days of award. Those who are hired within the first 90 days of performance will be listed on a report the contractor subsequently files with the contracting officer.

Solicitation Provision

FAR 52.207-1, Notice of Standard Competition, or FAR 52.207-2, Notice of Streamlined Competition.

FAR 52.207-3, Right of First Refusal of Employment, if conversion from Government performance to contract performance is possible. The 10-day period in the clause may be varied by the contracting officer up to 90 days.

2.9.6 Bundling

FAR 7.107

A special concern involves *bundling* services. This entails consolidating two or more procurement requirements for goods or services previously provided by separate contracts into a solicitation for a single contract that could be too large for a small business firm to perform. It also covers any procurement that is so large or diverse in terms of geography or skill sets that a small business (or team of small businesses) cannot expect to perform.

If an agency contemplates bundling, it consults with the local SBA procurement center representative with the anticipated benefits and cost savings. At least 30 days before solicitation or placing an order, the agency also notifies any affected incumbent small business concerns of the Government's intention to bundle the requirement, and how they can contact the SBA representative. Moreover, if the total value exceeds $2 million, the agency's senior procurement executive or chief acquisition officer must determine in writing that market research has been conducted, alternative approaches and negative impacts on small businesses have been considered, the SADBU or SBA representative have been consulted, and how small businesses will be included in the acquisition. At higher dollar values (which vary by agency), this determination requires further explanation of anticipated small business participation, since at this point we have substantial bundling. This determination is then posted on the agency's website.

Bundling may provide substantial benefits to the Government but requires market research to justify its use. Benefits are often received in terms of cost, delivery, quality, and contract terms and conditions. Contracting offices are tempted to bundle to reduce their workload. However, bundling gives rise to concern that small businesses will be unable to compete for the full requirement. Analysis should quantify and discuss cost savings or price reduction, improved terms and conditions, quality improvements, and reduced acquisition cycle times. Agencies may not consider savings in procurement operations or manpower to justify bundling. Ironically, this was the very reason why some agencies were blamed for promoting the use of bundling in the first place.

As a rule of thumb, bundling is justified if analysis reveals ten percent savings of estimated contract value if the total contract value is estimated to be below $94 million, or five percent savings (but not less than $9.4 million) if greater than $94 million. Reduced administrative or personnel costs are inadequate justification. The acquisition strategy must identify the benefits anticipated from bundling, strategies to reduce the scope of the bundling, and the rationale for not choosing these alternatives. The strategy must also address impediments to participation by small business concerns as contractors, and actions designed to maximize small business participation as (sub)contractors.

DFARS 205.205-70

If the acquisition is funded solely by DoD funds and could involve bundling, the contracting officer must publish in SAM a notification of the intent to bundle at least 30 days before solicitation. This notification must include any determination of measurably substantial benefits expected to be derived due to bundling.

DFARS 207.171

If a weapon system or major end item is bought without competition, then any component subcontracted without competition will be considered for breakout and purchase directly by the Government. This evaluation must consider cost savings as well as delivery, performance, quality, or reliability. Even when competition is present on either the prime or subcontract level, breakout can still occur for components exceeding $1 million in value if cost savings can be determined, such as quantity discounts or standardized design or spare parts.

This evaluation consists of assessing potential risks to the end item from possibilities such as delayed delivery and reduced reliability of the component, calculating estimated acquisition savings less any offsetting costs, and analysis of the factors involved (e.g., administrative, logistics, operational, and technical). If possible, the contractor should also assess the end item. Other considerations include:

- advance acquisition funding;
- alternative source;
- available data package;
- end item failure;
- financial risk;
- further design or engineering effort;
- future usage in Government-furnished equipment;
- impact on component standardization;
- logistic support needed for component breakout;
- need for developing specifications or testing or quality assurance requirements;
- production scheduling;
- projected cost savings in production oversight;
- quality control; and
- reliability.

2.9.7 Special Circumstances in Services

DFARS 237.270

Any offeror or contractor for financial statement auditing or remediation services must certify that it has not faced disciplinary proceedings within the past three years. If so, it must disclose the details.

DFARS 237.503

The agency head or designee must ensure that requirements for service contracts are properly vetted and approved to prevent unauthorized personal services. A certification in conjunction with service contract requirements must be placed in the contract file. The program manager or other agency-designated official responsible for the requirement must execute the certification.

DFARs 237.7001

DOD policy for mortuary services is mandatory for deceased military personnel within the United States and discretionary for deceased civilian and military personnel in areas outside the United States. One military activity in each geographical area will contract for the estimated requirements to care of remains for all military activities in the area. If the estimated annual requirements for the area are ten or more, a requirements contract is used. Where no contract exists, a purchase order may be used.

DFARs 237.72

An educational service agreement is not a contract, but rather an ordering agreement under which the Government may order educational services. The Government pays normal tuition and fees (but not for lodging or meals) for educational services provided to a student by the institution under its normal schedule of tuition and fees applicable to all students generally. Enrollment is at the institution under its normal rules and in courses and curricula which the institution offers to all students meeting admission requirements. No special courses or special fees for Government students are allowed.

Educational service agreements are for an indefinite duration and remain in effect until terminated. The issuing activity must establish procedures to review each educational service agreement at least once each year. Review dates should consider the institution's academic calendar and occur at least 30 days before the beginning of a term. The purpose of the review is to incorporate changes to reflect requirements of any statute, Executive Order, FAR, or DFARS. If the contracting officer and the institution do not agree on required changes, the agreement will be terminated.

DFARs 237.73

Generally, agencies will acquire services of students at institutions of higher learning by contract between a nonprofit organization employing the student and the Government, without regard to socioeconomic requirements. When it is in the best interest of the Government, contracts may be made directly with students. The institution must be located in the United States or its outlying areas, be fully accredited and offer studies beyond the high school level.

DFARS 237.74

The Defense Authorization Amendments and Base Closure and Realignment Act (Pub. L. 100-526) and the Defense Base Closure and Realignment Act of 1990 (Pub. L. 101-510) address noncompetitive contracting with local governments for police, fire protection, airfield operation, or other community services at military installations to be closed.[90] Contracts for these requirements must be implemented at least 180 days before the date the installation is scheduled to be closed. They require a determination by the head of the contracting activity that the services being acquired under contract with the local government are in the best interests of DoD. Employees are subject to the right of first refusal for employment unless it conflicts with the local government's civil service selection procedures.

DFARS 237.7602

Contractors providing essential services which support mission-essential functions must continue providing such services in accordance with the contract during periods of crisis. The designation as essential contractor services will not apply to an entire contract but will apply only to those service functions that have been specifically identified as essential contractor services by the functional commander or civilian equivalent. These contractors must provide a written plan to be incorporated in the contract to ensure the continuation of these services in crisis situations. Contracting officers consult with a functional manager to assess the sufficiency of the contractor-provided written plan. Contractors will activate such plans only during periods of crisis, as authorized by the contracting officer, who does so at the direction of the appropriate functional commander or civilian equivalent.

Solicitation Provision

DFARS 252.237-7012, Instruction to Offerors (Count-of-Articles), for laundry and drycleaning services to be provided on a count-of-articles basis. This provision is mandatory for effort within the United States and discretionary for services outside the United States.

DFARS 252.237-7013, Instruction to Offerors (Bulk Weight), for laundry services to be provided on a bulk weight basis. This provision is mandatory for effort within the United States and discretionary for services outside the United States.

DFARS 252.237-7025 Preaward Transparency Requirements for Firms Offering to Support Department of Defense Audits— Representation and Disclosure.

Solicitation Provisions and Contract Clauses

DFARS 252.237-7002, Award to Single Offeror, for mortuary services. Use the basic provision in all sealed bid solicitations for mortuary services. Use Alternate I in all negotiated solicitations for mortuary services. Use the following clauses:

- FAR 52.245-1, Government Property, with its Alternate I, when including port of entry requirements;
- DFARS 252.237-7003, Requirements, (insert activities authorized to place orders in paragraph (e) of the clause);

- DFARS 252.237-7004, Area of Performance. Do not use when including include port of entry requirements;
- DFARS 252.237-7005, Performance and Delivery;
- DFARS 252.237-7006, Subcontracting;
- DFARS 252.237-7007, Termination for Default;
- DFARS 252.237-7008, Group Interment;
- DFARS 252.237-7009, Permits; and
- DFARS 252.237-7011, Preparation History.

DFARS 252.237-7014, Loss or Damage (Count-of-Articles), for laundry and drycleaning services to be provided on a count-of-articles basis.

DFARS 252.237-7015, Loss or Damage (Weight of Articles), for laundry and drycleaning services to be provided on a bulk weight basis. Insert a reasonable per pound price in paragraph (b) of the clause, based on the average per pound value. When the contract requires laundry services per bag, insert reasonable per pound prices. Insert an appropriate percentage in paragraph (e) of the clause, not to exceed eight percent.

DFARS 252.237-7016, Delivery Tickets. Use the basic clause when services are not to be provided on a bulk weight basis. Use Alternate I clause when services are for bag type laundry to be provided on a bulk weight basis. Use Alternate II when services are unsorted laundry to be provided on a bulk weight basis.

DFARS 252.237-7017, Individual Laundry, for laundry and drycleaning services to be provided to individual personnel. Insert the number of pieces of outer garments in paragraphs (d)(1) and (2) of the clause. The number of pieces and composition of a bundle in paragraphs (d)(1) and (2) may be modified to meet local conditions.

DFARS 252.237-7018, Special Definitions of Government Property, in all solicitations and contracts for laundry and drycleaning services.

DFARS 252.237-7022, Services at Installations Being Closed.

DFARS 252.237-7023, Continuation of Essential Contractor Services, for services that are in support of mission-essential functions.

DFARS 252.237-7024, Notice of Continuation of Essential Contractor Services, for services that include DFARS 252.237-7023.

Contract Clauses

FAR 52.232-3, Payments Under Personal Services Contracts.

FAR 52.249-12, Termination (Personal Services).

DFARS 252.237–7026, Postaward Transparency Requirements for Firms that Support Department of Defense Audits.

2.9.8 Services Requirements Review Boards

DFARS 201.170

A Services Requirements Review Board (SRRB) process will be used to review, validate, prioritize, and approve services requirements.[91] They are chaired by senior leaders to assess and support trade-off decisions regarding the cost, schedule and performance for the acquisition of services. While SRRBs typically focus on contractor-provided services, they also help inform the decision to use organic capabilities (government civilians or military) instead of contracting for the required service by examining current mission needs, market research risk, and spend data and cost analysis. This process is conducted annually or more often, focusing on the requirements rather than a given contract, and identifies best practices and efficiencies. The SRRB should be conducted before a procurement request package is transferred over to the contracting office. This process is used for services acquisitions with an estimated total value $10 million or more, including any individual task order over this amount.

An SRRB will increase visibility and collaboration on services requirements, validating them before executing an approved acquisition strategy or a contract option. It will prioritize these requirements to increase collaboration among stakeholders on key strategy decisions and enable efficiencies, foster proactive management, identify and document opportunities for savings and cost avoidance due to reduction in service delivery levels or outright cancellation, and provide a process for senior leaders to assess, review, and validate services requirements. In addition, it could identify inherently governmental activities not suitable for contracted services, improved alignment of labor categories to work provided, and opportunities for strategic sourcing of services capabilities.

Documentation for the management and oversight process for the acquisition of services will consider:[92]

- Requirements development and management, which will include the source of the requirement, the outcomes to be achieved and what metrics will be used to measure the outcomes, how the requirement was previously satisfied, a summary of the market research conducted, consolidated, or bundled requirements, and a summary of the analysis of alternatives;
- Acquisition approach, which will include appropriate milestones, total cost/price estimate, funding sources(s), implementation of performance-based services acquisition or rationale for not doing so, opportunities for small business and socioeconomic concerns, proposed evaluation criteria and basis for award, the rationale for limited or no competition, multiyear service contracting, and any required waivers or deviations;

- Solicitation and contract award documentation, which may include contract type and duration of each business arrangement in terms of base period and all option periods;
- A management plan, to include potential impacts on cost, schedule, and performance, any acquisitions in which there is limited experience with the specific requirement and there is a moderate to high risk of not completing the acquisition successfully, incentive fees, a history of protests or performance problems, inherently governmental functions, externally or internally assisted acquisitions that intend to employ authority; and
- A summary of the plan for evaluating whether the metrics and any other measures identified to guide the acquisition have been achieved.

Requirements owners must plan appropriately before to avoid the use of a bridge contract to provide for continuation of a service to be performed through a services contract.[93] Such planning must include allowing time for a requirement to be validated and funded. For a services contract in an amount less than $10 million, any rationale for using a bridge contract must be provided to the commander or the senior civilian official of the Defense agency, field activity military installation concerned. For a services contract in an amount equal to or greater than $10 million, this information is provided to the SAE of the department, head of the agency concerned, the Combatant Commander, or the USD(A&S), as applicable. Upon the second use of a bridge contract to provide for continuation of a service to be performed through a services contract in an amount less than $10 million, notification of such use is submitted to the Vice Chief of Staff of the armed force concerned and the SAE of the MILDEP concerned, the head of the Defense Agency concerned, the Combatant Commander concerned, or the USD(A&S), as applicable. This approach does not apply to contingency operations, disaster relief, humanitarian assistance, international agreement, or national security emergency.

A major outcome of every SRRB should be a prioritized list of existing and anticipated requirements in terms of:

- industrial base;
- inherently or closely related governmental;
- marginal cost of performance;
- mission criticality;
- overall life cycle cost;
- personal services; and
- requirements management impacts.

Ultimately, the benefit of validating requirements via SRRBs is the active management of services to ensure cost-effective and efficient application of resources to meet mission requirements. SRRBs provide tools to assess relative values of services and to make cost-effective trade-offs without compromising mission capabilities.

2.10 INFORMATION TECHNOLOGY

Computers and digital information have become critical aspects of Government operations and contract support. Because regulatory guidance is limited, it is essential that today's contracting professionals have a basic understanding of some key concepts in this area.

2.10.1 Information Management

The Federal Government probably produces, collects and distributes more information than any other American entity. Because of the import and scope of these information activities, the management of Federal information resources is a critical and complex issue. In acquiring information technology products and services, agencies must comply with OMB Circular A-130, Managing Information as a Strategic Resource to consider:

- accommodations for individuals with disabilities;
- emergency preparedness;
- energy efficiency;
- environmental assessment of hardware;
- evolving information technology through market research and refreshment;
- national security;
- protection of privacy; and
- security of resources.

The Federal Government makes extensive use of *information systems* which process data, facts (often not for public release), opinions, and technology for a number of processes (e.g., audiovisual presentations, cartography, payment data, and reports). The output of these systems can be used by the office, other agency offices, elsewhere in the Federal Government, or to external sources (including contractors and the general public). These systems include a number of tangible *hardware* devices:

- input: mouse, keyboard, webcam, and microphone;
- network components: cables, circuits, displays, and power supplies;
- networking: routers and switches;

- output: monitor and printer; and
- storage: hard drive, thumb drive and optical disk.

Under the Information Technology Management Reform Act, the Department of Commerce issues standards, and guidelines for Federal computer systems to ensure security and interoperability.[94] Known as the *Federal Information Processing Standards (FIPS)*, they are approved by the Secretary of Commerce and issued by the National Institute of Standards and Technology (NIST). NIST is the organization which develops and maintains publications for national standards and measurements. These standards are issued as FIPS for use government-wide and within industry to promote interoperability and security.[95]

FIPS are compulsory and binding for Federal contractor performance and agency operations, which cannot waive their use. NIST has also issued a series of Special Publications which are gaining increasing utility throughout the Federal Government as de facto standards for information system security, as well as usage in the academic and corporate sectors. These standards provide technical controls to protect the confidentiality, integrity and availability of stored data, and prescribe automated procedures to analyze and remediate vulnerabilities and weaknesses. Contractors who manage Federal information systems must therefore:

- control connections to external information systems;
- control information posted or processed on publicly accessible or web-based information systems;
- identify and authenticate identities of devices, processes or users requesting access;
- identify, report and correct information and system flaws;
- limit physical access to authorized information equipment, systems and their operating environments;
- maintain subnetworks for publicly accessible system components so that they are logically or physically separated from internal networks;
- monitor and protect communications at the system's external boundaries and key internal boundaries;
- monitor visitor activity and maintain audit logs of physical access;
- periodically scan the system and files from external sources as applications are downloaded or executed;
- protect the system from malicious code and update mechanisms when new releases are available; and
- sanitize or destroy media before disposal or reuse.

Agencies must also follow OMB Circular A-123 Appendix D, Compliance with the Federal Financial Management Improvement Act of September 20,

2013, to acquire financial products and services. Any core financial management software to be acquired for Federal-only information systems (the Circular does not apply to contractor systems) must be certified by the Financial Systems Integration Office (formerly the Joint Financial Management Improvement Program) within the Department of the Treasury. This office manages the Federal Financial Management System Requirements, which tie into business processes and apply to administrative and programmatic systems supporting financial management systems.[96] These requirements cover data input, processing, and output, and are intended to focus on outcomes rather than process or technology.

In accordance with Section 508 of the Rehabilitation Act of 1973, Federal employees and citizens with disabilities must be able to access and use data to the same extent as their colleagues without disabilities.[97] However, these requirements do not apply to a project or effort incidental to a contract, repair or occasional monitoring of equipment, or any situation which would impose an undue difficulty or expense on the agency. Also, these requirements do not apply to a *National Security System* for information or telecommunications operated by an agency or its contractor or other organization. These functions involve command and control of military forces, integral components of a weapon system, or intelligence and cryptologic activities. This definition does not include routine administrative and business applications (e.g., finance, logistics, payroll, and personnel management).

Software itself comes in many forms and flavors. There are several types of software that could be bought in the marketplace:

- *commercial off-the-shelf software* is proprietary to the producer and readily available to the general public;
- *custom software* is developed specifically for the customer per his/her specifications;
- *embedded software* is part of a larger system and performs some system functions without user interface (e.g., an aircraft or traffic control system);
- *freeware* is copyrighted software available free of charge for an indefinite time period;
- *Government off-the-shelf software* is developed in-house by the agency's technical staff, or else by a contractor funded specifically under contract;
- *mobile code* is passed between systems to describe applets (e.g., Microsoft's ActiveX, Sun's Java, or Netscape's JavaScript) within web browsers, and is strictly controlled in many Government sites;
- *modifiable off-the-shelf software* means the *source code* (computer or application instructions, usually written in plain text, to be transcribed into binary code for the computer to execute) can be modified by the buyer, producer or third party to meet customer requirements;

- *open source software* has source code available under a copyright license for users to study, improve and redistribute it; and
- *shareware* is a trial version of commercial software distributed free and in advance of mass distribution, with payment due after a set number of days or uses.

Concerns over software vulnerabilities and malicious code, and the risks they introduce to information systems, have prompted the concept of *software assurance*. This approach provides a level of confidence that the software operates as intended and is free from defects. Pioneered by the Departments of Defense and Homeland Security, a working group developed guidance on how to include software assurance considerations in the acquisition process and build security into the software.[98] This has now become a paramount concern in software development and operations to mitigate risk. This guidance is also intended to minimize harm that may result from the loss, misuse or unauthorized access to (or modification of) the system itself or the information it manages.

FAR 39.103

As another recent development in this field, *modular contracting* is a technique using one or more contracts to acquire information technology systems in successive, interoperable increments. It is designed to acquire rapidly changing information technology while minimizing program risk and incentivizing contractor performance. Contracts are normally awarded within six months of solicitation. The effort may be divided into several smaller acquisitions to:

- address objectives incrementally to improve likelihood of achievement;
- isolate impact of custom-designed components from the rest of the system;
- leverage off technology innovation or requirements changes that occur during implementation; and
- test solutions without dependence on other increments.

To comply with the Privacy Act, any design, development or operation of a system of records that uses commercial information technology services must include agency rules of conduct for the contractor and its employees, Government inspection requirements, and safeguards for the contractor to implement.[99] The intent is to ensure the discovery and countermeasures of new threats and hazards. If a contractor is required to design, develop or operate a system of records, the contracting officer must ensure that the statement of work complies with agency requirements.

DFARs 239.101

A contracting officer may not enter into a contract above the simplified acquisition threshold for non-commercial information technology (IT) products or services unless the head of the contracting activity determines in writing that no commercial items are suitable to meet the agency's needs, as determined through market research.

2.10.2 Network Systems

A *network* is a collection of computers and related devices interconnected by communications channels allow users to perform tasks and share resources. Computer networks can be used for sharing:

- *communications* via email, instant messaging, chat rooms, and video conferencing;
- *files, data, and information* stored on other computers on the network;
- *hardware*, such as printing a document on a shared network printer; and
- *software and applications* stored on other computers.

Networked computers exchange information by cable or wireless connection between data links. As such, several aspects of networking become important to keep in mind. *Network architecture* is a framework to specify an information system's physical components and their configuration, data formats and operating principles and procedures. A telecommunications network architecture may also include a description of products and services delivered, and detailed rate and billing structures. Network architecture often includes the classification and structure of a distributed application architecture, which includes hardware that may be either physically collocated or remote.

Network management covers a myriad of activities, methods, procedures, and tools. They are designed to plan, allocate, deploy, coordinate, and monitor network features such as:

- bandwidth management;
- *configuration management* (document a system's physical and functional characteristics, and control and report any changes thereto);
- cryptographic key distribution authorization;
- equipment repair and upgrade;
- frequency allocation;
- network monitoring to spot problems rapidly to keep the network and its services up and running smoothly;

- performing corrective and preventive measures to improve network performance;
- predetermined traffic routing to support load balancing and associated analytics;
- security management; and
- tracking and assigning network resources.

Data for network management is collected through automated hardware agents installed at key points throughout the infrastructure. These hardware agents provide monitoring services to simulate activity logs, business transactions, sniffers to analyze data packets for illegal activity, and user activities.

Finally, *network monitoring* looks for slow or failing components and notifies the network administrator in case of outages. While an intrusion detection system monitors a network for threats from the outside, a network monitoring system looks internally for problems caused by overloaded and/or crashed servers or network connections. Commonly measured metrics in the network monitoring process are response time and availability. If a connection cannot be re-established or times out, or a document or message cannot be retrieved, the monitoring system sends an alarm email to the administrator. An automatic failover system may be activated to remove the troubled server from operation.

All information systems require qualified people to serve as network administrators to monitor their performance, respond to security incidents and update with patches. These services may be performed in-house or contracted out, since they are commercial in nature. In fact, many task orders under Federal schedules are for network administration or a subset thereof because of a plethora of qualified individuals available in the private sector. Hence, this is a major source of Federal contracting activity.

2.10.3 Telecommunications

Telecommunications involves transmitting communications over distances (whether across the room or cross-country). These communications entail sending and receiving (and related emissions of) images, intelligence, signals, signs, sounds, or writing. These emissions may be by means of cable, satellite, fiber optics, laser, radio, or satellite.

A basic telecommunications system includes a transmitter, physical channel, and receiver to translate the message into readable form. Communications signals can be either *analog* (the information is varied continuously) or *digital* (the information is encoded as a set of discrete values, such as ones and zeros). Some digital networks contain routers to transmit information to the correct user, whereas an analog communications network uses switches to establish a connection between users. Both types of network may use repeaters to amplify or recreate the signal when transmitted over long distances, and to combat physical noise.

Computer networks stack individual protocols to run independently of each other. This way, lower-level protocols can be customized for the network without changing how higher-level protocols operate. Most intercontinental communication uses the Asynchronous Transfer Mode protocol (or a modern equivalent) on top of optic fiber.

As the most common wireless network, the *Internet* is a worldwide network of computers that communicate with each other using the Internet Protocol (IP). It has become a critical resource for buyers and sellers to do research and communicate with each other. Any computer on the Internet has a unique IP address that can be used by other computers to route information to it, and to send a message to any other computer by using its IP address. For the World Wide Web, these IP addresses are derived from a human readable form using the Domain Name System. We have already seen examples of this (e.g., www.unicor.gov.) This service is usually provided under contract by a public utility or private telecommunications firm.

DFARS 239.74

DoD strives to acquire telecommunications services from common and noncommon telecommunications carriers competitively when possible. Common carriers (not to be confused with transportation companies) are regulated by the Federal Communications Commission or other governmental body, whereas noncommon carriers are not. DoD adopts the regulations, practices and decisions of the Federal Communications Commission, or else the generally accepted practices of the industry on those issues concerning common carrier services where no governmental regulatory body has exercised jurisdiction.

Purchase requests identify the nature and extent of information requiring security during telecommunications, and must identify the approved telecommunications security equipment, services or techniques with which the contractor must interoperate. (Sub)contractors provide all telecommunications security property, techniques or services required for performance of Government contracts. On rare occasions, the head of the agency may authorize provision of the necessary property as Government-furnished property or acquisition as contractor-acquired property.

The contracting officer may enter into a telecommunications service contract on a month-to-month basis or for any longer period(s), not to exceed a total of 10 years.

Common carriers are not required to submit certified cost or pricing data before award of contracts for tariffed services. Rates or preliminary estimates quoted by a common carrier for tariffed telecommunications services are deemed prices set by regulation within the provisions of 10 U.S.C. 2306a. This is true even if the tariff is set after execution of the contract. However, rates or preliminary estimates quoted by a common carrier for nontariffed telecommunications services or by a noncommon carrier for any telecommunications service are not considered prices set by law or regulation.

A common carrier may provide a special service or facility related to the performance of the basic telecommunications service requirements. Known as *special construction*, this may include expediting minimum service levels or providing facilities or moving equipment. Special construction costs may be a contingent liability for using telecommunications services for a shorter time than the minimum to reimburse the contractor for unamortized nonrecoverable costs. These costs are usually expressed in terms of a termination liability, either in the contract or by tariff.

When a common carrier submits a proposal which has special construction requirements, the contracting officer requires a detailed special construction proposal. (S)he will then determine the adequacy of the proposed construction, disclose excessive or duplicative construction and provide for the form of charge most advantageous to the Government. (S)he will try to analyze and approve special construction charges before receiving the service or else impose a ceiling on the special construction costs before authorizing the contractor to proceed, and certainly before final payment.

If the special construction includes construction, alteration, or repair of a public building or public work, the construction labor standards may apply. Otherwise, they do not.

Special assembly to design, manufacture, assemble, or wire equipment may be necessary to provide telecommunications services that cannot be provided with general use equipment. In such cases, special assembly rates and charges are negotiated based on estimated costs. If this is not possible, then provisional rates and charges subject to adjustment are imposed until final rates and charges are negotiated. Cancellation or termination charges may also need to be established.

Currently, contractors cannot obtain a telecommunications system or service pertaining to ballistic missile or nuclear defense that is produced by companies located in The People's Republic of China or Russia, unless waived by the Secretary of Defense.

FAR 4.22

The Federal Government cannot permit the use of the TikTok application or any service developed or provided by ByteDance Limited or any entity thereof.

Solicitation Provisions

FAR 52.204-24, Representation Regarding Certain Telecommunications and Video Surveillance Services or Equipment.

FAR 52.204-26, Covered Telecommunications Equipment or Services-Representation.

DFARS 252.239-7016, Telecommunications Security Equipment, Devices, Techniques, and Services, when performance of a contract requires secure telecommunications.

DFARS 252.239-7017, Prohibition on the Acquisition of Defense Telecommunications Equipment or Services, when performance of a contract requires secure telecommunications.

DFARS 252.239-7018, Prohibition on the Acquisition of Covered Defense Telecommunications Equipment or Services, when performance of a contract requires secure telecommunications.

Solicitation Provisions and Contract Clauses

FAR 52.204-23, Prohibition on Contracting for Hardware, Software, and Services Developed or Provided by Kaspersky Lab and Other Covered Entities.

FAR 52.204-25, Prohibition on Contracting for Certain Telecommunications and Video Surveillance Services or Equipment.

FAR 52.204-27, Prohibition on a ByteDance Covered Application.

DFARS 252.239-7002, Access.

DFARS 252.239-7004, Orders for Facilities and Services.

DFARS 252.239-7007, Cancellation or Termination of Orders.

DFARS 252.239-7008, Reuse Arrangements.

DFARS 252.239-7013, Obligation of the Government, in basic agreements for telecommunications services. Use Alternate I when the new agreement supersedes an existing agreement.

Contract Clauses

DFARS 252.239-7011, Special Construction and Equipment Charges, when using special construction charges.

DFARS 252.239-7012, Title to Telecommunication Facilities and Equipment, when using special construction charges.

2.10.4 System Enterprise Resource Planning

Enterprise Resource Planning is a method to manage both external and internal resources. Its goals are to improve the information flow between business functions in the organization, and manages the connections to outside stakeholders.

Such systems consolidate all business operations into an enterprise-wide system. Enterprise resource planning uses an integrated computer-based system to manage physical assets as well as financial and human resources. Some firms distribute the system across the network to minimize hardware expenses and communicate on a local area network. The system can either reside on a centralized server or be distributed across modular hardware and software units that communicate on a local area network. This second method lets a firm assemble modules from different vendors without buying expensive computer systems.

Enterprise resource planning is an adaptation of *integrated business planning* to technologically connect all stakeholders in the firm's planning functions. This approach integrates finance, marketing, and operations to identify their interdependencies and make informed purchase decisions regarding profitability and financial risk. Commercial ERP applications include:

- access control: managing user privileges;
- customer relationship management: call center support, customer contact, sales and marketing, service visits, and tracking commissions;
- data services: self-service interfaces for customers, employees and suppliers;
- financials: accounts payable, accounts receivable, cash management, fixed assets, and general ledger;
- human resources: employee benefits, payroll, time and attendance, and training;
- manufacturing: bills of material, capacity planning, engineering tasks, quality control, scheduling, and workflow and process management;
- project management: activity sequencing, billing, costing, performance tracking, and time and expense records;
- supply chain management: claim processing, inspection, inventory, order entry, product configuration, purchasing, and supplier scheduling; and
- translating contract requirements into usable instructions for internal compliance systems.

2.10.5 Seat Management

This initiative allows the management, operation and support of a distributed computing environment by a service provider firm. Performance is based on predetermined and negotiated service levels that are monitored by designated performance metrics. Examples of metric service level goals include:

- 98 percent or more availability;
- 80 percent customer satisfaction rating;
- answer help desk calls in 30 seconds or less;
- resolve 80 percent of problems on the first call;

- respond to hardware problems within one hour; or
- return hardware to service within two hours.

Critical to this concept are incentives to the contractor for exceeding key metrics and penalties for failing to meet these metrics. Also, a subscriber may elect to receive tiered services, opting to pay more money for higher levels of service. Thus, pricing is affected by asset distribution, infrastructure, refresh rate service levels required, and type of support.

The Clinger-Cohen Act requires Federal agencies to focus more on the results achieved through its IT investments, while streamlining the Federal IT procurement process.[100] It has revolutionized how Federal agencies manage IT acquisition. This legislation has also led the private sector to assess seat management to improve their cost performance, end-user satisfaction, environment, performance, and support. The departmental Chief Information Officer ensures the Department's IT systems are interoperable, justified, and secure, and contribute to mission goals. The head of each component is required to implement a process to maximize the value and assess and manage the risks of the agency's IT acquisitions. The prime guidance for DoD implementation is DoDI 5000.02T, Enclosure 11.

2.10.6 Cloud Computing

DFARS 239.76

Cloud computing is a model to enable ubiquitous, on-demand network access to a shared pool of configurable computing resources. These resources include applications, networks, servers, services, and storage. The intent is rapid provisioning and release of services with minimal management effort or service provider interaction. This includes commercial terms such as broad network access, measured service, on-demand self-service, rapid elasticity, and resource pooling. Commercial cloud service providers furnish virtual data storage and computing capabilities which are often more efficient and innovative than traditional approaches.

DoD usually acquires cloud computing services using commercial terms and conditions such as license agreements or terms of service. These services are normally bought from a cloud service provider that has been granted provisional authorization by Defense Information Systems Agency to provide the relevant cloud computing services in accordance with the Cloud Computing Security Requirements Guide.[101] This guide mandates baseline cybersecurity controls and information impact levels to host DoD missions in cloud service operators up to and including SECRET, based on the type of data to be hosted. Defense Information Systems Agency is the DoD Risk

Management Executive and uses the Guide to oversee cybersecurity assessment of cloud servicing operations and issues of a DoD Provisional Authorization. This will indicate that the cloud service operator is suitable for use up to an indicated impact level.[102]

An unauthorized provider may receive an award if the requirement is waived by the DoD Chief Information Officer or is for a private, on-premises version that will be provided from U.S. Government facilities. Under this circumstance, the cloud service provider must obtain a provisional authorization prior to operational use.

The requiring activity must describe *Government data*, which is any information, document, media, or machine-readable material regardless of physical form or characteristics, that is created or obtained by the Government during official business. It must also describe any *Government-related data* of the same nature that is created or obtained by a contractor through the storage, processing or communication of Government data. This does not include a contractor's financial or legal records or data such as operating procedures, software coding, or algorithms that are not uniquely applied to the Government data. The data descriptions must also address specific data ownership, licensing, delivery and disposition instructions. These instructions provide for the transition of data in commercially available, or open and non-proprietary format, and comply with guidance issued by National Archives and Record Administration. The data is subject to search and access capabilities as well as inspection and audit.

The contracting officer must provide written notification to the contractor when permitting it to maintain Government data at a location outside the 50 states, the District of Columbia and outlying areas of the United States.

NIST SP 800-145 describes three "service models," four "deployment models," and five "essential characteristics" a service should exhibit to be considered a cloud service.[103] The Service Models are:

- *Infrastructure as a Service (IaaS)*: basic computing resources such as networks, processing and storage. The customer generally still controls deployed applications, operating systems and storage, and limited control of certain networking components such as host firewalls.
- *Platform as a Service (PaaS)*: applications created using programming languages, libraries, services, and tools from the cloud service provider. The customer does not manage or control the underlying cloud infrastructure but does control the deployed applications and perhaps configuration settings for the environment.
- *Software as a Service (SaaS)*: applications run on a cloud infrastructure and are accessible through either a thin client interface (e.g., a web browser) or a program interface. The customer does not manage or control the

underlying cloud infrastructure other than limited user-specific application configuration settings.

The NIST-defined Deployment Models are as follows:

- *Public cloud infrastructures* operate in a multi-tenant environment with resources allocated for the public. They tend to be large to provide economies of scale for their customers. Privacy and security are issues because any individual or organization can potentially access the same cloud infrastructure.
- *Private cloud infrastructures* operate only for an individual organization. The organization can leverage both performance and scalability benefits of cloud computing, but the infrastructure is isolated from other organizations. This protection improves security and privacy but is specialized in nature and therefore can be just as costly as dedicated data centers.
- *Community cloud infrastructures* are private clouds provisioned for a specific community of interest with shared concerns, such as a government-only cloud.
- *Hybrid cloud infrastructures* combine two or more of the other cloud infrastructures.

NIST-defined Essential Characteristics are:

- *Broad network access:* capabilities are available over the network and accessed through thick or thin client platforms (e.g., laptops, mobile phones, tablets, and workstations). The DoD component mandates the access points over the Internet or the Defense Information Systems Network.
- *Measured service:* cloud systems automatically control and optimize resource use by a metering capability (e.g., bandwidth, processing or storage for active user accounts). Resource usage can be monitored, controlled and reported to provide transparency for both provider and user.
- *On-demand self-service:* the user can automatically provision network storage and server time without any human interaction with the service provider. The user can be an individual or a DoD organization that governs provisioning of the cloud service to their individual users. The provider may also use manual processes to internally provision the service.
- *Rapid elasticity:* capabilities can be provisioned and released, ideally automatically and near-real-time, to scale rapidly to match demand. To the user, the capabilities appear to be unlimited and in any quantity at any time. Components can govern use to ensure it does not exceed the financial and other resources obligated for the service.

Resource pooling: the provider's computing resources are combined to serve multiple consumers and dynamically assign different physical and virtual resources according to consumer demand. These resources include memory, network bandwidth, processing, and storage. The customer generally has no control or knowledge over the exact location of the provided resources.

DAG: Requirements for the Acquisition of Digital Capabilities Guidebook, 6.4.1

The requirements for cloud computing are extensive. The contractor must provide the ability to log actions to an immutable destination within the cloud offering with an audit trail.[104] DoD operators and auditors verify compliance with standards and policies.[105] Logical separation of unclassified infrastructure and encryption with cryptographic implementations is necessary for data both at rest and in transit and requires encryption with NSA-approved cryptography. Multi-factor authentication such as DoD PKI is required at the appropriate classification level. Account management, authentication and authorization services must be isolated from those used by other customers to prevent access to these services from the Internet and any other unauthorized network. The cloud service provider must support both Internet Protocol version 4 (IPv4) and Internet Protocol version 6 (IPv6) network addressing. The contractor must also support the Government cybersecurity test and evaluation process, including access to packet capture and system logs to support problem resolution and test results and reporting. This test environment must emulate the operational environment and be able to connect a DoD cyber test range emulation of its infrastructure to the test environment.

An agency acquiring cloud services will retain ownership of the data it acquires, as either a commercial, Governmental, or public asset. The contract must specify that the Government can select and migrate to another cloud service provider if it is not satisfied with the services it receives. The contract should also address data relationships, portability and records management. The contract should ensure that the cloud service provider is held accountable for data breaches, even if it does not own the data. Agencies with specific data location requirements must include contractual requirements identifying where data-at-rest (primary and replicated storage) shall be stored, which might be outside the United States.

Prior to pursuing cloud services, the program office must ensure a trade-off between cost and operational benefit and an informed approach to shape the acquisition strategy. To determine cost trade-off, PMs may conduct business case analysis to ensure a consistent approach to IT investment analysis. This analysis should facilitate comparison of alternatives and define expected benefits, costs, operational impacts, and risk.

A major cost driver is over-provisioning, when demand for an application is overestimated. Cloud service providers make it easy to max out and the costs become inflated. Although servers can be scaled back, this is often a slow process. To reduce costs, the site can shut down virtual instances when not in use, understand uptime requirements and scheduling, and monitor usage. In contrast, under-provisioning is when demand is underestimated, which is easier to detect and fix. Once again, costs can be saved and security improved by turning off resources that are no longer needed and by eliminating extra systems administrators.

Since cloud service providers offer different tiers of storage pricing based on data accessibility, the agency should consider which tier structure they need for specific data. Since storage grows and never shrinks, storage consumption must be actively managed by moving data to lower-cost services when they are no longer in constant use, and should cache and delete files as appropriate. Some carriers offer a "free tier" which becomes billable if thresholds are exceeded, and usually have an expiration date after which the full billing rate applies. Some commercial cloud service providers offer a menu of different virtual network and server instances that can be "rented" (e.g., databases, load balancers, and VPN concentrators). Troubleshooting is typically an overlooked cost that becomes more time consuming and expensive over time. The root cause of complex technical issues is hard to resolve because there is often no visibility into a cloud and in-house staff must work with the service provider to resolve issues. Hence, unless the exact frequency of usage is known, choosing a size and payment model can lead to unnecessary costs.

Generally, cloud computing is provided on an IDIQ contract. However, the contracting officer and PM should first check to see if current cloud cybersecurity policies are covered on an overarching contract; if so, the PM may not need to include these requirements on individual task orders or delivery orders. PMs should consider the use of time and materials type contracts, which allow for cloud resource units to be treated as fixed labor hour rates.

As for the NIST Service Models, for both IaaS and PaaS, the agency brings its own licenses and may or may not update them depending on funding. An FFP contract is often used. Contract risk should be relatively low and predictable within acceptable limits. However, agencies can be charged for services not used or are charged more than expected.

SaaS offerings vary from IaaS and PaaS in that vendors typically charge for active users or seat licenses that are permitted to access the service. In the SaaS model however, the cloud servicer provider is responsible for the application layer all the way down the stack. Also, the agency must budget for the service and consider seats and usage, as well as IT professional services. SaaS seats may be scaled up or down each month in keeping with the metered billing model. SaaS usually carries a perpetual and per-user license, paid monthly on an annual or multiyear term. Additional hidden costs include unanticipated development and maintenance costs due to customization, defining an integration architecture with a simple business process, testing the integrated services to understand capabilities and security features, and monitoring access, usually based on volume pricing to lower unit cost by purchasing more units.

There are a couple of models which the Government can use to obtain provisioning. Under the subscription model, a fixed amount of computing is bundled together for a recurring fixed monthly price. The agency may consume all or part of the bundled computing resources each month. If the agency does not use the entire bundle during the month, the remainder is lost. Most SaaS offerings include monitoring capabilities built into the service. Agencies can take advantage of the automation tools to control access, help provision, and provide cloud monitoring and reporting. Usually procured under a firm-fixed-price contract, each monthly invoice amount is clearly known. It is low risk due to a certainty of forecasted utilization and is relatively simple to execute.

Alternatively, the Government may pay with a "consumption-based" model using metered billing. It can move funds easily to cover costs of demand surges or quick scaling, but must obligate a set amount of funds that may not cover full demand or overestimate and overspend. In addition, if the licensing model requires that all available resources be considered even if not allocated, licensing costs will increase if migrated to a public-cloud platform. Similarly, if the application licensing is based per core and the cloud provider does not offer the ability to configure the cloud environment per core, this will increase licensing cost. This model is often procured under a time-and-materials contract.

The contract should define service level agreements that clearly define the contract performance standards, how the contractor measures and reports the service performance, and the enforcement mechanisms for compliance. They commonly include Monthly Uptime Percentage or Availability of Time percentage in a given period that the cloud service is accessible and usable. This can be easily measured, while storage resources are often described using transaction count. Cloud Service Response Time is another metric and should be measured at the edge of the consumer's IT system and includes the network transit time for both the request and the response.

The cloud service must interface with the appropriate DoD network via a DoD CIO-approved cloud access point and network boundary cybersecurity defense mechanism. If hosting unclassified data, approved cloud service offerings need not be classified. In either case, a supporting Cybersecurity Service Provider must be identified and confirmed, and have functional monitoring capabilities prior to operational use. If hosting unclassified data, approved cloud service offerings need not be classified. In either case, a supporting Cybersecurity Service Provider must be identified and confirmed, and have functional monitoring capabilities prior to operational use.[106]

DAG CH 6–3.9.2.3

The agency must consider mission risk before granting any authority to operate an information system or process. Any compensating controls must be reflected in the service level agreement or contract. Additional risks and concerns in contracting with a cloud service provider may include:

- acquiring a commercial service through a system integrator or value-added reseller, which means that they, not the cloud service provider, are accountable to the Government. This increases the risks to the Government due to lack of privity;
- any third-party ownership of assets that are applied for service provisioning;
- banner language which provides that consent to view any content on the system without a warrant may need to be displayed prior to allowing a user access;
- developing an interoperable strategy to move applications and/or systems from one cloud service provider to another;
- need for a change management and training program to implement security and cyber defense changes;
- need for the cloud service provider to indemnify the Government against lawsuits from third parties for a tort when the cloud service provider was liable;
- typical vendor contract terms and conditions may not be detailed enough once operations and services begin; and
- using insurance to pay for costs stemming from a breach of DoD data or to replace any damages to the DoD system, including credit monitoring.

It is a good idea to negotiate required service levels and expected performance with the cloud service provider to mitigate potential conflict. These agreements should also address performance measurement and enforcement. Sample requirements for such an agreement include:

- attestation and certification requirements to include FedRAMP Authorizations;
- availability requirements (e.g., percentage of time that the system or data will be available and usable);
- dates when the contract or service level agreement is active;

- enforceable penalties and remedies (e.g., termination or non-compliance with Service Level Agreement performance measures);
- exit details and procedures to ensure continuity with minimal disruption for catastrophic termination of service, failure to perform, or completion of contract. These procedures include level of contractor assistance and any associated fees, transitioning DoD data and networks back to the DoD, and transmitting and removing data from the contractor's environment;
- geographic locations that data may be processed and stored, and if the Government can specify location requests;
- glossary of the key performance and reliability terms (e.g., availability, breach of service agreement, continuity, emergency, outage (planned and unplanned), and recovery);
- how and when the contractor will retain or dispose of DoD records containing personally identifiable information or health records;
- how the contractor will isolate any co-located Government data into an environment where it may be scanned or forensically evaluated in a secure space, and how access will be limited to authorized Government personnel identified by the contracting officer;
- how service reliability measures with all responsible parties differ between IaaS, PaaS and SaaS services provided;
- list of accessibility standards, policies and regulations that must be met by the service;
- requirements for continuity of operations for SaaS providers and management of outages;
- requirements for service resilience, preservation, protection, and secure back up of all audit trails and transaction logs of the system/network operations;
- requirements for the identified personal identifiable/health information security controls associated with:
    - Access Control,
    - Audit and Accountability,
    - Authentication Enhancement,
    - Configuration Management,
    - Device Identification,
    - Incident Response,
    - Media Protection,
    - Personnel Screening,
    - Risk Evaluations,
    - Security Assessment and Authorization,
    - System and Communications Protection, and
    - System Interconnections Enhancement,
- roles and responsibilities for the parties:

  - contractor audit or forensic support,
  - contractor operations and maintenance support,
  - cybersecurity entities and service providers,
  - network operations,
  - program office system administrators, and
  - trusted internet connection support;
- service performance measures with all responsible parties including those that are responsible for measuring performance. These should include capacity and capability, elasticity, exception criteria, monitoring, and response time; and
- system quality measures for service performance including accuracy, agility, durability, fault tolerance, interoperability, portability, reliability, standards compliance, scalability, serviceability, and usability.

Solicitation Provision

DFARS 252.204-7008, Compliance with Safeguarding Covered Defense Information Controls, except for commercial items.

DFARS 252.239-7009, Representation of Use of Cloud Computing, for information technology services.

Solicitation Provisions and Contract Clauses

FAR 52.239-1, Privacy or Security Safeguards.

DFARS 252.204-7009, Limitations on the Use or Disclosure of Third-Party Contractor Reported Cyber Incident Information, for services that include support for the Government's activities related to safeguarding covered defense information and cyber incident reporting.

DFARS 252.204-7012, Safeguarding Covered Defense Information and Cyber Incident Reporting, for acquiring commercial items.

DFARS 252.239-7000, Protection Against Compromising Emanations, if information technology requires protection against compromising emanations.

DFARS 252.239-7001, Information Assurance Contractor Training and Certification, involving contractor performance of information assurance functions as described in DoD 8570.01-M.

DFARS 252.239-7010, Cloud Computing Services, for information technology services.

2.10.7 Cybersecurity

With our increasing dependency on information technology, adversaries can threaten the Government's ability to perform its missions. These adversaries can be amateur hackers, criminals, disgruntled employees, or enemies (both foreign and domestic). They can compromise Government computer systems and performance by inserting malicious programs or installing backdoors on systems for future access. These methods allow the adversary to modify data or system settings, misuse or damage hardware or software, or even steal data.

A *cybersecurity attack* refers to a disruption of digital network service to Federal information systems and those systems deemed by the President to be critical to the national infrastructure. These would include nationwide financial networks such as those used by the stock exchanges, the electrical power grid, and mass transportation systems. An attack prevents users from connecting to the Internet, or sending or receiving the lawful content of the user's choice over the Internet, as well as running applications or services of the user's choice.

Program office networks and systems, and supporting contractor facilities, are at risk of cyberattacks by state and individual threat actors. These malicious activities include remote unauthorized activity to subvert or compromise Federal networks, systems, support infrastructure, and employees through malicious actions. They can do so by compromising or disrupting operational and classified data, intellectual property or technical documentation to weaken technological advantage. They can also insert compromised hardware or software to disrupt or degrade system performance. Attention must be paid to cybersecurity at all acquisition category levels and all classification levels, including unclassified, throughout the entire life cycle.

Organizations institute cybersecurity countermeasures by using firewalls, trusted internet connections, system and software testing, intrusion detection and prevention tools, encryption, and monitoring. Employee training is also a significant measure to combat these threats. Federal agencies ensure that their desktops and laptops are configured in accordance with the Federal Desktop Core Configuration settings for Microsoft operating systems.[107]

The three key principles in an entity's security program are confidentiality, integrity and availability, commonly known as the "CIA triad." *Confidentiality* is the assurance that data secrecy is enforced at every junction of processing to prevent unauthorized disclosure. This includes when data is at rest in a database, in transmission and upon receipt at final destination. *Integrity* provides accurate and reliable information and systems, prevents unauthorized modification of data and protects the network from outside interference and contamination. *Availability* of systems and networks requires adequate capacity to perform predictably and acceptably to prevent disruption of service and productivity.

DFARs 239.7102

Statements of work and inspection and acceptance criteria must provide for information assurance to protect and defend information that is entered, processed, transmitted, stored, retrieved, displayed, or destroyed. They must also address information systems by ensuring their authentication, availability, confidentiality, integrity, and non-repudiation. This includes providing for the restoration of information systems by incorporating protection, detection, and reaction capabilities. The pertinent Government-wide directive is National Security Telecommunications and Information Systems Security Policy No. 11.[108] Pertinent DoD directives include:

- DoD Directive 8140.01, Cyberspace Workforce Management;
- DoD Directive 8500.01, Information Assurance;
- DoD Instruction 8500.01, Cybersecurity;
- DoD Instruction 8500.2, Information Assurance Implementation;
- DoD Manual 8570.01-M, Information Assurance Workforce Improvement Program; and
- National Security Telecommunications and Information Systems Security Policy No. 11.

For acquisitions requiring information assurance against compromising emanations, the requiring activity is responsible for providing to the contracting officer an established National TEMPEST standard. "TEMPEST" stands for Telecommunications Electronics Materials Protected from Emanating Spurious Transmissions. It is mandated by the National Security Council and NATO to protect information systems from leaking electromagnetic emanations such as electrical or radio signals, sounds or vibrations. The intent is to protect these systems and their communications and stored data against espionage. The activity must also furnish identification markings to include TEMPEST or other certified equipment (especially if to be reused), inspection and acceptance requirements addressing the validation of compliance with TEMPEST or other standards, and a date through which the accreditation is deemed current.

For acquisitions that include information assurance services for DoD information systems, or that require appropriately cleared contractor personnel to access a DoD information system, the requiring activity must provide the contracting officer a list of information assurance functional responsibilities for DoD information systems by category (e.g., technical or management) and level (e.g., computing environment, enclave or network environment). Thcy must also cite information assurance training, certification, certification maintenance, and continuing education or sustainment training required for the information assurance functional responsibilities. The certifications and certification status of all contractor personnel performing information assurance functions must comply with the DoD manual and are identified, documented and tracked.[109]

DFARS 204.7302 & 7602

All (sub)contractors must provide adequate security on all their information systems that are in any way involved with contract performance. They must implement all security controls mandated by NIST 800-171 and pass a DoD assessment of same within the past three years.[110] Of course, the contracting officer will need to verify this status by accessing the Supplier Performance Risk System before award or option exercise.[111] Similarly, the (sub)contractor may be required by the program office to meet the requirements for Cybersecurity Maturity Model Certification.[112] This requirement is discretionary for the program office until October 1, 2025, after which it becomes mandatory on all contracts and orders unless for COTS supplies. This provides a time period for contractors to become certified. This system helps to assess risk of contractors in terms of performance, price or unsuccessful performance.

They must also report cyber incidents directly to DoD, along with any available malicious software and host media.[113] Lower-tier subcontractors report the incident report number assigned by DoD to their higher-tier subcontractor, and so on until reaching the prime contractor. DoD may need to agree in writing to protect this information against unauthorized disclosure due to its sensitivity to the contractor and potential damage to its competitive position. The contracting officer will coordinate any action with the Chief Information Officer of the department or agency.

DoDI 5000.02, ENCLOSURE 14.1

DoD program office networks and systems, and supporting contractor facilities, are at risk of cyberattacks by state and individual threat actors. These malicious activities include remote unauthorized activity against DoD to subvert or compromise DoD networks, systems, support infrastructure, and employees through malicious actions. They can do so by compromising or disrupting operational and classified data, intellectual property or technical documentation to weaken DoD technological and military advantage. They can also insert compromised hardware or software to disrupt or degrade system performance. Attention must be paid to cybersecurity at all acquisition category levels and all classification levels, including unclassified, throughout the entire life cycle.

DoDI 5000.02, ENCLOSURE 14.2

The program manager's technical risk and opportunity management will consider potential exploitation of:

- contractor facilities: design, development and production environments, networks, supply chains, and personnel with access to government program organizations or fielded systems;
- degradation of configuration or poor cyber hygiene of fielded systems, which can expose system functionality to unauthorized access;
- equipment, facilities or services for design, development, manufacturing, maintenance, test, or training, which could provide unauthorized access to system functionality, information, or technology;
- program organization: classification of information, cybersecurity practices, detecting malicious insiders, dissemination control, information network security, and personnel training;
- software, firmware, and microelectronics used in the system or incorporated into spares, which can be deliberately compromised while in the supply chain for cyber-attacks; and
- system interface configuration, documentation, maintenance, and protection against unauthorized system access or malicious software or content.

DoDI 5000.82, Section 3.6 b.

All acquisitions of systems containing IT, including NSS, will have a Cybersecurity Strategy, in accordance with DoDI 8580.1. For mission essential and mission critical IT systems, this strategy may be an appendix to the program protection plan for applicable Adaptive Acquisition Framework pathways.[114]

Solicitation Provisions and Contract Clauses

FAR 52.204-21, Basic Safeguarding of Covered Contractor Information Systems.

DFARS 252.204-7012, Safeguarding Covered Defense Information and Cyber Incident Reporting, except for COTS items.

DFARS 252.204-7019, Notice of NIST SP 800-171 DoD Assessment Requirements, except for COTS items.

DFARS 252.204-7020, NIST SP 800-171 DoD Assessment Requirements, except for COTS items.

DFARS 252.204-7021, Cybersecurity Maturity Model Certification Requirements, except for COTS items.

2.11 RISK

2.11.1 Nature of Risk

Risk is a concept which addresses the impact of a given vulnerability. Risk measures future uncertainties by identifying events that are reasonably predicted and may threaten a mission and its successful performance. It can be mathematically calculated as the product of the probability and magnitude of the vulnerability's impact. Risk calculation is a method to envision this impact on future outcomes by first measuring how much the results deviate from expected values, then planning how to avoid or mitigate these risks. Although these deviations may be either positive or negative, most people focus on the negative ("downside risk") or failure to achieve sufficient beneficial outcome ("upside risk"). Risk can be measured in economic terms due to lower income or higher costs than anticipated, caused by such events as loss of key personnel or production stoppages. It should also reflect changing market conditions such as arrival of a new market competitor or higher prices for raw materials. A comprehensive risk definition should even consider external events such as a change in political party in power or natural disasters.

Risk is not always about a technical issue. It can also be financial in nature; perhaps an investment's actual return will differ from that expected. Competitors may introduce technological breakthroughs, or the marketplace may take a negative turn. Also, the possibility of external hacking or fraudulent employee behavior is ever-present.

A fundamental idea in the financial world is the relationship between risk and return. The greater the potential return sought, the greater the risk assumed. This is why demand for a safer investment drives its price higher and its return lower, while weak demand for a riskier investment drives its price lower and its potential return higher. Management will first address the risks with the greatest loss and probability of occurrence, then analyze risks with lower probability of occurrence and loss in descending order.

FAR 39.102

When planning an acquisition, agencies use the common security configurations available from NIST and agency guidance pertaining to information technology standards.[115] They analyze risks, benefits and costs during program investment and implementation. Examples of acquisition risk include:

- change implementation and organizational conflicts of interest;
- contract type;
- cost;

- dependencies between a new project and other projects or systems;
- environmental impact;
- funding availability;
- impact of lack of protection or a security breach;
- need for new processes to be implemented and sufficient time for contractors to propose;
- occupational health impact;
- program management;
- quantity of simultaneous high-risk projects to be monitored;
- residual risk after all mitigation actions are taken;
- safety;
- schedule;
- security (i.e., clearances, facility access and government property); and
- technical feasibility, maturity, obsolescence, and relevancy.

Evaluation criteria can include development knowledge, process maturity and use of testing tools and code vulnerability scanners. Proposals are rated on a scorecard using either qualitative or quantitative methods, or else by means of a "go-no go" decision. A due diligence questionnaire is often used as a tool to gain further input on offerors regarding the following:

- architecture and design,
- assurance claims and evidence,
- built-in software defenses,
- component assembly,
- concept and planning,
- development process management,
- financial history and status,
- foreign interests and influences,
- individual malicious behavior,
- installation and acceptance,
- licensing,
- operating environment for services,
- organizational history,
- past version support,
- security monitoring and performance history,
- security training and awareness,
- service confidentiality policies,
- software change management,
- software manufacturing and packaging,
- testing, and
- timeliness of vulnerability mitigation.

2.11.2 Risk Management

Risk management should be an integral part of a firm's decision-making processes. A systematic structured approach is necessary, such as that spelled out in ISO 31000, "Risk management—Principles and guidelines on implementation."[116] The decision process must consider the human factors and interests of all affected parties, respond to change and continuous process improvement, and be tailored to the firm.

The risk management process contains several steps:

- define a framework and agenda for risk identification;
- develop an analysis methodology;
- identify risks:
- develop mitigation or solution strategies using human, organizational and technological resources; and
- identify stakeholders, evaluation schemes and any constraints.

Critical to this process is *risk identification*, a process to isolate a problem or its source. Identifying risk areas requires considering relationships among all the risks and to identify potential areas of concern that would have otherwise been overlooked. Risk sources may be internal or external to the system, such as:

- application error (e.g., computation or input errors or buffer overflows);
- data loss or destruction;
- data misuse (e.g., espionage, fraud, sharing trade secrets, and theft);
- human error;
- inside or outside attacks (e.g., cracking or hacking);
- physical damage; and
- system or peripheral device malfunction.

Common risk identification methods are based on checklists, questionnaires, scenarios, or threats to objectives. Once risks have been identified, they must then be assessed for both their potential severity of loss and their probability of occurrence. The order of basic steps in the process are to:

- assign value to information and assets;
- perform a threat analysis;
- derive overall loss potential per risk;
- choose remedial measures to counteract each risk; and
- decide whether to accept, reduce or transfer the risk.

The risk management process can be either qualitative or quantitative in nature. A qualitative method identifies possible scenarios, ranks threat seriousness and asset sensitivity based on judgment and experience, and then derives a score for each scenario. Alternatively, the widely accepted formula for risk quantification is:

Risk = Rate of occurrence × Impact of event.

Adding all risk calculations results in a Composite Risk Index, a cumulative risk measure based on the probability and severity of the various areas of concern.

Risk analysis looks at the potential variation from the planned approach and its expected outcome. This assessment addresses both probability of future occurrence and its consequence or impact. The biggest difficulty in risk assessment could be determining the rate of occurrence if there is limited statistical information on past incidents. The impact of the risk event may be assessed on a scale of 0 to 10, and the probability of occurrence is on a percentage scale from 0 to 100. The overall risk assessment is then Low, Medium or High, depending on the calculated value of the Composite Index. For instance, Low could be classified as a score between 0 and 3.5, Moderate between 3.6 and 7.0, and High any score over 7.0.[117]

Risk management requires a top-level assessment of the impact on the requirement when all risk events are considered. This is not an easy process to execute, since risks must be correctly understood and cost effectiveness may not be acceptable. Moreover, an opportunity cost arises by not spending resources on more profitable activities. Hence, risk management strives to minimize resource consumption and avoid the negative impact of events.

DoDI 5000.02T ENCLOSURE E2: 6.d

It is easy to see that a key element of program management is to reduce or eliminate programmatic risk over the life of the program. A formal risk management program is therefore important to identify program risks and develop an associated risk mitigation approach. The following risk management techniques are commonly used:

- alternative designs that meet requirements but may reduce performance;
- independent risk assessments by outside subject matter experts;
- industrial base availability and capabilities;
- modeling and simulation to develop tools to support a comprehensive risk management and mitigation approach;
- multiple design approaches;

- phasing program activities or technology development to address high-risk areas as early as possible;
- prototyping the (sub)system or component (competitive where possible);
- schedule and funding margins; and
- technology demonstrations and decision points to insert planned technologies or select alternative technologies.

Once risks have been identified and assessed, they will be addressed by one of four treatment methods:

- avoidance;
- reduction;
- sharing; and
- retention.

The first treatment option is avoidance. The organization can refrain from performing an activity that could carry risk. For example, a firm could decide that the cost of complying with shock test standards so discourages a potential maritime product that it would rather forego a shipboard application for its commercial product. Avoidance also means losing out on the potential rewards and profits that could have resulted if the risk was accepted. If the elimination of hazards takes too long or is too costly, mitigation must be considered.

Second, the organization can reduce the severity or likelihood of the loss from occurring. However, it must carefully balance technical effectiveness with cost for the solution. Incremental development and delivery (also known as "build a little, test a little") is one method used in major system development to counteract this concern.

Third, the firm or organization can share or transfer risk by purchasing insurance or outsourcing, even though the buyer is still legally responsible. Risk retention pools are another example of sharing by retaining the risk for a group of entities without paying an upfront premium, but rather by assessing losses to all group members.

Finally, any risk that does not fall into the other categories is retained by definition. The organization can accept the benefit or loss from a risk when it occurs through self-insurance if the cost of purchased insurance exceeds the total losses sustainable. Uninsurable risks or those with unaffordable premiums are also retained, such as war.

A *Risk Management Plan* should document the decisions about how each of the identified risks should be handled. This plan should propose controls and countermeasures (with supporting rationales) to manage these risks (e.g., buying and installing an antivirus software program). The plan should also contain an implementation schedule and identify responsible parties. Practice and experience (perhaps even an actual event) will dictate changes in the plan and revised decisions in confronting risks. The plan should be reviewed at least annually to evaluate the effectiveness of the selected security controls and possible risk level changes in the environment. This evaluation should also identify new threats and reconsider the severity of ongoing threats.

For all its benefits, risk management is a process that can go off-track. Risks can be improperly assessed and prioritized, thereby wasting time with unlikely results and resources that could be used more profitably. Also, qualitative risk assessment is subjective and inconsistent, and could be mired in legal and bureaucratic processes. An organization must also take care not to prioritize risks so highly that it cannot complete a project.

An enterprise can also use risk management to address risks to its customers, existence, human and capital resources, products, and services, as well as from the external environment and society. The process includes the following activities:

- assign a risk officer to foresee potential project problems;
- create an anonymous risk-reporting channel;
- identify risk management activities, budget and responsibilities;
- maintain a current project risk database with an action officer, description, importance, probability, and due date for resolution;
- prepare a mitigation plan to describe how this particular risk will be handled; and
- summarize planned and faced risks, effectiveness of mitigation activities, and level of effort for risk management.

Risk mitigation techniques during contract performance include:

- acquisition planning tied to budgeting;
- continuous risk-based data collection and assessment;
- implementing identified security controls;
- modular contracting;
- post-implementation cost-benefit reviews;
- project management;
- prototyping before implementation;
- tradeoffs between cost, operational effectiveness and risk; and
- transfer to or sharing with a third party.

All risks cannot be fully avoided or mitigated due to financial and practical limitations; hence the organization must accept some level of residual risks. *Business continuity planning* addresses these accepted residual risks by considering infrastructure issues such as data, facilities, and hardware. This planning must also address less tangible elements such as crisis communication, key personnel, planning for resumption of applications, and reputation protection. Any of three types of control measures (preventive, detective, and corrective) can be implemented to reduce risk:

- *corrective*—restore the process or system back to its previous state, or mitigate the impact of the threat (e.g., anti-virus protection, backup data storage and operating system restoration);
- *detective*—monitor activity to determine where policies or procedures were not followed (e.g., audit trails, intrusion detection systems, job rotation, and network monitoring systems); and
- *preventive*—preclude the harm or loss from occurring (anti-virus protection, biometrics, firewalls, guards, and security awareness training).

As another planning tool, a *disaster recovery plan* should be created that includes metrics for the recovery point and time for business processes, information systems and supporting infrastructure. These metrics can then be used to develop budget justification to ensure an affordable level of protection. Basic data protection begins with the use of anti-virus software. However, hardware solutions are often used, such as fire alarms and extinguishers, surge protectors and uninterruptible power supply and/or backup generators. Common strategies for data protection in storage include local mirrors of data and/or systems, and disk protection technology (such as redundant array independent disks). An organization can also send tape backups off-site at regular intervals, say daily for critical data and weekly for more routine information. It can also invest in high availability systems to replicate both the data and system off-site, using storage area network technology to enable continuous access.

Continuity of operations (COOP) is a plan that outlines the steps needed to ensure that an agency can carry on all essential functions in case of a natural or manmade disaster. Agencies designate functions as either essential or nonessential, depending on how critical the need for performance is (e.g., communications, financial, health, safety, and security). This is why organizations ensure that resources or personnel involved in a critical function are geographically disbursed and not concentrated in one area should a disaster strike. Presidential Decision Directive 67, Enduring Constitutional Government and Continuity of Government Operations, requires agencies to develop COOPs, and the Federal Emergency Management Agency (FEMA) released Federal Preparedness Circular 65, Federal Executive Branch Continuity of Operations, to advise how they should develop their COOPs. These plans identify the order of succession for agency management (principally for their positions and responsibilities), alternate work locations, and internal and public communications. Agencies must conduct tests and training exercises to ensure that backup operations can support the regular workload if networks fail.

There is more Federal guidance to continuity planning. Homeland Security Presidential Directive 20, National Continuity Policy (also labeled as National Security Presidential Directive 51) mandates agencies to develop continuity plans to ensure that mission-critical functions continue during emergencies.[118] FEMA remains in charge of coordinating emergency activities under the National Response Framework, a plan to promote interdepartmental cooperation and continuity during a national emergency (such as attack or natural disaster).[119]

The Continuity Policy Implementation Plan provides guidance for agencies to identify those functions that are necessary to continue operating the government. FEMA's Federal Continuity Directive 1 sets criteria for continuity facility operations, communications requirements, and vital records management. FEMA's Federal Continuity Directive 2 provides guidance on how to identify mission-essential functions and the primary functions that must be resumed within 12 hours of a catastrophe. This directive requires agencies to conduct a risk management process to identify these functions and report them to the Department of Homeland Security.[120]

COOP also includes teleworking remotely from home or another location to perform critical job tasks at an alternate location. GSA has a goal of promoting more eligible Federal employees teleworking (25 percent or maybe even 50 percent).[121]

FAR 4.402

The National Industrial Security Program (NISP) safeguards Federal Government classified information that is released to contractors, grantees, and licensees of the U.S. Government. NISP's operating manual (NISPOM) chronicles the requirements of various executive orders into a coherent operating procedure. Identified within DoD as DoD 5220.22-M, and NISPOM, it requires use of the Contract Security Classification Specification, DD Form 254, to indicate security requirements of contract performance in terms of documentation, facility and personnel clearances. This form is attached to every contract that requires contractor access to classified or controlled unclassified information.

DFARS 204.470

Under the U.S.-International Atomic Energy Agency Additional Protocol, the United States Government must declare many public and private nuclear-related activities to the Agency. Agency inspectors may be given access to verify these activities. However, the Government can declare exclusions from these inspection requirements for activities or related information or locations with national security significance. If a contractor notifies a program manager that it must report an activity per the Protocol, the program manager conducts a security assessment to determine if and how access may be granted or else ask the agency treaty office to apply for exclusion of access.

Solicitation Provision and Contract Clause

DFARS 252.204-7010, Requirement for Contractor to Notify DoD if the Contractor's Activities are Subject to Reporting Under the U.S.-International Atomic Energy Agency Additional Protocol, for research and development or major defense acquisition programs involving fissionable or radiological source materials (e.g., uranium, plutonium, neptunium, thorium, americium) or technologies directly related to nuclear power production (e.g., nuclear or radiological waste materials).

Contract Clauses

FAR 52.204-2, Security Requirements, if classified work is involved. Use Alternate I for an educational institution and Alternate II for construction or architect-engineering contracts.

DFARS 252.204-7000, Disclosure of Information, if the contractor will have access to or generate sensitive unclassified information that should not be released to the public.

DFARS 252.204-7003, Control of Government Personnel Work Product.

2.12 SUPPLY CHAIN MANAGEMENT

Supply chain management is the process of furnishing products and services to customers. This approach integrates inventory, logistics, performance measurement, procurement, production, and transportation, along with forecasts of suppliers and clients. This process designs, plans and monitors the storage and transportation of raw materials and parts, converts these materials into finished goods, manages work supportability and in-process inventory, and transports finished goods to the point of consumption. Critical to the supply chain is *physical distribution*, a process which deals with packaging, shipping and warehousing.

2.12.1 Logistics

Logistics involves the flow management of goods and services (including people and data) between the points of origin and delivery to meet customer requirements. More colloquially, it means having the right item in the right quantity at the right time at the right place for the right price in the right condition to the right customer. Logistics integrates a great deal of information into the supply chain to add value, such as inventory, packaging, security, and transportation.

Logistics is closely tied with *production planning and control*, which coordinates supply and demand. The firm must tie together these functions so that finished goods are available from inventory, the production line or suppliers in time to fill orders. Whereas demand is a function largely filled by human performance (i.e., sales), the supply function lends itself to more automated means.

At the operational level, *production logistics* ensures that each machine and workstation is fed with the right product in the right quantity and quality at the right point in time. It strives to streamline and control the product flow and eliminate steps adding little or no value. Production logistics is a means to merge customer satisfaction with capital efficiency.

Even at the component level, logistics plays a key role in production planning. Each component must be compatible and interface with each other to ensure interchangeability. The firm can simplify this process by reducing the number and complexity of items in a product design, largely by eliminating unnecessary subitems or performance features. Another logistics technique is component redundancy, which utilizes multiple items or systems to overlap other parts or systems to increase *reliability* (the duration or probability of failure-free performance), though it also increases cost. Another technique is to standardize the number and size of parts and components used in production. This approach often leads to purchasing larger quantities, longer manufacturing runs and reduced setup costs. However, this approach suffers if customers do not want standard parts for their custom-made items.

Another approach is *Integrated Logistics Support*, largely used in military industries to ensure customer service at the lowest cost and maximum reliability, availability, and *maintainability* (using prescribed procedures and resources by skilled personnel to maintain and repair equipment or restore their working condition). This approach leads to systems components that function together effectively and efficiently, last longer with less support, increase customer value and contractor return on investment, and avoid proliferation of similar items. This process emphasizes off-the-shelf items produced and placed in stock by a manufacturer or distributor before receiving orders.

Needless to say, the distribution process is critical to effective logistics operations. *Physical distribution* is concerned with packaging, shipping and warehousing (both in-plant and in shipment). The basic modes of transportation are:

- commercial air transport: air freight and forwarders;
- motor freight: chartered motor carriage, contract carrier, private trucking, and small-shipment carriers;
- pipelines;
- railroads; and
- water transportation: non-contiguous operations, intercoastal service or coastal trade.

The traffic or transportation manager has four major concerns:

- *expediting*—facilitate movement of goods and trace lost shipments;
- *operations*—company-owned transportation assets, equipment scheduling, lease-or-buy analysis, and destination charges;
- *pricing*—most advantageous rate and special charges or discounts; and
- *routing*—carrier selection and mode of payment.

There are similarities between commercial and Government logistics problems. Both are concerned with efficiently acquiring material and services in the right price, quality, quantity, and time. Both want to ensure adequate training of personnel. However, the Government is also concerned with implementing socioeconomic issues, meeting more stringent requirements and properly accounting for spent public funds.

2.12.2 Supply Chain

The path by which these intermediary activities occur is the *supply chain*, since each link in the chain adds value to the process or final product. The supply chain is a bidirectional flow of products and services, funds and information among participating firms and customers. Some links represent in-house effort in different departments, but many links connect needs which are contracted to other firms. By focusing in-house effort on core competencies and outsourcing other activities to sources that can perform them more efficiently, the firm tends to increase both source and distribution channels, reduce management control of daily logistics operations, and improve trust and collaboration among partners within the chain. Again, these activities are all in an effort to ultimately create user satisfaction.

Possible scenarios that could disrupt the supply chain are created and resolved under *supply chain event management*. The increased amount of outsourcing as firms tend to specialize on core competencies will lead to more organizations involved in the supply chain, increased logistical coordination and a need to improve trust and collaboration among partners during inventory movement.

Supply chain management is clearly a complicated matter due to all its moving parts. Its challenges include:

- aligning organizational and supply strategies;
- cash-flow and payment terms among firms;
- communication of status updates and operational improvements;
- constraints imposed by customers, suppliers, manufacturers, and distribution centers;
- customer service;
- demand forecasting, including sharing the forecast with all suppliers;
- developing strategic partnerships and sourcing decisions;
- distribution plans and schedules, including location and size of inventory and distribution centers;
- globalization, which leads to issues of:
  - different tax laws,
  - different trading protocols,
  - international coordination and planning to achieve global optimums,
  - inconsistent treatment and lack of transparency of cost and profit,
  - longer lead time, and
  - multiple currencies;
- implementing best practices throughout the enterprise;
- inbound tracking and receipt from suppliers and receiving inventory;
- information technology expansion, sharing and updates;
- integrating new and current products into the supply chain and capacity management;
- long-lead procurements;
- make-or-buy and sourcing decisions;
- manufacturing flow;
- milestone payments;
- order fulfillment and shipments;
- product life cycle management to integrate supplies and services into the supply chain;[122]
- production operations and scheduling, including consumption of materials and flow of finished goods;
- returns and warranty management;
- security management system as described in ISO/IEC 28000 and ISO/IEC 28001;
- shared service centers for logistical and administrative functions;
- trade-offs to reduce total logistics cost; and
- transportation modes, routes, and frequency.

In an effort to address this myriad of challenges, several management initiatives have been developed. *Supply Chain Management 2.0 (SCM 2.0)* is a term used to describe today's world of global and specialized supply chains. SCM 2.0 emphasizes creativity and information sharing among partners in the supply chain by sharing processes, tools, and delivery options. This methodology emphasizes collaboration and feedback among all parties to improve customer service, product development and supplier relationships.

Enterprise Resource Planning is a method to manage both external and internal resources (tangible, financial and human) by improving the information flow, both inside the firm and to/from suppliers. It consolidates all related business processes into one central database, using common operating platforms throughout the enterprise. Some firms will distribute the system across the network on modular hardware and software configurations to communicate on a local area network, to minimize hardware expenses. This is an adaptation of *integrated business planning* to technologically connect all stakeholders in the firm's planning functions. This approach integrates finance, marketing, and operations to identify interdependencies among planning alternatives and make informed decisions regarding profitability and financial risk.

The most commonly-used model to depict the materiel management activities within the supply chain is the Supply-Chain Operations Reference model (SCOR) from the Supply Chain Council.[123] SCOR intends to improve and communicate management practices between all parties within the supply chain, treating them like an extended enterprise.[124] In this way, it strives to support both strategic planning and continuous improvement. SCOR focuses on relationships between physical material and service transactions processes within the supply chain and associated configuration alternatives. It emphasizes collaboration between supply chain members by highlighting a series of interactions. These include both customer interactions, from order entry through paid invoice, and market interactions, including understanding aggregate demand and fulfilling each order.

SCOR contains four basic pillars: process modeling, performance measurements, best practices, and people skills. The Process Modeling Pillar uses building blocks to model supply chains in a common set of definitions to describe its depth and breadth. This pillar is based on six distinct management processes:

- *Plan*—balance aggregate demand and supply to optimally meet sourcing, production and delivery requirements;
- *Source*—procure goods and services;
- *Make*—transform product to a finished state;
- *Deliver*—provide finished goods and services by managing transportation and distribution;

- *Return*—receiving returned products; and
- *Enable*—manage business rules, contracts, data, facilities, performance, regulatory compliance, resources, risk, and supply chain network management.

This pillar provides levels of detail to define scope, supply chain configuration, and process performance attributes. The firm defines its practices at this level to maximize its competitive advantage while adapting to changing business conditions.

The Performance Measurements Pillar reflects over 250 indicators of operations performance in conjunction with performance attributes that characterize a supply chain operation. This allows for evaluation with other supply chains to measure success within the marketplace against competitors. These indicators focus on agility, asset management, cost, reliability, and responsiveness.

The *Best Practices Pillar* contains over 430 executable methods that are current, structured with clear goal, scope and procedure or process, proven in a working environment, and repeatable in different environments. These practices show either a gain in a positive metric or reduction in an unfavorable metric.

The *Skills* pillar is concerned with managing talent by describing the expertise necessary to perform tasks and manage processes. Each individual skill is couched in terms of delivering predetermined results using standards of aptitudes, experience, and training, with minimized time and effort. The intent is to align people and their skills to individual processes.

SCOR modeling requires that a unit of supply engenders a unit of delivery, and vice versa. The model can be depicted in a labeled picture for a given supply chain operation.

Critical to success of supply chain management is the use of *strategic sourcing*. Instead of buying tactically to meet a specific need, this approach encourages planning collaborative acquisitions based on the other firm's spending trends and future requirements. This methodology conducts a total cost analysis of producing the required supplies and services. First, all requirements are collected and standardized. The firm must then identify suitable suppliers to develop a sourcing strategy. A level of competition must be defined, and perhaps a concept of operations should be established. After negotiating with the chosen suppliers, a supply structure is implemented and monitored. The firm may create permanent partnerships, and even centers of excellence based on core competencies or local practice. This approach should minimize dollar expenditure while maximizing use of resources and provision of support. The Federal Government is using this approach more often to increase enterprise transparency and enhance inter-agency collaboration.

A firm practicing supply chain management concentrates on those activities where it has knowledge and a distinctive advantage and outsources everything else. The manufacturer provides products to distribution channels based on past forecasts. Orders are filled just-in-time in minimum lot sizes, which leads to shorter cycle times and improved responsiveness to customer demand.

Another component of supply chain management addresses the customer. *Customer service* is designed to attain operational objectives or perform an activity of value to the customer. Customer service can be provided in both wholesale logistics (e.g., weapon systems) or retail logistics (e.g., base services). Typically, customer orientation and warranties are hallmarks of customer service. Properly managed customer service should ultimately increase revenue and enhance profitability.

After negotiating with the chosen supplier(s), a supply structure is implemented and monitored. The firm may create permanent partnerships, and even centers of excellence based on core competencies or local practice. This approach should minimize dollar expenditure while maximizing use of resources and support. The Federal Government uses this approach sometimes to enhance inter-agency collaboration.

2.12.3 Inventory

The *inventory* function is concerned with maintaining a proper level of hardware while minimizing costs. This function includes many aspects:

- available physical space;
- cost control (start-up, facilities, tools, labor, training, transportation, and location);
- defective goods or spoilage;
- demand forecasting;
- design of storage areas;
- disposal of excess items;
- materials requirements identification;
- ordering;
- packaging, storage, and delivery;
- planning production and sourcing;
- price forecasting;
- quality management;
- receiving and inspection;
- replenishment lead time; and
- visibility.

Products which need inventory management include the following:

- *raw materials*—substances and components scheduled for processing and consumption in the production process;
- *purchased parts*—components made by other firms to their own specifications;
- *subcontracted items*—components made by other firms to the customer's specifications;
- *work in process*—materials and components that are partially completed when transformed into finished goods. It allows production scheduling flexibility and provides a buffer against raw materials lead time and variation in demand;
- *safety stock*—a minimal amount of spare parts to cushion against stockout; used only if the cost of stockout exceeds carrying cost of the safety stock;
- *finished goods*—ready for sale to customers; and
- returned goods for resale.

Major materials functions are often assigned to a single materials management department. This unit manages cost control, production flow and control, use of capital resources, and interaction with vendors and suppliers. Many firms use a *material management and accounting system* to plan and control material acquisition, use and disposal. The system could be standalone, but often ties into other systems (e.g., accounting, engineering, estimating, planning, and purchasing). The materials system may be automated or manual.

A firm can use *materials requirements planning* to determine when and how much material to order based on customer demand. This methodology requires assessing delivery schedules, production activities and purchasing deadlines to ensure that materials are on hand when needed, though at minimal stocking levels. A computer program can use the master production schedule for a given item to estimate specific component or part requirements for the time period. Today's planning systems also consider capacities of labor, machine and suppliers. Of course, the firm must ensure that the inventory is available to the facility, rather than sitting in a warehouse across the country (if so, shipping cost and time must be included in the calculations).

The program office develops a *bill of material* to list all raw material, parts and assemblies needed to fabricate the product. The list can be developed as requirements are designed, fabricated, maintained, or ordered. The list is often hierarchical in nature, with each assembly broken down into subassemblies and parts. This list is then used by the procurement department to purchase supplies for inventory.

Models are used in *operations research*, which applies mathematics to decision making. Operations research is used to develop a minimum or maximum value for such issues as profit, performance, yield, loss, risk, or cost. It can also develop an economic order quantity, balance holding costs against replenishing inventory, or yield an optimal quantity to minimize cost. The material system then develops an *economic order quantity (EOQ)*, the number of units to be ordered that would minimize both ordering costs and carrying costs. The *ordering cost* covers procurement expenses, while the *carrying costs* include inventory storage costs (which are often expressed as a percentage of the value of the material costs).

Some people make the mistake of trying to equate these two values. That is not the goal of this ordering process; rather, the objective is to minimize *both* inventory carrying and ordering costs. EOQ is used to determine incremental impacts for both types of costs. This process assumes constant ordering cost and rate of demand, fixed lead time, instantaneous replenishment and delivery, and unit prices not wildly fluctuating.

This discussion means that the Total Cost of a given purchase is the sum of three cost components:

- *purchase price*: the product of unit price and demand quantity, or P × D;
- *ordering cost*: a fixed cost O for placing one order times the number of orders in a given time period (usually a year). This second number is derived by dividing the total annual demand quantity D by the order time frequency F. Hence, ordering cost = O × D / F;
- *holding cost*: carrying cost C times the average quantity in stock, which is midway between full and empty stock shelves, or C × D / 2.

Hence, TC = PD + (OD / F) + CD / 2.

As a result of mathematical manipulations beyond the scope of this book (by using basic calculus), EOQ = the square root of 2DO / C.

Maintaining an inventory costs money, but lack of an item can stop a production line. Hence, production forecasts should include EOQs and order points. There are several formulas that tie into this approach:

- Maximum inventory = quantity at delivery + units on hand;
- Average inventory = ½ × (beginning inventory + ending inventory);
- Reorder point = lead time × average usage in the same period of time (e.g., months or weeks).

The *reorder point* is the level of inventory at which a new order must be placed to procure enough material to return to the EOQ. Ordering at this point in time ensures that inventory is never totally depleted (stockout), which runs the risk of customer dissatisfaction and lost sales. Since the procurement office must have sufficient lead time to place an order, the firm can identify the normal consumption during this lead time and add it to the safety stock level to obtain a realistic reorder level.

Safety stock quantities escalate throughout the supply chain because each vendor adds its own buffer stock to inventory. Common causes of safety stock are:

- anticipated shortages;
- consolidated demands and quantity discounts from vendors;
- forecasting errors (e.g., replenishment lead time);
- lost synchronization between lot sizes and ordering;
- misperceptions of the production process;
- panic ordering after unmet demand; and
- revised inventory projections.

These conditions can lead to more than just excessive or insufficient inventory. It can also cause inefficient production, inferior customer service, and poor utilization of the distribution channel. They can also cause a *bullwhip effect*, where an action downstream causes a response throughout the upstream supply chain, where each entity up the chain wishes to carry its own safety stock. The effect grows with each link of the supply chain, leading to unnecessary inventory on hand throughout the distribution system.

The length of the manufacturing cycle also affects materials accounts. The acquisition lead time begins with identifying a materials requirement and continues until award is made. At that point, production lead time commences until the day of delivery. Therefore, the concept of *lead time risk* is a factor in program impact due to failure of material to arrive on time, regardless of whether the delay is due to the acquisition process or vendor performance. This item may need to be included in the risk assessment for program management consideration.

Advance buys of long-lead items can protect production schedule by avoiding lengthy delays awaiting components. Some major programs with known or predictable future needs will execute an *advance acquisition contract* solely to obtain long-lead items as well as production planning and engineering effort. These contracts cover items that are either needed upfront or take a long time to fabricate or locate and then deliver. The end-items will be fully funded in a future fiscal year; however long-lead funding is available in the current year. These long-lead contracts may then be converted into the final production contracts as funds become available and final end-item prices are definitized.

A controversial alternative is to order all raw material upfront, known as *forward buying*. Ordering upfront and receiving material only as needed will free up cash flow and minimize storage capacity used. However, this approach can lead to complex inventory management and higher storage costs, so it is usually practiced only in stable markets or when prices are rising.

The length of manufacturing time can also be a factor in deciding for forward buying. A long manufacturing cycle requires more complex management with a higher probability of schedule impacts. A short manufacturing cycle requires less complex management but does not afford as much time for rework. Even for finished goods inventory, the length of manufacturing cycle would impact the amount of inventory to satisfy demand. A long cycle would require more material and goods, while a short cycle would need less finished goods inventory.

Some entities may use a *systems contract* that authorizes designated employees (often from the user department) to place orders with the supplier for specific items at a specific time in a predetermined release system. Sometimes known as *stockless purchasing*, this approach reduces inventory to a minimal level while assuring continuity of supply.

As complicated as this process is, it is essential to expose customer demand back up the channel.[125] This requires investment in information technology and the embracement of flexibility and customer demand. It also requires all supply chain firms to share information with each other. Other explicit methods to address customer demand include:

- discourage low-price promotions;
- limit customer returns and cancellations;
- prioritize orders based on past sales data;
- provide more frequent replenishments;
- reduce batch sizes; and
- spread out vendor deliveries.

Upon receipt, each item is bar-coded with an identification number (known as a *store keeping unit* identifier, or *SKU*) to track its presence in storage. These are the same bar codes read by the cash register at your favorite retail store. Nontangible items such as warranties or delivery fees also bear SKUs on their written terms of service. SKUs are entered into a database for an information system to track physical features (e.g., size and color), as well as destination of a particular unit and stock on hand.

Inventory systems use barcodes and Radio Frequency Identification (RFID) tags to automate identification of inventory items (e.g., capital equipment, fixed assets, goods for sale, material, tools, etc.). A barcode scanner or RFID reader identifies the unit to collect information for display on terminals or mobile computers. This automates the process of filling sales orders. The system can also be programmed to alert managers when products reach a predetermined low level in order to prompt reordering.

Per DFARS 211.275, RFID is required for cases and palletized unit loads packaging levels and any additional consolidation level(s) deemed necessary by the requiring activity for shipments of items that will be shipped to one of the locations listed at http://www.acq.osd.mil/log/sci/RFID_ship-to-locations.html or a location outside the contiguous United States when the shipment has been assigned Transportation Priority 1, or contain items in any of the following classes of supply:[126]

- Subclass of Class I—Packaged operational rations;
- Class II—Clothing, individual equipment, tentage, organizational tool kits, hand tools, and administrative and housekeeping supplies and equipment;
- Class IIIP—Packaged petroleum, lubricants, oils, preservatives, chemicals, and additives;
- Class IV—Construction and barrier materials;
- Class VI—Personal demand items (non-military sales items);
- Subclass of Class VIII—Medical materials (excluding pharmaceuticals, biologicals, and reagents—suppliers should limit the mixing of excluded and non-excluded materials); or
- Class IX—Repair parts and components including kits, assemblies and subassemblies, reparable and consumable items required for maintenance support of all equipment, excluding medical-peculiar repair parts.

This requirement does not apply to shipments of bulk commodities or to locations other than Defense Distribution Depots when the contract includes FAR 52.213-1, Fast Payment Procedures. Nor does it apply for humanitarian or peacekeeping missions.

Two major models to track inventory are *fixed-order quantity* to initiate an order at a specified reorder level, and *fixed-order period* (also known as *periodic, or interval system*) to order at a predetermined point in time. Both inventory models strive to minimize costs by either *deterministic* (where demand is certain) or *probabilistic* methods (where demand varies daily and requires either setting safety stock to meet customer desire, or else minimizing carrying cost of additional inventory). Input necessary to manipulate these models includes:

- frequency of review;
- order placement cost;
- order size;
- production setup cost;
- reorder point;
- shipping costs;
- storage cost; and
- vendor identity, lead time and pricing.

Firms will record inventory using either a periodic or perpetual system. A *perpetual* system tracks inventory items on hand daily, updated whenever a unit is added or subtracted. By contrast, a *periodic inventory method* will physically count at discrete times the units in raw material, work-in-process, and finished goods states, then records inventory at the end of the year to derive cost of goods sold.

Other management methods can be used to track inventory. *Price-break models* measure quantity changes when unit price changes with order size, while *single-period models* (or *static models*) present a cost tradeoff for every order and stocking action.

Another option involves *ABC classification*, an implementation of the Pareto Rule (20 percent of the quantity provides 80 percent of the benefit) by stratifying inventory items. This approach is intended to set priorities among a number of issues, then focus priorities and resources on the most important ones. The technique lists the items into several categories, say A, B and C. We can see the Pareto principle reflected in this scheme: Category A reflects the largest 80 percent of cost, B represents the next 15 percent or so, and C includes the rest of the items. We can see the Pareto principle reflected in this scheme: 80 percent of the cost applies to a few items (category A), so they are the cost drivers and require more attention. Category B items require less attention and will undoubtedly be more numerous in number. Depending on the level of confidence in the firm's inventory management process, Category C items may be accepted without further review, or at most a sanity check. This process can also be used for customer prioritization, since for many firms, roughly 20 percent of the customers provide about 80 percent of the revenue.

After deriving the ABC data, a *Pareto diagram* can be prepared to graphically depict the results from this stratification. A bar chart can be developed to display a value for each object (e.g., number of times a problem occurs, sales per customer, or usage of an inventory item) in descending order to identify the most important problems. Then a line chart can display all bars to visually reflect the sum results of the data collection.

Commonality is another method to make inventory as efficient as possible. When separate materials or systems have similar and interchangeable characteristics, they may be charged out of stock for use on the other system. However, personnel who are trained to use one system may not work equally well with the other, so cross-training may be necessary.

Inventory costs include a variety of components:

- breakage and spoilage;
- depreciation;
- insurance;
- line cost for each item;
- obsolescence;
- *opportunity cost of capital*;[127]
- ordering cost;
- production setup;
- stockout;
- storage space; and
- taxes.

An obvious method to minimize inventory is to promote productivity. *Cost of Goods Sold* (CoGS) is a prime measure of a factory's productivity. It is calculated by deriving the cost of goods produced:

Cost of Beginning Inventory + Inventory Purchases + Production Cost
= Cost of Goods Produced

This number absorbs production overhead and raw material costs into an inventory value. Then,

Cost of Goods Produced – Cost of Ending Inventory
= Cost of Goods Sold

CoGS can then be subtracted from sales price to determine a sales margin figure.

Manufacturing management also uses formulas to measure inventory levels. One approach can derive a value for *inventory turnover*; that is, the number of times inventory is sold and replaced over a given time period:

Inventory turnover ratio =
Cost of Goods Sold / Average Inventory

where Average Inventory is the average of Beginning Inventory and Ending Inventory levels. This number tells us how much cash or goods are tied up waiting for the process and is a critical measure of process effectiveness and reliability. The timeframe for turnover can be defined as follows:

Average Days to Sell Inventory =
Number of Days in a Year / Inventory Turnover Ratio

When an item is issued from inventory, the value of the inventory account is reduced by CoGS.

Common methods to adjust inventory value are:

- *First in—first out* (FIFO) matches the price of the first unit that arrived in inventory to the cost of the first unit sold. Many stock units actually do operate this way to avoid spoilage. Under this method, older costs are assigned to CoGS and newer costs are assigned to Inventory. Since costs generally rise over time, FIFO tends to increase the value of inventory and reduce CoGS.
- *Last in—first out* (LIFO) matches the last arriving unit with the first one sold. As the mirror image of FIFO, LIFO tends to reduce the value of inventory and increase CoGS. Because material prices tend to rise over time, LIFO accounting often leads to lower *net income* (also called *net profit* or, more colloquially, *the bottom line*), the sum of total revenue and gains, minus expenses and losses for the accounting period. It is often paid out as dividends or else classified as retained earnings. LIFO also tends to result in lower *book value* (cost less depreciation, which is the asset value carried in the accounting books) because of inflation, and hence lower taxes.
- *Average Cost* of a unit in beginning inventory plus purchases made during the period helps to derive both the cost of sales and the ending inventory value.
- *Weighted Average Method* derives a unit average cost as follows:

$$\frac{\text{Cost of purchases + Cost of beginning inventory}}{\text{\# Units bought year-to-date + Beginning \# units}}$$

- Then,

Unit cost × Number of units in ending inventory = Inventory cost

Just-in-time inventory management was developed in Japan to ensure that inventory materials arrive at the plant only when needed for use on the production line. Parts and materials are bought in an exact quantity just as needed. It has changed the procurement function through:

- contingent liabilities if production is cancelled;
- frequent specification changes;
- increased transportation costs due to frequent delivery cycles;
- less inventory in the plant;
- multiyear relationships with fewer suppliers to promote their timely delivery; and
- price escalation protection.

Manufacturing firms are impacted by shortages of critical materials. They reconsider their inventory decision models and the significance of *make-or-buy* decisions (deciding whether to perform or make in-house or subcontract the effort to another firm). They strive to improve cooperation between purchasing and production departments, develop alternate sources of supply, consider backward and forward integration, and increase efficiencies.

There are several methods which a firm can employ to improve the inventory system. It can use agreements for recurring purchases or accept partial deliveries on EOQs. A firm can also select local suppliers or negotiate shorter lead times. Some firms can also set aside stocks at supplier facilities to reduce costs and leverage off suppler advantages.

Quality assurance is another method to improve inventory management. It includes testing parts and material, both before ordering and during use. All parts and materials must be tested to ensure that a specific level of quality is met. This is typically completed before a purchase order is issued to a supplier, to ensure that the supplier has met the requirements.

Material attrition is a net loss to the firm and can manifest itself in several ways. *Shrinkage* is the loss of materials once they have reached the firm due to loss or damage. To reduce this risk, firms take loss prevention measures (e.g., bar coding, itemized product inventory, and security cameras). Other causes of material attrition include obsolescence and spoilage. *Loss through misplacement* is common in large organizations or warehouses where material is received at the entry point and then moved to an incorrect location by the distribution staff (or worse, stolen). This condition can be reduced through bar code scanning and a tracking system which records when and where items are stored.

Inventory that is not included in deliverable items is known by several names. *Rejects* are products or raw material that did not meet production standards. *Scrap* is material left over or discarded, but can be reprocessed, whereas *waste* is useless material created as a byproduct and must be disposed. *Surplus material* is inventory remaining after contract completion. Surplus material can be disposed by return to the supplier or use within the firm. If these are not possible, it can donate to an educational or nonprofit institution or sell the material to employees or another firm.

Inventory management also addresses:

- available physical space;
- cost control (start-up, facilities, tools, labor, training, transportation, and location);
- defective goods;
- demand forecasting;
- price forecasting;
- quality management;
- replenishment lead time; and
- visibility.

Methods to improve the inventory system include:

- accept partial deliveries on EOQs;
- negotiate shorter lead times;
- select local suppliers;
- set aside stocks at supplier facilities; and
- use formal agreements for recurring purchases.

DFARs 242.7203

DoD reviews a contractor's material management and accounting system if the firm has contracts exceeding the simplified acquisition threshold that are for non-commercial items and are either cost-reimbursement or fixed-price contracts with progress payments based on costs incurred by the contractor as work progresses. The review does not apply to small businesses, educational institutions or nonprofit organizations.

The system should reasonably forecast material requirements, ensure the costs of purchased and fabricated material charged or allocated to a contract are based on valid time-phased requirements, and logically track costing of material transactions. The cognizant contracting officer, in consultation with the auditor and functional specialist, shall determine the acceptability of the contractor's system and approve or disapprove the system and pursue correction of any deficiencies.

A system review is conducted when a contractor has $40 million of qualifying sales to the Government during the contractor's preceding fiscal year and the ACO, with advice from the auditor, determines a system review is needed based on a risk assessment of the contractor's past experience and current vulnerability. Qualifying sales require certified cost or pricing data or are priced on other than a firm-fixed-price or fixed-price with economic price adjustment basis.

The auditor or functional specialist documents findings and recommendations in a report to the contracting officer. Any significant deficiencies are described in sufficient detail to allow the contracting officer to understand the deficiencies. The contracting officer in turn describes to the contractor in writing each significant deficiency in sufficient detail, requests a written response within 30 days, and evaluates the response in consultation with the auditor or functional specialist. (S)he makes a final determination that either the material system is acceptable and approved and no deficiencies remain, or else identifies any remaining significant deficiencies, and indicate the adequacy of any proposed or completed corrective action. The contracting officer shall request that the contractor, within 45 days of receipt of the final determination, either correct the deficiencies or submit an acceptable corrective action plan showing milestones and actions to eliminate the deficiencies. However, the contracting officer may instead elect to disapprove the system or withhold payments.

Solicitation Provisions and Contract Clauses

DFARS 252.211-7003, Item Unique Identification and Valuation, for supplies, and for services involving the furnishing of supplies, when item unique identification is required. Identify in paragraph (c)(1)(ii) of the clause the contract (sub)line or exhibit line item number and description of any covered item(s) below $5,000 in unit acquisition cost. Identify in paragraph (c)(1)(iii) of the clause the applicable attachment number, when DoD item unique identification or a DoD recognized unique identification equivalent is required.

DFARS 252.211-7007, Reporting of Government-Furnished Property, when including FAR 52.245-1, Government Property.

DFARS 252.211-7008, Use of Government-Assigned Serial Numbers, when using DFARS 252.211-7003, Item Unique Identification and Valuation, and require the contractor to mark major end items.

DFARS 252.242-7004, Material Management and Accounting System, when exceeding the simplified acquisition threshold, but not for the acquisition of commercial items.

2.13 INTERNATIONAL CONTRACTING

2.13.1 Agreements and Restrictions

FAR 25

The *Buy American Act* advocates the purchase of *domestic end products*, as defined below.[128] The Act restricts the purchase of non-domestic end products for use within the United States, unless the contracting officer determines that the price of the lowest domestic offer is unreasonable or if another exception applies. The Buy American Act uses a two-part test to define a domestic end product: it must be manufactured in the United States, and the cost of domestic content must exceed 55 percent of the cost of all the components.[129] This second test is waived to acquire COTS items. Within DoD, at least 95 percent of the cost of iron and steel must be domestic (excluding refining steel additives).[130]

There are three key exceptions to the Buy American Act for supplies. The head of the agency may determine that domestic preference would be inconsistent with the public interest, such as an agreement with a foreign government that provides a blanket exception to the Buy American Act. Second, the Act does not apply to end items or components that are not mined or produced in the United States in sufficient commercial quantities and quality. Also, the Act does not apply to micro-purchases.

A nonavailability determination has been made for a variety of items listed in FAR 25.104, meaning that domestic sources can only meet half or less of total domestic demand. However, before acquiring an article on the list as either an end product or a component comprising over half the value of all components within an end product, the procuring agency must first conduct market research to seek domestic sources.

When the lowest offer in a competition is not a domestic item, the contracting officer must determine cost reasonableness by adding to its price any duty, plus a premium differential. The duty must be identified in the offer. The socioeconomic status of the respective offerors is not relevant in this situation. Even if the acquisition is conducted under a small business set-aside, and even if the low offer is from a small business concern offering a non-domestic end product from another small business concern, a premium must be applied to the price. If the domestic offer does not exceed this adjusted price, it is deemed reasonable (a tie is decided in favor of the domestic product). The evaluation factor does not provide a preference for one foreign offer over another.

Prohibitions against certain countries often exist in Federal contracting. At the time of this book, no firm conducting business operations in Sudan may obtain a Federal contract. Nor can it export sensitive technology to Iran or participate in its petroleum or weapons programs.

DFARS 225.1

For DoD, any manufactured end product is a domestic end product if manufactured in the United States and the cost of its U.S. and qualifying country components exceeds 50 percent of the cost of all its components. This threshold is lower for items which are deemed critical or contain critical components: 20 percent if the low offeror is a large business or 30 percent if a small business. Additionally, exceptions are made in the public interest for certain countries listed in DFARS 225.872-1, for procurements covered by the World Trade Organization Government Procurement Agreement, and when USD(AT&L) determines that it is inconsistent with the public interest to apply the Buy American statute to end products that are substantially transformed in the United States. Examples of a public interest exception are to:

- accept the low domestic offer will involve substantial foreign expenditures, or accept the low foreign offer will involve substantial domestic expenditures;
- ensure access to advanced state-of-the-art commercial technology; or
- maintain the same source of supply for spare and replacement parts for a domestic end product or to avoid impairing integration of the military and commercial industrial base.

A determination for a public interest exception must be approved:

- at a level above the contracting officer for acquisitions valued at or below the simplified acquisition threshold;
- by the head of the contracting activity for acquisitions with a value greater than the simplified acquisition threshold but less than $1.5 million; or
- by the agency head for acquisitions valued at $1.5 million or more.

A determination bearing the same dollar thresholds can be made that a material or supply is not reasonably available when domestic offers are insufficient to meet the requirement and award is to be made on other than a qualifying country or eligible end product. However, this second instance can be signed by the chief of the contracting office and the third instance by the head of the contracting activity or immediate deputy for acquisitions.

DoD has already determined that spare or replacement parts that must be acquired from the original foreign manufacturer or supplier are not reasonably available from domestic sources. The same permission is granted for certain specific foreign drugs.

DFARS 225.871 through .873

Departments and agencies (that have authority to do so) may enter into cooperative project agreements with NATO or with one or more member countries of NATO under DoDD 5530.3, International Agreements. These agreements are undertaken to further the objectives of standardization, rationalization, and interoperability of the armed forces of NATO member countries. One or more of the other participants may share with the United States the cost of research and development, testing, evaluation, or joint production (including follow-on support) of certain defense articles. Departments and agencies may enter into contracts, or incur other obligations, on behalf of other participants without charge to any appropriation or contract authorization. A waiver of certain laws and regulations may be obtained if required by the terms of a written cooperative project agreement, will significantly further NATO interoperability, rationalization, and standardization, and approved by the appropriate DoD official.

For (sub)contracts placed outside the United States, the Deputy Secretary of Defense may waive any provision of law that specifically prescribes:

- procedures for the formation of contracts;
- requirements or preferences for goods grown or manufactured in the United States or in U.S. Government-owned facilities, or services to be performed in the United States;
- requirements regulating the performance of contracts; or
- terms and conditions for inclusion in contracts.

There is no authority for waiver of any provision of:

- Arms Export Control Act (22 U.S.C. 2751);
- 10 U.S.C. 2304;
- cargo preference laws of the United States, including the Military Cargo Preference Act of 1904 and the Cargo Preference Act of 1954;[131] or
- financial management responsibilities administered by the Secretary of the Treasury.

The Director of DPAP may authorize the direct placement of subcontracts with specific firms. Directed subcontracting is not authorized unless specifically addressed in the cooperative project agreement. If this is not feasible, the agreement must state the general provisions for work sharing at the prime and subcontract level.

Congressional notification is required when DoD makes a determination to award a contract or subcontract to a particular entity before the time of contract award. The proposed notice shall include the reason it is necessary to use the authority to designate a particular (sub)contractor.

DoD has determined it is inconsistent with the public interest to apply restrictions of the Buy American statute or the Balance of Payments Program to the acquisition of qualifying country end products from the countries (currently 26) listed at DFARS 225.872-1. Procurements excepted from this requirement are those subject to the National Disclosure Policy implemented by DoDD 5230.11 (Disclosure of Classified Military Information to Foreign Governments and International Organizations), non-Canadian defense mobilization base requirements, other U.S. laws or regulations, national security requirements, and construction contracts.

In reviewing contractor subcontracting procedures, the contracting officer ensures that the contract does not preclude qualifying country sources from competing for subcontracts, except when restricted by national security interest reasons, mobilization base considerations, or applicable U.S. laws or regulations.

DoD and the Government of the United Kingdom (U.K.) have agreed to waive U.K. commercial exploitation levies and U.S. nonrecurring cost recoupment charges on a reciprocal basis. For U.K. levies to be waived, the offeror or contractor must identify the levies and the contracting officer requests a waiver before award of the contract or subcontract under which the levies are charged.

Solicitation Provision

FAR 52.225-18, Place of Manufacture, for manufactured end products whose estimated value exceeds that of other items to be acquired as a result of the solicitation.

FAR 52.225-20, Prohibition on Conducting Restricted Business Operations in Sudan—Certification, except for commercial items.

FAR 52.225-25, Prohibition on Contracting with Entities Engaging in Certain Activities or Transactions Relating to Iran-Representation and Certifications.

DFARS 252.206-7000, Domestic Source Restriction, when foreign sources are restricted.

Solicitation Provisions and Contract Clauses

FAR 52.215-2, Audit and Records—Negotiation, and paragraph (d) of the clause at 52.212-5, Contract Terms and Conditions Required to Implement Statutes or Executive Orders—Commercial Items, with foreign contractors to authorize examination of records by the Comptroller General. If they object, the contracting officer may use 52.215-2 with its Alternate III or 52.212-5 with its Alternate I after negotiations fail, no other sources of supply can be found in a reasonable time at reasonable cost, and the head of the agency has executed a D&F with the concurrence of the Comptroller General. Such concurrence is not required if the contractor is a foreign government or agency or prevented by native law from providing records for examination.

FAR 52.225-1, Buy American Act—Supplies and 52.225-2, Buy American Act Certificate, when greater than $25,000 and no alternative clauses apply. The clauses are not used if restricted to domestic end products, for supplies for use outside the United States, or for supplies to be used within the United States and an exception to the Buy American Act applies (e.g., nonavailability, public interest, or information technology that is a commercial item).

FAR 52.225-7, Waiver of Buy American Act for Civil Aircraft and Related Articles, for civil aircraft and related articles, if the acquisition value is less than $191,000.

FAR 52.225-14, Inconsistency Between English Version and Translation of Contract, if anticipating translation into another language.

2.13.2 Buy American Act—Construction Materials

FAR 25

The Act also generally requires the use of domestic construction materials in contracts for construction within the United States. *Construction material* is an article or supply brought to the construction site by a (sub)contractor to be incorporated into the building or work. It could be either preassembled or incorporated on the site. However, there are special exceptions for safety systems:

- impracticability or inconsistency with the public interest, such as an agreement with a foreign government that bears a blanket exception to the Buy American Act;
- information technology that is a commercial item;
- materials bought directly by the Government, since they are considered supplies rather than construction material;
- nonavailability within the United States (the same exception as for supply contracts);

- safety systems: audio evacuation, emergency lighting and fire alarm systems (all evaluated as a single construction material regardless of when or how the individual parts or components are delivered to the site); or
- unreasonable cost.

A D&F is necessary to invoke any of these exceptions.

The contracting officer reviews any allegations of Buy American Act violations. If a positive finding results, the contracting officer notifies the contractor of the apparent unauthorized use of foreign construction material and requests a reply, to include a proposed corrective action (unless fraud is suspected, in which case the contracting officer must follow agency procedures). The contracting officer may:

- direct replacement of the foreign material without causing delay;
- determine not to remove the material but not waive the Act, thereby preserving the right to further punitive action;
- reduce the contract price;
- suspend or debar the (sub)contractor; or
- terminate for default.

Certain trade agreements waive the Act below a specified dollar value. In these cases, end products and construction materials from specified countries receive nondiscriminatory evaluation.

Solicitation Provision

FAR 52.225-10, Notice of Buy American Act Requirement—Construction Materials, if including the clause at 52.225-9. Use the provision with Alternate I if insufficient time is available before receipt of offers to process a determination of inapplicability of the Buy American Act.

FAR 52.225-12, Notice of Buy American Act Requirement—Construction Materials under Trade Agreements, if containing the clause at 52.225-11. Use the provision with its Alternate I if insufficient time to process a Buy American Act determination. Use the provision with its Alternate II for acquisitions between $7,358,000 and $10,079,365.

Solicitation Provisions and Contract Clauses

FAR 52.225-9, Buy American Act—Construction Materials, for construction that is performed in the United States valued at less than $7,358,000.

FAR 52.225-11, Buy American Act—Construction Materials under Trade Agreements, for construction that is performed in the United States and valued at $7,358,000 or more. Use the clause with Alternate I if the acquisition value is between $7,358,000 and $10,079,365. When using funds appropriated under the Recovery Act for construction, use the following (with appropriate Alternates) in lieu of the provisions and clauses 52.225-9, 52.225-10, 52.225-11, or 52.225-12, respectively:

- FAR 52.225-21, Required Use of American Iron, Steel, and Manufactured Goods—Buy American Statute—Construction Materials.
- FAR 52.225-22, Notice of Required Use of American Iron, Steel, and Manufactured Goods—Buy American Statute—Construction Materials.
- FAR 52.225-23, Required Use of American Iron, Steel, and Manufactured Goods—Buy American Statute—Construction Materials Under Trade Agreements. List all foreign construction materials excepted from the Buy American Act or Section 1605 of the Recovery Act.
- FAR 52.225-24 Notice of Required Use of American Iron, Steel, and Manufactured Goods—Buy American Statute—Construction Materials Under Trade Agreements.

2.13.3 Performance Outside the United States

FAR 25.3

Contractors usually provide their own logistic and security support. The Government can do so if it has available resources to ensure continuation of contract performance and the contractor cannot obtain them at a reasonable cost. This would occur most often in contingency, housekeeping or peacekeeping missions. The contracting officer must specify in the solicitation what support it will provide and whether the contractor shall reimburse the Government.

The contract may require contractor personnel to perform in a designated operational area during contingency operations (including humanitarian, peacekeeping, or military operations), or when supporting a diplomatic or consular mission designated by the Department of State as a danger pay post. If so, the contracting officer will inform the contractor that the Synchronized Predeployment and Operational Tracker is the appropriate automated system to use for the list of contractor personnel.

Contractors providing security services overseas have the additional responsibility of informing their employees about compliance with relevant directives, instructions, and orders, including those of the theater military commander. These directives cover such topics as accounting for weapons, keeping appropriate personnel records, registering, and identifying military vehicles (e.g., armored trucks and helicopters), and reporting accidents and other incidents.

There is normally a 2 percent tax of the amount of a specified Federal procurement payment on any foreign person receiving such payment, although the IRS will permit certain exemptions. An IRS Form W-14, Certificate of Foreign Contracting Party Receiving Federal Procurement Payments, must be included with the invoice. Currently, this exemption also applies to any citizen or resident of Afghanistan.

Failure to comply with the above could lead to a negative report in the past performance database and reduced award fee. If the failure is long-term, suspension or debarment may be called for.

DFARS 225.371

Contracts to support U.S. Armed Forces deployed outside the United States in contingency, humanitarian, or peacekeeping operations, or when designated by the combatant commander, may be necessary to maintain a safe and secure environment. They are also used to provide emergency infrastructure reconstruction, humanitarian relief, or essential governmental services until feasible to transition to local government. The agency may provide logistical or security support only when the appropriate agency official determines in coordination with the combatant commander that such Government support is available and necessary to ensure continuation of essential contractor services and cannot be obtained from other sources at a reasonable cost. The contracting officer must specify in the solicitation and contract valid terms that specify the responsible party to provide protection to the contractor personnel performing in the designated operational area, any other Government support to be provided, and whether this support will be provided on a reimbursable basis (with the authority for the reimbursement). The contracting officer must also sign a Synchronized Predeployment and Operational Tracker–generated letter of authorization to process through a deployment center or to travel to, from or within the designated operational area.

Basic war training at a military or alternative training facility may be required for private security contractor personnel, security guards in or near areas of military operations, or persons who will come into contact with enemy prisoners of war. The solicitation and contract must specify the types of personnel subject to advanced law of war training requirements and whether the training will be provided by the Government or the contractor. If the Government provides the training, its source must be provided to the contractor. If a contractor provides the training, the content must be coordinated with the servicing DoD legal advisor to ensure that it is commensurate with the duties and responsibilities of the personnel to be trained.

PGI 225.370 through .371

A contracting officer's representative may approve a letter of authorization. Contractor travel orders will be prepared by the supporting installation. The letter will state the intended length of assignment in the theater of operations and will identify planned use of Government facilities and privileges in the theater of operations, as authorized by the contract. Authorizations may include such privileges as access to the exchange facilities and the commissary and use of Government messing and billeting. The letter must include the name of the approving Government official.

The geographic combatant commander or subordinate is authorized to control the assignment of contract administration during contingency operations, for contracts requiring delivery of items or performance within the area of operations.[132] These operations must be consistent with the combat support agency's established core competencies, mission functions and responsibilities. This responsibility may establish such things as a contracting command and control structure, head of contracting activity responsibilities, local clauses and policies, and roles and responsibilities of DoD components and supporting agencies in contract formation and execution. These procedures and requirements often cover contract clearance and administration requiring delivery of items and performance within the area of operations.

If the acquisition requires the performance of services or delivery of supplies in an area outside the United States, the contracting officer must ensure that the solicitation and contract include any applicable host country and designated operational area performance considerations. This precaution permits the contractor to fulfill the contract terms and conditions, avoid undue support burdens being placed on the Government in a theater of operations, and preclude contractor personnel from conflicting with theater operations or a theater commander's directives or host country laws. The contractor must also comply with any theater business clearance and contract administration delegation requirements set forth in memorandum with the Joint Contingency Contracting System Platform and established by the geographic combatant commander. This business clearance ensures that contracted effort is visible to the combatant commander and consistent with his/her in-country plans, properly overseen in designated area(s) of operation, and addresses in the contract any Government-furnished support requirements associated with contractor personnel.[133] The contracting officer uses a checklist at PGI 225.370 to assist in document consideration of each listed issue and retain a copy in the contract file.[134]

Solicitation Provisions and Contract Clauses

FAR 52.225-19, Contractor Personnel in a Designated Operational Area or Supporting a Diplomatic or Consular Mission outside the United States. Do not use for personal service contracts with individuals, or when all contractor personnel performing outside the United States and will be covered by DFARS 252.225-7040.

FAR 52.225-26, Contractors Performing Private Security Functions Outside the United States, for performance in a combat area or in support of foreign military operations. Do not use if the contract supports intelligence activities or temporarily uses indigenous personnel unaffiliated with a local security company.

FAR 52.229-11, Tax on Certain Foreign Procurements—Notice and Representation.

FAR 52.229-12, Tax on Certain Foreign Procurements.

FAR 52.229-13, Taxes—Foreign Contracts in Afghanistan.

FAR 52.229-14, Taxes—Foreign Contracts in Afghanistan (North Atlantic Treaty Organization Status of Forces Agreement).

DFARS 252.225-7039, Defense Contractors Performing Private Security Functions Outside the United States, instead of FAR 52.225-26, Contractors Performing Private Security Functions Outside the United States, when private security functions are to be performed outside the United States in combat, contingency, peacekeeping, or other military operations designated by the Combatant Commander or Secretary of Defense.

DFARS 252.225-7040, Contractor Personnel Supporting U.S. Armed Forces Deployed Outside the United States, instead of the clause at FAR 52.225-19, Contractor Personnel in a Designated Operational Area or Supporting a Diplomatic or Consular Mission Outside the United States, for performance in a designated operational area that authorize contractor personnel to support U.S. Armed Forces deployed outside the United States in contingency or peace operations or other military operations or exercises, when designated by the combatant commander or as directed by the Secretary of Defense. The following clauses might also be applicable:

- DFARS 252.225-7043, Antiterrorism/Force Protection Policy for Defense Contractors Outside the United States;
- FAR 52.228-3, Workers' Compensation Insurance (Defense Base Act), or FAR 52.228-4, Workers' Compensation and War-Hazard Insurance Overseas;
- FAR 52.228-7, Insurance—Liability to Third Persons, in cost-reimbursement contracts;
- DFARS 252.228-7003, Capture and Detention;
- DFARS 252.237-7019, Training for Contractor Personnel Interacting with Detainees;
- FAR 52.249-14, Excusable Delays;
- FAR 52.251-1, Government Supply Sources; and
- DFARS 252.251-7000, Ordering from Government Supply Sources.

DFARS 252.225-7043, Antiterrorism/Force Protection Policy for Defense Contractors Outside the United States, if requiring performance or travel outside the United States, except for contracts with foreign governments or their representatives or wholly owned corporations.

DFARS 252.225-7980, Contractor Personnel Performing in the United States Africa Command Area of Responsibility, in lieu of DFARS 252.225-7040, Contractor Personnel Supporting U.S. Armed Forces Deployed Outside the United States, when requiring contractor personnel to perform in the United States Africa Command.

DFARS 252.225-7981, Additional Access to Contractor and Subcontractor Records (Other than USCENTCOM), if more than $50,000 and to be performed outside the United States and its outlying areas, in support of a contingency operation in which members of the armed forces are actively engaged in hostilities, except for contracts that will be performed in the United States Central Command (USCENTCOM) theater of operations.

DFARS 252.225-7987, Requirements for Contractor Personnel Performing in USSOUTHCOM Area of Responsibility, if requiring performance in the USSOUTHCOM Area of Responsibility, unless the clause at DFARS 252.225-7040 applies.

DFARS 252.225-7993, Prohibition on Providing Funds to the Enemy, if awarded before December 31, 2019, with an estimated value in excess of $50,000 that are being, or will be, performed outside the United States and its outlying areas, in support of a contingency operation in which members of the Armed Forces are actively engaged in hostilities.

DFARS 252.225-7995, Contractor Personnel Performing in the United States Central Command Area of Responsibility, in lieu of DFARS 252.225-7040, when requiring performance in the United States Central Command Area of Responsibility.

2.13.4 Trade Agreements

FAR 25.4 and 5

This subpart does not apply to acquisitions:

- from UNICOR and SourceAmerica;
- in support of national security (including war materiel);
- of end products for resale;
- of goods and services specifically excluded under trade agreements;
- of sole-source or limited-source nature; or
- under small business set-asides.

The Trade Agreements Act authorizes the President to waive the Buy American Act and other provisions for eligible products from countries with which the United States has an international trade agreement or designation of preference.[135] This provision extends to the World Trade Organization Government Procurement Agreement and our nation's Free Trade Agreements. Offers of these eligible products receive equal consideration with domestic offers. However, the country of origin must be where material incurs "substantial transformation" into a new and different article, with a different character, name or use. Dollar thresholds are revised by the U.S. Trade Representative for different nations roughly every other year and are summarized at FAR 25.402.

The contracting officer must determine the origin of supplies or services by the country in which the firm is established, though (s)he may rely on the offeror's certification of end product origin. To evaluate offers, the contracting officer first eliminates offers deemed unacceptable due to non-price issues, such as nonresponsiveness or prohibited sources. Then the remaining offers are ranked by price. Any other non-price evaluation factors are then considered. To break any ties, preference is given to a domestic offer if non-price factors were considered, or drawing lots if no such preferences were involved.

To derive the evaluated price of the domestic product, the contracting officer adds the value of all options and invokes the following rules:

- If a fixed-term contract of 12 months or less is contemplated, use the total estimated value of the acquisition.
- If a fixed-term contract of more than 12 months is contemplated, use the total estimated value of the acquisition plus the estimated residual value of any leased equipment at the end of the contract.
- If an indefinite-term contract is contemplated, use the estimated monthly payment multiplied by the total number of months for ordering (i.e., the initial ordering period plus any optional ordering periods).
- If there is any doubt as to the contemplated term of the contract, use the estimated monthly payment multiplied by 48.
- If, in any 12-month period, recurring or multiple awards for the same type of product or products are anticipated, use the total estimated value of these projected awards. The acquisition should not be divided with the intent of reducing the estimated value of the acquisition below the dollar threshold of the Agreement.

Should one or more offers call for award by lot or on an all-or-none basis, the contracting officer may need to first apply evaluation factors by line item for any portion that does not so restrict award, then evaluate the lots which are restricted. Unless the restricted lot price is lower overall, award is made to the most favorable unrestricted offer. For offers of both domestic and foreign items, whichever constitutes the majority of the price for the given lot determines whether to treat the offer as domestic or foreign.

Solicitation Provision

FAR 52.214-34, Submission of Offers in the English Language.
FAR 52.214.35, Submission of Offers in U.S. Currency.

Solicitation Provisions and Contract Clauses

FAR 52.225-3, Buy American Act—Free Trade Agreements—Israeli Trade Act, and 52.225-4, Buy American Act—Free Trade Agreements—Israeli Trade Act Certificate for use within the United States, and the acquisition value is between $25,000 and $191,000. Use both clauses with Alternate I if the acquisition value is between $25,000 and $50,000. Use both clauses with Alternate II if the acquisition value is between $50,000 and $77,533. Use both clauses with Alternate III if the acquisition value is between $77,533 and $100,000. Do not use for information technology that is a commercial item.

FAR 52.225-5, Trade Agreements, and 52.225-6, Trade Agreements Certificate, if valued at $194,000 or more, the acquisition is covered by the WTO GPA, and the Buy American Act does not apply.

2.13.5 American Recovery and Reinvestment Act

FAR 25.6

The American Recovery and Reinvestment Act (7 U.S.C. 2036, previously introduced as the Recovery Act) is intended to finance a project to alter, construct, maintain, or repair a public building or work that is located in the United States. It includes only manufactured goods such as iron and steel that are produced or manufactured in the United States. This restriction does not apply if the:

- contracting officer determines that a certain construction material is not mined, produced or manufactured in the United States in sufficient and available commercial quantities of a satisfactory quality;
- cost of domestic construction material is unreasonable (i.e., would raise the evaluated contract price more than 25 percent for a manufactured item or 20 percent for unmanufactured material);
- steel or iron is used as a component of other manufactured construction material (such as a window frame), which need not be domestic; or
- restriction would be impracticable or inconsistent with public interest.

Allowable countries of origin are a World Trade Organization Government Procurement Agreement country, a Free Trade Agreement country, or at least developed country as designated in FAR 25.003. Current prohibited sources are Cuba, Iran, Sudan, Myanmar (imports only), and North Korea (imports only).[136] Any instances of contractor noncompliance with the Recovery Act are handled by the contracting officer in the same manner as the Buy American Act.

An offeror may request from the contracting officer a determination concerning the inapplicability of section 1605 of the Recovery Act or the Buy American Act for specifically identified construction materials. FAR 52.225-22 or -24 (whichever applies to the solicitation) paragraph (b) describes the timing for such a request, and FAR 52.221-21 or -23 (whichever applies to the solicitation) paragraphs (c–d) describes the information to be furnished.

If the contracting officer has determined that an exception applies because the cost of certain domestic construction material is unreasonable, then (s)he adds an evaluation factors to the offered price in the same manner as described earlier for the Buy American Act. The factor is 25 percent to the offer including foreign iron, steel, or other manufactured goods, or 6 percent to the cost of foreign unmanufactured construction material. Once again, if two or more offers are equal in price, the contracting officer gives preference to an offer that does not include foreign construction material.

Offerors may submit alternate offers based on use of equivalent domestic construction material to avoid possible rejection of the entire offer, in case the Government determines that no exception permits use of a particular foreign construction material. The alternate offer may not be a very attractive price, but at least the firm is still under consideration for award.

Although uncommon, the contracting officer might grant a request to determine inapplicability after award. However, (s)he must negotiate adequate consideration in this case and modify the contract to allow use of the foreign construction material. Again, the 25 and 6 percent factors may be used if a domestic material is found to be unreasonably priced.

Solicitation Provisions and Contract Clauses

FAR 52.225-13, Restrictions on Certain Foreign Purchases, unless an exception applies.

2.13.6 Customs and Duties

FAR 25.9

United States laws impose duties on foreign supplies imported into the customs territory of the United States, as implemented at 19 CFR 10.100. Certain exemptions from these duties are available to Government agencies by contracting officer petition to the Commissioner of Customs. Subchapters VIII and X of Chapter 98 of the Harmonized Tariff Schedule of the United States list supplies for which exemptions may be obtained.[137]

The solicitation will specify the currency of offers and payment, either U.S. dollars or local currency. If offers come in terms of multiple currencies, the contracting officer must convert the offered prices to U.S. currency for evaluation purposes. This requires using the current market exchange rate from a commonly used source in effect on the date of bid opening for sealed bidding, or the date specified for receipt of offers or any final revisions for negotiated acquisitions.[138]

DFARS 225.901

DoD will issue duty-free entry certificates for qualifying country end products and components, eligible end products (not components) under contracts covered by the World Trade Organization Government Procurement Agreement or a Free Trade Agreement, and other foreign supplies for which the contractor estimates that duty will exceed $300 per shipment into the customs territory of the United States. However, DoD will not issue a duty-free certificate if the supplies are entitled to duty-free treatment under a special category in the Harmonized Tariff Schedule of the United States (e.g., the Caribbean Basin Economic Recovery Act or a Free Trade Agreement), or if the supplies already have entered into the customs territory of the United States and the contractor already has paid the duty.

Solicitation Provision

FAR 52.225-17, Evaluation of Foreign Currency Offers, to permit the use of an unspecified currency. Insert in the provision the source of the rate to be used in the evaluation of offers.

DFARS 252.225-7000, Buy American—Balance of Payments Program Certificate, instead of FAR 52.225-2, Buy American Certificate, if including the basic or the alternate of DFARS 252.225-7001, Buy American and Balance of Payments Program. Do not use if the solicitation includes FAR 52.204-7. Use the basic provision when the solicitation includes DFARS 252.225-7001. Use Alternate I when the solicitation includes Alternate I of DFARS 252.225-7001.

DFARS 252.225-7003, Report of Intended Performance Outside the United States and Canada—Submission with Offer, if the value exceeds $13.5 million.

DFARS 252.225-7010, Commercial Derivative Military Article—Specialty Metals Compliance Certificate, when using DFARS 252.225-7009 and expecting competition.

DFARS 252.225-7018, Photovoltaic Devices—Certificate, if including DFARS 252.225-7017.

DFARS 252.225-7020, Trade Agreements Certificate, instead of FAR 52.225-6, Trade Agreements Certificate, in solicitations that include the basic or alternate II of DFARS 252.225-7021, Trade Agreements. Do not use if the solicitation includes FAR 52.204-7. Use the basic provision if the solicitation includes DFARS 252.225-7021. Use Alternate I provision if the solicitation includes Alternate II of DFARS 252.225-7021.

DFARS 252.225-7023, Preference for Products or Services from Afghanistan, as required. The contracting officer may modify the 50 percent evaluation factor in accordance with contracting office procedures.

DFARS 252.225-7024, Requirement for Products or Services from Afghanistan, if including DFARS 252.225-7023, Preference for Products or Services from Afghanistan.

DFARS 252.225-7031, Secondary Arab Boycott of Israel, unless an exception or waiver applies. Do not use if the solicitation includes FAR 52.204-7.

DFARS 252.225-7032, Waiver of United Kingdom Levies—Evaluation of Offers, if a U.K. firm is expected to submit an offer or receive a subcontract exceeding $1 million.

DFARS 252.225-7035, Buy American—Free Trade Agreements—Balance of Payments Program Certificate, instead of FAR 52.225-4, Buy American—Free Trade Agreements—Israeli Trade Act Certificate, when including the basic or an alternate of DFARS 252.225-7036, Buy American—Free Trade Agreements—Balance of Payments Program. If the solicitation includes FAR 52.204-7, do not separately list DFARS 252.225-7035 in the solicitation. Do not include the corresponding basic or alternate clause if DFARS 252.225-7036 or the corresponding alternate is used.

DFARS 252.225-7037, Evaluation of Offers for Air Circuit Breakers, if requiring air circuit breakers for naval vessels unless an exception applies.

DFARS 252.225-7046, Exports by Approved Community Members in Response to the Solicitation, if including DFARS 252.225-7047.

DFARS 252.225-7049, Prohibition on Acquisition of Commercial Satellite Services from Certain Foreign Entities—Representations, to acquire commercial satellite services. Do not use if the solicitation includes FAR 52.204-7.

DFARS 252.225-7050, Disclosure of Ownership or Control by the Government of a Country that is a State Sponsor of Terrorism, if expected to result in contracts of $150,000 or more. Do not use if the solicitation includes FAR 52.204-7.

Solicitation Provisions and Contract Clauses

FAR 52.225-8, Duty-Free Entry, for supplies that may be imported into the United States and for which duty-free entry may be obtained, if the value of the acquisition exceeds the simplified acquisition threshold, or if the savings from waiving the duty exceed the administrative cost of the duty.

DFARS 252.225-7001, Buy American and Balance of Payments Program, instead of FAR 52.225-1, Buy American—Supplies, unless all line items will be acquired from a particular source or sources or require domestic or qualifying country end products. This exception does not apply if manufacture of the end product must be in the United States or without a corresponding requirement for use of domestic components. Do not use this clause for supplies for use within the United States and an exception to the Buy American statute applies, or for supplies for use outside the United States and an exception to the Balance of Payments Program applies. Either or both of the following DFARS clauses or alternates must be used: DFARS 252.225-7021, Trade Agreements, or DFARS 252.225-7036, Buy American—Free Trade Agreements—Balance of Payments Program. Use the basic clause if the acquisition is not of end products listed in DFARS 225.401-70 in support of operations in Afghanistan. Use Alternate I when the acquisition is of end products listed in DFARS 225.401-70 in support of operations in Afghanistan.

DFARS 252.225-7002, Qualifying Country Sources as Subcontractors, when including the basic or one of the alternates of the following clauses:

- DFARS 252.225-7001, Buy American and Balance of Payments Program;
- DFARS 252.225-7021, Trade Agreements; and
- DFARS 252.225-7036, Buy American—Free Trade Agreements—Balance of Payments Program.

DFARS 252.225-7004, Report of Intended Performance Outside the United States and Canada—Submission after Award, with a value exceeding $13.5 million.

DFARS 252.225-7008, Restriction on Acquisition of Specialty Metals, when exempt from the specialty metals restrictions that exceed the simplified acquisition threshold and require the delivery of specialty metals as end items.

DFARS 252.225-7009, Restriction on Acquisition of Certain Articles Containing Specialty Metals, exempt from the specialty metals restrictions that exceed the simplified acquisition threshold and require delivery of ammunition, military vehicles or weapon systems containing specialty metals.

DFARS 252.225-7011, Restriction on Acquisition of Supercomputers, to acquire supercomputers unless a waiver has been granted.

DFARS 252.225-7013, Duty-Free Entry, instead of FAR 52.225-8. Do not use to acquire supplies that will not enter the customs territory of the United States.

DFARS 252.225-7016, Restriction on Acquisition of Ball and Roller Bearings, except for commercial items other than ball or roller bearings acquired as end items, the items being acquired do not contain ball and roller bearings, or a waiver has been granted.

DFARS 252.225-7017, Photovoltaic Devices, if expected to exceed the simplified acquisition threshold and calls for a photovoltaic device that will be installed in the United States on DoD property or in a facility owned by DoD or reserved for the exclusive use of DoD in the United States.

DFARS 252.225-7019, Restriction on Acquisition of Anchor and Mooring Chain, when requiring welded shipboard anchor or mooring chain four inches or less in diameter.

DFARS 252.225-7021, Trade Agreements, instead of FAR 52.225-5, Trade Agreements, if the World Trade Organization Government Procurement Agreement applies (i.e., the acquisition is of end products listed at DFARS 225.401-70, the value of the acquisition equals or exceeds $180,000, and none of the exceptions at FAR 25.401(a) applies). Use the basic clause except for end products in support of operations in Afghanistan, or that include DFARS 252.225-7024, Requirement for Products or Services from Afghanistan. Use Alternate II clause when not including DFARS 252.225-7024, Requirement for Products or Services from Afghanistan, when the acquisition is of end products in support of operations in Afghanistan. Do not use the basic or an alternate of the clause if purchase from foreign sources is restricted, unless the contracting officer anticipates a waiver of the restriction, or DFARS 252.225-7026, Acquisition Restricted to Products or Services from Afghanistan, is included in the solicitation and contract.

DFARS 252.225-7025, Restriction on Acquisition of Forgings, for any forgings unless an exception applies.

DFARS 252.225-7026, Acquisition Restricted to Products or Services from Afghanistan, when acquiring products or services from Afghanistan or directed to a particular source or sources from Afghanistan.

Do not use any of the following DFARS provisions or clauses in solicitations or contracts that include the provision at DFARS 252.225-7023, 252.225-7024 or 252.225-7026:

- DFARS 252.225-7000, Buy American Act—Balance of Payments Program Certificate.
- DFARS 252.225-7001, Buy American Act and Balance of Payments Program.
- DFARS 252.225-7002, Qualifying Country Sources as Subcontractors.

- DFARS 252.225-7035, Buy American Act—Free Trade Agreements—Balance of Payments Program Certificate.
- DFARS 252.225-7036, Buy American Act—Free Trade Agreements—Balance of Payments Program.
- DFARS 252.225-7044, Balance of Payments Program—Construction Material.
- DFARS 252.225-7045, Balance of Payments Program—Construction Material Under Trade Agreements.
- Do not use DFARS 252.225-7020, Trade Agreements Certificate or 252.225-7021, Trade Agreements, in solicitations or contracts that include DFARS 252.225-7026.

DFARS 252.225-7027, Restriction on Contingent Fee, for Foreign Military Sales. Insert in paragraph (b)(1) of the clause the name(s) of any foreign country customer(s).

DFARS 252.225-7028, Exclusionary Policies and Practices of Foreign Governments, to purchase supplies and services for international military education training ad FMS.

DFARS 252.225-7029, Acquisition of Uniform Components for Afghan Military or Afghan National Police, for textile components that DoD intends to supply to the Afghan National Army or the Afghan National Police for purposes of production of uniforms.

DFARS 252.225-7030, Restriction on Acquisition of Carbon, Alloy, and Armor Steel Plate, when requiring delivery to the Government of these items that will be used in a Government-owned or rented facility, unless a waiver has been granted.

DFARS 252.225-7033, Waiver of United Kingdom Levies, if a U.K. firm is expected to submit an offer or receive a subcontract exceeding $1 million.

DFARS 252.225-7036, Buy American—Free Trade Agreements—Balance of Payments Program, instead of FAR 52.225-3, Buy American—Free Trade Agreements–Israeli Trade Act, for the items listed at DFARS 225.401-70, when the estimated value equals or exceeds $25,000 but is less than $180,000 unless an exception applies. Use the basic clause within the same thresholds unless the acquisition is of end products in support of operations in Afghanistan. Use Alternate I when the estimated value equals or exceeds $25,000, but is less than $80,317, except for end products in support of operations in Afghanistan. Use Alternate II when the estimated value equals or exceeds $100,000, but is less than $180,000, and the acquisition is of end products in support of operations in Afghanistan. Use Alternate III when the estimated value equals or exceeds $25,000, but is less than $80,317, and the acquisition is of end products in support of operations in Afghanistan. Use Alternate IV when the estimated value equals or exceeds

$80,317 but is less than $100,000, except if the acquisition is of end products in support of operations in Afghanistan. Use Alternate V when the estimated value equals or exceeds $80,317 but is less than $100,000 and the acquisition is of end products in support of operations in Afghanistan. Do not use the basic or an alternate of the clause if purchase from foreign sources is restricted (unless the contracting officer anticipates a waiver of the restriction), acquiring information technology that is a commercial or providing a preference for products or services from Afghanistan, limiting competition to products or services from Afghanistan or using procedures other than competitive procedures to award a contract to a particular source or sources from Afghanistan.

DFARS 252.225-7038, Restriction on Acquisition of Air Circuit Breakers, for air circuit breakers for naval vessels unless an exception applies.

DFARS 252.225-7044, Balance of Payments Program—Construction Material, for construction to be performed outside the United States, including acquisitions of commercial items or components, with an estimated value greater than the simplified acquisition threshold but less than $6,932,000. Use the basic clause unless the acquisition is in support of operations in Afghanistan. Use Alternate I clause if the acquisition is in support of operations in Afghanistan. Do not use if the entire acquisition is exempt from the Balance of Payments Program.

DFARS 252.225-7045, Balance of Payments Program—Construction Material Under Trade Agreements, for construction to be performed outside the United States with an estimated value of $6,932,000 or more, including acquisitions of commercial items or components. Use the basic clause for an estimated value of $10,441,216 or more unless the acquisition is in support of operations in Afghanistan. Use Alternate I clause in for an estimated value of $6,932,000 or more, but less than $10,441,216 unless the acquisition is in support of operations in Afghanistan. Use Alternate II clause for an estimated value of $10,441,216 or more and is in support of operations in Afghanistan. Use Alternate III clause for an estimated value of $6,932,000 or more, but less than $10,441,216, and is in support of operations in Afghanistan. Do not use if the entire acquisition is exempt from the Balance of Payments Program.

2.13.7 Export Controls

An *export* is a product, software or technology sent from the United States to a foreign nation. An item is also considered an export if it leaves the United States to a wholly-owned U.S. subsidiary in a foreign country. Even a foreign-origin item is treated as an export if it is trans-shipped through the United States, or returns from the United States to its foreign country of origin.

License requirements depend on an item's technical characteristics, destination, end-user, and purpose. If an exported item has both commercial and military or space usage, it requires a validated license to protect a national security or foreign policy interest. The item is given a specific Export Control Classification Number that describes both the item and the controls placed on that item. All such numbers are listed in the Commerce Control List.[139]

PGI 225.79

The International Traffic in Arms Regulations (ITAR), issued by the Department of State, control the export of defense-related articles and services, including technical data, ensuring compliance with the Arms Export Control Act.[140] The United States Munitions List identifies defense articles, services, and related technical data that are inherently military in character and could, if exported, jeopardize national security or foreign policy interests of the United States. This list is part of the ITAR.[141] Contracting officers should not answer any questions a contractor may ask regarding how to comply with the ITAR and instead refer them to the Department of State.

All other exports are controlled by the Department of Commerce through the Export Administration Regulations (EAR), usually under a general license. The EAR, issued by the Department of Commerce, controls the export of dual-use items, (items that have both commercial and military or proliferation applications) and purely commercial items. These items include commodities, software, and technology. Releasing technology or source code to a foreign national within the United States is considered an export to the home country of the foreign national under the EAR. Many items subject to the EAR are set forth by Export Control Classification Number on the Commerce Control List.[142] Contracting officers should not answer any questions a contractor may ask regarding how to comply with the EAR and instead refer them to the Department of Commerce.

Government approvals are often necessary for companies to hold discussions about potential projects, pursue joint activities, ship hardware, or transfer know-how to one another, and even sometimes to move engineers and other personnel within branches of the same company located in different countries. This process can be challenging for U.S. exporters and for foreign firms in their supply chains. Bilateral DTC Treaties with both Australia and the United Kingdom establish permissions for export without export licenses for each country if an export meets the DTC Treaty requirements. Other exports remain under the AECA and the ITAR. The DTC Treaties are intended solely to waive certain requirements of the ITAR for specific transactions within the scope of the DTC Treaties not remove any requirements for contractors to comply with domestic U.S. law.[143]

Solicitation Provisions and Contract Clauses

DFARS 252.225-7047, Exports by Approved Community Members in Performance of the Contract, when export-controlled items are expected to be involved in the performance of the contract and DFARS 252.225-7048 is used; and at least one contract line item is intended to satisfy a U.S. DoD Treaty-eligible requirement. The contracting officer will complete paragraph (b) of the clause using information the program manager provided.

DFARS 252.225-7048, Export-Controlled Items.

2.13.8 Inverted Domestic Corporations

FAR 9.108

An *inverted domestic corporation* is a firm currently incorporated in another country but was once incorporated in the United States. The definition includes subsidiaries and partnerships in the same situation. The concern with inverted firms is that they continue to do most of their business in the United States but have relocated overseas in a tax haven nation to mitigate or eliminate paying Federal taxes. Government agencies are prohibited from contracting with such firms unless the agency head grants a waiver. Offerors must execute a representation to the effect that they are not an inverted domestic corporation. They must also notify the contracting officer if during performance they become inverted, or if their parent becomes inverted. This is one of several issues in federal procurement which has nothing to do with performance or pricing, but is totally a result of a political decision. Congress and the President use the power of the public purse to implement such decisions, and they represent implemented contracting policy.

Solicitation Provision

FAR 52.209-09, Representation, Prohibition on Contracting with Inverted Domestic Corporations.

Contract Clause

FAR 52.209-10, Prohibition on Contracting with Inverted Domestic Corporations.

2.13.9 Foreign Military Sales (FMS)

The DoD runs a *Foreign Military Sales* (FMS) program to facilitate sales of U.S. arms and defense equipment (including from defense stockpiles), services and military training to foreign governments. This program implements the Foreign Assistance Act of 1961 and the Arms Export Control Act.[144] The foreign buyer does not deal directly with the defense contractor. Rather, the Defense Security Cooperation Agency serves as an intermediary for procurement, logistics and delivery support, and often provides product support and training. FMS requires the foreign nation to place a deposit in a U.S. Trust Fund or else demonstrate appropriate credit and approval. Funding can also come from Congressional appropriation or grants under the Military Assistance Program.[145]

The foreign nation can dictate a sole source. The United States charges the foreign nation an administrative fee and nonrecurring costs to place and administer the contract. Note that any unusual costs of doing business in the foreign country (e.g., government brokerage fees) could raise the price.

In addition to goods, knowledge may also be shared with foreign nations. A good example is *international coproduction*, a method by which technical information and procedures are transferred to other nations to produce or assemble military items domestically.

2.13.10 Priority Delivery

Mutual interdependence of supplies is necessary to achieve national security, interoperability and timely delivery between the United States and its allies. DoD has entered into arrangements with several NATO nations to request priority delivery for (sub)contracts or orders from companies in these countries. DoD program managers and contractors acquiring materials and services from participating firms may request priority delivery for their (sub)contract or order to meet U.S. defense requirements. Partner nations are instituting government-industry codes of conduct for firms to help provide priority support on a voluntary basis.

2.13.11 Contracting with Canada

DFARS 225.870

The Canadian government guarantees to the U.S. Government all commitments and covenants of the Canadian Commercial Corporation (CCC) under any contract or order issued to the CCC by any contracting office of the U.S. Government. The CCC is the prime contractor. To indicate acceptance of offers by individual Canadian companies, the CCC issues a letter supporting the Canadian offer and provides its name, endorsement of the firm and 100 percent subcontract with the firm. The CCC will award and administer contracts with contractors located in Canada, except for negotiated acquisitions for experimental, developmental or research work under projects (other than the Defense Development Sharing Program), urgency, at or below the simplified acquisition threshold, or made by DoD activities located in Canada.

If requested, contracting offices will routinely furnish a solicitation to the CCC even if no Canadian firm is solicited. If a Canadian offer cannot be processed through the CCC in time to meet the date for receipt of offers, the CCC may permit Canadian firms to submit offers directly. However, the CCC's endorsement is still required before contract award.

The CCC will submit all sealed bids in terms of U.S. currency. Hence, fluctuation in exchange rates is not an issue. For negotiated procurements, however, offers will be in terms of Canadian currency. The CCC may choose to quote and receive payment in terms of U.S. currency, again ignoring fluctuation in exchange rates. If the award is priced in Canadian dollars, the contract should note "CN" by the price and include the U.S./Canadian conversion rate at the time of award and the U.S. dollar equivalent of the Canadian dollar contract amount.

Direct communication with the Canadian supplier is encouraged for all technical aspects of the contract, provided the CCC's approval is obtained on any matters involving changes to the contract. DoD has waived the requirement for submission of certified cost or pricing data for the CCC and its subcontractors. However, it is not exempt from the requirement to submit data other than certified cost or pricing data.

No further approval is required to request data other than certified cost or pricing data from the CCC if the acquisition is cost-reimbursement over $700,000 or fixed-price over $500 million if sole-source or the only respondent. Nor is approval required for modifications that exceed $150,000 in these types of contracts, nor for competitive solicitations in which data other than certified cost or pricing data are required from all offerors.

Otherwise, the contracting officer must only require data other than certified cost or pricing data if an official at least two levels above the contracting officer determines that such data are needed. Such data must be submitted by the firm through the CCC.

PGI 225.870

The CCC uses provisions in contracts with Canadian or U.S. concerns that give DoD the same production rights, data, and information that DoD would obtain in contracts with U.S. concerns. It provides the following services without charge to DoD:

- accountability and disposal of Government property;
- compliance with Canadian labor laws;
- cost and price analysis;
- customs documentation;
- industrial security;
- processing disputes and appeals;
- processing termination claims; and
- production expediting.

The Public Works and Government Services Canada (PWGSC) performs audits when needed, for contracts overseen by the Canadian Commercial Corporation in accordance with international agreement. The audit agency will perform audits without charge to DoD, including accounting system and interim voucher reviews, when needed for DoD contracts awarded directly to Canadian firms, and subcontracts with Canadian firms under such direct contracts with either U.S. or Canadian firms.

The Department of National Defence (Canada) provides inspection personnel, services, and facilities, at no charge to DoD departments and agencies. The PWGSC approves invoices on a provisional basis for cost-reimbursement basis pending completion of the contract and final audit. Moreover, for all contracts placed in Canada, the Department of National Defence (Canada) will perform any necessary contract quality assurance and/or acceptance, as applicable.

Solicitation Provision

DFARS 252.215-7003, Requirement for Submission of Data Other Than Certified Cost or Pricing Data—Canadian Commercial Corporation.

DFARS 252.215-7004, Requirement for Submission of Data Other Than Certified Cost or Pricing Data—Modifications—Canadian Commercial Corporation.

2.13.12 The Berry Amendment

DFARS 225.7002

10 U.S.C. 2533a (the "Berry Amendment") precludes DoD from acquiring any of the following items, either as end products or components, unless grown, produced, reprocessed, or reused in the United States:

- a flag of the United States (does not apply to flagpoles and accessories);
- canvas products;

- clothing and the materials and components thereof, other than items such as electronics or sensors added to clothing and the materials and components thereof;
- cotton and other natural fiber products;
- food;
- hand or measuring tools;
- individual equipment manufactured from or containing designated fabrics, fibers, materials, or yarns;
- spun silk yarn for cartridge cloth;
- synthetic fabric, textile fibers and yarns;
- tents, tarpaulins, or similar covers;
- wool fiber or yarn; and
- woven silk or woven silk blends.

This restriction does not apply to acquisitions at or below the simplified acquisition threshold, nor for items if the Department Secretary (or Director of DLA) determines that items grown, produced, reprocessed, or reused in the United States cannot be acquired as and when needed in a satisfactory quality and sufficient quantity at U.S. market prices. This determination requires an analysis of alternatives that would not require a domestic nonavailability determination and a written certification by the requiring activity why such alternatives are unacceptable.

The Berry Amendment also does not apply to acquisitions of:

- chemical warfare protective clothing under an agreement with a qualifying country;
- emergency actions by activities located outside the United States for personnel of those activities;
- fibers and yarns that are for use within synthetic fabric (but not the purchase of the synthetic or coated synthetic fabric itself), if the fabric is to be a component of a non-textile end product (e.g., apparel, bedding, draperies, flags, floor coverings, furnishings, furs, leather, para-aramid fibers and yarns manufactured in a qualifying country, parachutes, tents, textiles, and upholstered seats);
- food or hand or measuring tools in support of contingency operations or for which the use of other than competitive procedures has been approved on the basis of unusual and compelling urgency;
- foods manufactured or processed in the United States, except for fish, shellfish or seafood;
- incidental amounts of cotton, other natural fibers, or wool incorporated in an end product, for which the estimated value is not more than 10 percent of the total price of the end product and does not exceed the simplified acquisition threshold;

- Interagency, State or local purchases that are executed by DoD as a result of the transfer of contracts from the General Services Administration or for which DoD serves as an item manager for products on behalf of the General Services Administration;
- items deemed to be nonavailable and listed in FAR 25.104(a);
- items specifically for commissary resale;
- items manufactured outside the United States in support of combat operations;
- perishable foods by or for activities located outside the United States for personnel of those activities;
- requirements by vessels in foreign waters; and
- waste and byproducts of cotton or wool fiber for use in the production of explosives and propellants.

2.13.13 Restrictions on Foreign Contracting

Each annual DoD Appropriations Act seems to bring new limitations on DoD contracting for foreign operations or foreign-produced items. Though many are highly specific, they are intended to reflect Congressional thinking on these matters. A number of these restrictions do permit Canadian sources and supplies in an effort to support North American defense. The list of limitations is quite lengthy, and seems to grow every year.

DFARS 209.104-1

Per 10 U.S.C. 2536(a), DoD cannot award a contract to an entity controlled by a foreign government if that entity requires access to proscribed information to perform the contract.[146] The Undersecretary of Defense for Intelligence may waive the prohibition upon determining that the waiver is essential to the national security interests of the United States. Waiver requests, prepared by the requiring activity in coordination with the contracting officer, include a proposed national interest determination that:

- describes the acquisition and performance requirements;
- includes the national security interests involved and how award of the contract helps advance those interests;
- lists the proposed awardee and its foreign ownership and any other entity with the capability, capacity, and technical expertise to satisfy the requirements; and
- sets forth methods available to satisfy the requirement (e.g., substitute products or technology, or alternate approaches to meet program objectives).

The Secretary of Defense may, in the case of a contract awarded for environmental remediation, restoration or waste management at a DoD facility, waive the prohibition upon determining that the waiver will advance these objectives and will not harm the national security interests of the United States. The foreign government controlling the entity must be authorized to exchange Restricted Data with DoD under section 144 c. of the Atomic Energy Act of 1954 (42 U.S.C. 2164(c)). The Secretary must notify Congress of the decision to grant the waiver, then wait at least 45 days to make award.

DFARS 225.502

Whenever the acquisition is in support of operations in Afghanistan, the offers of end products from South Caucasus or Central and South Asian states listed in DFARS 225.401-70 are treated the same as qualifying country offers.

For acquisitions subject to the World Trade Organization Government Procurement Agreement, in lieu of FAR 25.502(b), the contracting officer will consider only offers of U.S.-made, qualifying country, or designated country end products, and award to the low offeror.

For acquisitions subject to the Buy American statute or the Balance of Payments Program or a Free Trade Agreement, in lieu of FAR 25.502(c), only qualifying country end products are exempt from application of the Buy American or Balance of Payments Program evaluation factor. If the low offer is a foreign offer that is exempt, it receives the award. If the low offer is a foreign offer that is not exempt, and there is another foreign offer that is exempt and is priced below the lowest domestic offer, award goes to the low foreign offer. Otherwise, the 50 percent evaluation factor is applied to the low foreign offer to determine award.

If price is not the determining factor and there are domestic offers, the contracting officer will apply the 50 percent Buy American or Balance of Payments Program evaluation factor to all foreign offers unless an exemption applies. Then (s)he will evaluate in accordance with the criteria of the solicitation. If these procedures will not result in award on a domestic offer, (s)he will proceed with award only after executing a determination that domestic preference would be inconsistent with the public interest.

DFARS 225.770

DoD personnel are authorized to make emergency acquisitions in direct support of U.S. or allied forces deployed in military contingency, humanitarian or peacekeeping operations in a country or region subject to economic sanctions administered by the Department of the Treasury, Office of Foreign Assets Control.

DoD will not acquire supplies or services covered by the United States Munitions List, including a subcontract at any tier, from any Communist Chinese military company.[147] This prohibition does not apply to components and parts of covered items unless the components and parts are themselves covered by the List. The prohibition can be waived for national security reasons by the USD(AT&L), the Secretaries of the military departments or the Acquisition Executive of the Defense Logistics Agency. However, the waiver must include recommendations to develop alternative sourcing capabilities in the future. The prohibition does not apply to supplies or services acquired in connection with a visit to the People's Republic of China by a vessel or an aircraft of the U.S. armed forces, or for testing or intelligence gathering.

The contracting officer shall not award a contract of $150,000 or more to a firm when a foreign government that is a state sponsor of terrorism owns or controls, either directly or indirectly, a significant interest in the firm, subsidiary of controlling firm. This requirement may be waived if the Secretary of Defense determines that a waiver is not inconsistent with the national security objectives of the United States.

The contracting officer shall not award a contract for commercial satellite services to a foreign entity in which the government of a covered foreign country has an ownership interest that enables it to affect satellite operations, launch a satellite or offer commercial satellite services. USD(AT&L) or USD(Policy) can determine at least seven days before contract award that it is in the national security interest of the United States to enter into such a contract.

Award cannot be made for Afghanistan operations if Government personnel or their representatives cannot safely access the project. To waive this requirement, a D&F is necessary to justify the need and document safeguards in place. The contracting officer may approve the D&F if below $1 million, obtain the signature of a theater commander if up to $40 million, or else obtain Secretary of Defense approval with Congressional notification if at least $40 million in life-cycle value.

DFARS 225.7003

DoD cannot acquire ammunition, military vehicles or weapon systems, or any components thereof, unless any specialty metals contained in the items or components or as individual end items are melted or produced in the United States. This restriction does not apply to the following acquisitions:

- ammunition, military vehicles and weapon systems manufactured in or containing specialty metals melted or produced in a qualifying country;
- at or below the simplified acquisition threshold;
- COTS items containing specialty metals, except for:
  - fasteners not incorporated into COTS end items, subsystems, or assemblies; or are commercial items acquired under a (sub)contract with a

manufacturer who has certified that it will purchase, during the calendar year, an amount of domestically melted or produced specialty metal for use in producing fasteners for sale that is at least 50 percent of the total amount of the specialty metal purchased to carry out the production;
    - forgings or castings;
    - high-performance magnets; and
    - specialty metal mill products (e.g., bar, billet, slab, wire, plate, and sheet) not incorporated into end items, subsystems, assemblies, or components;
- electronic components, unless the Secretary of Defense determines that the domestic availability of a particular electronic component is critical to national security;
- end items where not more than two percent of total weight of specialty metals are not domestic. This exception does not apply to high-performance magnets containing specialty metals;
- for which the use of noncompetitive procedures has been approved based on unusual and compelling urgency;
- in support of contingency operations;
- items for test and evaluation under the foreign comparative testing program, but not under follow-on production contracts;
- items specifically for commissary resale;
- outside the United States in support of combat operations;
- specialty metal if an authorized official determines that specialty metal melted or produced in the United States cannot be acquired as and when needed at a fair and reasonable price in a satisfactory quality, a sufficient quantity, and the required form (i.e., a domestic nonavailability determination);
- the offeror has certified that it and its subcontractor(s) will individually or collectively enter into a contractual agreement(s) to purchase a sufficient quantity of domestically melted or produced specialty metal; or
- USD(AT&L) or the Secretary of the military department concerned determines that the item is a commercial derivative military article.

The specialty metal exception above needs further explanation. The Secretary of the department is authorized, without power of redelegation, to make such a determination that applies to only one contract. The supporting documentation for the determination includes an analysis of alternatives that would not require a domestic nonavailability determination and written documentation by the requiring activity why such alternatives are unacceptable. A domestic nonavailability determination that applies to more than one contract (i.e., a class domestic nonavailability determination), requires the approval of the USD(AT&L). But at least 30 days before making this determination, USD(AT&L) will publish a notice to SAM of the intent to make the domestic nonavailability determination and solicit information relevant to such notice from interested parties, including producers of specialty metal mill products.

DFARS 225.7004

Per 10 U.S.C. 2534, DoD cannot acquire a multipassenger motor vehicle (bus) unless it is manufactured in the United States, Australia, Canada, or the United Kingdom. This restriction does not apply for temporary use if buses manufactured in these nations are not available to satisfy requirements that cannot be postponed. Buses manufactured in other nations can be obtained at no cost or at or below the simplified acquisition threshold.

DFARS 225.7006

In accordance with 10 U.S.C. 2534, DoD cannot acquire air circuit breakers for naval vessels unless they are manufactured in the United States, Australia, Canada, or the United Kingdom. This restriction does not apply if the acquisition is for an amount at or below the simplified acquisition threshold or for spare or repair parts needed to support air circuit breakers manufactured outside the United States.

DFARS 225.7007

DoD cannot acquire welded shipboard anchor and mooring chain, four inches or less in diameter, unless manufactured in the United States and the cost of the components manufactured in the United States exceeds 50 percent of the total cost of components. The Secretary of the department may waive the restriction if sufficient domestic suppliers are not available to meet DoD requirements on a timely basis and the acquisition is necessary to acquire capability for national security purposes. The written determination and findings must be provided to the House and Senate Committees on Appropriations.

DFARS 225.7008

The restrictions on certain foreign purchases under 10 U.S.C. 2534(a) may be waived if USD(AT&L) determines that domestic producers would not be jeopardized by competition from a foreign country, and that country does not discriminate against defense items produced in the United States to a greater degree than the United States discriminates against defense items produced in that country. Another acceptable basis for waiver is that the restriction would impede cooperative programs entered into between DoD and a foreign country or a reciprocal procurement of defense items under a memorandum of understanding. The determination must be published in the Federal Register and submitted to the congressional defense committees at least 15 days before its effective date. The effective period of the waiver shall not exceed one year. The waiver can also be applied to subcontracts or options exercised into on or after the effective date.

The head of the contracting activity may waive a restriction on a case-by-case basis upon execution of a determination and findings that the restriction would cause unreasonable delays, satisfactory quality items manufactured in the United States, Australia, Canada, or the United Kingdom are not available from at least two sources, or else the restriction is not in the national security interests of the United States or would adversely affect a U.S. company. The restriction is also waived when it would cause unreasonable costs by exceeding 150 percent of the offered price, inclusive of duty, of items that are not of U.S. or Canadian origin.

DFARS 225.7009

DoD cannot acquire ball and roller bearings unless manufactured in the United States or Canada and the cost of the bearing components manufactured in the United States or Canada exceeds 50 percent of the total cost of the bearing components of that ball or roller bearing. This does not apply to (sub)contracts to acquire commercial items, unless acquired as end items.

The Secretary of the Department or Component Acquisition Executive may waive this restriction by certifying to the House and Senate Committees on Appropriations that adequate domestic supplies are not available to meet DoD requirements on a timely basis or to acquire capability for national security purposes.

DFARS 225.7010

Per 10 U.S.C. 2534, the following unique components of naval vessels must be manufactured in the United States or Canada:

- electronic navigation chart systems;
- gyrocompasses;
- propulsion and machinery control systems;
- pumps;
- steering controls; and
- totally enclosed lifeboats.

This restriction does not apply to (sub)contracts that do not exceed the simplified acquisition threshold or to spare or repair purchase of these items if those from alternate sources are not interchangeable. Waiver criteria are the same as for air circuit breakers. No contract clauses or certifications implement this restriction.

DFARS 225.7011

DoD cannot acquire carbon, alloy, or armor steel plate for use in a Government-owned facility or a leased facility unless it is melted and rolled in the United States or Canada. This restriction does not apply to the acquisition of an end product (e.g., a machine tool), to be used in the facility, that contains carbon, alloy, or armor steel plate as a component.

The Secretary of the Department responsible for acquisition may waive this restriction, on a case-by-case basis, by certifying to the House and Senate Committees on Appropriations that adequate U.S. or Canadian supplies are not available to meet DoD requirements on a timely basis for national security purposes.

DFARS 225.7012

DoD cannot purchase a supercomputer unless it is manufactured in the United States. The Secretary of Defense may waive this restriction, on a case-by-case basis, after certifying to the Armed Services and Appropriations Committees of Congress that adequate U.S. supplies are not available to meet requirements on a timely basis for national security purposes.

DFARS 225.7013

Per 10 U.S.C. 7309 and 7310, DoD cannot contract to construct in a foreign shipyard a military vessel or a major component of the hull or superstructure of same. Nor can DoD overhaul, repair, or maintain in a foreign shipyard, a naval vessel homeported in the United States (but can contract for voyage repairs).

DFARS 225.7017

Photovoltaic devices that convert light directly into electricity through a solid-state, semiconductor process must be domestic in origin if installed in the United States on DoD property or in a facility owned by DoD or otherwise used exclusively by DoD. This means they must be manufactured in the United States and over half the cost of the components must be, too (including any duty, scrap or transportation cost). The exceptions are if obtained under a Free Trade Agreement and worth at least $25,000 or more, or under a World Trade Organization—Government Procurement Agreement valued at $180,000 or more. The product must be either manufactured in whole or else transformed within the Free Trade or World Trade Organization country. The head of the contracting activity is authorized to waive this restriction on a case-by-case basis in the public interest (e.g., over the dollar threshold or from a qualifying country) or unreasonable cost (e.g., under the threshold and at least 50 percent less expensive than any domestic product).

DFARS 225.7018

No samarian-cobalt or neodymium iron-boron magnets either melted or produced in a designated country may be acquired for use within the United States unless at or below the simplified acquisition threshold or commercially available as COTS (with certain exceptions).[148] This restriction also applies to tungsten metal powder and heavy alloy, including any component containing same. Any such acquisition requires a written determination signed by the service secretary or Director of DLA, which must include a written and certified analysis of nonavailability by the requiring activity should address whether nonavailabilty, unreasonable price and/or insufficient quantity.

No energy sourced from inside Russia can be used on a military installation. However, energy converted by a third party into another form of energy is allowed. A waiver can be approved by the head of the contracting activity based on lack of adequate supply and national security requirements, and notification of same to Congressional oversight committees within 14 days. DoD must also take steps to mitigate the risk of using Russian-furnished energy.

DFARS 225.7020

DoD cannot contract for products or services with a firm that operated with the authority of the government of Venezuela not recognized by the United States unless for consular or diplomatic operations or licensed by the Department of the Treasury. The Secretaries of Defense and State must jointly determine any acquisition to provide disaster or humanitarian assistance to the Venezuelan people or vital to the interests of the United States.

DFARS 225.7021

No award over $5 million in value may be awarded to a firm performing work or leasing or owning real property in the People's Republic of China unless so disclosed by the firm. The senior procurement executive can waive disclosure requirements if deemed in national security interests of the United States.

DFARS 225.7022

No award can be made above the micropurchase level for a product produced by forced labor in the Xinjiang Uyghur Autonomous Region of the People's Republic of China.

DFARS 225.72

No award over $5 million can be made to a firm which performs work or leases or owns real property in the People's Republic of China.

DFARS 225.7102

Forging items, whether as end items or components, must be of domestic manufacture to the maximum extent practicable. Forgings used for periscope tubes, ring forgings for bull gears and ship propulsion shafts should be bought from domestic sources unless using simplified acquisition procedures. They can be of foreign manufacture if for overseas use or the quantity acquired exceeds the amount needed to maintain the U.S. defense mobilization base (provided the excess quantity is an economical purchase quantity). Upon request from a contractor, the contracting officer may waive the requirement for domestic manufacture.

DFARS 225.7201

10 U.S.C. 2410g requires offerors and contractors to notify DoD of any intention to perform a DoD contract outside the United States and Canada if the contract could be performed inside either country. This policy does not apply to contracts for commercial items, construction, ores, natural gas, utilities, petroleum products and crudes, timber (logs), or subsistence.

DFARS 225.7501

Construction material must be domestic products when used outside the United States, including end products and construction material for foreign military sales, unless the:

- acquisition is covered by the World Trade Organization Government Procurement Agreement;
- acquisition of foreign end products or construction material is required by a treaty or executive agreement between governments;
- contracting officer determines that a requirement can best be filled by a foreign end product or construction material, including determinations that:
  - a particular domestic construction material is not available;
  - a subsistence product is perishable and delivery from the United States would significantly impair the quality at the point of consumption;
  - an end product or construction material, by its nature or as a practical matter, can best be acquired in the geographic area concerned, e.g., ice; bulk material, such as sand, gravel, or other soil material; concrete masonry units; fired brick; or stone;

- ◦ the cost of domestic construction material would exceed the cost of foreign construction material by more than 50 percent, calculated based on a particular construction material or the comparative cost of applying the Balance of Payments Program to the total acquisition; or
  - ◦ use of a particular domestic construction material is impracticable;
- end product or particular construction material is:
  - ◦ a brand drug specified by the Defense Medical Materiel Board;
  - ◦ a petroleum product;
  - ◦ a spare part for foreign-manufactured vehicles, equipment, machinery, or systems, provided the acquisition is restricted to the original manufacturer or its supplier;
  - ◦ acquired for commissary resale;
  - ◦ an industrial gas;
  - ◦ information technology that is a commercial item; or
  - ◦ listed in FAR 25.104;
- estimated cost of the acquisition or the value of a particular construction material is at or below the simplified acquisition threshold; or
- local preference for an acquisition in support of operations in Afghanistan is used.

The requirement for domestic end products applies after receipt of offers unless the evaluated low offer is an offer of an end product or construction material that is eligible, a non-construction material from a qualifying country, or if the acquisition is in support of operations in Afghanistan, a South Caucasus/Central and South Asian state end product, or a nonqualifying country end product, but application of the Balance of Payments Program evaluation factor would not result in award on a domestic offer. At any time during the acquisition process, the head of the agency may determine that it is not in the public interest to apply the restrictions of the Balance of Payments Program to the end product or construction material.

DFARS 225.770

Items included on the Commerce Control List or United States Munitions List may not be acquired from a Communist Chinse military company.

DFARS 225.772

No contract for satellite services may be awarded to Communist China, North Korea, Russia, or any state which sponsors terrorism.

Solicitation Provision

DFARS 252.225-7012, Preference for Certain Domestic Commodities, when exceeding the simplified acquisition threshold.

DFARS 252.225-7049, Prohibition on Acquisition of Certain Foreign Commercial Satellite Services—Representations.

DFARS 252.225–7055, Representation Regarding Business Operations with the Maduro Regime.

DFARS 252.225-7056, Prohibition Regarding Business Operations with the Maduro Regime.

DFARS 252.225-7057, Preaward Disclosure of Employment of Individuals Who Work in the People's Republic of China.

DFARS 252.225–7059, Prohibition on Certain Procurements from the Xinjiang Uyghur Autonomous Region–Certification

Solicitation Provisions and Contract Clauses

DFARS 252.209-7004, Subcontracting with Firms that are Owned or Controlled by the Government of a Country that is a State Sponsor of Terrorism, if over $150,000 in value.

DFARS 252.225-7005, Identification of Expenditures in the United States, when exceeding the simplified acquisition threshold for supplies or services (including construction) for use outside the United States.

DFARS 252.225-7006, Acquisition of the American Flag, for the acquisition of the American flag, with an estimated value that exceeds the simplified acquisition threshold.

DFARS 252.225-7007, Prohibition on Acquisition of United States Munitions List Items from Communist Chinese Military Companies, involving the delivery of items covered by the United States Munitions List, unless an exception in DFARS 225.770-3 applies.

DFARS 252.225-7015, Restriction on Acquisition of Hand or Measuring Tools, when exceeding the simplified acquisition threshold and requiring delivery of hand or measuring tools.

DFARS 252.225-7041, Correspondence in English, when contract performance will be wholly or in part in a foreign country.

DFARS 252.225-7042, Authorization to Perform, in solicitations when contract performance will be wholly or in part in a foreign country. Do not use if the solicitation includes FAR 52.204-7.

DFARS 252.225-7053, Representation Regarding Prohibition on Use of Certain Energy Sourced from Inside the Russian Federation.

DFARS 252.225-7054, Prohibition on Use of Certain Energy Sourced from Inside the Russian Federation.

Contract Clause

DFARS 252.225-7051, Prohibition on Acquisition of Certain Foreign Commercial Satellite Services.

DFARS 252.225-7052, Restriction on the Acquisition of Certain Magnets and Tungsten.

DFARS 252.225–7056, Prohibition Regarding Business Operations with the Maduro Regime.

DFARS 252.225-7058, Postaward Disclosure of Employment of Individuals Who Work in the People's Republic of China.

DFARS 252.225–7060, Prohibition on Certain Procurements from the Xinjiang Uyghur Autonomous Region.

DFARS 252.225-7061, Restriction on the Acquisition of Personal Protective Equipment and Certain Other Items from Non-Allied Foreign Nations.

2.14 INNOVATIVE CONTRACTING METHODS

2.14.1 MultiYear Contracting

FAR 17.1

A *multiyear contract* allows for supplies or services purchases for up to five years. Performance during the second and subsequent years of the contract may be contingent upon the appropriation of funds, with a cancellation payment to the contractor if appropriations are not made. There is no need to exercise an option for each program year.

The contracting officer may enter into a multiyear contract if the head of the contracting activity determines that the need for the supplies or services is reasonably firm and continuing over the period of the contract, and that a multiyear contract will encourage full and open competition or promote economy in agency administration and operation. For DoD, the head of the agency must further determine that the:

- contract will lead to substantial program cost savings over annual contracts;
- design is stable and the technical risks are not excessive;
- estimates of both the cost and its avoidance through the use of a multiyear contract are realistic;
- head of the agency plans to have sufficient funding to avoid contract cancellation; and
- minimum procurement quantity is expected to remain substantially unchanged during the contract period.

Use of multiyear contracting can provide many benefits, such as:

- broadened competitive base for firms not otherwise willing or able to compete for lesser quantities (often due to high startup costs);
- enhanced standardization;
- established quality control techniques and procedures;
- incentives to improve productivity through investment in capital facilities, equipment and technology;
- realistic estimates of contract cost and savings (and hopefully, lower costs);
- reduced administrative burden in contract placement and administration;
- stabilized contractor planning and work forces;
- stable design and funding; and
- substantial continuity of production or performance (thus avoiding annual startup, preproduction testing and phase-out costs).

If funds are not appropriated to support the succeeding years' requirements, the agency must cancel the contract. This means that all program years after the first are subject to cancellation. This cancellation must occur within a contractually specified time. The contracting officer either notifies the contractor of nonavailability of funds, or else declines to notify the contractor that funds are available for performance of the succeeding program year.

For each program year subject to cancellation, the contracting officer establishes a *cancellation ceiling*. This represents the Government's maximum liability to the contractor should the contract be cancelled. This ceiling amount (also called *cancellation charges*) covers the contractor's nonrecurring costs (and perhaps some recurring costs, such as economic order quantities) which would have been recouped through amortization over the full term of the contract. Ceilings exclude amounts for requirements included in prior program years because they are prospective only. They decrease for each program year in direct proportion to the remaining requirements which are subject to cancellation. This concept differs from *termination costs*, which can be imposed at any time during the life of the contract and can apply to partial or total quantities.

The Government can fully fund this ceiling and hold the funds in reserve, or it can create an unfunded contingent liability that must nonetheless be covered if termination occurs. The cancellation ceiling is not an evaluation factor in source selection.

In determining cancellation ceilings, the contracting officer estimates preproduction or startup costs, labor learning and other nonrecurring costs which can be amortized across multiyear requirements. Here a distinction in cost categorization is necessary. *Recurring costs* include operating and maintenance costs that vary with production operations and recur repeatedly during the life cycle of the product or service. By contrast, *nonrecurring costs* are generally incurred on a one-time basis, such as:

- facilities to be acquired or established;
- pilot runs;
- plant or equipment relocation or rearrangement;
- preproduction engineering;
- special tooling and special test equipment;
- specialized work force training and transportation to/from the work site; and
- spoilage and rework.

Nonrecurring costs exclude any labor, material or other expenses which might be incurred to perform subsequent program year requirements. The total estimate of these costs is then compared with the contract cost estimate (based on in-house engineering cost estimates and the effect of labor learning) to arrive at a reasonable percentage or dollar figure to derive a cancellation ceiling.

Solicitations for multiyear contracts reflect all the factors to be considered for evaluation, specifically including the Government's:

- acknowledgement that award cannot be made for less than the first program year requirements;
- administrative costs of annual contracting, if known upfront;
- criteria to compare the lowest evaluated proposal for the first-year requirements to that for the multiyear requirements;
- evaluated price or estimated cost and fee for the first year only;
- requirements for the first program year and estimates for the total multiyear period; and
- separate cancellation ceiling on a percentage or dollar basis for each program year subject to cancellation.

Funding of multiyear contracts must conform to OMB Circular A-11, Preparation and Submission of Budget Estimates, which is the Government's "cookbook" on developing budget projections for upcoming fiscal years.[149] Multiyear contracts to acquire fixed assets are either funded in full or in economic or programmatic stages. When the period of production is likely to warrant a labor and material cost contingency in the contract price, the contracting officer uses an economic price adjustment clause.

A multiyear contract which includes a cancellation ceiling in excess of $114.5 million may not be awarded until the head of the agency gives written notification of the proposed contract and cancellation ceiling to the

Appropriations and Armed Services Committees of the Senate and House of Representatives, and allows 30 days before award.

Contract Clauses

FAR 52.217-2, Cancellation Under Multiyear Contracts.

2.14.2 Options

FAR 17.2

An *option* is a unilateral contract right for a specified time during which the Government may elect to obtain additional quantities of supplies or services or extend the period of performance. Options are used when the foreseeable requirements involve minimum economic quantities which are large enough to permit recovery of startup and production costs at a reasonable price. Options are also appropriate when future requirements permit competitive acquisition, production, and delivery. Service contracts may use options when the Government needs continuity of operations and the potential cost of disrupted support is unacceptable. Options are not appropriate when procuring architect-engineer services or the contractor will incur undue risks, such as uncertain availability or pricing of necessary materials or labor. Nor are they used when known firm requirements are funded. If the basic quantity is for learning or testing purposes and competition for the option is impracticable after initial contract award, then an option amount may not be appropriate. Options are also not appropriate in risky situations, such as when market prices for the supplies or services are likely to change substantially or the contractor will incur undue risks, such as uncertain availability or pricing of necessary materials or labor. Solicitations containing option provisions state whether evaluation excludes or includes the option, and inform offerors that the Government may exercise the option at time of award. In this case, solicitations specify how the Government will evaluate the option (e.g., highest option price offered, or option price for specified requirements).

Solicitations normally allow option quantities to be offered without price restriction. However, the solicitation may instead require that options be offered at prices no higher than those for the initial requirement, such as when future competition for the option is impracticable. Such solicitations specify that the Government will accept an option price higher than the base price only if it does not prejudice any other offeror. Solicitations also limit option quantities to 50 percent or less of the initial quantity of the line item (a level above the contracting officer may approve a greater percentage).

The contract specifies the period within which the option may be exercised. This provides the contractor adequate lead time to ensure continuous production. This period may extend beyond the contract completion date for service contracts when the option requires obligation of funds that are not yet available in the future fiscal year. Unless otherwise approved in accordance with legislation or agency procedures, the total of the basic and option periods cannot exceed five years of requirements (though information technology contracts may run for a longer period of time).

Contracts may include options for increased amounts of supplies or services in terms of percentage, quantity, or additional numbered line items. Contracts may express extensions of the contract length as a later completion date or additional time for performance. The contracting officer justifies in writing the quantities or the term under option, the notification period for exercising the option, and any limitation on option pricing.

In awarding the basic contract, the contracting officer evaluates offers for any option quantities or periods contained in a solicitation if (s)he determines prior to soliciting offers that the Government is likely to exercise the options. This determination is mandatory under sealed bidding and customary for negotiation, unless determined at a level above the contracting officer that evaluation would not be in the best interests of the Government (e.g., funds will likely be unavailable to permit exercise of the option).

When exercising an option, the contracting officer provides written notice to the contractor within the time period specified in the contract (usually 30 or 60 days before expiration of the current year). If the contractor requests an economic price adjustment per contract terms, the contracting officer must consider the effect of the adjustment on competitive pricing. The contracting officer may exercise options only after determining in writing that:

- a new solicitation fails to produce a better price or a more advantageous offer than that included in the option;
- an informal price analysis or market survey indicates that thc option price is better than prices available in the market (often used when the option date is shortly after initial award);
- exercise of the option is the most advantageous method of fulfilling the Government's need (considering continuity of operations, costs of disrupting operations, effect on small business, and price);
- funds are available;
- the contractor is not listed on the Excluded Parties List System;
- the option was synopsized; and
- the requirement covered by the option fulfills an existing Government need.

DoD has several special requirements for option evaluation and exercise. Per 10 U.S.C. 2305(a)(5), sealed bid solicitations cannot include provisions for evaluating options unless the contracting officer determines that there is a reasonable likelihood that the options will be exercised.[150] Before exercising an option, the contracting officer must determine that the contractor's records in SAM, DUNS and CAGE codes, name and physical address are accurate. Also, before exercising an option for firm-fixed-price contracts containing spare parts (except micro-purchases), the contracting officer must analyze the cost or price of the proposed spare parts by an appropriate sampling technique or request field pricing assistance.

PGI 217.2

The first two options for major systems should normally be priced at time of award. If quantities are not firm, range option pricing may be appropriate.

Solicitation Provisions

FAR 52.217-3, Evaluation Exclusive of Options.

FAR 52.217-4, Evaluation of Options Exercised at Time of Contract Award, if the option clause will probably be exercised.

FAR 52.217-5, Evaluation of Options, if firm-fixed-price with an option clause that will probably be exercised after contract award.

Solicitation Provisions and Contract Clauses

FAR 52.217-6, Option for Increased Quantity, for supplies with an option quantity expressed as a percentage of the basic contract quantity or an additional quantity of a specific line item.

FAR 52.217-7, Option for Increased Quantity—Separately Priced Line Item, for supplies with an option quantity identified as a separately priced line item having the same nomenclature as the basic contract line item.

FAR 52.217-8, Option to Extend Services.

FAR 52.217-9, Option to Extend the Term of the Contract, if the Government must give the contractor either a preliminary written notice of its intent to extend the contract or else a specified limitation on the total duration of the contract.

DFARS 252.217-7000, Exercise of Option to Fulfill Foreign Military Sales Commitments, when an option may be used for foreign military sales requirements. Do not use the basic or alternate clause to establish or replenish DoD inventories or stocks, or acquisitions made under DoD cooperative logistics support arrangements. Use the basic clause when the foreign military sales country is known at the time of solicitation or award. Use Alternate I when the foreign military sale country is not known at the time of solicitation or award.

DFARS 252.217-7001, Surge Option, when a surge option is needed in support of industrial capability production planning. Insert the percentage of increase the option represents in paragraph (a) of the clause to ensure adequate quantities are available to meet item requirements. As appropriate, change 30 days in paragraphs (b)(2) and (d)(1) to longer periods, and the 24-month period in paragraph (c)(3).

2.14.3 Leader Company Contracting

FAR 17.4

The Government may designate a developer or sole producer of a product or system as the *leader company* to furnish assistance and knowledge under contract to one or more designated *follower* companies, so they can become a future source of supply. This approach may be used to develop a second source for production. The objectives of this technique can include:

- economies in production;
- eliminating problems with proprietary data;
- equipment compatibility, reliability and uniformity, as well as interchangeable and standardized components;
- geographic dispersion of suppliers;
- maximized use of scarce tooling or special equipment;
- reduced delivery time; and
- transition from development to production and subsequent competitive acquisition of major end items or components.

Leader company contracting is to be used only when:

- assistance is limited to that necessary to enable the follower(s) to produce the items;
- no other source could meet the Government's requirements without the aid of a leader company;
- the contract contains a disclosure agreement of any proprietary data or software, trade secrets, and technical concepts or designs;
- the firm has the production knowledge and can furnish assistance to the follower(s);
- the Government reserves the right to approve subcontracts between the leader company and the follower(s); and
- use is authorized in accordance with agency procedures.

The contracting officer may award a contract to a leader company, obligating it to subcontract a designated portion of the end items to a specified follower company and to assist it in production. Alternatively, the contract may require the leader company to assist a follower company, and the follower to produce the items. There can also be a contract awarded to the follower company, obligating it to subcontract with a designated leader company for required assistance.

2.14.4 Interagency Acquisitions

FAR 17.5

The Economy Act authorizes agencies to enter into mutual agreements to obtain supplies or services on an inter-agency basis.[151] *Interagency acquisition* is a procedure by which an agency needing supplies or services (the *requesting agency*) obtains them from another agency (the *servicing agency*), or from a different unit within the same department or agency. Agency regulations prescribe procedures for such transactions.[152]

The Economy Act is not used for acquisitions conflicting with any other agency's authority or responsibility, especially to circumvent conditions and limitations imposed on the use of funds. It cannot be invoked to contract out inherently Governmental functions or for procurements which have separate statutory authority (e.g., Federal Supply Schedule contracts or Government-wide acquisition contracts).

The requesting agency writes a D&F which concludes that the use of an interagency acquisition represents the best procurement approach. It then obtains the concurrence of the requesting agency's contracting office in accordance with internal agency procedures. The determination for a *directed acquisition* (where an agency places an award against another agency's indefinite delivery contract) further includes an analysis that the acquisition services of another agency:

- has prudent procurement approaches;
- is cost effective with its servicing fees;
- satisfies the requesting agency's:
  - customer satisfaction,
  - delivery requirements,
  - performance, and
  - schedule; and
- will legally use funds in accordance with appropriation restrictions and the requesting agency's laws and policies.

The D&F also states that the servicing agency has an existing contract, or has capabilities or expertise not available within the requesting agency to contract for such supplies or services, or is specifically authorized by law or regulation to purchase such supplies or services on behalf of other agencies. This D&F is included in the package sent to the servicing agency.

For an *assisted acquisition* (where one agency asks another to procure on its behalf), the analysis also addresses the expertise of the requesting agency to place orders and administer them, against the other agency's selected contract vehicle throughout the acquisition lifecycle. The analysis must also assess the contract's suitability and value in terms of lower prices and administrative cost savings, as well as increasing the number of potential vendors.

Before solicitation, the two agencies sign a written interagency agreement to establish the terms and conditions of their relationship, such as roles and responsibilities for acquisition planning, contract execution and administration. The requesting agency provides any unique terms or conditions, laws or regulations, directives, and requirements for the order or contract.[153] The two agencies should agree to procedures for resolving disputes between them. If they agree on third-party resolution, the third party should agree in writing. Work placed with an FFRDC is subject to acceptance by the sponsor and must fall within the mission, scope of effort or competency of the FFRDC without placing the FFRDC in direct competition with domestic private industry.

The servicing agency must also develop a D&F that provides a business case that its use is in the best interest of the Government, and that the supplies or services cannot be obtained as conveniently or economically by contracting directly with a private source. The D&F also addresses the following:

- costs to award and administer the contract;
- impact of award on Government purchasing power;
- need for the contract;
- roles and responsibilities of contract administration; and
- strategies for promoting the use of small businesses.

The servicing agency is responsible for generating any required J&A or additional D&F for the procurement action.

The order may be placed on any form or document that is acceptable to both agencies, and includes the acquisition authority, delivery requirement(s), description of the supplies or services, funds citation, and payment provision. Several specific procedures apply to contractor payment. The servicing agency may direct the requesting agency to fully fund the procurement in advance, with adjustment based on negotiated or actual cost. Or instead, the servicing agency may ask for reimbursement after contract completion. Advance payment requests and bills may not be audited or certified before payment. In addition, the servicing agency may charge the requesting agency the actual cost of award or administration, but not an arbitrary fixed fee. In fact, the servicing agency cannot compel the requiring agency to pay any fee in excess of the actual cost (or estimated cost if the actual cost is not known) of entering into and administering the contract.

If a civilian agency is asked to place an order on behalf of a Defense activity, it is still bound to comply with FAR, DFARS and class deviations. Further, the civilian agency must certify its compliance in writing to the Under Secretary of Defense (Acquisition, Technology and Logistics) (AT&L).

Often, interagency acquisitions simply utilize indefinite-delivery contracts for task and delivery orders. Most often, these are FSS, GWACs and multi-agency contracts. In the past, agencies used an interagency acquisition to circumvent funding conditions and limitations. Certain restrictions are now in place to prevent this abuse; however, it is still allowed routinely for orders of $600,000 or less issued against Federal Supply Schedules.[154]

PGI 217.502

Before any DoD contracting activity provides acquisition assistance to deployed units or personnel from another DoD Component, a written inter-agency agreement between components is documented on the DD Form 1144, Support Agreement, with procurement support provided on a non-reimbursable basis (unless the parties mutually agree otherwise) and use a DD Form 448, Military Interdepartmental Purchase Request to document a description of the supplies/services and certification of funds.

PGI 217.770

Departments and agencies establish and maintain procedures to review and approve orders placed under non-DoD contracts for supplies and services in excess of the simplified acquisition threshold. These reviews evaluate whether using a non-DoD contract for the acquisition is in the best interest of DoD by considering customer satisfaction, schedule, cost effectiveness, and contract administration. The reviews collect and analyze data to examine whether the tasks or supplies to be provided are within the scope of the contract to be used and if funding is within appropriation limitations.

2.14.5 Management and Operating Contracts

FAR 17.6

A *management and operating contract* (also known as a *facilities* contract) covers effort to operate, maintain or support a Government-owned or -controlled research, development, special production, or testing establishment. These are known as *Government-owned contractor-operated (GOCO)* facilities. They differ from COCO or GOGO facilities, where the acronym identifies the owner and operator of the facilities. Hence, contractors own and operate COCOs and the Government does both duties for GOGOs.

This facility is often owned by either the Department of Defense or Energy, but could be statutorily assigned to other agencies. These Government-owned or -controlled facilities are utilized to promote the national defense or mobilization readiness, or because private enterprise is unable or unwilling to use its own facilities for the work. The conduct of the work is separate from the contractor's other business, and is of a long-term or continuing nature. These precautions ensure both continuity of operations and an orderly transition of personnel and work should there be a change in contractors.

The Government is often limited in its ability to effect competition or to replace a contractor. Hence, contracting officers must ensure that the prospective contractor's technical and managerial capacity are sufficient, resolve organizational conflicts of interest, and retain for the Government continuing rights in technical and managerial decision-making regarding performance.

Management and operating contracts are not authorized for functions involving:

- authorizing use and rental of Government property;
- daily agency staff or management functions;
- determining Government policies;
- direction or control of Government personnel (unless incidental to training); or
- exercise of police or regulatory powers, other than guard services or plant protection.

The contracting officer reviews each management and operating contract at least once every five years to determine whether meaningful improvement in performance or cost might reasonably be achieved. Any extension or renewal is authorized at the same level within the agency as where the original contract was authorized. When reviewing contractor performance, contracting officers consider the incumbent contractor's overall performance (administrative, cost and technical) and the potential impact of a change in contractors or program needs (e.g., mobilization, national defense and safety) through completion.

2.14.6 Emergency Acquisitions

FAR 18

Emergency acquisitions are determined by the head of an executive agency in support of a contingency operation to facilitate the defense against or recovery from biological, chemical, nuclear, or radiological attack against the United States. They can also occur when the President declares an incident of national emergency or a major disaster (such as a hurricane) under the Robert T. Stafford Disaster Relief and Emergency Assistance Act.[155]

Contractors are not required to be registered in SAM to obtain a contract to support unusual and compelling needs or emergency acquisitions. However, they must register with SAM in order to gain access to the Disaster Response Registry.[156] Contracting officers will consult the Registry to determine the availability of contractors for debris removal, distribution of supplies, reconstruction, and other disaster or emergency relief activities inside the United States and outlying areas. The following changes to normal procurement procedures occur:

- agencies may limit the number of sources;
- agencies need not enforce qualification requirements;
- authorization under the North American Free Trade Agreement prior to use of a patented technology may be waived;
- contracting officers are not restricted to an AbilityOne notification if changes in specifications or descriptions are required;
- contracting officers may solicit from only one source for purchases not exceeding the simplified acquisition threshold;
- contracting officers need not submit a synopsis notice;
- contracts may be awarded on a sole-source basis to HUBZone and Service-Disabled Veteran-owned small business concerns;
- contracts to the SBA for 8(a) firms may be awarded on either a sole-source or competitive basis;
- electronic funds transfer payments may be waived;
- interagency acquisitions are authorized;
- letter contracts may be used;
- oral requests for proposals are authorized;
- overtime approvals may be retroactive if justified;
- preference in the form of local area set-asides or evaluation preference will be given to local firms, individuals, and organizations;
- purchase from UNICOR is not mandatory and a waiver is not required;
- rental requirements do not apply to certain items of Government production and research property if approved by FEMA;
- the chief of the contracting office may waive the requirement to obtain a bid guarantee when a performance bond is required;
- the contracting officer has the authority under PL 85-804 to amend contracts without consideration, authorize advance payments, correct or mitigate non-fraudulent mistakes in a contract, or formalize informal commitments in the interest of national defense;

- the head of the contracting activity may determine that the contracting process may continue after GAO has received a protest;
- the no-setoff provision for assignment of claims may be used; and
- trade agreement policies need not apply to acquisitions awarded noncompetitively.

The head of the contracting agency may determine in writing to increase the thresholds for micro-purchases, simplified acquisitions, or the commercial items test program to facilitate defense against or recover from such attacks. Using the same procedure, the same official can also treat any acquisition of supplies or services as commercial items, or else waive the provisions of the Cargo Preference Act of 1954 that require use of American-flagged vessels to carry cargo.[157]

On a broader scale, the National Response Framework establishes a comprehensive, national approach to domestic incident response by identifying key response principles, roles and structures. It describes how communities, state and Federal governments, the private sector, and nongovernmental partners apply these principles for a coordinated, effective national response. It also describes when the Federal Government exercises a larger role, such as catastrophic incidents where a state would require significant support.[158]

DFARs 218.201

There are numerous requirements that do not apply to DoD-unique emergency contracting scenarios. These scenarios include attack or disaster or emergency assistance. The contracting officer qualification requirements for a baccalaureate degree and 24 semester credit hours of business related courses do not apply to DoD employees or members of the armed forces who are in a contingency contracting force.

Government-wide commercial purchase cards are not required for purchases valued at or below the micro-purchase threshold for an overseas transaction to support either a contingency operation or for training exercises in preparation of emergency, humanitarian, or peacekeeping operations. The purchase card can be used to make a purchase that exceeds the micro-purchase threshold but does not exceed the simplified acquisition threshold if certain conditions are met. Imprest funds are used without further approval for overseas transactions at or below the micro-purchase threshold in support of a contingency operation or a humanitarian or peacekeeping operation. The Standard Form (SF) 44, Purchase Order-Invoice-Voucher, may be used for purchases not exceeding the simplified acquisition threshold for overseas transactions by contracting officers in support of these operations. Upon declaration of the emergency, the simplified acquisition threshold is raised to $300,000 for DoD purchases that are awarded and performed outside the United States in support of that operation.

The head of the agency may waive certain limitations for undefinitized contract actions upon determination that the waiver is necessary to support a contingency operation or a humanitarian or peacekeeping operation. Contractors need not provide DoD-unique item identification if the head of the agency determines the items will be used to facilitate defense against or recovery from biological, chemical, nuclear, or radiological attack. Contractors need not submit payment requests in electronic form for contracts awarded by deployed contracting officers these operations.

In these emergency situations, the usual restrictions on food, clothing, fabrics, specialty metals, and hand or measuring tools, does not apply to acquisitions:[159]

- at or below the simplified acquisition threshold,
- by activities located outside the United States for personnel of those activities in emergencies;
- for food, specialty metals, or hand or measuring tools in support of contingency operations, or for which the use of other than competitive procedures has been approved based on unusual and compelling urgency in accordance with FAR 6.302-2;
- for vessels in foreign waters;
- of perishable foods for personnel located outside the United States; or
- outside the United States in support of combat operations.

PGI 218.271

Use of electronic business (e-business) acquisition tools greatly enhances the efficiency of the contracting process in a contingency business environment to quickly obtain goods and services for the warfighter in an operational area. One example is the 3in1 Tool to automate the field order, receipt and purchase processes in lieu of the paper Standard Form 44. This handheld device records and transmits "cash-and-carry" purchases and payment data to the prime database for remote reconciliation and review. It is useful when conducting on-the-spot and over-the-counter field purchases where use of the Government Purchase Card is not feasible. The 3in1 database may be accessed on the Joint Contingency Contracting Systems (JCCS) website.[160]

Another tool is the Acquisition Cross-Servicing Agreements Global Automated Tracking and Reporting System (AGATRS). This is an automated tool that tracks and provides visibility into worldwide agreements that may satisfy a requirement through support from the host nation or other nations supporting the contingency. Such transactions used in support of contingency or humanitarian or peacekeeping operations must be documented and tracked in AGATRS per the Chairman of the Joint Chiefs of Staff Instruction 2120.01C, Acquisition Cross Servicing Agreements.[161]

2.14.7 Alpha Contracting

Alpha contracting is an acquisition process adopted to reduce the cycle time of sole-source acquisitions. It promotes use of contractor and government teaming without compromising acquisition goals. An approved acquisition plan is required. A Joint Government/Industry Team develops requirements, conducts an audit, determines the price, and drafts the contract. There is no solicitation or proposal; rather, the team addresses the technical and cost details to draft a model contract prior to final pricing. The team may even recommend changes to the program baseline to improve performance or to reduce cost or risk. The model contract is revised as technical and price details are resolved, and then becomes the official contract document.

Success requires open communications early in the process, mutual understanding of the statement of work, and agreement on appropriate scope and hours. The contractor and Government negotiating teams use the same cost and pricing data spreadsheet format and software version to facilitate negotiations and documentation.

2.14.8 Pilot Mentor-Protégé Program

DFARS Appendix I, I-100

The Pilot Mentor-Protégé Program motivates major DoD contractors to assist protégé firms to enhance their capabilities and participation for DoD (sub) contract requirements and establish long-term business relationships between protégé firms and such contractors. Under the Program, eligible companies approved as mentor firms will enter into agreements with eligible protégé firms to provide appropriate developmental assistance. DoD may provide the mentor firm with either cost reimbursement or credit against applicable subcontracting goals established under contracts with DoD or other Federal agencies.

Mentors are generally large businesses, whereas the protégés tend to small or socially disadvantaged business. Mentor firms will be solely responsible for selecting protégé firms and have no limit on how many protégés it helps. By contrast, a protégé firm may have only one active DoD mentor-protégé agreement.

Prospective mentors and their protégés may choose to execute letters of intent prior to negotiation of mentor-protégé agreements. The agreements should be structured after assessing and the developmental assistance to be provided to enhance the protégé's ability to perform successfully under (sub) contracts. The mentor-protégé agreement may provide for the mentor firm to furnish any or all of the following types of developmental assistance:

- advance payments under such subcontracts;
- assistance by mentor firm personnel in general business management, production inventory control and quality assurance;
- award of subcontracts on a noncompetitive basis;
- investment(s) in the protégé firm in exchange for an ownership interest of up to 10 percent in the protégé firm;
- loans; and
- progress payments for the performance of subcontracts in amounts as provided for in the subcontract; but in no event may any such progress payment exceed 100 percent of the costs incurred by the protégé firm for the performance of the subcontract, unless unusual progress payments are approved by the head of the contracting activity.

Pursuant to FAR 31.109, approved mentor firms seeking credit or reimbursement should enter into an advance agreement with the contracting officer responsible for determining final indirect cost rates. This agreement will establish the accounting treatment of the costs of the developmental assistance before the mentor firm incurs any costs. Otherwise, mentor firms will establish the accounting treatment of such costs and any necessary changes to their cost accounting practices.

A program participation term for the agreement that does not exceed 3 years, although a two-year extension may be approved by the agency small business director. The protégé firm must comply with reporting requirements review the agreement up to two years after the expiration date.

A mentor firm may voluntarily terminate its mentor-protégé agreement(s) with 30 day-notice only if it no longer wants to be a participant in the Program as a mentor firm. Otherwise, a mentor firm must terminate a mentor-protégé agreement for cause. It can terminate the mentor-protégé agreement for cause with 30 days' notice, allowing the protégé 30 days to respond. The mentor's final decision is not reviewable by DoD.

The mentor-protege agreement must be approved by the agency small business director, prior to incurring costs eligible for credit. The cognizant DoD component will execute a contract modification or a separate contract prior to the mentor's incurring costs eligible for reimbursement. The total amount reimbursed to a mentor firm for costs of assistance furnished to a protege firm in a fiscal year may not exceed $1,000,000 without approval by the same official. Developmental assistance costs that are incurred pursuant to an approved reimbursable mentor-protege agreement, and have not been reimbursed through a separate contract, is not reimbursable. There are a few very specific exceptions.

Mentors must submit progress reports semiannually covering costs, expenditures, credits toward applicable subcontracting goals, the developmental assistance provided, and capabilities enhanced, certifications received, and/or technology transferred. The protégé must provide an annual progress report covering employment, revenues, and participation. These reports will be reviewed by DCMA for cot reasonableness and data accuracy.

2.14.9 Economic Order Quantities

FAR 7.2

An *economic order quantity* is that amount which minimizes all associated costs by equating carrying and acquisition costs. Each solicitation for supplies invites the offeror to indicate if the solicited quantity of supplies is economically advantageous to the Government, and, if not, to recommend an alternative quantity which includes a unit price and total amount.

Contracting officers take no action to revise quantities to be acquired on the instant procurement unless a significant price variation is evident from the offers and a potential for significant savings has arisen. Then, the contracting officer consults with the cognizant inventory manager or requirements development activity before proceeding.

Solicitation Provision

FAR 52.207-4, Economic Purchase Quantity—Supplies, except for a GSA multiple award schedule, or if the data is already available to the Government.

2.14.10 Telecommuting

FAR 7.108

Telecommuting is actually a controversial subject in Government performance, especially in terms of contractor performance and Government oversight. Government managers will disagree on whether contract workers can be allowed to perform from home or a nearby telework center, or whether they must sit in Government owned or rented spaces (which are not free and raise the specter of personal services). Congress has stepped into this dispute by prohibiting an agency from discouraging a contractor who wishes to allow its employees to telecommute in the performance of Government contracts.[162] However, the contracting officer can determine that the requirements of the agency, such as frequent meetings or security requirements, cannot be met if telecommuting is permitted. There is no current program for either the Government or the contractor to either encourage or discourage telecommuting among contract employees.

2.14.11 Equipment Lease versus Purchase

Agencies consider whether to lease or purchase equipment based on a case-by-case evaluation of comparative costs and other factors, such as:

- availability of a servicing capability;
- availability of purchase options;
- cumulative rental payments for the estimated period of use;
- estimated length and extent of usage;
- financial and operating advantages of alternative types and makes of equipment;
- imputed interest;
- maintenance and other service costs;
- net purchase price;
- potential future use of the equipment by other agencies;
- potential obsolescence of equipment due to imminent technological improvements;
- trade-in or salvage value; and
- transportation and installation costs.

Generally, purchase is preferable to rental if the equipment will be used beyond the point in time when cumulative leasing costs exceed the purchase price. Alternatively, the lease method may be better when circumstances require immediate use of equipment to meet program or system needs but do not justify purchase for the long term. If a lease is justified, an option to purchase is preferable, specified in the contract as either a firm price or a formula for how the purchase price will be established at the time of purchase. Generally, a long-term lease should be avoided, unless an option to purchase or other favorable terms are included.

DFARS 207.401

If the lease will exceed 60 days, the requiring activity must prepare and provide the contracting officer with the justification supporting the decision to lease or purchase.

DFARS 207.470

No aircraft, combat vehicle or vessel may be leased or chartered for 18 months or more unless the head of the contracting activity so determines in writing by considering all costs (including termination liability). Commercial vehicles and associated equipment can be leased by contracting officer determination that leasing is both efficient and practicable.

Solicitation Provision and Contract Clause

FAR 52.207-5, Option to Purchase Equipment.

2.14.12 Outsourcing

Outsourcing is the process of subcontracting effort to an outside firm. Outsourcing provides the prime contractor with benefits to:

- access intellectual property;
- develop a core business;
- improve quality with a new service level agreement;
- make variable costs more predictable;
- manage a change in production level;
- promote risk management through a more capable source of supply;[163]
- reduce overall cost of the service;
- reduce time to market;
- standardize business processes and information technology services, especially when too difficult or time-consuming to develop in-house;
- supplement limited in-house capacity by accessing a larger talent pool of science and engineering skills; or
- use a contract with financial penalties and legal redress, which cannot be done if retained in-house.

The prime contractor must decide how to align its interests with its subcontractor to promote their common goals. This should lead to a governance structure that facilitates discussions between the parties to thoroughly understand the interests of both. A contract manager may be dedicated on a full-time basis to attend meetings, monitor operations for compliance with contract terms, review and maintain procedures, and track communications.

As a critical element of outsourcing, quality of service is measured through a service level agreement. Quality can be measured through customer satisfaction questionnaires which are professionally designed to capture an unbiased view of quality tracked over time and to identify corrective action to be taken.

Foreign sources provide challenges for outsourcing. Laws and taxes in foreign nations, as well as administrative procedures, must be followed. Labor unions, workforce structure and management control may also be different. Language barriers, especially where words may have different meanings, could be a problem (even between English-speaking countries).

Sometimes, public opinion in the United States opposes offshoring because it leads to job displacement and workforce insecurity. This could become especially critical as public opinion seems to be turning against sending jobs out of the country. Offshore outsourcing solely to save cost could diminish the real productivity of a company. Firms may reduce employment and outsource work to firms offshore that appear to be more productive simply because the workers are paid less. This may be illusory however, since increased productivity often results from more productive tools or operating methods that make it possible for a worker to do more work in a given time period. Yet offshore outsourcing may reduce prices and provide greater economic benefit, so the controversy continues.

2.14.13 E-Procurement

E-procurement is a paperless, electronic form of procurement that involves B2B, B2C or B2G purchase and sale over the Internet. Typically, e-procurement websites allow registered users to look for buyers or sellers to invite or submit offers. Repetitive purchases may qualify customers for volume discounts. E-procurement allows vendors to control inventories, reduce purchasing payroll and manufacturing cycles, and obtain real-time information of customer needs. Both Government (through simplified acquisitions) and contractors may use e-procurement for commercial products.

There are at least seven versions of e-procurement:

- *e-informing*: gather and distribute purchasing information both from and to internal and external parties;
- *e-market sites*: buyers access suppliers' websites, add to shopping carts, create and approve requisitions, receive purchase orders, and process invoices;
- *e-MRO* (Maintenance, Repair and Overhaul): order goods and services that are not product-related;
- *e-reverse auctioning*: buy goods and services from a number of suppliers;
- *e-sourcing*: identify new suppliers;
- *e-tendering*: send and receive requests for information and prices to suppliers; and
- *Web-based Enterprise Resource Planning*: create and approve requisitions, place purchase orders, track deliveries, manage inventory, and receive goods and services.

Electronic contracting contains three main methods of transactions. A *shrink-wrap contract* purchases off-the-shelf products such as software, delivered with documented terms and conditions. This type of transaction has been around for some years and exists in both paper and electronic environments. Secondly, a *click-wrap agreement* made on a website requires the buyer to click "I agree" before the transaction continues or the user gains access to the website. In the *browse-wrap transaction*, the user accesses a website where terms and conditions are posted but does not require the user to click assent to these terms before paying for the product.

All three methods have raised fundamental questions about what types of conduct constitute assent to terms and conditions. There have been concerns about how to treat terms that are not proposed or disclosed until after the user has already agreed to go forward with the transaction and made payment. One can also question whether there was assent, when it was manifested, and whether it covers terms about which the user had no knowledge or understanding. Fortunately, the incidence of unexpected terms should diminish as lawyers work to improve the focus of the terms and conditions which are acknowledged before purchase is completed.

Electronic Data Interchange is a structured transmission of business data in a standardized format between systems (known as *trading partners*) without human intervention. The documents are transmitted between sender and receiver via telecommunications over a third-party value-added network, or else via electronic storage media. The sending computer connects to the Internet through a modulator-demodulator (*modem*) which converts computer-stored information into an audio tone that can pass over the telephone wire. Then at the receiving end, the tone can be reconverted into computer-readable data. This process is used for electronic commerce for a variety of business functions such as solicitation, award, modification, billing, and shipping.

The Government can also do electronic funds transfer between bank accounts to pay contractors via electronic bill payment or payment card. Although several sets of standards prescribe formats, character sets and data elements, the predominant formatting in North America is the American Standard Code for Information Interchange (X12).

These electronic transactions use an *encryption* algorithm to make the information in the electronic transfer unreadable to anyone who does not have the key to decrypt the cipher. Most firms encrypt data transfers and stored data. Messages use a message authentication code or digital signature to ensure they are genuine and to protect the validity of the data.

2.14.14 Communications Among Stakeholders

There are several opportunities during the acquisition cycle when communications can effectively save money and time. Early focus on developmental planning efforts enables program offices to understand refresh and replacement cycle timelines for various technologies. This enables inclusion of life-cycle opportunities for technology insertion into program plans. These opportunities can include commercial technologies, industry efforts funded through Independent Research and Development programs, military technologies maturing through rapid prototyping, and science and technology transitioning from government laboratories.

Much of the Defense acquisition community's program results are attained in relationship with industry. Several specific efforts can improve acquisition outcomes by leveraging a strong and open relationship with industry. One is to provide draft technical requirements to industry early, and iteratively if necessary. This avoids the program teams from operating under misconceptions. A typical Request for Proposal (RFP) will give industry 30–60 days to provide a proposal, even for large-scale systems developments. However, short timelines are beneficial if RFPs and industry proposals have had the benefit of previous sharing of thinking on issues such as cost and performance drivers, risks and technology opportunities. Examples of this approach include draft RFPs, formal Requests For Information, and Program Industry Days with one-on-one meetings.

Beyond early communications, a program office can fund competitive concept definition studies (such as early design trade studies and operations research) to support decisions about requirements and as inputs to the formal Analyses of Alternatives. Although this is an up-front expense, it can boost net buying power by fueling industry innovations, which can enable improved user requirements that enable more responsive capability solutions.

2.14.15 Other Transaction Agreements

The use of "*other transactions agreements*" (OTAs) dates back to the creation of NASA in 1958 (Pub. L. 85-568). This term covers any transaction that is not a contract, grant, or formal agreement. In 1989, Congress permitted the Defense Advanced Research Projects Agency to use OTAs for basic, applied or advanced research projects. Pub. L. 114-92 permitted expansion of the usage to any research and development project or prototype project.[164] Today, most OTAs are issued by DoD; however certain other departments and agencies are authorized to issue them. The goal is to broaden DoD's ability to access commercial and cutting-edge technology from companies or individuals which are unable or unwilling to enter into Federal procurement contracts.

A prototype project is intended to enhance or improve mission effectiveness of the warfighter and supporting components, material, platforms, or systems. It is intended to evaluate the technical or manufacturing feasibility or military utility of a particular idea, process, product, or technology. It can be a proof of concept, pilot or novel application of commercial technologies for defense purposes. All significant commercial participants in the transaction must be small businesses or nontraditional defense awardees, and at least one of them must be the latter (either as prime or subawardee). The significant contribution expected of the nontraditional defense contractor(s) must be documented in the agreement file. These nontraditional awardees often voice reservations about Government auditing power, cost accounting standards and intellectual property rights. They would also include firms that have not had any DoD (sub)contract opportunities within the past year which were subject to full cost accounting standards.

As awardees, the commercial participants must fund at least 1/3 of the total project cost; the balance may come from the Government (similar to a cost-sharing contract arrangement). A greater Government cost share is only permitted if the agency senior procurement executive determines in writing that exceptional circumstances justify the use of a transaction that either innovative business arrangements or structures are necessary or else the opportunity to expand the defense supply base would not be practical or feasible.

The officials who decide whether a project qualifies under the prototype designation are the Directors of DARPA and the Missile Defense Agency, the Secretaries of the military departments and any other official designated by USD (AT&L) who is under a different chain of command. These officials approve in writing any program between $50 and $250 million; projects of a greater amount must be approved by USD (AT&L) with 30-day Congressional notification. There is no maximum threshold for an OTA, nor does DoD have a maximum amount for the total OTA program.

Traditional FAR and DFARS guidance does not apply to OTAs. Many related statutes do not apply to OTAs, so it is essential that legal counsel be involved in their creation. Competition is sought as much as possible, but without the legislative or regulatory direction under traditional procurements. However, each OTA over $5 million must permit the Comptroller General to examine the records of each participants for up to three years after completion of performance. Review of accounting systems is not necessary for a fixed-price arrangement, but may be appropriate when payment is based on incurred costs reported from financial records.

OTAs generally end when the product enters low-rate initial production. Follow-on opportunities are usually issued under FAR and DFARS coverage. The follow-on contract may be awarded noncompetitively upon completion of the OTA effort only if the OTA itself was competitively awarded.

The role of contracting officer is deemed as an *agreements officer* within the same authority as the warrant conveys. The agreements officer is free to use innovation and good business sense to develop the agreement, but must still ensure that the pricing structure is fair and reasonable.

Agencies who solicit OTAs may create their own process to solicit and fairly assess potential solutions while documenting the rationale for making the Government investment decision. This includes commercial methods beyond the traditional www.sam.gov website. One example of a solicitation method is a Commercial Solutions Opening, similar to a Broad Agency Announcement, to identify particular Government problem areas and solicit solution ideas from industry. This means that market research is key to a successful OTA. Upon receiving solution ideas, the Government can select an offeror to demonstrate its solution or submit a proposal. If a proposal is deemed a good investment for the Government to pursue, the agreements officer can negotiate and award an OTA to the company for the prototype project.

An acquisition approach must be documented early in the process. It should address:

- authority to use an OTA;
- rationale (e.g., how to attract nontraditional defense awardees, benefits to cost-sharing commercial entities);
- technical objectives, milestones, project metrics, and testing;
- Government team, management plan and program structure;
- program schedule;
- risk assessment of cost, schedule and technical aspects;
- expected sources, publicizing the opportunity, source selection process, extent of competition;
- pricing structure (related to project risk), method to determine reasonableness, and how to ensure compliance with the agreement;
- terms and conditions; and
- follow-on activities (e.g., intellectual property requirements, life cycle costs, sustainability, test, and evaluation), based on successful prototyping and obtaining future competition.

The pricing arrangement may be either for a fixed amount or on an expenditure basis. The latter requires the awardee to provide its best effort to complete the project for an estimated cost and payments are based on amounts generated from the awardee's financial or cost records (or that require at least one third of the total costs to be provided by non-Federal parties pursuant to statute). This includes interim and final milestone payments that may be adjusted for actual costs incurred.

Agreements officers can negotiate intellectual property terms and conditions which differ from those typically used in procurement contracts. However, in negotiating these clauses, the agreements officer must consider the laws that affect the Government's use and handling of intellectual property. Moreover, licenses and restrictions on portability of property rights may hinder future competitive opportunities or adaptability to future program needs (especially follow-on production). Foreign source licensing might also be a consideration. Hence, the Government's rights, as well as future needs of (sub)awardees, must be well thought-out and established upfront, spelled out in agreement clauses.

It is common for the participant to retain ownership of the subject invention while the Government reserves a nonexclusive, nontransferable, irrevocable, paid-up license to practice or have practiced for or on behalf of the United States the subject invention throughout the world. The Government may also obtain rights to any background invention, as well as march-in rights to encourage further commercialization of the technology. Some companies may insist that the invention remain a trade secret; if so, the Government must consider whether its interest in use of the technology is protected, including allowing a third party to use the technology. Hence, three topics which should be covered by clause are:

- Authorization and Consent (to shift liability for patent infringement from the awardee to the Government, provided that performance and delivery are within the United States and its possession);
- Indemnity (mitigate the Government's risk of cost increases caused by infringement of a patent owned by a third-party); and
- Notice and Assistance (the awardee notifies the Government of all infringement claims and assists with evidence and information).

The Government can negotiate rights in technical data and computer software that are developed under the agreement, regardless of whether it is delivered, based on the instant and future needs of both parties, the technology at issue, and any commercialization strategies. Both executable and program code may be desired for delivery, and deferred delivery or escrow arrangements may be negotiated. Of course, restrictive markings and legends should be agreed to upfront. Since the software and data are commercial in nature, the Government may insist on greater rights than normal.

Any proposal and supporting documentation, business plan or confidential technical information is exempt from disclosure under a FOIA request for five years after receipt. Confidential financial information and trade secrets may be protected for a longer period of time.

Agreements officers must ensure the legal authority of the party which is signing the agreement to ensure a binding agreement. This is especially important in dealing with an unincorporated consortium. (S)he may need to review with legal counsel the articles of collaboration which the consortia members have agreed upon.

There are other special issues to consider when establishing an OTA. It may require the awardee to pay DoD or another Federal department or agency to receive support by means of a clause which specifies the amount to be collected. Most ethics requirements apply to OTAs except for the Procurement Integrity Act. GAO has no authority over protests, but the U.S. Court of Federal Claims does. The agreement should include a Changes clause, especially if the Government wishes to retain the right to a unilateral change and equitable adjustment. Use of an Alternative Disputes Resolution process should be included to minimize court involvement.

If awardee costs are based on internal financial records or comprise at least 1/3 of total agreement amount (minimum of $500,000), the agreement officer must consider the validity of the financial system as part of the evaluation process. Direct costs must be attributed to applicable contracts by a job order accounting system, and indirect costs must be collected and allocated per generally accepted accounting procedures. This methodology should be spelled out in a contract clause. Revisions to the awardee's accounting system are discouraged if it fulfills these requirements, which is why Cost Accounting Standards and Cost Principles are not typically implemented. Audits of OTAs are uncommon, usually reserved for large milestone payments or early terminations, and may be performed by either DCAA or an independent public auditor (at awardee expense).

If the awardee is unable to fund 1/3 of the project cost, the Government may nonetheless proceed with negotiating a cost-sharing arrangement (such as third-party financing) if it would effectively incentivize and encourage the project's outcomes, but not merely to cover a program shortfall. Preaward costs must be justified as necessary for performance to be recognized. Any part of the cost share that includes an amount for a fully depreciated asset should be limited to a reasonable usage charge. Generally, Government financing should represent its cost share as the work progresses, rather than front-loading Government contributions. There should be an adjustment of Government or private sector investment or some other remedy if the awardee is not able to make its required investment. Such Federal or third-party financing should be reflected in financial reports.

The payment method must be set forth in the agreement. This includes methods of payment adjustment and final payment conditions and procedures. Payment milestones may be either fixed or adjustable. Advance payments may be needed for large up-front expenditures or ensuring sufficient cash flow for small companies. An interest-bearing checking account may be established.

The Government should not take title to property unless deliverable and spelled out on the agreement. If title does revert to the Government, then the parties should spell out in the agreement who is responsible for property accountability, control, damage, or destruction (including if resulting from its use), disposal, loss or theft, maintenance, repair or replacement. If reverting to the awardee and included in its cost share, then property values must be agreed to. Government-furnished property should be listed in the agreement along with suitability for its intended use, the condition in which the property should be returned, and any limitations on how or when the property may be used.

Termination clauses for both Convenience and Default should be included. Additionally, perhaps the awardee should have a similar right is it discovers that the expected commercial value of the prototype technology does not justify continued investment or the Government fails to provide funding. Perhaps the clause can provide for no payment beyond the last completed payable milestone, especially in a fixed-price agreement. On the other hand, it may be appropriate to require recoupment of Government investment or to obtain unlimited or Government purpose license rights to intellectual property created during performance.

The parties must agree on whether some or all of the consortium members receive copies of performance reports. An appropriate amount should be withheld if a report is not delivered.

NOTES

1. For more discussion on marketing to Government officials, see Dan Lindner, *An Insider's Guide to Working for the Federal Government*, Bernan Press, Lanham, MD, 2020, p. 98.
2. A *broker* is a third-party entity authorized to negotiate with potential vendors but not authorized to make a commitment or contract.
3. Because subsets of the data may not behave the same as the entire data set, not all behaviors and relationships may apply in all subsets.
4. This theory was first developed by David Ricardo in his 1817 work, *On the Principles of Political Economy and Taxation*, in which he demonstrated that it was in the best interest of his native England to trade with Portugal for wine and cloth because the latter could produce them at a lower labor cost than could his native land, thereby leading to lower prices for English consumers.
5. This theory was first advanced by Adam Smith in his 1776 classic, *An Inquiry into the Nature and Causes of the Wealth of Nations.*
6. Otto B. Martinson et al., "Profit '76," Logistics Management Institute, Washington, D.C., 1976, https://apps.dtic.mil/sti/pdfs/ADA038334.pdf.
7. The company's own annual (10K) and quarterly (10Q) reports are a good place to start.
8. An excellent information source of service contractors is "Market Research/ Market Intelligence" at https://www.acq.osd.mil/asda/dpc/cp/policy/docs/sa/2017_Market_Research_Guide_(Final).pdf.

9. https://piee.eb.mil. This website is limited to DoD offices and contractors, not the general public.

10. Source Selection Procedures, 2.1.2 and Appendix D.

11. 15 U.S.C. 637(e) and 41 U.S.C. 416, respectively.

12. https://SAM.gov.

13. The format exception must be determined in writing by the senior procurement executive.

14. Rewards or penalties may be involved with the original vendor in second source development.

15. FOIA stands for Freedom of Information Act.

16. www.unicor.gov.

17. In such a case, it will be listed at http://www.acq.osd.mil/dpap/cpic/cp/specific_policy_areas.html#federal_prison.

18. 41 U.S.C. 46.

19. A Procurement List of items is at www.abilityone.gov.

20. Some agencies may establish procedures to obtain advance approval, on a case-by-case basis.

21. 40 U.S.C. 501.

22. Schedules are stored at www.gsa.gov/elibrary.

23. https://www.gsa.gov/tools-overview/buying-and-selling-tools/acquisition-gateway.

24. www.ebuy.gsa.gov/ebuy.

25. https://www.dau.edu/tools/Documents/SAM/home.html.

26. This requirement can be waived due to undue burden, fundamental alteration or nonavailability. See FAR 39.205.

27. National Institute of Standards and Technology, *Special Publication 500-267B: A Profile for IPV6 in the U.S. Government.* National Institute of Standards and Technology, Gaithersburg, MD, 2022.

28. See OMB Memorandum M-05-22, Transition Planning for Internet Protocol Version 6, dated August 2, 2005. The agency Chief Information Officer may waive the requirement.

29. EIA Standard-748-D, Earned Value Management Systems, dated January 8, 2019, is available for a fee from SAE International, Inc., Warrendale, PA., or www.sae.org.

30. See MIL-STD-1840C, Automated Interchange of Technical Information.

31. Support Anti-terrorism by Fostering Effective Technologies Act of 2002 (6 U.S.C. 441).

32. This requirement is found in USD (AT&L), "DoD Business Rules for the Synchronized Predeployment and Operational Tracker (SPOT)," May 10, 2018, and is available at https://www.acq.osd.mil/log/PS/.spot.html/SPOT_DoD_Business_Rules_May2018.pdf.

33. 50 U.S.C. 4501.

34. This program is fully discussed at www.dodmantech.com.

35. 42 U.S.C. 12101.

36. This is done through quantitative and qualitative analysis to determine the probability that a specific interaction of performance, schedule and cost will or will not be attained due to a planned course of action.

37. Air Force Institute of Technology, "Interpretive Guide to the Evaluation/ Demonstration Review Checklist for C/SCSC (Appendix E, Joint Information Guide)," Air Force Institute of Technology, Wright-Patterson Air Force Base, Ohio, September 1991.

38. The process is sometimes called *benefit-cost analysis*. For our purposes, the terms are synonymous.

39. John Stuart Mill, *Principles of Political Economy*, John W. Parker, London, UK, 1859.

40. In fact, it is commonly believed that the discount rate actually declines over time as people lose interest in a particular initiative.

41. DoD is planning to split this function into two separate Under Secretaries, one for Research and Engineering and one for Acquisition and Sustainment. At the time of this book however, this split has not been finalized and it remains unclear how responsibilities will be allocated. The author has therefore been compelled to continue referring to just one authority figure.

42. These dollar thresholds were established in 1990 and never adjusted; hence they are still measured in FY90 dollars, allowing for inflation. We will see this convention of constant dollars used elsewhere in the Federal Government.

43. Governing documents are CJCSI 5123.01I, Implementation of the JCIDAS (October 2021), JCIDS Manual (also October 2021), DODD 7045.14 PPBE Process (August 2017), and DOD 7000-14R DOD Financial Management Regulation (May 2019).

44. CJCS Instruction 5123.01 describes the roles and responsibilities of the JROC.

45. The JCIDS Manual is at http://www.acqnotes.com/wp-content/uploads/2014/09/Manual-for-the-Operationsof-the-Joint-Capabilities-Integration-and-Development-System-JCIDS-18-Dec-2015.pdf.

46. Business systems validate capability requirements using processes described in DoDI 5000.75, Business Systems Requirements and Acquisition, dated February 2, 2017.

47. The PPBE process is well explained at https://www.dau.mil/acquipedia/Pages/ArticleDetails.aspx?aid=10fdf6c0-30ca-43ee-81a8-717156088826.

48. Numerous DOD directives govern various components of the pathways. They are separately noted in the Bibliography. See also *A Guide to Program Management Business Processes*, pp. 1-2.

49. DoDI 5000.81, "Urgent Capability Acquisition," December 31, 2019.

50. DoD 5000.87, Operation of the Software Acquisition Pathway, October 2, 2020.

51. Once again, we see an instance of constant dollar thresholds. These dollar amounts were established in 2020 and never adjusted; hence they are still measured in FY20 dollars, allowing for inflation.

52. Public Law 114-92 Section 806.

53. The governing document is Office of the Secretary of Defense, Analysis of Alternatives Cost Estimating Handbook, July 2021.

54. DoD Instruction 5000.88, “Engineering of Defense Systems,” November 18, 2020.

55. DoD Instruction 5000.91, “Product Support Management for the Adaptive Acquisition Framework,” November 4, 2021.

56. Engineering of Defense Systems Guidebook, 3.2.1.3.5.

57. Small Business Administration, Office of Advocacy, “Frequently Asked Questions About Small Businesses,” Washington, D.C., September 2019, page 1.

58. www.census.gov/eosd/www/naics.

59. The industry size standards are published by the SBA at http://www.sba.gov /content/table-small-business-size-standards.

60. Detailed guidance is found at PGI 217.7506.

61. A partial set-aside cannot be used in construction contracts because there is only one prime contractor per job.

62. http://www.pro-net.sba.gov/textonly/pro-net/search.html.

63. Specific results must be reported for subcontracts exceeding $150,000 in value.

64. www.esrs.gov.

65. Per DFARS 219.705-4, a small disadvantaged business goal of less than five percent in a subcontracting plan must be approved one level above the contracting officer.

66. This class deviation requires submission of the Standard Form 294 in lieu of Individual Subcontract Reports in the Electronic Subcontracting Reporting System for orders against basic ordering agreements and blanket purchase agreements.

67. 15 U.S.C. 637(a).

68. DFARS Appendix I to Chapter 2, I-101.

69. *Rothe Development Corp. v. Dept. of Defense* (545 F. 3d 1023).

70. 15 U.S.C. 657f.

71. Despite any concerns over political correctness, the term “Indian” was used in the original statute and has never been changed by Congress; hence the term will be used in this book.

72. 43 U.S.C. 1601.

73. 42 U.S.C. 5150.

74. The incredibly long title of this Executive Order is “Promoting Procurement With Small Businesses Owned and Controlled by Socially and Economically Disadvantaged Individuals, Historically Black Colleges and Universities, and Minority Institutions.”

75. Public Law 110-247.

76. 15 U.S.C. 631.

77. This program was inspired by E.O. 13005, Empowerment Contracting, May 24, 1996.

78. http://www.sba.gov/hubzone.

79. 42 U.S.C. 12101.

80. Its website is https://www.ntis.gov.

81. PL 95-224.

82. More information on the SBIR program can be found at https://www.sbir.gov/.

83. This is not to be confused with the Stevenson-Wydler Technology Innovation Act (15 U.S.C. 3701), which sets aside 0.5 percent of each agency's research budget to fund technology transfer between laboratories and industry.

84. A complete list of these centers is found on the National Science Foundation's website at www.nsf.gov/statistics/ffrdclist.

85. This dollar threshold was imposed in the legislation (41 U.S.C. 351) when it was written in 1965 and has never been modified by Congress. Hence, we have the odd situation where requirements for service employees might fall below the simplified acquisition threshold, but still require a formal contract and wage determination.

86. However, the installation is subject to the Davis-Bacon Act if the services are obtained from the manufacturer or supplier of the equipment on a sole-source basis.

87. This Executive Order does not apply to apprentices, executives and professionals, seasonal recreation services (except for food and lodging), and students.

88. See the OASD (Readiness and Force Management) memorandum entitled "Private Sector Notification Requirements in Support of In-sourcing Actions," dated January 29, 2013, for further information.

89. Although these projects may include energy savings or purchased utility service due to such a project for periods not to exceed 25 years.

90. *Military installation* means a base, camp, post, station, yard, center, or other activity under the jurisdiction of the Secretary of a military department or, in the case of an activity in a foreign country, under the operational control of same.

91. DoDI 5000.74, January 10, 2020, Change 1, June 24, 2021, Section 4.3. Specific focus areas are listed in DoDI 5000.74, Enclosure 5, section 3 that allow each organization to tailor the process to meet unique missions and needs.

92. DoDI 5000,74, Section 4.4.

93. DoDI 5000.74, Section 4.7.

94. 40 U.S.C. 25.

95. FIPS standards are located at https://csrc.nist.gov/publications/fips or purchased from the Superintendent of Documents, U.S. Government Printing Office.

96. Department of the Treasury periodically updates these requirements for annual reporting purposes. The current version is in the Treasury Financial Manual, Chapter 9500, found at http://tfm.fiscal.treasury.gov/v1/p6/c950.pdf.

97. 29 U.S.C. 794d. See also Department of Energy, Architectural and Transportation Barriers Compliance Board Electronic and Information Technology (EIT) Accessibility Standards (36 CFR 1194), Department of Energy, Washington, D.C., June 2005.

98. Detailed guidance is found in Mary Linda Polydys and Stan Wisseman, "Software Assurance in Acquisition: Mitigating Risks to the Enterprise." This document was generated by the Software Enterprise Institute and is managed by the United States Computer Emergency Readiness Team within the Department of Homeland Security.

99. 5 U.S.C. 552a.

100. Title 40 U.S.C. Subtitle III.

101. https://public.cyber.mil/dccs.

102. Additional policy and guidance that must be followed when acquiring and implementing cloud services include DoD Memorandum, "Updated Guidance on the Acquisition and Use of Commercial Cloud Computing Services," December 15, 2014, and DoD Instruction 5000.74, "Defense Acquisition of Services," Enclosure 7, January 5, 2016.

103. NIST SP 800-145, "The NIST Definition of Cloud Computing," September 2011.

104. DoD Instruction 8530.01, Cybersecurity Activities Support to DoD Information Network Operations, July 25, 2017.

105. Both FedRamp and The DoD Cloud Computing Security Requirements Guide, Version 1 Release 4, 14 January 2022.

106. The Federal Risk and Authorization Program (FedRAMP) requires all Federal departments and agencies to formally assess and authorize their secure access to cloud computing resources and services. Lists of cloud services with FedRAMP authorizations and provisional authorizations are available at https://marketplace.fedramp.gov and https://disa.deps.mil/org/RMED/cas/SitePages/CSOCatalog.aspx respectively.

107. Available at http://nvd.nist.gov/fdcc/download_fdcc.cfm.

108. Committee on National Security Systems, "National Security Telecommunications and Information Systems Security Policy No. 11," June 10, 2013.

109. DoD 8570.01-M, Information Assurance Workforce Improvement Program.

110. The NIST 800-171 DoD methodology is at https://www.acq.osd.mil/dpap/pdi/cyber/strategically_assessing_contractor_implementation_of_NIST_ SP_800-171.html.

111. https://www.sprs.csd.disa.mil.

112. https://www.acq.mil/cmmc/index.html.

113. https://dibnet.dod.mil.

114. As identified in Enclosures 3 and 13 of DoDI 5000.02T

115. http://checklists.nist.gov.

116. Published in 2009 by ISO in Geneva, Switzerland. *ISO* stands for the International Organization for Standardization, a multinational collection of quality and safety experts. They combine their knowledge to develop voluntary consensus-based standards to promote international trade.

117. The prime guidance for risk assessment is DoD Instruction 8510.01, "Risk Management Framework."

118. FEMA, "Homeland Security Presidential Directive 20, National Continuity Policy," Washington, D.C., May 4, 2007.

119. Department of Homeland Security (May 2013). "National Response Framework." Retrieved March 3, 2021, from www.fema.gov/emergency-managers/national-preparedness/frameworks/response.

120. FEMA, Federal Continuity Directive 1, "Federal Executive Branch National Continuity Program and Requirements," updated July 14, 2014, and "Federal Continuity Directive 2, Federal Executive Branch Mission Essential Functions and

Candidate Primary Mission Essential Functions Identification and Submission Process," updated December 9, 2013.

121. An OPM report to Congress, "Status of Telework in the Federal Government," dated December 2022, says that only about 47 percent of all employees in the Executive Branch regularly telework, primarily non-supervisors. This number is certainly influenced by the COVID pandemic, but will undoubtedly continue to some extent to reduce both absenteeism and commuting cost. For further discussion, see Dan Lindner, *An Insider's Guide to Working for the Federal Government*, Bernan Press, Lanham, MD, 2020.

122. This work can be done by an *integrator*, a third-party firm that combines products of multiple other firms to produce a final product or system. They are often used to assemble information systems, but they can be used in other types of endeavors.

123. Also in common use is the American Productivity & Quality Center (APQC) Process Classification Framework from the Council of Supply Chain Management Professionals.

124. "Supply Chain Operations Reference Model: SCOR 12.0 Quick Reference Guide," Association for Supply Chain Management, Chicago, IL, 2017. Retrieved May 7, 2021, from www.apics.org/scor.

125. One method to send demand upchannel is *kanban*, a Japanese approach to schedule what, when and how much to produce. This approach gained prominence in Toyota Motor Corp. and is now used by other distributed firms such as Wal-Mart, where point-of-sale information is sent to a central data point to assess customer demand and inventory movement.

126. These classes are defined in DoD Manual 4140.01, Volume 6, DoD Supply Chain Materiel Management Procedures: Material Returns, Retention, and Disposition.

127. This is the maximum alternative earnings that might have been obtained if the item had been put to another use. It is the real cost of an alternative that is not pursued.

128. 41 U.S.C.8301.

129. This threshold is 55 percent for civilian agencies. It raises to 75 percent for products delivered on or after January 1, 2029. For construction materials, the threshold is and will remain at 55 percent.

130. DFARS 225.003.

131. 10 U.S.C. 2631 and 46 U.S.C. 1241(b), respectively.

132. Joint Chiefs of Staff. JCS 3170.01I, "Joint Capabilities Integration and Development System and Manual." August 31, 2018. Retrieved March 9, 2023, from https://www.acq.osd.mil/asda/jrac/docs/2018-JCIDS.pdf.

133. Further guidance is contained on the respective combatant commander's operational contract support webpage, which is linked to the procedures at http://www.acq.osd.mil/asda/dpc/cp/cc/aor.html. These pages list combatant commander's directives, host nation laws, policies, regulations, requirements, and unique clauses, necessary to solicit and award a contract to perform in or deliver items to that combatant commander's area of responsibility.

134. DoDI 3020.41, Operational Contract Support, establishes policy, assigns responsibilities, and provides procedures such as program management, contract

support integration, and integration of defense contractor personnel into contingency operations outside the United States.

135. 19 U.S.C. 2501, *et seq.*

136. Prohibited sources of supply are listed at https://www.treasury.gov/about/organizational-structure/offices/Pages/Office-of-Foreign-Assets-Control.aspx.

137. U.S. International Trade Commission, *Harmonized Tariff Schedule of the United States*. 19 U.S.C. 1202. U.S. International Trade Commission, Washington, D.C., May 16, 2023, at https://hts.usitc.gov/current. Although the Trade Commission publishes and maintains the schedule, the actual legwork and rulings are performed by the Customs and Border Protection unit out of the Department of Homeland Security.

138. e.g., http://www.federalreserve.gov/releases/g5/current.

139. www.bis.doc.gov/index.php/regulations/commerce-control-list-ccl.

140. 22 U.S.C. 2751 *et seq.* The official version of the ITAR is maintained at http://www.gpoaccess.gov/cfr/index.html. The Department of State also maintains an online version at http://www.pmddtc.state.gov/regulations_laws/itar_official.html.

141. The United States has signed treaties with Australia and the United Kingdom to sometimes waive these controls to promote sharing of mutual defense information.

142. The EAR is available at https://www.bis.doc.gov/index.php/regulations/export-administration-regulations-ear. The Commerce Control List is Part 774 of the EAR and is available at the same site.

143. Defense Trade Cooperation Treaties are accessible at http://pmddtc.state.gov.

144. 22 U.S.C. 2301 and 22 U.S.C. 2778, respectively.

145. Guidance is at Under Secretary of Defense (Comptroller), DoD Financial Management Regulation 7000.14-R, Volume 15, DoD, Washington, D.C., September 2017.

146. At the time this book was written, the list of states sponsoring terrorism consisted of Iran, North Korea, Sudan, and Syria.

147. 22 CFR Part 121.

148. The current designated countries are Iran, North Korea, People's Republic of China, and Russia.

149. OMB Circular A-11, Preparation and Submission of Budget Estimates, December 23, 2020, OMB, Washington, D.C.

150. DFARS 217.207 and .208 and PGI 217.207.

151. 31.U.S.C. 1535.

152. Government-wide guidance comes from Office of Management and Budget, "Improving the Management and Use of Interagency Acquisitions," June 6, 2008, retrieved March 3, 2021, from www.gsa.gov/cdnstatic/Integrated_Technology_Services/OMB%20Memo%2020080608%20iac_revised.pdf.

153. An excellent resource to do this is the OFPP document "Interagency Acquisitions" available at http://www.whitehouse.gov/omb/assets/procurement/iac_revised.pdf.

154. These agreements are listed at https://www.contractdirectory.gov/contractdirectory, which is managed by GSA.

155. 42 U.S.C. 5121.

156. www.acquisition.gov.

157. 46 U.S.C. 55305.

158. The Framework is available at https://www.fema.gov/media-library-data/20130726-1914-25045-1246/final_national_response_framework_20130501.pdf.

159. DFARS 225.7002.

160. https://www.jccs.gov/olvr.

161. The Agreements are available at (http://dtic.mil/cjcs_directives/cdata/unlimit/2120_01.pdf). AGATRS is accessible on the JCCS website at https://www.jccs.gov/olvr.

162. National Defense Authorization Act, Section 1428, 41 U.S.C. 403.

163. This is generally referred to as *acquisition risk*, the chance that a (sub)contract will produce an unintended impact on system availability, cost, effectiveness, or maintainability.

164. 10 U.S.C. §2371b. An excellent resource is Department of Defense, "Other Transactions Guide for Prototype Projects," January 2017.

Chapter 3

Placement

Procurement operations commence when the program office or requirements office submits a procurement package with all information and technical description necessary to commence the solicitation process. This includes a purchase request that describes the requirement to tell prospective offerors what is required, as well as financial data citing funds to pay for performance.

3.1 SOURCE SELECTION PLAN

The *Source Selection Plan* documents how the Government will conduct a competition and find a contractor that fully meets its needs. The plan lists the organization, membership, and responsibilities of the source selection team, and contains the process and evaluation criteria for selection. It is prepared by the program manager, reviewed by the contracting officer, and approved by the source selection authority. This may well be the contacting officer on routine procurements, but on major acquisitions it will be a designated agency official.

The content and format of the source selection plan are dictated by agency directive. Often, this information comes straight out of the acquisition plan.

The evaluation factors may be tailored to the particular acquisition, but must have meaningful impact on source selection. Cost or price is always included, along with any of the following as appropriate:

- cost realism,
- experience,
- management capability,
- past performance,

- personnel qualifications,
- schedule, and
- technical excellence.

Usually these criteria are grouped into Technical, Management and Cost categories. Once the criteria have been selected, their relative importance must be measured. This process can be based on criteria, judgment, priority, or tradeoff. Importance can be scored by several methods:

- adjectives—excellent, good, fair, poor (with a narrative description of findings);
- binary—either acceptable or unacceptable;
- lowest-priced technically acceptable offer;
- numerically—by score;
- tradeoffs—score the management and technical proposals, then trade off the differences against the prices offered; or
- varied—cost becomes more important as technical proposals become more equal to each other.

The solicitation must state the relative importance of the factors by list, order of importance or adjectival description.

DAG: Source Selection Procedures, 2.2

A written SSP is required for all competitive acquisitions that use these major source selection procedures. The SSA must approve the SSP before the final solicitation is issued. At a minimum, the SSP shall describe:

- the requirement, objectives, and any applicable guidance;
- how the specific acquisition fits into the entire program;
- the Source Selection Team organizational structure, roles and responsibilities, individual names, and delegated responsibilities of the source selection team;
- communications process and controls with Industry and internal Government team during the source selection;
- security measures to protect source selection information, including the networks on which such information is stored or shared;
- evaluation (sub)factors;
- types of documents that will be prepared during the course of the source selection, such as an SSEB Report, an SSAC Report, and the SSDD; and
- nongovernment advisors and how to secure source selection materials throughout the evaluation process.

3.2 DESCRIBING AGENCY NEEDS

3.2.1 General Specifications

FAR 11.0 through 11.1

Specifications are particulars that describe technical requirements for the deliverable item or service. There are four basic types. *Functional specifications* describe performance characteristics and intended use of a product with only a general end result, including the minimum essential characteristics to satisfy the product's intended use. In contrast, *performance specifications* describe operational characteristics and end results of the item, allowing contractor use of judgment and discretion to design and engineer the product as it sees fit to meet the performance requirements. They tend to be more restrictive than functional specifications because they limit alternatives and set definite performance standards that the contractor must meet, or else risk non-performance. This type of specification is best left to experienced contactors or special-use military items of high performance and low volume, but also fit well with commercial items.

Design specifications prescribe key characteristics of the item to be produced or delivered. They include measurements and tolerances for inspection and quality control, or mandatory material composition requirements. This approach leaves the Government responsible for any errors and omissions, as well as accepting the risk of non-performance if the product is built to specification. In effect, the Government provides an implied warranty through its design specifications that the contractor will deliver an acceptable product by following these specifications.[1] Hence, the Government must take care that the specifications are current, reasonably flexible, and specific, and do not limit competition.

DoD has *military specifications* which depict standards and requirements that are unique to military application and needs. They can be either design or performance in nature, and are stored in the DoD Index of Specifications and Standards.[2] This index works in conjunction with the Military Standard Requisitioning and Issue Procedures (MILSTRIP) to issue material by standardized methods.[3] DoD accepts Single Process Initiative (SPI) processes in lieu of specific military or Federal specifications or standards that specify a management or manufacturing process. However, contracting officers must first obtain approval of the requiring activity for any proposed substitutions prior to contract award and, if a competitive procurement, must permit offerors to verify that an SPI process is an acceptable replacement for a military or Federal specification or standard prior to the date specified for receipt of offers.[4] Any determination that an SPI process is not acceptable must be approved by the head of the contracting activity or program executive officer.

As often as possible, requirements for contractor performance must be expressed in a way to encourage offerors to supply commercial or nondevelopmental items, and to require (sub)contractors to incorporate such items as components of their deliverable products. Specifications should not be more restrictive or detailed than necessary to meet the minimum needs of the Government. Too many detail or "gold-plated" specifications could restrict competition and frustrate the most reasonable pricing. To avoid this problem, the specifications should not contain unnecessary design requirements, arbitrary requirements unrelated to needs, or bias toward a specific product. However, they can be tailored to meet specific needs of the requestor or to adjust minimum requirements. In fact, there is a prioritization scheme for setting requirements:

- statute-specified documents;
- performance work specifications and statements of objectives;
- design specifications and Federal or DoD standards or specifications; and
- non-mandatory standards and specifications.

The Metric Conversion Act of 1975 and the Omnibus Trade and Competitiveness Act of 1988 designate the metric system of measurement as the preferred system of weights and measures for United States commerce.[5] Each agency uses the metric system of measurement in its acquisitions unless impracticable or likely to cause significant inefficiencies or loss of market. Whenever possible, agencies use voluntary consensus standards in lieu of Government-unique standards, unless they are impractical or illegal. The private sector manages and administers consensus standards (e.g., ISO 9000 and IEEE 1680).[6,7] Solicitations should specify the document version and effective date.

Potential offerors may recommend including and tailoring requirements documents and alternative approaches. Requiring agencies should then make a final decision on the use or modification of these documents for the design and development process. For a negotiated procurement, this process may continue through the proposal and evaluation steps.

An agency may require offerors to demonstrate that the items offered have either achieved commercial market acceptance (except for new or evolving items) or been supplied to an agency under current or recent contracts for the same or similar requirements.[8] Otherwise, offered items must meet the item description or specifications prescribed in the solicitation. This means that the contracting officer must ensure that the solicitation criteria:

- are supported by market research;
- consider items supplied satisfactorily under prior contracts;

- consider the entire relevant commercial market, including small business concerns;
- reflect minimum needs of the agency; and
- show an item's performance and intended use rather than an offeror's capability.

Solicitations citing requirements documents listed in the GSA Index of Federal Specifications, Standards and Commercial Item Descriptions, the DoD Acquisition Streamlining and Standardization Information System[9] or other agency index must identify each document's approval date and any applicable amendments and revisions.[10] Contracting offices will not normally furnish these cited documents with the solicitation. Any other documents not listed in these indices are furnished with the solicitation, or else specific instructions to obtain or examine them are included.

When acquiring commercial items, the contracting officer considers the customary practices in the industry. (S)he may require offerors to provide information on any proposed supplies that are used, reconditioned, or remanufactured, as well as unused former Government surplus property. When acquiring information and communications technology, the requirements submission must address how users with disabilities will perform required functions, related development and configuration, appropriate maintenance, and accessibility standards.

Section 505 of Executive Order 13101, "Greening the Government through Waste Prevention, Recycling, and Federal Acquisition," establishes minimum recovered material content standards to purchase printing and writing paper. It includes *postconsumer fiber* such as used corrugated boxes, old newspapers and magazines, paper, paperboard, and other fibrous materials.[11] The fiber definition also includes *manufacturing wastes* (dry paper and paperboard waste generated after completion of the papermaking process, and obsolete inventories of commercial paper and paperboard). Agencies do not normally require supplies composed of virgin material unless directed by law or regulation, or if vital for safety or performance requirements. If so, the offeror must acknowledge the presence of virgin material in the proposal.

FAR 11.104

Sometimes, commercial needs are met only when a particular brand name(s) is known to be acceptable. *Brand name or equal* purchase descriptions include functional, performance or physical characteristics of the brand name item that an "equal" item must meet to be acceptable. Offerors submit literature describing their offered product, and the Government determines whether the product meets the needed characteristics.

The use of brand name or equal purchase descriptions may be advantageous under certain circumstances. They include a general description of those "salient" or prominent functional, performance or physical characteristics of the brand name item that another make-and-model item must meet to be acceptable for award. However, care must be taken that requirements are not written to require a specific brand name, feature, or product peculiar to one manufacturer, thereby precluding consideration of a competitor's product. Brand names are only used if it is essential to the government's requirements and market research indicates competitors' products (or products lacking the particular feature) do not or cannot be modified to meet the agency's needs.

Solicitation Provisions

FAR 52.211-1, Availability of Specifications Listed in the GSA Index of Federal Specifications, Standards and Commercial Item Descriptions, FPMR Part 101-29.

FAR 52.211-2, Availability of Specifications, Standards, and Data Item Descriptions Listed in the Acquisition Streamlining and Standardization Information System (ASSIST).

FAR 52.211-3, Availability of Specifications Not Listed in the GSA Index of Federal Specifications, Standards and Commercial Item Descriptions.

FAR 52.211-4, Availability for Examination of Specifications Not Listed in the GSA Index of Federal Specifications, Standards and Commercial Item Descriptions.

FAR 52.211-5, Material Requirements, for supplies that are not commercial items.

FAR 52.211-6, Brand Name or Equal.

FAR 52.211-7, Alternatives to Government-Unique Standards, if using Government-unique standards when the agency reports its use of voluntary consensus standards to NIST per OMB Circular A-119, "Federal Participation in the Development and Use of Voluntary Consensus Standards and in Conformity Assessment Activities" (2016).

Solicitation Provision and Contract Clause

DFARS 252.211-7005, Substitutions for Military or Federal Specifications and Standards, when exceeding the micro-purchase threshold to obtain previously developed items.

3.2.2 Statements of Work

FAR 37.6

A method of acquiring services by emphasizing output is known as *performance-based acquisition.* Initially defined in OFPP Policy Letter 91-2 (since rescinded), this approach is objective, measurable and mission-related. The solicitation describes what must be done, not how it will be done. This approach is intended to provide several benefits:

- better contractor performance;
- innovation;
- lower prices due to fewer government-unique specifications;
- reduced contract administration; and
- shorter procurement lead time.

Performance-based acquisition is not used to acquire architect-engineer services or construction, utility services, or any services that are incidental to a supply or purchase.

There are seven prescribed steps to this process, most of which are already familiar from prior discussion:

- establish the acquisition team;
- decide what problem needs solving;
- examine private- and public-sector solutions;
- develop a performance work statement or statement of objectives;
- decide how to measure and manage performance;
- select the correct contractor(s); and
- manage their performance.

DAG CH 1–4.2.11.6

There are several approaches to describing what a contractor must accomplish. A *statement of work* (SOW) establishes and defines all non-specification requirements for contractor's efforts.[12] This document describes the actual work that is to be performed by the contractor and often refers to specifications and compliance or reference documents. Some of these documents can be presented in full text while others may be incorporated by reference. The SOW sets forth the work to be done to develop or produce the supplies to be delivered or services to be performed by a contractor in specific performance-based, qualitative or quantitative terms. This specificity enables offerors to clearly understand the government's requirements. A review board or "murder board" may review the SOW before solicitation to ensure compliance with policy and procedures.

Alternatively, a *Performance Work Statement* (PWS) is used for a performance-based acquisition to describe the required results in specific and objective terms with measurable outcomes. These are often used for services but can also be used in supply contracts. This document states requirements in general terms of what is to be done (result), rather than how it is done (method). The contractor now has maximum flexibility to devise the best method to accomplish the required result. Proposals for performance-based services include a PWS that describes the effort to be performed in detail, measurable performance benchmarks or standards (e.g., quality, quantity, and timeliness) and the method of assessing contractor performance (including any performance incentives). The proposal also includes any data deliverables and needed Government-furnished property and facilities. The offerors may select any performance method, so long as they emphasize outcomes rather than procedures. The statement should focus on factors that the contractor controls without relying on Government processes or procedures. Agencies evaluate the proposed performance standards to determine if they meet agency needs.

Preparing a PWS begins with a job analysis that examines the agency's requirements. It tends to be a bottom-up assessment with re-engineering potential. This analysis is the basis for establishing performance requirements and standards, writing the PWS and producing the quality assurance plan.

A third option is a *Statement of Objectives* (SOO), a summary of key agency goals and/or outcomes that is incorporated into a performance-based acquisition to provide competitors with maximum flexibility to propose their own original solutions. These solutions may include a technical approach, performance standards and a quality assurance surveillance plan, which may be based on commercial business practices. Usually, a SOO states the agency goals in the most general sense, allowing vendors more creativity in proposing a solution. It is a common axiom that the SOO is intended to tell the contractor what to do, such as performance objectives and constraints such as availability or security, not how to do it. It provides performance objectives and constraints such as availability or security, but does not specify how the work should be accomplished. It is usually shorter than a PWS or SOW. This is a good approach to use when the agency can provide usage statistics and has no mandated or preferred way of providing the service, or when there are very specific requirements and constraints that limit potential solutions.

The SOO describes the work through required results rather than how the work is to be accomplished or the number of hours to be provided. The SOO enables assessment of work performance against measurable standards. It also encourages competitors to develop and implement innovative and cost-effective methods to perform the work. These standards are usually written agreements among multiple organizations that define characteristics or specifications of specific operations. The SOO does not become part of the contract. The SOO sets forth:

- purpose;
- scope or mission;
- period and place of performance;
- background;
- performance objectives results; and
- any operating constraints.

SOO content depends both on the type of supplies or services and on the program phase. It is possible that a "mature" program, such as a software product in the maintenance phase could require more detail in the SOO to properly integrate with other software programs under development or operation. The key is to keep the document short and concise. The SOO does not specifically address each Work Breakdown Structure (WBS) element, but each WBS element is traceable to the SOO.[13] For example, a SOO may instruct the offerors to address an engineering approach. That is not a particular WBS element, but several WBS elements might be created to break out the engineering tasks. In so doing, end users get the best supplies or services, and competition is enhanced if dissimilar solutions are submitted in response to the solicitation.

The following actions provide the conceptual process for developing the SOO:

- complete a risk assessment that highlights the high and moderate risks of business, programmatic and technical aspects of the program based on the requirements and objectives;
- conduct market research to determine if commercial or non-developmental items are available to meet program requirements;
- prepare a bibliography citing all applicable governing directives, instructions, specifications, and standards with which the program is required to comply; and
- review the requirements documents that authorize the program and any international acquisition documents that impact the program.

There is no mandatory format for the PWS or the SOO—each agency may develop its own format and procedures. Acceptable quality levels may need to be defined in the document. It is critical that the requirement not be defined so tightly that each offeror proposes the same solution. If all offerors provide the same solution, there will be no creativity or innovation in the proposals. How the PWS is written will either empower or stifle the private sector to craft innovative solutions.

As much as possible, the PWS should:

- avoid specifying the number of contractor employees or their educational and skill levels required to perform the work (except when necessary);

- describe the outcomes or results rather than how to do the work;
- encourage the contractor to focus on continuous improvement;
- include disincentives to handle poor performance;
- include incentives to motivate the contractor to improve performance or to reduce costs;
- minimize constraints that restrict the contractor's ability to perform;
- permit the contractor to implement new technology to improve performance or to lower cost;
- prescribe the AQL levels that are clearly defined, realistic, and achievable;
- use commercial performance standards that are easy to measure and timely; and
- use performance standards that address quantity, quality, and/or timeliness.

The Government may either prepare a *quality assurance surveillance plan* (*QASP*), or require the offerors to submit a proposed plan for Government review.[14] This plan describes a methodology to verify that the contractor's quality control efforts are effective and timely, and deliver the specified results. It should spell out the roles and responsibilities of the various parties to performance, desired outcomes, performance rating levels and their definitions, and reporting and resolution processes. The plan indicates how contractor performance will be measured and what performance standards will be used, ideally in a matrix format. During performance, the contractor appraises its performance against these standards. These standards are known as *acceptable quality levels* and must be realistic, represent minimum acceptable performance levels, and consider cost trade-offs and market research. If a quality level is breached, the contractor calculates the number of errors as a percentage of total measured events during the time period, then applies it to the task value to derive the amount to be deducted from the price.

The QASP should be reviewed and modified whenever necessary, principally because the method and degree of performance assessment may change over time, depending on the level of confidence in the contractor. The theory is to make the contractor rather than the Government responsible for managing the QASP quality controls and ensuring that the performance meets the terms of the contract. A different approach to the analytical process is described in the *Guidebook for the Acquisition of Services*.[15] It describes the Requirements Roadmap Process and the availability of a database PWS and Quality Assurance Surveillance Plan authoring tool known as the Acquisition Requirements Roadmap Tool (ARRT).[16] The ARRT provides authoring question-and-answer "wizards" to guide users through the requirements roadmap process. The ARRT allows an author to use standardized templates to create a PWS and QASP tailored to a specific requirement. It also includes some default text and includes tools for requirements definition, cost estimation evaluation factors, and performance assessment. The requirements roadmap process is designed to define and analyze the desired outcomes to identify what tasks must be accomplished to arrive at the desired outcomes.

A few ways to assess a contractor's performance that can properly monitor performance and quality include checklists, customer feedback, metrics, periodic or 100 percent inspection, sampling, and third-party audits. Sometimes, decision tables can identify different examples of unsatisfactory performance, probable cause factors, and resulting consequences. When a service has failed to meet performance standards, a decision must be made as to who is at fault by using a decision table.[17]

Based on the market research results, the program office develops the Independent Government Cost Estimate (IGCE) which supports the requirement. The IGCE is the estimates the resources and their projected costs that a contractor will incur in the performance of the contract. The IGCE helps determine what legal, policy and regulation requirements are necessary to release a Request for Proposal.[18]

3.2.3 Delivery or Performance Schedules

The time of delivery or performance is stated in solicitations and must meet the realistic requirements of the Government. The contracting officer may express contract delivery or performance schedules in terms of specific calendar dates, periods of time after the date of award, receipt of award by the contractor, or effective date of the contract.

Short or difficult schedules tend to restrict competition, conflict with small business policies, and may increase contract prices. Hence, the solicitation may also allow for the offeror to propose an alternative delivery schedule. The solicitation must then inform bidders or offerors how their bids or proposals will be evaluated with respect to time of delivery or performance.

The contracting officer evaluates the bid by adding five calendar days for arrival through ordinary mail. The solicitation states if the contract or notice of award will be transmitted electronically, and the contracting officer adds one working day to the proposed delivery schedule based on the date of contract receipt or notice of award.

Solicitation Provisions and Contract Clauses

FAR 52.211-8, Time of Delivery, other than construction and architect-engineering, if the Government requires delivery by a particular time and the delivery schedule is based on the contract date. Use the clause with its Alternate I if the delivery schedule is expressed in terms of specific calendar dates or specific periods and is based on an assumed date of award. Use the clause with its Alternate II if the delivery schedule is expressed in terms of specific calendar dates or specific periods and is based on an assumed date the contractor will receive notice of award. Use the clause with its Alternate III if the delivery schedule is to be based on the actual date the contractor receives a written notice of award.

FAR 52.211-9, Desired and Required Time of Delivery, other than construction and architect-engineering, if the Government desires delivery by a certain time but requires delivery by a specified later time, and the delivery schedule is to be based on the date of the contract. The Alternate versions are used in the same manner as FAR 52.211-8.

FAR 52.211-10, Commencement, Prosecution, and Completion of Work, when a fixed-price construction contract is contemplated. Use the clause with its Alternate I if the completion date is expressed as a specific calendar date, based on the contractor receiving the notice to proceed by a certain day.

3.2.4 Variation in Quantity

A fixed-price supply contract may authorize Government acceptance of a variation in the quantity of items called for if caused by loading, packing, or shipping, or by allowances in manufacturing processes. Any permissible variation is stated as a percentage increase, decrease or both. It is based upon the normal commercial practices of a particular industry for a particular item. The permissible variation does not exceed plus or minus 10 percent unless a different limitation is established in agency regulations. Excess quantities of items totaling up to $250 in value may be retained without compensating the contractor, and excess quantities over $250 in value may, at the Government's option, be either returned at the contractor's expense or retained and paid for at the contract unit price.

Construction contracts may authorize a variation in estimated quantities of unit-priced items. If the variation between the estimated and actual quantity of a unit-priced item is more than plus or minus 15 percent, an equitable adjustment in the contract price is made upon the demand of either the Government or the contractor. The contractor may request an extension of time if the quantity variation requires it to complete performance. However, the contracting officer may extend this time limit before the date of final settlement of the contract.

Solicitation Provisions and Contract Clauses

FAR 52.211-16, Variation in Quantity, for fixed-price supplies or services.

FAR 52.211-17, Delivery of Excess Quantities, for fixed-price supplies.

FAR 52.211-18, Variation in Estimated Quantity, for fixed-price construction.

3.2.5 Liquidated Damages

The contracting officer considers the potential impact on pricing, competition, and contract administration before using a liquidated damages clause. When delivery or timely performance is so important that the Government expects to suffer damage if the contractor is delinquent, and the damage would be difficult or impossible to estimate accurately or prove, then liquidated damages may be prudent. Liquidated damages are neither punitive nor negative performance incentives, but rather are compensation to the Government for probable damages. The liquidated damages rate reasonably forecasts compensation for these damages. The contracting officer may use more than one liquidated damages rate when the probable damage to the Government may change over the contract period of performance. However, the contracting officer must realize that offerors may reflect the amount of such damages by means of a price increase.

Construction contracts with liquidated damages provisions describe the rate(s) of liquidated damages assessed per day of delay, the estimated daily cost of Government inspection and superintendence, and an amount for other expected expenses associated with delayed completion (e.g., renting substitute property, or paying additional allowance for living quarters).

Solicitation Provisions and Contract Clauses

FAR 52.211-11, Liquidated Damages—Supplies, Services, or Research and Development, if fixed-price for supplies, services, or research and development when the contracting officer determines that liquidated damages are appropriate.

FAR 52.211-12, Liquidated Damages—Construction, for construction (other than cost-plus-fixed-fee) when the contracting officer determines that liquidated damages are appropriate. It can be modified to reflect multiple liquidation rates for multiple stages of work.

FAR 52.211-13, Time Extensions, for construction that use the Liquidated Damages—Construction clause, when FAR 52.211-12 has been revised.

3.3 ACQUISITION OF COMMERCIAL ITEMS

3.3.1 Nature of Commercial Items

FAR Part 12

A commercial item is offered, sold, and used in substantial quantities in the commercial marketplace by the general public or by nongovernmental entities (domestic and foreign) for nongovernmental purposes, including any minor modifications thereto. A nondevelopmental item can be deemed commercial if developed exclusively at private expense and sold in substantial quantities on a competitive basis to the same parties. Similarly, *commercial services* are offered and sold competitively to the same markets for specific tasks or intended outcomes under standard commercial terms and conditions. Examples include installation, maintenance, repair, and training services.

Pricing for commercial items must be based on established catalog or market prices. A *catalog price* is included in a published catalog, price list or schedule that is regularly maintained by the manufacturer or vendor, with prices at which sales are currently or recently made to a significant number of buyers constituting the general public. *Market prices* are established in the course of ordinary trade between buyers and sellers based on competition or independent sources.

Commercial products, as opposed to specially designed and manufactured items, are often faster to acquire and travel quickly through established distribution systems. They usually cost less due to competition. Because commercial items are plentiful, they tend to reduce inventory costs because fewer items need to be stocked.

However, commercial items will not meet all requirements and may require additional contractor maintenance. Items bought commercially include auto parts, drugs, food, office supplies and tools. Items least susceptible to commercial acquisition include MIL-SPEC or Government-only items and military aircraft components.

Agencies conduct market research to determine whether commercial or nondevelopmental items could meet the agency's requirements. They also require prime contractors and subcontractors at all tiers to incorporate, to the maximum extent practicable, commercial or nondevelopmental items as components of deliverable items. This policy does not apply to acquisitions at or below the micro-purchase threshold or from another Federal agency.

Contracting officers may treat, as an acquisition of commercial items, supplies or services to facilitate defense against or recovery from nuclear, biological, chemical, or radiological attack. However, a sole-source contract over $16 million for such an item or service which does not meet the definition of a commercial item is not exempt from cost accounting standards or cost or pricing data requirements.

A statement of need for a commercial item describes the product or service to be acquired, how the agency plans to use it, and its functionality, performance requirement or essential physical characteristics. The contracting officer uses the Standard Form 1449, Solicitation/Contract/Order for Commercial Items, for an acquisition exceeding the simplified acquisition threshold (and may use it for lower-value acquisitions) and usually allows 15 days to notify the marketplace before soliciting.

Offers are evaluated in accordance with the criteria contained in the solicitation. For many commercial items, the criteria need not be more detailed than technical, price and past performance. Technical capability may be evaluated by how well the proposed products meet the Government requirement and their intended use. A technical evaluation would normally include examination of such things as product literature describing product characteristics or operation, product samples, technical features, and warranty provisions. If an agency decides during their market research that technical information is necessary to evaluate offers, agencies review literature of products available in the industry to determine its adequacy. Offerors may propose more than one product that will meet a Government need in response to solicitations for commercial items, and each product is evaluated as a separate offer.

Where technical information is necessary for evaluation of offers, agencies include in their market research a review of existing product literature available in the industry to determine its adequacy to evaluate offers. Offerors may propose more than one product that will meet a Government need in response to solicitations for commercial items, and each product is evaluated as a separate offer. The contracting officer may require offerors to provide information on proposed supplies that are used, reconditioned, or remanufactured, or else unused former Government surplus property.

Contracts for commercial items rely on contractors' existing quality assurance systems instead of Government inspection and testing, unless customary market practices for the commercial item include in-process inspection.

The parties presume that data delivered under a contract for commercial items was developed exclusively at private expense. Commercial computer software and documentation are acquired under licenses customarily provided to the public if consistent with Federal law and otherwise satisfy the Government's needs. Generally, offerors and contractors need not furnish non-customary technical information or provide the Government any further rights to such software or documentation.

Firm-fixed-price contracts or fixed-price contracts with economic price adjustment are normally used for the acquisition of commercial items. A time-and-materials contract or labor-hour contract (including an indefinite-delivery contract) may be used to acquire commercial services; however the contracting officer must write a D&F justifying the contract type and establish a ceiling price that can only be changed by writing another D&F. The D&F describes the market research, explains the impossibility of estimating work extent or duration and/or cost uncertainty, and discusses the likelihood of using the preferred contract types in future acquisitions for the same supplies or services. These alternative contract types may also include an award fee using performance or delivery incentives rather than cost.

Contracting officers may use a combined synopsis/solicitation procedure to streamline the process. In this case, no separate written solicitation is used. Because the synopsis and solicitation are contained in a single document, it is not necessary to separately synopsize 15 days before the issuance of the solicitation. A reasonable response time must be set based on availability, commerciality, complexity, and urgency.

FAR 15.403-1

Services that are offered and sold competitively in substantial quantities in the commercial marketplace may be considered commercial items regardless of quantity actually sold. The contracting officer must sign a D&F stating that the offeror has submitted sufficient information to evaluate (through price analysis) that the price of such services is reasonable. The contracting officer may request price information (or if not available, then cost information) from the offeror to make this determination. If so determined, then the contractor is not required to certify cost or pricing data. This requirement does not apply to any modifications of a commercial item that do not exceed five percent of total contract price (up to the certified cost or pricing data threshold).

DFARS 234.7

A DoD major weapon system may be treated as a commercial item only if the Secretary of Defense (or Deputy) determines that the major weapon system is a commercial item, such treatment is necessary to meet national security objectives, and the congressional Armed Services Committees are notified at least 30 days before such treatment or acquisition occurs. A subsystem or any component or spare part of a non-commercial major weapon system is treated as a commercial item and acquired under commercial procedures if the contracting officer so determines in writing. However, any such components and spare parts must be acquired by DoD through a prime contract or modification, or through a subcontract for which the prime contractor adds negligible value.

To determine price reasonableness, the contracting officer requires the offeror to submit prices paid for the same or similar commercial items under comparable terms and conditions by both commercial and Government customers. If this is not possible, then the offeror can submit information on prices paid for the same or similar items or services under different terms and conditions or for alternative solutions or approaches. Failing that, uncertified cost data may be required unless there are sufficient nongovernment sales of the same item to establish price reasonableness. An offeror may be required to submit such information for any other item that was developed exclusively at private expense only after the head of the contracting activity determines in writing that the information submitted to date is not sufficient to determine price reasonableness.

DFARS 212.102

When using commercial procedures for acquisitions exceeding the simplified acquisition threshold in value (except to facilitate defense against or recovery from biological, chemical, nuclear, or radiological attack), the contracting officer must sign a determination that the procurement is for a commercial item (or get approval at a higher level in certain cases) based on competitive sales (including lease or license) of products or services in substantial quantities offering to the general public with pricing based on established catalog or market prices. This requirement can also be fulfilled with commercial modifications or minor non-commercial modifications made to meet Federal Government requirements, usually of small size or value which do not change the nongovernmental function or essential physical characteristics of an item or process.

The contracting officer may rely on past determinations of commerciality for the same supplies or services. Alternatively, the contracting officer may request the head of the contracting activity to review the nature of the supplies or services within 30 days to determine whether it is commercial in nature.

Contracting officers may deem supplies and services provided by nontraditional defense contractors as commercial items. Any services must use the same pool of employees and priced the same way as commercial services. This approach may enhance innovation and investment by acquiring nontraditional items from new contractors. No commercial item determination is required in this situation.

DFARS 212.7002

If a procurement valued up to $100 million was previously procured based on a commercial item determination, then the contracting officer cannot unilaterally convert the procurement from commercial to noncommercial acquisition procedures. The head of the contracting activity must first determine in writing that the earlier use of commercial acquisition procedures was in error or based on inadequate information and that DoD will realize a cost savings by not using commercial acquisition procedures. This involves analysis of any changes in quantities, the estimated cost of research and development by the existing contractor to improve future products or services, Government assessment and responses to data requests to convert to noncommercial acquisition procedures, and delays due to the conversion.

3.3.2 Commercial Warranties

FAR 12.404

The Federal Acquisition Streamlining Act of 1994 requires contracting officers to use commercial warranties whenever possible.[19] Solicitations for commercial items require offerors to furnish the same warranty terms offered to the general public in commercial practice. However, they may also include express warranties (perhaps covering a minimum duration) appropriate for the Government's intended use of the item. However, the express warranty must be cost-effective, protect the Government's needs, and allow postaward administration (e.g., collect product performance information, identify warranted items, and set forth procedures to return warranted items to the contractor for repair or replacement).

In some markets, contractors may customarily exclude or limit the implied warranties. If so, the contracting officer must ensure that the express warranty provides for repair or replacement of defective items discovered within a prescribed time period after acceptance.

The Government relies on the contractor's assurances that the commercial item tendered for acceptance conforms to the contract requirements. Government inspection of commercial items does not prejudice its other rights, since it always has the right to refuse acceptance of nonconforming items.

3.3.3 Impact on Regulations

FAR 12.5

The following laws do not apply to contracts for commercial items:

- 41 U.S.C. 43, Walsh-Healey Act;
- 41 U.S.C. 254(a) and 10 U.S.C. 2306(b), Contingent Fees;
- 41 U.S.C. 65, Contracts for Materials, Supplies, Articles, and Equipment Exceeding $15,000;
- 41 U.S.C. 416(a)(6), Minimum Response Time for Offers under Office of Federal Procurement Policy Act;
- 41 U.S.C. 701, *et seq.*, Drug-Free Workplace Act of 1988;
- 31 U.S.C. 1354(a), Limitation on use of appropriated funds for contracts with entities not meeting veterans' employment reporting requirements;
- 31 U.S.C. 6101 note, Public Law 109-282, Federal Funding Accountability and Transparency Act of 2006, requirement to report subcontract data;
- Section 806(a)(3) of Public Law 102-190, as amended by Sections 2091 and 8105 of Public Law 103-355, Payment Protections for Subcontractors and Suppliers; and

- 41 U.S.C. 254d(c)(1) and 10 U.S.C. 2313(c)(1), GAO Access to Contractor Employees, Section 871 of Public Law 110-417.

Certain requirements of the following laws are not applicable to contracts for commercial items:

- 40 U.S.C. 3701 *et seq.*, requirement for a certificate and clause under the Contract Work Hours and Safety Standards Act;
- 41 U.S.C. 57(a)-(b) and 58, requirements for a clause and other issues related to the Anti-Kickback Act of 1986; and
- 49 U.S.C. 40118, requirement for a clause under the Fly American provisions.

Certain laws have been modified for contracts for the acquisition of commercial items:

- 41 U.S.C. 253g and 10 U.S.C. 2402, Prohibition on Limiting Subcontractor Direct Sales to the United States; and
- 41 U.S.C. 254(d) and 10 U.S.C. 2306a, Truth in Negotiations Act 41 U.S.C. 422, Cost Accounting Standards (48 CFR chapter 99).

The following laws do not apply to subcontracts for commercial items or components:

- 10 U.S.C. 2631, Transportation of Supplies by Sea, except that the clause does apply to items resold or distributed to the Government without adding value, shipped either under f.o.b. destination or in direct support of U.S. military contingency operations, exercises, or humanitarian or peacekeeping operations;
- 15 U.S.C. 644(d), requirements for labor surplus areas under the Small Business Act;
- 41 U.S.C.43, Walsh-Healey Act;
- 41 U.S.C. 253d, Validation of Proprietary Data Restrictions;
- 41 U.S.C. 254(a) and 10 U.S.C. 2306(b), Contingent Fees;
- 41 U.S.C. 254d(c) and 10 U.S.C. 2313(c), Examination of Records of Contractor, when a subcontractor is not required to provide cost or pricing data, unless using funds appropriated or otherwise made available by the American Recovery and Reinvestment Act of 2009;
- 41 U.S.C. 416(a)(6), Minimum Response Time for Offers under Office of Federal Procurement Policy Act;
- 41 U.S.C. 418a, Rights in Technical Data;
- 41 U.S.C. 701, *et seq.*, Drug-Free Workplace Act of 1988;

- 46 U.S.C. App. 1241 (b), Transportation in American Vessels of Government Personnel and Certain Cargo (except for the types of subcontracts listed under the Transportation of Supplies by Sea clause above);
- 49 U.S.C. 40118, Fly American provisions;
- Section 806(a)(3) of Public Law 102-190, as amended by Sections 2091 and 8105 of Public Law 103-355, Payment Protections for Subcontractors and Suppliers (10 U.S.C. 2302);
- 41 U.S.C. 10a, portion of first sentence that reads "substantially all from articles, materials, or supplies mined, produced, or manufactured, as the case may be, in the United States," Buy American Act—Supplies, component test;
- 41 U.S.C. 10b, portion of first sentence that reads "substantially all from articles, materials, or supplies mined, produced, or manufactured, as the case may be, in the Unites States," Buy American Act—Construction Materials, component test; and
- 42 U.S.C. 6962(c)(3)(A), Certification and Estimate of Percentage of Recovered Material.

The requirements for a certificate and clause under the Contract Work Hours and Safety Standards Act, 40 U.S.C. 3701, *et seq.*, do not apply to subcontracts for commercial items or commercial components.

The applicability of the following laws has been modified in regard to subcontracts for commercial items or components:

- 41 U.S.C. 253g and 10 U.S.C. 2402, Prohibition on Limiting Subcontractor Direct Sales to the United States;
- 41 U.S.C. 254(d) and 10 U.S.C. 2306a, Truth in Negotiations Act; and
- 41 U.S.C. 422, Cost Accounting Standards (48 CFR chapter 99).

The contracting officer may include in solicitations and contracts by addendum other FAR provisions and clauses, and agency-unique statutes as approved by the agency senior procurement executive. Any tailoring of the above clauses is by addendum to the solicitation and contract, and must be approved by the head of the contracting activity.

When acquiring commercial items, contracting officers use only these provisions and clauses:

Solicitation Provisions

FAR 52.212-1, Instructions to Offerors—Commercial Items.

FAR 52.212-2, Evaluation—Commercial Items, when the use of evaluation factors is appropriate.

FAR 52.212-3, Offeror Representations and Certifications—Commercial Items. Use the provision with its Alternate I. Use the provision with its Alternate II for small, disadvantaged business procurements on a regional basis.

DFARS 252.213-7000, Notice to Prospective Suppliers on Use of Past Performance Information Retrieval System—Statistical Reporting in Past Performance Evaluations.

DFARS 252.215-7003, Requirements for Submission of Data Other Than Certified Cost or Pricing Data—Canadian Commercial Corporation.

DFARS 252.215-7004, Requirement for Submission of Data other Than Certified Cost or Pricing Data—Modifications—Canadian Commercial Corporation.

DFARS 252.215-7007, Notice of Intent to Resolicit.

DFARS 252.215-7008, Only One Offer.

DFARS 252.215-7010, Requirements for Certified Cost or Pricing Data and Data Other Than Certified Cost or Pricing Data. Do not use FAR 52.215-20, Requirements for Certified Cost or Pricing Data and Data Other Than Certified Cost or Pricing Data. Use the basic provision when submission of certified cost or pricing data is required to be in the FAR Table 15-2 format, or if it is anticipated, at the time of solicitation, that the submission of certified cost or pricing data may not be required. Use Alternate I to specify a format for certified cost or pricing data other than the format required by FAR Table 15-2.

DFARS 252.215-7011, Requirements for Submission of Proposals to the Administrative Contracting Officer and Contract Auditor, when using DFARS 252.215-7010 and copies of the proposal are to be sent to the ACO and contract auditor.

DFARS 252.215-7012, Requirements for Submission of Proposals via Electronic Media, when using DFARS 252.215-7010 and submission via electronic media is required.

DFARS 252.215-7013, Supplies and Services Provided by Nontraditional Defense Contractors.

Solicitation Provisions and Contract Clauses

FAR 52.203-3, Gratuities.

FAR 52.212-4, Contract Terms and Conditions—Commercial Items. Use this clause with its Alternate I when a time-and-materials or labor-hour contract will be awarded. The contracting officer may tailor this clause except for such requirements as assignments, disputes, invoicing, and payments.

FAR 52.212-5, Contract Terms and Conditions Required to Implement Statutes or Executive Orders—Commercial Items. DFARS 252.203-7000, Requirements Relating to Compensation of Former DoD Officials.

DFARS 252.203-7003, Agency Office of the Inspector General.

DFARS 252.203-7005, Representation Relating to Compensation of Former DoD Officials.

DFARS 252.204-7008 Compliance with Safeguarding Covered Defense Information Controls.

DFARS 252.204-7009, Limitations on the Use or Disclosure of Third-Party Contractor Reported Cyber Incident Information.

DFARS 252.204-7012, Safeguarding Covered Defense Information and Cyber Incident Reporting.

DFARS 252.204-7014, Limitations on the Use or Disclosure of Information by Litigation Support Contractors.

DFARS 252.204-7015, Notice of Authorized Disclosure of Information for Litigation Support.

DFARS 252.205-7000, Provision of Information to Cooperative Agreement Holders.

DFARS 252.211-7003, Item Unique Identification and Valuation.

DFARS 252.211-7006, Passive Radio Frequency Identification.

DFARS 252.211-7007, Reporting of Government-Furnished Property.

DFARS 252.211-7008, Use of Government-Assigned Serial Numbers.

DFARS 252.219-7000, Advancing Small Business Growth.

DFARS 252.219-7003, Small Business Subcontracting Plan (DoD Contracts). Use the basic clause when using the basic or either alternate of FAR 52.219-9. Use the Alternate I clause when using Alternate III of FAR 52.219-9.

DFARS 252.219-7004, Small Business Subcontracting Plan (Test Program).

DFARS 252.223-7008, Prohibition of Hexavalent Chromium.

DFARS 252.225-7000, Buy American—Balance of Payments Program Certificate. Use the basic provision when the solicitation includes DFARS 252.225-7001. Use Alternate I when the solicitation includes Alternate I of DFARS 252.225-7001.

DFARS 252.225-7001, Buy American and Balance of Payments Program. Use the basic clause if the acquisition is not of end products listed in DFARS 225.401-70 in support of operations in Afghanistan. Use the Alternate I clause when the acquisition is of end products listed in DFARS 225.401-70 in support of operations in Afghanistan.

DFARS 252.225-7006, Acquisition of the American Flag.

DFARS 252.225-7008, Restriction on Acquisition of Specialty Metals.

DFARS 252.225-7009, Restriction on Acquisition of Certain Articles Containing Specialty Metals.

DFARS 252.225-7010, Commercial Derivative Military Article—Specialty Metals Compliance Certificate.

DFARS 252.225-7012, Preference for Certain Domestic Commodities.

DFARS 252.225-7015, Restriction on Acquisition of Hand or Measuring Tools.

DFARS 252.225-7016, Restriction on Acquisition of Ball and Roller Bearings.

DFARS 252.225-7017, Photovoltaic Devices.

DFARS 252.225-7018, Photovoltaic Devices—Certificate.

DFARS 252.225-7020, Trade Agreements Certificate. Use the basic provision if the solicitation includes the basic clause at DFARS 252.225-7021. Use the Alternate I provision if the solicitation includes Alternate II of the clause at DFARS 252.225-7021.

DFARS 252.225-7021, Trade Agreements. Use the basic clause for other than end products in support of operations in Afghanistan, or if including DFARS 252.225-7024, Requirement for Products or Services from Afghanistan. Use Alternate II clause for end products in support of operations in Afghanistan and if not including DFARS 252.225-7024.

DFARS 252.225-7023, Preference for Products or Services from Afghanistan.

DFARS 252.225-7024, Requirement for Products or Services from Afghanistan.

DFARS 252.225-7026, Acquisition Restricted to Products or Services from Afghanistan.

DFARS 252.225-7027, Restriction on Contingent Fees for Foreign Military Sales.

DFARS 252.225-7028, Exclusionary Policies and Practices of Foreign Governments.

DFARS 252.225-7029, Acquisition of Uniform Components for Afghan Military or Afghan National Police.

DFARS 252.225-7031, Secondary Arab Boycott of Israel.

DFARS 252.225-7035, Buy American—Free Trade Agreements—Balance of Payments Program Certificate, instead of FAR 52.225-4, Buy American—Free Trade Agreements—Israeli Trade Act Certificate. Use the basic provision in solicitations when the basic of the clause at DFARS 252.225-7036 is used. Use the same Alternate provision when the solicitation includes an Alternate of DFARS 252.225-7036.

DFARS 252.225-7036, Buy American—Free Trade Agreements—Balance of Payments Program instead of the clause at FAR 52.225-3, Buy American—Free Trade Agreements–Israeli Trade Act. Use the basic clause when the estimated value equals or exceeds $100,000, but is less than $180,000, except if the acquisition is of end products in support of operations in Afghanistan. Use the Alternate I clause when the estimated value equals or exceeds $25,000, but is less than $80,317, except if the acquisition is of end products in support of operations in Afghanistan. Use the Alternate II clause when the estimated value equals or exceeds $100,000, but is less than $180,000, and the acquisition is of end products in support of operations in Afghanistan. Use the Alternate III clause when the estimated value equals or exceeds $25,000, but is less than $80,317, and the acquisition is of end products in support of operations in Afghanistan. Use the Alternate IV clause when the estimated value equals or exceeds $80,317 but is less than $100,000, except if the acquisition is of end products in support of operations in Afghanistan. Use the Alternate V clause when the estimated value equals or exceeds $80,317 but is less than $100,000 and the acquisition is of end products in support of operations in Afghanistan. Do not use the basic or an alternate of the clause if purchase from foreign sources is restricted (unless the contracting officer anticipates a waiver of the restriction), acquiring information technology that is a commercial item, or using a preference for products or services made in Afghanistan.

DFARS 252.225-7037, Evaluation of Offers for Air Circuit Breakers.

DFARS 252.225-7038, Restriction on Acquisition of Air Circuit Breakers.

DFARS 252.225-7039, Defense Contractors Performing Private Security Functions Outside the United States.

DFARS 252.225-7040, Contractor Personnel Supporting U.S. Armed Forces Deployed Outside the United States.

DFARS 252.225-7043, Antiterrorism/Force Protection Policy for Defense Contractors Outside the United States.

DFARS 252.225-7049, Prohibition on Acquisition of Commercial Satellite Services from Certain Foreign Entities—Representations.

DFARS 252.225-7050, Disclosure of Ownership or Control by the Government of a Country that is a State Sponsor of Terrorism.

DFARS 252.226-7001, Utilization of Indian Organizations, Indian-Owned Economic Enterprises, and Native Hawaiian Small Business Concerns.

DFARS 52.227-7013, Rights in Technical Data–Noncommercial Items. Use the clause at DFARS 252.227-7013 with its Alternate I for research procurements when the contracting officer determines, in consultation with counsel, that public dissemination by the contractor would be in the interest of the Government, and facilitated by the Government relinquishing its right to publish the work for sale, or to have others publish the work for sale on behalf of the Government. Use the clause at DFARS 252.227-7013 with its Alternate II for the development or delivery of a vessel design or any useful article embodying a vessel design.

DFARS 252.227-7015, Technical Data–Commercial Items. Use the clause at DFARS 252.227-7015 with its Alternate I, for the development or delivery of a vessel design or any useful article embodying a vessel design.

DFARS 252.227-7037, Validation of Restrictive Markings on Technical Data.

DFARS 252.232-7003, Electronic Submission of Payment Requests and Receiving Reports.

DFARS 252.232-7006, Wide Area WorkFlow Payment Instructions.

DFARS 252.232-7009, Mandatory Payment by Government-wide Commercial Purchase Card.

DFARS 252.232-7010, Levies on Contract Payments.

DFARS 252.232-7011, Payments in Support of Emergencies and Contingency Operations.

DFARS 252.237-7010, Prohibition on Interrogation of Detainees by Contractor Personnel.

DFARS 252.237-7019, Training for Contractor Personnel Interacting with Detainees.

DFARS 252.239-7009, Representation of Use of Cloud Computing.

DFARS 252.239-7010, Cloud Computing Services.

DFARS 252.239-7017, Notice of Supply Chain Risk.

DFARS 252.239-7018, Supply Chain Risk.

DFARS 252.243-7002, Requests for Equitable Adjustment.

DFARS 252.244-7000, Subcontracts for Commercial Items.

DFARS 252.246-7003, Notification of Potential Safety Issues.

DFARS 252.246-7004, Safety of Facilities, Infrastructure, and Equipment for Military Operations.

DFARS 252.246-7008, Sources of Electronic Parts.

DFARS 252.247-7003, Pass-Through of Motor Carrier Fuel Surcharge Adjustment to the Cost Bearer.

DFARS 252.247-7022, Representation of Extent of Transportation by Sea.

DFARS 252.247-7023, Transportation of Supplies by Sea. Use the basic clause unless any of the supplies to be transported are commercial items that are shipped in direct support of U.S. military contingency operations, exercises, or forces deployed in humanitarian or peacekeeping operations, or for commissary or exchange cargoes transported outside of the Defense Transportation System, when the contract is not for construction. Use the Alternate I clause if any of the supplies to be transported are commercial items that are shipped in direct support of U.S. military contingency operations, exercises, or forces deployed in humanitarian or peacekeeping operations when the contract is not a construction contract. Use the Alternate II clause if any of the supplies to be transported are commercial items that are commissary or exchange cargoes transported outside of the Defense Transportation System (10 U.S.C. 2643), when the contract is not a construction contract.

DFARS 252.247-7025, Reflagging or Repair Work.

DFARS 252.247-7026, Evaluation Preference for Use of Domestic Shipyards—Applicable to Acquisition of Carriage by Vessel for DoD Cargo in the Coastwise or Noncontiguous Trade.

DFARS 252.247-7027, Riding Gang Member Requirements.

DFARS 252.247-7028, Application for U.S Government Shipping Documentation/Instructions.

3.4 UNIFORM CONTRACT FORMAT

3.4.1 Section Arrangement

FAR 14.201

The Uniform Contract Format is as follows:

Part I—The Schedule

A. Solicitation/contract form
B. Supplies or services and prices
C. Description/specifications
D. Packaging and marking
E. Inspection and acceptance
F. Deliveries or performance
G. Contract administration data
H. Special contract requirements

Part II—Contract Clauses

I. Contract clauses

Part III—List of Documents, Exhibits, and Other Attachments

J. List of documents, exhibits, and other attachments

Part IV—Representations and Instructions

K. Representations, certifications, and other statements of bidders
L. Instructions, conditions, and notices to bidders
M. Evaluation factors for award

The contracting officer prepares the Schedule as follows:

- *Section A, Solicitation/contract form.* Use Standard Form (SF) 33, Solicitation Offer and Award, or 1447, Solicitation/Contract. The alphanumeric contract number will follow a format prescribed in agency regulations, beginning with a six-digit identifier of the procurement office which issues the contract or agreement, the last two digits of the fiscal year of award, a single letter from a list which indicates the type of procurement instrument, and a serial number of between four and eight digits assigned by the department or agency. It then depicts such basic information as name and address or issuing office and bid room, dates of issuance and bid opening, and address blocks for the bidder and payment.

- *Section B, Supplies or services and prices.* Include a brief description of the supplies or services (e.g., item or part number, national stock number, title or name, and quantities).[20] Use Optional Form 336 or Continuation Sheet.
- *Section C, Description/specifications.*
- *Section D, Packaging and marking.* Include packing and preservation requirements.
- *Section E, Inspection and acceptance.* Include quality assurance and reliability requirements.
- *Section F, Deliveries or performance.* Specify the requirements for time, place and method of delivery or performance.
- *Section G, Contract administration data.* Include accounting and appropriation data and instructions.
- *Section H, Special contract requirements.* Include requirements not listed elsewhere. These are usually written in free-form text within this section.
- *Section I, Contract clauses.*
- *Section J, List of documents, exhibits, and other attachments.* List the title, date, and number of pages for each attached document.
- *Section K, Representations, certifications, and other statements of bidders.* Include solicitation provisions that require bidders to fill in representations and certifications.
- *Section L, Instructions, conditions, and notices to bidders.* Insert the time and place for bid openings, and submission information.
- *Section M, Evaluation factors for award.* Include price related factors to be considered in evaluating bids and awarding the contract.

All information is traced back to the specific line item(s) to which it applies. Each line item defines specific deliverable(s) and associated pricing and quantity. Multiple subline items may be used for similar deliverables that nonetheless have distinct differences, such as separate funding citations or delivery destinations. Line items are numbered sequentially with a four-digit code (i.e., 0001, 0002, etc.). Subline items will bear a two-digit alphabetic suffix (e.g., 0001AA) if they are separately priced, or else a two-digit numeric suffix (e.g., 000101) if they are not separately priced.

The contracting officer may use the simplified contract format instead, consisting of:

- *Solicitation/contract form.* Standard Form (SF) 1447.
- *Contract schedule.* Include the following for each contract line item:
  - contract line item number;
  - description of supplies or services;
  - quantity and unit of issue;
  - unit price and amount;
  - packaging and marking requirements;
  - inspection and acceptance, quality assurance, and reliability requirements;
  - place of delivery, performance and delivery dates, period of performance, and f.o.b. point; and
  - other item-specific information (e.g., individual fund citations).
- *Clauses.* Include only the clauses required by FAR and agency supplement, adding clauses only when considered absolutely necessary to the particular acquisition.
- *List of documents and attachments.*
- *Representations and instructions—*
  - *Representations and certifications.* Insert provisions that require representations, certifications, or other information by offerors.
  - *Instructions, conditions, and notices.* Include the required provisions and any other instructions to guide offerors.
  - *Evaluation factors for award.*

Upon award, the contracting officer need not include the representations and certifications in the resulting contract, but does retain them in the contract file.

The clauses and provisions below are required for all Federal solicitations or contracts:

Solicitation Provisions

FAR 52.252-3, Alterations in Solicitation, to revise or supplement, as necessary, other parts of the solicitation that apply to the solicitation phase only, except for any provision authorized for use with a deviation.

FAR 52.252-5, Authorized Deviations in Provisions, including any FAR or supplemental provision with an authorized deviation. The contracting officer identifies the deviation by the same number, title, and date assigned to the provision when it is used without deviation, include regulation name for any supplemental provision, but inserts "(DEVIATION)" after the date of the provision.

Solicitation Provisions and Contract Clauses

FAR 52.252-1, Solicitation Provisions Incorporated by Reference.

FAR 52.252-4, Alterations in Contract, to revise or supplement, as necessary, other parts of the contract, or parts of the solicitations that apply to the contract phase, except for any clause authorized for use with a deviation.

FAR 52.252-6, Authorized Deviations in Clauses, if including any FAR or supplemental clause with an authorized deviation. The contracting officer identifies the deviation by the same number, title, and date assigned to the clause when it is used without deviation, include regulation name for any supplemental clause, but inserts "(DEVIATION)" after the date of the clause.

Contract Clauses

FAR 52.252-2, Clauses Incorporated by Reference.

3.4.2 Line Items

FAR 4.10

Line items are used to define deliverables and associated price and quantity information about them. Separate line items are required for supplies with unique identification such as a part number or national stock number, or a unique item description. Services are separated if they have a unique statement of work or performance work statement. A separate line item is also required for a first article requiring separate approval (but not if the first article is part of a lot that must be approved in its entirety).

A line item must bear a single unit price or total price and be of one contract type. If a cost-type contract, it must bear an estimated cost and fee amount rather than unit and total prices. It usually contains one funding citation, although a single deliverable may be funded by multiple accounting classifications when the deliverable effort cannot be otherwise subdivided. A line item usually has a single delivery schedule, destination, period of performance, or place of performance.

Line items may be subdivided into separate subline items if they have different characteristics such as appearance, delivery (date, destination, or method), place of performance, or accounting data. In such a case, the line item itself contains only information common to all subline items thereunder. All subline items must be the same contract type as the line item.

Terms and conditions in other sections or clauses of the contract which do not apply to the entire contract must specify to which individual line items they do apply.

Delivery or task orders under indefinite-delivery contracts must specify accounting data and either delivery date and destination or period and place of performance. Quantities may also be necessary in each order if they are not specified in the basic contract.

Offerors are permitted to restructure the line item arrangement by proposing subline items or combining them into a group or a single line item.

DFARS 204.7103

A single unit price or total price is not required if the item is not separately priced because the cost is included in the unit price of another contract line item. Often this method is used to obtain technical data. If the line item refers to an exhibit or an attachment, the price may be set forth in the exhibit's item description block. If the contract involves a test model or a first article (either individual unit or lot) to be submitted for approval, a separate contract (sub) line item can be established.

Informational subline items can be used to track performance or ease administration. They are not normally separately priced, nor do they bear separate quantities or shipping details (unless in parenthesis for management tracking purposes). They may be used to identify accounting data in case of multiple items. However, per DFARS 204.7104-1, payment on the priced line item can be withheld until all subline items are delivered.

DFARS 207.7002 and .7003

DoD may obtain a greater quantity of an end item than authorized if the head of the agency determines that this end item is an established requirement that is expected to remain substantially unchanged throughout the period of the acquisition.[21] No additional funding is allowed due to production efficiencies or other cost reductions. Each unit is fully funded as a complete end item. For a sole-source contract however, the increased quantity may not exceed 10 percent of the base amount.

Solicitation Provisions

FAR 52.204-22, Alternative Line Item Proposal.

DFARS 252.204-7006, Billing Instructions, if including a DoD payment instruction that requires contractor identification of the contract line item(s) on the payment request.

DFARS 252.204-7011, Alternative Line Item Structure, when using FAR Part 12 procedures for the acquisition of commercial items or for initial provisioning spares.

Solicitation Provision and Contract Clause

DFARS 252.2004-7002, Payment for Contract Line or Subline Items Not Separately Priced, when using (sub)items not separately priced.

3.5 CONTRACT TYPES

A wide variety of contract types is available to provide flexibility in cost management and profit incentive. The objective in selecting contract type is to negotiate a price arrangement that will result in reasonable contractor risk and maximize incentive for efficient and economical performance. The best contract type is one that appropriately shares the risk between government and contractor.

The contract types are grouped into two broad categories: *fixed-price* and *cost-reimbursement*. Fixed-price contracts establish a ceiling beyond which the Government is not responsible for payment, no matter what the contractor's cost incurrence is. By contrast, cost-reimbursement contracts pay a contractor's allowable incurred costs based on an upfront estimate of total cost to establish a maximum amount that the contractor exceeds at its own risk. They are used when uncertainties in performance do not permit cost estimates sufficient to use a fixed-price contract. Government surveillance during performance provides reasonable assurance that efficient methods and cost controls are used. Once the money runs out, the contractor may stop performance unless the Government provides additional funds to cover further costs on a no-fee basis. No further consideration is needed because the original contact amount was merely an estimate.

Fixed-price and cost-reimbursement contracts may also be divided into Completion and Term forms. The Completion form normally requires the contractor to complete and deliver the specified product within the estimated cost, if possible. However, in the event the work cannot be completed within the estimated cost, the Government may require more effort without increase in fee, provided it increases the estimated cost and has sufficient funding. The Term form describes the scope of work in general and obligates the contractor to devote a specified level of effort for a stated time period. Fixed-price type contracts are generally of the Completion form, except for level-of-effort term contracts, which require the contractor to provide a specified level of effort over a specified period of time, on work that can be stated only in general terms. The Completion form of contract type is generally preferred over the Term form because it better ensures that the Government will receive its deliverable(s).

There is a preference in contract type for fixed-price contracts over cost-reimbursement contracts. Firm-fixed-price contracts, which best utilize the basic profit motive of business enterprises, are used when the risk involved can be predicted with an acceptable degree of certainty. When that is not the case, other contract types may be more suitable. Under a fixed-price contract, the contractor commits to delivering an acceptable product at a fixed price regardless of actual cost. Thus, under a fixed-price type contract, the possibility exists that the contractor could ultimately end up losing money on the effort.

Under a cost-reimbursement type contract, the Government reimburses all allowable costs up to the specified limit. Hence the risk to the Government is high, with no guarantee that a usable product will be delivered. The contractor merely agrees to use its best efforts to perform the specified work within the estimated cost. The risk to the contractor is low because all allowable costs are reimbursed by the Government.

FAR 16.1 through 16.3

There are many factors that the contracting officer considers in selecting and negotiating contract type. Major risk elements will influence the selection of contract type. Consideration must be given to the three program management parameters (cost, performance and schedule). Risk can also be caused by unique situations such as exotic specifications, first-time usage, hazardous components, or sophisticated hardware. Complex requirements usually result in greater cost risk assumption by the Government (e.g., research and development), whereas a recurring requirement or production shifts cost risk of monetary loss or gain to the contractor and a fixed-price contract is more appropriate. Urgency of the requirement may lead the Government to assume more risk or offer incentives to ensure timely performance. The period of performance or length of production run may require economic price adjustment terms or even a more flexibly-pried contract. Also, the extent of proposed subcontracting could reduce risk to the prime contractor.

Contract type can also result from the chance of program termination, which can be mitigated by multiyear contract or diversification. Multiyear contracting is a means to obtain quantity price discounts for requirements lasting up to four outyears after the base year without full funding by issuing a contract with a cancellation cost for each year should the funding not come through.

The contractor's pricing ability is also a key factor in contract type selection. Cost analysis of the offeror's proposal and the Government estimate provides baselines to negotiate contract pricing in the absence of price competition and price analysis, to ensure the contractor bears a fair degree of cost responsibility. Hence, the adequacy of the contractor's accounting system to develop valid cost data is critical to instill confidence in a cost proposal. Other key factors to consider include any concurrent contracts and their pricing arrangements, the contractor's technical capability and financial responsibility, and the stability of labor and material prices.

Many, though not all, contract types require the contracting officer to develop a sign a D&F to justify use of the chosen contract type. The D&F must identify added risks in terms of their mitigation and management, complexity of requirements, cost analysis if competition is limited or nonexistent, contractor's technical capability and financial responsibility (including its accounting system), contract administration, and effort to make follow-on contracts of a more favorable type. This document must be executed before solicitation.

A contract for up to 10 years may be used to purchase electricity from sources of renewable energy. The head of the contracting activity must determine that this approach is cost effective.

One can relate contract type to the acquisition stage of a given major program. During the material solution analysis stage, any contract type may be used. After Milestone A however, a cost-plus-fixed-fee contract is common. After Milestone B, incentive contracts are most likely used. After Milestone C, production will occur under a fixed-price contract (often incentivized). Operational support will then occur within a fixed-price environment, which might be incentivized.

Solicitation Provision

FAR 52.216-1, Type of Contract, except for a fixed-price acquisition made under simplified acquisition procedures, or for information or planning purposes.

3.5.1 Firm Fixed Price

FAR 16.202

A *firm-fixed-price contract* cannot be adjusted due to the contractor's cost experience. The contractor bears total cost risk and responsibility, and therefore a maximum incentive to control costs and perform effectively. Therefore, care should be taken before award to ensure there is reasonable certainty of cost, product performance and schedule achievement.

A firm-fixed-price contract is used to acquire commercial items and other supplies or services with definite functional specifications. Prior cost history is usually available. There is usually adequate price competition or comparison with prior competitive purchases of the same or similar supplies or services. Nearly all contracts resulting from sealed bidding are firm-fixed-price contracts. A written D&F that justifies contract type is not required.

Both parties have minimal administrative burden. The contractor need not have an approved cost accounting system; hence firms which are primarily commercial without an approved accounting system are compelled to use this contract type. The contract can include an award-fee incentive to address performance or delivery incentives rather than cost.

3.5.2 Firm Fixed Price with Economic Price Adjustment

FAR 16.203

A *fixed-price contract with economic price adjustment* is set up like a firm-fixed-price contract, but with a twist. The contract provides for up-or-down price revision upon the occurrence of specified contingencies. The price adjustment is based on a prescribed level in published industry prices, labor or material cost standards or indexes beyond the contractor's control. This contract type may include an award-fee adjustment based on performance or delivery incentives rather than cost. The contractor need not have an approved cost accounting system, though the contracting officer must execute a D&F justifying the use of a price adjustment clause to protect the Government and/or contractor from market fluctuations.

Use of an adjustment based on cost indexes of labor or materials may be appropriate when the period of performance exceeds one year and the economic variables for labor and materials are too unstable to equitably divide risk between Government and contractor (such as purchasing basic commodities subject to price fluctuation). The agency prepares and approves the price adjustment clause. It specifies labor rates and material unit prices subject to adjustment, and their quantities allocable to each deliverable unit. If adjustment is only to a unit price, then the catalog or price list (plus any discount) must be included in the contract file.

PGI 216.203-4

Adjustment provisions can result in significant and unanticipated price increases. They should be used only when general economic factors make the estimating of future costs too unpredictable within a fixed-price contract. These factors include volatility of labor and/or material costs and contract length. The provision must be carefully crafted to ensure an equitable adjustment to the contract. Hence, contracting officers should always request assistance from their local pricing office, DCMA or DCAA when considering use of an EPA provision.

The clause should not provide either a ceiling or a floor for adjustment unless based on indices below the six-digit level of the Bureau of Labor Statistics Producer Price Index, Employment Cost Index for wages and salaries, benefits and compensation costs for aerospace industries, or NAICS Product Code. A blended index can be used (e.g., labor and materials or labor and benefits, based on rate of expenditure by percentage). The clause should cover potential economic fluctuations using a trigger band. The clause must establish and identify a base period as a reference point for application of an index. The clause should not provide for an adjustment beyond the original contract performance period, including options. The adjustment clause should not apply to labor costs covered by a union agreement or uninvolved subcontract or overhead costs, nor to profit. Adjustments should be frequent enough to afford the contractor appropriate economic protection without creating a burdensome administrative effort, such as quarterly to annually. Paid adjustments must be subtracted from the total allowable costs to calculate any incentive arrangement. Likewise, profit and any costs not subject to economic fluctuation should be excluded. After labor and material allocations and contract price have been adjusted, they remain fixed through the life of the contract and can be modified only for significant changes in the scope of the contract, such as revised delivery schedule or labor or material cost adjustments.

Solicitation Provision

DFARS 252.216-7007, Economic Price Adjustment—Basic Steel, Aluminum, Brass, Bronze, or Copper Mill Products—Representation, in solicitations that include DFARS 252.216-7000, Economic Price Adjustment—Basic Steel, Aluminum, Brass, Bronze, or Copper Mill Products.

Solicitation Provisions and Contract Clauses

FAR 52.216-2, Economic Price Adjustment—Standard Supplies, for standard supplies with catalog or market prices.

FAR 52.216-3, Economic Price Adjustment—Semistandard Supplies, for semistandard supplies related to the prices of standard supplies with catalog or market price.

FAR 52.216-4, Economic Price Adjustment—Labor and Material, when labor or material cost factor(s) are subject to change.

DFARS 252.216-7000, Economic Price Adjustment—Basic Steel, Aluminum, Brass, Bronze, or Copper Mill Products, for basic steel, aluminum, brass, bronze, or copper mill products, such as sheets, plates, and bars, bearing an established catalog or market price. The 10 percent figure in paragraph (d)(1) of the clause can be exceeded only if approved at a level above the contracting officer.

DFARS 252.216-7001, Economic Price Adjustment—Nonstandard Steel Items, may be used for a steel producer which actually manufacturers the standard steel mill item (even if the items being acquired are nonstandard steel items, they must be made all in in part of standard steel mill items). For sealed bidding, omit Note 6 of the clause and all references thereto. Any proposed price that is not an established price must be verified.

DFARS 252.216-7003, Economic Price Adjustment—Wage Rates or Material Prices Controlled by a Foreign Government, if performed wholly or in part in a foreign country where the government controls wage rates or material prices and may impose a mandatory change during contract performance.

DFARS 252.216-7008, Economic Price Adjustment–Wage Rates or Material Prices Controlled by a Foreign Government—Representation, in solicitations that include DFARS 252.216-7003, Economic Price Adjustment—Wage Rates or Material Prices Controlled by a Foreign Government. If the solicitation includes the provision at FAR 52.204-7, do not separately list the provision 252.216-7008 in the solicitation.

3.5.3 Firm Fixed Price, Level-of-Effort Term

FAR 16.207

A *firm-fixed-price, level-of-effort term contract* is used to investigate a specific research and development area and produce a report showing the results achieved by the level of effort. Payment is based on the effort expended rather than on the results achieved. This contract type is usually at a price below $100,000, unless the chief of the purchasing officer agrees to a higher amount. The contractor will accept cost risk in this instance because it is confident in its cost estimate and willing to accept what little risk exists.

3.5.4 Fixed-Price Incentive

FAR 16.205-206 and 16.402-403

Incentive contracts are used to obtain supplies or services (often with improved delivery or technical performance) by relating the amount of profit or fee to contractor performance.[22] An incentive arrangement includes predefined relationships of cost, schedule and/or technical performance to motivate the contractor to meet or even exceed the Government's desired outcomes. Increased profit or fee dollars are earned for exceeding performance targets (not just minimum requirements), and decreases are imposed for missing targets. The contractor is thereby motivated to improve performance and mitigate waste and inefficiency. The contracting officer must first execute a D&F to justify contract type. This and other flexibly-priced contracts contain *framework pricing arrangements*, which are definitive in all respects except final pricing. They include a predetermined framework (e.g., algorithm, formula or index) to calculate price at time of completion.

Incentives are used when costs are not stable and cannot be projected with reasonable certainty. They should be structured to motivate the contractor toward a desired level of performance. They must clearly communicate what is desired, be quantitatively measurable and yet be realistic for contractor performance.

Many incentive contracts include only cost incentives, which take the form of a profit adjustment formula to motivate the contractor to effectively manage costs. No incentive contract may provide for other incentives without also providing a cost incentive or constraint to avoid paying more than the value of a performance or technical improvement. The parties negotiate a *share ratio* which shows the relative level of responsibility of costs which deviate from the target. If the ratio is 80/20 for example, the Government pays every dollar of cost overrun but reduces the profit by 20 cents for each dollar of overrun. If the contractor underruns, the government accepts the cost savings and adds to the profit amount 20 cents for each dollar underrun. In effect, the Government bears 80 percent of the cost risk and the contractor bears 20 percent.

To implement this pricing approach, in lieu of a firm fixed price, these contracts include a target cost, a target profit, and an adjustment formula. This formula is designed to ensure that actual cost at target will result in the target profit, cost overruns will result in downward adjustment of profit, and cost underruns will result in a higher final profit. The final price is subject to a negotiated price ceiling; however there is no limit on the final profit rate. This contract type ensures that the contractor's assumption of some cost responsibility will motivate a profit incentive to manage cost and performance. Billing prices are established as an interim basis for payment and are adjusted within the ceiling limits upon request of either party, once it is obvious that final negotiated cost will differ from target cost.

Added incentives on technical performance and/or delivery can positively impact the contractor's management of the work. Performance incentives may be used in connection with performance characteristics in major systems contracts (e.g., missile range, aircraft speed, engine thrust, or vehicle maneuverability), both in development (when performance objectives are known and fabrication of prototypes for test and evaluation is required) and in production (if improved performance is desired and attainable). Positive and negative performance incentives can also be considered for service contracts to perform objectively measurable tasks. Because technical performance incentives may involve a variety of characteristics that contribute to the overall performance of the end item, the incentives must be balanced to avoid exaggerating one characteristic to the detriment of overall performance.

The contract establishes test criteria (e.g., conditions, data interpretation, instrumentation precision, etc.) and performance standards (such as the quality levels of services to be provided). The incentive itself is calculated based on a formula included in the contract (e.g., a test speed which is ten miles per hour faster than specification earns one percent extra profit, whereas a speed which is ten miles slower loses one percent of profit).

Delivery incentives are used when the Government desires improvement from its required delivery schedule (e.g., earliest possible delivery or earliest quantity production). The contract specifies the rewards and penalties for Government-caused delays or other delays beyond the control of the contractor or subcontractor. A delivery incentive might reward one percent of profit for delivery 30 days early, or deduct one percent for every ten days late.

A properly structured multiple-incentive arrangement should motivate the contractor to strive for outstanding results in all incentive areas. It will compel trade-off decisions among the incentive areas, consistent with the Government's overall objectives for the acquisition. The incentive plan includes the *point of total assumption* (PTA), where the sum of actual cost and earned profit will equal the ceiling price. Beyond this point, the contractor absorbs total responsibility for cost growth.

For example, suppose the parties negotiate a target cost of \$100,000, a target profit of \$10,000 and a ceiling price of \$125,000, plus a share ratio of 70/30. The *point of total assumption* (PTA) is where the sum of actual cost and earned profit equals the point where final profit erodes to zero. Or,

$$\text{PTA} = \frac{\text{Ceiling Price} - \text{Target Price}}{\text{Government Share}} + \text{Target Cost}$$

$$\text{PTA} = \frac{\$125{,}000 - (100{,}000 + 10{,}000)}{0.70} + \$100{,}000$$

$$= \frac{\$15{,}000}{0.70} + \$100{,}000 = \$121{,}429.$$

This allows the contractor to incur a cost overrun of over 21 percent before all profit erodes; beyond that point, the contractor earns no more profit dollars and has no motivation to control costs. However, since delivery is required in a fixed-price environment, the contactor is now unable to cover any additional costs, but must still perform. However, the PTA shows that there is still plenty of room for cost growth, which hopefully will result in better technical performance and/or early delivery. Note however that the final price can never exceed the ceiling price of \$125,000, regardless of contractor performance, at which point it must complete performance with its own funding and no further help from the Government.

Now, assume that final cost is $95,000, a 5 percent underrun. Then the contractor receives its share of the underrun plus target profit:

$$\text{Final Profit} = (\text{Underrun} \times \text{Contractor Share}) + \text{Target Profit}$$
$$= (\$5{,}000 \times 0.30) + \$10{,}000 = \$13{,}500.$$

Then the final price is $95,000 + $13,500 = $108,500. The effective profit rate is

$$\frac{\$13{,}500}{\$95{,}000} = 14.21\%, \text{ as opposed to a } 10\% \text{ goal.}$$

Notice that the final profit exceeds the target profit in both value and rate of return. This provides a reward to the contractor for effective cost performance.

Because performance incentives present complex problems in contract administration, the contracting officer negotiates them in full coordination with Government engineering and pricing specialists. The parties must also remain aware of the effect that any contract changes pursuant to the Changes clause will have on performance incentives.

There are four different methods used to price changes in FPI contracts. The *Individual Adjustment* method means the parties negotiate separately each component of the incentive package. This approach maximizes tailoring the change to the circumstances but is time-consuming and administratively burdensome, and could permit a poorly performing contractor to get well. The *Severable Change* method negotiates price adjustment separately to be added to the contract as a package, but the costs must be segregable. The *Constant Dollar* method increases ceiling price by the same dollar amount as target price. This approach significantly increases profit at the point of total assumption, and is used when small changes do not greatly affect program uncertainty. The *Constant Percentage* method ignores the dollar relationships of these values by adjusting the ceiling price to be the same percentage of target cost, and can be used to combine multiple changes.

Objective criteria are commonly used with both cost-plus-incentive-fee and fixed-price-incentive contracts. Contractor performance incentives should relate to specific performance areas of milestones, such as delivery or test schedules, quality controls and reliability and maintenance standards. If the contracting officer determines that it is in the best interest of the Government to also incentivize subjective elements of performance, the contract should include multiple incentives (both objective and subjective), with either an award or incentive cost criterion.

To further complicate the subject of fixed-price incentive contracts, there are several different variations that are authorized for use. Each will now be examined.

3.5.4.1 *Fixed-Price Incentive (Firm Target) Contract*

FAR 16.403-1

A *fixed-price incentive (firm target) contract* includes a target cost, target profit, price ceiling (but not a profit ceiling or floor), and profit adjustment formula. This is the predominant form of fixed-price incentive contract and incorporates the features just discussed. The price ceiling is the maximum that may be paid to the contractor. As we saw in the mathematical example above, once the contractor completes performance, the parties negotiate the final cost and apply the formula to establish the final price. If the final cost is less than the target cost, the final profit will exceed the target profit, whereas a final cost above the target cost results in a final profit below the target profit. If the final negotiated cost exceeds the price ceiling, the contractor absorbs the difference as a loss and earns no profit. Because profit varies inversely with cost, this contract type provides a profit incentive for the contractor to control costs.

PGI 216.403-1

Fixed-price incentive (firm target) contracts are encouraged for acquisitions moving from development to production. However, the cost risk cannot be so great that establishing a ceiling price is unrealistic. As a rule of thumb, if actual costs on prior FFP contracts have varied by more than four percent from the costs negotiated, then incentives may be appropriate. Remember that actual costs on prior contracts for the same item are cost and pricing data on the pending contract, regardless of contract type or data reporting requirements of the prior contract. As another rule of thumb, the typical incentive arrangement for FPI contracts in production mode would be a 120 percent ceiling and a 50/50 share ratio.

The analysis of risk is essential. For the contractor, technical and schedule risk also have financial ramifications because they lead to increased effort and therefore increased cost. Therefore, all risk can be translated into cost risk and quantified. Risk always has two components that must be considered in the quantification: the magnitude of the impact and the probability that it will occur.

Many fixed-price production contracts include many FFP subcontracts. The subcontractor is obligated to deliver at the negotiated price, so the risk to the prime contractor is the supplier's failure to perform satisfactorily or on time. This risk is considered low by both the prime and the subcontractor as evidenced by the FFP contract type. In addition, the prime contractor will normally have priced effort (either as direct labor or within overhead) for material management or subcontract administration to ensure performance by suppliers. If the majority of the target cost is comprised of FFP subcontracts, then the majority of the prime contractor's cost risk is minimal. This argues for a lower ceiling price. On the other hand, if a subcontract is not yet negotiated, then the risk is essentially limited to the difference between the subcontractor proposal and the subcontract value within the prime contractor's proposal.

For subcontracts that are not FFP, the risk to the prime results from the risk represented by the subcontractors' contractual relationship with the prime. If the subcontract is FPIF and has a 60/40 share ratio and 120 percent ceiling, the prime's risk is 40 percent of each dollar of overrun up to the ceiling amount. The subcontractor's risk must then be analyzed to determine the probability of reaching the ceiling price.

The risk in direct labor involves the hours needed to perform the effort, since there is little risk to the labor rates paid to employees. This risk can be driven by several factors including technical complexity or schedule constraints or the availability of labor, parts, or tooling. Generally, any schedule slip can only affect the prime contractor's in-house cost, so schedule risk primarily consists of the impact on the prime contractor's performance. On the other hand, a production schedule assumes optimal task sequencing which presumes the timely arrival and quality of parts from suppliers or in-house. Any delay in receiving parts as planned could require task resequencing and could impact the efficiency of performing some tasks but will not cause the entire workforce to be idle during the delay.

Indirect costs provide either cost growth or cost reduction opportunities. Proposed overhead rates are based on forecasts of overhead expenses and their base amounts. The final overhead rate charged to a contract will be based on the actual overhead expenses and the actual base, perhaps significantly different than estimated (higher or lower). Since a significant portion of the indirect expenses are fixed in nature (such as depreciation), the base fluctuations are more likely to create risk.

The contracting officer should also consider the contractor's ability to predict overhead rates by comparing proposed and actual rates for prior years. If the contractor overruns direct labor hours, that rate would be applied to a higher base and therefore increased overhead expenses, and vice versa.

Contract Clause

FAR 52.216-16, Incentive Price Revision—Firm Target. Use the clause with its Alternate I to order supplies or services under a provisioning document or Government option and include the prices in the incentive arrangement.

3.5.4.2 *Fixed-Price Incentive (Successive Targets) Contract*

FAR 16.403-2

A *fixed-price incentive (successive targets) contract* specifies an initial target cost and profit, and a ceiling price as above, but adds an initial profit adjustment formula to establish the firm target profit (including a ceiling and floor), and the production point at which the firm targets (cost and profit) will be negotiated (usually before delivery or completion of the first item). When the production point is reached, the parties negotiate the firm target cost based on cost experience under the contract to date. Applying the formula establishes the firm target profit. The parties may decide to negotiate a firm fixed price at this point by adding together the firm target cost and target profit, or else negotiate a formula to establish the final cost at completion and then apply the formula to set the final profit. This contract type is appropriate when enough information becomes available early in contract performance to negotiate either a firm fixed price or firm targets and a final profit formula to incentivize the contractor.

Contract Clause

FAR 52.216-17, Incentive Price Revision—Successive Targets. Use the clause with its Alternate I for the same circumstance as FAR 52.216-16.

3.5.4.3 *Fixed Price with Prospective Price Redetermination*

FAR 16.205

A *fixed-price contract with prospective price redetermination* provides a firm fixed price for an initial period of contract performance, and prospective redetermination at a stated time(s) (at least annually) to price-out subsequent periods of performance. The contract may provide for a ceiling price based on evaluation of performance uncertainties and their possible cost impact, and assumption of a reasonable amount of risk by the contractor. However, the ceiling price may be revised only by equitable adjustment or as specified in the contract.

Contract Clause

FAR 52.216-5, Price Redetermination—Prospective.

3.5.4.4 *Fixed Price with Retroactive Price Redetermination*

FAR 16.206

A *fixed-price contract with retroactive price redetermination* provides for price adjustment within the ceiling price after contract completion. It is used for research and development contracts valued at $150,000 or less when a firm fixed price cannot be negotiated at the outset and the short performance period make the use of any other contract type impracticable. The contract requires a negotiated billing price. The ceiling price is adjusted equitably or as specified in the contract. The ceiling price is really the only cost control motivator for the contractor in this variation.

Table 3.1 identifies various sample performance evaluation criteria which can be used in incentive contracts.

Contract Clause

FAR 52.216-6, Price Redetermination—Retroactive.

3.5.4.5 Fixed-Price Contract with Award Fees

FAR 16.404

Award-fee provisions may be used in fixed-price contracts when the Government wishes to motivate a contractor but contractor performance cannot be measured objectively to allow for other incentive arrangements. Such contracts establish a fixed price for satisfactory contract performance, and an award fee for above-target performance. A special board of Government officials is convened to determine the award fee. This variation uses award fee provisions to be discussed thoroughly in an upcoming section.

3.5.5 Labor Hour and Time-and-Materials Contracts

FAR 16.601

A *time-and-materials contract* is based on direct labor hours at specified fixed hourly rates for each labor category. It reimburses actual costs for materials, subcontracts and other direct costs. It is not possible at the time of placing the contract to either estimate accurately the extent or duration of the work, or to anticipate costs with any reasonable degree of confidence. It is commonly used for engineering and design services, repair and maintenance and overhaul, and emergency work. In a related vein, a *fixed rate contract* requires product delivery for a period of time at a fixed price.

The contract specifies separate fixed hourly rates for each labor category. These rates can also cover services transferred between divisions, subsidiaries or affiliates of the contractor under a common control. Materials are covered by a separately priced line item. These contracts do not include profit for the transferring organization, but may include profit for the prime contractor. Any commercial services carry the established catalog or market rate per the

Table 3.1 Incentive Performance Criteria

		Unsatisfactory	*Acceptable*	*Good*	*Excellent*
Time of Delivery	Adherence to plan schedule	Late on 10% plans without prior agreement.	Occasional late plan without justification.	Meets plan schedule.	Delivers all plans on schedule and meets production change requirements on schedule.
	Action on Anticipated delays	Slow to resolve plans.	Anticipates changes and advises program office, but misses completion of design plans 10% of time.	Keeps program office posted on delays and resolves plans independently.	Anticipates in time, advises program office, resolves plans independently and meets schedule.
	Plan Maintenance	Work plan changes delayed.	Major work plans coordinated in time to meet production schedules.	Design changes from studies and interrelated plant issued in time to meet product schedules.	Design changes and studies resolved and test data issued ahead of production requirements.
Quality of Work	Work Appearance	80% of drawings are compatible with program office processes and use.	90% are compatible with program office processes and use.	100% are compatible with program office processes and use.	100% are compatible with program office processes and use.
	Thoroughness and Accuracy of Work	Occasional problems in following guidance, type, and standard drawings.	Has followed guidance, type, and standard drawings. Questions and resolves doubtful areas.	Work complete with notes and thorough explanations for anticipated questionable areas.	Work of highest caliber incorporating all pertinent data required including related activities.

(*Continued*)

Table 3.1 (Continued)

	Unsatisfactory	*Acceptable*	*Good*	*Excellent*
Engineering Competence	Inadequate engineering ability to use and adapt existing designs to suit job on hand for routine work.	Engineered to satisfy specifications, guidance plans and material provided.	Displays excellent knowledge of subject matter. Requirements consider systems aspect, cost, shop capabilities and procurement problems.	Exceptional knowledge of subject matter and adaptability to work processes incorporating knowledge of future planning in Design.
Liaison Effectiveness	Dependent on program office to force resolution of problems without constructive recommendations to subcontractors or vendors.	Maintains normal contract with associated activities depending on program office for problems requiring military resolution.	Maintains independent contact with all associated activities, keeping them informed to produce compatible design with little assistance for program office.	Maintains expert contact, keeping program office informed, obtains info from equipment supplies without prompting of program office.
Tenacity	Requires occasional prodding to stay on schedule and expects program office resolution of most problems.	Normal interest and desire to provide workable plans with average assistance and direction by program office.	Complete and accurate job. Free of incompatibilities with little or no direction by program office.	Develops complete and accurate plans, seeks out problem areas and resolves ahead of schedule.

Cost Control	Utilization of Personnel	Poor supervision to set and review goals for designers.	System planning by supervisory personnel, studies checked by engineers.	Design parameters established by system engineers and held in design plans.	Modifications to design plans limited to less than 5% due to lack of engineering system correlation.
	Control Direct Charges (Except Labor)	Expenditures reviewed occasionally by supervision.	Direct charges set and accounted for on each work package.	Provides services as part of normal design function without extra charges.	No cost overruns on original estimates absorbs service demands by program office.
	Performance to Cost Estimate	Does not meet cost estimate for original work or changes 20% time.	Exceeds original estimate on change orders 10% time.	Exceeds original estimate on change orders 5% time.	Never exceeds estimates of original package or change orders.

established pricing practice of the transferring organization. Material handling costs are excluded from the labor-hour rate and allocated to direct materials per the contractor's usual accounting procedures. In a related vein, a *fixed rate contract* requires product delivery for a period of time at a fixed price.

The contract includes a ceiling price that the contractor exceeds at its own risk. Contractors under this contract type are not motivated toward effective cost control. It is commonly used for engineering and design services, repair and maintenance and overhaul, and emergency work.

The contracting officer's D&F of contract type must be approved by the head of the contracting activity if total length (including option periods) exceeds three years. The D&F reports on efforts to develop a firm-fixed-price contract.

This contract type provides no positive profit incentive to the contractor for cost control or labor efficiency, so Government surveillance of contractor performance must give reasonable assurance that efficient methods and effective cost controls are being used.

FAR 16.602

A *labor-hour contract* is a variation of the time-and-materials contract, differing only in that materials are not supplied by the contractor. The same restrictions for usage apply.

DFARS 212.207

DoD cannot use a time-and-materials or labor hour contract to buy commercial supplies, and can buy commercial services only in support of a commercial item or emergency repairs. However, the head of the agency can approve a written determination for commercial services if the offeror has submitted sufficient information to demonstrate that the services are commonly sold to the public through use of time-and-materials or labor-hour contracts, and that such a contract is in the best interest of the Government.

DFARS 216.601

For contracts and orders where the portion performed on a time-and-materials or labor-hour basis exceeds $1 million, the approval authority for the determination and findings must be the senior contracting official within the contracting activity. If below $1 million, the approval authority is one level above the contracting officer. These approval levels do not apply to contracts that support contingency or peacekeeping operations or provide humanitarian assistance, disaster relief, or recovery from conventional, nuclear, biological, chemical, cyber, or radiological attack.

The determination and findings must describe the market research conducted, state that the extent or duration of the work or cost estimate is not certain, justify contract type, limit the use of time-and-materials (by fixed-price subcontracts) and labor-hour requirements (by limiting the value or length of the effort), and describe how the Government will minimize the use of time-and-materials and labor-hour contracts on future acquisitions for the same requirements.

Solicitation Provisions

FAR 52.216-30, Time-and-Materials/Labor-Hour Proposal Requirements—Non-Commercial Item Acquisitions without Adequate Price Competition.

FAR 52.216-31, Time-and-Materials/Labor-Hour Proposal Requirements—Commercial Item Acquisitions.

DFARS 252.216-7002, Alternate A, with FAR 52.216-29, Time-and-Materials/Labor-Hour Proposal Requirements—Non-Commercial Item Acquisition with Adequate Price Competition, in competitive solicitations contemplating the use of a time-and-materials or labor-hour contract type for non-commercial items.

Contract Clause

FAR 52.216-29, Time-and-Materials/Labor-Hour Requirements—Non-Commercial Item Acquisitions With Adequate Price Competition, for noncommercial items where price is based on adequate price competition.

3.5.6 Cost-Plus-Incentive-Fee Contract

FAR 16.304 & 16.405

Once we encounter contracts without a ceiling price, we introduce the concept of fee. A *fee* is the same as profit, namely the amount of revenue that exceeds cost. It is merely a change in terminology to differentiate from fixed-price contracts, which include profit rather than fee. Also, cost-plus contracts do not use the term "price," but rather talk in terms of estimated cost and fee. Within DoD, the D&F for any cost-type contract over $25 million must be approved by the head of the contracting activity. Otherwise, the D&F for this contract type can be approved at any level above the contracting officer.

A *cost-plus-incentive-fee contract* has a negotiated fee to be adjusted later by a formula based on the relationship of total allowable costs to total target costs. This contract type specifies a target cost and three different fee numbers (target, minimum and maximum), and a fee adjustment formula. Note the differences from fixed-price incentive contracts: the firm ceiling price concept is gone (replaced by an estimate), and now we see minimum and maximum restrictions on the fee rate.

After contract performance, the final fee is determined in accordance with the formula. The fee amount increases above target when total allowable costs are less than the target cost, and decreases below target when total allowable costs exceed the target cost. When total allowable cost is greater than the range of costs within which the fee-adjustment formula operates, the contractor is paid total allowable costs, plus the minimum fee. By contrast, if total cost is below the cost range, the contractor receives all allowable costs plus maximum fee.

Assume a target cost of \$500,000, target fee of 10% (\$50,000), minimum fee of 5% (\$25,000), maximum fee of 15% (\$75,000), and an 80/20 share ratio. Now let us assume a 2% overrun, which means the final cost is

\$500,000 + 2% = \$500,000 + \$10,000 = \$510,000.

The contactor's share of the overrun is 20% × \$10,000 = \$2,000. Subtracting this result from the target fee of \$50,000 leaves a final fee of \$48,000. Added to the final cost of \$510,000, this yields a final contract amount of \$558,000. The final fee rate is:

$$\frac{\$48{,}000}{\$510{,}000} = 9.4\%.$$

Note that this total amount is below the maximum possible amount of \$500,000 + \$75,000 = \$575,000, so it is allowable. Also, note that the final fee rate is below the target of 10 percent because the contractor incurred cost growth and was therefore penalized.

Alternatively, assume the contractor underruns cost estimate by 15 percent. Then,

\$500,000 − \$75,000 = \$425,000 final cost

Contractor share = 20% × \$75,000 = \$15,000
Final fee = \$50,000 + \$15,000 = \$65,000
Final amount = \$425,000 + \$65,000 = \$490,000
Final fee rate = $\frac{\$65{,}000}{\$425{,}000} = 15.3\%$.

Note the higher calculated fee rate because the contractor is rewarded for a significant cost underrun.

But wait! Now we have another problem! This result exceeds the legally permitted maximum fee rate of 15 percent for a research and development contract; hence the final fee rate must be restricted to 15% × $425,000 = $63,750. This is because the actual result lies outside the *range of incentive effectiveness*, the set of probable costs over which the incentive arrangement works. The delta of $65,000 − $63,750 = $1,250 is not recovered by the contractor, not as lost cost but rather as unrealized profit. In this example, that would equate to a maximum cost figure of $600,000 (plus $30,000 fee) and a minimum cost figure of just under $428,000.

In this example, the range of incentive effectiveness lies between the outcomes which produce a 5 and 15 percent final fee. It equates to a maximum allowable cost figure of $547,619 (plus $27,381 fee) and a minimum allowable cost figure of $478,261 (plus a 15 percent fee of $71,739). This concept also applies to some extent to fixed-price incentive contracts, where the point of total assumption coincides with the top end of the range (one could argue that there is no bottom end).

Notice that there is more room for the incentive fee to work for an overrun than underrun. This is due to the cost uncertainty of a cost contract environment being reflected in this example, where the target fee is midway between the minimum and maximum fees. These numbers can be adjusted in negotiations if the Government wishes a different result, such as more seriously motivating the contractor to control costs.

Notice that in this example, there is more room for the incentive fee to work for an overrun than underrun:

$600,000 − $500,000 = $100,000 overrun

$500,000 − $428,000 = $72,000 underrun

This is due to the cost uncertainty of a cost contract environment being reflected in this example, where the target fee is midway between the minimum and maximum fees.

As with fixed-price incentives, the contract may include technical performance incentives if required development of a major system is feasible, and the use of both cost and technical performance incentives is desirable. Schedule performance incentives may also be used to reward early and/or penalize late delivery. The fee adjustment formula provides an incentive over the full range of foreseeable variations from target cost. If a high maximum fee is negotiated, the contract also provides for a low minimum fee that could conceivably be zero or negative.

Changes can be priced out using the same methods as FPI contracts. The *Constant Dollar* method maintains the dollar relationships between minimum, maximum and target fees (and therefore the range of incentive effectiveness), with a certain increase in minimum fee, but assumes little technical uncertainty associated with the changed effort. The *Constant Percentage* method ignores the dollar relationships of these values and instead preserves the percentage relationships between minimum and maximum fees. This method increases the minimum fee less than the Constant Dollar method and thereby increases the range of incentive effectiveness due to greater uncertainty for cost overrun, and can also be used to combine multiple changes.

PGI 216.405-1

In an initial product development contract on a cost-plus-incentive-fee basis, it may be appropriate to provide for relatively small adjustments in fee tied to the cost incentive feature, but significant adjustments if the contractor meets or surpasses performance targets. Then subsequent development and test contracts may include an incentive formula tied to the contractor's success in cost control.

DFARS 216.301-3

For contracts in connection with a military construction project or a military family housing project, contracting officers shall not use cost-plus-fixed-fee, cost-plus-award-fee, or cost-plus-incentive-fee contract types.[23] This applies notwithstanding a declaration of war or the declaration by the President of a national emergency under section 201 of the National Emergencies Act that includes the use of the Armed Forces.[24]

Solicitation Provisions and Contract Clauses

FAR 52.216-7, Allowable Cost and Payment, for a cost-plus-incentive-fee or a cost-plus-award-fee contract.

FAR 52.216-10, Incentive Fee, for cost-plus-incentive-fee arrangements.

3.5.7 Cost-Plus-Award-Fee Contract

FAR 16.305 & 16.401

A *cost-plus-award-fee contract* provides two fees: a base amount (which may be zero, but generally not more than 3 percent of estimated cost) fixed at contract inception, and an award fee based upon a judgmental evaluation by the Government to motivate excellence in contract performance. It may be used in combination with other types of incentive fee contacts. Periodic evaluations by the Government help determine award amounts by providing feedback to the contractor to enable improved contractor performance. This contract type can improve contractor communications, motivation, responsiveness, and visibility. Or it can lead to contractor frustration at perceived Government unfairness, since the contractor has no basis for appeal of award fee decisions. Within DoD, the D&F for this contract type can be approved at the level below the head of the contacting activity.

Performance factors must be meaningful, demonstrate effective management control over each factor and its results, and clearly described with measurement criteria. Evaluation may include assessment of personnel usage or ability to plan work, as well as timely and acceptable test results. Management controls could include business and cost management, corporate support, customer relationships, mission enhancement, and planning and scheduling. Award-fee contracts are used when predetermined objective incentive targets are not possible. The contract arrangement should motivate the contractor toward exceptional performance and provide the Government with the flexibility to evaluate both performance and the conditions under which it was achieved. The Government bears additional administrative effort and cost to monitor and evaluate performance, so the D&F justifying contract type addresses the expected benefits by a risk and cost-benefit analysis. Award fee is not earned if the contractor's overall performance is unsatisfactory. The Government determination and its methodology are documented in the contract file. The determination is a unilateral decision solely within the discretion of the Government and not subject to dispute or appeal.

All contracts providing for award fees are supported by an award-fee plan that establishes the procedures to evaluate award fee. There may also be a formal award review board. An *Award-Fee Board* is a team identified by name or position in the award-fee plan to evaluate performance and recommend the award-fee amount. The *Fee-Determining Official* reviews the Board's recommendations to determine the amount of award fee to be earned by the contractor for each evaluation period. Award-fee plans are approved by the Fee Determining Official and identify the award-fee evaluation criteria and how they link to the acquisition objectives in terms of contract cost, schedule, and technical performance. They describe how the contractor's performance will be measured against the award-fee evaluation criteria. The plan defines the total award-fee pool amount and its allocation across each evaluation period.

Award fee pools use an adjectival rating and award-fee pool earned percentages such as in table 3.2 (contracting officers may supplement the adjectival rating description). The plan should provide for evaluation period(s) at stated intervals during the period of performance (e.g., quarterly, every 6 or 12 months, or at specific milestones) to inform the contractor of performance quality and the areas in which improvement is expected. It should specifically prohibit earning any award fee when a contractor's overall cost, schedule and technical performance is below satisfactory.

Table 3.2 Award-Fee Pool Percentages

Award-Fee Rating	*Award-Fee Pool Available to Be Earned*
Excellent	91%–100%
Very Good	76%–90%
Good	51%–75%
Unsatisfactory	50% or less

The Government may unilaterally change evaluation weights during the contract, to take effect with the subsequent rating period, if it desires to change management emphasis as the contract progresses. A significant amount of the fee pool must be retained however, for the final evaluation period to maintain contractor incentive.

The Government does not rollover unearned award fee dollars, which is a process that would transfer unearned fee in one evaluation period to a subsequent period to allow the contractor an additional opportunity to earn fee dollars. Prohibiting rollover imposes a penalty of sorts in terms of lost fee dollars, but alerts the contractor to improve performance in future evaluation periods. Similarly, any award fee plan must allow for the possibility of zero fee dollars when a contractor's overall cost, schedule and technical performance is below satisfactory.

Each agency collects data on award fee, incentive fees, and performance measures to determine their effectiveness as a tool to improve contractor performance and achieve desired program outcomes. This information should be included in the acquisition planning process to determine the appropriate type of contract for future acquisitions.

DFARS 216.405-2

The award-fee pool is the total available award fee for each evaluation period for the life of the contract. The contracting officer must ensure that at least 40 percent of the award fee is available for the final evaluation and appropriately distributes award fee over all evaluation periods to incentivize the contractor throughout performance of the contract. To set this below 40 percent requires a contracting officer determination approved by the head of the contracting activity. The fee-determining official's rating for award-fee evaluations is provided to the contractor within 45 calendar days of the end of the period being evaluated. In situations where there may be no identifiable milestone for a year or more, consideration should be given to apportioning some of the award-fee pool for a predetermined interim period of time based on assessing progress toward milestones. This contract type is not used for engineering development or operational system development acquisitions with specifications suitable for simultaneous research and development and production. However, it is permitted for individual development effort associated with a major weapon system or equipment if more advantageous and intended to determine or solve specific problems associated with the system or equipment.

Weighted guidelines are not used for deriving either the base (fixed) fee or the award fee. The base fee cannot exceed three percent of the estimated cost of the contract exclusive of the fee.

The D&F for award-fee contracts must be signed by the head of the contracting activity or designee one level below. The D&F for all other incentive contracts may be signed at one level above the contracting officer.

DFARS 216.405-2-70

A mandatory evaluation criterion of any award-fee plan is a review of (sub) contractor actions that jeopardized the health or safety of Government personnel and gross negligence or reckless disregard for the safety of such personnel, such as conviction in a criminal proceeding, finding of fault and liability in a civil or administrative proceeding or DoD investigation. If such an event occurs, the contracting officer may consider reducing or denying award fees for a period or even recovering all or part of award fees previously paid for such period. A similar punitive action applies if private security functions in an area of contingency operations, complex contingency operations, or designated military operations or exercises.

PGI 216.405-2

The contracting activity may establish a board to evaluate contractor performance and either determine the amount of the award or recommend an amount to the contracting officer. The board can afford the contractor an opportunity to present information on its own behalf.

PGI 216.470

Award fees can be used in other types of contracts if the:

- administrative costs of evaluation do not exceed the expected benefits;
- award review board conducts the evaluation;
- base fee is not used;
- chief of the contracting office approves the use of the award amount; and
- Government wishes to motivate and reward a contractor to buy capital assets (including machine tools) manufactured in the United States or

perform in areas which cannot be measured objectively, and where normal incentive provisions cannot be used (e.g., logistics support, quality, timeliness, ingenuity, and cost effectiveness).

Contract Clauses

DFARS 252.216-7004, Award Fee Reduction or Denial for Jeopardizing the Health or Safety of Government Personnel, when containing award-fee provisions.

3.5.8 Cost-Plus-Fixed-Fee Contract

FAR 16.306

A *cost-plus-fixed-fee contract* has a negotiated fee that does not vary with actual cost, but may be adjusted as a result of changes in the work to be performed under the contract. This arrangement covers efforts that present great risk to contractors but only a minimum incentive to control costs. It is suitable for research, preliminary exploration, or study, or for development and test, provided that the required *level of effort* (the quantity of hours to be procured over a stated period of time) is unknown. It is not used to develop major systems after preliminary exploration, studies and risk reduction indicate that development can be achieved and reasonably firm performance objectives and schedules are available. All allowable costs are reimbursed up to the estimated cost level. There is no guarantee of results, only the contactor's best efforts. The fee dollars are fixed regardless of cost performance. The Government is free to add funding to cover additional cost, but the fee dollars remain unchanged (hence the final fee rate would drop). There is no guarantee of results, only the contactor's best efforts. This contract type will generate unpopularity with some members of the public and Congress due to many past instances of cost growth and overrun.

A cost-plus-fixed-fee contract may take either the completion or term format. The *term* form describes the scope of work in general terms and requires the contractor to devote a specified level of effort for a stated time period. If performance is satisfactory to the Government, the fixed fee is paid at the end of the contract period. The *completion* form contains a definite goal or target and end product, and normally requires the contractor to complete and deliver the specified end product (often a final research report) as a condition for payment of the entire fixed fee. If the end item is not delivered in time, the contractor may be directed by the Government to continue performance until delivery is made, and if additional is necessary and provided, the work must be under a cost-only basis without additional fee dollars. Because the delivery requirement imposes a certain amount of risk on the contractor, fee rates tend to be slightly higher under this method than the term format.

For both contract forms, if performance is satisfactory to the Government, the fixed fee is paid at the end of the contract period. Should the work not be completed within the estimated cost, the Government may increase the contract amount to require more effort and cover the cost without increasing fee.

The cost-plus-a-percentage-of-cost contract would guarantee the contractor a set percentage of fee dollars regardless of contract performance. This means that the contractor would be motivated to overrun the contract cost in order to make more profit. Once permitted and used by the Federal Government during wartime, it is now prohibited in all prime and subcontracts (except under firm-fixed-price contracts).

DFARS 216.306

Annual military construction appropriations acts prohibit the use of cost-plus-fixed-fee contracts over $25,000 that are performed within the United States (except Alaska). The Secretaries of the military departments can approve such contracts if for environmental work that is not classified as construction. Any other waiver requests must be approved by the Secretary of Defense or designee.

Solicitation Provisions and Contract Clauses

FAR 52.216-7, Allowable Cost and Payment. Use the clause with Alternate I for a construction contract. Use the clause with Alternate II for an educational institution contract. Use the clause with Alternate III for a contract with a state or local government. Use Alternate IV for a nonprofit organization if it is not an educational institution, is a state or local government, or is exempted under OMB Uniform Guidance at 2 CFR Part 200, Appendix VIII.

FAR 52.216-8, Fixed Fee, for other than a construction contract.

FAR 52.216-9, Fixed-Fee—Construction, for a cost-plus-fixed-fee construction contract.

3.5.9 Cost-Only Contract

FAR 16.302

In a *cost-only contract*, the contractor receives no fee. It is used for research and development work with nonprofit educational or other nonprofit organizations.

FAR 16.303

A variation of this contract type is a *cost-sharing contract*. Here the contractor receives no fee and is reimbursed only for an agreed-upon portion of its allowable costs (less than 100 percent). It is used when the contractor expects compensating benefits in future business, either Government or commercial, and wishes to obtain defrayment of its development costs. Again, this would most likely be an educational or nonprofit organization.

Solicitation Provisions and Contract Clauses

FAR 52.216-11, Cost Contract—No Fee. Include Alternate I for a research and development contract with an educational institution or nonprofit organization and no withhold of allowable costs.

FAR 52.216-12, Cost-Sharing Contract—No Fee. Include Alternate I for research and development with an educational institution or a nonprofit organization and no withhold of allowable costs.

FAR 52.216-15, Predetermined Indirect Cost Rates, for a research and development contract with an educational institution using predetermined indirect cost rates.

3.5.10 Letter Contract

FAR 16.603

A *letter contract* is a written preliminary contractual instrument that authorizes the contractor to begin immediately to manufacture supplies or perform services. A letter contract is used when the contractor receives a binding commitment to start work immediately, and negotiating a definitive contract is not yet possible. However, a letter contract is as complete and definite as possible. If award is based on price competition, the contracting officer includes an overall price ceiling in the letter contract.

Each letter contract contains a negotiated definitization schedule including three dates for: submission of the contractor's price proposal and required cost or pricing data, the start of negotiations, and definitization of final price. This date must be within 180 days after the date of the letter contract or before completion of 40 percent of the work to be performed, whichever occurs first. However, a separate date after proposal submission may be established for any required make-or-buy and subcontracting plans.

If the contracting officer and the contractor cannot reach agreement as to price or fee, the contractor proceeds with the work and the contracting officer may, with the approval of the head of the contracting activity, determine a reasonable price or fee, subject to appeal under the Disputes clause.

A letter contract requires the head of the contracting activity or a designee to determine in writing that no other contract is suitable. Letter contracts do not commit the Government to a definitive contract in excess of the funds available at the time of execution. The maximum liability of the Government is the estimated amount necessary to cover contractor requirements for funds before definitization, but not over 50 percent of the estimated cost of the definitive contract, unless approved in advance by the official that authorized the letter contract.

A letter contract is an example of a *gap filler*, an interim agreement to define the rights and obligations of the parties and the basis to conduct business before establishing a formal contract. Other examples of gap fillers are memoranda of understanding and teaming or short-term agreements.

Letter contracts and similar undefinitized instruments contain at least a preliminary basic plan and will negotiate a final plan within 90 days after award or before definitization, whichever occurs first. Per DFARS 217.7404, undefinitized FMS contracts may allow up to 180 days after receipt of proposal (later for a contingency, humanitarian, or peacekeeping mission or if over $50 million in value, with prior approval from the head of the contracting activity).

DFARS 217.7404

The contracting officer may withhold up to 5 percent of subsequent financing requirements if no definitization proposal is submitted.

PGI 217.74

The contracting officer must obtain written approval to enter into an undefinitized contracting action. This justification must discuss the urgency of need prior to definitization, adverse impact on the Government due to delays in performance, the contracting instrument to be used, funding limitation, and the schedule to definitize. A maximum not-to-exceed price is necessary for any fixed-price instrument.

Contract Clauses

FAR 52.216-23, Execution and Commencement of Work.

FAR 52.216-24, Limitation of Government Liability.

FAR 52.216-26, Payments of Allowable Costs Before Definitization, if cost-reimbursement, except for ship conversion, alteration, or repair.

DFARS 252.217-7027, Contract Definitization, instead of FAR 52.216-25, Contract Definitization.

3.5.11 Indefinite Delivery/Indefinite Quantity Contract

3.5.11.1 Policy

Indefinite delivery contracts provide for issuing orders during the contract period without specifying a firm delivery schedule. Likewise, *indefinite quantity contracts* have no firm quantities in the contract, other than a minimum or maximum quantity. *Delivery order contracts* cover supplies, while *task order contracts* cover services. These contracts have the following advantages:

- limit the Government's obligation to the minimum quantity specified in the contract;
- may provide for any appropriate cost or pricing arrangement;
- permit flexible quantity and delivery scheduling after requirements are firm; and
- permit Government stocks to be maintained at minimum levels and ship directly to users.

An *indefinite-quantity/indefinite-delivery* contract is used when the Government can only guess how much it will need or when it will need it. The contracting officer does not synopsize orders under indefinite-delivery contracts, unless funded in whole or in part by the Recovery Act. Performance-based acquisition methods are used whenever possible for services orders.

Delivery and task orders contain the following information:

- accounting and appropriation data;
- contract line item number, description, quantity, and unit price or estimated cost and fee;
- contract number and order number;
- date of order;
- delivery or performance schedule;
- method of payment and payment office, if not specified in the contract;
- packaging, packing and shipping instructions; and
- place of delivery or performance.

FAR 16.5

Some agencies issue *Government-wide Agency Contracts (GWAC)* for multiple agencies to place orders against. These are multiple-award procurements to promote competition and reduce delivery times for repetitive or common requirements, both supplies and services. Orders placed under an indefinite delivery contract awarded by another agency or a GWAC still have an acquisition plan if otherwise required, and cannot circumvent regulations for bundling requirements or funding obligations. Orders placed under multi-agency contracts for architect-engineer services require direct supervision by a professional architect or engineer licensed in the state or area where the services are to be performed.

Protests for an order are only allowed if the order increases the scope, period of performance or maximum value of the contract. Protests of orders in excess of $10 million may only be filed with the Government Accountability Office.

The Government may place multiple contracts with different firms for the same family of supplies or services, with the intent of generating competition among these firms. The contracting officer provides each awardee a *fair opportunity* to submit an offer for each order exceeding $10,000 (below that amount, a sole-source award is acceptable). The contracting officer has broad discretion to develop order placement procedures, including streamlined procedures such as oral presentations. The contracting officer need not contact any awardee which does not respond to the fair opportunity notice.

For task or delivery orders in excess of $5 million, the requirement to provide all awardees a fair opportunity for each order includes:

- a notice of the agency's requirements;
- a reasonable response period;
- evaluation factors and subfactors, including cost or price, and their relative importance;
- the basis for award if best value; and
- an opportunity for a postaward debriefing.

The concept of *best value* contracting entails trading off evaluation factors to obtain the best contract performance, including but not limited to cost. It reflects a life cycle cost analysis and a marginal analysis of cost versus technical performance tradeoff for each offeror. Price and related factors cannot be the dominant concern in best value procurements. Evaluators compare proposals and look for relative advantages (*discriminators*) held by one or more proposals that tie into specified evaluation factors or system capabilities. Discriminators should be quantified in dollar terms whenever possible, so that a cost-benefit tradeoff may be conducted.

A common way to conduct a trade-off is to estimate cost if the lowest-priced offeror provided the benefit, adjusted for cost realism, and discounted cash flow, and add to its evaluated price. If the lowest priced offer is still low, then the added benefit is not cost-effective. Another approach is to quantify the benefit using an index, methodology or model. A third way is to compare benefits between a specific pair of offers, and then rank the results ordinally.

Assigning price points and technical points is an old approach which does not quantify the benefits and still requires using the second or third option. Consequently, point systems are not recommended.

Each agency has an ombudsman (often the agency's competition advocate) to review complaints from contractors and ensure they are afforded a fair opportunity for consideration. The fair opportunity process is not required when:

- a single source is required by statute;
- only one awardee is capable of providing the required quality of supply or service;
- the agency need for the supplies or services is too urgent to permit delay;
- the order satisfies a minimum guarantee; or
- the requirement is a logical follow-on to an order already issued under the contract and must be awarded on a sole-source basis to promote economy and efficiency.

The ordering period of a task-order contract for advisory and assistance services, including all options or modifications, normally may not exceed five years unless specifically authorized by a statute. The contracting officer may extend the contract on a sole-source basis only once for a period not to exceed six months. This action requires a determination that the award of a follow-on contract is delayed by unforeseeable circumstances and extension is necessary to ensure continuity of services. Within DoD, this determination must be approved by the senior procurement executive of the department or agency.

There are dollar limits on these contracts. If any indefinite contract covers advisory and assistance services, it normally cannot exceed three years in length and $13.5 million in value unless multiple awards are made.

DFARS 216.501-2-70

Indefinite-delivery type contracts can, for items with a shelf-life of less than six months, allow orders to be placed either directly by the users or by central purchasing offices with deliveries direct to users.

PGI 216.505

If an order exceeds the simplified acquisition threshold and is a follow-on to a prior order based on a justification for an exception to fair opportunity, the new justification must include a copy of the prior justification. The intent is to see if the Government can remove or overcome any barriers that led to the previous exception to fair opportunity and if they have been resolved. If the actions were not completed, the justification for the follow-on action must be approved one level above the approval authority for the previous justification.

DFARS 217.204

The ordering period of a task order or delivery order contract may be for up to five years, extendable for successive periods in accordance with an option provided in the contract or modification and may not exceed 10 years unless the head of the agency determines in writing that exceptional circumstances require a longer ordering period. The senior procurement executive must approve if performance under the order is expected to extend more than eleven years. There are exceptions:

- advisory and assistance service task order contracts that are limited by statute to five years;
- contracts awarded under statutory authority;
- definite-quantity contracts;
- GSA schedule contracts; and
- multi-agency contracts awarded by agencies other than NASA, DoD, or the Coast Guard.

There are three varieties of indefinite-delivery contracts: definite-quantity, requirements, and indefinite-quantity contracts. They are used when the exact times and/or exact quantities of future deliveries are not known at the time of contract award, and will now be discussed in turn.

Solicitation Provisions

FAR 52.216-27, Single or Multiple Awards, if solicitation may result in multiple contract awards.

FAR 52.216-28, Multiple Awards for Advisory and Assistance Services, instead of FAR 52.21-27 for advisory and assistance services that exceed three years and $11.5 million (including all options). The estimated number of awards must be specified.

Solicitation Provisions and Contract Clauses

FAR 52.216-18, Ordering.

FAR 52.216-19, Order Limitations.

3.5.11.2 Definite-Quantity Contract

FAR 16.502

A *definite-quantity contract* provides for specific supplies or services to be delivered over a fixed period scheduled at designated locations upon order. It is used when a firm quantity of supplies or services will be required during the contract period, and the supplies or services are regularly available or will be available after a short lead time.

Solicitation Provisions and Contract Clauses

FAR 52.216-20, Definite Quantity.

FAR 52.216-32, Task Order and Delivery Order Ombudsman. Include Alternate I when the contract is for multi-agency use.

3.5.11.3 Requirements Contract

FAR 16.503

A *requirements contract* provides for a contractor to fill all actual purchase requirements of designated Government activities for supplies or services during a specified contract period. The contract guarantees the contractor all orders and obligates some funding upfront to motivate the contractor to keep a quantity on hand for the Government customer. Requirements contracts encourage faster deliveries for long-lead-time items because a contractor is more willing to maintain limited stocks when it has status as sole source of supply. This contract type is used when the Government cannot predetermine the precise quantities of supplies or services that designated activities will need during a definite period. Alternatively, an agency can issue a *letter of intent* to obligate funds while protecting price and availability of long-lead items, then convert the letter to another contract type upon definitization.

The contracting officer develops a realistic estimated total quantity based on records of previous requirements and consumption. The contract states the maximum quantity for the contract, the maximum or minimum quantities for each order, and the maximum amount to be ordered during a specified period of time. Usually, a minimum dollar amount is obligated with the contract award to guarantee the contractor will be interested in fulfilling the requirements (and also as a good-faith gesture).

No requirements contract over $100 million (including all options) may be awarded to a single source unless the agency head so determines in writing and notifies Congress within 30 days.

When a requirements contract is used to repair, modify, or overhaul Government property, the Government furnishes such items in "estimated" or "maximum" amounts and will not entitle the contractor to any equitable adjustment in price under the Government Property clause.

Any requirements contract principally for advisory and assistance services in excess of three years and $11.5 million (including all options) requires a contracting officer determination that the services required are so unique or highly specialized that it is not practicable to make multiple awards. DoD requirements contracts cannot exceed $112 million in total estimated value.

Solicitation Provisions and Contract Clauses

FAR 52.216-21, Requirements. Use the clause with Alternate I for nonpersonal services and related supplies. Use the clause with Alternate II to acquire subsistence products for both Government use and resale on a brand-name basis. Use the clause with Alternate III for a partial small business set-aside. Use the clause with Alternate IV if both conditions for Alternates II and III apply.

3.5.11.4 Indefinite-Quantity Contract

FAR 16.504

An *indefinite-quantity contract* provides for the Government placing orders for individual requirements, stating quantity limits as number of units or as dollar values. The contract requires the Government to order (and the contractor to furnish) at least a stated minimum quantity of supplies or services. The contracting officer establishes a maximum quantity based on market research, trends on recent contracts for similar supplies or services, or a survey of potential users. The minimum quantity must be more than a nominal quantity, but not in excess of the amount that the Government is fairly certain to order. The contract may also specify maximum or minimum quantities that the Government may order under each task or delivery order and the maximum that it may order during a specific period of time.

An indefinite-quantity solicitation and contract specifies:

- a description of the activities authorized to issue orders;
- a statement of work or specifications to describe the scope, nature, complexity, and purpose of the supplies or services;
- authorization for placing oral orders, if appropriate;
- contact information of the agency task and delivery order ombudsman;
- if multiple awards may be made, how the Government will provide awardees a fair opportunity to be considered for each order;
- procedures that the Government will use in issuing orders, and the ordering media;
- the period of performance, number of options and the period for which the Government may extend the contract under each option; and
- the total minimum and maximum quantity of supplies or services the Government will acquire under the contract.

An indefinite-quantity contract is used when the Government cannot predetermine, above a specified minimum, the precise quantities of required supplies or services for the contract period, but the Government is willing to commit itself for more than a minimum quantity.

The Government prefers to make multiple awards of indefinite-quantity contracts for the same or similar supplies or services, except for advisory and assistance services. The number of contracts to be awarded is a function of scope and complexity, expected duration and frequency of orders, mix of contractor resources, and ability to maintain competition among the awardees. The multiple award approach is not appropriate if:

- more favorable terms and conditions and pricing will be provided for a single award;
- only one contractor is capable of performance due to unique or highly specialized supplies or services;
- the projected orders are integrally related (in which case a requirements contract would be more appropriate);
- the administrative cost of multiple contracts outweighs their expected benefits; or
- the total estimated value of the contract is below the simplified acquisition threshold.

No task or delivery order contract in excess of $100 million (including all options) may be awarded to a single source unless the head of the agency determines in writing that only one source is qualified and capable of performing the work at a reasonable price to the Government, or else the task or delivery orders are so integrally related that only a single source can reasonably perform the work. Of course, exceptional circumstances may arise and need to be cited within this determination.

Unless incidental to contract performance, an indefinite-quantity contract for advisory and assistance services exceeding three years and $11.5 million, including all options, requires multiple awards unless the sole-source conditions outlined above are present or only one offer is received.

Solicitation Provision and Contract Clause

FAR 52.216-22, Indefinite Quantity.

3.5.12 Multiyear Contracting

FAR 17.1

One way to mitigate risk is by use of multiyear contracting. *Multiyear contracting* is a means to obtain quantity price discounts for requirements lasting up to four outyears after the base year without full funding. This is accomplished by issuing a fixed-price contract with a cancellation ceiling for each year should the funding not come through. This ceiling should bear some relationship to the proportionality of estimated contract cost, such that the ceiling rises in any given year with anticipated heavy expenditures, and drops in a year with lighter expenditures. Calculation for ceiling amounts may also need to reflect such considerations as startup and learning costs and amortization of facilities and equipment. Civilian agencies may use cost-type or fixed-price contracting methods for multiyear contracts, but DoD must stay with fixed-price methods only. Benefits of multiyear contracting include:

- broaden the competitive base with firms not otherwise willing or able to compete for lesser quantities, particularly in cases involving high startup costs;
- incentivize contractors to improve productivity through investment in capital facilities, equipment, and advanced technology;
- lower costs;
- maintain the same quality control techniques and procedures each year;
- reduce contract administrative burden;
- stabilize contractor work forces;
- standardization; and
- substantial continuity of production or performance, thus avoiding annual startup costs, preproduction testing costs and phaseout costs.

DFARS 217.1

Before awarding a multiyear contract, the head of the agency must compare its cost to that of an annual procurement approach by using present value analysis and show dollar savings. The agency head must provide written notice to the congressional Appropriations and Armed Services Committees at least 30 days before terminating any multiyear contract. Similar notification is required before entering into a multiyear contract with an unfunded contingent liability or economic order quantity in excess of $20 million or a cancellation ceiling in excess of $135.5 million. Moreover, the DoD component must request authority to enter into any multiyear contract as part of the component's budget submission for the fiscal year.

A multiyear contract for up to five years is permitted for these services and related supplies:

- base services (e.g., ground maintenance, in-plane refueling, bus transportation, and refuse collection and disposal);
- environmental remediation services for a military installation either active or inactive;
- maintenance or modification of highly complex military equipment (aircraft, ships and other vehicles);
- operation, maintenance and support of facilities and installations; and
- specialized training with high quality instructors (e.g., pilot and aircrew training or foreign language training).

The cost of any amortized plant or equipment cost may not exceed the ratio between the period of contract performance and the anticipated useful commercial life (not the physical life) of the plant or equipment. Alternatively, the contracting officer may obtain an option to extend the term of the contract for up to three years at prices that do not include charges for plant, equipment or other nonrecurring costs already amortized. In the extreme case, it could be desirable to reserve the right to take title to the plant or equipment upon payment of the unamortized portion of the cost.

The head of the agency must make a written determination before award that there is a continuing requirement for the services, which require either a substantial initial investment in plant or equipment or incurrence of substantial contingent liabilities for the assembly, training, or transportation of a specialized work force, and that using a multiyear contract will promote the best interests of the United States by encouraging effective competition and promoting economies in operations. The value of any multiyear contract may not exceed $678.5 million unless specifically authorized by law.[25]

Before entering into a multiyear supply contract, the Secretary of Defense must request in the budget full funding of units to be procured. To procure aircraft, the budget request must include full funding for production beyond any advance procurement activities of aircraft units to be produced in the fiscal year. Cancellation provisions in the contract should not consider recurring manufacturing costs pertaining to the production of unfunded units, nor may payments be made in advance of incurred costs on funded units. Finally, no price adjustment based on a failure to award a follow-on contract is allowed. Nonetheless, advance procurement of long-lead components, parts, and materials necessary to manufacture a weapon system, especially to achieve economic lot purchases or more efficient production rates, is allowed on a fixed-price basis (including any incentive arrangements).

Multiyear contracts may run up to four years for supplies and services to maintain, manage and operate military family housing. These contracts may be paid from annual appropriations for that year.

A contract for up to 10 years may be used to purchase electricity from sources of renewable energy. The head of the contracting activity must determine that this approach is cost effective.

Solicitation Provisions and Contract Clauses

FAR 52.217-2, Cancellation Under Multiyear Contracts.

FAR 52.222-43, Fair Labor Standards Act and Service Contract Labor Standards—Price Adjustment (Multiple Year and Option Contracts), if the contract is subject to the Service Contract Act.

3.6 AGREEMENTS

3.6.1 Basic Agreement

FAR 16.702

A *basic agreement* is not a contract, but rather a written instrument of understanding between an agency and a contractor that contains contract clauses to be applied to future contracts between the parties by reference or attachment. Also known as a *master agreement*, it is used when numerous separate contracts may be awarded to a contractor during a particular period and significant recurring negotiating problems may have been experienced. These separate orders or contracts contain the specifics as to performance and price. Basic agreements may be used with negotiated fixed-price or cost-reimbursement contracts. Each basic agreement is reviewed annually before the anniversary of its effective date and modified as necessary to conform to regulations. Either party may cancel the agreement with 30 days written notice. Modifying an agreement does not retroactively affect orders previously issued under it. Contracting officers often obtain and use existing basic agreements of another agency.

Each contract incorporating a basic agreement includes a scope of work and price, and delivery and other terms that apply to the particular contract. The basic agreement is incorporated into the contract by specific reference or attachment. A basic agreement does not cite appropriations or obligate funds, but rather states an agreement by the Government to place future contracts or orders with the contractor.

This concept was born overseas. European governments use a *framework pricing agreement* between contracting authority and contractor to establish terms (especially price and quantity) for the parties to enter into contracts with each other during a specified time period.

3.6.2 Basic Ordering Agreement

FAR 16.703

A *basic ordering agreement* is likewise not a contract, but rather an agreement with terms and clauses applying to future orders between the parties during its term, a description of supplies or services to be provided, and methods for pricing and issuing future orders under the basic ordering agreement. It contains the same qualities and restrictions as a basic agreement. Each basic ordering agreement specifies the point where each order becomes a binding contract (e.g., date of issuance, acceptance of order or specified number of days afterward to allow for rejection by the contractor). A basic ordering agreement may be used to expedite contracting for uncertain requirements when specific items, prices and quantities are unknown at the time the agreement is executed, but numerous requirements are anticipated to be purchased from the contractor. These procedures can reduce administrative lead time, inventory investment and obsolescence from design changes. Basic Ordering Agreements may not exceed five years in length.

The contracting officer cannot make any final commitment or authorize the contractor to begin work on an order under a basic ordering agreement until prices have been established, unless the order establishes a ceiling price limiting the Government's obligation. In this case, either the basic ordering agreement provides adequate procedures for timely pricing of the order early in its performance period, or else the need for the supplies or services is unusually urgent. The contracting officer prices the order as soon as practical, but not retroactively. Failure to reach agreement on negotiated price for any order is a dispute under the Disputes clause.

3.7 SIMPLIFIED ACQUISITION PROCEDURES

3.7.1 Theory

FAR Part 13

Simplified acquisition procedures reduce administrative costs, increase socioeconomic contracting opportunities, and create a more efficient and economic contracting process. They are used for purchases above the micro-purchase threshold of $3,500 ($20,000 for contingency or emergency operations domestically and $30,000 overseas) up to $150,000 ($300,000 for the same exceptions). The threshold for contingency operations contracts awarded and performed outside the United States has been raised to $1 million. The agency head must approve any such increases above the basic threshold.

All simplified acquisitions are reserved for small businesses. They may be further set-aside for HUBZone or service-disabled veteran-owned small business concerns within the contracting officer's discretion, without further review by the procurement center representative.

The contracting officer may not break up a requirement greater than the simplified acquisition or micro-purchase threshold into multiple purchases below the applicable threshold merely to avoid using formal contracting procedures.

An agency that has specific statutory authority to acquire personal services may use simplified acquisition procedures to do so if within the dollar thresholds above. Agencies use the Government-wide commercial purchase card and electronic purchasing techniques to the maximum extent practicable in conducting simplified acquisitions. Drawings and lengthy specifications can be provided off-line in hard copy.

An agency may issue a Request for Quotation using SF18; however a *quotation* is not an offer. It is instead a statement of price, either oral or written, issued by a seller at the request of the buyer. It may describe the product or service, delivery, period of performance, and/or terms of payment or sale. It cannot be accepted by the Government to form a binding contract, but may be used as the basis for an ensuing contract or for obtaining market information.

At its simplest, only price needs to be evaluated for simplified quotations or offers. However, the contracting officer needs to make known the basis of award. If the contracting officer may decide to use factors in addition to price, however solicitations are not required to state the relative importance assigned to each evaluation factor and subfactor, nor are they required to include subfactors. Contracting officers are encouraged to use best value and are permitted to use oral solicitations.

Offers can be evaluated in an efficient and minimally burdensome fashion. Formal evaluation plans, establishing a competitive range, conducting discussions, and scoring quotations or offers are not required. Contracting officers may conduct comparative evaluations of offers. Before making award, the contracting officer must determine that the price is fair and reasonable. Documentation should be kept to a minimum.

The following laws and clauses do not apply to (sub)contracts at or below the simplified acquisition threshold:

- 41 U.S.C. 57(a) and (b) (Anti-Kickback Act of 1986) (except requirements to incorporate contractor procedures to prevent and detect violations, and to cooperate in investigations are applicable);
- 40 U.S.C. 3131 (Miller Act). Alternative forms of payment protection for suppliers of labor and material are still required if the contract exceeds $30,000);
- 40 U.S.C. 3701 *et seq.* (Contract Work Hours and Safety Standards Act—Overtime Compensation);
- 41 U.S.C. 701(a)(1) (Section 5152 of the Drug-Free Workplace Act of 1988), except for individuals;
- 42 U.S.C. 6962 (Solid Waste Disposal Act), (unless the contract value exceeds $100,000);
- 10 U.S.C. 2306(b) and 41 U.S.C. 254(a) (Contract Clause Regarding Contingent Fees);
- 10 U.S.C. 2313 and 41 U.S.C. 254(c) (Authority to Examine Books and Records of Contractors);
- 10 U.S.C. 2402 and 41 U.S.C. 253g (Prohibition on Limiting Subcontractor Direct Sales to the United States);

- 15 U.S.C. 631 note (HUBZone Act of 1997), 15 U.S.C. 657a(b)(2)(B) is optional;
- 31 U.S.C. 1354(a) (Limitation on use of appropriated funds for contracts with entities not meeting veterans' employment reporting requirements);
- FAR 52.203-5, Covenant Against Contingent Fees;
- FAR 52.203-6, Restrictions on Subcontractor Sales to the Government;
- FAR 52.203-7, Anti-Kickback Procedures;
- FAR 52.215-2, Audits and Records—Negotiation, except when used with its Alternate I if funds are appropriated or available by the American Recovery and Reinvestment Act of 2009 (Public Law 111-5);
- FAR 52.222-4, Contract Work Hours and Safety Standards Act—Overtime Compensation;
- FAR 52.223-6, Drug-Free Workplace, except for contracts with individuals; and
- FAR 52.223-9, Estimate of Percentage of Recovered Material Content for EPA-Designated Items.

3.7.2 Procedures

FAR 13.1

Contracting officers use the System for Award Management database to find vendor information. Offices who maintain additional vendor source files or listings should identify the status of each source in the following categories:

- HUBZone small business;
- service-disabled veteran-owned small business;
- small business only;
- small disadvantaged business;
- veteran-owned small business; and
- women-owned small business.

The contracting officer does not solicit quotations based on personal preference or restrict solicitation to suppliers of well-known and widely distributed makes or brands. (S)he considers solicitation of at least three sources to promote competition to the maximum extent practicable, and tries to request quotations or offers from two sources that were not included in the previous solicitation.

The public display and synopsis requirements apply, although a combined synopsis and solicitation may be used for commercial items or supplies or services.

In soliciting competition, the contracting officer considers whether the requirement is highly competitive and readily available in several brands. The contracting officer will also assess dollar value, past experience concerning specific dealers' prices, and urgency. The contracting officer notifies potential offerors of the basis on which award will be made (price alone or price and other factors). Contracting officers may solicit from one source upon determination that the circumstances of the contract action deem only one source is available.

If obtaining electronic or oral quotations is uneconomical or impracticable, the contracting officer issues paper solicitations for contract actions likely to exceed $30,000 (or construction requirements exceeding $2,000).

The contracting officer has broad discretion in establishing evaluation procedures. Such a solicitation does not require formal evaluation plans, competitive ranges, discussions, or scoring quotations. Past performance evaluation may be based on contracting officer knowledge and prior experience with the supply or service being acquired, customer surveys, past performance questionnaire replies, and the Government-wide Performance Assessment Reporting System (CPARS).

Before making award, the contracting officer must determine that the proposed price is fair and reasonable. Whenever possible, competition should be the basis for reasonableness. If only one response is received, the contracting officer must include a statement of price reasonableness in the contract file that is based on market research, comparison with prices found reasonable on previous purchases, current price lists or catalogs, comparison with similar items in a related industry, personal knowledge of the item being purchased, or comparison to an independent Government estimate. If award is based on non-price factors, an explanation must be included.

Notification to unsuccessful suppliers is given only if requested, subcontracting opportunities are present, or the procurement is subject to the World Trade Organization Government Procurement Agreement or a Free Trade Agreement.

DFARS 212.209

If market research of existing products, services and technologies proves insufficient to determine price reasonableness, the contracting officer reviews any information submitted by the offeror of recent prices paid by the Government and commercial customers for the same or similar commercial items under comparable terms and conditions. If this information is not sufficient to determine reasonableness of price, the contracting officer next requests the offeror to submit price information for the same or similar items sold under different terms and conditions, similar levels of work or effort on related products or services or alternative solutions or approaches. If this is still insufficient, the contracting officer needs to request any other relevant information regarding the basis for price or cost, including uncertified cost data such as labor, material, and other direct and indirect costs.

3.7.3 Actions at or Below the Micro-Purchase Threshold

FAR 13.2

The Government-wide commercial purchase card is the preferred method to purchase and to pay for micro-purchases. These purchases do not require provisions or clauses. The supplier must be listed in the Central Contractor Registry and be able to accept electronic funds transfer for payment. The DoD threshold for micro-purchases is $5,000, with certain exceptions. For research and development effort, the threshold is raised to $10,000. For service contracts, the threshold is lowered to $2,500, and to $2,000 for construction contacts, to comply with specific statutes. The threshold limit for contingency operations or in defense or recovery from attack is $20,000 for domestic award or performance and $30,000 for international award or performance. U.S. Government fuel cards may be used to buy fuel or oil or related products.

To the extent practicable, micro-purchases are distributed equitably among qualified suppliers. Micro-purchases may be awarded without soliciting competitive quotations if the price is reasonable. Action to verify price reasonableness need only be taken if the contracting officer believes that the price may not be reasonable (e.g., comparison to the previous price paid or personal knowledge of the supply or service), or no comparable pricing information is readily available.

3.7.4 Purchase Orders

FAR 13.302

Once it makes a decision to award, the Government issues to the supplier an offer in the form of a purchase order to buy certain supplies or services upon specified terms and conditions.[26] A contract is established only when the supplier accepts the offer. The contracting officer may ask the supplier to indicate acceptance of an order by written notification to the Government. Otherwise, the supplier indicates acceptance of the order by furnishing the supplies or services ordered, or else proceeding with the work until substantial performance has occurred (i.e., the contractor has complied with all major aspects of contract performance requirements). In this case, the contracting officer signs the order without contractor signature. In effect, the purchase order is not a contract because the supplier did not sign it, but instead manifests agreement by performance. The Government may by written notice to the supplier withdraw, amend or cancel its offer at any time before acceptance.

Purchase orders are usually firm-fixed price instruments. They specify the quantity of supplies or scope of services ordered, contain a definite delivery date or period of performance, and include any offered trade and prompt payment discounts. Generally, inspection and acceptance should be at destination. Shipping costs are typically included for supplies delivered within the continental United States. Facsimile and electronic signatures are both allowed, and electronic funds transfer is required.

An unpriced purchase order is used when the price is not established at the time of the order. This is fairly common for equipment maintenance and repairs requiring disassembly to determine the nature and extent of repairs, or repair parts items for which exact prices are not known. A monetary limitation is placed on each unpriced purchase order (either in total or by line item), which is adjusted when a firm price is established. The contracting officer reviews the invoice price for reasonableness and processes it for payment.

Contract Clauses

FAR 52.213-2, Invoices, to authorize advance payments for subscriptions for newspapers, magazines, periodicals, or publications.

FAR 52.213-3, Notice to Supplier, in unpriced purchase orders.

FAR 52.213-4, Terms and Conditions—Simplified Acquisitions (Other Than Commercial Items), if exceeding the micro-purchase threshold for non-commercial items.

DFARS 252.225-7001, Buy American and Balance of Payments Program, in lieu of FAR 52.225-1, Buy American—Supplies.

DFARS 252.225-7036, Buy American—Free Trade Agreements—Balance of Payments Program, in lieu of FAR 52.225-1, Buy American—Supplies.

DFARS 252.243-7001, Pricing of Contract Modifications, in all bilateral purchase orders.

3.7.5 Blanket Purchase Agreements

FAR 13.3

If the supplies or services are repetitive in need, the ordering activity may decide to establish an unpriced blanket purchase agreement with each supplier. *Blanket Purchase Agreements* (BPAs) are designed to fill repetitive needs for supplies or services by establishing charge accounts with qualified sources of supply for office or project operations. BPAs are useful when the quantities and delivery requirements are not known in advance and may vary considerably, and for offices that do not have the authority to purchase. The BPA process avoids the need to write numerous purchase orders.

The number of BPAs to establish is a function of administrative costs within the purchasing office, contractor technical qualifications, requirement scope and complexity, and need for technical or price completion. BPAs set forth terms for:

- authorized ordering agencies;
- delivery locations and times;
- discounts;
- estimated quantities;
- invoicing instructions;
- ordering frequency and procedures; and
- type of work.

If the ordering activity has only one BPA, authorized users may place orders directly under it to fill requirements. If the ordering activity awards multiple BPAs however, any order exceeding the micro-purchase threshold requires solicitation among multiple BPA holders for competitive quotes and a best value determination before award.

BPAs generally run a maximum of five years, but may go longer to meet program requirements. However, the ordering activity reviews the BPA annually to verify that the schedule contract is still in effect and represents best value, that estimated amounts have not been exceeded, and whether additional price reductions can be obtained. The office should pursue price reductions when the supply or service is available elsewhere at a lower price, or if the potential volume of orders (regardless of the size of individual orders) could lead to greater discounts. Any price reductions obtained on a single order are not binding on either the contractor or customer for future orders.

Although BPAs may fall outside the socioeconomic preference programs, orders placed against schedule contracts may be credited toward the ordering activity's small business goals. Small business set-asides are encouraged. Ordering activities rely on the small business representations made by schedule contractors. Hence, socioeconomic status may be a factor when selecting a source for award of an order or BPA, especially for orders exceeding the micro-purchase threshold when two or more items at the same delivered price will satisfy the requirement. Nonetheless, an ordering activity must still justify its action when considering only one source for any acquisition above the micro-purchase level.

For brand-name purchases between $25,000 and $100,000, the contracting officer will post to e-Buy the RFQ and the reason(s) for restricting competition. For actions over $100,000, the J&A information is also posted. As with delivery orders, posting is not necessary in case of national security or file size or format, or if the agency's senior procurement executive determines that access through e-Buy is not in the Government's interest.

The ordering activity contracting officer refers any disputes regarding contract terms and conditions to the schedule contracting officer for resolution under the Disputes clause, and so notifies the schedule contractor. Ordering activities also evaluate contractor performance for each order that exceeds the simplified acquisition threshold.

An ordering activity contracting officer may terminate individual orders for cause, and so notify the schedule contracting office. Only the schedule contracting officer may terminate a BPA for cause, in which case no further orders may be placed for those items. Nonetheless, orders placed prior to termination must still be fulfilled by the contractor.

FAR 13.303

Contracting officers establish any necessary parameters to limit purchases to individual items or commodity groups or classes. They also consider suppliers of proven past performance with consistently lower prices, especially at or below the simplified acquisition threshold. Sources include multiple suppliers to provide maximum practicable competition, including Federal Supply Schedule contractors, or a single firm from which numerous individual purchases at or below the simplified acquisition threshold will likely be made in a given period. Additional benefits of BPAs include maximum discounts and periodic billings. BPAs require the supplier to furnish supplies or services, described in general terms, if and when requested during a specified period and within any stipulated aggregate amount. The Government is obligated only to the extent of authorized purchases made under the BPA. The dollar limitation for each individual purchase under the BPA must be included. A list is set forth of individuals authorized to purchase under the BPA, identified either by title of position or by name of individual, organizational component, and the dollar limitation per purchase for each. All shipments under the agreement (except periodicals such as newspapers or magazines) must be accompanied by delivery tickets or sales slips.

Purchases generally are made electronically or orally. Individual purchases cannot exceed the simplified acquisition threshold unless for commercial items. A paper purchase document may be issued only to ensure that the supplier and purchaser agree on the transaction. An informal memorandum records the date, supplier, supplies or services, price, delivery date, and accounting data on the purchase requisition. Upon delivery or performance, the supplier's sales or delivery document or invoice may record receipt and acceptance of the supplies or services.

The contractor must submit either a summary or itemized invoice monthly for all deliveries made during a billing period by listing the delivery tickets, total dollar value, and receipt copies of the tickets. Alternatively, an itemized invoice can be submitted monthly for all deliveries during a billing period for which payment has not been received (copies of delivery tickets are not required). All individual invoices for a delivery may be accumulated if a single payment is made for each specified period. The discount period begins on either the last date of the billing period or receipt of invoices for accepted deliveries, whichever occurs later. For subscriptions or other periodicals, an invoice can show the starting and ending dates and state that ordered subscriptions are in effect, or will be upon receipt of payment.

If the fast payment procedure is used, supplies must be shipped prepaid, and invoices must be submitted directly to the finance office designated in the order (or in the case of unpriced purchase orders, to the contracting officer).

The ordering officer reviews a random sample of the BPA files at least annually to ensure that authorized procedures are being followed. This review includes updating the BPA and maintaining awareness of changes in market conditions and sources of supply. The results of this review may require making new arrangements with different suppliers or modifying existing arrangements.

An individual BPA is considered complete when the purchases under it equal any total dollar limitation or when its stated time period expires.

FAR 8.405-3

Ordering activities may establish BPAs to fill repetitive needs with one or more schedule contractors. The number of BPAs to establish is a function of requirement scope and complexity, need for technical or price completion, administrative costs, and contractor technical qualifications. BPAs set forth terms for:

- authorized ordering agencies,
- delivery locations and times,
- discounts,
- estimated quantities,
- invoicing,
- ordering frequency and procedures, and
- type of work.

If the ordering activity has only one BPA, authorized users may place orders directly under it to fill requirements. If the ordering activity awards multiple BPAs however, any order exceeding the micro-purchase threshold requires solicitation among multiple BPA holders for competitive quotes and a best value determination before award.

BPAs generally run a maximum of five years, but may go longer to meet program requirements. However, the ordering activity reviews the BPA annually to verify that the schedule contract is still in effect and represents best value, that estimated amounts have not been exceeded, and whether additional price reductions can be obtained. Price reductions are pursued when the supply or service is available elsewhere at a lower price, or the potential volume of orders (regardless of the size of individual orders) could lead to greater discounts. Price reductions obtained on a single order are not binding on either the contractor or customer for future orders.

Although BPAs may fall outside of the socioeconomic preference programs, orders placed against schedule contracts may be credited toward the ordering activity's small business goals. Ordering activities rely on the small business representations made by schedule contractors at the contract level. Hence, socioeconomic status may be a factor when selecting a source for award of an order or BPA, especially for orders exceeding the micro-purchase threshold when two or more items at the same delivered price will satisfy the requirement. However, an ordering activity must justify its action when restricting consideration to one source.

Brand-name purchases between $25,000 and $100,000 post to e-Buy the RFQ and the reason(s) for restricting competition. For actions over $100,000, the J&A information is also posted. As with delivery orders, posting is not necessary in case of national security or file size or format, or if the agency's senior procurement executive determines that access through e-Buy is not in the Government's interest.

An ordering activity contracting officer may terminate individual orders for cause, and so notify the schedule contracting office. Only the schedule contracting officer may terminate a BPA for cause, in which case no further orders may be placed for those items, but orders placed prior to termination for cause are fulfilled by the contractor.

The ordering activity contracting officer refers all disputes regarding contract terms and conditions to the schedule contracting officer for resolution under the Disputes clause, and so notifies the schedule contractor. Ordering activities also evaluate contractor performance for each order that exceeds the simplified acquisition threshold.

Contract Clause

FAR 52.213-4, Terms and Conditions—Simplified Acquisitions (Other Than Commercial Items).

3.7.6 Imprest Funds and Third-Party Drafts

FAR 13.305

An *imprest fund* is a cash fund of a fixed amount without appropriation, established by an advance of funds from a financial or disbursing officer to a duly appointed cashier. They are used to pay cash for relatively small dollar amounts for incidental items. Each agency using imprest funds and third party drafts periodically reviews accounts to determine whether there is a continuing need for each fund or third-party draft account established. They also designate personnel authorized to make purchases using imprest funds or third party drafts, receive and accept supplies and services for the Government, receive cash or third party draft payments by suppliers, and make cash advances and reimbursements.

Imprest funds may be used for purchases up to $500, and third party drafts up to $2,500, or as set by agency or Treasury restrictions. Each purchase using these methods is based upon an authorized purchase requisition or contracting officer funds verification statement. These purchases are placed orally and without soliciting competition if prices are considered reasonable. No clauses are involved because ordering and delivery are simultaneous.

DFARS 213.305

Imprest funds are authorized for use without further approval for overseas transactions in support of a contingency, humanitarian or peacekeeping operation, or classified transactions.

3.7.7 Fast Payment Procedure

FAR 13.4

The fast payment procedure allows payment under limited conditions before verification that supplies have been received and accepted. This procedure provides for payment based on the contractor's invoice that certifies delivery to a common carrier, post office or point of first receipt by the Government (with transportation prepaid). The invoice also certifies that the contractor shall repair or replace supplies not received at destination, damaged in transit or not conforming to the agreement, with the contracting officer determining any debt due from the contractor. The conditions for use are as follows:

- documentation exists of contractor prior performance under fast payment purchases;
- Government receiving and disbursing activities are apart from each other and lack communications to make timely payment;
- individual actions do not exceed $30,000, unless increased by agency regulations;
- invoices are submitted directly to the finance or other office designated in the order, or in the case of unpriced purchase orders, to the contracting officer;

- suppliers with a current history of abusing the fast payment procedure are identified;
- supplies are shipped transportation or postage prepaid;
- the consignee notifies the purchasing office within 60 days after the date of delivery of supplies not received, damaged in transit or not conforming to specifications;
- the purchase instrument is a firm-fixed-price contract, purchase order or delivery order; and
- timely feedback of any deficiency is provided to the contracting officer.

DFARS 213.4 and PGI 213.201

Individual orders may exceed the simplified acquisition threshold for brand-name commissary resale subsistence and medical supplies for direct shipment overseas. Moreover, orders may reach the contingency contracting thresholds of $20,000 domestically and $30,000 if the ordering office is also outside the United States.

Solicitation Provision and Contract Clause

FAR 52.213-1, Fast Payment Procedure.

3.7.8 Forms

Forms used in Department of Defense contracting carry a prefix of either SF or DD. *SF* indicates a Standard Form which is used throughout the Federal Government and managed by GSA. *DD* reflects a Department of Defense form which is authorized by use in all DoD contracting offices. Forms commonly used in solicitations and contracting actions include:

- SF 1449, Solicitation/Contract/Order for Commercial Items;
- SF 18, Request for Quotations;
- OF 336, Continuation Sheet, when additional space is needed;
- OF 348, Order for Supplies or Services Schedule—Continuation, when additional space is needed for clauses;
- SF 30, Amendment of Solicitation/Modification of Contract;
- SF 44, Purchase Order—Invoice—Voucher, for on-the-spot or over-the-counter purchases of supplies and services while away from the purchasing office or at isolated activities. It also can be used as a receiving report, invoice, and public voucher;
- DD Form 1155, Order for Supplies of Services, for delivery and purchase orders; and
- SF 1165, Receipt for Cash—Subvoucher, for purchases using imprest funds or third party drafts.

3.8 SEALED BIDDING

FAR 14.101 and .201

Sealed bidding is a contracting method that uses public solicitation, bid opening and award. *Invitations for bids* are publicized by mailing to prospective bidders, posting in public places, and transmission to SAM. The Government provides enough time for prospective bidders to prepare and submit bids, which are opened publicly at the time and place stated in the solicitation. Bids are evaluated without discussions between parties or permitting the offeror to revise its offer. Award is made to the responsible bidder whose bid is most advantageous to the Government, considering only price and other factors specified in the invitation. An *Order of Precedence* provision sets priorities to resolve any contradictions within the solicitation.

There are several pre-conditions which must be met to use sealed bidding procedures. Only firm-fixed-price contracts (with or without economic price adjustment clauses) are subject to sealed bidding. There must be sufficient time to permit the solicitation, submission, and evaluation of sealed bids. Since award will be made on the basis of price and other price-related factors only, discussions with the responding offerors are not permitted. Also, there must be a reasonable expectation of receiving more than one sealed bid.

Award is made by acceptance of a bid on the award portion of Standard Form 33, 26 or 1447, incorporating the bidder's Representations and Certifications, and other statements of the bidder.

DFARS 214.201-5

An evaluation factor is used for supply chain risk when acquiring information technology as a service or a supply for a national security information system.

DFARS 214.209

If an invitation for bids allowed fewer than 30 days for receipt of offers and results in only one offer, the contracting officer must cancel and resolicit, allowing at least 30 days for receipt of offers.

Solicitation Provision and Contract Clause

FAR 52.214-29, Order of Precedence—Sealed Bidding, if the uniform contract format applies.

3.8.1 Preparation of Bids

FAR 5.3

The procurement must be advertised through SAM by means of a brief write-up known as a *synopsis*. This step is important to broaden competition and assist small businesses in obtaining Government contracts and subcontracts. A synopsis is required for all solicitations exceeding the simplified purchase threshold unless:

- awarded under the Small Business Innovation Development Act;
- for perishable subsistence supplies;
- for utility services to one source (although telecommunications services must still be synopsized);
- national security precludes public announcement of the requirement;
- the result of an unsolicited proposal with a unique and innovative research concept; or
- to support the Government in a dispute or litigation.

A bidding time between issuance of the solicitation and opening of bids is at least 30 calendar days when synopsis is required. To avoid unduly restricting competition or paying higher prices, the following factors are considered to set a reasonable bid time:

- anticipated extent of subcontracting,
- complexity of requirement,
- degree of urgency,
- geographic distribution of bidders,
- transmittal time for invitations and bids, and

As a rule, solicitations estimated between $15,000 and $25,000 can be synopsized for up to 10 days. Such a notice may go to SAM or can be posted at a convenient public location near the Procurement office. Synopsis for solicitations below this amount is discretionary. Presolicitation notices are often considered as well.

Telegraphic bids and mailgrams are authorized only when the opening date will not allow bidders enough time to submit bids in the prescribed format, or if prices change frequently (e.g., bulk fuels).

Solicitation Provisions

FAR 52.214-3, Amendments to Invitations for Bids.

FAR 52.214-4, False Statements in Bids.

FAR 52.214-6, Explanation to Prospective Bidders.

FAR 52.214-10, Contract Award—Sealed Bidding (except for construction contracts).

FAR 52.214-12, Preparation of Bids.

FAR 52.214-14, Place of Performance—Sealed Bidding, unless the place of performance is specified by the Government.

FAR 52.214-15, Period for Acceptance of Bids, for non-construction solicitations not issued on SF 33 or SF 1447, unless the Government specifies a minimum acceptance period.

FAR 52.214-16, Minimum Bid Acceptance Period, for non-construction solicitations when a minimum acceptance period must be specified.

FAR 52.214-18, Preparation of Bids—Construction, for construction work.

FAR 52.214-19, Contract Award—Sealed Bidding—Construction, for construction work.

FAR 52.214-20, Bid Samples, if bid samples are required. Use the provision with its Alternate I if the nature of the required product permits a waiver to a product produced at a different plant from where the product previously acquired or tested was produced. Use the provision with its Alternate II if the waiver must restrict award to a product produced at the same plant in which the product previously acquired or tested was produced.

FAR 52.214-21, Descriptive Literature, if the required descriptive information will not be readily available unless it is submitted by bidders. Use the provision with its Alternate I if the contracting officer may waive the requirement for furnishing descriptive literature for a bidder offering a previously supplied product that meets current specification requirements.

FAR 52.214-22, Evaluation of Bids for Multiple Awards, if multiple awards might be made if economically advantageous to the Government.

FAR 52.214-23, Late Submissions, Modifications, Revisions, and Withdrawals of Technical Proposals under Two-Step Sealed Bidding, for technical proposals in step one of two-step sealed bidding.

FAR 52.214-24, Multiple Technical Proposals, for technical proposals in step one of two-step sealed bidding if the contracting officer permits the submission of multiple technical proposals.

FAR 52.214-25, Step Two of Two-Step Sealed Bidding, for step two of two-step sealed bidding.

FAR 52.214-31, Facsimile Bids, if authorized.

DFARS 252.215-7007, Notice of Intent to Resolicit, for commercial items.

DFARS 252.215-7008, Only One Offer, for commercial items.

Solicitation Provisions and Contract Clauses

FAR 52.214-26, Audit and Records—Sealed Bidding, if submission of cost or pricing data is required. Use the clause with its Alternate I if the acquisition will use funds appropriated by the Recovery Act.

FAR 52.214-27, Price Reduction for Defective Cost or Pricing Data—Modifications—Sealed Bidding, if cost or pricing data are required, unless waived by the head of the contracting activity for a contract with a foreign government or agency.

FAR 52.214-28, Subcontractor Cost or Pricing Data—Modifications—Sealed Bidding, if cost or pricing data are required, unless waived by the head of the contracting activity for a contract with a foreign government or agency.

FAR 52.214-29, Order of Precedence—Sealed Bidding, if the uniform contract format applies.

3.8.2 Rules for Solicitation

FAR 14.2

The time frame between issuance of the solicitation and opening of bids is at least 30 calendar days when synopsis is required. To avoid unduly restricting competition or paying higher prices, the following factors are considered to set a reasonable bid time:

- anticipated extent of subcontracting;
- complexity of requirement;
- degree of urgency;
- geographic distribution of bidders;
- transmittal time for invitations and bids; and
- use of presolicitation notices.

The Government may require bid samples to assess a product's balance, color, ease of use, or feel if these characteristics cannot be described adequately in the specification.[27] Invitations for bids set forth the number and size of sample submissions, and also state the characteristics to be examined. The requirement for bid samples may be waived when a bidder offers a product previously or currently contracted for or tested by the Government and found to comply with current specifications. Invitations for bids set forth the number and size of sample submissions. They also state all characteristics for examination. Bid samples merely determine the responsiveness of the bid, not a bidder's ability to produce the required items. Bids will be rejected as nonresponsive if the sample fails to conform to each of the characteristics listed in the invitation. Unrequested bid samples are usually disregarded, unless the bid is qualified for their acceptance.

Bidders need not furnish descriptive literature unless required before award to determine whether the products offered meet the specification. The invitation states what descriptive literature to furnish and why it is needed. Further, the solicitation must specify the extent of consideration in bid evaluation and the impact of any failure to furnish the literature before bid opening or not complying with the requirements of the invitation.

As with bid samples, the contracting officer may waive the requirement to furnish descriptive literature if the bidder states that the product being offered is the same as one previously or currently furnished to the contracting activity, and the product complies with the current requirement. The bid may be based on either descriptive literature or a previously furnished product, but not both. Unsolicited descriptive literature is treated the same as unsolicited bid samples.

Contracting officers may authorize facsimile bids based on urgency, price change frequency or administrative inability to handle bid volume and protection. Contracting officers will then request the apparently successful offeror to provide the complete, original signed bid subsequent to the opening date. Contracting officers may authorize use of electronic commerce to submit bids, but must specify in the solicitation the electronic method(s) to use.

In lieu of initially forwarding complete bid sets, the contracting officer may send presolicitation notices to potential bidders. The notice specifies the final date for receipt of requests for a complete bid set and describes the requirement. It also furnishes other information for firms to determine whether they have an interest in the invitation. Bid sets are sent to concerns that request them in response to the notice.

A pre-bid conference may be used before bid opening in a complex acquisition to brief prospective bidders and explain complicated requirements and clear up any ambiguities. This ensures that all potential bidders have a common understanding of the goods or services required. However, it is not a substitute for amending a defective or ambiguous invitation.

Any changes in opening date, quantity, schedule, specifications, or a defective or ambiguous invitation are accommodated by amending the invitation for bids using Standard Form 30. Amendments are sent before bid opening to every solicited firm and are also displayed in the bid room. If it is appropriate to extend the period of time remaining until bid opening, bidders should be notified by telegram or telephone and confirmed in the amendment.

Any information given to a prospective bidder is furnished promptly to all other prospective bidders as an amendment to the invitation, especially if the lack of such information would be prejudicial to uninformed bidders. This provides prospective bidders with enough time to decide on or modify their bids. General information that would not be prejudicial to other prospective bidders may be furnished upon request (e.g., explaining a clause or a condition in the invitation for bids).

Invitations for bids should never be cancelled unless the requirement ends or the amendment is so extensive that a new solicitation package is cleaner. The reason for cancellation is announced electronically, any electronic bids received are deleted without viewing, and any paper bids are returned unopened.

Information concerning proposed acquisitions is not released outside the Government before solicitation except for presolicitation notices, long-range acquisition estimates or synopses. Within the Government, such information is restricted to those with a legitimate interest. Releases of information are made simultaneously to all prospective bidders, so that one prospective bidder does not have an unfair advantage over another.

3.8.3 Submission of Bids

FAR 14.3

To be considered for award, a bid must comply in all material respects with the invitation for bids. This approach places all bidders on an equal footing and maintains the integrity of the sealed bidding system. Bids are filled out, executed, and submitted in accordance with the instructions in the invitation. A bidder's own bid form or letter may be considered only if the bidder accepts all terms and conditions of the invitation and does not vary from the invitation.

Bids may be modified or withdrawn by any method authorized by the solicitation, if notice is received in the designated bidding office not later than the exact time set for opening of bids. If no time is specified in the solicitation, the time for receipt is 4:30 p.m. local time, on the date that bids are due. Otherwise, the bid is late and will not be considered unless received before award is made without unduly delaying the acquisition, and it was received either at the initial point of entry to the Government infrastructure by 5:00 p.m. on the working day prior to the date specified for receipt of bids, or at the Government installation and under Government control prior to the hour set for receipt of bids.

A late modification of a successful bid that makes its terms more favorable to the Government will be considered at any time it is received and may be accepted. Evidence to establish the time of receipt at the Government installation includes the time/date stamp on the bid wrapper or oral testimony or statements of Government personnel. If an emergency or unanticipated event (e.g., a snowstorm or natural disaster) interrupts normal Government processes to prevent bid receipt at the Government office by the exact time specified in the solicitation, the time specified for receipt of bids will be extended to the same hour on the first work day on which Government processes resume.

Late bids and modifications that are not considered are held unopened (except for identification) until after award and then retained with other unsuccessful bids. However, any bid bond or guarantee is returned.

Solicitation Provisions

FAR 52.214-5, Submission of Bids.

FAR 52.214-7, Late Submissions, Modifications, and Withdrawals of Bids.

FAR 52.214-31, Facsimile Bids, if facsimile bids are authorized.

FAR 52.214-34, Submission of Offers in the English Language, if including any Buy American Act clause.

FAR 52.214-35, Submission of Offers in U.S. Currency, if including any Buy American Act clauses unless the Evaluation of Foreign Currency Offers clause is included.

3.8.4 Opening of Bids

FAR 14.4

All bids received before the time set for opening are securely stored. Envelopes that do not identify the bidder or the solicitation are opened solely for identification by a designated official. This official immediately writes on the envelope an explanation of the opening, the date and time opened, the invitation number and signature, then reseals the envelope.

The bid opening officer announces when the time set for opening bids has arrived and informs attendees of same. These events are open to the general public, but are usually attended only by representatives of the bidder organization. The contracting officer personally and publicly opens all bids received by that time, reads the bids aloud, and records them on an abstract sheet. The original copy of each bid is examined by the public only under the immediate supervision of a Government official to prevent alteration or substitution in the bid.

The general public may not attend bid openings for classified acquisitions; only a bidder or representative with the appropriate security clearance may attend. No public record is made of bids or bid prices received in response to classified invitations for bids.

Abstracts of offers for unclassified acquisitions are available for public inspection but do not reveal failure to meet minimum standards of responsibility, apparent collusion of bidders, or information exempt from public disclosure.

3.8.5 Rejection of Bids

FAR 14.404 through 14.406

Award is made to the responsible bidder who submitted the lowest responsive bid, unless there is a compelling reason to reject all bids and cancel the invitation. The contracting officer tries to anticipate requirement changes before the opening date and notifies all prospective bidders of any resulting modification or cancellation, so they can change their bids and avoid unnecessary exposure of bid prices.

Sometimes delivery is expressed in terms of days after award. In such cases, the contracting officer evaluates the bid by adding five calendar days for arrival through ordinary mail. If the solicitation states that the contract or notice of award will be transmitted electronically, the contracting officer adds one working day to the proposed delivery schedule based on the date of contract receipt or notice of award. Solicitations also inform bidders or offerors how their bids or proposals will be evaluated with respect to time of delivery or performance.

Cancelling an invitation for bids is discouraged because it means lost time, effort and money by both Government and bidders. Moreover, it defeats the publicized desire to issue an award. Invitations may only be cancelled, and all bids rejected after opening, when the agency head determines in writing that any of the following events has occurred:

- a cost comparison as prescribed in OMB Circular A-76 shows that performance by the Government is more economical;
- all bids received are at unreasonable prices or else the contracting officer cannot determine the reasonableness of the bid price;
- bids indicate that the needs of the Government can be satisfied by a less expensive article than specified;
- bids were not independently arrived at in open competition or were submitted in bad faith;
- cancellation is clearly in the public's interest;
- inadequate or ambiguous specifications were cited in the invitation;
- no bidder is deemed responsible;
- specifications were ambiguous or inadequate or have been revised;
- the invitation did not provide for all cost evaluation factors; or
- the supplies or services are no longer required.

Bids are returned unopened to the bidders and notice of cancellation is sent to all prospective bidders to whom invitations were issued. Electronic bids remain unopened and are purged from data storage systems. The cancellation notice identifies the solicitation number and subject matter, states the reason for cancellation, and assures prospective bidders that they will have an opportunity to bid on any resolicitation or future requirements for the same type of supplies or services.

Should administrative difficulties be encountered after bid opening that may delay award beyond bidders' acceptance periods the several lowest bidders whose bids have not expired are requested to extend in writing the bid acceptance period (with consent of sureties, if any) to avoid resolicitation.

When the agency head determines that an invitation for bids should be canceled in favor of negotiations, the contracting officer may award without a new solicitation if each responsible bidder is given notice that negotiations will be conducted and an opportunity to participate in negotiations.

A bid must be rejected when it:

- comes from a bidder determined to be not responsible (but if a bidder is a small business concern, a certificate of competency could be in order);
- comes from any person or firm that is debarred, proposed for debarment, suspended, or otherwise declared ineligible as of the bid opening date;
- contains materially unbalanced prices for any line items or subline items;
- fails to conform to the delivery schedule or any alternates stated in the invitation;
- fails to conform to the essential requirements of the invitation for bids, unless it authorized submission of alternate bids and the supplies offered meet the requirements specified in the invitation;
- fails to furnish a required bid guarantee;
- imposes conditions that would modify requirements of the invitation or limit the bidder's liability to the Government, since to allow the bidder to impose such conditions would be prejudicial to other bidders;
- is from a firm which transfers its assets during the time period between the bid opening and the award, unless the transfer is effected by merger or operation of law;
- is unreasonable as to price in total amount or by individual item;
- limits the rights of the Government under any contract clause;
- prohibits the disclosure of information to permit competing bidders to know the nature and type of the products offered or those elements of the bid that relate to quantity, price and delivery terms;
- protects against future changes in conditions, such as increased costs;
- qualifies the bid by stating that it is to be considered only if, before date of award, the bidder receives (or does not receive) award under a separate solicitation before date of award;
- qualifies its price as being subject to what is in effect at time of delivery; or
- requires the Government to determine that the bidder's product meets applicable Government specifications.

The originals of all rejected bids, and any written findings with respect to such rejections, will be preserved with the official contract file.

The contracting officer may request a low bidder to delete objectionable conditions from a bid if they do not go to the substance of the bid (i.e., not affect price, quantity, quality, or delivery, or create injustice on other bidders).

Unless the solicitation provides otherwise, a bid may be responsive notwithstanding that the bidder specifies that award will be accepted only on all, or a specified group, of the items.

Per DFARS 227./7103-10, information provided by offerors may be used to evaluate the impact on evaluation factors due to restrictions on·the Government's ability to use or disclose technical data. However, offerors may offer products for which they are entitled to provide the Government with limited data rights. If so, they cannot be required, either as a condition of being responsive to a solicitation or as a condition for award, to sell or otherwise relinquish any greater rights in technical data.

3.8.6 Mistakes in Bids

FAR 14.407

Contracting officers examine all bids for mistakes before award. If any are found, the contracting officer requests from the bidder a verification of the bid and calls attention to the suspected mistake.

A *minor informality* or irregularity is merely a matter of form and not of substance, an immaterial defect in a bid or a variation of a bid that can be corrected or waived without prejudicing other bidders. The defect or variation has no impact on delivery, price, quality, or quantity compared with the total cost or scope of the supplies or services acquired. The contracting officer either gives the bidder an opportunity to cure any deficiency resulting from a minor informality or irregularity in a bid or else waives the deficiency, whichever is to the Government's advantage. Examples include failure of a bidder to:

- acknowledge receipt of an amendment to an invitation for bids if the bid clearly indicates its acceptance by another action (e.g., only a matter of form or has no or negligible effect on the item bid upon);
- execute the representations with respect to Equal Opportunity and Affirmative Action Programs, Previous Contracts and Compliance Reports, and Affirmative Action Compliance;
- furnish required information concerning the number of its employees;
- return the number of copies of signed bids required by the invitation; or
- sign its bid a cover letter or bid guarantee indicates the bidder's intention to be bound by the unsigned bid.

If a bid received at the Government facility by electronic data interchange is so unreadable that conformance to the essential requirements of the invitation for bids cannot be ascertained, the contracting officer immediately notifies the bidder that the bid will be rejected unless the bidder provides clear and convincing evidence of the original bid's content. The unreadable condition of the bid must be caused by Government software or hardware error, malfunction, or mishandling.

Any obvious clerical mistake may be corrected by the contracting officer before award after obtaining from the bidder a verification of the bid intended (e.g., misplaced decimal point, reversed discounts or FOB prices, etc.). The verification must be attached to both copies of the bid and included in the award, but the Government may not change the face of the submitted bid.

If a bidder requests permission to correct a mistake and evidence clearly establishes both the existence of the mistake and the bid actually intended, the agency head may determine that the bidder may correct the mistake. However, if the correction displaces any lower bids, the existence of the mistake and the bid actually intended must be obvious from the invitation and the bid itself.

If a bidder requests permission to withdraw rather than correct a bid, and the evidence of the mistake is clear and convincing, and the bid is still the lowest price, the agency head may determine to correct the bid and not permit its withdrawal. If on the other hand, the evidence of a mistake is clear and convincing but not as to the intended bid, an official above the contracting officer may determine to allow the bidder to withdraw the bid. If the evidence does not warrant any determination, the agency head may decide to neither correct nor withdraw the bid.

If the bid is verified, the contracting officer considers the bid as originally submitted. If the time for acceptance of bids is likely to expire before a decision can be made, the contracting officer requests all bidders eligible for award to extend the acceptance time for their bids. If the bidder whose bid is believed erroneous does not extend the time, the bid shall be considered as originally submitted.

On the other hand, if the bidder admits a mistake, the contracting officer shall advise the bidder to make a written request to withdraw or modify the bid, including evidence that establishes the existence of the error, how it occurred, and the intended bid. If the bidder fails or refuses to furnish evidence in support of a suspected or alleged mistake, the contracting officer considers the bid as submitted.

3.8.7 Mistakes After Award

FAR 14.407-4

When a mistake in a contractor's bid is not discovered until after award, it may be corrected by contract modification if favorable to the Government without changing the essential requirements of the specifications. The contracting officer may also rescind the contract or reform it to delete the items involved in the mistake or increase the price if it does not exceed that of the next lowest acceptable bid under the original invitation for bids. The mistake must be either mutual or else so obvious that the contracting officer should have noticed it.

The contracting officer requests the contractor to support the alleged mistake by submitting written statements and pertinent evidence (e.g., contractor's file copy of the bid, original worksheets and other data used in preparing the bid, subcontractor quotes, published price lists, etc.). The case file concerning an alleged mistake contains this contractor evidence plus a signed statement by the contracting officer that describes the action taken.

FAR 14.408-4

When a solicitation does not contain an economic price adjustment clause but a bidder proposes one with a ceiling that the price will not exceed, the bid is evaluated on the basis of the maximum possible economic price adjustment of the quoted base price. Prior to award, the contracting officer requests the bidder to agree to the inclusion in the award of an approved economic price adjustment clause subject to the same ceiling, or else award the bid as originally submitted. If the proposed clause has no ceiling, the bid must be rejected.

When a solicitation contains an economic price adjustment clause and no bidder takes exception to the provisions, bids are evaluated on the basis of the quoted prices without the allowable economic price adjustment being added. The bid is rejected if the bidder increases the maximum percentage of adjustment or deletes the clause. If the bidder proposes decreasing the maximum percentage, the bid is evaluated at the base price and if awarded, reflects the lower ceiling.

3.8.8 Price Related Factors

FAR 14.201-8

If bids are on an f.o.b. origin basis, transportation costs to the designated points must be considered in determining the lowest cost to the Government. Changes made or requested by the bidder in any of the provisions of the invitation for bids may be considered if the change does not constitute a ground for rejection. The contracting officer may also need to consider taxes and origin of supplies and, in case of foreign origin, application of the Buy American Act or any other prohibition on foreign purchases.

The contracting officer considers advantages or disadvantages to the Government that might result from making more than one award. The norm is to use $500 as the cost to the Government for issuing and administering each separate award.

It is very uncommon that cost or pricing data is requested in formal advertising, since the presence of competitive pricing is relied upon to determine price reasonableness. However, such information is not prohibited if deemed necessary to understand the pricing structure, especially if only one bidder responds. Similarly, certified cost or pricing data could be required for pricing out contract modifications. Solicitation provisions and contract clauses must be included to address this situation.

Solicitation Provisions and Contract Clauses

FAR 52.214-26, Audit and Records—Sealed Bidding, if submission of cost or pricing data is required. Use the clause with its Alternate I if the acquisition will use funds appropriated by the American Recovery and Reinvestment Act of 2009.

FAR 52.214-27, Price Reduction for Defective Cost or Pricing Data—Modifications—Sealed Bidding, if cost or pricing data are required, unless waived by the head of the contracting activity for a contract with a foreign government or agency.

FAR 52.214-28, Subcontractor Cost or Pricing Data—Modifications—Sealed Bidding, if cost or pricing data are required, unless waived by the head of the contracting activity for a contract with a foreign government or agency.

3.8.9 Award

FAR 14.408

The contracting officer issues a contract award by written or electronic notice within the time for acceptance specified in the bid or extension to that responsible bidder whose bid, conforming to the invitation, will be most advantageous to the Government, considering only price and the price-related factors included in the invitation. All solicitation provisions and changes made by a bidder in the bid are set forth (either expressly or by reference) in the award document. Because the award is an acceptance of the bid, both the bid and the award constitute the contract. Award is generally made by using SF33 or 1447.

Prompt payment discounts are not considered in evaluating bids. However, any discount offered will form a part of the award, and will be taken by the payment center if payment is made within the discount period specified by the bidder.

If two or more bids are equal in all respects, then the first tie-breaking criterion favors a small business concern that are also labor surplus area concerns. If no such firm bids, then the second criterion favors any other small business concern. If a tie remains, the contracting officer draws lots to determine a winner.

The contracting officer notifies each unsuccessful bidder in writing or electronically within three days after contract award that its bid was not accepted. When award is made to other than a low bidder, the notice states the reason for rejection in the notice to each of the unsuccessful low bidders. When a non-bidder requests information of an unclassified award, the contracting officer may furnish the names of successful bidders and the award prices.

DFARS 205.301

Per 10 U.S.C. 2533a(k), contracting officers also must synopsize through SAM awards exceeding the simplified acquisition threshold for any clothing, fiber, fabric, or yarn items if determined that domestic items are not available. They must also synopsize chemical warfare protective clothing if the contracting officer determines that a foreign item must be procured to comply with an agreement with a qualifying country. The synopsis must be made within seven days after contract award and state the basis for the exception.

DFARS 215.371

If only one offer is received from a competitive solicitation that allowed less than 30 days for receipt of proposals, the contracting officer must consult with the requiring activity to consider revising the requirements document to promote more competition and resolicit by allowing 30 days or more for receipt of proposals. The head of the contracting activity is authorized to waive this requirement and can lower the approval authority to the level above the contracting officer. If more than one potential offeror expressed an interest in an acquisition where only one offer was ultimately received, the contracting officer should seek feedback from potential offerors and document the file. Receipt of only one offeror in this case is not considered to be adequate price competition unless so determined at a level above the contracting officer. If the solicitation did allow for at least 30 days or exceeds the simplified acquisition threshold, then the contracting officer must use cost or price analysis either from the offeror or past purchase history to justify the offered price is fair and reasonable and that adequate price competition exists (with approval of the determination at a level above the contracting officer) or another exception to the requirement for certified cost or pricing data applies. The cost or pricing data will need to be certified if it exceeds the threshold for same. Negotiations may be necessary to establish a fair and reasonable price.

These steps are not necessary for the following acquisitions:

- architect-engineer services;
- at or below the simplified acquisition threshold;
- basic or applied research or development that use a broad agency announcement;
- in support of contingency, humanitarian, or peacekeeping operations, or to facilitate defense against or recovery from biological, chemical, cyber, nuclear, or radiological attack; or
- socioeconomic set-asides.

DFARS 205.303

All DoD awards over $7 million must be announced. This includes not-to-exceed amounts but not unexercised options. The synopsis should include the following data, preferably in this order:

- contract number, modification or delivery order number (if any), dollar value of this action, cumulative value of the contract, description of product or service bought, contract type, and identification of the foreign customer (if applicable);
- number of solicitations sent and number of offers received;
- name, address and place of performance (if performed at a different location);
- type of appropriation and fiscal year of the funds, and if the contract is multiyear; and
- identification of the contracting office and its point of contact, known congressional interest, and the information release date.

This information is also submitted to members of Congress in whose state or district the contractor is located and the work is to be performed.

Solicitation Provision

DFARS 252.215-7007, Notice of Intent to Resolicit, in competitive solicitations that will be solicited for fewer than 30 days, unless an exception applies or the requirement is waived.

DFARS 252.215-7008, Only One Offer, when in excess of the simplified acquisition threshold.

Solicitation Provision and Contract Clause

DFARS 252.205-7000, Provision of Information to Cooperative Agreement Holders, if expected to exceed $1,000,000.

3.8.10 Two-Step Sealed Bidding

FAR 14.5

Two-step sealed bidding permits a description of the Government's requirements, including a technical data package, so that future acquisitions may be made by conventional sealed bidding. This method is used in acquisitions for complex items requiring technical proposals. Step One consists of solicitation, submission, evaluation, and any discussion of an unpriced technical proposal. This step determines the acceptability of the proposed supplies or services and clarifies technical questions (e.g., engineering approach, manufacturing processes and testing techniques). The Government may request no further information from any offeror, request additional information from offerors of proposals that it considers reasonably susceptible of being made acceptable, or discuss proposals with all offerors. The contracting officer notifies any offeror if its proposal is deemed unacceptable. When specifications permit different technical approaches, the Government often permits multiple proposals.

Proposals are categorized as Acceptable, Reasonably susceptible of being made acceptable, or Unacceptable. Any proposal which modifies or does not conform to the essential requirements or specifications of the solicitation is considered nonresponsive and rejected as unacceptable. When a technical proposal is found unacceptable, the contracting officer notifies the offeror of the basis of the determination and that a revision of the proposal will not be considered. The contracting officer debriefs unsuccessful offerors at their written request.

The contracting officer may proceed directly with Step Two if sufficient acceptable proposals ensure adequate price competition and the Government lacks the time or desire to make additional proposals acceptable. The contracting officer requests any bidders whose proposals may be made acceptable to submit additional clarifying information, fixing a time for bidders to conclude discussions.

Sealed bidding procedures continue throughout Step Two except that invitations for bids are issued only to those offerors submitting acceptable technical proposals in Step One, and are not synopsized through SAM. However, the names of firms that submitted acceptable proposals in Step One will be listed through SAM for the benefit of prospective subcontractors.

Step Two is the submission of sealed priced bids by those who submitted acceptable technical proposals in Step One. These bids are evaluated and awards are made in the same manner as sealed bidding. Each bid in the second step is based on the bidder's own technical proposals. The Government could decide to accept an initial proposal, so the bidder must bid its most favorable terms. If Step One results in no acceptable technical proposal or only one acceptable technical proposal, the acquisition may be continued by negotiation.

Two-step sealed bidding is preferred to negotiation when:

- a firm-fixed-price contract or a fixed-price contract with economic price adjustment will be used;
- at least two technically qualified sources are available;
- available specifications or purchase descriptions are not definite or complete, or may be too restrictive without technical evaluation;
- definite criteria exist for evaluating technical proposals; and
- sufficient time will be available for use of the two-step method.

Solicitation Provisions

FAR 52.214-23, Late Submissions, Modifications, Revisions, and Withdrawals of Technical Proposals under Two-Step Sealed Bidding, for technical proposals in step one of two-step sealed bidding

FAR 52.214-24, Multiple Technical Proposals, for technical proposals in step one of two-step sealed bidding if the contracting officer permits the submission of multiple technical proposals

FAR 52.214-25, Step Two of Two-Step Sealed Bidding, for step two of two-step sealed bidding.

3.9 COMPETITIVE NEGOTIATIONS

3.9.1 Solicitation of Proposals

The secret to success in competitive negotiations involves the exchange of information between parties. Information should be freely shared, from the earliest identification of a requirement through receipt of proposals, among all interested parties (e.g., potential offerors, end users, Government acquisition and supporting personnel). This improves understanding of both Government requirements and industry capabilities, so that potential offerors may judge whether or how they can satisfy the Government's requirements. An early exchange of information among industry, the program manager and contracting officer can identify and resolve concerns regarding the acquisition planning schedules and strategy, contract type and terms and conditions, feasibility of the requirement, reference documents, and suitability of the proposal instructions and evaluation criteria. A common technique to promote early exchanges of information is to use presolicitation or preproposal conferences with potential offerors to discuss technical problems and ascertain the level of market interest. Other common techniques include:

- draft solicitations;
- industry or small business conferences;
- market research;
- one-on-one meetings with potential offerors;
- prequalification of offerors;
- presolicitation notices;
- public hearings;
- Requests for Information; and
- site visits.

A *Request for Information* (RFI) is used when the Government does not intend to award a contract, but rather wants to obtain information regarding market capabilities, delivery or pricing for planning purposes. Responses to these notices are not offers and cannot be the basis for a binding contract. There is no required format for RFIs.

The agency may publish a presolicitation notice to invite potential offerors to submit information so that the Government may advise the offerors about their potential as viable competitors (and if not, why not). The presolicitation notice includes a general description of the scope or purpose of the acquisition, information that must be submitted, and the criteria to make the initial evaluation. Information sought may be limited to a statement of qualifications, proposed technical concept, past performance, and limited pricing information. All respondents may participate in the resultant acquisition, even if advised by the Government that they are not viable competitors.

Formal *Requests for Proposals* (RFPs) are used in negotiated acquisitions to submit Government requirements to prospective contractors and to solicit proposals. If facsimile proposals are authorized, contracting officers may request offeror(s) to provide the complete, original signed proposal at a later date. Letter RFPs may be used in sole-source acquisitions. Oral RFPs are authorized when processing a written solicitation would delay the acquisition to the detriment of the Government (e.g., perishable items and support of contingency operations or other emergency situations).

In addition to the Uniform Contract Format used for formal bids, two more sections are added to the solicitation. Section L, Instructions to Offerors, may require organization of proposals into sections (e.g., Administrative, Management, Technical, Past Performance, and Cost and Pricing Data). The government should develop and include in Section L a matrix requiring offerors' to cross-reference CLINs/Contract Data Requirements Lists (CDRLs)/Statement of Work paragraph/Sections L & M/Offerors Proposal Paragraph and WBS references. This crosswalk can be used as a tool during negotiations to make sure all requirements are accounted for in an offerors' proposal and used as a tool to track across offerors during negotiations. A government-developed cross-reference matrix will preclude each offeror having a different format and streamline the evaluation.

DAG: Source Selection Procedures, 2.3

Section M, Evaluation Factors for Award, will identify all factors used to evaluate offers. They may be qualitative, quantitative, or both, but cannot use numerical or percentage weighting of the relative importance of evaluation (sub)factors. However, assigning monetary value to enhanced performance characteristics under the VATEP methodology is permitted. The solicitation may prescribe minimum "go/no go" or "pass/fail" gates as criteria that an offeror's proposal must meet before receiving further evaluation, which saves both the Government and the offeror time and money. The solicitation should also notify offerors that the contracting officer may also limit the number of proposals in the competitive range to permit efficient competition among the most highly rated proposals.

More than one technical factor can be used and titled to match the specific evaluation criteria appropriate for the RFP. The technical factor(s) will assess the offeror's proposed approach to satisfy the Government's requirements. Examples include technical approach, risk, management approach, personnel qualifications, and facilities. The technical factor may be divided into sub-factors that represent the specific areas that are significant enough to be discriminators and to have an impact on the source selection decision.

All evaluations that include a technical evaluation factor shall also consider risk, separately or in conjunction with technical factors, unless the technical proposal is evaluated only for acceptability based on stated criteria. Risk assesses the degree to which the offeror's proposed technical approach may disrupt schedule, increase costs, degrade performance, create increased Government oversight, or increase likelihood of unsuccessful contract performance. A separate risk rating can be assigned at the technical (sub)factor level or be inherent in the technical evaluation factor.

The past performance evaluation factor assesses the degree of confidence the Government has in an offeror's ability to supply products and services that meet Government needs, based on its demonstrated record of performance. Past performance need not be evaluated if the PCO documents the reason. Similarly, the SSEB may evaluate the extent of participation of small business concerns by establishing a separate small business participation evaluation (sub)factor. Small Business participation may be evaluated using an acceptable or unacceptable rating.

The solicitation shall state, at a minimum, whether all evaluation factors other than cost or price, when combined, are (1) significantly more important than cost or price; (2) approximately equal to cost or price; or (3) significantly less important than cost or price. The individual factors' relative importance in relation to each other shall also be stated clearly in the solicitation. Nonetheless, cost or price must be evaluated in every source selection.

The Government may issue a *master solicitation* with clauses and provisions essential for repetitive procurements of supplies or services. An agency may decide to maintain a master solicitation by updating it with changes in laws, regulations, or policies.

3.9.2 Amending the Solicitation

After release of a solicitation, the contracting officer is the focal point of any exchange with potential offerors. Any information about a proposed acquisition disclosed to one or more potential offerors is furnished to all as soon as practicable to avoid creating an unfair competitive advantage.

If the Government changes its requirements or terms and conditions, the contracting officer amends the solicitation by issuing amendments to all parties solicited or still under consideration for award.

If a proposal of interest to the Government departs from the stated requirements, the contracting officer may amend the solicitation but must withhold from the other offerors the alternate solution proposed. The solicitation may be cancelled if this amendment would so greatly change the solicitation as to permit additional firms to propose. Oral notices may be used in case of urgency. The amendment may revise the solicitation closing date. Proposals and RFI responses are always safeguarded from unauthorized disclosure throughout the source selection process.

Any proposal or modification received at the designated Government office after the exact time specified for receipt of proposals is late and generally not considered. Nevertheless, the Government will accept the proposal if it is received before award is made, the contracting officer determines that accepting the late proposal would not unduly delay the acquisition, or a late modification of an otherwise successful proposal makes its terms more favorable to the Government.

Proposals may be withdrawn by written notice at any time before award. Oral proposals in response to oral solicitations may be withdrawn orally.

Prescribed forms are not required for RFPs, but generally are the SF30, SF33 and Optional Form (OF)-17.

DFARS 215.370

In accordance with Section 819 of Pub. L. 109-163, the contracting officer may use an evaluation factor to assess offerors' intent to use employees or individual subcontractors who are members of the Selected Reserve. As defined at 10 USC 10147, these reservists attend at least 48 training sessions per year, comprising between 14 and 30 days (plus travel time).

Solicitation Provisions

FAR 52.215-1, Instructions to Offerors—Competitive Acquisition, where the Government intends to award a contract without discussions. Use the provision with its Alternate I if the Government intends to make award after discussions with offerors within the competitive range. Use the provision with its Alternate II if the Government would be willing to accept alternate proposals.

FAR 52.215-3, Request for Information or Solicitation for Planning Purposes.

FAR 52.215-5, Facsimile Proposals.

FAR 52.215-6, Place of Performance, unless the place of performance is specified by the Government.

DFARS 252.215-7005, Evaluation Factor for Employing or Subcontracting with Members of the Selected Reserve, when including an evaluation factor considering whether an offeror intends to perform the contract using employees or individual subcontractors who are members of the Selected Reserve.

DFARS 252.215-7006, Use of Employees or Individual Subcontractors Who are Members of the Selected Reserve, when including DFARS 252.215-7005. Include the clause in the resultant contract only if the contractor stated in its proposal that it intends to perform the contract using employees or individual subcontractors who are members of the Selected Reserve, and that statement was used as an evaluation factor in the award decision.

Solicitation Provisions and Contract Clauses

FAR 52.215-2, Audit and Records—Negotiation, unless below the simplified acquisition threshold, utility services at rates not exceeding those established to apply uniformly to the general public (plus any applicable reasonable connection charge), or commercial items where cost or pricing data submission is exempted. Use the basic provision with its Alternate I when using funds appropriated or otherwise made available by the American Recovery and Reinvestment Act of 2009. Use the clause with its Alternate II for cost-reimbursement contracts with state and local Governments, educational institutions, and other nonprofit organizations. Use the clause with its Alternate III when the head of the agency has waived the examination of records by the Comptroller General.

FAR 52.215-8, Order of Precedence—Uniform Contract Format.

3.9.3 Bid or No-Bid Decision

Every contractor has its own methodology to develop proposals. In general however, major proposals follow these steps:

- evaluate the opportunity;
- decide to bid or no-bid;
- develop a capture strategy;
- develop a compliance matrix;
- draft a proposal outline;
- prepare a storyboard outline;
- write and edit proposal;
- review proposal; and
- submit proposal.

Upon receipt of the solicitation, a firm thoroughly reads it (especially the statement of work or specifications, and special provisions) and decides whether it makes sense to submit an offer by examining the evaluation factors, risk and potential benefits. The bid-no bid decision is critical because it preserves resources for those opportunities with a higher win probability and thereby raises the firm's win-ratio of winning to total proposals. Factors which the firm must consider in this decision include:

- ambiguities;
- availability of resources;
- capability and qualifications to perform;
- competitiveness and probability of winning;
- contract type;
- difficulty of performance;
- importance to firm's business line and market posture;
- incumbency or presence of competitor incumbent contractor;
- need to maintain workforce employment;
- possibility of cost overrun;
- potential for follow-on work;
- potential gains (experience, financial and knowledge);
- prior customer dealings;
- profitability;
- program stability;
- restrictive provisions or specifications; and
- schedule.

A firm must decide whether the solicited requirement is aligned with its corporate strategy and benefit its product or service line. Therefore, the requirement should appeal to one of the company's strengths. It helps if the customer is well-known to the company, either by reputation or as a current client. The firm must have the necessary resources, which is especially important for services contracts because a lack of desired talent skills will prove fatal to its proposal. It must also decide if performance risks are worth the potential rewards. Of course, the opportunity must also be profitable.

As a rule of thumb, a firm would like at least a one-in-three chance of winning to decide to develop an offer. If the firm decides not to offer, it should notify the agency in writing, either by letter or by filling out the cover page of the SF-18, with a brief reason why (such as inability to meet the requirements), and that it wishes to remain on the mailing list to compete for future agency requirements.

Some corporate managers will use a "gut feel" approach to a decision whether to bid. Others will employ a formal checklist or matrix with a mechanistic scoring process requiring formal evaluation and grading of these criteria. Either way leads to a decision with which corporate management feels more comfortable.

Once a firm decides to submit a proposal, it will adopt a capture strategy based on assessing the customer's objectives and evaluation criteria. It will map its approach and solution to the customer's needs, identify any gaps therein, and spell out any discriminators that it feels a need to emphasize. It must highlight its own strengths and overcome any weaknesses it identifies. It will also emphasize such strengths as its comprehensive capability, experience, financial strength, price, quality, and responsiveness. This effort will serve to improve its positioning to win.

3.9.4 Technical/Management Proposal

The Instructions to Offerors will specify the content structure of the submission, as well as more mundane but still critical directions such as maximum page count. More complicated requirements and evaluations will require more detailed proposals with multiple binders, whereas more routine requirements may require nothing more than a handful of pages stapled together.

The *technical proposal* is designed to convince the Government that the firm understands what the Government wants and has developed an effective and efficient solution. It often includes a detailed description of the firm's background and approach, related past performance, task breakdown, and biographies of key personnel and consultants.

The *management proposal* (if one is required) explains how the firm will manage the work and organize human and materiel resources to reach a successful conclusion. It should also identify any necessary facilities or equipment to be furnished by the Government. The *cost proposal* is submitted in a separate volume and contains all cost and pricing information requested in the solicitation. The entire proposal also includes:

- binders and covers,
- executive summary of the highlights,
- index to cross-reference the proposal to the statement of work,
- introduction stating corporate commitment to performance,
- page numbers consistent with the solicitation's instructions to offerors,
- reference documents,
- section dividers, and
- table of contents and list of exhibits.

Many contracting offices will impose a page limit on the proposal length. The offeror exceeds this limit at its own peril, since pages beyond the limit will be disregarded. Some offices may even reject a proposal due to excessive length.

Offerors will develop a compliance matrix to list all solicitation requirements, specifications and evaluation criteria. A compliance matrix can cross-reference requirements, reveal inconsistencies in the solicitation, provide organization to the proposal writers, and ensure responsiveness to requirements. They will also use the matrix to assess their competitive strengths and weaknesses, as well as to ensure completeness of their proposal. A storyboard serves to focus the proposal team on the objective of the exercise—a winning proposal. The review is sometimes called "white glove" because it not only reviews the writeup but also adds polish.

DAG: Source Selection Procedures, 3.1.6

If subcontractor experience is submitted for consideration as part of the proposal, the offeror should include a commitment signed by offeror and subcontractor certifying that if a contract is awarded resulting from the proposal, the parties commit to joint performance as proposed. If the signed commitment is not fully executed by both parties and provided with the Past Performance Proposal, subcontractor references will not be evaluated or considered. This includes affiliate companies, sister companies, teaming arrangements, joint venture agreement. Documentation includes a copy of the signed arrangement such as documented affiliation, a copy of the teaming agreement, a copy of the joint venture agreement, etc.

3.9.5 Unsolicited Proposal

FAR 15.6

An *unsolicited proposal* occurs when the business concern submits a proposal on its own initiative rather than in response to a solicitation. Knowledge of an unannounced need may result from work on another contract, broad agency announcement or knowledge of a contractor employee. An unsolicited proposal must be innovative and unique, individually developed without Government assistance or endorsement, and demonstrate benefit to the agency (especially in research or development). It cannot be merely an advance proposal for a future known requirement. The proposal must be detailed enough to permit a determination that Government support could benefit the agency's research and development or other mission responsibilities. Ideally, it leads to sole-source negotiation.

The Government encourages the submission of new and innovative ideas in response to Broad Agency Announcements, Small Business Innovation Research, Small Business Technology Transfer Research, Program Research and Development Announcements and unsolicited proposals. However, unsolicited proposals often represent a substantial investment of time and effort by the offeror to provide its unique and innovative ideas or approaches to the Government with the intent to enter into contract to support the Government mission.

Agencies are free to announce submission procedures and furnish potential offerors of unsolicited proposals with the following information:

- agency points of contact for information;
- anticipated results and how the proposed approach helps accomplish the agency mission;
- definition and content of an unsolicited proposal acceptable for formal evaluation;
- guidance on preferred methods to submit ideas to the Government;
- information sources on agency objectives and areas of potential interest;
- instructions to identify and mark proprietary information;
- procedures to submit and evaluate unsolicited proposals; and
- requirements concerning responsible prospective contractors and organizational conflicts of interest.

Unsolicited proposals should contain the following information:

- concise title and abstract (approximately 200 words) of the proposed effort;
- date of submission;
- description of the organization, previous experience, relevant past performance, and facilities to be used;
- identification of proprietary data to be used only for evaluation purposes;
- names and biographical information on the offeror's proposed key personnel;

- names and telephone numbers of technical and business personnel for evaluation or negotiation;
- names of other Federal, State or local agencies receiving the proposal or funding the proposed effort;
- objectives of the effort, method of approach, and extent of effort;
- offeror's name and address and type of organization (e.g., profit, nonprofit, educational, small business, etc.);
- organizational conflicts of interest, security clearances and environmental impacts;
- period of time for proposal validity;
- preferred contract type;
- proposed duration of effort;
- proposed price or total estimated cost;
- required Government property or personnel resources; and
- signature of a person authorized to represent and contractually obligate the offeror.

Before initiating a comprehensive evaluation, the agency contact point shall determine if the proposal truly is unsolicited, related to the agency mission and responsive to an existing agency requirement. The proposal must be approved by a responsible official to obligate the offeror contractually and comply with marking requirements. It must promote overall scientific, technical, or socioeconomic merit and contain sufficient technical information and cost or price information for evaluation. Evaluators will review the unique, innovative and meritorious approaches, concepts and methods proposed to contribute to the agency's mission, assessing the proposal's overall scientific, technical or socioeconomic merits. They will also assess the offeror's capabilities, experience, facilities, or techniques that are integral to achieving the proposal objectives. The proposed principal investigator, team leader or key personnel must be highlighted in the proposal so their capabilities, experience and qualifications can be evaluated. Finally, cost realism of the proposal must be considered.

The evaluators notify the agency point of contact of their recommendations upon completion of evaluation. The agency point of contact will return an unsolicited proposal to the offeror with reasons when it:

- does not demonstrate an innovative and unique approach, concept or method;
- does not relate to the activity's mission;
- is not deemed a meritorious proposal;

- its substance is available to the Government without restriction from another source; and
- resembles a pending competitive acquisition requirement.

The contracting officer may commence negotiations on a sole-source basis only after an unsolicited proposal has received a favorable comprehensive evaluation, a J&A has been signed, funding has been provided, and the requirement has been synopsized.

Government personnel may not use any data or concept of an unsolicited proposal as the basis to solicit or negotiate with any other firm unless the offeror is notified of and agrees to the intended use.

3.10 RESPONSIBLE OFFERORS

3.10.1 Responsibility

FAR 9.104

The contracting officer must determine responsibility for any contractor other than another government entity, source furnished through NIB or NISH, or one covered by an SBA Certificate of Competency. To be determined responsible, an offeror must have (or be able to obtain):

- a satisfactory performance record (lack of relevant performance history is not a basis for nonresponsibility);
- a satisfactory record of integrity and business ethics;
- adequate financial resources to perform the contract, or the ability to obtain them;
- commitment at the time of contract award to acquire or rent the necessary equipment, facilities and personnel;
- compliance with all applicable laws and regulations;
- fulfillment of the delivery or performance schedule, considering all existing commercial and governmental business commitments;
- necessary construction, production and technical equipment and facilities, and
- necessary construction, production and equipment and facilities, experience, skills, and controls (accounting, operations, production, property, quality assurance, and safety).

A prospective contractor seriously deficient in past or present contract performance is presumed to be nonresponsible, unless the contracting officer determines that the circumstances were beyond the contractor's control, or that the contractor has taken appropriate corrective action. Past failure to apply perseverance and tenacity to perform acceptably or meet quality requirements is strong evidence of nonresponsibility. Compliance with subcontracting plans under recent contracts is also considered.

If a small business concern is to be rejected because of a determination of nonresponsibility, the contracting officer refers the matter to the SBA, which will decide whether or not to issue a Certificate of Competency.

A prospective contractor may be required to provide written evidence of a proposed subcontractor's responsibility. The contracting officer may directly determine a prospective subcontractor's responsibility by using the same standards as for a prime contractor's responsibility.

The contracting officer notifies the agency official responsible for initiating debarment or suspension action if an offeror indicates the existence of an indictment, charge, conviction, civil judgment, or Federal tax delinquency that exceeds $3,000.

In making the determination of responsibility, the contracting officer considers relevant past performance information, including:

- business and trade associations;
- commercial sources of supplier information;
- Contract Performance Assessment Reporting System (CPARS);[28]
- financial institutions;
- Government agencies;
- preaward survey reports;
- proposal certifications, questionnaire replies, and other data on financial, personnel and production equipment;
- publications;
- records within the contracting, contract administration and audit offices;
- suppliers and customers of the prospective contractor; and
- the Excluded Parties List System.

If a prospective contractor is a joint venture, the venture's past performance is reviewed. If not available, then past performance of each party to the venture is considered.

The contracting officer's signing of a contract constitutes a determination that the prospective contractor is responsible with respect to that contract. If the offeror is found to be nonresponsible, the contracting officer signs and places in both the contract file and the Federal Awardee Performance and Integrity Information System (FAPIIS) a determination of nonresponsibility. Per PGI 219.602-1, any nonresponsibility determination of a small business must be reported to the small business specialist.

A preaward survey is normally required only when available information is not sufficient to make a determination regarding responsibility. It is usually performed by the contract administration office which is cognizant of the offeror's geographic area. This entails examining the firm's physical, technical, managerial, and financial capability, as well as its systems, procedures and past performance record. When a preaward survey discloses previous unsatisfactory performance, the surveying activity specifies the extent to which the prospective contractor plans or has taken corrective action. The report addresses any persistent pattern of need for costly and burdensome Government assistance (e.g., technical, testing or excessive inspection assistance).

DFARS 209.104

For a flexibly priced contract or for progress payments or a percentage-of-completion contract, the contractor's accounting system and controls must be reviewed to ensure legal and regulatory compliance, data reliability, minimal risk of misallocation and mischarges, and consistency with invoiced contract allocations and charges.

DFARS 209.104-4

The Canadian Commercial Corporation vets its subcontractors to such a degree that it is deemed a sufficient basis for affirmatively determining responsibility. However, when this determination is not consistent with other information available to the contracting officer, the contracting officer shall request from CCC and any other sources whatever additional information is necessary to make the responsibility determination.

DFARS 209.105-2-70

If a (sub)contractor not subject to U.S. courts is determined to be so negligent or reckless in disregard for the safety of civilian or military personnel that serious bodily injury or death results, the contracting officer shall enter this determination into FAPIIS.

Solicitation Provisions

FAR 52.209-5, Certification Regarding Responsibility, where the estimated value exceeds the simplified acquisition threshold.

FAR 52.209-7, Information Regarding Responsibility Matters, where the estimated value exceeds $600,000.

FAR 52.209-9, Updates of Information Regarding Responsibility Matters, where the total estimated value exceeds $600,000.

FAR 52.209-11, Representation by Corporations Regarding Delinquent Tax Liability or a Felony Conviction under any Federal Law.

FAR 52.209-12, Certification Regarding Tax Matters, for any offer exceeding $5.5 million.

DFARS 252.209-7002, Disclosure of Ownership or Control by a Foreign Government, when access to proscribed information is necessary for contract performance. Do not use if the solicitation includes FAR 52.204-7.

3.10.2 Teams and Pools

FAR 9.6 and 9.7

Partnering is a frequent technique used by contractors who cannot provide all deliverables in-house, and needs one or more firms to join them to develop a top-notch team. It entails a voluntary cooperative agreement to work together and share the resources, responsibilities, and rewards of performance. Successful partnering creates a synergistic arrangement where each party can leverage off its own strengths to succeed beyond its own capabilities. Partners generally aim to reduce costs and increase their competitive advantage. There are several varieties of partnership.

A *team arrangement* involves at least two firms that form a partnership to act as a single entity (either prime or subcontractor) to perform a contract. They can leverage their respective strengths to maximize performance abilities and cost. Often used in complex research and development projects, such an arrangement is established before the offer is made. A teaming arrangement can be mutually exclusive, where the parties pledge neither to seek other sources for the work kept in-house nor to remove resources to work on other projects. They can be of either a repetitive or one-time-only nature. Prospective team members must consider several factors about each other before entering agreement:

- bonding capability and track record;
- compensating strengths in terms of:
  - past performance with the same customer;
  - personnel resources;
  - possession of required equipment;
  - proximity to the project site;
  - technical knowledge; and
  - unique capabilities;
- cultural fit and values;
- customer satisfaction;
- Dun & Bradstreet rating;

- ethics compliance;
- financial resources;
- OSHA safety record;
- past performance, and
- willingness to take risks.

A *joint venture* is an association of persons or concerns engaged in a specific business venture for joint profit, but not on a continuing or permanent basis. They combine their efforts, money, property, and skills or knowledge. It is considered a business entity with the power of management.

A *pool* is a group of firms (often small businesses) that agree to perform together by formally chartering their organization and procedures. Formal approval must be obtained from the SBA. The pool submits an offer in its own name with written concurrence of all pool members. The contracting officer verifies pool status with the SBA and obtains from each pool member a certified power of attorney of signature status, which is physically attached to the signed copy of the contract. Any pool member is free to submit an independent offer on any solicitation on which the pool is not offering, but any such proposal is rejected if submitted for the same requirement where the pool is offering.

A *memorandum of agreement* (*MOA*) or *cooperative agreement* is a written agreement between parties to cooperatively work together on a project or meet an objective. An MOA can be used between agencies, or between agencies on different government levels. An MOA can set forth the cooperative procedures, terms and responsibilities of the partner entities, sometimes with an obligation of funds.

Solicitation Provision

FAR 52.207-6, Solicitation of Offers from Small Business Concerns and Small Business Teaming Arrangements or Joint Ventures (Multiple-Award Contracts).

3.10.3 Prohibition on Contracting With Inverted Domestic Corporations

Controversy surrounds firms which have moved across the border or overseas. An *inverted domestic corporation* was incorporated in the United States or in a partnership in the United States at one time, but now is either incorporated in a foreign country or is a subsidiary whose parent corporation is incorporated in a foreign country. A foreign corporation is treated as an inverted domestic corporation if at least 80 percent of the stock is now held by former shareholders or partners of the domestic entity, and the foreign entity does not have substantial business activities in the foreign country. Contracting with such a corporation is prohibited. Any agency head may waive the requirement for a specific contract by determining in writing that the waiver is required in the interest of national security, documents the determination, and reports it to the Congress.

Solicitation Provision

FAR 52.209-2, Prohibition on Contracting with Inverted Domestic Corporations—Representation.

FAR 52.209-5, Certification Regarding Responsibility Matters, if the contract value is expected to exceed the simplified acquisition threshold.

3.10.4 Qualifications Requirements

FAR 9.2

Before establishing a preaward qualification requirement, the agency head or designee justifies in writing the need and reason to establish the qualification requirement, estimates testing costs to be incurred by the potential offeror to become qualified, and specifies all requirements that a potential offeror (or its product) must satisfy in order to become qualified. Potential offerors are provided upon request all requirements to satisfy the qualification and a prompt opportunity to demonstrate their abilities to meet these standards. A potential offeror seeking qualification is promptly informed of qualification results and reasons for any failure. If successful, the offeror is placed on a Qualified Bidders List (QBL), Qualified Manufacturers List (QML) or Qualified Products List (QPL), and is not denied the opportunity to submit and receive consideration of its offer for a contract. The qualification decision and its requirements are not subject to a certificate of competency. Nor is the qualification process an opportunity to delay an award merely because a potential offeror wishes to be qualified for the instant procurement. Qualification requirements are reviewable every seven years.

If a qualification requirement applies, the contracting officer need consider only those offers identified as meeting the requirement or included on the applicable QBL, QML or QPL, unless an offeror can satisfactorily demonstrate to the contracting officer that it or its product or its subcontractor's product can meet the standards established for qualification before the date specified for award.

A QPL lists by specification the manufacturers and products that have passed qualification tests. It saves time, provides a quick reference list, eliminates the need to qualify for new procurement, is tightly controlled, and gives a high degree of confidence that the product will meet requirements. Testing can be a lengthy process, however, could lead to protests due to limiting competition, takes time to maintain, and has high laboratory costs.

The contracting officer promptly reports to the agency activity which established the qualification requirement any conditions which may merit removal or omission from a qualified list, such as:

- a condition of meeting the qualification requirement was violated;
- a manufacturer of a qualified product has discontinued its manufacture;
- a revised specification imposes a new qualification requirement;
- a source requests removal from a QBL, QML or QPL;
- a supplier fails to request reevaluation after moving or changing ownership of the plant where the product was manufactured;
- manufacturing or design changes are made to the qualification requirement;
- performance of a contract subject to a qualification requirement is unsatisfactory;
- products or services previously rejected and the defects were not corrected;
- products or services submitted for inspection or acceptance do not meet the qualification requirement; or
- the source is on the Excluded Parties List System.

DFARS 209.270-4

The head of the design control activity must approve any source and qualification requirements for an aviation or ship critical safety item before its purchase.

Solicitation Provisions and Contract Clauses

FAR 52.209-1, Qualification Requirements.

DFARS 252.209-7010, Critical Safety Items, if the acquisition includes an item(s) so designated by the design control activity.

3.10.5 First Article Testing and Approval

FAR 9.3

First article testing and approval ensures that the contractor can furnish a product that conforms to all contract requirements for acceptance. This idea entails preproduction models, test and initial production samples, and first lots. The contracting officer considers the impact on cost or time of delivery, risk of foregoing such a test, and availability of less costly methods to ensure desired quality before requiring such a test. First article testing is appropriate when the contractor has not previously furnished the product to the Government, specifications or manufacturing processes have changed, production has been discontinued for a long time, or the tested product performed below expectation. First article testing is also appropriate if a manufacturing standard must be established. First article testing is not appropriate for commercial items, product qualification, research or development, or technical specifications. The solicitation provides performance characteristics, technical requirements, and deliverable data, as well as a delivery schedule. Failure to pass the test is treated as a case of missed delivery.

When the Government is responsible for the first article approval testing, the solicitation includes performance characteristics and tests necessary to obtain approval. An offeror may submit alternate offers with an unapproved product. The delivery schedule can provide for earlier delivery when testing and approval is waived and the Government desires earlier delivery (though this cannot be an evaluation factor). However, the Government's estimated testing costs will be a factor for use in evaluating offers. Prices for first articles and tests in relation to production quantities may not be materially unbalanced when separately priced.

Solicitation Provisions and Contract Clauses

FAR 52.209-3, First Article Approval—Contractor Testing, for a fixed-price contract and the contractor will be required to conduct the first article testing.

FAR 52.209-4, First Article Approval—Government Testing, for a fixed-price contract that requires first article approval under Government test.

For either First Article Approval clause, use the clause with its Alternate I if the contractor is required to produce the first article and the production quantity at the same facility. Use the clause with its Alternate II to authorize the contractor to purchase material or commence production before first article approval.

3.10.6 Excluded Parties List System

GSA operates the web-based Excluded Parties List System of names and addresses of all contractors debarred, suspended, proposed for debarment, or ineligible, with cross-references when more than one name is involved in an action. They could also be ineligible through the *Nonprocurement Common Rule,* the procedures used by Executive Agencies to suspend, debar or exclude individuals or firms from participation in nonprocurement transactions.[29] Examples of nonprocurement transactions are:

- contracts of assistance;
- cooperative agreements;
- donation agreements;
- fellowships;
- grants;
- insurance;
- loan guarantees;
- loans;
- payments for specified use;
- scholarships; and
- subsidies.

Any debarment, suspension or other Government-wide exclusion of an offeror applies to all Federal executive agencies.[30] Contractors debarred, suspended, or proposed for debarment may not receive contracts, represent other contractors, act as a surety, or be solicited unless the agency head determines that there is a compelling reason for such action. Otherwise, any offers from such firms are not considered. Immediately prior to award, the contracting officer again reviews the List to ensure that no award is made to a listed contractor. Agencies may continue (sub)contracts in existence at the time the contractor was debarred, suspended, or proposed for debarment unless the agency head directs otherwise. Contractors may not enter into any subcontract in excess of $30,000 with a contractor that has been debarred, suspended, or proposed for debarment unless there is a compelling reason to do so.

3.10.7 Suspension

FAR 9.407

Suspension is imposed on the basis of adequate evidence, pending investigation or legal proceedings (including appeals) when necessary to protect the Government's interest. Agencies consider the amount of available information, its credibility, corroboration of allegations, and drawn inferences. The suspending official (the agency head or designee) may consider remedial measures or mitigating factors. A contractor has the burden of promptly presenting evidence of remedial measures or mitigating factors when it has reason to know that a cause for suspension exists.

Suspension covers all divisions or organizational elements of the contractor, unless limited by its own terms. The suspending official may extend the suspension decision to include any affiliates of the contractor if they are given written notice of the suspension and an opportunity to respond. *Affiliates* are business concerns, organizations, or individuals where either one controls or has the power to control the other, or a third party controls or has the power to control both. Common indications of control include interlocking management or ownership, especially among family members, or common use of employees or equipment or facilities. Another red flag is a business entity organized following the debarment, suspension, or proposed debarment of a contractor, bearing the same or similar management, ownership or principal employees.

A business entity organized after the debarment, suspension, or proposed debarment of a contractor, which bears the same or similar management, ownership or principal employees is probably an instance of control that would lead to suspension.

Agencies establish procedures governing the decision-making process that are as informal as practicable, while maintaining fairness. Suspension is for a temporary period pending the completion of investigation and any legal proceedings. If legal proceedings are not initiated within 12 months after the date of the suspension notice, the suspension ends automatically unless an Assistant Attorney General requests a six-month extension. A suspension cannot exceed 18 months without legal proceedings underway.

DFARS 209.405

The contracting officer must notify GSA in writing before awarding to a suspended or debarred source. Possible reasons for such action include a requirement for national defense, sole source of supply or urgency. It is possible that the contractor and department or agency have an agreement not to suspend or debar the contractor for previous events.

Should a contractor be found guilty of violating the Clean Air Act or Clean Water Act and receive a "Code H" annotation within the SAM to indicate ineligibility for performance at that facility, a flag officer or member of the Senior Executive Service can nonetheless grant an exemption for award after consulting with the debarring official of the Environmental Protection

Agency. This exemption if only valid for one year and must be renewed for any further awards.

Solicitation Provisions and Contract Clauses

FAR 52.209-6, Protecting the Government's Interests when Subcontracting with Contractors Debarred, Suspended, or Proposed for Debarment, where the contract value exceeds $35,000, except for COTS items.

DFARS 252.209-7004, Subcontracting with Firms that are Owned or Controlled by the Government of a Country that is a State Sponsor of Terrorism, when the value is at least $150,000.

3.10.8 Debarment

FAR 9.4

Debarred firms are listed in the SAM. Once a firm is debarred or proposed for same, it can no longer receive solicitation or awards, nor can it act as a surety. Subcontracts can only be awarded for standard commercial items or for awards below $35,000 in value. This is why the contracting officer must check SAM before award. However, ongoing contracts continue to completion unless the agency head determines otherwise.

Agencies establish their own debarment procedures. Debarment is a more serious event than suspension because it precludes the firm from Federal contracting. The debarring official may debar a contractor for:

- a knowingly false statement of a material element of a certification concerning the foreign content of an item of supply;
- commission of an offense indicating a lack of business integrity or honesty, such as an unfair trade practice;
- conviction of or civil judgment for committing fraud, or a criminal offense to obtain or attempt to obtain a federal contract or subcontract;[31]
- delinquent Federal taxes exceeding $3,000;
- embezzlement, theft, forgery, bribery, falsification or destruction of records, making false statements, tax evasion, violating Federal criminal tax laws, or receiving stolen property;
- failure by a principal, until three years after final payment, to timely disclose to the Government evidence of bribery, conflict of interest, fraud, or gratuity; False Claims Act violations; or significant contract overpayments (other than from contract financing payments);
- failure to comply with the requirements of FAR 52.223-6, Drug-Free Workplace;[32]

- intentionally affixing a label bearing a "Made in America" inscription to a product sold in or shipped to (but not made in) the United States or its outlying areas;
- non-compliance with Immigration and Nationality Act employment provisions based on a determination by the Secretary of Homeland Security or the Attorney General of the United States;[33]
- violation of any agreement of the Coordination Committee under the Export Administration Act of 1979 or any similar bilateral or multilateral export control agreement;[34]
- violation of Federal or State antitrust statutes relating to the submission of offers;
- violation of Section 337 of the Tariff Act of 1930 as determined by the International Trade Commission;[35] or
- willful failure to perform in accordance with the terms of one or more contracts.

Before arriving at any debarment decision, the debarring official designated by the agency head considers if the contractor:

- brought the activity to the attention of the Government agency in a timely manner;
- cooperated fully with Government agencies during the investigation and any court or administrative action;
- fully investigated the circumstances and provided the results to the debarring official;
- had adequate time to eliminate the circumstances within the contractor's organization;
- had effective standards of conduct and internal control systems in place at the time of the activity under investigation;
- implemented or agreed to implement remedial measures and revised review and control procedures and ethics training;
- paid or agreed to pay all criminal, civil, and administrative liability for the improper activity, including any investigative or administrative costs incurred by the Government, and has made or agreed to make full restitution;
- recognizes and understands the seriousness of the misconduct; and
- took appropriate disciplinary action against the individuals responsible for the activity.

If a cause for debarment exists, the contractor has the burden of demonstrating, to the satisfaction of the debarring official, its present responsibility and that debarment is not necessary. Debarment applies to all divisions or other organizational elements of the contractor, unless limited by its terms to specific commodities, divisions, or organizational elements.

Debarment is for a period commensurate with the seriousness of the cause(s), not to exceed three years, except five years for Drug-Free Workplace Act of 1988 violations and one year where no conviction is involved. The debarring official may extend the debarment for an additional period if necessary to protect the Government's interest. The debarring official may reduce the period or extent of debarment upon contractor request for reasons such as:

- bona fide change in ownership or management;
- elimination of causes for which the debarment was imposed;
- newly discovered material evidence; or
- reversal of the conviction or civil judgment.

The criminal, fraudulent or improper conduct of any employee, officer, partner, or shareholder associated with a contractor may be imputed to the contractor when the conduct occurred in connection with the individual's performance of duties for or on behalf of the contractor, or with the contractor's acquiescence, approval or knowledge. Contractor acceptance of the benefits derived from this conduct is evidence of such acquiescence, approval, or knowledge.

DFARS 209.406

As an alternative to debarment, the contractor may be directed to agree in writing that it will establish and maintain the standards of conduct and internal control systems set forth in FAR 52.204-13 concerning a code of ethics, plus report any employees who violate Federal law on the job. If an indictment or conviction for a felony occurs, the debarring official must determine that the contractor has addressed the circumstances that caused the misconduct and implemented appropriate standards of ethics and integrity.

DFARS 209.471

Section 8118 of Pub. L. 105-262 prohibits award or extension of a (sub) contract to any entity that, within the preceding 15 years, has been convicted under 18 U.S.C. 704 of unlawfully manufacturing or selling the Congressional Medal of Honor.

3.10.9 Prohibited Sources

FAR 9.110

The Government cannot enter into a contract over the simplified acquisition threshold with an institution of higher education which prohibits ROTC units or students participating in an ROTC unit, or military recruiting at the institution, unless it has a historical or religious identity of pacifism.

DFARS 237.102-70

Per 10 U.S.C. 2465, the DoD cannot contract for firefighting or security-guard functions at any military installation or facility unless performance is located outside the United States and its outlying areas on a Government-owned but privately operated installation and members of the armed forces would have to be used for performance at the expense of unit readiness. Moreover, the contract may not exceed one year and can cover only firefighting functions.

Pub. L. 103-160 and 107-56 exempt any contract that is for:

- a proximately located local or State government or combination of same;
- effort supporting Operation Enduring Freedom up to 180 days thereafter;
- performance of security functions at any military installation or facility in the United States;
- prescribing standards for the training and other qualifications of local government law enforcement personnel who perform security functions under the contract; or
- services at installations being closed.

DFARS 237.102-71

Pub. L. 109-364 and 110-181 prohibit DoD from contracting to acquire a military (non-commercial) flight simulator. However, the Secretary of Defense may waive this prohibition by determining that a waiver is in the national interest and providing a best-value analysis of alternatives to the congressional defense committees at least 30 days before the waiver takes effect.

DFARS 237.102-72

Pub. L. 110-181 requires that DoD may award a contract for acquisition support functions with respect to the development or production of a major system only if the contract prohibits the contractor from performing inherently governmental functions or recommending the award of a (sub)contract to develop or produce the major system to an entity owned in whole or in part by the prime contractor.

DFARS 237.102-73

DoD is prohibited from entering into contracts for the services of senior mentors.

DFARS 237.270

DoD cannot contract for audit services unless the cognizant DoD audit organization determines that expertise required to perform the audit is not available within the DoD audit organization or temporary audit assistance is required to meet audit reporting requirements mandated by law or DoD regulation. Except in unusual circumstances, contracts for recurring audit services must be for a one-year period with at least two option years. The requiring activity must provide evidence that the cognizant DoD audit organization has approved the statement of work. The requiring agency must obtain the same evidence of approval for subsequent material changes to the statement of work.

Solicitation Provision

DFARS 252.237-7000, Notice of Special Standards of Responsibility, for audit services.

Solicitation Provisions and Contract Clauses

FAR 52.209-14 Reserve Officer Training Corps and Military Recruiting on Campus.

DFARS 252.237-7001, Compliance with Audit Standards, for audit services.

DFARS 252.237-7010, Prohibition on Interrogation of Detainees by Contractor Personnel for the provision of services.

Contract Clause

DFARS 252.237-7026, Postaward Transparency Requirements for Firms that Support Department of Defense Audits.

3.11 EVALUATION OF OFFERS

3.11.1 Source Selection Team

DAG: Source Selection Procedures, 1.4

Teams for larger, more complex source selections generally consist of the SSA, Source Selection Advisory Council (SSAC), Source Selection Evaluation Board (SSEB), Advisors, Cost or Pricing Experts, Legal Counsel, Small Business Professionals/Specialists, and other subject-matter experts. All members of the team are designated early in the source selection process and receive appropriate training from the agency. All persons receiving source selection information must sign a Nondisclosure Agreement and a Conflict of Interest statement.

Discussions are expected if the estimated value is at least $100 million, and encouraged if under $100M.[36] If the solicitation states the Government intends to award without discussions and discussions are deemed necessary after reviewing proposal evaluation results, the SSA must review and approval. Prior to conducting discussions, the PCO must determine the competitive range, document the basis for excluding any offeror from the competitive range, submit it to the SSA for review and approval, and provide in writing to the unsuccessful offeror(s). The PCO should obtain offeror organizational conflict of interest plans as part of proposals and examine the particular facts of the contracting situation and exercise common sense, good judgment, and sound discretion in deciding whether a significant conflict of interest exists and determining the appropriate means for resolution.

The SSAC provides functional area expertise to support the SSA for acquisitions with a total estimated value of $100 million or more unless a waiver is approved. An SSAC is optional but encouraged for special interest acquisitions of a lesser dollar amount. The SSAC provides a written comparative analysis of offers and recommendation to the SSA and to provide oversight to the SSEB. The SSA may convene the SSAC at any stage in the evaluation process as needed.

The SSEB is comprised of a chairperson and evaluators, frequently organized into functional teams corresponding to specific evaluation criteria with a Functional Team Lead to consolidate the evaluation findings of the team and serve as the primary team representative to the SSEB Chairperson. Technical Team members will review proposal elements within their areas of specialty and coordinate with cost/pricing experts to ensure consistency across non-cost/price portions of the proposal and proposed cost/prices. The SSEB Chairperson ensures that the evaluation process follows the evaluation criteria and ratings are applied consistently, provides consolidated evaluation results in an SSEB Report to the SSA and/or the SSAC, and may attend any postaward debriefings and meetings. Legal Counsel advises the SSA, PCO, SSAC, and SSEB, as required, on matters related to the legal aspects of the source selection process. Advisors may assist functional teams in their areas of expertise, however use of nongovernment personnel as voting members of the SSEB is prohibited.[37]

Cost/pricing team members will review the cost or pricing aspects of the source selection process, consider materiality and risk to the Government when making decisions on how much information to request from offerors, use external Government resources such as DCAA and DCMA to perform cost modeling, augment non-cost/price evaluations, and provide assist audits or rate recommendations. Small Business Advisors may assist the SST by providing organizational small business goals, identifying market capabilities, and developing small business participation evaluation factors. Past Performance Advisors may assist the SST by compiling past performance information and developing past performance evaluation factors. Legal counsel provide review and support as required.

The SSA's decision regarding which proposal is most advantageous to the Government is based on a comparative analysis of proposals against all source selection criteria in the solicitation. Beyond this, the SSA has broad discretion in making the source selection decision. In fact, the SSA is not bound by the evaluation findings of the SSEB or the recommendations of the SSAC as long as the SSA has a rational basis for the differing opinion. The SSA will issue a Source Selection Decision Document continuing the rationale for any tradeoffs made or relied upon by the SSA, including benefits associated with additional costs, and for any business and independent judgments.

The Source Selection Evaluation Board contains a variety of specialists who advise the contracting officer in developing the source selection plan. They evaluate proposals in accordance with this plan. Most boards contain three subgroups for evaluation: one for technical aspects of the proposal, one to assess any management proposal, and one to analyze proposed cost and price.

Evaluators must be free of conflict of interest and *bias*, the intent and act of favoring or disfavoring a particular offeror. The Government takes great care in educating its evaluators and protecting against conflicts and biases. All reviewers must sign an agreement to not disclose any offeror's technical solutions, prices and past performance references without permission of the contracting officer. Unless it can prove that the agency maliciously intended and in fact did cause it injury, an offeror will have great difficulty gaining relief from GAO.

3.11.2 Evaluation Process

FAR 15.3

The contracting officer is designated as the SSA unless the agency head appoints another individual for a particular acquisition(s), principally due to dollar value or technical complexity.[38] The source selection authority will:

- approve the source selection strategy or acquisition plan before solicitation release;
- consider the recommendations of any advisory boards or panels;
- ensure consistency among the solicitation requirements, notices to offerors, proposal preparation instructions, data requirements, evaluation factors and subfactors, solicitation provisions, and contract clauses;
- ensure that proposals are evaluated based solely on the (sub)factors contained in the solicitation;
- establish a comprehensive evaluation team that includes appropriate contracting, legal, logistics and technical expertise; and
- select the source(s) proposing the best value to the Government.

After release of a solicitation, the contracting officer serves as the focal point for inquiries from actual or prospective offerors.

The award decision is based on evaluation factors and subfactors that are tailored to the acquisition. Evaluation factors represent the key areas of importance in the source selection decision, and support meaningful comparison and discrimination between and among competing proposals. The quality of the product or service is addressed in every source selection through consideration of past performance, compliance with solicitation requirements, technical excellence, management capability, personnel qualifications, and/or prior experience.

Past performance is evaluated in all source selections for negotiated competitive acquisitions expected to exceed the simplified acquisition threshold, unless the contracting officer documents why it is not an appropriate evaluation factor. Past performance need not be evaluated for construction contracts below $550,000 in value (and architect-engineering services below $30,000 in value) unless the offeror was previously terminated for default. For solicitations involving bundling that offer a significant opportunity for subcontracting, the contracting officer includes a factor to evaluate past performance that assesses the extent to which the offeror attained applicable goals for small business participation. The extent of participation of small, disadvantaged business concerns in performance of the contract is normally evaluated in unrestricted acquisitions expected to exceed $550,000 ($1,000,000 for construction).

The currency and relevance of past performance information, its source, context, and general trends in contractors' performance are considered. This comparative assessment of past performance information is separate from the responsibility determination. The solicitation describes the approach for evaluating past performance, including evaluating offerors with no relevant performance history, and allows offerors to identify past or current contracts (including Federal, State, and local Government and private customers) for efforts similar to the Government requirement. The solicitation authorizes offerors to provide information on problems encountered on the identified contracts and corrective actions. The evaluation may consider past performance information regarding predecessor companies, key personnel who have relevant experience, or subcontractors that will perform major or critical aspects of the requirement. The evaluation includes the past performance of offerors in complying with subcontracting plan goals for small, disadvantaged business concerns. An offeror without relevant past performance may not be evaluated either favorably or unfavorably on past performance. All factors, significant subfactors and their relative importance are stated in the solicitation.

Proposal evaluation assesses the offeror's ability to perform the prospective contract successfully based solely on the (sub)factors specified in the solicitation. The applicability and sufficiency of the proposed approach is reviewed to determine if it will meet contract requirements. Evaluations may use any rating method or combination of methods (e.g., adjectives, colors, numerical weights, or ordinal rankings). The relative strengths, deficiencies, weaknesses, and risks supporting proposal evaluation are documented in the evaluation team's report. The rating method need not be disclosed in the solicitation, though the general approach for evaluating past performance is revealed.

When tradeoffs are performed, the source selection team assesses each offeror's ability to accomplish the technical requirements and summarizes (both quantitatively and in words), each technical proposal using the evaluation factors.

DAG: Source Selection Procedures, 3.2

Following the initial round of evaluations, the SSEB Chairperson consolidates the inputs from each of the evaluation teams into a consolidated SSEB report and submit to the SSA. All evaluation records and narratives are reviewed by the contracting officer, legal counsel and the SSEB Chairperson for completeness and compliance with the solicitation. If the SSEB members do not reach a consensus opinion on evaluating a particular proposal, the SSEB Chairperson will document the basis of disagreement and raise it to the SSAC Chairperson or the SSA to resolve. The SSAC will review the results of the SSEB to see if additional areas of evaluation are required. The SSA then decides to either approve award without discussions or enter into discussions.

When contracting on a firm-fixed-price or fixed-price with economic price adjustment basis, comparison of the proposed prices usually satisfies the requirement to perform a price analysis by examining the price itself without evaluating separate cost elements, and a cost analysis need not be performed. On the other hand, there are times when a cost analysis may establish reasonableness of the otherwise successful offeror's price. When contracting on a fixed-price incentive or cost-reimbursement basis, evaluations include a cost realism analysis to determine what the Government should realistically expect to pay for the proposed effort, the offeror's understanding of the work, and the offeror's ability to perform the contract.

There are several techniques used to estimate cost without obtaining detailed breakdowns from offerors. A *bottoms-up* estimate can be made at the lowest possible level (provided that detailed data exists at such a level) using engineering expertise, then aggregate and adjust to account for integration and indirect expenses. One could draw an *analogy* by collecting cost data on similar systems and modify to reflect variations in the evaluated system. A third method is to *extrapolate* from actual costs. Finally, *parametric analysis* of cost data can develop cost estimating relationships between cost elements and system or process characteristics. The bottoms-up approach is most accurate but consumes more time and labor than the others. The two comparison methods establish an initial baseline and calibrate other methods. Parametric analysis will be more accurate based on data quality, representative cost estimating relationships and the strength of the derived relationships, and should be conducted early in the program lifecycle.

The total cost is evaluated as well as its *reasonableness* (level of proposed effort) and *realism* (acceptable risk without fear of contractor buy-in at low cost in hopes of getting well during performance or receiving follow-on contracts on a sole-source basis at artificially high prices). Cost information may be provided to the technical evaluation team in accordance with agency procedures.

The SSA may reject all proposals received in response to a solicitation, if doing so is in the best interest of the Government.

DFARS 203.170

Legal review of documentation of major acquisition system source selection is required before contract award, including documentation of the source selection evaluation board, advisory council, and authority.

DFARS 215.404

If there is no adequate price competition, pricing based on market prices is the preferred method to establish a fair and reasonable price. If market price information is inadequate or nonexistent, the contracting officer must next consider recent prices paid for the same or similar commercial items under comparable terms and conditions. However, the contracting officer must be satisfied that these previous prices remain a valid reference for comparison, especially considering the time elapsed and quantities purchased. If this technique does not determine price reasonableness, the contracting officer should next ask the offeror to submit pricing information for the same or similar items sold under different terms and conditions, similar levels of work or effort on related products or services, or for alternative solutions or approaches. If this does not succeed and no commercial sales data is sufficient, then cost data will be necessary. The contracting officer shall consider the following factors when evaluating the relevance of the information available:

- age of data (e.g., evolving technologies, product maturity and stability, and new sellers in the marketplace);
- nature of transactions, such as customer type (government, distributor, retail end-user, etc.), maintenance agreements, and preferred customer rewards;
- pending sale if probable at the anticipated price; and
- sales transaction data of different customers, date, quantity sold, part number and nomenclature, and sales price.

The contracting officer will consider catalog prices to be reliable when they are regularly maintained and supported by relevant sales data (including any related discounts, refunds, rebates, or offsets). The contracting officer may request that the offeror support differences between the proposed price(s), catalog price(s), and relevant sales data.

DFARS 215.203-70

Consideration shall be given to the tiers of small businesses (e.g., 8(a), HUBZone small business, service-disabled veteran-owned small business, small business) before evaluating offers from other than small business concerns. Before solicitation, the contracting officer conducts market research to determine if the criteria in FAR Part 19 are met for setting aside the acquisition for small business. For a task or delivery order, the contracting officer may instead consider if there are a sufficient number of qualified small business concerns available to justify limiting competition. If the contracting officer cannot determine if either of these topics are true, (s)he must enter a written explanation in the contract file.

For spare parts or support equipment, price analysis includes line items which are offered at excessive prices for the requirement, and more than 25 percent of the lowest price the Government has paid within the most recent 12-month period. Generally, the Government will analyze significant high-dollar-value items and a random sample of the remaining low-dollar-value items.

DFARS 215.304

Procurements to charter ocean-going vessels for transportation services must include the following preferences as evaluation factors:

- involvement in the Voluntary Intermodal Service Agreement;
- manufacturing readiness and associated processes of (sub)contractors;
- overhaul, repair and maintenance work performed in a U.S. shipyard (if done in a foreign shipyard, whether the work was due to an accident or emergency and reimbursed by the U.S. Government);
- supply chain risk when acquiring information technology service or supply for an emergency or contingency situation; and
- U.S.-flagged vessels.

PGI 217.7103-3

A master solicitation for repair and alteration of vessels must include the:

- date the vessel will be available to the contractor;
- date the work is to be completed;
- nature of the work to be performed; and
- notice if bulk ammunition is aboard the vessel.

Unless the solicitation states otherwise, performance occurs at the contractor's site. If a negotiated acquisition, offerors must include a cost breakdown. Offerors have an opportunity when possible to inspect the item needing repair or alteration.

If the repairs extent and probable cost cannot be determined, the solicitation should request offers for determining the nature and extent of the repairs. Upon request by the contracting officer of what work is necessary, the contractor will negotiate prices for performance of the repairs, and provide that the prices will be set forth in a modification of the job order.

PGI 217.77

"Over and above" work requirements are common in overhaul and repair contracts. They require the contractor to identify necessary repairs and corrective actions. These requirements must be separately priced but may contain a dollar limitation. Approval procedures normally required for undefinitized contract actions do not apply to these requirements.

Contract Clauses

Include the following in master agreements to alter or repair vessels:

DFARS 252.217-7003, Changes.
DFARS 252.217-7004, Job Orders and Compensation.
DFARS 252.217-7005, Inspection and Manner of Doing Work.
DFARS 252.217-7006, Title.
DFARS 252.217-7007, Payments.
DFARS 252.217-7008, Bonds.
DFARS 252.217-7009, Default.
DFARS 252.217-7010, Performance.
DFARS 252.217-7011, Access to Vessel.
DFARS 252.217-7012, Liability and Insurance.
DFARS 252.217-7013, Guarantees.
DFARS 252.217-7014, Discharge of Liens.
DFARS 252.217-7015, Safety and Health.
DFARS 252.217-7016, Plant Protection.
DFARS 252.217-7026, Identification of Sources of Supply.
DFARS 252.217-7028, Over and Above Work.

3.11.3 Exchanges with Offerors

FAR 15.3

Clarifications are limited exchanges between the Government and offerors that may occur when award without discussions is contemplated. If award will be made without discussions, offerors may be given the opportunity to clarify aspects of proposals or resolve minor or clerical errors. Award may be made without discussions if the solicitation states the Government intends to make award without discussions.

However, care must be taken not to share information between offerors regarding technical or technological information. Such *technical transfusion* would expose a firm's confidential approach and information to other offerors, which is expressly forbidden in Government contracting. Similarly, the contracting officer may not help an offeror upgrade its proposal to match other offerors by conducting multiple rounds of negotiations. This would be the result of discussing the offeror's lack of competence, diligence or inventiveness, and is also expressly forbidden in Government contracting.

A *competitive range* must be established by the contracting officer to include all offerors who have a reasonable chance of receiving award (when in doubt, include them in the range) based on responsiveness, technical acceptability, and possible price reductions. Communications are limited to the offerors within the range, and any offerors facing elimination due solely to past performance. Such communications may be conducted to enhance Government understanding of proposals or facilitate the Government's evaluation process. These communications are not used to cure proposal deficiencies or material omissions, or materially alter the technical or cost elements of the proposal. These communications may address ambiguities in the proposal or other concerns (e.g., perceived deficiencies, weaknesses, errors or mistakes, omissions, and past performance information).

If the solicitation permits, the contracting officer may limit the number of proposals in the competitive range to permit an efficient competition among the most highly rated proposals. For competitive acquisitions estimated value of $100 million or more, contracting officers should conduct discussions with all offerors within the competitive range.[39] If the contracting officer decides that an offeror's proposal should no longer be included in the competitive range, the proposal is eliminated by written notice to the offeror, who may then request a debriefing.

When negotiations are conducted in a competitive acquisition, they take place after establishment of the competitive range and are called *discussions*. These are tailored to each offeror's proposal, and must be conducted by the contracting officer with each offeror within the competitive range to maximize the Government's ability to obtain best value, based on the requirement and the evaluation factors set forth in the solicitation. The contracting officer must discuss with each offeror under consideration for award any deficiencies, significant weaknesses, and adverse past performance information to which the offeror has not yet had an opportunity to respond, but need not discuss every area where the proposal could be improved. The scope and extent of discussions are a matter of contracting office judgment. (S)he may negotiate for increased performance beyond any mandatory minimums, and may suggest to offerors that have exceeded any minimums that their proposals would be more competitive if the excesses were removed and the offered price decreased. If discussions result in an offeror originally in the competitive range no longer considered to be among the most highly rated offerors, that offeror may be eliminated from the competitive range even if all material aspects of the proposal were not discussed, and whether or not the offeror has been afforded an opportunity to submit a proposal revision.

Auctioneering is a controversial part of contracting. Modeled after the method of a descending pricing process used in the Netherlands to buy tulips, a contracting officer shops around among offerors trying to obtain lower prices than bid in the hope that somebody will lower their price. However, care must be taken that the offeror does not sacrifice quality or delivery terms merely to obtain the contract. When used in Government contracting, it gives rise to two competing schools of thought. On the one hand, it reflects the sworn duty of the contracting officer as a wise steward of the tax dollar to obtain as low a price as possible. On the other hand, it raises concern about the integrity of the competitive procurement process and could make a mockery of the system by which the Federal Government spends its money. Because this philosophical argument has no resolution, the Government takes the position that it cannot discourage the use of auctioneering. However, DFARS 217.7801 precludes auctions when buying aviation critical or personal protective equipment.

Government personnel involved in the acquisition may not engage in conduct that favors one offeror over another, or reveals an offeror's technical solution, price or intellectual property to another offeror. The contracting officer may inform an offeror that its price is considered to be too high or too low, and may reveal the results of the analysis supporting that conclusion, including a Government cost or price estimate. The Government may not reveal the names of individuals providing reference information about an offeror's past performance. The contracting officer may request or allow proposal revisions to clarify and document understandings reached during negotiations.

If discussions are to be conducted, the PCO will, upon consultation with the SSEB and with the approval of the SSA, establish the competitive range based on the ratings of each proposal against all evaluation criteria. The criteria used for establishing the competitive range and an analysis of what will be discussed with each offeror is documented in a competitive range decision document. Discussions are tailored to each offeror's proposal and must be conducted by the PCO with every offeror within the competitive range. The scope and extent of discussions are a matter of PCO judgment. This will include any deficiencies or significant weaknesses that have been identified during the evaluation, including adverse past performance information. The contracting officer can also discuss weaknesses, excesses, and price that could enhance materially the proposal's potential for award. Although not mandatory, it is a best practice to discuss proposal weaknesses with prospective offerors. It is also a best practice for the PCO to require offerors to submit written proposal changes resulting from discussions before requesting Final Proposal Revisions, which would be pricing updates only.

If, during discussions, the PCO decides an offeror's proposal should no longer be included in the competitive range, the PCO shall obtain SSA approval to eliminate the proposal from consideration for award and update the competitive range decision document. Written notice of this decision shall be provided to unsuccessful offerors. If an offeror's proposal is eliminated or otherwise removed from the competitive range, no further revisions to that offeror's proposal are accepted or considered.

At the conclusion of discussions, each offeror still in the competitive range has an opportunity to submit a *best and final offer*, with the contracting establishing a common cut-off date only for receipt of final proposal revisions. Requests for final proposal revisions advise offerors that the final proposal revisions be in writing and that the Government intends to make award without further revisions.

The SSA decision is based on a comparative assessment of proposals against all source selection criteria in the solicitation. While the SSA may use reports and analyses prepared by others, the source selection decision represents the SSA's independent judgment. The source selection decision is documented, including the rationale for any business judgments and tradeoffs made or relied on by the SSA. The documentation need not quantify the tradeoffs that led to the decision.

3.11.4 Best Value Continuum

FAR 15.1

In acquisitions where the requirement is clearly definable and the risk of unsuccessful contract performance is minimal, cost or price may play a dominant role in source selection. Prospective pricing decisions made prior to contract performance are based on analyzing comparative prices, price estimates, past costs, or all of the above. Where the requirement is less definitive, more development work is required, or more performance risk is present, then technical or past performance considerations will be more significant in source selection. A *tradeoff process* is used when it may be in the best interest of the Government to consider award to other than the lowest priced or highest technically rated offeror. All evaluation factors and significant subfactors that will affect contract award and their relative importance are stated in the solicitation. This process permits tradeoffs among cost or price and non-cost factors, and allows the Government to accept other than the lowest priced proposal. However, the perceived benefits of the higher priced proposal must merit the additional cost and be documented in the file.

DAG: Source Selection Procedures, Appendix B

Tradeoffs are improved by stating in the solicitation the Government "value" placed on above-threshold performance or capabilities. Although the relative importance of evaluation factors are revealed in the solicitation, offerors still do not know the boundaries of how much more the Government may be willing to pay if an offeror exceeds a mandatory minimum. The commonly used methodologies are the Subjective Tradeoff and Value Adjusted Total Evaluated Price (VATEP) Tradeoff techniques, although others will be discussed below. These tradeoff processes permit the SSA to consider award to other than the lowest evaluated priced offeror or other than the highest technically rated offer.

The Subjective Tradeoff process identifies in the RFP all evaluation (sub) factors and state their relative importance. The solicitation should state whether all evaluation factors other than cost or price, when combined, are significantly more important, approximately equal in importance, or significantly less important than cost or price.

In contrast, the VATEP technique monetizes different levels of performance that defines both threshold (minimum) and objective (maximum) performance and capabilities. It identifies in the RFP the percentage price increase or dollar amount the Government is willing to pay for measurable levels of performance between threshold and objective criteria, such as operational range and weapon accuracy. This process will balance price with capability and performance above threshold requirements to maximize the achievement of program objectives. Offerors may be more likely to propose innovative solutions with this information spelled out in the RFP.

Proposals are further evaluated to determine if the specified above-threshold criteria are met technically and are below the affordability cap. If a technically acceptable above-minimum performance level or capability is proposed for a valued requirement, the offeror's TPP will be adjusted, for evaluation purposes only, in accordance with the methodology specified in the solicitation to quantify the importance the Government places on the additional capability. This balancing decision should consider affordability and operational benefits and risk. An affordability cap may be established by the program office, which an offeror may not exceed without losing the award. Award is made to the offeror whose proposal represents the best value to the Government based on the evaluation criteria set forth in the solicitation. The specification, Statement of Work, or performance work statement in the awarded contract document will reflect all above-minimum performance levels or capabilities for which evaluation credit was given in the source selection process.

DAG: Source Selection Procedures, Appendix C

Using a third tradeoff process, a Lowest-Priced Technically Acceptable approach requires that minimum requirements can be described clearly and comprehensively, expressed in terms of performance objectives, measures and standards that will be used to determine the acceptability of offers. No real value will be realized from a proposal that exceeds the minimum technical or performance requirements, and no subjective judgment is needed to the desirability of one offer over another. Supplies to be procured are usually expendable in nature, nontechnical or have a short life expectancy. Well-defined standards of performance and quality of services must be available to support the use of LPTA. In order to be considered awardable, there must be an acceptable rating in every non-price (sub)factor. The contracting officer documents the contract file describing the circumstances justifying the use of the lowest-price technically acceptable source selection process, ensuring that the lowest price reflects full life-cycle costs of the products or services being acquired. However, this approach should not be used for:

- an aviation critical safety item or personal protective equipment, when the requiring activity advises the contracting officer that the level of quality or failure of the equipment or item could result in combat casualties;
- auditing services;
- engineering and manufacturing development for a major defense acquisition program for which budgetary authority was requested beginning in FY 2019;
- knowledge-based professional services, such as cybersecurity, electronic testing information technology, systems engineering, and technical assistance services; and
- knowledge-based training or logistics services in contingency operations or other operations outside the United States, including in Afghanistan or Iraq;

DAG: Source Selection Procedures, Appendix D

Several other processes are sometimes employed. The Highest Technically Rated Offeror Approach can be used in competitions for multiple award IDIQ contracts that establish ceiling rates or prices subject to additional negotiation or competition for delivery or task orders. It allows awards to the highest technically rated proposals that are also found to have a reasonable price without using trade-offs between cost or price and technical. This approach selects the highest rated/ranked offeror based on non-price factors, then awarding to the highest-rated proposals that also offer fair and reasonable prices. The SSA has discretion in awarding to higher-rated performers over lower-rated performers if the price differential is warranted and considered to be the best value. Since reasonableness of proposed prices is not established by competition, price analysis or cost analysis is required.

The Performance-Price Tradeoff process is commonly used with IDIQ contracts. This approach allows the Government to reject offerors with marginal to unsatisfactory performance and include offerors with stronger present and past performance records. The SSA has the discretion to award to offerors with a higher Performance Confidence rating if the price differential is warranted. It is often used with a technically acceptable/unacceptable technical factor. However, this approach is not appropriate for acquisitions that require varying levels of technical merit among proposals.

Award Without Technical Factors can be used in less complex actions, such as replenishment spares or aviation critical safety items, where competition is limited to named companies that have undergone required qualification processes and have been certified as approved sources. The assessment of recent and relevant past performance, resulting in a performance confidence assessment rating, is based on the results of information from offerors and survey questionnaires sent to customers identified by the respective offerors. This approach simplifies the source selection process by reducing acquisition timelines and manpower requirements and eliminates the technical evaluation if an offeror has demonstrated relevant experience sufficient to show they can perform the work. This approach also has the benefit of addressing actual experience versus a promise to perform.

Oral presentations by offerors may be requested by the Government to replace or supplement written information. Oral presentations may occur at any time in the acquisition process, and are subject to the same restrictions as written information regarding timing and content. Oral presentations provide an opportunity for dialogue among the parties. Pre-recorded videotaped presentations that lack real-time interactive dialogue are not considered oral presentations, although they may be included in offeror submissions. Representations and certifications are submitted with a signed offer sheet (including any exceptions to the Government's terms and conditions). Additional information (e.g., an offeror's capability, past performance, work plans or approaches, staffing resources, transition plans, or sample tasks) may be suitable for oral presentations. In deciding what information to obtain through an oral presentation, the contracting officer considers the Government's ability to adequately evaluate the information, incorporate any information into the resultant contract, impact efficiency of the acquisitions, and impact (including cost) on small businesses. The solicitation may specify the date, location, and time of the presentation, though this is often arranged by the contracting officer based on the number of offerors and progress in technical evaluations. The solicitation may describe the types of information to be presented orally, restrictions on time length, and requirements for, and any limitations or prohibitions on the use of written material or other media. Personnel qualifications on presenters may be included. Also important are the scope and content of exchanges between the Government's and offeror's representatives, including whether or not discussions will be permitted during oral presentations.

The contracting officer maintains a record of oral presentations to document what the Government relied upon in making the source selection decision. The source selection authority will determine the level of detail for the record. When an oral presentation includes information that the parties intend to include in the contract as material terms or conditions, the information is then put in writing. Incorporation by reference of oral statements is not permitted.

3.12 NEGOTIATION

3.12.1 Strategy and Tactics

The Government maintains the initiative throughout negotiations since it has the power of the purse. Negotiations are led by the contracting officer or a procurement specialist. Technical specialists may participate, especially in sole-source negotiations. After non-price issues are resolved, the Government makes a counteroffer within its approval threshold. Over time, the goal is to reach an agreement on a fair and reasonable price, as individual cost elements need not be agreed to by the parties.

Sole-source negotiations for major procurements often include fact-finding meetings, either at the contracting office or at the contractor's facility. Cost auditors and program engineers may be present to lend their expertise. Assumptions and judgments made by the contractor will be questioned and either accepted or contested. Afterward, the contractor may need to revise its proposal assumptions and costing, while the contracting officer digests all this input to develop a coherent position, either as a counteroffer or justification for the proposed amount. The wise contracting officer will develop a range of acceptable positions to provide negotiating room, and will also brief office management on the proposal, recommendations received from other team members and an objective position.[40]

To prepare for negotiations, one must decide how the other party will use the negotiation to satisfy its needs and both accomplish its own goals and identify joint goals. The contracting officer should review previous negotiations to identify past problems and identify negotiation flexibility, then prioritize negotiation objectives to separate must-haves (e.g., funding and time constraints) from give points. Sometimes mock negotiations are performed before actual sessions. Opponent motivations should be identified regarding time constraints, management demands, and technical and funding constraints. The parties will often strive to negotiate agreeable items before differences.

Negotiation techniques vary depending on the situation. In a sole-source environment, the negotiator must evaluate the proposal in depth and take care not to authorize work until price agreement is reached. In a competitive environment, no single firm can influence the market price, so the buyer uses the supply-demand force to drive closer to the market price, considering non-price aspects of competition for a standardized product. In an oligopoly with few firms that each consider reactions of the others to their pricing policy, the buyer will focus on their mutual interdependence, inflexible prices and critical non-pricing competition. In a regulated market, the buyer will try to maximize benefits such as price breaks, quantity buys, longer terms, and free services.

Negotiation features bargaining or discussion, flexibility, a lack of competition, and a time deadline. They may be written or oral, or both. Some specific stratagems and tactics that are commonly used (not always successfully or even wisely) include:

- adopt and maintain high aspiration levels;
- ask for an additional concession;
- ask questions to uncover any avoided topic;
- announce all your demands at once;
- avoid controversy;
- avoid showing any weaknesses;
- be patient, polite and respectful;
- be prepared to walk away, but also to return;
- concede slowly in small amounts, in trade for a concession from the other side;
- create doubts in the other party's mind to lower their expectations;
- create options for mutual gain through brainstorming ideas aloud;
- derive the true cost of a concession rather than conceding a given quantity;
- describe the problem in one's own words before offering a solution;
- display respect for the other party;
- discuss each other's perceptions;
- do not blame the other party;
- establish a deadline to pressure other party;
- focus on interests rather than positions;
- imagine yourself in other party's position to understand their concerns, interests and constituents;
- have room to compromise;
- insist that everything is negotiable;
- invite criticism and advice rather than defending your ideas;
- list and prioritize the other party's interests;
- listen actively;

- maintain room to compromise;
- narrow down the issues to learn what is essential to the other party;
- negotiate agreeable items before differences;
- never volunteer weaknesses;
- do not yield to perceived prestige of other side;
- pause to create an effective silence;
- prioritize negotiation objectives to separate must-haves from give points;
- provide counteroffers which contain new conditions or prices, in effect rejecting the previous offer by the other party;
- recognize emotions of both parties;
- review previous negotiations to identify past problems and negotiation flexibility;
- satisfy the other side without sacrificing one's own goals;
- separate the people from the problem;
- speak in first rather than second person;
- stand firm on your position without anger or fear;
- stay calm and professional;
- think before you speak;
- trade a decoy for a concession of value;
- use alternative pricing packages; and
- wait out a party who breaks off negotiations to see how they respond.

Parties should identify the opportunity cost of not reaching agreement (known as the *best alternative to a negotiated agreement*). Hopefully, this won't lead to a breakdown in negotiations and no resulting contract, though this does sometimes happen. The desired solution for both parties should reflect a mutual agreement which satisfies both their interests.

After negotiations conclude, the contracting officer writes a post-negotiation memorandum that explains why the price is fair and reasonable. It discusses what facts were relied on, what new data was presented by the offeror during negotiations, and how these new facts changed the Government's judgment. The memorandum explains why the contracting officer considers the price to be fair and reasonable. Format for this memorandum is dictated by the agency and procurement office.

3.12.2 Cost/Price Analysis

FAR 15.4

Contracting officers must purchase supplies and services from responsible sources at fair and reasonable prices. In establishing the reasonableness of the offered prices, the contracting officer must not obtain more information than is necessary. Unless cost or pricing data are required, the contracting officer usually uses the following order of preference in determining the type of information required:

- no additional information required from the offeror if the price is based on adequate price competition;
- established catalog or market prices or previous contract prices;
- information available within the Government;
- information obtained from external sources other than the offeror;
- information obtained from the offeror on the prices at which the same or similar items have been sold previously;
- cost information; and
- age of data, as well as a sufficient number of transactions to represent the range of relevant sales to all types of customers.

The contracting officer prices each contract separately without using proposed price reductions under other contracts as an evaluation factor, or considering losses or profits realized or anticipated under other contracts. Nor does (s)he include in a contract price any amount for a specified contingency if the contract provides for a price adjustment based upon the occurrence of that contingency.

Cost or pricing data is not authorized to be obtained for acquisitions in any of the following circumstances:

- a reasonable expectation that adequate price competition would exist, even though only one offer is received from a responsible offeror. Based on the offer received, the contracting officer could reasonably conclude that the offer was submitted with the expectation of competition, approved at a level above the contracting officer;
- based on adequate price competition. This means at least two responsible offerors compete independently and submit priced offers that satisfy the Government's expressed requirement. The winning price must still be reasonable;
- commercial items, if the offeror has submitted sufficient information to evaluate, through price analysis, price reasonableness. The contracting officer may request the offeror to submit prices paid for the same or similar commercial items under comparable terms and conditions by both Government and commercial customers. The contracting officer may also consider information on labor costs, material costs and overhead rates;
- price analysis demonstrates that the proposed price is reasonable in comparison with current or recent prices for the same or similar items, adjusted to reflect changes in market or economic conditions, quantities or terms and conditions under contracts that resulted from adequate price competition;

- priced at or below the simplified acquisition threshold; or
- prices set by law or regulation, based on review or ruling by a governmental body or embodied in law. A firm need not charge the same price for intrastate commerce when it does not limit competition, market conditions change, manufacturing or sales or delivery changes, or lower prices are established in good faith.

The head of the contracting activity may waive the requirement for submission of cost or pricing data in exceptional cases if the price can be determined to be fair and reasonable without submission of cost or pricing data. Award of any lower-tier subcontract expected to exceed the cost or pricing data threshold requires the submission of cost or pricing data unless an exception waiver specifically includes that subcontract and rationale. If the contracting officer has sufficient information available to determine price reasonableness, then (s)he should consider requesting a waiver if the price does not exceed $650,000. On the other hand, the same official may authorize the contracting officer to obtain cost or pricing data for pricing actions below this threshold but over the simplified acquisition threshold. Within DoD, all such waivers in excess of $19.5 million will be reported to Congress on an annual basis.[41]

When cost or pricing data are required, the offeror includes a certificate of current cost or pricing data that to the best of its knowledge and belief, the cost or pricing data were accurate, complete and current as of the date of agreement on price, or an earlier date agreed upon between the parties that is as close as practicable to the date of agreement on price. This disclosure ensures compliance with the Truth in Negotiations Act to ensure the Government does not pay excessive prices.

The exercise of an option at the price established at contract award or initial negotiation does not require submission of cost or pricing data. Cost or pricing data are not required for proposals used solely for overrun funding or interim billing price adjustments.

DFARS 215.403

DoD has waived the requirement for submission of certified cost or pricing data for the Canadian Commercial Corporation and its subcontractors on all contract types. It also exempts educational and nonprofit organizations on cost-reimbursement-no-fee contracts. The contracting officer should still obtain data other than certified cost or pricing data, as well as certified cost or pricing data from subcontractors that are not nonprofit organizations if their proposal exceeds the certified cost or pricing data threshold. Also, certification is not needed for offset costs negotiated by the contractor to provide a benefit or obligation to induce foreign military sales.

Forward pricing rate proposals should be submitted to the Government at least 90 days prior to the proposed effective date of the rates, along with the Contractor Forward Pricing Rate Proposal Adequacy Checklist at DFARS Table 215.403-1. This submission should provide the location of requested information or explain why the requested information is not provided. This checklist covers such topics as:

- basis of each estimate;
- judgmental factors and explanation of the estimating processes and methods used;
- known or anticipated changes in business activities or processes that could impact the proposed rates;
- reconciliation to the supporting data referenced; and
- trends and budgetary data.

Direct labor rates must include the methodology and basis of each estimate, escalation factors for the out-year labor rates, location of supporting documents (e.g., payroll records), planned or anticipated changes in the composition of labor rates or categories, and any union agreements.

Indirect labor rates must include the same information as for direct labor rates, identification of each burden center and cost element by year, allocated costs and intermediate cost pools such as corporate office or shared services, contingencies, development of the allocation base, and how they reconcile with plans and budgets.

Cost of money factors must include net book value of assets, comparison of prior forecasted costs to actual results, and a summary of changes or the facts requiring a rate change.

DFARS 215.470

DoD requires estimates of the prices of data to evaluate the cost to the Government of data items in terms of their engineering value, management or product. This information is reflected in the DD Form 1423, Contract Data Requirements List. The contract cannot require data that the contractor has delivered or is obligated to deliver to the Government under another (sub) contract, and that the successful offeror identifies any such data required by the solicitation. However, where duplicate data are desired, the contract price shall include the costs of duplication, but not of preparation, of such data.

The solicitation requests the offeror to state what portion of the total price is due to the production or development of the listed data requirements for the Government, though not for the sale of rights in the data. Data price estimates must be analyzed before used for contract pricing.

PGI 215.403

The head of the contracting activity is authorized to determine that a waiver to the Truth in Negotiations Act is appropriate in an exceptional case. If the procurement exceeds $100 million, it must be coordinated with the senior procurement executive before granting the waiver. However, (s)he must be certain that the supplies or services could not be obtained without the waiver and that the determination is clearly documented. A prime example would be when a firm is the only source to offer an item essential to DoD's mission but refuses to submit certified cost or pricing data. Per DFARS 215.403-3, the waiver must discuss availability from other sources, company rationale for not submitting the data, price reasonableness, risk due to non-award, and urgency of need. Historical analysis of past purchases must discuss time elapsed and quantities procured.

However, the procuring agency must develop a strategy for future procurement that will not require such a waiver, such as developing a second source or an alternative product that satisfies the department's needs, or even producing the item in-house. A waiver can be issued for part of an offeror's proposed price when it is identified as separate and distinct from the balance of the proposal, given that the offeror has no objection to certifying to the balance of its cost proposal.

If certified cost or pricing data are not required and there is no basis for the contracting officer to determine that prices are fair and reasonable, the offeror must submit "data other than certified cost or pricing data," such as the prices at which the same or similar items have previously been sold, adequate for determining the reasonableness of the price.

Sales data must be comparable to the product or service proposed in terms of capability and specifications. Data related to prior sales (or "offered for sale") may help. If not, cost data may be necessary. However, the contracting officer must verify and document that sufficient analysis was performed to determine that the prior price was fair and reasonable. The contracting officer also must verify that the prices previously paid were for quantities consistent with the current solicitation. Failure to verify that a previous analysis was performed, or the consistencies in quantities, has been a recurring issue on sole-source commercial items reported by oversight organizations. Hence, the contracting officer must discuss the basis of previous prices paid with the contracting organization that previously bought the item and document the contract file accordingly.

Contracting officers may rely on the confirmation and endorsement of the offer from the Canadian Commercial Corporation as an endorsement of the cost/price as no more than would be charged to the Canadian government.

PGI 215.404-2

The contracting officer may request field pricing assistance for any single-offeror proposals exceeding the certified cost or pricing data threshold. For offerors without significant estimating system deficiencies, cost-type proposals need only exceed $10 million for a field pricing report. Procurements of a lower dollar amount can lead to such reports if the contracting officer lacks knowledge of the particular offeror or there is a change in, or unusual problems with, an offeror's internal systems.

The contracting officer should consider requesting audit assistance from DCAA for fixed-price proposals exceeding $10 million and cost-type proposals exceeding $100 million. DCAA rarely accepts field pricing report requests for a lower dollar amount, but will furnish direct and indirect rate recommendations telephonically upon request by the contracting officer.

PGI 215.404-3

The contracting officer should consider the need for field pricing analysis of subcontractor proposals, including assistance to prime contractors when they are being denied access to subcontractor records. (S)he should request audit or field pricing assistance to analyze and evaluate a proposal of a subcontractor at any tier if the contractor or higher-tier subcontractor has a poor business relationship with the subcontractor which is not conducive to independence and objectivity, or has been denied access to the subcontractor's records. Pricing assistance should also be requested if the proposed (sub)contractor is a sole-source supplier, and the subcontract costs represent a substantial part of the contract cost. Also, field pricing support is necessary if the (sub)contractor was cited for significant estimating system deficiencies in subcontract pricing, such as failure to perform adequate cost analyses of proposed subcontract costs prior to negotiation of the prime contract with the Government.

When performing the subcontract analysis itself, DoD obtains consent of the subcontractor reviewed and furnishes to the prime contractor or higher-tier subcontractor, with a summary of the analysis which identifies any unacceptable costs included in the subcontract proposal. If the subcontractor withholds consent, DoD furnishes a range of unacceptable costs for each element but prevents disclosure of subcontractor proprietary data to the prime contractor.

When repricing a price redeterminable or fixed-price incentive contract, even if the contractor has not yet established final prices for the subcontracts, the contracting officer may negotiate a firm contract price if certified cost or pricing data on the subcontracts show the amounts to be reasonable and realistic. If certified cost or pricing data on the subcontracts are too indefinite to determine whether the amounts are reasonable and realistic, final prices can still be established if circumstances require. The contract modification must then require the contractor to submit firm subcontractor prices upon settlement and an equitable adjustment is then executed.

PGI 215.406-1

If the contracting officer does not sustain at least 75 percent of the auditor's findings (excluding unsupported or unresolved costs) for a contract action worth at least $10 million, (s)he notifies the audit office in writing and allows three days to elevate the issues within the contracting officer's activity. Failure to reach agreement could lead to escalation up the respective chains of command, ultimately to USD(AT&L) and the Comptroller.

Cost estimates developed for baseline descriptions and other program purposes by the Director of Cost Assessment and Program Evaluation pursuant to its functions, do not meet the criteria useful for cost or price reasonableness.

PGI 215.406-2

If the contractor submits revised cost or pricing data after certifying the previous submission, it must be either dealt with after award or else require reopening negotiations and obtaining a new certificate after settlement.

PGI 215.406-3

The price negotiation memorandum must discuss significant deviations from the prenegotiation profit objective, include the DD Form 1547, Record of Weighted Guidelines Application (or rationale why it was not used). It is then uploaded into the Contract Business Analysis Repository to share negotiation experience with other contracting officers preparing to negotiate.[42] This is required for all noncompetitive actions valued over $25 million for all definitized or awarded actions over $100 million. For a basic initial indefinite-delivery indefinite-quantity task or delivery order contract, the estimated value of the contract (e.g. ceiling price) governs the threshold to decide whether to upload.

3.12.3 Notifications to Unsuccessful Offerors

FAR 15.503

The contracting officer notifies offerors promptly in writing when their proposals are excluded from the competitive range, with the basis for the determination, and that no proposal revision will be considered. For a socio-economic set-aside (other than 8(a) set-asides), the contracting officer notifies each unsuccessful offeror of the identity of the successful offeror, and that they may challenge the firm's socioeconomic status. This notice is not required when the contracting officer determines in writing that the urgency of the requirement necessitates award without delay. Also, this does not apply to 8(a) set-asides because the SBA has already affirmed the successful offeror's status.

Within three days after the date of contract award, the contracting officer notifies each offeror whose proposal was in the competitive range but was not selected for award:

- number of offerors solicited;
- number of proposals received;
- name and address of each offeror receiving an award;
- items, quantities, and any stated unit prices of each award; and
- reason(s) the offeror's proposal was not accepted, unless the price of the successful offeror is clearly the reason for award.

The same information may be provided to unsuccessful offerors where simplified acquisition procedures are used only upon request of the offeror(s), as well as to unsuccessful offerors that received a preaward notice of exclusion from the competitive range.

The contracting officer awards a contract to the successful offeror by furnishing the executed contract or other notice of the award. If the award document includes information that is different than the latest signed proposal, both the offeror and the contracting officer sign the contract, creating a *bilateral award.*

3.12.4 Debriefing

FAR 15.505 and .506

Offerors excluded from the competitive range or before award may request a debriefing before award by written request to the contracting officer within three days after receipt of the notice of exclusion from the competition.[43] At the offeror's request, this debriefing may be delayed until after award. The contracting officer may refuse the request for a debriefing if, for compelling reasons, it is not in the best interests of the Government to conduct a debriefing at that time. Debriefings may be done orally or in writing. Preaward debriefings include the agency's evaluation of the offeror's proposal, the rationale for eliminating the offeror from the competition, and answers to questions about whether source selection procedures contained in the solicitation and applicable regulations were followed. Preaward debriefings do not disclose:

- confidential commercial and financial information (e.g., cost breakdowns, indirect cost rates and profit);

- content of other offerors proposals;
- identity of other offerors;
- names of individuals providing reference information about an offeror's past performance;
- point-by-point comparisons of the debriefed offeror's proposal with other offerors;
- privileged or confidential manufacturing processes and techniques;
- ranking and evaluation of other offerors; or
- trade secrets.

Postaward debriefings do include:

- a summary of the rationale for award;
- evaluation of the significant weaknesses or deficiencies in the offeror's proposal,
- for acquisitions of commercial items, the make and model of the item to be delivered by the successful offeror;
- overall evaluated cost or price (including unit prices), and any technical rating of the successful offeror and the debriefed offeror,
- overall ranking of all offerors;
- past performance information on the debriefed offeror;
- the make and model of the commercial item to be delivered by the successful offeror; and
- whether source selection procedures contained in the solicitation and applicable regulations were followed.

DFARS 215.506

Postaward debriefings are required for any award of at least $10 million. A small business or nontraditional defense contractor may request a copy of the written source selection decision, although confidential and proprietary information of other offerors must be redacted.

Any debriefed offeror may submit written questions within two business days thereafter, which must be answered by the contracting officer within five business days after receipt.

3.13 PROTESTS

FAR 33.1

A *protest* is a written objection by an interested party to a solicitation or award, or cancellation thereof. It may be submitted to either the contracting officer or GAO. Contracting officers consider all protests and seek legal advice. Protests based on alleged apparent improprieties in a solicitation must be filed before bid opening or the closing date for receipt of proposals. If the head of an agency determines that a solicitation or proposed award does not comply with the requirements of law or regulation, the head of the agency may reimburse the protestor for costs and require the awardee to reimburse the Government's costs due to the awardee's intentional or negligent misstatement, misrepresentation or miscertification. The Government may collect this debt by offsetting the amount against any payment due the awardee under any contract. Protests usually claim either improper or illegal procedures or unfair treatment.

The impact of a protest is delayed award with mission impact, administrative time and expense, and notice that the process did not flow smoothly (either the agency of the protestor is wrong). The protestor may fear informal blacklisting for causing trouble.

The contracting officer must suspend performance of a contract within 10 days after contract award or within five days after a debriefing date offered to the protester upon a written determination that a protest is likely to be filed by an interested party, and delay of performance is in the best interests of the United States.[44] An *interested party* is an actual or prospective offeror whose direct economic interest would be affected by the award of a contract or the failure to award a contract. The contracting officer may also issue a stop work order or even terminate the award until the protest is resolved.

3.13.1 Protests to the Agency

FAR 33.103

The agency provides for protest resolution that is expeditious, inexpensive, informal, and procedurally simple. All protests filed directly with the agency are addressed to the contracting officer. Alternative dispute resolution techniques or third-party neutrals are both acceptable protest resolution methods. All protests filed directly with the agency are addressed to the contracting officer. Interested parties may request an independent review of their protest at a level above the contracting officer. Any agency appellate review of the contracting officer's decision on the protest will not extend GAO's timeliness requirements, so any subsequent protest to the GAO must be filed within 10 days of knowing an initial adverse agency action.

Upon receipt of a protest before award, a contract may not be awarded, pending agency resolution of the protest, unless contract award is justified in writing for urgent and compelling reasons or is determined to be in the best interest of the Government. Such justification or determination is approved at a level above the contracting officer. The contracting officer informs the offerors who might become eligible for award of the protest. If appropriate, the offerors should be requested to extend the time for acceptance. In the event of failure to obtain such extension of offers, consideration should be given to proceeding with award. Upon receipt of a protest within 10 days after contract award or within five days after a debriefing date offered to the protester under a timely debriefing request, whichever is later, the contracting officer suspends performance pending resolution of the protest, unless continued performance is justified, in writing at a level above the contracting officer, for urgent and compelling reasons or to be in the best interest of the Government.

Agencies try to resolve protests within 35 days after the protest is filed. To the extent permitted by law and regulation, the parties may exchange relevant information. The protest decision is provided to the protester with evidence of receipt.

PGI 233.170

For a protest of a competitively awarded Major Defense Acquisition Program or of an acquisition of services valued at $1 billion or more, the agency must brief DPAP within 10 days of the filing of the protest. The briefing must outline the basis of the protest and the agency's position.

3.13.2 Protests to GAO

FAR 33.104

An interested party may protest directly to the GAO in accordance with GAO regulations, since it is a Congressional office and Congress has the authority to observe how its appropriated funds are spent and GAO acts as its watchdog.[45] GAO will only consider a protested delivery or task order if it exceeds a prescribed dollar amount and alleges an increase in maximum value, period of performance or scope of work. GAO, for its part, does encourage the party to seek resolution with the agency first, including formally protesting in writing to the contracting officer. However, no protest may be filed at GAO for a procurement integrity violation unless that person reported the incident to the contracting officer within 14 days after first discovering the possible violation. The agency, for good cause or when a protest raises a significant issue, may consider the merits of any protest which is not timely filed.

GAO has four options in a decision:

- declare the contract illegal and void;
- direct termination for convenience and award to the proper offeror;

- direct a letter of criticism to the agency; or
- direct a letter to the protestor that the award was properly made.

A protester furnishes a copy of its complete protest to the official and location designated in the solicitation or the contracting officer within one day after the protest is filed with the GAO. The GAO may dismiss the protest if it is late. Immediately after receipt of the GAO's written notice of a protest, the agency notifies the contractor (if award has been made) or all parties who appear to have a reasonable prospect of receiving award. The contracting officer immediately begins compiling the information necessary for a report to the GAO within 30 days after the GAO notifies the agency that a protest has been filed, or within 20 days after receipt from the GAO of a determination to use the express option.

When a protest is filed with the GAO, and an actual or prospective offeror so requests, the procuring agency provides actual or prospective offerors reasonable access to the protest file. At least five days prior to the filing of the report, the agency provides to all parties and the GAO a list of those documents that the agency has released to the protester or intends to produce in its report, and those documents that the agency intends to withhold from the protester with the reasons. Any objection to the scope of the agency's proposed disclosure for nondisclosure of the documents must be filed with the GAO and the other parties within two days after receipt of this list. At the same time the agency submits its report to the GAO, the agency furnishes copies of its report to the protester and any interveners. The GAO process for adjudicating protests is the same as for agencies, both before and after award.

The GAO may issue protective orders which establish terms, conditions and restrictions to provide any document to an interested party, especially for procurement sensitive information, trade secrets, proprietary research or development, or commercial information that is contained in such document. Protective orders do not authorize withholding any documents or information from Congress or an executive agency.

In accordance with agency procedures, the head of the contracting activity may authorize contract performance, notwithstanding the protest, upon a written finding that contract performance will be in the best interests of the United States, or based on urgent and compelling circumstances. Contract performance shall not be authorized until the agency has notified the GAO of same. When it is decided to suspend performance or terminate the awarded contract, usually because an award may be invalidated and a delay in receiving the supplies or services is not prejudicial to the Government's interest, the contracting officer attempts to negotiate a no-cost mutual agreement. The contracting officer also gives written notice of the decision to the protester and other interested parties.

GAO issues its recommendation on a protest within 100 days from the date of filing of the protest with GAO, or within 65 days under the express option. The head of the contracting activity must report any failure to implement the GAO findings within five days of the expiration of a 60-day period.

If the GAO determines that a solicitation or award does not comply with a statute or regulation, it may recommend that the agency pay to an appropriate protester the cost, exclusive of profit, of filing and pursuing the protest, including reasonable attorney, consultant, and expert witness fees, and bid and proposal preparation costs. The agency uses funds available for the procurement to pay the costs awarded. The protester files its claim for costs with the contracting agency within 60 days after receipt of the GAO's recommendation that the agency pay the protester its costs. Failure to file the claim within that time may result in forfeiture of the right to recover its costs. If the agency and the protester are unable to agree on the amount to be paid, the GAO may, upon request of the protester, recommend to the agency the amount of costs that the agency should pay.

Solicitation Provisions and Contract Clauses

FAR 52.233-2, Service of Protest, if expected to exceed the simplified acquisition threshold.

FAR 52.233-3, Protest After Award. Use the clause with its Alternate I if a cost reimbursement contract is contemplated.

DFARS 252.215-7016, Notification to Offerors—Postaward Debriefings.

DFARS 252.216-7010, Postaward Debriefings for Task Orders and Delivery Orders.

3.14 CONSTRUCTION CONTRACTS

3.14.1 Policy

FAR 36.2

Contracts to erect real property such as buildings, roads or other public works have a mindset all their own. *Design-bid-build* is the traditional delivery method, where design and construction are sequential and contracted for separately with two contracts and two contractors. The design process defines the construction requirement, functional relationships, and technical systems to be used (e.g., architectural, electrical, environmental, fire protection, mechanical, and structural), producing the technical specifications and drawings, and preparing the construction cost estimate. Offers are then solicited to obtain a separate builder firm. A construction contract is not awarded to the firm that designed the project or its subsidiaries or affiliates, except with the approval for the head of the agency or authorized representative.

Design-build is an alternative method which combines design and construction into a single contract with one contractor. This approach means one award instead of two, which saves the contracting office much time and effort. However, it is not very popular with contractors because so much design work must be done before realistic build costs can be derived.

An independent Government cost estimate is prepared and furnished to the contracting officer for each proposed contract or modification anticipated to exceed the simplified acquisition threshold, or greater if requested by the contracting officer. The estimate is prepared in such detail as though the Government were competing for award. When two-step sealed bidding is used, the independent Government estimate is prepared when the contract requirements are definitized. Access to information concerning the Government estimate is limited to authorized Government personnel, although the contracting officer might need to disclose the associated cost breakdown figures in the Government estimate of a specialized task during negotiations. The overall amount of the Government's estimate is not disclosed except as permitted by agency regulations.

Advance notices and solicitations state the magnitude of the requirement in terms of physical characteristics and estimated price range, but not the Government's actual cost estimate, as follows:

- under $25,000;
- $25,000 to $100,000;
- $100,000 to $250,000;
- $250,000 to $500,000;
- $500,000 to $1,000,000;
- $1,000,000 to $5,000,000;
- $5,000,000 to $10,000,000;
- $10,000,000 to $25,000,000;
- $25,000,000 to $100,000,000;
- $100,000,000 to $250,000,000;
- $250,000,000 to $500,000,000; and
- Over $500,000,000.[46]

Any small-business set-aside solicitation submitted to the GPE must include a description of policies and procedures for definitizing equitable adjustments to change orders, with data on the time frame consumed over the past three years to so definitize.

Contracts for construction must comply with any statutory cost limitations (with allowances for Government-imposed contingencies and overhead), unless applicable limitations are waived in writing for the contract.[47] Solicitations containing one or more items subject to statutory cost limitations specify the applicable cost limitation for each affected item in a separate schedule, and that an offer which does not contain separately-priced schedules will not be considered. The solicitation also states that the price on each schedule shall include an approximate apportionment of all estimated direct costs, allocable indirect costs, and profit.

The Government rejects an offer if its prices are materially unbalanced, even if within statutory limitations. An offer is unbalanced if its prices are significantly below cost for some work, and overstated for other work. This situation may occur with startup work or when option items are priced out with the initial quantity.

Firm-fixed-price contracts are usually used to acquire construction. They may be priced on either a lump-sum or unit-price basis, or both. Lump-sum pricing is preferred, meaning that all contractor work and risk is aggregated into one price. Unit-price basis is used only when:

- estimated quantities of work may change significantly during construction;
- large quantities of work such as building outside utilities, grading, paving, or site preparation are involved;
- offerors would have to expend unusual effort to develop adequate estimates; or
- quantities of work, such as excavation, cannot be estimated to develop a lump-sum offer without a substantial contingency.

Fixed-price contracts with economic price adjustment may be used if customary in contracts for the type of work being acquired, or when omission of an adjustment provision would either preclude many firms from submitting offers or cause offerors to include unwarranted contingencies in proposed prices. Cost-type or price-incentive contracts are not permitted concurrently at the same work site with firm-fixed-price contracts (to avoid concerns over mischarging costs to the wrong contract) without the prior approval of the head of the contracting activity.

The contracting officer arranges for prospective offerors to inspect the work site and to examine available data which may provide information concerning the performance of the work (e.g., boring samples and records, plans of previous construction, utilities to be furnished during construction, etc.). A record is maintained of the identity and affiliation of all offerors' representatives who attend a site visit or examine the data.

Advance notices and solicitations are distributed to as many prospective offerors as practicable. Contracting officers may send notices and solicitations to organizations that maintain free display rooms for prospective offerors, subcontractors, and material suppliers. If requested by such organizations, this may be done for construction projects on an annual or semiannual basis. Contracting officers may determine the geographical extent of distribution of advance notices and solicitations on a case-by-case basis.

FAR 36.5

To assure adequate interest in and supervision of all work involved in larger projects, the contractor must perform a significant part of the contract work with its own workforce. The contract states a minimum percentage of work that must be performed in-house. This percentage is as high as the contracting officer considers appropriate for the project, consistent with customary or necessary specialty subcontracting and the complexity and magnitude of the work. This number is usually at least 12 percent unless a greater percentage is required by law or agency regulation. Specialties such as electrical, heating, and plumbing work are usually subcontracted, and should not normally be considered in establishing the amount of work required to be performed in-house.

The contracting officer must approve the machinery and mechanical equipment to be incorporated into the work. The contractor will provide the manufacturer's name and model number, as well as performance information such as capacity, nature, and rating. Similar information must be furnished for any other articles or material which the contractor contemplates incorporating into the work. The contractor may be directed to submit samples for approval at its own expense, including shipping charges. Failure to obtain approval will result in usage at the risk of subsequent rejection.

If a contractor discovers *differing site conditions* that are latent (not obvious) or subsurface, it is entitled to equitable adjustment of price and/or schedule. Such conditions are categorized as either I or II. Category I conditions differ from what is specified in the contract, while Category II conditions differ from what is usually encountered in such work.

Construction contractors will need to perform the following duties during performance, and will therefore need to consider them in its pricing structure:

- adapt scheduling and work to accommodate other contractors performing work in the area;
- attend any preconstruction conference called by the contracting officer;
- be responsible for damages to equipment, persons, property, roads (including curbs and sidewalks), and vegetation;
- erect temporary buildings and roadways and tear them down at the end of performance unless the contracting officer says otherwise;
- have an on-site superintendent;

- keep a copy of drawings and specifications on the work site;
- keep the area free of trash;
- lay out work based on any base lines and benchmarks in Government-furnished drawings;
- obtain any necessary permits;
- provide safety barricades, lights, and signs;
- provide utility connections and pay for consumed utilities at the same rate as the Government pays;
- submit a progress chart of scheduled work within five days of beginning work;
- submit a safety plan for contracting officer approval before commencing work if the area has hazardous material; and
- submit any shop drawings to the contracting officer for approval.

When unit pricing of effort is used in a fixed-price contract, the Government can perform quantity surveys to determine level of completion.

Executive Order 13502, Use of Project Labor Agreements for Federal Construction projects, encourages the use of project labor agreements to promote economy and efficiency in the performance of Federal construction projects where the total cost is more than $25 million. The agency may require that every contractor and subcontractor engaged on a construction project agree, for that project, to negotiate or become a party to a project labor agreement with one or more labor organizations.

Forms used for construction, demolition, dismantling, or removal of improvements contracts are:

- Standard Form 1442, Solicitation, Offer, and Award (Construction, Alteration, or Repair), if expected to exceed the simplified acquisition thresholds;
- Optional Form 347 (Order for Supplies or Services) or SF 1442 if at or below the simplified acquisition threshold; or
- Optional Form 1419, Abstract of Offers—Construction, and Optional Form 1419A, Abstract of Offers—Construction, Continuation Sheet, for sealed bidding (and optional for negotiations).

DFARS 236.270

10 U.S.C. 2858 requires agency head approval to expedite the completion date of a contract funded by a Military Construction Appropriations Act if additional costs are involved. The approval authority must certify that the additional expenditures are necessary to protect the national interest, and establish a reasonable completion date for the project. The contracting officer may approve an expedited completion date if no additional costs are

involved. In any event, CPFF (cost-plus-fixed-fee) contracts are often forbidden by annual DoD Appropriations Acts for military construction.

DFARS 236.272

Prequalification procedures may be used when necessary to ensure timely and efficient performance of critical construction projects. Prequalification results in a list of sources determined to be qualified to perform a specific construction contract and limits offerors to those with proven competence to perform in the required manner.

The head of the contracting activity must authorize the use of prequalification by determining, in writing, that a construction project is of an urgency or complexity that requires prequalification and approve the prequalification procedures.

For small businesses, the prequalification procedures must require the qualifying authority to request a preliminary recommendation from the appropriate Small Business Administration regional office, if the qualifying authority believes a small business is not responsible. The contracting officer must permit the small business to submit a bid or proposal if the preliminary recommendation is that the small business is responsible.

DFARS 236.273

In accordance with Section 112 of the Military Construction and Veterans Affairs and Related Agencies Appropriations Act, 2015 and the same provision in subsequent military construction appropriations acts, certain military construction contracts funded with military construction appropriations that are estimated to exceed $1,000,000 shall be awarded only to United States firms.[48] The lowest responsive and responsible offer of a United States firm may not exceed the lowest responsive and responsible offer of a foreign firm by more than 20 percent. This restriction only applies to work performed in the United States, its outlying areas in the Pacific and on Kwajalein Atoll, or in countries bordering the Arabian Gulf. If the contract is for military construction on Kwajalein Atoll, the lowest responsive and responsible offer must be submitted by a Marshallese firm.

DFARS 236.274

In accordance with military construction appropriations acts, the contractor may not acquire, or allow a subcontractor to acquire, steel for any construction project or activity for which American steel producers, fabricators, or manufacturers have been denied the opportunity to compete for such acquisition.

Solicitation Provisions

FAR 52.236-27, Site Visit (Construction), if using the Differing Site Conditions and Site Investigations and Conditions Affecting the Work clauses. Use Alternate I if a site visit will be conducted.

FAR 52.236-28, Preparation of Offers—Construction, for negotiated construction.

DFARS 252.236-7006, Cost Limitation, if the solicitation's bid schedule contains one or more items subject to statutory cost limitations, and if a waiver has not been granted.

DFARS 252.236-7007, Additive or Deductive Items, if such procedures are being used.

DFARS 252.236-7008, Contract Prices—Bidding Schedule, if the contract will contain only unit prices for some items.

DFARS 252.236-7010, Overseas Military Construction—Preference for United States Firms, for military construction contracts that are funded with military construction appropriations and are estimated to exceed $1,000,000 and when contract performance will be in a United States outlying area in the Pacific or in a country bordering the Arabian Gulf.

DFARS 252.236-7012, Military Construction on Kwajalein Atoll—Evaluation Preference, for military construction contracts that are funded with military construction appropriations and are estimated to exceed $1,000,000 and when contract performance will be on Kwajalein Atoll.

Solicitation Provisions and Contract Clauses

FAR 52.236-1, Performance of Work by the Contractor, if fixed-price unless awarded under socioeconomic preference programs, when the contract amount is expected to exceed $1,500,000.

FAR 52.236-2, Differing Site Conditions, if fixed-price and exceeding the simplified acquisition threshold.

FAR 52.236-3, Site Investigation and Conditions Affecting the Work, if fixed-price and exceeding the simplified acquisition threshold.

FAR 52.236-4, Physical Data, if fixed-price construction and physical data (e.g., test borings, hydrographic data, weather conditions data) will be furnished or made available to offerors.

FAR 52.236-5, Material and Workmanship, for construction only.

FAR 52.236-6, Superintendence by the Contractor, if fixed-price and exceeding the simplified acquisition threshold.

FAR 52.236-7 Permits and Responsibilities, if fixed-price (or cost-reimbursement for construction only).

FAR 52.236-8, Other Contracts, if fixed-price and exceeding the simplified acquisition threshold.

FAR 52.236-9, Protection of Existing Vegetation, Structures, Equipment, Utilities, and Improvements, if fixed-price and exceeding the simplified acquisition threshold.

FAR 52.236-10, Operations and Storage Areas, if fixed-price and exceeding the simplified acquisition threshold.

FAR 52.236-11, Use and Possession Prior to Completion, if fixed-price construction and exceeding the simplified acquisition threshold.

FAR 52.236-12, Cleaning Up, if fixed-price and exceeding the simplified acquisition threshold.

FAR 52.236-13, Accident Prevention, if fixed-price and exceeding the simplified acquisition threshold. Use the clause with its Alternate I if the work is of a long duration or hazardous nature. Alternate I is optional if services will be performed at Government facilities and technical representatives advise that special precautions are appropriate.

FAR 52.236-14, Availability and Use of Utility Services, if fixed-price and exceeding the simplified acquisition threshold, the existing utility system(s) is adequate for both the Government and the contractor (and listed in the contract), and furnishing it is in the Government's interest.

FAR 52.236-15, Schedules for Construction Contracts, if fixed-price construction and exceeding the simplified acquisition threshold. The period of actual work performance usually exceeds 60 days.

FAR 52.236-16, Quantity Surveys, if fixed-price construction with unit pricing of items and payment based on quantity surveys. Use the clause with its Alternate if determined at a level above the contracting officer that Government personnel cannot perform the original and final surveys, and the contractor must do so.

FAR 52.236-17, Layout of Work, if fixed-price construction and an accurate work layout and site verification during work performance are necessary.

FAR 52.236-18, Work Oversight in Cost-Reimbursement Construction Contracts, if cost-reimbursement construction.

FAR 52.236-19, Organization and Direction of the Work, if cost-reimbursement construction.

FAR 52.236-21, Specifications and Drawings for Construction, if fixed-price and exceeding the simplified acquisition threshold. When the Government needs *record drawings* (drawings submitted by a contractor or subcontractor to show the construction of a particular structure or work as actually completed under the contract), use the clause with its Alternate I if reproducible shop drawings are needed, or with its Alternate II if reproducible shop drawings are not needed.

FAR 52.236-26, Preconstruction Conference, if fixed-price and a preconstruction conference is desired.

FAR 52.237-4, Payment by Government to Contractor, for demolition, dismantling or removal of improvements if the Government will pay the contractor and take title to any property it received under the contract.

FAR 52.237-5, Payment by Contractor to Government, for demolition, dismantling or removal of improvements whenever the contractor is to receive title to dismantled or demolished property and a net amount of compensation is due to the Government.

FAR 52.237-6, Incremental Payment by Contractor to Government, for demolition, dismantling or removal of improvements if the contractor is to receive title to dismantled or demolished property and a net amount of compensation is due the Government. The contracting officer must determine that it would be advantageous for the contractor to pay in increments and the Government to transfer title to the contractor for increments of property only upon receipt of those payments.

DFARS 252.236-7000, Modification Proposals—Price Breakdown, if fixed-price.

DFARS 252.236-7001, Contract Drawings and Specifications, if fixed-price.

DFARS 252.236-7002, Obstruction of Navigable Waterways, if fixed-price and the contract will involve work near or on navigable waterways.

DFARS 252.236-7003, Payment for Mobilization and Preparatory Work, for major construction contracts that require major or special items of plant and equipment or large stockpiles of material which are in excess of the type, kind, and quantity which would be normal for a contractor qualified to undertake the work. The head of the contracting activity must first approve use of a separate bid item for mobilization and preparatory work. Generally, allocate 60 percent of the lump sum price in paragraph (a) of the clause to the cost of mobilization. Vary this percentage to reflect the circumstances of the particular contract, but in no event should mobilization exceed 80 percent of the payment item.

DFARS 252.236-7004, Payment for Mobilization and Demobilization, if involving major mobilization expense, or plant equipment and material made necessary by the location or nature of the work. The head of the contracting activity must approve use of a separate bid item for mobilization and preparatory work. Generally, allocate 60 percent of the lump sum price in paragraph (a) of the clause to the cost of mobilization. Vary this percentage to reflect the circumstances of the particular contract, but in no event should mobilization exceed 80 percent of the payment item.

DFARS 252.236-7005, Airfield Safety Precautions, when construction will be performed on or near airfields.

DFARS 252.236-7013, Requirement for Competition Opportunity for American Steel Producers, Fabricators, and Manufacturers, for military construction that may require the acquisition of steel as a construction material.

3.14.2 Sealed Bidding Procedures

FAR 36.213

Contracting officers may use sealed bid procedures when appropriate for a construction contract performed within the United States and its outlying areas. The contracting officer issues presolicitation notices on any construction requirement exceeding the simplified acquisition threshold, and may do so below the threshold. These notices are issued in advance of the invitation for bids to stimulate the interest of prospective bidders. They include the:

- amount (if any) to be charged for solicitation documents;
- deadline to submit requests for the invitation for bids;
- location of the work;
- nature and volume of work (i.e., physical characteristics and estimated price range);
- place where plans will be available for inspection without charge;
- publication through a GPE;
- restriction to small businesses (if any); and
- tentative dates for issuing invitations, opening bids and completing contract performance.

Each invitation for bids includes the following information, when applicable:

- any facilities (e.g., utilities, office, or storage space) to be furnished during construction;
- appropriate wage determination, or a notice that the schedule of minimum wage rates to be paid under the contract will be issued as an amendment to the invitation for bids before the opening date for bids;
- arrangements for bidders to inspect the site and examine data concerning performance of the work;
- instructions concerning bids and award;
- magnitude of the proposed project;
- period of performance;
- prebid conference information;
- reporting requirements; and
- special qualifications or experience requirements to be considered in determining the responsibility of bidders.

If any proposed cost element differs significantly from the Government estimate (e.g., material estimates, wage rates, etc.), the contracting officer requests the offeror to submit cost information concerning that element. When a proposed price is significantly lower than the Government estimate, the contracting officer ensures that both the offeror and the Government estimator completely understand the scope of the work. If negotiations reveal errors in the Government estimate, the estimate is corrected and the changes are documented in the contract file. Proposed prices may be compared to current prices for similar types of work, adjusting for differences in the work site and the specifications. Rough yardsticks may be used (e.g., cost per cubic foot for structures, cost per linear foot for utilities, and cost per cubic yard for excavation or concrete).

3.14.3 Two-Phase Design-Build Selection

FAR 36.303

Two-phase design-build selection procedure is used to select a limited number of offerors during Phase One to submit detailed proposals for Phase Two. These procedures are used for the design and construction of a public building, facility, or work, if the contracting officer makes a determination that the procedures are appropriate for use. These procedures are used based on the following:

- at least three offers are anticipated from capable offerors;
- design work must be performed by offerors before developing price or cost proposals;
- offerors will incur a substantial amount of expense in preparing offers;
- project requirements are adequately defined;
- the delivery schedule allows for an extra phase of evaluation; and
- the agency is capable of managing a two-phase selection process.

The agency develops a scope of work that defines the project and states the Government's requirements. The scope of work may include criteria and preliminary design, budget parameters, and schedule or delivery requirements.

One solicitation may be issued covering both phases or two solicitations may be issued in sequence. Proposals will be evaluated in Phase One to determine which offerors will submit proposals for Phase Two, if only one contract will be awarded.

Phase One of the solicitation(s) includes:

- scope of work;
- Phase-One evaluation factors, including:

    - technical approach (but not detailed design or technical information);
    - technical qualifications:
        - specialized experience and technical competence;
        - capability to perform;
        - past performance of the offeror's team (including the architect-engineer and construction members); and
    - other appropriate factors (excluding cost or price related factors);
- Phase-Two evaluation factors; and
- the maximum number of offerors that will be selected to submit Phase-Two proposals.

After evaluating Phase One proposals, the contracting officer selects the most highly qualified offerors (usually not more than five) and requests that only those offerors submit Phase-Two proposals. Examples of potential Phase-Two technical evaluation factors include design concepts, key personnel, management approach, and proposed technical solutions. Phase Two requires submission of technical and price proposals, which are evaluated separately. A D&F is required if the contracting officer desires to consider more than five offerors for Phase Two. If the acquisition exceeds $4 million, the D&F must be approved by the head of the contracting activity or designee, such as the competition advocate.

3.14.4 Davis-Bacon Act

FAR 22.404

The *Davis-Bacon Act* requires any laborer or mechanic employed at the worksite on a Federal construction contract over $2,000 within the United States to receive at least the prevailing local wage rate.[49] To implement the Davis-Bacon Act, the Department of Labor issues *wage determinations* for individual contracts to reflect prevailing wages and fringe benefits, applied only to laborers and mechanics employed by a contractor on the worksite, including drivers who transport materials and equipment to or from the site. A *general wage determination* contains prevailing wage rates for the types of construction (e.g., building, heavy, highway, and residential) designated for the contract and specific geographical area. General wage determinations do not expire until canceled, modified, or superseded by the Department of Labor, or the contracting officer exercises an option to extend the period of performance. The determinations are published online at https://SAM.

A *project wage determination* is issued at the specific request of a contracting agency when no general wage determination applies, and is effective for 180 calendar days. However, if a determination expires before contract award, an extension to the 180-day determination is possible to cover the life of the contract, unless the contracting officer exercises an option to extend the term of the contract.

If a general wage determination on the SAM website applies to the project, the agency may use it without notifying the Department of Labor. Otherwise, the contracting agency submits requests for project wage determinations on SF 308 to the Department of Labor at least 45 days before issuing the solicitation or exercising an option to extend the term of a contract. Subsequently, some very situation-specific procedures come into play.

In a sealed bid process, bids are not opened until after the wage determination (or modification) for the primary worksite is furnished to all bidders. If necessary, the contracting officer postpones the bid opening date to obtain the determination, amends the solicitation and permits bidders to revise their bids. If the new determination does not change the wage rates, the amendment merely cites the number and date of the new determination.

If a project wage determination expires after bid opening but before award, the contracting officer requests an extension of the current wage determination expiration date, and if necessary, delays award to permit receipt. Otherwise, the contracting officer may award the contract and incorporate the new determination (or modification) to take effect on the contract award date, with an equitable adjustment to the contract price for any change in resultant cost.

In negotiated acquisitions, the contracting officer may open proposals and conduct negotiations before obtaining the wage determination (or modification), but must incorporate it before submission of best and final offers. If a project wage determination expires before contract award, the contracting officer requests a new determination and delays award until obtained, requesting offerors to extend the period for acceptance of proposal if necessary. If the new determination (or modification) changes any wage rates, the contracting officer amends the solicitation to incorporate the new determination and provide offerors an opportunity to amend their proposals. If the new determination (or modification) does not change any wage rates, then (as with sealed bidding) the amendment only includes the number and date of the new determination.

The Department of Labor may modify a wage determination by either specifying only the items being changed or else reissuing the entire determination. The need to modify a general wage determination for a solicitation is based on either the date the modified wage determination is published on the SAM website, or the date the agency (not the contracting officer) receives actual written notice of the modification from the Department of Labor, whichever occurs first. During the course of the solicitation, the contracting officer monitors the SAM website to determine whether the applicable wage determination has been revised, and amends the solicitation if warranted.

The contractor must post a copy of the applicable wage determination and any added classifications at the worksite so the workers can easily see it.

The Secretary of Labor has established an Administrative Review Board to hear appeals concerning Davis-Bacon Act wage determinations. A contracting agency or other interested party may file a petition for review if reconsideration by the Administrator has been sought and denied.

Whenever the contracting officer exercises an option to extend the term of a construction contract, (s)he modifies the contract and any task orders to incorporate the most current wage determination, which becomes effective for the complete period of performance of those task orders. However, the contracting officer may not further adjust the contract price or extend the term of the contract. Generally, this method is used in construction-only contracts with options to extend the term up to three years.

The contract may include a method to adjust the price upon exercise of each option. At the time of option exercise, the contracting officer incorporates a new wage determination into the contract and applies the specific pricing method to calculate the contract price adjustment. One such method is to include a clause which designates what percentage of the contract is subject to the provision of the Davis-Bacon Act (the default portion is 50 percent), then apply a percentage rate using a published economic indicator to that portion of the contract. Another technique is to arithmetically adjust the price to reflect the contractor's actual increase or decrease in wages and fringe benefits due to the new or revised wage determination upon exercise of the option.

In computing wages paid, the contractor may include only the amounts paid in cash to the laborer or mechanic, and irrevocable contributions to a trustee or a third party under a plan or program to provide a *fringe benefit*. Examples of such benefits include compensation for occupational injuries or illness, life insurance, medical or hospital care, pensions for accident disability or sickness, and unemployment benefits.

The contractor computes required overtime payments (i.e., 1 1/2 times the basic hourly rate of pay) using either the wage determination basic hourly rate or the actually paid rate, if higher. The basic rate of pay includes employee contributions to fringe benefits, but excludes the contractor's contributions or costs of cash equivalents for fringe benefits. The contracting officer rejects any misclassified apprentices or helpers, and requires the contractor to pay the affected employees at the rates for the classification of the work actually performed.

Within seven calendar days after the payment date of each payroll week, the contractor submits copies of weekly payrolls for itself and all subcontractors, along with statements of compliance. The contracting officer withholds funds from any payment should the contractor fail to do so. The contracting agency retains payrolls and statements of compliance for three years after contract completion and furnishes them upon request to the Department of Labor, the (sub)contractor who submitted them, or any higher-tier (sub) contractor.

The contracting officer periodically checks to ensure compliance with the labor standards requirements of the contract. Regular compliance checks look at daily inspector's report and logs of construction, to ensure consistency and payroll reviews to ensure timely submissions and completeness. On-site inspections are frequently conducted to check type of work performed, number and classification of workers, and posting of notices. These inspections may also include employee interviews to determine correctness of classifications, fringe benefits payments, hours worked, and pay rates.

The contracting officer reports to the Wage and Hour Division of the Department of Labor on SF 1446, Labor Standards Investigation Summary Sheet, upon finding the (sub)contractor has committed aggravated or willful violations, or otherwise disregarded its legal obligations to employees and subcontractors. If the prime contractor underpays its subcontractor by $1,000 or more, even if inadvertent, it will be reported. Failure to assure future compliance or make restitution will also cause a report.

If a (sub)contractor fails or refuses to comply with the Davis-Bacon Act and related statutes, the agency suspends payment or guarantee until either the violations cease or the agency has withheld sufficient funds to compensate employees for back wages and any liquidated damages.

Executive Order 13502, Use of Project Labor Agreements for Federal Construction Projects, encourages the use of a *project labor agreement* to promote economy and efficiency in the performance of Federal construction projects where the total cost is more than $25 million. The agency may require that every (sub)contractor engaged on a construction project agree, for that project, to negotiate or become a party to a project labor agreement with one or more labor organizations. This approach is appropriate if:

- a project labor agreement will promote the agency's long-term program interests, such as facilitating the training of a skilled workforce to meet the agency's future construction needs;
- completion of the project will require an extended period of time;
- project labor agreements have been used on comparable projects undertaken by Federal, State, municipal, or private entities in the geographic area of the project;
- the agreement may be developed with the input of potential bidders and labor union officials;
- the project will require multiple construction (sub)contractors employing workers in multiple crafts or trades; or

- there is a shortage of skilled labor in the region in which the construction project will be sited.

The agreement will:

- allow all (sub)contractors to compete for (sub)contracts without regard to whether they are otherwise parties to collective bargaining agreements;
- bind all (sub)contractors engaged in construction on the project to comply with the project labor agreement;
- contain guarantees against job disruptions such as lockouts and strikes;
- include any additional requirements as the agency deems necessary to satisfy its needs;
- provide other mechanisms for labor-management cooperation on matters of mutual interest and concern, including health, productivity, quality of work, and safety; and
- set forth effective, prompt, and mutually binding procedures for resolving labor disputes arising during the term of the project labor agreement.

Solicitation Provision

FAR 52.222-33, Notice of Requirement for Project Labor Agreement. Use the provision with its Alternate I if the agency decides to require the submission of a project labor agreement, from only the apparent successful offeror, prior to contract award. Use the provision with its Alternate II if an agency allows submission of a project labor agreement after contract award.

Contract Clauses

The following FAR clauses are used in solicitations and contracts over $2,000 for construction within the United States:

- 52.222-5, Davis Bacon Act—Secondary Site of the Work;
- 52.222-6, Davis-Bacon Act;
- 52.222-7, Withholding of Funds;
- 52.222-8, Payrolls and Basic Records;
- 52.222-9, Apprentices and Trainees;
- 52.222-10, Compliance with Copeland Act Requirements;
- 52.222-11, Subcontracts (Labor Standards);
- 52.222-12, Contract Termination-Debarment;
- 52.222-13, Compliance with Davis-Bacon and Related Act Regulations;
- 52.222-14, Disputes Concerning Labor Standards;

- 52.222-15, Certification of Eligibility; and
- 52.222-16, Approval of Wage Rates, except for contracts with a State or political subdivision.

FAR 52.222-30, Davis-Bacon Act—Price Adjustment (None or Separately Specified Pricing Method), if subject to the Davis-Bacon Act and option provisions may extend the term of the contract.

FAR 52.222-31, Davis-Bacon Act—Price Adjustment (Percentage Method), if fixed-price, subject to the Davis-Bacon Act, and contains option provisions to extend the term of the contract and adjust the price for a revised age determination.

FAR 52.222-32, Davis-Bacon Act—Price Adjustment (Actual Method), if fixed-price, subject to the Davis-Bacon Act, and contains option provisions to extend the term of the contract and adjust the price for a revised age determination.

FAR 52.222-34, Project Labor Agreement Use the clause with its Alternate I if an agency allows submission of the project labor agreement after contract award.

3.15 ARCHITECT/ENGINEERING SERVICES

FAR 36.6

Architect-engineer services are professional services which are associated with design or construction of real property, or else performed by registered architects or engineers or their employees (sometimes so mandated by state law), such as:

- comprehensive planning;
- conceptual designs;
- construction services;
- consultations;
- drawing reviews;
- mapping;
- preparing operating and maintenance manuals;
- program management;
- soils engineering;
- specifications development;
- studies and investigations;
- surveying;
- tests and evaluations; and
- value engineering.

3.15.1 Source Selection

FAR 36.602 through .603

Agencies evaluate each offeror for its:

- capacity to accomplish the work in the required time;
- location in and knowledge of the geographical area of the project;
- past performance in terms of cost control, compliance with performance schedules, and quality of work;[50]
- professional qualifications necessary for satisfactory performance; and
- specialized experience and technical competence in the type of work required (e.g., energy conservation, pollution prevention, use of recovered materials, or waste reduction).

For facility design contracts, the statement of work requires the architect-engineer to maximize use of recovered materials (consistent with the performance requirements, availability, price reasonableness, and cost-effectiveness) and if appropriate, energy conservation, pollution prevention and waste reduction. The contractor must identify hazardous material and use safety data sheets.

To be considered for architect-engineer contracts, a firm must file with the appropriate office or board a SF 330, "Architect-Engineer Qualifications," using Part I to provide information about the firm's specific qualifications for the contract and Part II to discuss the firm's general professional qualifications. These offices or permanent evaluation boards maintain an architect-engineer qualifications data file. After reviewing the SF 330, they classify the firm with respect to capacity of work that can be undertaken, experience in computer-assisted design, location, professional capabilities, and specialized experience.

Agencies may evaluate firms on the basis of their conceptual design of the project. Design competition may be used for prestige projects (e.g., memorials), when sufficient time is available for the production and evaluation of conceptual designs, and when beneficial to the project.

The architect-engineer evaluation board is composed of representatives from the acquisition, architecture, construction, and engineering fields. Members are appointed from among highly qualified professional employees of the agency or other agencies, and (if authorized by agency procedures) private practitioners. One Government member of each board is designated as the chairperson. No firm may be awarded an architect-engineer contract during the period in which any of its principals or associates are participating as members of the awarding agency's evaluation board. The evaluation board will evaluate the responding firms and their current data files, then hold discussions with at least three of the most highly qualified firms about concepts and relative utility of alternative methods of furnishing the required services. Upon completion of discussions, they will prepare a selection report for the agency head or designated selection authority recommending, in order of preference, at least three firms that are the most highly qualified to perform the required services. The report describes the board's discussions and evaluation.

The selection authority reviews the recommendations of the evaluation board and makes the final selection by listing, in order of preference, the firms (s)he considers most highly qualified to perform the work. If the firm listed as the most preferred is not the firm recommended as the most highly qualified by the evaluation board, the selection authority explains in writing the reason for the preference. All firms on the final selection list are considered "selected firms" with which the contracting officer may negotiate.

The selection authority cannot add firms to the selection report. If the firms recommended in the report are not deemed to be qualified or the report is considered inadequate, the selection authority records the reasons and returns the report to the evaluation board for revision.

Two shorter selection processes may be used to select firms for contracts not expected to exceed the simplified acquisition threshold. In one method, the board's selection report becomes the final selection list and is provided directly to the contracting officer. Or, if the board decides that formal action is not necessary for selection, the board chairperson performs the selection functions, submits a report to the agency head or designated selection authority and upon approval, sends the report to the contracting officer as authorization to begin negotiations.

3.15.2 Negotiations

FAR 36.606

Architect-engineering services are always acquired by negotiation, not by sealed bidding. An independent Government estimate of the cost of architect-engineer services is prepared and furnished to the contracting officer before beginning negotiations for each proposed contract or contract modification expected to exceed the simplified acquisition. The Government estimate is based on a detailed analysis of the required work as though the Government were submitting its own proposal.

Unless otherwise specified by the selection authority, the final selection authorizes the contracting officer to begin negotiations with the most preferred firm in the final selection. The contracting officer should seek advance agreement on any charges for computer-assisted design, and discuss with the offeror appropriate modern and cost-effective design methods (e.g., computer-assisted design) if not addressed in the proposal. Subcontractors must be specifically agreed to at this time since qualifications are a critical element of selection.

If a mutually satisfactory contract cannot be negotiated, the contracting officer obtains a written final proposal revision from the firm, and notifies the firm that negotiations have been terminated. The contracting officer then initiates negotiations with the next firm on the final selection list. This procedure is continued until a mutually satisfactory contract has been negotiated. If negotiations fail with all selected firms, the contracting officer refers the matter to the selection authority, who may direct the evaluation board to recommend additional firms.

Contracting officers solicit offers using SF 1442 and award using either Optional Form 347 (if under the simplified acquisition threshold) or SF 252, Architect-Engineer Contract, to award fixed-price contracts for architect-engineer services if performed in the United States or its outlying areas. Standard Form 330, Architect-Engineer Qualifications, is used to evaluate firms before awarding a contract for architect-engineer services, using Part I to obtain information about the firm's specific qualifications for the contract and Part II to obtain information about the firm's general professional qualifications.

DFARS 236.601

Written notification to the congressional defense committees is required if the total estimated contract price for architect-engineer services or construction design, in connection with military construction, military family housing, or restoration or replacement of damaged or destroyed facilities, exceeds $1.5 million. For military construction or military family housing, the notification must include the scope of the project and the estimated contract price and provide at least 21 days before the initial obligation of funds (14 days if provided by electronic medium).

For restoration or replacement of damaged or destroyed facilities, the notification must include the justification for the project, the estimated contract price, and the source of the funds for the project; and provide at least 21 days before the initial obligation of funds (7 days if provided by electronic medium). The notification must also include the evaluation criteria and their relative order of importance in the announcement.

PGI 236.602

The evaluation criteria should be project specific. The contracting officer should use performance evaluation data from CPARS. The primary factor in architect-engineer contractor selection is the determination of the most highly qualified firm. Secondary factors include geographic proximity and equitable distribution of work, but are not attributed greater significance than to qualifications and past performance. The overall most highly qualified firm is not rejected solely in the interest of equitable distribution of contracts. Also considered will be superior performance evaluations on recently completed DoD contracts.

The contracting officer will consider the volume of work awarded by DoD during the previous 12 months. This includes equitable distribution of work among architect-engineer firms, small business concerns, historically black colleges and universities and minority institutions, firms that have not had prior DoD contracts, and small disadvantaged business concerns and joint ventures with small, disadvantaged business participants. Similar success in subcontracting will also be considered.

In this regard, the contracting officer will not consider awards to overseas offices for projects outside the United States, its territories, and possessions. Nor will (s)he consider awards to a subsidiary not normally subject to bookkeeping, management decisions and policies of a holding or parent company or an incorporated subsidiary that operates under a firm name different from the parent company. This allows greater competition.

DFARS 236.602-70

Architect-engineer contracts funded by military construction appropriations that are estimated to exceed $500,000 and are to be performed in Japan, NATO nation or a country bordering the Arabian Gulf shall be awarded only to United States firms or to joint ventures of United States and host nation firms.

DFARS 236.606-70

10 U.S.C. 4540, 7212 and 9540 limit the contract price (or fee) for architect-engineer services for the preparation of designs, plans, drawings, and specifications to six percent of the project's estimated construction cost. The six percent limit also applies to contract modifications, including modifications involving work not initially included in the contract.

For redesign effort, add the estimated construction cost of the redesign features to the original estimated construction cost, then add the contract cost for the original design to the contract cost for redesign, and finally divide the total contract design cost by the total estimated construction cost. The resulting percentage may not exceed the six percent statutory limitation.

If a contract or modification also includes other services, the part of the price attributable to the other services is not subject to the six percent limit.

Solicitation Provision

DFARS 252.236-7011, Overseas Architect-Engineer Services—Restriction to United States Firms, if funded with military construction appropriations; estimated to exceed $500,000, and to be performed in Japan, in any North Atlantic Treaty Organization member country, or in countries bordering the Arabian Gulf.

3.15.3 Responsibility for Design Errors or Deficiencies

FAR 36.609-2

Architect-engineer contractors make necessary corrections at no cost to the Government when their designs, drawings, specifications, or services contain any deficiencies, errors or inadequacies. If the Government does not require a firm to correct such errors, the contracting officer documents the contract file with the reasons for that decision.

Architect-engineer contractors may also be liable for Government costs resulting from problems in designs furnished under its contract. When a construction contract must be modified because of a deficiency or error in the services provided, the contracting officer considers the extent to which the contractor may be reasonably liable. The contracting officer then issues a demand for payment of the amount due, if the recoverable cost will exceed the administrative cost involved or is otherwise in the Government's interest.

Contract Clauses

FAR 52.236-22, Design Within Funding Limitations, in fixed-price architect-engineering contracts unless the design effort involved is minimal or for a standard structure and is not intended for a specific location. The head of the contracting activity or a designee determines in writing that cost limitations are secondary to performance considerations and additional project funding can be expected, if necessary.

FAR 52.236-23, Responsibility of the Architect-Engineer Contractor, if fixed-price.

FAR 52.236-24, Work Oversight in Architect-Engineer Contracts.

FAR 52.236-25, Requirements for Registration of Designers, unless the design is to be performed outside the United States and its outlying areas, or in a state or outlying area of the United States that does not require registration for the particular field.

NOTES

1. This concept is based on the *Spearin Doctrine* set forth by the Supreme Court in *United States v. Spearin*, 248 U.S. 132 (1918), which holds the contractor without liability in such cases.

2. Department of Defense, "DoD Index of Specifications and Standards," 41 CFR 101-29.216, DoD, Washington, D.C., 2012.

3. Defense Logistics Management Standards Office, "Military Standard Requisitioning and Issue Procedures," Defense Logistics Agency, Alexandria, VA, DLM 4000.25-1 dated April 2, 2019.

4. PGI 211.273-3.

5. Both at 15 U.S.C.205a, *et. seq.*

6. *ISO* stands for the International Standards Organization. Based in Geneva, Switzerland, it is composed of representatives from many national standards organizations to develop and issue worldwide industrial and commercial standards. *IEEE* is the Institute of Electrical and Electronics Engineers and develops standards in a variety of technological fields (e.g., energy, health, information technology, and transportation) to foster innovation and excellence.

7. The Federal specifications that do exist are available from GSA's Index of Federal Specifications, Standards and Commercial Item Descriptions https://www.gsa.gov/acquisition/purchasing-programs/requisition-programs/gsa-global-supply/supply-standards/index-of-federal-specifications-standards-and-commercial-item-descriptions, and DoD specifications are available online at quicksearch.dla.mil.

8. 41 U.S.C. 22 section 8002(c).

9. ASSIST, http://assist.daps.dla.mil.

10. General Services Administration, Federal Management Property Regulation, Part 101-29, General Services Administration, Washington, D.C., 1992.

11. This definition does not include converter scrap, over-issue publications, and printer over-runs.

12. Additional guidance on preparing these solicitation documents can be found in MIL-HDBK-245D, Department of Defense Handbook: Preparation of a Statement of Work (SOW), 03 April 1996.

13. The Work Breakdown Structure is described in MIL-STD-881C, DoD Work Breakdown Structure Standard.

14. Each contracting agency is free to develop its own template.

15. The Guidebook is found at https://www.acq.osd.mil/asda/dpc/cp/cc/docs/corhb/ref/Guidebook_for_Acquisition_of_Services_24March2012.pdf.

16. ARRT is available at http://sam.dau.mil/ARRTRegistration.aspx.

17. Additional QASP information, such as the recommended document format, template, and training courses, is available at https://www.dau.mil/acquipedia/Pages/ArticleDetails.

18. Additional information on IGCEs is available from DPAP, DoD IGCE Handbook for Services Acquisition, February 2018.

19. 41 U.S.C. 264.

20. A *National Stock Number* is a 13-digit number assigned to each part in a Government inventory.

21. 10 U.S.C. 2308.

22. The Defense Acquisition University hosts the Award and Incentive Fees Community of Practice to house relevant policies and training courses, as well as sample incentive plans. It can be accessed at https://acc.dau.mil/awardandincentivefees.

23. 10 U.S.C. 2306(c).

24. 50 U.S.C. 1621.

25. 10 U.S.C. 2306c(d)(2).

26. This is accomplished on a Form DD1155. If the order is signed by the contractor to form a bilateral contract, it is deemed an 1155R.

27. However, when these characteristics are extensive, two-step sealed bidding or negotiation is used.

28. The contracting officer must use some judgment in evaluating PPIRS data, since it is up to five years old and contains contracts irrelevant to the current acquisition.

29. Executive Order 12549, Debarment and Suspension, of February 18, 1986.

30. Public Law 103-355, Section 2455 (31 U.S.C.6101), and Executive Order 12689.

31. The list of specified felonies is long: bribery, embezzlement, falsification or destruction of records, forgery, illegally obtaining or attempting to obtain a federal contract or subcontract, making false statements, receiving stolen property, tax evasion, theft, or violating Federal criminal tax laws.

32. This also applies if a number of contractor employees are convicted of violations of criminal drug statutes occurring in the workplace, which indicates that the contractor has failed to make a good faith effort to provide a drug-free workplace.

33. Such a determination is automatically accepted without further review in the debarment proceedings.

34. 50 U.S.C. App. 2401, *et seq.*

35. 19 U.S.C.1337.

36. DFARS 215.306(c)(1).

37. FAR 7.503[c][12][ii].

38. 10 UCC 2305.

39. DFARS 215.306.

40. It is a proven axiom that these presentations, either oral or written, provide the negotiator and contracting officer with an opportunity to demonstrate their talents to management and enhance their careers.

41. DFARS 215.403-1.

42. https://eadf.dcma.mil/ewam2/registration/setup.do.

43. Source Selection Procedures, Appendix A, sets forth requirements for conducting debrief sessions.

44. This requirement is permissive within civilian agencies; however per DFARS 233.104, it is mandatory within DoD.

45. 4 CFR Part 21.

46. Thresholds over $10,000,000 are unique to DoD and are set forth at DFARS 236.204.

47. For example, 33 U.S.C. 624 prohibits the Army Corps of Engineers from awarding a contract for harbor or river improvement that exceeds the Government cost estimate by more than 25 percent.

48. Division I of Pub. L. 113-235.

49. 40 U.S.C. 3141 *et seq.*

50. The contracting officer then enters these evaluations into the Contractor Performance Assessment Reporting System at www.cpars.gov.

Chapter 4

Pricing

Pricing defines what a firm will receive for its products. Pricing factors include competitor's prices, interaction of supply and demand, manufacturing or services cost, market position, profit goal, and promotion strategy.

4.1 MARKET-BASED PRICING

Price should match market reality in terms of competitor prices and how much customers value the products and services that it provides. This requires the firm to set an *efficient price* (the highest amount that customers are willing to pay) to maximize its return. Pricing is a balancing act, striving for equilibrium between a price floor (below which the organization loses money) and a price ceiling (beyond which demand sinks toward zero).

To achieve this objective, one can imagine three different pricing levels. Pricing at the *industry* level focuses on changes in both supplier prices and customer demand. This activity is often based on raw material or commodity futures, or else economic trends. The price we pay at the gasoline pump behaves in this manner. By contrast, pricing at the *market* level focuses on competitive pricing rather than competitor products. This results in matching competitor pricing behavior, either raising or lowering prices based on what the competition does. Retail stores operate on this approach. Finally, pricing at the *transaction* level focuses on discounts from list price, and is unique to each customer based on frequency or quantity of purchase, or importance of retaining its business. Volume discounts such as in public warehouses are a classic example of transaction pricing.

A firm will estimate the potential market price of its offering (also known as its *fair value*) by examining those features that enhance profits and help it maintain a competitive advantage in the marketplace. It will consider such factors as:

- cost of close substitute products;
- costs of acquisition, production, and distribution;
- interaction of supply and demand;
- perceived utility by customer;
- return on capital; and
- risk.

Several different types of markets can be described in economic terms. A *monopoly* involves one supplier with so much market control that it in effect dictates the terms of sale to multiple customers, who find no effective alternative source of supply. A regulated utility or raw material supplier can be an example, and there is not much the Government or prime contractor can do to obtain a price reduction. In fact, any firm guilty of price-fixing can be accused of being a monopoly. However, even a complete monopoly must be aware of potential alternative products that could cost it customers, such as a regulated landline telephone utility facing the challenge of wireless telephone carriers. Moreover, the act of maintaining or expanding a large market share illegally or through threats is called *monopolization*, and is often the subject of investigation by the Federal Trade Commission.

Government policies can be invoked to combat monopoly. Barriers to entry can be minimized, antitrust policy can be invoked at the first sign of price collusion, and large firms can be broken up (which rarely happens today). To assess whether any of these conditions might exist in a given market, economists use a *concentration ratio* to analyze barriers to market entry or exit. This ratio compares the firm's percentage of business or market share to the number of firms in the market. The higher the ratio, the stronger a firm's market share, and the more attractive the opportunity to remain in the market.

A *monopsony* is the opposite of a monopoly, in which one customer has control of the marketplace. For example, the Federal Government has monopsonistic control over the American aircraft carrier and submarine industries. In all Federal contracts in fact, certain clauses are truly monopsonistic (e.g., Cost Accounting Standards, disputes, socioeconomics clauses, and termination for convenience). Also, some laws and regulations seem monopsonistic (e.g., percentage of profit limits, restrictive bidding rules, and truth in negotiation). One could argue that the Government tends to rely heavily on certain product lines, perhaps because commercial competitors refuse Government contract terms, which also leads to monopsonistic tendencies.

In contrast, an *oligopoly* is an industry with a few firms producing most of the industry output in identical form. Basic commodity industries such as aluminum or nylon would be oligopolies because they contain a few large firms producing homogeneous products. An oligopoly would also describe markets with a few sellers of differentiated products such as automobiles, cigarettes, and heavy machinery. Government contracting officers may obtain some competition within an oligopoly market, but the number of offerors will be limited.

The contrasts between oligopolies and monopolies are significant. Oligopolies include interdependent decision-making, price stability and intense competition. If one firm lowers its price, others match the reduction in a "price war." Alternatively, a price increase by one may not create any response from competitors other than price maintenance to gain any customers upset with the price increase. Hence the actions of one firm can influence the behavior of other firms in the industry.

Comparatively, monopolies and oligopolies have significant barriers of entry due to control of natural resources, high startup costs or technological superiority, intellectual property rights, and/or lack of substitute goods. They tend to be price-setters and can run abnormally high profits over a long term. By contrast, monopsonistic markets have more price-takers and lower barriers to entry.

Another market type involves *differentiated sellers*. Here there may be many sellers who try to create an impression in the minds of potential customers that their products are better than their competitors. This market includes common consumer items in stores and is the market type we deal with in our everyday lives.

Another economic concept plays a big part in market pricing. The change in income due to increasing output by one unit is called *marginal revenue*. This item will increase if demand is elastic, decrease if inelastic, and hardly change if demand is fluctuating between the two. Maximum-profit equilibrium is achieved where marginal revenue equals marginal cost (the change in cost by producing one extra unit). A firm that strives to maximize profit will outperform others in terms of marginal revenue. A monopolist will strive to achieve this position and maximize its profit, even to the point of reducing production to introduce an artificial scarcity of its product.

4.2 COST-BASED PRICING

4.2.1 Managerial Accounting

Unlike market-based pricing, the cost-based method makes heavy use of accounting. Individual cost elements must be projected and tracked. A bottoms-up approach is used to project prices. It identifies both direct costs assignable to a specific contract and indirect costs allocated across several contracts.

Management is heavily involved in reviewing reports of these numbers. This is why cost-based pricing feeds directly into *managerial accounting* to develop numbers for reports which management can then use to assess performance, develop strategies, and make decisions.

Two managerial uses of cost analysis are activity-based and life-cycle costing. *Activity-based costing* correlates costs of each production activity based on their actual consumption. It sums direct and indirect costs to help estimate the total costs of products or services. This method emphasizes production efficiency such as scheduling production runs or equipment idle time when no useful work is performed. Activity-based accounting helps to identify inefficient activities and departments, so it can be used to support resource allocation and cost control initiatives. It is quite useful in production plants where multiple products share common costs.

Life-cycle (or *whole-life*) *costing* is more comprehensive in scope because it examines total costs over the life of the program or asset, sometimes colloquially referred to as "cradle-to-grave" cost. Frequently used in Federal programs, this process recognizes that the best time to influence the cost of manufacturing is in the design stage, since small changes to the product design may lead to significant savings in manufacturing cost. Individual cost components of life-cycle costing may include:

- acquisition;
- basic and advanced research;
- construction;
- depreciation;
- design;
- development;
- financing;
- maintenance;
- operations;
- planning;
- production;
- renewal or rehabilitation;
- replacement or disposal; and
- training.

Total life cycle cost is the sum of the costs for all phases of a program. Lower life cycle costs reduce proposed price and thereby increase the chance for award, although losses may result if cost projections are too low. This process can also be used to assess lease-or-buy options by considering cost elements rather than price to derive total cost of ownership.

Life cycle costing can also be used to cost out alternative purchase choices, which are then used in a benefit-cost analysis to select the best option. The benefit and cost of each option is calculated and then discounted into a present value. Each option (including the null option of doing nothing) receives a benefit-cost ratio, and the highest ratio is chosen.

4.2.2 Cost Accounting

Cost accounting is used to determine budgeted and actual costs of departments, operations, and products. Managers use cost accounting to support decisions to cut costs and improve profitability. Cost accounting is primarily used for internal managers rather than outside users, and management decides what to compute based on its own objectives. There are so many varieties of cost accounting in use that even managers can become confused (let alone you, the reader). Nonetheless, some of the common techniques will be described here.

Small firms use a simple process known as *cash accounting*, which recognizes revenues when they are received, regardless of when the sale actually took place. So an end-of-year sale that results in revenue after the end of the year is recognized in the following year. Many small and individual businesses use this method due to its simplicity.

A more complex method is *accrual accounting*, where revenues are recorded when services are rendered or supplies or products are delivered. Expenses related to production and delivery are recorded as if they were incurred in the same period as in a cause-and-effect basis. This is known as the *matching* principle of accounting. It does not matter whether payment is received the same or a later period. If they will arrive in a later accounting period, they are listed as *accrued revenue* and will be deducted from that account once received. On the other hand, advance revenue receipts are not truly revenue under the accrual method, but rather are considered liabilities in a deferred income account, since they are not yet considered to be a firm sale. From the buyer's point of view, such prepayments are actually *deferred expenses* and adjusted after the goods or services have arrived.

If the collection of receivables involves a high risk, a firm often opts to defer revenue recognition. There are three methods which deal with this situation. The *cost recovery method* records uncollectable payment, but profit is not recognized until total cash receipts exceed cost of goods sold. The *deposit method* recognizes cash receipts before transfer of ownership, but not until the risks and rewards of ownership have transferred to the buyer. Finally, the *installment sales method* recognizes gross profit in proportion to the amount received. If the customer pays monthly over four months, then the seller books 25 percent of the sales price each month.

Revenue from inventory sales is usually recognized at the point of sale, but there are several exceptions. *Buyback agreements* allow a firm to sell a product and agree to buy it back after some time. If the buyback price covers inventory costs plus related holding costs, then the inventory remains on the seller's books. Alternatively, firms which cannot estimate the amount of future returns, or have high rates of returns, may choose to recognize revenues only when the right to return expires. Otherwise they must deduct estimated future returns from revenue.

Long-term contracts for aircraft, construction, space, and weapon systems may contain a clause that allows the contractor to bill at designated contract milestones. Otherwise, the *completed-contract method* is used if the contract involves high risks by recognizing costs, revenues, and gross profit only after the project is fully completed. However, it does recognize any expected loss immediately. Finally, the *completion-of-production* basis recognizes revenues even if no sale was made. This approach is intended for agricultural products and minerals with a ready market, certain prices and insignificant selling and distributing costs.

The nature of a given cost depends on the reason for its incurrence. *Fixed costs* are incurred without regard to production volume, whereas *variable costs* are caused by production activities. Fixed costs are often a function of time because they are incurred to maintain operations (e.g., depreciation, insurance, and property taxes). Over time, the law of diminishing returns will tend to reduce the extra output produced when adding more variable production factors such as labor and material. Hence, although the cost of further production increases for each succeeding item, the marginal cost of production falls. This is why quantity discounts are often feasible.

Costs are collected through the life of the project and summarized at its endpoint. Costs are collected either by job order or by process. *Job order costing* collects costs assigned to a specific job by reference number. Direct costs are recorded at their actual value. In contrast, *process costing* collects costs continuously for high-volume, homogeneous, standardized products when unit costs cannot be developed until after the work is completed. Dividing total costs by units of work performed yields a process cost. Both of these methods collect historical costs of the product, which can then be adjusted to allow for changes in such factors as equipment, manufacture methods, materials, plant layout, working conditions and efficiency, and even uncontrollable factors such as time and weather. Alternatively, the firm can develop *cost estimating relationships* to apply historical costs to a performance or physical feature of the end product, such as cost per pound. Use of these relationships is quick and easy, and quite objective; however they do not allow history to reflect the factor changes cited above, and could be too simplistic or even inaccurate.

To project what a cost should be, the department may develop *standard costs,* which are expected values used as goals or baselines. Standard costs are derived through engineering studies, efficiency reviews and actual working conditions. The accounting system captures and analyzes differences from standards for material, labor hours and overhead costs. The difference between planned and actual cost is a *variance*, which can be analyzed by dividing the actual cost into its components (e.g., labor, material, etc.) to determine why costs differ from their planned level. The standard costs for each factor of production are then added to overhead to derive the cost of the finished unit. Note that overhead is not a standard cost, but rather a period cost for a set time frame, often a month.

Yet another choice for product costing is to use either the absorption or direct costing method. *Absorption costing* assigns costs to production units as they progress through stages, from Work in Progress through Finished Goods to Cost of Goods Sold. Indirect costs are added to direct labor and material costs to yield the total unit cost. If standard costing is used, then the product cost is the sum of standard allowances for each factor of production. This method recognizes that unit cost will vary with production volume. A variation of this approach is the *normal cost* approach, which takes the actual labor and material costs of a production item and adds a predetermined estimate of overhead cost derived from the average production schedule.

By contrast, *direct costing* classifies all costs as either fixed or variable regardless of volume or production stage. It assigns all variable costs to production accounts and all fixed costs to an expense account which is then allocated across all production units. Because the direct costing method separates fixed and variable costs from overhead, it can more easily identify key pricing factors and ignore any variations in overhead costs. Direct costing data is especially useful to determine lot sizes and economical production runs, and is typically used in pricing proposals. However, direct costing may miss some production and inventory costs and does not consider charges against revenue for the period, and is therefore not widely used to measure earnings.

Accountants use several more terms to describe types of costs. *Discretionary or managed costs* are fixed costs which reflect management policies, such as advertising or research and development. The opposite would be *avoidable costs,* those not incurred due to management decision to change or delete a given operation (e.g., shutting down a department to avoid salary expenses). *Joint costs* are common to multiple business segments of the firm and must be allocated to a collection pool. Joint costs could be assigned to multiple units without identification to a specific unit until they reach a later *split-off point* where the individual units can again be identified.

Time is an element that is reflected in several costing terms. *Unexpired costs* are carried forward to a future accounting period and treated as an asset, such as inventory. *Recurring costs* occur period after period. *Nonrecurring costs* are one-time expenses such as plant or equipment setup or moving, preproduction engineering, special tooling and test equipment, spoilage and rework, and workforce training. *Normal cost* adds to the actual labor and material costs of a production item a predetermined estimate of overhead cost based on average production schedule.

Some other terminology is useful to understand accounting techniques. *Capital expenditures* benefit future periods, such as investing in new equipment or plant, whereas *revenue expenditures* only benefit the current period (such as maintenance of equipment). An expenditure which requires current or future resource utilization is an *out-of-pocket cost* and thus an impending cash outflow. By contrast, a *sunk cost* is a past commitment of funds (e.g., depreciation) and may be irrelevant to future decision-making.

Incremental costs result from a decision to do or not do something, such as to increase or change production. Incremental costing can be used for quantity buys or options where fixed costs were covered during the initial production run. This process can also be used in make-or-buy decisions to provide an alternative method to decide whether to preserve labor or a production line, such as to fabricate a component when demand is down and buy it when demand is up.

A firm can also use *throughput accounting* to allocate variable costs to products and services, which are then deducted from sales revenue to determine actual throughput. This method is based on cash receipts and may not allocate all fixed costs or overhead. It seeks to maximize throughput (and reduce inventory and operating costs) rather than profit.

Finally, *lean accounting* is a new approach that eliminates traditional costing procedures and budgeting, instead focusing on:

- box scores for decision-making;
- desire to free up capacity;
- eliminating transactional control systems;
- eliminating waste;
- performance measurements;
- simple financial reports;
- speeding up the processes;
- summarizing direct costs; and
- value-based pricing.

4.2.3 Corporate Budget

For a firm, a budget documents the various targets for costs, financing, growth, investment, and sales. Long-term budgets have a time horizon of at least five years to provide vision, while short-term annual budgets control operations in a specific year. If the actual figures come close to the budget, the managers have achieved their goals. But if the figures diverge wildly from the budget, the situation may need the attention of higher management.

Budgets are management plans used to acquire future resources. There are many different types of budgets used, including:

- *capital budget*: lists fixed asset requirements and their financing, often adjusted annually;[1]
- *cash budget*: shows all expected sources and uses of cash (e.g., cash on hand, collections, disbursements, and borrowings). It predicts short-term cash receipts and expenditures to anticipate when income will cover expenses. An unfavorable outcome will lead the firm to decide to seek outside financing;
- *expenditure budget*: identifies spending items (e.g., manufacturing expense, sales, and marketing, general and administrative, research and development). Synonymous titles are *flexible* or *variable budget*;
- *marketing budget*: estimates the funds needed to cover advertising and public relations of the product or service;
- *master operating budget*: prepared from earnings and sales forecasts;
- *production budget*: basis for developing material, labor, and overhead budgets. It projects the number of units to be produced to meet sales objectives;
- *project budget*: estimates the labor, materials, and other expenses of a project; and
- *sales budget*: estimates future sales, often by both units and dollars. The Federal Government has a related concept, a *revenue budget*, identifying tax and tariff income projections.

When program managers prepare and submit budgets, they may use the concept of *zero-based budgeting*. This elaborate and lengthy process is often performed by program office staff or support contractors to justify the program's plans and actions on a continuing basis. The manager defines the anticipated output of each expenditure, and the necessary inputs for that output. This requires as much effort as developing the initial program budget. This process is most helpful where costs are discretionary in nature, especially with nonprofit and Government organizations. This process is not often used in commercial firms.

Budgets can be compared over time to identify how well past performance mirrored budget plans. Budgets are also used to project current needs into out-years. Project managers or firms can also use incremental budgets to highlight differences from last year to current year. Budget figures can be expressed in *current-year dollars* to reflect today's dollar values, or *then-year dollars* to apply an escalation factor to historical values to reflect inflation.

4.2.4 Auditing

An *audit* systematically evaluates a firm, system, process, or project. Audits review the validity and reliability of information by developing a formal written opinion based on testing (often statistical sampling) and then assessment of the results. Audits adhere to generally accepted standards set by governing bodies to provide sufficient confidence that the opinions are arrived at professionally and reasonably error-free. Auditors can review financial systems and records, information system performance and security risks. An *integrated audit* goes one step further, in that auditors express a written opinion on a firm's internal control over financial reporting. Auditors validate reported cost savings and cost reduction reports by selectively reviewing the reports and supporting documents.

The accountant for the firm is under a professional obligation for *full disclosure* of all relevant information to promote a clear understanding and avoid errant implications. Accountants use the *objectivity test* to ensure that information is verifiable and can be reproduced for independent reviewers who use the same set of facts and assumptions.

Quality audits review a quality management system, usually in accordance with ISO 9001 (which will be discussed later), and assess if processes achieve their targets, are properly implemented, and reduce problem areas. Such audits can also look at monitoring procedures, but are primarily concerned with program effectiveness.

Audits should not be confused with assessments. Audits are independent evaluations involving quantitative and qualitative analysis, whereas an *assessment* tends to be less independent and more consultative in nature. Generally, consultants conduct assessments and independent third parties run audits.

When an audit reveals possible criminal activity, the Federal Government may step in. The *Securities and Exchange Commission* (SEC) is authorized to bring civil enforcement actions against firms or persons for accounting fraud, providing false information, or insider trading (dealing in stocks or bonds by using information that is not disclosed to the general public). Firms which are publicly traded on a stock exchange submit quarterly and annual reports to the SEC, which maintains an online database called EDGAR (the Electronic Data Gathering, Analysis, and Retrieval system) for investor access. EDGAR is accessible to the general public without charge, and handles some 3000 actions per day.[2]

4.2.5 Chart of Accounts

Every firm keeps a list of the various accounts in which it accumulates costs. This is necessary for both proposals and cost accounting. Assets, liabilities, and expenses are maintained in separate numbered sections, with numerous accounts treated as "buckets" into which accountants drop specific debits and credits ("plusses" and "minuses"). Table 4.1 is a sample chart listing typical accounts with assigned code numbers. Note the broad headings in the table. Assets include permanent physical attributes such as equipment, facilities, and land. Liabilities include payable accounts such as material inventory, prepaid benefits, and work in process. Next come accrued liabilities such as payroll and associated taxes due, then loans and mortgages which raise operating capital. Equity such as stock and bond issues, as well as net earnings, are treated as liabilities by accountants. The rest of the accounts address operating expenses such as labor, selling and other administrative activities.

A *directly associated cost* is generated solely because of incurring another cost (e.g., salary of personnel incurred while generating unallowable costs). When an unallowable cost is incurred, its directly associated costs are also unallowable and so identified in any billing, claim or proposal to the Government. If a directly associated cost is included in a cost pool allocated over a base that includes an unallowable cost, the Government will disallow both the unallowable costs and their allocable share of costs from the indirect cost pool if they are material. *Materiality* is a function of the actual dollar amount, cumulative effect of all directly associated costs in a cost pool, and ultimate effect on total contract cost.

Statistical sampling is a valid way to account for unallowable costs if it results in an unbiased sample of the universe that permits audit verification. Any large dollar value or high-risk transaction is removed from the universe and separately reviewed. An advance agreement specifies the basic characteristics of the sampling process, or else the burden of proof is on the contractor to establish that its method meets these criteria. The sampling process may be *probability sampling* (selecting sample units according to chance) or *nonprobability sampling* (selecting sample units based on personal choice or expert judgment).

4.3 COST PRINCIPLES

FAR 31

Federal contractors use cost accounting procedures governed by *generally accepted accounting procedures (GAAP)* issued by the Financial Accounting Standards Board, a private institution of the accounting trade. GAAP is not accounting theory, but rather a collection of agreements based on custom, experience, practical necessity, and reason. These practices have

Table 4.1 Chart of Accounts

ASSETS (0-199)
CASH (100-129)
101 Petty Cash
110 Bank Savings Account
112 Payables Checking Account
115 Payroll Checking Account
120 Money Market Account
RECEIVABLES (130-139)
131 Customer Accounts Receivable
INVENTORIES (140-149)
140 Purchased Materials
145 Subassembly Inventory
146 Work-in-Process Inventory
147 Finished Product Inventory
PREPAID EXPENSES (150-159)
151 Rent
154 Advertising
155 Insurance
FIXED ASSETS (160-199)
161 Land
162 Buildings
169 Buildings Depreciation
170 Machinery & Equipment
179 Machinery & Equipment—Depreciation
180 Furniture & Fixtures
188 Leasehold Improvements
189 Furniture & Fixtures—Depreciation
190 Transportation Equipment
199 Transportation Equipment—Depreciation
LIABILITIES & EQUITY (200-299)
PAYABLES (200-229)
220 Accounts Payable
225 Commissions Payable
229 State Sales/Use Tax Payable
PAYROLL & WITHHOLDINGS (230-239)
231 Accrued Wages
232 Vacation
234 Withholdings—FIT (federal income tax)
235 Withholdings—FICA (social security)
236 Withholdings—FICM (Medicare)
237 Withholdings—SIT (state income tax)
ACCRUED EXPENSES (240-249)
240 Federal Unemployment Tax
241 State Unemployment Tax
249 Property Tax
OTHER LIABILITIES (250-259)
250 Bank Loan
251 Mortgage

(Continued)

Table 4.1 (Continued)

EQUITY (280-289)
280 Common Stock
285 Paid-In Capital
289 Retained Earnings
NET EARNINGS (290-299)
290 Domestic Revenue
297 Exports
EXPENSES (300-999)
MANUFACTURING EXPENSE (300-399)
320 Labor—General
325 Overtime
326 Bonuses
335 Vacation
336 Holidays
340 Material Discounts
349 Manufacturing Supplies
355 Heat, Light, Power
361 Freight Out
362 Freight In
370 Outside Services
ENGINEERING EXPENSE (400-499)
420 Labor
425 Overtime
426 Bonuses
435 Vacation
436 Holidays
460 Supplies
470 Outside Services
495 Royalties
SELLING EXPENSE (600-699)
620 Labor
625 Overtime
626 Bonuses
629 Commissions
635 Vacation
636 Holidays
640 Air Travel
641 Auto Expense
642 Parking and Tolls
650 Advertising
660 Supplies
669 Postage
670 Outside Services
680 Travel & Entertainment
690 Bad Debts
696 Sales Allowances

(Continued)

Table 4.1 (Continued)

ADMINSTRATIVE EXPENSE (700-799)
720 Labor
725 Overtime
741 Workers Compensation
745 Employee Insurance
751 Sick Leave
752 Vacation
753 Holidays
760 Benefits
765 Commissions
771 Equipment Maintenance
772 Facility Maintenance
775 Office Supplies
778 Telephone
780 Outside Services
782 Legal & Audit
785 Travel & Entertainment
789 Corporate Insurance
792 Real Property Tax
793 Personal Property Tax
795 Sales/Use Tax
OTHER EXPENSE (900-999)
940 Loan Interest

the authoritative support of the accounting trade and are accepted practices within the profession.

The United States Government does not impose any financial reporting regulations on its contractors, believing that the private sector is in a better position to understand the needs of the users of financial information. The Board issues *statements of financial accounting standards* (now known as *financial standards codification*) which describe how to prepare and represent financial reports. Currently, there are many statements in force (covering about 90 topic areas) and incorporated within the new codification scheme.

An audit of the financial statements is usually required by financiers, investors, and tax authorities. Audits are usually performed by independent accountants or auditing firms, using the rules and conventions of GAAP to ensure consistency in financial statements across all firms. Auditing results are summarized in a report that provides an opinion of the fairness and accuracy of the financial statements, which is then included in the firm's annual report.

In view of GAAP, the Government issues *cost principles* to equitably treat similar firms doing similar work.[3] Cost principles and procedures are used in contracts with commercial firms to negotiate indirect cost rates. This is necessary to calculate the cost-reimbursement portion of time-and-materials contracts and revise fixed-price incentive contracts. They are also used to definitize changes and contract modifications and terminations.

The accounting profession has a mindset of exactitude which is reflected in its treatment of costs. Accountants generally use a policy of conservatism to avoid overstating assets and income. Costs must be treated the same in successive years to ensure consistency over time.

If a contractor wishes to make a change to its accounting process, it submits a description of the proposed change at least 60 days before implementation to the cognizant contracting officer. If the description is adequate and compliant with cost accounting principles, the contracting officer requests the contractor to submit a general dollar magnitude proposal of the estimated overall impact on affected (sub)contracts based on the previous cost accounting practice, or else the fiscal year(s) in which the costs are incurred. The parties then negotiate any cost or price adjustments. If the request is denied, the change might still be implemented unilaterally by the contractor.

The Government often will not object as long as the change complies with GAAP, and will certainly be happy if it deems the change to be desirable. A *desirable change* is any unilateral change to a disclosed cost accounting practice that the contracting officer finds beneficial to the Government. To be deemed desirable, the contracting officer must consider how the change will maintain compliance with cost accounting principles and promote cost savings through forward pricing rates. If the change leads to a cost increase, availability of funds is necessary. If the proposed change is not approved, the contractor may still elect to make the change voluntarily and the Government pays no aggregate increased costs.

Any deviations concerning cost principles require advance approval of the agency head or designee. Class deviations require advance approval of USDA.

Administrative contracting officers and contractors may seek advance agreement on the treatment of special or unusual costs. Advance agreements are negotiated before incurrence of these costs. The agreements must be in writing and executed by both parties before being incorporated into applicable current and future contracts. Advance agreements may cover a single contract or group of contracts, or for all the contracts of a contracting office or agencies. Examples for which advance agreements may be useful are:

- compensation (e.g., incentive pay, living differential, relocation, severance, or termination of defined benefit pension plans);
- construction plant and equipment costs;
- deferred maintenance costs;
- general and administrative costs for architect-engineer, construction or job site, facilities, and GOCO plant contracts;

- idle facilities and idle capacity;
- independent research and development, and bid and proposal costs;
- plant reconversion;
- precontract costs;
- professional services (e.g., accounting, engineering, or legal);
- public relations and advertising;
- royalties;
- selling and distribution costs;
- statistical sampling methods;
- training and education;
- travel; and
- usage charges for fully depreciated assets.

Any generally accepted method to determine or estimate future costs may be used if it is equitable and consistently applied. The contractor must account for costs and maintain supporting documentation. To be acceptable, a cost must be allocable, allowable, and reasonable.

A cost is *allocable* if appropriately assignable or chargeable to one or more cost objectives based on relative benefits received or other equitable relationship. This is sometimes referred to as a *separable cost.* The cost must be necessary to the overall operation of the business or contract performance. Allocation includes both direct assignment of cost and the reassignment of a share from indirect cost pools. A direct cost is allocable if incurred specifically for the contract, while an indirect cost must benefit both the contract and other work. In either event, the cost must be distributed to work in reasonable proportion to the benefits received.

A cost is *allowable* only when allocable, compliant with GAAP, permitted by contract terms (including the cost principles outlined below), and reasonable. The contracting officer may disallow any unsupported cost or portion thereof. This is why flexibly priced contracts require certification of the indirect cost rates to initiate final payment. If unallowable costs are included in final indirect cost settlement proposals after contract termination, penalties may be assessed.

A cost is *reasonable* if it does not exceed that which would be incurred by a prudent person in the conduct of competitive business. No presumption of reasonableness is attached to a cost just because it was incurred. Once challenged by the contracting officer, the burden of proof is upon the contractor to establish that the cost is reasonable. What is reasonable depends upon:

- contractor responsibilities to employees, the Government, other customers, owners, and the public;
- deviations from the contractor's established practices;

- Federal and State laws and regulations;
- general recognition of a cost as ordinary and necessary to conduct business or perform the contract; and
- generally accepted sound business practices and arm's-length bargaining.

All costs specifically identified with other final cost objectives of the contractor are direct costs of those cost objectives and allocated to them, rather than being not charged to the contract, either directly or indirectly. If a cost was previously incurred for the same purpose in like circumstances and included in an indirect cost pool, the contractor must treat the cost as indirect to be consistent with past practice. Of course, the contractor may treat any small direct cost as indirect if the accounting treatment is consistently applied to all final cost objectives and results in the same outcome as if it were treated as a direct cost. For example, a company may decide that office expenses below $500 are not worth the trouble of separately reporting and tracking, and instead will charge them to an overhead account.

After direct costs have been determined and charged directly to the contract, indirect costs must then be allocated to intermediate or multiple final cost objectives. To do this, the contractor accumulates these indirect costs by logical cost groupings (known as *cost pools*) based on the reasons for their incurrence. The contractor then determines an allocation base that is common to all cost objectives. The base must then allocate the pool to intermediate and final cost objectives based on the accrued benefits.

Once an appropriate base for allocating indirect costs has been accepted, the contractor cannot remove individual elements. All items includable in an indirect cost base must bear a pro rata share of indirect costs, regardless of whether they are acceptable as Government contract costs. If unallowable, the Government will recalculate the rate by excluding these costs and then negotiate a lower rate.

The base period for allocating indirect costs is the same as the accounting period during which the costs are incurred and accumulated. The base period is usually the contractor's fiscal year used for financial reporting purposes. The fiscal year will normally be 12 months, but a different period may be appropriate (e.g., a change in fiscal year due to a business combination).

The Government receives a credit for the applicable portion of any income, rebate or allowance relating to any allowable cost that is received by or accrues to the contractor. This credit is taken either as a cost reduction or a cash refund.

PGI 242.71

Generally, the contracting officer requests voluntary refunds only after determining that no contractual remedy is readily available to recover the amount sought. Acceptance of unsolicited refunds does not prejudice remedies otherwise available to the Government. Before soliciting a voluntary refund or accepting an unsolicited one, the contracting officer should have legal counsel review the contract and related data to confirm that there are no readily available contractual remedies and advise whether the proposed action would jeopardize or impair the Government's rights.

The contracting officer will request voluntary refunds only when the contractor overcharged under a contract, or inadequately compensated the Government for the use of Government-owned property, or inadequately compensated the Government in the disposition of contractor inventory and retention of the amount in question by the contractor or subcontractor would be contrary to good conscience and equity. The head of the contracting activity must usually concur with the request for a voluntary refund. They may be requested during or after contract performance. A contract modification, rather than a check, is the preferred means of effecting a solicited or unsolicited refund transacted before final payment. If a check is nonetheless to be accepted, it should be payable to the agency that awarded the contract, forwarded to the procuring or administrative contracting officer, and then sent to the office responsible for control of funds.

4.3.1 Advertising and Public Relations Costs

FAR 31.205-1

Advertising costs cover use of communications media to promote sales. These media include billboards, broadcasting, business cards, conventions, magazines, and samples. These costs cover not only the actual expense of buying time and space, but also associated salaries, fringe benefits and travel. Advertising costs are allowable if required by (or arising from) the contract to acquire scarce items or dispose of scrap or surplus materials acquired for contract performance. Costs to promote exports of products sold to the U.S. Government, including trade shows, are allowable except for alcoholic beverages, entertainment, and memorabilia.

Public relations expenses are incurred to promote a favorable image of the company and its products among the public. Clearly, communications (e.g., creditors, customers, press, stockholders, etc.) and responding to inquiries on company policies and activities are allowable public relations costs. Moreover, plant tours and open houses, as well as roll-out ceremonies specifically provided for by contract (e.g., keel laying, ship launching or commissioning, etc.) are allowable. Another permissible activity for cost recoupment is participation in community services such as blood bank, charity and savings bond campaigns, and disaster assistance.

Other advertising and public relations costs not listed above are disallowed. This includes corporate celebrations, donation of excess food, dues for joining community activities, product promotional material, and special events that do not disseminate technical information.

DFARS 231.205-1

Unallowable public relations and advertising costs include payments to the Government associated with the leasing of Government equipment, including reimbursements for support services, except for foreign military sales contracts.

4.3.2 Bad Debts

FAR 31.205-3

Bad debts, collection costs and legal costs from uncollectable accounts receivable are unallowable.

4.3.3 Bonding Costs

FAR 31.205-4

Bonding costs are allowable when the Government requires assurance against financial loss to itself or others caused by contractor act or default. This covers bid, payment, and performance bonds. Any bonding costs to cover general conduct of a business are also allowable where customary for the trade.

4.3.4 Compensation for Personal Services

FAR 31.205-6

Compensation covers the total amount of wages, bonuses, deferred compensation, and employer contributions to defined contribution pension plans. Allowable compensation costs must be for work performed by the employee in the current year, not a retroactive adjustment of prior years' wages. The total compensation must conform to the terms and conditions of the contractor's implemented compensation plan or practice. Distribution of profits is not an allowable cost. Table 4.2 is a comparison of allowable and unallowable costs. Reasonable tests for compensation involve looking at similar firms of the same size and industry, perhaps in the same geographic area, engaged in similar nongovernment work.

Incentive pay systems which offer more money for more labor are controversial because they could create several problems. They may tend to

Table 4.2 Allowable and Unallowable Costs

Allowable Costs	*Unallowable Costs*
Compensation costs established under "arm's length" labor-management agreements.	Compensation costs unjustified by the nature of the work, discriminatory, or exceeding that paid for similar commercial work by other firms of the same size, industry, and geographic area.
Corporate stocks and bonds assessed at the fair market value on the date when the number of shares awarded is known.	—
	Differential income tax allowances from domestic assignments.
Income taxes and reimbursed relocation costs due to foreign assignments.	—
Bonuses and incentive compensation paid or accrued under an agreement pre-dating the services rendered, or pursuant to an established plan or policy.	
Severance pay to workers if involuntarily terminated, required by law, employer-employee agreement, established contractor policy, or circumstances of employment.	Payments to a replacement contractor to continue employment at another facility or entity of the firm.
Normal turnover severance payments based on past experience at the contractor's plant.	Mass severance pay, though case-by-case exceptions may be granted.
Severance payments to foreign nationals employed under a service contract performed outside the United States.	Severance payments to the same foreign nationals that exceed amounts typically paid to domestic employees providing similar services in the same industry within the United States, or if the facility is closed by direction of the host government.
Backpay (a retroactive adjustment of prior years' salaries or wages) for underpaid work required by a negotiated settlement or court decree, or to union employees (and to nonunion employees under a firm's policy or practice) incurred during labor-management negotiations while no labor agreement is in force.	All other forms of backpay, including changes in the price of corporate securities, dividend or cash payments to an employee in lieu of receiving or exercising an unallowable benefit, option, or right.
Year-end accruals for salaries, wages, or bonuses paid within a reasonable time after the end of a cost accounting period.	Deferred compensation to award an employee in a future cost accounting period(s) for services rendered in a prior period.
—	Termination payments to employees after a change in management control or ownership of the firm or its assets.

(*Continued*)

Table 4.2 (Continued)

Allowable Costs	*Unallowable Costs*
—	Payments to employees under plans introduced by a management change which are contingent upon the employee remaining with the firm for a specified period of time.
An early retirement incentive plan if the plan benefits only active employees. The firm must measure, assign, and allocate the costs in accordance with its accounting practices.	The present value of the total incentives in excess of the employee's annual salary for the fiscal year before retirement.
Fringe benefits—allowances and services provided by the firm to its employees in addition to regular wages and salaries (e.g., insurance, holidays, vacations, sick and military leave, and supplemental unemployment benefit plans). These costs must be required by law, employer-employee agreement, or the firm's established policy.	The cost of company-furnished automobiles for personal use by employees, including transportation to and from work.
—	Rebates and purchase discounts granted to employees on products or services produced by the firm or its affiliates.
Employee stock ownership plans (ESOP)—a stock bonus plan designed to invest primarily in the stock of the employer. Pension costs must be funded by the time set for filing the Federal income tax return or any extension.	Contributions by the firm in any one year that exceed the deductibility limits of the Internal Revenue Code* for that year.
ESOP stock contributions limited to the fair market value of the stock on the date that title is effectively transferred to the trust.	Stock purchases by the ESOP in excess of fair market value. The excess amount must be credited to the same indirect cost pools charged for the ESOP contributions in the year in which the stock purchase occurs.

* 26 U.S.C. et seq.

sacrifice quality for quantity, can lead to friction between labor and management, and may divert the latter's attention from improving organization and operations. Incentive rates are rather inelastic and hard to charge as fixed time rates. Incentive plans may be unusable in new operations or by beginning workers. They could increase supervision of employees. Finally, it is hard to change from time rates to incentive wage system. They are however permissible if in accordance with an agreement or plan previously agreed to by the employee(s) and management.

Post-retirement benefit plans are very complicated in their cost treatment, yet are a critical element in an employee's compensation package and therefore require some discussion. A *pension plan* is a deferred compensation method established and maintained by employers to pay benefits to plan participants after their retirement. They may include additional benefits (e.g., permanent and total disability payments, and survivorship payments to beneficiaries of deceased employees). A *pension plan participant* is a current or former employee or beneficiary who is or may become eligible to receive a benefit from a pension plan by meeting its participation requirements. A *qualified pension plan* is a written program to benefit employees that meets the Internal Revenue Code criteria for preferential tax treatment regarding contributions, investments and distributions. Any other plan is deemed a *nonqualified pension plan.*

For most pension plans, the contractor must fund pension costs by the deadline to file the Federal income tax return or any extension thereto. Traditionally, most companies fund these costs within 30 days of the end of the quarter. But for defined-contribution pension plans, where the company sets aside a specific amount or percentage every year, allowable pension cost is limited to the net contribution for the cost accounting period (after considering dividends and other credits).

Pension payments require an agreement between the contractor and employees before the work is performed. Most one-time-only pension supplements unavailable to all participants of the basic plan are not allowable unless they represent a separate pension plan, and the benefits are payable for life at the employee's option. However, the Government will allow increased payments for cost-of-living adjustments to previously retired plan participants.

A firm may use the pay-as-you-go method by allocating pension costs in the cost accounting period to which they are assigned. Any excess funded amount is assigned to a future period. For defined-benefit plans, a pension cost exceeding the amount required to be funded pursuant to a waiver granted under the Employee Retirement Income Security Act of 1974, is allowable in those future accounting periods to which the funding is assigned.[4]

Indemnifying the Pension Benefit Guaranty Corporation due to terminating an employee-deferred compensation plan is allowable if the indemnification payment is not recoverable under insurance.

An advance agreement is required to recognize increased pension costs if assets are withdrawn from a pension fund and transferred to another employee benefit plan fund or related account. The advance agreement states the portion of the Government's equitable share in the amount withdrawn or transferred. Unless otherwise specified by law or regulation, the Government may direct refund or credit of its equitable share of any assets that revert to the contractor. Excise taxes on pension plan asset reversions or withdrawals are unallowable.

Certain fringe benefits are strictly disallowed. Deferred bonuses are not allowable—only a bonus paid in the current year is recognized. Payments to terminated workers in excess of normal company severance payments are also disallowed. In the opposite sense, a payment to remain with the company when taken over by new management will be disallowed. Use of company cars is allowable to the extent they are used for company business, but not that part attributed to personal use. Employee rebates and purchase discounts are also unallowable.

Postretirement benefits other than pensions (*PRB*) cover all benefits (other than cash and life insurance paid by pension plans) provided to employees, their beneficiaries and covered dependents during the period following the employees' retirement. Examples of PRB include day care, health care, housing subsidies, legal services, life insurance, and tuition assistance. PRB costs must be incurred pursuant to law, employer-employee agreement, or an established contractor policy. There are three different types of PRB plans:

- *Accrual basis.* PRB costs are accrued during the working lives of employees and are paid to an insurer or trustee to establish and maintain a fund or reserve solely to provide PRB to retirees. They are measured and assigned in accordance with either GAAP or the Internal Revenue Code.
- *Pay-as-you-go.* This is the opposite approach—PRB costs are not accrued during the working lives of employees. Costs are assigned to the period in which benefits are actually provided or paid to an insurer or provider for current year benefits or premiums.
- *Terminal funding.* Again, PRB costs are not accrued during the working lives of the employees. The entire PRB liability is paid in a lump sum upon employee termination (or conversion to a terminal-funded plan) to an insurer or trustee to establish and maintain a fund reserve for PRB payments to retirees. Terminal funded costs are amortized over a period of 15 years.

As with pension plans, PRB costs must be funded or paid to the insurer or provider by the time set for filing the Federal income tax return or any extension thereof, and are not allowable in any subsequent year. Similarly, increased PRB costs due to delay of more than 30 days after each quarter are not allowable. The Government receives a fair share of any previously funded PRB costs which revert or inure to the firm.

Compensation in excess of the benchmark amount determined for the fiscal year by OFPP is unallowable. Although this policy at one time applied just to the most highly compensated executives, it now applies across the board to all employees.

DFARS 231.205-6

Costs for bonuses or other payments in excess of the normal salary paid by the contractor to an employee that are part of restructuring costs associated with a business combination, are unallowable under DoD contracts. This limitation does not apply to severance payments or early retirement incentive payments.

Fringe benefit costs that are contrary to law, employer-employee agreement, or an established policy of the contractor are unallowable.

DFARs 242.73

The ACO is responsible for determining the allowability of insurance/pension costs in Government contracts and for determining the need for a Contractor/Insurance Pension Review. DCMA insurance/pension specialists and DCAA auditors assist ACOs in making these determinations and conduct Pension Reviews when needed. A Review provides an in-depth evaluation of a contractor's insurance programs, pension plans and other deferred compensation plans. These in-depth reviews are conducted only when a contractor has $50 million of (sub)contracts and modifications to the Government during the contractor's preceding fiscal year for which certified cost or pricing data were required. A more limited review that concentrates on specific areas of a contractor's insurance programs, pension plans or other deferred compensation plans is performed if the contractor:

- has a deficiency in its insurance and/or pension program;
- is involved in an acquisition, divestiture or merger;
- proposes or implements changes in its insurance, pension, or deferred compensation plans; or
- receives word that the Government needs to follow up on contractor implementation of prior Pension Review recommendations.

Solicitation Provisions and Contract Clauses

FAR 52.215-15, Pension Adjustments and Asset Reversions, when cost or pricing data will be required.

FAR 52.215-18, Reversion or Adjustment of Plans for Postretirement Benefits (PRB) Other Than Pensions, when cost or pricing data will be required.

4.3.5 Contingencies

FAR 31.205-7

A *contingency* is a possible future event or condition arising from presently known or unknown causes, with an unknown outcome. Such costs are generally unallowable except for contract termination, where a contingency factor may be recognized for a past period to recognize minor unsettled factors. This is permitted to expedite contract settlement.

Future cost contingencies may arise from presently known and existing conditions, such as anticipated costs of rejects and defective work, in which case they are included in the estimates of future costs. They could also arise from presently unknown conditions that cannot be measured precisely, such as results of pending litigation. These contingencies are excluded from cost estimates and separately disclosed, including their basis of computation.

4.3.6 Contributions or Donations

FAR 31.205-8

Contributions or donations of cash, property, and services (other than charity drives) are unallowable.

4.3.7 Cost of Money

FAR 31.205-10

Facilities capital reflects the net book value of depreciable capital assets, both tangible and intangible. Because actual interest cost is unallowable, *facilities capital cost of money* is recognized as an imputed cost of borrowings to finance facilities and other capital assets used in contract performance. It is considered an "incurred cost" under cost-reimbursement contracts and for progress payments under fixed-price contracts. The cost of money rate is established by the Department of the Treasury and adjusted twice a year.

The *cost of capital* is the expected return on the portfolio of securities that reflects the cost of debt and equity. This is a technique to evaluate potential new projects by deriving the minimum return that investors expect for providing capital to the company. This is the logic behind Facilities Capital Cost of Money used in DoD contracts and occasionally in civilian production contracts.

4.3.8 Depreciation

FAR 31.205-11

Depreciation is a common fixed cost that is based on the *going-concern concept* that a firm will continue indefinitely and therefore use up the depreciable asset over its full lifetime. Depreciation allocates an asset's cost over its useful life on an annualized basis. American firms use the Modified Cost

Recovery System to recover the capitalized cost of tangible property over a specified period of years that represents its usable lifetime. This calculation need not consider the asset's level of output. Annual depreciation rates are specified in tables issued and maintained by the Internal Revenue Service.

Capital costs are one-time expenditures to purchase land and improvements thereto (i.e., buildings and equipment) and will be depreciated over 15 to 20 years for the equipment, 27.5 years for real property, and 39 years for business property. Personal property lifetimes range between 3 and 20 years.

A *tangible capital asset* has physical substance and is expected to be held for continued use beyond the current accounting period. Generally, only estimated residual values that exceed 10 percent of the asset's capitalized cost are used to establish depreciable costs, and are not deducted from capitalized cost.

Depreciation on a contractor's plant, equipment and other capital facilities is allowable. However, depreciation cost is disallowed if it significantly reduces the book value of a tangible capital asset below its residual value.

Four common methods of depreciation are used. A common one is known as *straight-line*, deriving equal periodic charges during the life of the item. The depreciation amount for each period equals the cost of salvage or service life. So if a lathe costs $40,000 and is expected to last five years, and has a $4,000 salvage value, the annual depreciation cost is

$$\frac{\$40{,}000 - \$4{,}000}{5} = \$7{,}200.$$

Second, the *unit of production* method relates an item's depreciation to estimated productive capacity. The purchase cost less salvage value is divided by the number of production units expected during its lifetime to derive a depreciable cost per unit. The unit cost is multiplied by total production volume for a given year. If our lathe can process 9,000 items, then:

$$\frac{(\$40{,}000 - 4{,}000)}{9{,}000 \text{ units}} = \$4 \text{ per unit.}$$

And if the 9,000 units are equally spread over the five-year service life mentioned above, then 9,000 / 5 = 1,800 units per year can be expected. So, 1,800 units × $4/unit = $7,200. This is not a remarkable result and indicates that the purchase price is fair related to its productive value.

The *sum-of-the-years digits* approach is an accelerated method that charges depreciation heavily to the early years, providing greater income tax savings in early years. The years of service life are added up and used as the denominator, which in our case is 1 + 2 + 3 + 4 + 5 = 15. The numerator will be the sum of the years of remaining life. So in the first year of operation:

$$\frac{5}{1+2+3+4+5} = 33.3\%.$$

Using this method, the second year would be 4/15 or 26.7%, the third year is 20%, year four is 13.3%, and the final year is 6.7%. Note as a check that these percentages do add up to 100%. This demonstrates how this method to value depreciation starts out high in early years, then diminishes over time.

Finally, *double declining balance* is another accelerated method based on twice the number derived in straight line method. For our lathe, 2 × $7,200 = $14,400 per year.

One concern with buyers is that using an accelerated method means they bear the brunt of investment, while subsequent buyers pay less for the same item. Nonetheless, it is an accepted accounting practice to reflect greater value of an asset early in its life cycle, and to treat depreciation accordingly.

The value of an asset or liability is based on its current market price, known as *fair value accounting*. This approach requires an unbiased estimate of an asset's market price based on alternatives cost, its utility and the interaction of supply and demand. Whenever market conditions affect the value of the asset or liability, the firm changes the balance sheet entry. However, this approach is not accurate if the market price differs greatly from the *book value* (historical or purchase cost). This problem occurs if the marketplace cannot value future assets and liabilities (due to excessive optimism or pessimism), or else lacks information to make informed pricing decisions. However, unless the Government can demonstrate that the book value or purchase price is unreasonable, it will accept the asset price.

Depreciation, rental or use charges are unallowable on property acquired from the Government at no cost. Allowable depreciation for contractor-owned property usually does not exceed the amount used for financial accounting purposes, and is determined by the same depreciation policies and procedures used on nongovernment business.

No depreciation or rental is allowed on property which is already fully depreciated. However, a usage charge may be allowed based on cost, decreased efficiency due to age, increased maintenance charges, or total estimated useful life.

A lease of capital equipment is usually capitalized as a purchased asset and distributed over either the asset's useful life as a depreciation charge, or over the leased life as an amortization charge. Should the contractor reacquire property in a sale and leaseback arrangement, allowable depreciation is based on the asset's net book value on the date of its first lease.

4.3.9 Economic Planning Costs

FAR 31.205-12

Economic planning costs for the contractor's future overall business development, including market changes and resultant company changes, are allowable.

4.3.10 Employee Activity Costs

FAR 31.205-13

Costs to improve employee working conditions, employer-employee relations, morale, and performance (excluding any income generated by these activities) are allowable. For example, this includes company-sponsored employee counseling services, fitness centers, health clinics, in-house publications, and sports teams. Contributions to an employee organization and vending machine receipts are allowable only as if directly incurred by the firm. Cost of gifts is disallowed, though the cost of performance awards is allowable. Food and dormitory services are only allowable if the company tries to break even in their operation, so undercharging for a company cafeteria and residence is a clear sign that such costs should be disallowed.

4.3.11 Entertainment Costs

FAR 31.205-14

Entertainment costs such as gratuities, lodging or meals (aside from authorized travel) are unallowable because they are not directly related to production or services. Costs of other social activities such as equipment rental for summer picnics will not be allowed. Similarly, membership dues in country, dining or social clubs are not reimbursable. Tickets to shows or sports events and transportation related to entertainment are also expressly disallowed.

4.3.12 Fines, Penalties, and Mischarges

FAR 31.205-15

Costs of fines and penalties resulting from violations of Federal, State, local, or foreign laws and regulations are unallowable unless incurred to comply with contract terms and conditions, or under written instructions from the contracting officer.

Effort related to mischarging costs on Government contracts is unallowable when the costs result from alteration, destruction, falsification, or reconstruction of records. Effort to determine the magnitude of the improper charge is also disallowed.

4.3.13 Disposition or Impairment of Depreciable Property or Other Capital Assets

FAR 31.205-16

Gains and losses from the sale or retirement of depreciable property are assigned in the year incurred to the applicable cost grouping(s). However, no gain or loss is recognized from transfer of assets in a business combination.

When costs of depreciable property are subject to sale and leaseback limitations, the gain or loss is the difference between the net amount realized and the asset's undepreciated balance on the date the lease begins. Of course, if the fair market value exceeds the undepreciated balance, no cost is allowable.

Gains and losses on disposition of tangible capital assets are measured the same as other depreciation costs. The amount realized is the difference between the acquisition cost of the asset and its undepreciated balance (or for assets acquired under a capital lease, the value at which the leased asset is capitalized). If the asset is replaced, the contractor can either adjust the basis of the new asset by the amount of the gain or loss, or else can recognize the gain or loss in the period of disposition. If the asset is not replaced, the gain or loss is recognized in the period of disposition.

An insurance award is allowable if property is destroyed by uncontrollable events (e.g., accident, fire, flood, theft, windstorm, etc.). However, a contractor cannot reflect a loss for assets written-down from carrying value to fair value due to environmental damage.

FAR 31.205-52

Depreciation and cost of money for tangible capital assets, when the purchase method of accounting for a business combination is used, is allowable if based on the capitalized asset values. *Intangible capital assets* have no physical substance or substantial value, and will be held by an enterprise for continued use beyond the current accounting period for the benefits it yields. For intangible capital assets under the purchase method of accounting, amortization and cost of money is limited to what would have been allowed had the combination not taken place.

4.3.14 Idle Facilities and Idle Capacity Costs

FAR 31.205-17

The costs of idle facilities cover equipment, land, and plant in terms of:

- depreciation;
- housing;
- insurance;
- maintenance;
- property taxes;
- rent; and
- repair.

These costs are unallowable except to meet fluctuations in workload or due to unforeseen changes in production economies and requirements, or company reorganization. Even these costs are normally allowable for one year only.

Idle capacity occurs when the facilities are not used for a work shift (or multiple shifts if customary for the facility). These costs are allowable if full capacity was necessary or reasonable under normal circumstances and cannot be rented out or sold. A separate agreement is necessary to cover reimbursement for any idle capacity reserved for defense mobilization production.

4.3.15 Independent Research and Development and Bid and Proposal Costs

FAR 31.205-18

Independent research and development (*IR&D*) is effort that is not sponsored by a grant or contract, and is categorized as basic research, applied research, development, or *systems and other concept formulation studies* (analyses and study efforts related to specific IR&D efforts, or effort to identify or modify systems [current or new] or their components or equipment). IR&D does not include technical effort to develop and prepare technical data specifically to support a bid or proposal.

IR&D costs incurred in previous accounting periods are normally unallowable, unless a contractor has developed a specific product at its own risk in anticipation of recovering the development costs in the sale price of the product. To be allowable in such a case, the contractor must have either had no Government business during the time of cost incurrence, or else did not allocate IR&D costs to Government contracts. If this is true, then the total amount of IR&D costs applicable to the product must be prorated over time. When deferred costs are recognized, the contract (except firm-fixed-price and fixed-price with economic price adjustment) specifies the allocable amount of deferred IR&D costs.

IR&D costs may be incurred by contractors working jointly with non-Federal entities pursuant to a cooperative arrangement (e.g., collaboration and consortium arrangements, joint ventures, limited partnerships, teaming arrangements). In these cases, IR&D costs are allowable if the work performed would have been allowed as contractor IR&D.

Bid and proposal (*B&P*) costs are incurred to prepare, submit, and support bids and proposals (whether or not solicited) on potential contracts. The term does not include any effort sponsored by a grant or cooperative agreement, or required by contract (they might be allowable as an IR&D expense if for a collaboration or consortium). This concept is intended to motivate Federal contractors to maintain continued interest in the industrial base.

IR&D and B&P costs are allocated to final cost objectives on the same basis used for the G&A expense grouping of the profit center. A *profit center* is the smallest organizationally independent segment charged by management with profit and loss responsibilities. If the expenses benefit other profit centers or the entire company, they are allocated through either their own G&A or corporate G&A.

DFARS 231.205-18

DoD restricts IR&D/B&P costs for any contractor whose product division allocated a total of more than $11,000,000 in IR&D/B&P during the preceding fiscal year to DoD (sub)contracts exceeding the simplified acquisition threshold, except for any fixed-price contract without cost incentives. In the case of a contractor that has no product divisions, the term means that contractor as a whole. For major contractors, the amount of IR&D/B&P costs allowable under DoD contracts shall not exceed the lesser of their allocable share of total incurred IR&D/B&P costs or the amount of incurred IR&D/B&P costs for projects having potential interest to DoD. Allowable IR&D/B&P costs are limited to projects that are of potential interest to DoD, including activities intended to accomplish any of the following:

- enable superior performance of future U.S. weapon systems and components;
- enhance the industrial competitiveness of the United States;
- increase the development and promotion of efficient and effective applications of dual-use technologies;
- promote the development of technologies identified as critical under 10 U.S.C. 2522;
- provide efficient and effective technologies for achieving such environmental benefits as cleanup and restoration, conservation, improved data gathering, pollution reduction in manufacturing, and safe management of facilities;
- reduce acquisition costs and life-cycle costs of military systems; and
- strengthen the defense industrial and technology base of the United States.

For annual IR&D costs to be allowable, the IR&D projects generating the costs must be reported to the Defense Technical Information Center (DTIC).[5] The inputs must be updated at least annually and when the project is completed, and shared with the cognizant administrative contracting officer and the cognizant Defense Contract Audit Agency auditor to support the allowability of the costs.

The contractor discusses its plans with a technical or operational DoD Government employee before IR&D costs are generated so that contractor plans and goals for IR&D projects benefit from DoD awareness and feedback of related ongoing and future potential interest opportunities. The contractor may contact the Office of the Assistant Secretary of Defense for Research and Engineering (OASD R&E). Contractors not meeting the threshold of a major contractor are encouraged to use the DTIC online input form to report IR&D projects to provide DoD with visibility into the technical content of the contractors' IR&D activities.

For major contractors, the ACO or corporate ACO determines whether IR&D/B&P projects are of potential interest to DoD and provide the results of the determination to the contractor. This includes guidance on financial information needed to support IR&D/B&P costs and on technical information needed from major contractors to support the potential interest to DoD determination.

4.3.16 Insurance and Indemnification

FAR 31.205-19

Insurance is the undertaking of one party to indemnify another against a certain eventuality, in exchange for a premium payment. There is a transfer of risk manifested in a bilateral contract, namely the insurance policy itself. Purchased insurance costs are allowable. Actual losses are unallowable unless expressly provided for in the contract, incurred under the deductible provisions of purchased insurance, or minor losses in the ordinary course of business. In fact, losses might not be covered by insurance (e.g., spoilage, breakage, disappearance of hand tools, etc.).

Insurance by purchase or self-insurance includes coverage that the contractor is required to carry under the contract terms. A *self-insurance charge* is the projected average loss under a self-insurance plan, and allowable if not exceeding the cost of comparable purchased insurance (including associated insurance administration expenses). Self-insurance is allowable unless paid insurance is available, in which case self-insurance is disallowed. Even if the latter is the case, charges for risks of catastrophic losses are unallowable.

Insurance administration expenses include operating an insurance or risk-management department. This also includes such costs as actuarial fees, processing claims and service fees paid to insurance companies, technical consultants, or trustees. Costs of insurance maintained by the contractor in connection with the general conduct of its business are allowable. Business interruption insurance costs are also allowable except for coverage of profit.

Many property insurance costs are allowable. If property insurance premiums exceed the assets' acquisition cost, the written policy must state that the new asset bears the book value of the replaced asset, adjusted for insurance proceeds and actual replacement cost. Costs of insurance for the risk of loss, damage, destruction, or theft of Government property are allowable only if the contractor is liable, the contracting officer has not revoked Government assumption of risk, and the insurance excludes willful misconduct or lack of good faith by contractor management. Costs of insurance on the lives of officers, owners or employees are allowable as additional compensation.

Several insurance costs are unallowable. The expense of insurance to correct the contractor's own defects in materials and workmanship is unallowable, except for fortuitous or casualty losses. Premiums for retroactive or backdated insurance written to cover known losses are unallowable. Late premium payment charges for employee-deferred compensation plan insurance are also unallowable.

4.3.17 Interest on Other Financial Costs

FAR 31.205-20

Unless assessed by State or local taxing authorities, bond discounts and interest on borrowings are unallowable. The costs of capital financing, including legal and professional fees to prepare a prospectus and issue stock rights, are also unallowable.

4.3.18 Labor Relations Costs

FAR 31.205-21

Costs to maintain satisfactory relations between the contractor and its employees, including costs of employee publications, labor management committees and shop stewards are allowable. However, costs dealing with efforts to persuade employees to either create or turn down the right to collective bargaining are not allowable (e.g., information materials, legal counsel, and meetings).

4.3.19 Lobbying and Political Activity Costs

FAR 31.205-22

The Government takes a hard line against political activities and their associated costs, on the theory that contractors must secure and perform contracts in an unbiased mode. Efforts to influence the introduction or outcome of any Federal, State, or local election or referendum are unallowable. This includes cash or in-kind contributions, endorsements or publicity with a legislator or Government official. Similarly, costs incurred to influence a Federal employee on a contract or regulatory matter are unallowable. Also prohibited are costs to operate or contribute to a political campaign, party or political action committee. Also, a contractor must disclose any person hired or expected to be hired with private funds.[6]

The Government is more lenient if the contractor is addressing contract matters before a legislature. In response to a documented request, contractor costs will be allowed when incurred to present information regarding contract performance in a formal statement or testimony, or in a letter to the Congress or a state legislature member or cognizant staff member. Costs for transportation, lodging or meals are allowable only if incurred to offer testimony at a scheduled Congressional hearing, again pursuant to a written request by the Chairman or Ranking Minority Member of the Committee or Subcommittee.

Lobbying costs are allowable only to influence state or local legislation to directly reduce contract costs or avoid material impairment of contractor authority to perform the contract.

DFARS 231.205-22

Costs associated with preparing any list, material, report, or analysis on the actual or projected economic or employment impact in a particular state or congressional district of an acquisition program for which all research, development, testing, and evaluation has not been completed also are unallowable.

4.3.20 Losses on Other Contracts

FAR 31.205-23

Any cost in excess of income under any other contract is unallowable. A contractor cannot charge for a loss incurred on another contract.

4.3.21 Manufacturing and Production Engineering Costs

FAR 31.205-25

Costs to analyze, develop and deploy new or improved production methods and pilot production lines (e.g., materials, systems, processes, methods, equipment, tools and techniques) are allowable. This includes plant layout, production scheduling and control. Also allowable are inspection techniques, tooling design and improvements, and analyses to optimize manufacturing suitability.

4.3.22 Material Costs

FAR 31.205-26

Material costs include components, parts, raw materials, sub-assemblies, and supplies, whether purchased or manufactured by the contractor, plus inbound transportation, in-transit insurance overruns, spoilage, and defective work. The contractor adjusts the material costs for income credits, trade discounts from list price, refunds, rebates, allowances, cash discounts, and credits for scrap, salvage, and material returned to vendors. Credits are charged either directly to the material account or to material overhead. Differences between periodic physical inventories and book inventories may be included.

Allowance for all materials, services and supplies sold or transferred between any affiliates, divisions or subsidiaries is normally on a cost-incurred basis, but may be included at price for a commercial item or service, or as a competitive award.

4.3.23 Organization Costs

FAR 31.205-27

Costs are unallowable to plan, execute or resist a business reorganization or takeover (including mergers and acquisitions). Such expenditures include changes in the contractor's financial structure, costs of employees or outside experts and incorporation fees. However, administrative costs of short-term borrowings for working capital are allowable, regardless of whether additional capital is raised.

4.3.24 Other Business Expenses

FAR 31.205-28

The costs of preparing and publishing shareholder reports and forms to regulatory and taxing bodies are allowable. This includes registration and transfers for changes in ownership of contractor-issued securities. Similarly, the incidental costs of directors, committee and shareholder meetings, including proxy solicitations, are allowable.

4.3.25 Plant Protection Costs

FAR 31.205-29

Guard equipment, uniforms and wages are allowable. Depreciation on plant protection capital assets, and compliance with military requirements, are likewise allowable.

4.3.26 Patent Costs

FAR 31.205-30

Allowable costs include those to prepare invention disclosures and reports, search for invention disclosures, file and prosecute a United States patent application to convey title or a royalty-free license to the Government, and general counseling services on patent laws and employee agreements.

4.3.27 Plant Reconversion Costs

FAR 31.205-31

Plant reconversion costs restore or rehabilitate contractor facilities to the same approximate condition as before the contract start, except for fair wear and tear. Reconversion costs are unallowable except to remove Government property and associated restoration or rehabilitation costs.

4.3.28 Precontract Costs

FAR 31.205-32

Precontract costs are incurred before the effective date of the contract when necessary to comply with the proposed contract delivery schedule. These costs are allowable as if incurred after the date of contract. However, a clause must be included in the contract expressly allowing precontract costs, along with a not-to-exceed amount. Agencies may require advance approval at a level above the contracting officer before authorizing precontract costs.

4.3.29 Professional and Consultant Services

FAR 31.205-33

Professional and consultant services are rendered by members of a profession who possess a special skill and are not contractor employees. Usually economic, financial, legal, or technical in nature, they furnish analyses, evaluations, information, recommendations, studies, or training. They may also include liaison with Government officials. These costs are generally allowable. Factors to help determine cost reasonableness and allowability include:

- impact of Government contracts on the contractor's business;
- nature and scope of the service rendered;
- past pattern of acquiring such services and their costs;
- qualifications of the individual or firm rendering the service and the customary fee charged on nongovernment contracts;
- terms of the contract (e.g., description, estimate of time required, compensation rate, termination provisions); and
- whether the service can be performed more economically in-house.

Professional and consultant services to illegally use protected data, implement an improper business practice or conflict of interest, or influence solicitation content or source selection, are unallowable.

Retainer fees are allowable only if:

- consultants submit work products and related documents (e.g., meeting minutes, trip reports, etc.);
- invoices submitted by consultants include the time expended and nature of the actual services provided;
- supported by evidence that the services are necessary and customary;
- the level of any past services justifies the amount of the retainer fees;
- the retainer fees are reasonable compared to maintaining an in-house capability to perform the covered services; and
- work requirements and rate of compensation are documented.

4.3.30 Recruitment Costs

FAR 31.205-34

Expenses to operate an employment office, including help-wanted advertising and operating an aptitude and educational testing program are allowable. Similarly, the costs of employment agencies are allowed. Associated travel costs are also allowable, both for applicants to interviews and employees to recruit personnel.

4.3.31 Relocation Costs

FAR 31.205-35

Relocation costs arise from an employee's permanent change of work location for at least a year, or upon recruitment of a new employee. The following relocation costs are allowable:

- advance trips by employee and/or spouse to locate living quarters;
- canceling an unexpired lease;
- closing costs to sell the employee's residence (i.e., appraisal, broker, financing, and legal fees, and points), up to 14 percent of the sales price;
- costs of family and personnel movements of a special or mass nature;
- home acquisition costs in the new work location for previous homeowners only, up to five percent of the purchase price;
- increased employee income or Federal Insurance Contributions Act taxes incident to allowable reimbursed relocation costs;
- mortgage interest differential payments for previous homeowners only;
- mortgage title insurance policy if the employee had a policy in the former home;
- ownership costs of a vacant residence (e.g., maintenance of building and grounds, mortgage interest, property insurance, taxes, and utilities) after the settlement or lease date of a new permanent residence, up to 14 percent of the sales price;
- relocation expenses (e.g., automobile registration, cutting and fitting rugs and draperies, (dis)connecting household appliances, driver's license and use taxes, forfeited utility fees and deposits, and insurance premiums for loss or damage to personal property);
- rental differential payments when retaining ownership in the old location and renting at the new location;
- spouse employment assistance;
- temporary lodging during the transition period for the employee and immediate family; and
- travel of the employee, immediate family members, and household and personal effects to the new location.

To be allowable, moving costs must be for the benefit of the employer and in accordance with its established policy or practice designed to motivate employees to relocate promptly and economically. The moving costs must be incurred to find a new home, travel to the new location (but not to transport household goods) and furnish temporary lodging, and cannot exceed the employee's actual expenses. No other costs to acquire a home in the new location will be recognized, such as brokers' fees and commissions, litigation, mortgage life insurance, operating or maintenance costs, property insurance against damage or loss, and property taxes. The Government will not recognize continuing mortgage principal payments on a residence being sold, or any loss on sale of a home. Likewise, the Government will not recognize furnishing equity loans to employees or arranging with lenders for employees to obtain below-market rate mortgage loans.

If relocation costs for an employee have been allowed and the employee resigns within 12 months for reasons within the employee's control, the contractor refunds or credits the relocation costs to the Government. Companies may in turn impose this same policy on their employees.

4.3.32 Rental Costs

FAR 31.205-36

Rental costs under operating leases are allowable. Rental costs under a sale and leaseback arrangement are limited to the net book value of the asset on the lease date, adjusted for any gain or loss. Rental charges for property between any divisions or subsidiaries are allowable up to the annual ownership costs as of the valuation date, excluding any unfunded actuarial liability.

4.3.33 Royalties and Other Patent Use Costs

FAR 31.205-37

Royalties or amortization of patent cost or rights for the contract are allowable unless the Government has a license or the right to free use of the patent. Costs are unallowable if the patent is expired, invalid or unenforceable. A royalty for a patent formerly owned by the contractor cannot exceed the cost which would have been allowed had the contractor retained title.

4.3.34 Selling Costs

FAR 31.205-38

Direct selling efforts are those acts or actions to induce particular customers to purchase particular products or services of the contractor. Direct selling is characterized by person-to-person contact and familiarizing a potential customer with the contractor's products or services, conditions of sale, service capabilities, etc. It also includes individual demonstrations, liaison, negotiation, technical and consulting discussions, and any other efforts intended to apply or adapt the contractor's products or services to a particular customer's use. The cost of these direct selling efforts is allowable.

Sellers' or agents' compensation, fees, commissions, percentages, retainers or brokerage fees are allowable only when paid to bona fide employees or established commercial or selling agencies.

4.3.35 Service and Warranty Costs

FAR 31.205-39

Allowable service and warranty costs include installation, refunds for inadequate performance, repair of product defects, replacing defective parts, and training.

4.3.36 Special Tooling and Special Test Equipment Costs

FAR 31.205-40

The cost of special tooling and test equipment is allowable and allocated to the specific Government contract or contracts for which acquired. Special tooling includes items such as dies, fixtures, gauges, and molds that can only be used (unless greatly modified) for development or production of particular items or parts. Special test equipment is designed to assess interconnected and interdependent items or assemblies. The cost of items acquired by the contractor before the effective date of the contract, and items which the contract schedule specifically excludes, are allowable only as depreciation or amortization. The cost of adapting the items for use under the contract and returning them to their prior configuration is also allowable.

4.3.37 Taxes

FAR 31.205-41

Federal, State and local taxes paid or accrued in accordance with GAAP are allowable. If the contracting officer directs the contractor not to pay a given tax for any reason, then interest or penalties incurred by the contractor for non-payment is allowable. However, the following taxes are not allowable:

- accruals for the differences between taxable income and pretax income;
- excise tax (e.g., qualified pension plans, welfare plans, and deferred compensation plans);

- Federal income and excess profits taxes;
- financing, refinancing, refunding operations, or reorganizations;
- real or personal property (including possession, sales, usage, or value taxes) used solely in connection with nongovernment contracts;
- special land assessments that represent capital improvements; and
- taxes where exemptions are available to the contractor.

Property taxes must directly apply to the respective work category to be allowable, except for insignificant amounts or if comparable results would otherwise be obtained. Tax or penalty refunds that were previously allowed must be remitted to the Government.

4.3.38 Termination Costs

FAR 31.205-42

The costs of items which are usable on other contract work are only allowable if the contractor submits evidence that the items could not be retained at cost without sustaining a loss (e.g., contemporaneous purchases of common items by the contractor).

Costs which cannot be discontinued immediately after the effective date of termination are generally allowable, unless due to negligent or willful failure of the contractor to discontinue the costs.

Starting load costs are also recognized. They result from inexperienced labor (such as spoilage and subnormal production and techniques) and training. Unless fully absorbed because of termination, these costs are allowable as nonrecurring labor, material and related overhead costs.

Initial plant rearrangement and alterations, personnel organization and production planning costs are allowable. Loss of useful value of special equipment, machinery and tooling is generally allowable if not capable of use in other work. However, title must be transferred to the Government if the contracting officer requests. Loss of acquisition cost is limited to the percentage of contract value terminated.

Rental costs under unexpired leases less residual value are generally allowable if the contractor makes all reasonable efforts to assign, reduce, settle, or terminate the lease. The cost of alterations and restorations required by the lease may be allowed.

Accounting, clerical, and legal costs are allowable to prepare and present settlement claims to the contracting officer. This includes protection, storage, transportation, and disposition of property acquired or produced for the contract. Indirect costs related to salary and wages are limited to fringe benefits, occupancy, payroll taxes, and supervision costs.

Subcontractor claims are generally allowable. A share of the contractor's indirect expense may be allocated to the subcontractor claim, but not claimed as settlement expenses.

4.3.39 Trade, Business, Technical, and Professional Activity Costs

FAR 31.205-43

Memberships in these organizations are allowable, as are subscriptions to their periodicals. Also allowable are certain costs of a conference, convention, meeting, seminar, or symposium to disseminate business, professional, technical or trade information or stimulate production or productivity. Allowable costs include attendance, organization, rental of meeting facilities, setup, sponsorship, subsistence, transportation, and travel costs by contractor employees. Also allowable is attendance by non-employees if they are not reimbursed by the employing company or organization and the individual's attendance is essential to the event.

4.3.40 Training and Education Costs

FAR 31.205-44

Costs of training and education related to the field in which the employee is working are generally allowable, including contributions to college savings plans for employee dependents. However, the following costs are unallowable:

- contributions to college savings plans for employee dependents;
- grants to educational or training institutions, including donation of facilities, fellowships and scholarships;
- overtime compensation for training and education;
- payments for full-time graduate education (e.g., fees, materials and textbooks, subsistence, salary, and tuition) after two school years;
- salary cost for attending undergraduate level classes or part-time graduate level classes during working hours, except when unusual circumstances do not permit attendance outside of regular working hours; and
- training or education costs for non-employees, except for employee dependents in a foreign country where public education is not available (these costs may be included in overseas differential pay).

4.3.41 Travel Costs

FAR 31.205-46

Costs incurred by contractor personnel on official company business are allowable and may be based on mileage rates and/or actual costs incurred. Costs for lodging, meals, and incidentals may be based on actual expenses and/or maximum per diem rates set forth in DoD's *Joint Travel Regulations*.[7]

Higher amounts must be approved by an officer of the contractor's organization per established practice, and all expenditures over $75 must be supported by receipt. Contracting officer approval is necessary if this is done on a continual basis. Airfare costs above the lowest-priced rates are only allowable when avoiding excessive delays or physical impact to the traveler. So a more expensive direct flight to make a meeting is allowable, as is a first-class ticket for a physically challenged passenger. Costs of contractor-owned or -leased automobiles (including lease, operation, maintenance, depreciation, insurance) are allowable.

4.3.42 Legal and Other Proceedings Costs

FAR 31.205-47

Legal costs are incurred before, during and after a judicial or administrative proceeding which bears a direct relationship to the proceeding. They include accountants or consultants retained by the contractor, administrative and clerical expenses, employee and director salaries, and legal services (either in-house or private counsel).

Costs incurred in connection with any government proceeding or investigation for violation of or failure to comply with law or regulation are unallowable if the result is a finding of contractor liability with penalty. Should the proceeding result in a consent agreement or compromise between the contractor and United States, such costs are allowable as agreed to between the parties. Costs incurred in an action brought under the False Claims Act by a third party that would have failed on its merits are allowable.

Up to 80 percent of legal costs are allowable if an action is brought by a state, local or foreign government due to a Federal contract's terms and conditions, or by specific written direction of the cognizant contracting officer. This reflects the *Boyle Rule*, which allows a Government contractor to escape liability from state law that conflicts with a unique federal interest, provided the contractor conformed to precise contract specifications approved by the Federal Government, and warned the Government of potential damages.[8]

The following actions will create legal costs that are unallowable:

- defense of suits for antitrust claims or the False Claims Act, or brought by employees or ex-employees of the contractor, any Government entity on any level, or a whistleblower complaint, where the contractor was found liable or settled;
- defense or prosecution against Federal Government claims or protests;
- lawsuits or appeals between contractors arising from joint or teaming arrangement, dual sourcing or coproduction (unless in accordance with the contract or agreed to in writing by the contracting officer);
- organization, reorganization or resisting mergers and acquisitions;
- patent infringement litigation; or
- representing or assisting groups, individuals or legal entities convicted of violating a law or regulation, or found liable in a civil or administrative proceeding.

Legal costs which may be unallowable are segregated and separately accounted for by the contractor. The contracting officer generally withholds payment of such costs until the legal proceeding is concluded.

4.3.43 Goodwill

FAR 31.205-49

Goodwill is an unidentifiable intangible asset arising during a business combination when the price paid by the acquiring company exceeds the fair value sum of identifiable individual assets acquired, less liabilities assumed. Any costs for amortization, expensing, write-off, or write-down of goodwill are unallowable.

4.3.44 Costs of Alcoholic Beverages

FAR 31.205-51

Costs of alcoholic beverages are unallowable.

4.3.45 Contracts with Nonprofit Entities

OMB Circular A-21, Cost Principles for Educational Institutions, provides rules to determine the costs for research and development, training, and other work performed by educational institutions under contracts with the Government. OMB Circular A-122, Cost Principles for Nonprofit Organizations sets forth all principles to determine the costs applicable to work performed by nonprofit organizations under contracts and grants with the Government.

These nonprofit organizations exist for charity, education, or science instead of private gain.

FAR 31.6

OMB Circular A-87, Cost Principles for State and Local Governments, Revised, provides principles to determine allowable contract and subcontract costs with State, local and Indian tribal governments. The following costs are unallowable:

- advertising designed to promote the contractor or its products;
- alcoholic beverages;
- civil, criminal or administrative proceedings commenced by the United States or a state;
- commercial insurance that protects against the costs to correct the contractor's own defects in materials or workmanship;
- contributions or donations;
- defense of any civil or criminal fraud proceeding brought by the United States where the contractor is found liable or pleads *nolo contendere* to a charge of fraud;
- entertainment, amusement, diversion, and social activities;
- fines and penalties resulting from violations of, or failure to comply with, laws and regulations, unless incurred to comply with contract terms and conditions or written instructions from the contracting officer;
- influencing legislative action before Congress or a state legislature;
- membership in any dining or social organization, including a country club;
- payment to an employee in excess of normal severance pay upon termination of employment (also known as a *golden parachute* payment) after a change in management control over the firm or assets;
- promotional items such as gifts, memorabilia, models, and souvenirs;
- severance pay to foreign nationals under a service contract performed outside the United States which exceeds the customary or prevailing practice for firms in that industry providing similar services in the United States. This also applies if employment termination of the foreign national is due to the closing or curtailment of activities at a United States facility;
- tickets to shows or sports events;
- travel by commercial aircraft which exceeds the standard commercial fare; and
- travel costs such as gratuities, lodging, meals, rentals, and transportation.

4.3.46 External Restructuring Costs

DFARS 231.205-70

Restructuring activities are nonroutine or nonrecurring activities which combine facilities, operations or workforce to eliminate redundant capabilities, improve operations and reduce overall costs. They do not include routine redeployments of productive facilities or workforce, nor do they include other routine expenses such as planning and analysis, or administration and financial support. Some restructuring activities occur after a business combination where assets or operations of two or more companies not previously under common ownership or control are combined by acquisition, merger or sale/purchase of assets. These external restructuring activities affect the operations of two or more companies not previously under common ownership or control, usually within three years of the combination.

Restructuring costs that may be allowed include severance pay for employees, early retirement incentive payments for employees, employee retraining costs, relocation expense for retained employees, and relocation and rearrangement of plant and equipment. However, an audit must first be performed of projected restructuring costs and restructuring savings (cost reductions, not reassignments to future accounting periods), including both direct and indirect cost reductions, which result from restructuring activities. The cognizant ACO reviews the audit report and the projected costs and projected savings, looking for assurance that the audited projected savings, on a present value basis, for DoD resulting from the restructuring will exceed either the costs allowed by a factor of at least two to one, or else the costs allowed and the business combination will result in preserving a critical capability that might otherwise be lost to DoD. If the amount of restructuring costs is expected to exceed $25 million over a five-year period, the USD(AT&L), Principal Deputy or an Assistant Secretary of Defense must determine these findings in writing. If the costs are between $2.5 and $25 million, the Director of DCMA is the determining official. If costs associated with external restructuring activities allocated to DoD contracts are less than $2.5 million, they are not subject to the audit, review and determination requirements and instead, the normal rules for determining cost allowability apply.

Information needed to obtain a determination includes the:

- audit report;
- contractor's restructuring proposal;
- novation agreement (if one is required); and
- proposed advance agreement.

Upon completion of analysis and written determination, the ACO will negotiate an advance agreement. The procuring contracting officer may wish to consider including a repricing clause in noncompetitive fixed-price contracts that are negotiated during the period between the date a business combination is announced, and the date the contractor's forward pricing rates are adjusted to reflect the impact of restructuring. This decision is a function of timing of the restructuring, contract performance period, reasonableness of the estimated impact of restructuring on the contract and size of the potential dollar impact of restructuring on the contract. Any repricing clause must provide for a downward-only price adjustment to ensure that DoD receives its appropriate share of restructuring net savings.

4.3.47 Counterfeit Electronic Parts

DFARS 231.205-71

The costs of counterfeit electronic parts and suspect counterfeit electronic parts, including rework or corrective action required to remedy their use or inclusion, are unallowable. The only exceptions are if the contractor has an operational system to detect and avoid real or suspected counterfeit electronic parts that has been reviewed and approved by DoD and the parts are Government-furnished property, or else the parts were obtained by the contractor in accordance with DFARS 252.246-7008, Sources of Electronic Parts. Moreover, the contractor must become aware of the apparent counterfeiting through authentication efforts such as inspection or testing by itself or its subcontractors, or through a Government Industry Data Exchange Program (GIDEP) alert. It must provide written notice within 60 days after the contractor becomes aware to the contracting officer(s) and GIDEP unless it is a foreign corporation or partnership with no presence or fiscal paying agent in the United States, or the counterfeit electronic part is the subject of an ongoing criminal investigation.

4.3.48 Institutions of Higher Learning

DFARS 231.303

The National Defense Authorization Act for Fiscal Year 1994 prohibits any limitation on reimbursing otherwise allowable indirect costs incurred by an institution of higher education under a DoD contract unless that same limitation is applied uniformly to all other organizations performing similar work under DoD contracts.[9] The 26 percent limitation imposed on administrative indirect costs by OMB Circular No. A-21 does not apply to institutions of higher education because the same limitation is not applied to other organizations performing similar work.

The cognizant administrative contracting officer may waive this prohibition if the governing body of the institution of higher education requests the waiver to simplify the institution's overall management of cost reimbursements under DoD contracts.

4.4 COST ACCOUNTING STANDARDS

FAR 30

Public Law 100-679 requires that the policies and procedures to apply the Cost Accounting Standards Board (CASB) rules and regulations apply to negotiated contracts and subcontracts with large businesses.[10] Whereas cost principles determine *what* costs are allowable, cost accounting standards dictate *how* costs are accumulated and allocated. A firm which only contracts on a firm-fixed-price basis does not need to comply with CASB. However, any large firm using a more flexibly priced contract does. Unlike cost principles, small businesses are exempt from compliance with cost accounting standards.

CASB is established to promote uniform accounting procedures and cost treatment by contractors. It is not affiliated with the Financial Accounting Standards Board, which develops generally accepted accounting practices for commercial firms. The CASB is chaired by OFPP and has representatives from Defense Contract Audit Agency (DCAA), GSA, industry, and the private sector. The Cost Accounting Standards (CAS) issued by CASB are shown in table 4.3. Applicability of CAS rules and regulations is governed by a CAS clause in the contract and the requirements of the standards themselves.

The contractor develops a *Disclosure Statement*, a written description of a contractor's cost accounting practices and procedures. Completed Disclosure Statements are required for any business unit that receives a CAS-covered (sub)contract of $50 million or more (for educational institutions, the threshold is $25 million). A separate Disclosure Statement is submitted for each segment whose costs included in any CAS-covered (sub)contract exceed $650,000, unless the (sub)contract is exempted or the segment's CAS-covered awards are less than 30 percent of total segment sales and less than $10 million.

Federal agencies assign a contacting officer to determine if a Disclosure Statement has adequately disclosed the practices required to be disclosed by CASB rules and Standards. In the case of a contractor that has no product divisions, the term means that contractor as a whole. This contracting officer determines when a proposed contract may require CAS coverage and ensures

Table 4.3 Cost Accounting Standards

CAS Number	*CAS Title*
401	Consistency in Estimating, Accumulating, and Reporting Costs
402	Consistency in Allocating Costs Incurred for the Same Purpose
403	Allocation of Home Office Expenses to Segments
404	Capitalization of Tangible Assets
405	Accounting for Unallowable Costs
406	Cost Accounting Period
407	Use of Standard Costs for Direct Material and Direct Labor
408	Accounting for Costs of Compensated Personal Absence
409	Depreciation of Tangible Capital Assets
410	Allocation of Business Unit General and Administrative Expenses to Final Cost Objectives
411	Accounting for Acquisition Costs of Material
412	Composition and Measurement of Pension Cost
413	Adjustment and Allocation of Pension Cost
414	Cost of Money as an Element of the Cost of Facilities Capital
415	Accounting for the Cost of Deferred Compensation
416	Accounting for Insurance Costs
417	Cost of Money as an Element of the Cost of Capital Assets under Construction
418	Allocation of Direct and Indirect Costs
419	Reserved (not in use)
420	Accounting for Independent Research and Development and Bid and Proposal Costs

that Disclosure Statements have been submitted and audited to verify compliance with CAS and cost principles. Either party may submit amendments and revisions to Disclosure Statements at any time, along with a general dollar magnitude or detailed cost impact proposal. Revisions could be due to an accounting system or CAS change, and could result in a net cost benefit to the Government. The assigned contracting officer reviews proposed changes for adequacy and materiality, and has the right to review ledger books and accounting records. Any decision of noncompliance must be returned to the contractor within 15 days, after which it has 60 days for rebuttal. The process to approve a request often takes longer.

To change a cost accounting practice or disclosure statement, the contractor submits a written description of the change at least 60 days before implementation. If the description is adequate and compliant, the contracting officer requests the contractor to submit a general dollar magnitude proposal of the estimated overall impact in cost accounting practice on affected CAS-covered contracts and subcontracts awarded based on the previous cost accounting practice, or the fiscal year(s) in which the costs are incurred. The parties then negotiate any cost or price adjustments. If the request is denied, the change may be implemented unilaterally.

The contractor or higher tier subcontractor is responsible for administering the CAS requirements contained in subcontracts.

The head of the agency may waive the applicability of CAS for a particular (sub)contract, and may delegate this waiver authority to the senior contract policymaking level. The (sub)contract value must be less than $15 million, and the firm must be primarily engaged in the sale of commercial items with no (sub)contracts that are subject to CAS.

FAR Appendix B—9903.201

The following categories of (sub)contracts are exempt from all CAS requirements:

- contractors or business units not currently performing any CAS-covered (sub)contracts valued at $7.5 million or greater;
- firm-fixed-priced and fixed-price with economic price adjustment contracts and subcontracts for commercial items;
- firm-fixed-price (sub)contracts awarded on the basis of adequate price competition without submission of cost or pricing data;
- foreign governments or their agents;
- foreign subcontractors under the NATO PHM Ship program if performance outside the United States negotiated contracts and subcontracts not in excess of $650,000;
- prices set by law or regulation;
- sealed bid contracts; and
- small businesses.

Full coverage requires that the business unit comply with all CAS in effect on the date of the contract award and with any CAS that become applicable because of subsequent award of a CAS-covered contract. Full coverage applies to contractor business units that receive a CAS-covered award of at least $50 million, or received at least $50 million in net CAS-covered awards during its preceding cost accounting period.

Modified CAS coverage may be applied to a covered contract below the monetary thresholds for full coverage. Modified CAS coverage requires only that the contractor comply with the standards for:

- 401—Consistency in Estimating, Accumulating, and Reporting Costs;
- 402—Consistency in Allocating Costs Incurred for the Same Purpose;
- 405—Accounting for Unallowable Costs; and
- 406—Cost Accounting Period.

Once a business entity receives a contract with modified coverage, all CAS-covered contracts awarded to that business unit during that cost accounting period must also have modified coverage until it receives a $50 million award, in which case both the award and all subsequent contracts will be subject to full CAS coverage. However, no current contract is upgraded from modified to full coverage.

Coverage for educational institutions applies to business units that receive negotiated contracts in excess of $650,000; however FFRDCs operated by an educational institution are subject to the full or modified CAS coverage.

Subcontracts subject to CAS require the same type of CAS coverage as would prime contracts awarded to the same business unit.

Contracts with foreign concerns are only subject to Standards 401: Consistency in Estimating, Accumulating, and Reporting Costs; and 402: Consistency in Allocating Costs Incurred for the Same Purpose.

The head of an executive agency may waive CAS applicability for a (sub) contract with a value of less than $15 million upon written determination that the business unit would not otherwise be subject to CAS, or when necessary to meet the needs of the agency.

Within 15 days of receiving a report of alleged CAS noncompliance from the auditor, the contracting officer either notifies the auditor of disagreement stating the reasons for same, or else issues a notice of potential noncompliance to the contractor, allowing 60 days for the contractor to agree or submit rationale of immateriality. The contracting officer reviews the contractor's response and notifies both the contractor and auditor in writing of the determination of compliance or noncompliance.

Naturally, there are several criticisms of CAS. The contractor may in fact be compelled to use different methods for commercial and Government business. Most standards were unilaterally developed by the Government with limited industry input. Often expensive to implement, CAS arguably reflects Government intervention in contractor business management, and may encourage firms to leave the Government supplier base.

DFARS 230.201-5

The military departments and the Director, DPAP, may grant a waiver upon determination that the property or services cannot reasonably be obtained under the (sub)contract or modification without granting the waiver, the price can be determined to be fair and reasonable without the application of the Cost Accounting Standards, and there are demonstrated benefits to granting the waiver. The military departments shall not delegate Cost Accounting Standards waiver authority below the individual responsible for issuing contracting policy for the department.

DFARS 242.7502

The cognizant contracting officer, in consultation with the auditor or functional specialist, determines the acceptability of a contractor's accounting system who receives flexibly-priced contracts and approve or disapprove the system and pursue correction of any deficiencies.

The auditor will document findings and recommendations in a report to the contracting officer. If there are no significant deficiencies, the contracting officer promptly notifies the contractor in writing that the accounting system is acceptable and approved. If the contracting officer finds that there are one or more significant deficiencies due to the contractor's failure to meet one or more criteria, the contracting officer will provide the contractor a written description of each significant deficiency in sufficient detail to allow the contractor to understand the deficiency. The contacting officer will request a written response within 30 days, evaluate the contractor's response to the initial determination, and make a final determination. The contracting office will then notify the contractor in writing either hat the accounting system is acceptable and approved or that significant deficiencies remain and indicate the adequacy of any proposed or completed corrective action. The contracting officer provides the contractor 45 days to either correct the deficiencies or submit an acceptable corrective action plan showing milestones and actions to eliminate the deficiencies. The contracting officer can also disapprove the system or withhold payments. Once the contractor resolves any deficiencies, the contracting officer will approve the accounting system.

The contracting officer responsible for negotiation of a proposal generated by an accounting system with an identified deficiency must evaluate whether the deficiency impacts the negotiations. If it does, the contracting officer should consider other alternatives, such as allowing the contractor additional time to correct the accounting system deficiency and submit a corrected proposal, consider another type of contract, use additional cost analysis techniques to determine the reasonableness of the affected cost elements, reduce the negotiation objective for profit or fee, or include a contract (reopener) clause that provides for adjustment of the contract amount after award. Any reopener clause necessitated by an accounting system deficiency should identify the amounts and items that are in question at the time of negotiation, indicate a specific time or subsequent event by which the contractor will submit a supplemental proposal, including certified cost or pricing data, identifying the cost impact adjustment necessitated by the deficient accounting system, provide for the contracting officer to adjust the contract price unilaterally if the contractor fails to submit the supplemental proposal and provide that failure of the Government and the contractor to agree to the price adjustment shall be a dispute under the Disputes clause.

PGI 242.75

Within 10 days of receiving the report, if the contracting officer makes a determination that there is a significant deficiency, the contracting officer should provide an initial determination of deficiencies and a copy of the report to the contractor and require the contractor to submit a written response. Within 30 days of receiving the contractor's response, the contracting officer, in consultation with the auditor or cognizant functional specialist, should evaluate the contractor's response and make a final determination.

In the event that a contractor's accounting system contains deficiencies, even if disapproved, a cost reimbursement contract is not prohibited if the contracting officer determines that the contractor's accounting system is adequate for determining costs applicable to the contract or order.

A couple of specific standards need additional explanation. CAS 409 alters accounting depreciation of plant and equipment to be based on expected service life. Like IRS regulations, it permits assets to be combined and depreciated as a group, derives a service life based on past experience, and allows changes in expected usefulness. Unlike IRS regulations however, the estimated service life must be used and recorded, and the depreciation method must reflect a pattern of consumption of services to be provided.

CAS 414 recognizes the cost of money required for facilities capital investments, which are not otherwise recognized as allowable or as a profit factor. DoD specifically recognizes this as an allowable cost but also as a profit setoff. However, only contractors with heavy facilities investment benefit from this process. Reimbursement rates are based on age and value of contractor assets. Calculations do not consider the source of contractor financing (whether borrowed or equity) and does not reimburse interest expense because it is treated as an imputed expense based on the prevailing Treasury rate.

FAR 30.603–605

Offerors state in their proposal whether contract award requires a change to an established cost accounting practice affecting existing (sub)contracts. They will then submit a description of the changed cost accounting practice as pricing support for the proposal.

Solicitation Provisions

FAR 52.230-1, Cost Accounting Standards Notices and Certification.

FAR 52.230-7, Proposal Disclosure—Cost Accounting Practice Changes.

Solicitation Provision and Contract Clause

DFARS 252.242-7006, Accounting System Administration, when contemplating a cost-reimbursement, incentive type, time-and-materials, or labor-hour contract, or with progress payments made on the basis of costs incurred by the contractor or on a percentage or stage of completion.

Contract Clauses

FAR 52.230-2, Cost Accounting Standards, unless the contract is exempted or subject to modified coverage.

FAR 52.230-3, Disclosure and Consistency of Cost Accounting Practices, if over $750,000 but less than $50 million, and the offeror certifies it is eligible for and elects to use modified CAS coverage.

FAR 52.230-4, Disclosure and Consistency of Cost Accounting Practices for Contracts Awarded to Foreign Concerns, with foreign concerns (not including foreign governments or their agents), unless the contract is otherwise exempt from CAS. FAR 52.230-2 and -3 are not included in these contracts.

FAR 52.230-5, Cost Accounting Standards—Educational Institution, if awarded to educational institutions, unless the contract is exempted or performed by an FFRDC.

FAR 52.230-6, Administration of Cost Accounting Standards, except for contracts which do not contain FAR 52.230-2, 3, 4, and 5.

DFARS 252.231-7000, Supplemental Cost Principles, when subject to the principles and procedures, except for educational institutions.

4.5 COST PROPOSAL

FAR 15.408

FAR Table 15-2—Instructions for Submitting Cost/Price Proposals When Cost or Pricing Data Are Required, provides instructions to prepare a pricing proposal when cost or pricing data are required. The offeror submits cost or pricing data that are verifiable and factual to explain the estimating process, including judgmental factors and mathematical or other methods used in the estimate, and those used to project from known data. It also discusses the nature and amount of any contingencies included in the proposed price. The offeror shows the relationship between contract line item prices and the total contract price, and attaches cost-element breakdowns for each proposed line item. When more than one contract line item is proposed, summary total amounts covering all line items for each element of cost are included. The proposal identifies any incurred costs for work performed before proposal submission.

Use of forward pricing rates/factors negotiated with the Government is described in the proposal. Contracting officers use forward pricing rates for pricing all contracts, modifications and other contractual actions to be performed during the period covered by the agreement. These agreements with major Federal contractors or offerors reflect current and complete cost or pricing data to establish rates to price out proposals. They can be cancelled by either party at any time. Certification is not required at the time of agreement for data supplied in support of advance agreements.

If the offeror intends to subcontract more than 70 percent of the total cost, it must identify the amount of its indirect costs and profit/fee applicable to the subcontracted effort, and describe the added value it provides to the subcontracted effort. The same requirements apply to any subcontractor proposing to send more than 70 percent of its effort to lower-tier subcontractor(s). In this case, the contracting officer must investigate whether direct contracting with one or more subcontractors is feasible. If not, (s)he prepares a written D&F to the file.

The proposal must include both direct and indirect costs associated with the proposed effort. *Direct costs* (or *prime costs*) are traced logically and entirely to a final cost objective (e.g., job or contract), such as direct labor or material. This reflects the matching concept in accounting theory that aligns expenses with the revenue they generate. After direct costs have been determined and charged appropriately, *indirect costs* are those remaining to be allocated to intermediate or multiple final cost objectives. Indirect costs cannot be identified with just one final cost objective and are therefore collected into *cost centers* or expense pools. At the end of the accounting period, they are allocated based on logical and causal relationships that reflect the department responsible for their incurrence. The logic here is that the department would not have incurred the expense if it did not wish to receive the benefit.

DAG: Source Selection Procedures, 3.12.3

The cost proposal should discuss:

- all intermediate cost pools and provide a reconciliation to show where the costs will be allocated;
- corporate, home office, shared services, or other incoming allocated costs and the source for those costs, including location and point of contact (custodian) name, phone number, and email address;
- cost of money factors submitted on Form CASB-CMF must include net book value of assets, comparison of prior forecasted costs to actual results, and a summary of changes or the facts requiring a rate change;

- details of the development of the allocation base;
- explanation of how the trend and budgetary data, as well as any adjustments to the data, were used;
- explanation of the estimating processes and methods used for proposed costs based on judgmental factors, including those used in projecting from known data;
- how the proposed allocation bases reconcile with its long-range plans, strategic plan, operating budgets, sales forecasts, program budgets, etc.;
- indirect expenses identified by burden center, by cost element, by year (including any voluntary deletions, if applicable) in a format that is consistent with the accounting system used to accumulate actual expenses;
- known or anticipated changes in business activities or processes that could materially impact the proposed rates, such as management initiatives to reduce costs or changes due to economic conditions and increased competitiveness; changes in accounting policies and procedures including reclassification of expenses from direct to indirect or vice versa, new methods of accumulating and allocating indirect costs and the related impact, and advance agreements; company reorganizations (including acquisitions or divestitures); facility shutdown; and changes in business volume and/or contract mix/type;
- planned or anticipated changes in the nature, type, or level of indirect costs, including fringe benefits;
- supporting data for the allocation base such as program budgets, negotiation memoranda, proposals, contract values, etc.;
- the basis of each estimate and provide an explanation of the methodology used to develop the indirect rates;
- the escalation factors used to escalate indirect costs for the out-years, the costs to which escalation is applicable, and the basis of each factor used; and
- the location of the supporting documents for the proposed rates.

The offeror must provide in the cost proposal breakdowns for the following basic cost elements, along with any profit or fee dollars.

4.5.1 Direct Material

Material costs are frequently spelled out in a *bill of materials* that describes and quantifies by listing all items necessary to fabricate the final end-item. Each item on the list includes a part number and name or similar identification, required quantity per unit and in total, unit price, and extended cost (quantity multiplied by unit price). This list draws from engineering drawings and specifications. Raw material quantities should allow for scrap, shrinkage, and spoilage factors due to manufacturing operations and errors. Shrinkage should drop as processes become more automated, although some material will still be wasted as machine tolerances are set up and tested. Contractors might propose a separate obsolescence factor since this results from technological progress rather than process mistakes. Cost or price analysis is required for all subcontracts and included with the offeror's cost or pricing data submissions.

Material can be issued from stock using either a First-In-First-Out (FIFO) or Last-In-First-Out (LIFO) method. For most firms, the actual flow of materials follows FIFO, where the oldest items are sold first while newer items are kept in stock. If costs are increasing, the first items sold are therefore the least expensive, so the cost of goods sold decreases, thereby increasing profits (and income taxes). Under LIFO, the newer items are more expensive, so as the cost of goods sold increases, both profits and income taxes decrease. Of course, if costs are decreasing, the opposite effects occur.

Material costs consist of four different types. *Raw material* includes the purchase of any substance that is transformed during manufacture into a different form, such as aluminum, bar stock or solder. Raw material quantity estimates must allow for scrap and shrinkage incurred during production. Parts may be consumed during trial-and-error testing during machine setup. Machine tolerance and sheet cutting may create unusable overage and hence scrap. In the case of a contractor that has no product divisions, the term means that contractor as a whole. Material shrinkage may be present as a result of machine tolerance and level of automation in the shop, as well as evolving automation and technology. The proposal should include these considerations in the form of percentage allowance factors when developing individual material quantities and the basis for pricing (e.g., vendor quotes and invoice prices) for items and services procured from subcontractors.

Purchased parts are standard commercial items listed in a vendor catalog or price list and built to the supplier's specifications. This would include such common hardware as fasteners, integrated circuitry, printing supplies, reducers and capacitors, and wire. The subcontractor is therefore responsible for any design flaws. They are often listed and priced in a vendor's catalog. If they prove defective during contract performance, the subcontractor bears the responsibility to remedy the problem at its own cost.

Subcontracted items are bought from vendors based on the buyer's specifications, often made to order rather than pulled from stock. These are usually precision and costly assemblies and components. If they prove defective, the buyer bears the responsibility for correction and may need to fund any rework out of its own pocket. This is another manifestation of the *contra preferentum* concept which we have seen before.

Finally, *interorganizational transfers* consist of work obtained from another division or profit center within the same corporate entity. Also known as *interdepartmental transfers or work authorizations*, they may include profit if they are standard commercial items; otherwise they are transferred at cost (to avoid paying profit on top of profit).

4.5.2 Direct Labor

Direct Labor comprises the hours that will be charged directly to the contract. *Labor* costs are the salaries paid to employees who charge to a given job. Often these are engineers who develop solutions to specific issues on a contract, manufacturing people on the assembly line, or professional and technical personnel who provide services as subject matter experts.

Labor categories may be accrued into several clusters, each to bear its own overhead rate. This occurs when overhead expenses vary widely between clusters. This approach also serves to make services contracts more competitive by eliminating the need to include manufacturing costs that are unrelated to the end objective of a services contract. Common cluster names are engineering, field engineering or onsite support, manufacturing, and quality assurance.

There are several broad categories of *engineering labor*, such as design and sustaining engineering labor, quality assurance, and reliability and maintainability effort. These people have bachelor's or advanced degrees in electrical, industrial or mechanical engineering. Engineers develop drawings with exact dimensions, specify material needs, plan manufacturing labor and machine setup activities, develop visual assembly aids and process sheets. This labor will be higher for new products or those with constant changes due to advances in the state of the art. As the product matures, this effort should diminish.

This category often includes quality assurance labor to develop and perform inspections and tests of assemblies and final products, though some manufacturing firms opt to set up a separate method of allocation for this type of labor. Reliability and maintainability engineers ensure that end products are designed and manufactured to meet longevity requirements and function properly through their life cycles by designing and monitoring testing and training, develop preventive maintenance schedules and work with design engineers to modify designs as necessary. Complexity factors may be applied to past work experience to derive proposed hours. The amount of engineering labor is a function of product complexity and age (state-of-the-art products require much more work than proven products) as well as the manufacturer's technology and previous production experience. Design engineers are paid to turn concepts into drawings and procedures.

They specify the physical characteristics of the product and develop drawings (assemblies and tooling), parts lists, schematics, and technical manuals (installation, repair, training, and users). This may also include engineers that develop reliability and repair documentation, and schedules to ensure maintainability. Engineers must also develop documentation deliverables such as installation instructions, users' guides, training manuals, and provisioning documents.

Proposed hours may be based on assigning individuals to specific work packages, or developing level-of-effort estimates for each package. When estimating hours for such a man-loaded function, the time may be expressed in terms of man-hours, man-days, man-weeks, man-months, or man-years. Sometimes ratios can be developed for engineering-to-manufacturing hours by reviewing payroll records, labor analysis reports or industrial engineering surveys. Line managers and their dedicated administrative personnel also are normally charged directly to the contract they support.

Manufacturing labor includes effort to fabricate parts from raw material, assemble parts or insert them into components, and test an end item. Scrap and spoilage rates are also included here in terms of impacting labor hours. These hours are often estimated based on labor standards, the amount of time that a qualified worker would need to perform the task under capable supervision at a normal pace (known as *leveled time*), allowing for personal fatigue and needs and production delays. The leveled time is based on time studies or work sampling of randomly selected workers (though generally not as accurate as time studies). Manufacturing labor includes employees who assemble components, fabricate parts from raw material, inspect same, operate machines, paint and engrave hardware, and test mechanical equipment and systems.

Manufacturing engineers plan labor activities to produce the item by writing manufacturing instructions and process sheets, workstations, assigning tools and machines, and scheduling production activities.

Some job-shop factories collect costs under a *job order* system against a specific contract or production run. This technique is chosen because the runs are short-term and designed to customer specifications, which makes cost forecasting a difficult task. By contrast, continuous manufacturers and mass producers of a single product use a *process cost* system which collects all costs over an accounting period (usually a month). Costs travel with the product from one process center to another until recorded in the final center.

Labor can be of a recurring nature if the process is identical to that done on prior contracts, or nonrecurring (such as preproduction effort). Actual hours of past effort can be used to project future operations. Sometimes a complexity factor can be used to increase or decrease prior experience to reflect the change in projected workload. Alternatively, labor standards can be developed from historical data and studies.

Quality assurance engineers develop specifications for test equipment and procedures to test the end product for compliance and performance. *Field engineers* support deployed end items through a variety of maintenance and testing tasks.

Sometimes, direct laborers support multiple contracts in the course of a week or month, and therefore may be charging their time to several contracts. Because it is often impossible to predict who will charge how much time to a specific contract, much less track their actual payroll cost to each contract, firms will create *labor categories* of similar labor types and responsibilities in which to accumulate salary expenses. Within a given project or contract, there may be different labor categories. The projected salaries for the upcoming year are averaged out to create an hourly *labor rate* for each category, which is then used to price out labor projections in proposals and to bill for hours incurred on contracts.

The proposal should include a time-phased (e.g., monthly, quarterly, etc.) breakdown of labor hours, rates, and cost by appropriate category, with bases for estimates.

4.5.3 Other Direct Costs

Other direct costs sometimes appear in proposals. These are direct charges which pass through the company's accounting system without bearing any overhead. Examples include:

- computer processing time at a corporate or independent server;
- consultant services;
- federal excise taxes;
- interdivisional transfers from another unit in the corporation;
- preservation, packaging and packing;
- royalties;[11]
- special tooling and test equipment; and
- travel at customer direction (e.g., field engineering and meetings and seminars).

The bases for pricing are included in the proposal. Although really another type of Material, interdivisional transfers do not bear labor overhead and are therefore listed as an Other Direct Cost. The exception is if they are stored with other material in a stockroom, in which case they bear Material Overhead expense and are properly deemed Direct Material.

4.5.4 Overhead

Many costs cannot be specifically tied to a particular contract or product. Hence, they cannot be matched to a single final cost objective. These *indirect costs* are incurred to support direct costs and remain to be allocated to intermediate or multiple final cost objectives. Indirect costs cannot be identified with just one final cost objective and are therefore collected into *cost centers* or expense pools. At the end of the accounting period, they are allocated based on logical and causal relationships that reflect the department responsible for their incurrence. The logic here is that the department would not have incurred the expense if it did not wish to receive the benefit. These cost pools serve as intermediate cost objectives and are then allocated in some consistent manner to final cost objectives, thereby serving the same purpose as if they had been treated as direct costs. Examples of indirect costs include:

- building maintenance and repair;
- depreciation;
- insurance:
  - accident,
  - fire,
  - flood, and
  - personal liability;
- office equipment and furniture;
- rent;
- travel not charged directly to the contract;
- utilities:
  - electricity,
  - fuel,
  - telephone, and
  - water and sewage.

Depreciation requires a definition of what constitutes a capital expense, since one could go crazy depreciating every ballpoint pen or coffee maker in the plant. So most firms use a rule of thumb that they will only capitalize and depreciate major items (usually over $5,000 in purchase price) and expense the smaller-value items to current-year cost centers. In fact, the contractor may treat any small direct cost as an indirect cost if consistently applied to all final cost objectives and resulting in substantially the same results as if it treated the cost as direct.

A *base period* must be established to allocate indirect costs is the timeframe when costs are incurred and accumulated to allocate work performed. This is usually a 12-month period of time coinciding with the contractor's *fiscal year*, the accounting period for which annual financial statements are regularly prepared. The company defines the start and end dates of the fiscal year, which may or may not coincide with the calendar year.

The firm cannot split the overhead base by removing individual elements; all items within the base bear a pro rata share of indirect costs. The allocation method may be revised due to change in the business, extent of subcontracting, fixed-asset improvements, inventory, manufacturing processes, and sales and production volume. The end result is a series of rates to equitably allocate costs. Equitability is important because a pool which is either under- or overabsorbed could cause the firm's competitive posture to suffer. Moreover, indirect costs are harder to control in the short run than direct costs because so many of them are fixed costs in nature.

Indirect rates are established by first estimating the total dollar amount for the year for both the labor or material base and its respective indirect pool. The indirect rate is calculated by dividing the projected pool amount into the projected base amount. This rate is then applied to total labor or material dollars within the proposal to develop an estimated dollar amount of overhead for each pool to be allocated to the specific contract. Hence, each of the direct cost bases bears its own indirect rate.

Material overhead comprises those expenses covering direct material charged to contracts:

- inspection;
- insurance;
- inventory;
- issuance;
- procurement operations;[12]
- receiving; and
- stockroom storage.

This pool includes associated labor costs such as forklift operators, guards and stockroom workers, and their payroll taxes and benefits. It would also include warehouse and loading dock charges and insurance. Scrap sales credits and inventory adjustments are customarily included as well. Receipt and inspection of incoming material and products are additional components of this cost pool. Vendor quality assurance may be included in this cost pool, though some companies will charge it as direct labor. Some companies will include procurement personnel in this cost pool; others will charge them directly to the contract or else include them in a corporate overhead cost pool.

Engineering overhead includes all labor and material costs pertaining to engineering effort which cannot be directly allocated to a specific contract, but rather must be spread across multiple contracts. This usually means supervisory engineer salaries and benefits, plus any engineering material costs.

Manufacturing overhead works on the same principle, applying the manufacturing overhead pool to total direct manufacturing labor dollars to derive a percentage, which is then applied to the proposed manufacturing labor amount to derive the manufacturing overhead amount for the proposal. Again, supervisory labor and material costs are included in this pool, along with employee downtime due to schedule openings. In addition however, plant and property expenses must be included, such as maintenance and utilities personnel (with attached benefits), depreciation, insurance, perishable tooling, rent, small consumable supplies, and taxes. This generally makes for a larger pool than engineering overhead (which includes little or no facilities costs), and often a much higher percentage rate.

Some companies will have a separate pool for *field engineering overhead.* This labor is located at or near a customer site to provide hands-on maintenance and repair and train military users. Because they are not located at the manufacturing or headquarters facility, they will not bear any allocation of facilities or supervisory labor, and will therefore bear a lower overhead rate.

The proposal will include the basis for computing and applying indirect costs, including cost breakdowns. The proposal should also include trends and budgetary data to evaluate the reasonableness of proposed rates.

4.5.5 General and Administrative Expenses

General and Administrative (G&A) expenses are incurred to manage and administer the whole business unit. They are collected in a separate indirect cost pool for allocation to final cost objectives through a G&A base. Examples of G&A costs include:

- accounting;
- bids and proposals;
- computer operations;
- conventions and seminars;
- depreciation;
- entertainment;
- executive management;
- Federal income tax;
- home office;
- human resources;
- independent research and development;
- insurance;
- interest;
- legal;
- memberships and professional society dues;
- office equipment and supplies;
- parking;

- postage;
- printing;
- recruiting;
- relocation;
- rent;
- salaries and benefits;
- sales;
- subscriptions;
- telephone;
- tools;
- training;
- transportation; and
- utilities.

The cost input base to allocate G&A expense includes all elements of the business unit's activity. The cost input base may use a total cost, value-added or single-element method. However, any changes from one type of input base to another due to a business circumstance are subject to equitable adjustment, provided that the contractor has notified the contracting officer of the change.

Total cost is the most common method since it simply adds up all the direct and overhead costs of the business unit. However, the other two methods can be used if a particular final cost objective or contract would receive a disproportionate allocation of G&A expenses by using the total cost input base. This is because the cost accounting standard does not permit the use of an abated or reduced rate for many costs.

Large subcontracts that do not require close supervision by the prime contractor could absorb G&A on a *value-added* base, which includes only labor and its overhead costs and excludes material and subcontract costs. Service contractors with major purchasing and subcontracting responsibility on a pass-through basis could allocate G&A as either the value-added or single-element method. Remember, the offeror must report to the contracting officer whenever more than 70 percent of contract charges are subcontracted, and the contracting officer has the right to disallow such additional charges.

A *single-element* cost input base may be used only when the base dollars are significant. This could occur with a services contractor which has heavy labor costs but very little material expense or other direct costs.

Any work on stock or product inventory items is considered a productive activity and therefore receives a G&A allocation only for the period(s) in which the items are produced or worked on. No additional G&A is applied when these items are finally issued.

Solicitation Provision

FAR 52.215-20, Requirements for Cost or Pricing Data or Information Other Than Cost or Pricing Data, in solicitations if cost or pricing data will be required. This provision also provides instructions to offerors on how to request an exception. The contracting officer uses Alternate forms in the same manner and conditions as FAR 52.215-21.

Solicitation Provisions and Contract Clauses

FAR 52.215-9, Changes or Additions to Make-or-Buy Program, when a make-or-buy program is contemplated for the contract. If a less economical "make" or "buy" categorization is selected for one or more items of significant value, use the clause with Alternate I for a fixed-price incentive contract, or Alternate II for a cost-plus-incentive-fee contract.

FAR 52.215-14, Integrity of Unit Prices, if greater than the simplified acquisition threshold except for:

- commercial items;
- construction or architect-engineer services;
- petroleum products;
- services where supplies are not required; and
- utility services.

Use the clause with its Alternate I when contracting without adequate price competition or when prescribed by agency regulations.

FAR 52.215-19, Notification of Ownership Changes, when cost or pricing data will be required.

FAR 52.215-21, Requirements for Cost or Pricing Data or Information Other Than Cost or Pricing Data—Modifications, if cost or pricing data or other information will probably be required for contract modifications. This clause also provides instructions to contractors on how to request an exception. Use the clause with its Alternate I to specify an alternative format for cost or pricing data. Use the clause with its Alternate II if copies of the proposal are to be sent to the contract administration office and contract auditor. Use the clause with its Alternate III if submission via electronic media is required. Replace the basic clause with its Alternate IV if cost or pricing data are not expected to be required because an exception may apply, but other pricing information is required.

FAR 52.215-22, Limitation on Pass-Through Charges—Identification of Subcontract Effort, for a cost-reimbursement contract over the simplified acquisition threshold.[13]

FAR 52.215-23, Limitations on Pass-Through Charges, when using FAR 52.215-22. Use the clause with its Alternate I when the prospective contractor has demonstrated that its functions provide added value to the contracting effort and there are no excessive pass-through charges.

DFARS 252.215–7014, Exception from Certified Cost or Pricing Data Requirements for Foreign Military Sales Indirect Offsets, when including FAR 52.215–20.

4.6 COST ANALYSIS

4.6.1 Analysis Techniques

FAR 15.404

The contracting officer evaluates the reasonableness of the offered prices. The complexity and circumstances of each acquisition determines the level of detail of analysis required.[14] The objective is to determine if the proposed amount is fair and reasonable. *Fair and reasonable price* is based on current market conditions, fairness to the seller because it covers full costs plus a reasonable profit, and fairness to the buyer based on value and utility.

The purpose of performing cost or price analysis is to develop a negotiation position that permits the contracting officer and the offeror an opportunity to reach agreement on a fair and reasonable price. A fair and reasonable price does not require that agreement be reached on every element of cost, nor is it mandatory that the agreed price be within the contracting officer's initial negotiation position. The contracting officer is responsible for exercising the judgment to reach a negotiated settlement with the offeror and is solely responsible for the final price agreement. However, when significant audit or other specialist recommendations are not adopted, the contracting officer provides rationale to support the result in the price negotiation documentation.

Price analysis is the process of examining and evaluating a proposed price without evaluating its separate cost elements and proposed profit. Analysis techniques include comparisons (more or less in order of preference):

- of proposed prices from all offerors (competition is always the first choice);
- of previous Government and commercial contract prices with current proposed prices for the same or similar items (the preferred technique if no competition exists);
- with prices obtained through market research for the same or similar items;
- with independent Government cost estimates; and
- by parametric estimating methods (e.g., dollars per pound or per horsepower) to highlight inconsistencies that warrant additional pricing inquiry.

The contracting officer can also measure any variance between the actual and standard prices, multiplied by the number of units to be bought. Traditionally, this term applies to direct materials and "rate variance" is used for assessing labor rates.

Except for commercial items, contracting officers require that offerors identify in their proposals those items of supply that they will not manufacture or contribute significant value to, unless adequate price competition is expected. Such information is used to determine whether the intrinsic value of an item was distorted through application of overhead and should be considered for breakout.

Cost analysis is the review and evaluation of the separate cost elements and profit in a proposal and the application of judgment to determine how well the proposed costs represent what the cost of the contract should be, assuming reasonable economy and efficiency. The Government may use various cost analysis techniques and procedures to ensure a fair and reasonable price, including:

- analysis of make-or-buy program reviews to evaluate subcontract costs;
- audited or negotiated indirect cost rates, labor rates and cost of money factors;
- comparison with actual costs previously incurred by the same offeror;
- comparison with previous cost estimates from the same or other offerors for same or similar items;
- evaluating cost necessity allowing for contingencies;
- evaluating the effect of the offeror's current practices on future costs;
- fact-finding sessions in face-to-face meetings with contractor and Government support personnel;
- forecasts of planned expenditures;
- independent Government cost estimates by technical personnel;
- necessity and reasonableness of proposed costs and allowances for contingencies;
- projection of the offeror's cost trends based on current and historical cost or pricing data;
- reasonableness of estimates generated by parametric models or cost-estimating relationships;
- trend analysis of basic labor and materials;
- verification of cost data;
- verification that the offeror's cost submissions are in accordance with the contract cost principles and procedures; and
- whether any cost or pricing data necessary to make the contractor's proposal accurate, complete and current have not been either submitted or identified by the contractor.

The contracting officer's objective is to negotiate a contract type and price that provides the contractor the greatest incentive for economical and efficient performance. Therefore, the contracting officer does not become preoccupied with any single element and should balance the contract type, cost and profit or fee to achieve a total price that is fair and reasonable to both parties. Because profit or fee is only one of several interrelated variables, the contracting officer does not agree on profit or fee without concurrent agreement on cost and type of contract.

Several variations of cost analysis are employed by the Government or higher-tier contractors. *Parametric cost estimating* involves collecting historical cost data and using mathematical and statistical methods to relate to the contemplated work output. An estimating relationship must be derived to connect a physical characteristic of the work output to the cost or labor hours needed to produce it. Examples of these characteristics include power, size, volume, or weight. They can provide a quick estimate even when nothing is known about the work output other than its physical characteristics. Similarly, *cost estimating relationships* compare historical costs with performance or technical characteristics. The danger is that reliance on historical experience could lead to false cost trends. However, these methods can help determine a realistic cost in these days where weapon system overruns are common.

There are other cost analysis methods that can be useful. *Value analysis* objectively and systematically evaluates a product's function to its cost, in an effort to derive the product's inherent worth. *Will cost* is a different technique that evaluates a cost estimate for a future task by the best estimate that uses current methods, historical costs and forecasting future costs.

Cost realism analysis is the process of independently reviewing and evaluating specific elements of the proposed cost estimate to determine whether they are sensible for the work to be performed, reflect a clear understanding of the requirements, and are consistent with the materials and methods of performance described in the offeror's technical proposal. The *probable cost* reflects the Government's best estimate of the most likely cost of the offeror, and is used to determine the best value. The probable cost is determined by adjusting each offeror's proposed cost and fee to reflect any additions or reductions in cost elements to realistic levels based on the results of the cost realism analysis. Cost realism analyses may also be used on competitive fixed-price incentive contracts when new requirements may not be fully understood by competing offerors, or past experience indicates that proposed costs have resulted in quality or service shortfalls.

Except for commercial items, contracting officers require that offerors identify in their proposals those items of supply that they will not manufacture or contribute significant value to, unless adequate price competition is expected. Such information is used to determine whether the intrinsic value of an item was distorted through application of overhead and should be considered for breakout.

Unbalanced pricing may increase performance risk and could result in payment of unreasonably high prices. Unbalanced pricing exists when, despite an acceptable total evaluated price, the price of one or more contract line items is significantly over- or understated. No method to distribute costs to line items may distort unit price. The greatest risks associated with unbalanced pricing occur with separate line items for startup work, mobilization or first articles. Likewise, when base quantities and option quantities are separate line items, or the evaluated price is the aggregate of estimated quantities to be ordered under separate line items of an indefinite-delivery contract, unbalanced pricing may result. An offer may be rejected if the contracting officer determines that the lack of balance poses an unacceptable risk to the Government. Except for adequate price competition or catalog or market price, unit prices must reflect the intrinsic value of an item or service and be proportionate to an item's manufacturing or acquisition costs.

Any proposal exceeding $10 million (fixed-price) or $100 million (cost-plus) will be sent to the local office of DCAA via the cognizant contract administration office for a field pricing report. Consequently, any subcontract proposal exceeding these amounts will be sent out for an assist audit to the DCAA office cognizant of the subcontractor. DCAA will review the cost proposal for consistency, accuracy and rates.

DAG: Source Selection Procedures, 3.1.1

All offers with separately priced line items or subline items shall be analyzed to determine if the prices are unbalanced, meaning that the prices of one or more line items are significantly overstated or understated, despite an acceptable total evaluated price. The contracting officer may reject offers if the lack of balance poses an unacceptable risk to the Government.

When FAR 52.222-46, Evaluation of Compensation for Professional Employees, is included in the contract, the Government evaluates whether an awardee understands the contract requirements and has proposed a compensation plan appropriate for those requirements.

4.6.1.1 Work Breakdown Structure

The proposal for a complex project will include a *work breakdown structure* (WBS) to decompose the project into specific component activities and tasks with their own separate task budgets (e.g., subsystems, subtasks, components, or work packages) into a tree-like structure or hierarchical chart.[15] The WBS is used both to describe the statement of work and to create work packages for the cost proposal.

A work breakdown structure dictionary describes the content of each box in the breakdown, namely task output, requirements from organizational elements, activities, and milestones. The contractor will use the work breakdown structure to:

- complete a cost estimate,
- determine needed experience,
- develop equipment and facilities requirements,
- prepare a technical proposal, and
- schedule resources.

The WBS is based on program products or outcomes rather than inputs or actions. The lowest level of work, that which cannot be further subdivided, is known as a *work package* (sometimes also called a *terminal element*). A work package at any level is a task that can produce a measurable deliverable and be realistically estimated. The task can be completed either in-house or by contract. However, it may not be capable of being broken down any further. This approach permits a limited and stable set of categories to collect costs.

Each program activity is assigned to only one WBS element. All work packages must be designed to be mutually exclusive. No two elements may share any effort, in order to avoid duplication and confusion over responsibility or authority. However, WBS elements can cross-reference to design or functional documents or specifications.

The WBS must cover all the work and deliverables within the scope of the contract, without overlap between work packages. This means that each package should depict a desired outcome or result, without dwelling on actions or methods. Each package must be estimated realistically, not subject to further breakdown, and be measurable and unique.

The specific categories were first established in 1968 with MIL-STD-881C, "Work Breakdown Structures for Defense Materiel Items," and are perpetuated in the associated MIL-HDBK-881A of the same name. The handbook contains instructions, descriptions, templates and several common elements for all systems and subsystems:[16]

- data;
- industrial facilities;
- initial spares and repair parts;

- integration, assembly, test, and checkout;
- operational and site activation;
- program management;
- support equipment;
- system test and evaluation;
- systems engineering; and
- training.

A key tenet of WBS creation is known as the *100% Rule*. It holds that the WBS includes 100 percent of the work within the project scope and 100 percent of all deliverables (both internal and external). This rule is true at all levels of the hierarchy, so all work at the parent level equals the sum of 100 percent of all work among the child sublevels. No work outside of project scope is included in the WBS.

The WBS is broken down several levels through a process of progressive elaboration. The numbering schema for a WBS is the same as used in this book, broken down into successively lower levels (though not usually more than four levels). Less complicated tasks such as project management may only need two levels. Hence, element 2 consists of 2.1 and 2.2, and 2.1 further breaks down into 2.1.1, 2.2.2, and 2.2.3. The greater the level of detail, the more likely that the author will begin to specify the process.

A heuristics rule can help determine the duration of an activity necessary to produce a specific deliverable. The *80 hour rule* limits any activity to produce a single deliverable to 80 hours of effort. Another common rule is that no activity should be longer than a single reporting period, usually monthly. One should always use common sense to create a single activity's duration to produce a deliverable.

A WBS describes project scope. It is not a list of tasks to perform or a schedule to perform to, nor is an organizational chart. It is subject to change control because processes do change over time, which is another reason why it must be outcome-oriented. As a management tool, it can be used to combine the budgets of various cost accounts and higher-level levels of the work breakdown structure, plus any undistributed amounts, to encompass the entire work scope of the program and to develop the program budget. It is a dynamic tool that can be updated as necessary by the program manager to develop and maintain technical, cost and schedule performance and reporting.

4.6.1.2 Direct Material Analysis Techniques

For Material, the analysts would look at:

- bill of material;
- catalog or market prices;

- competition obtained among suppliers;
- duplication of costs;
- effective planning and use of material;
- estimating methods;
- kinds and quantities;
- make-or-buy decisions;
- prior purchase history (quantities and prices);
- price breaks and economic purchase sizes;
- residual inventory;
- shrinkage or scrap factor, compared to industry average and past actuals; and
- subcontractor proposals.

There are several additional considerations when evaluating proposed material costs. Past experience could show that the prime contractor negotiates reductions in subcontractor proposals; if so, then applying an appropriate percentage reduction across-the-board or to specific proposals could be appropriate. Large-dollar proposals are especially appropriate for individual review and price reductions. Quantities should be reviewed by the program office and compared to past actual purchases. Any surplus material should not be included in the proposal, but rather sent to the stockroom or else returned to the vendor for credit. Also, any special clauses or options proposed by subcontractors should be evaluated.

4.6.1.3 Direct Labor Analysis Techniques

The analysis of direct labor would assess:

- actual hours incurred for previous effort;
- complexity factor applied to previous similar effort;
- design data package for engineering drawings and product specifications;
- estimating methodology;
- experience or learning curve data;
- historical costs;
- job descriptions;
- labor efficiency and performance factors;
- labor mix and types;
- labor standards compared to industry norms for fabrication and assembly hours;
- management ratio;
- number of hours;
- organization chart;

- process sheets;
- redundancy of effort and double-charging; and
- rework history.

Proposed hourly rates should be based on past or projected payroll data, segregated into individual rates for each cluster of labor pay grades.

Engineering labor is often proposed on a level-of-effort basis, meaning it is man-loaded by projecting the number of people or hours to accomplish the task. This effort is a function of product complexity and prior production, as well as the contractor's readiness and technology. Time is expressed in terms of man-hours (60 minutes of effort), man-months or man-years. The latter two measures are impacted by fatigue, personal leave, training, weekends and other reasons for absenteeism or nonproductivity. These reasons vary with each company so there is no set standard definition of either term, though a good rule of thumb is 168 hours for a man-month and 1600–2000 for a man-year.

Manufacturing labor is largely non-recurring in nature and therefore may be more difficult to analyze. It covers operating machinery such as drills, lathes, mills, and punch presses. It also includes associated tools such as clamps, gages, vises, and wrenches. Also, cutting machines must be not only operated, but also removed and replaced or sharpened.[17] This type of effort consists of:

- machine setup and teardown time and housekeeping;
- measuring;
- operation time for machine positioning, part handling and cutting;
- personal allowance, fatigue and delay; and
- tool changing and sharpening.

The material to work with also impacts labor hour projections. Steel is heavier than copper and much heavier than aluminum, and therefore takes longer to cut or fabricate. Both cut length and feed rate also affect labor hours. Hence, a manufacturing outline sheet or routing sheet is compiled by an industrial estimator from blueprints to detail the operations in sequence and select the machine and needed tools.

Manufacturing labor may be estimated in several ways by using labor standards. One option is to collect historical actual amounts for continuous observations of a person of average talent under average conditions without a break, known as *leveled time*. Another method is to break down a process into basic motions and time several iterations of each, calculating an average time for the process. A hybrid of these methods is the *predetermined-leveled-time technique*, used in high-volume production plants. A *work sampling* technique uses random sampling rather than continuous observations of an individual, especially if work cycles are lengthy in time. Finally, standards may be derived from external sources such as trade journals, manufacturer specifications or other departments.

The problem with leveled time is that it does not allow for personal breaks, so an industrial engineer would increase the calculated time by adding a *personal, fatigue and delay* allowance to cover bathroom breaks, drinking water, material replenishment, minor repairs to equipment and tools, oiling machinery, and end-of-day cleanup. When all this idle time is added up, it is expressed as a percentage of either 60 minutes or 8 hours to derive an allowance, which is then added to estimated work hours to derive a proposed amount. Similarly, a rework factor may be added based on historical data for inspection-rejected components. Also, test station setup time may need to be added as a discrete number, again based on historical data.

Yet another option is to create a *realization factor* by deriving the ratio of actual time to standard time, thereby reflecting the effects of such factors as fire, flood or obsolete equipment. The reciprocal of this factor is an *efficiency factor*. So if a process has a standard time of 10 minutes but actually takes 12½ minutes, the realization factor is 1.25 and the efficiency factor is 0.8. If the factor calculations show a wide gap between standard and actual times, inefficiency is present and should be investigated, such as cramped work stations, employee abuse or morale, excessive housekeeping or personal breaks, lack of storage space, or poor tool crib management.

To project the difference between standard and actual performance into the future for proposal purposes, the firm will develop an *experience curve* (better known as a *learning curve*). The theory here is that performance improves with repetition because machines are broken in, designs are stabilized, workers become efficient, and material handling methods improve. In theory, the labor or product cost decreases by a constant amount as the quantity of product doubles. By recording historical data, this relationship can be plotted on a graph to develop a learning curve whose slope represents an experience curve. The steeper the slope, the greater the learning. So if we have a curve of 80 percent and a cost at unit 1 of \$10, the cost for unit 2 will be 10 × 0.8 = \$8, for unit 4 will be \$6.40, and for unit 8 will be \$5.12. Note that the difference between these cost figures is shrinking, which means that the curve slopes toward an asymptote with a long tail when it reaches a certain point. This shows us that the impact of learning is ever present but shrinking as experience grows.

Alternatively, the contractor might develop cost estimating relationships to project labor hours. If a task has been done before but will be a measurable level more or less complex this time, perhaps a factor can be developed to reflect this change. For instance, an item which required 100 hours of work before will be 20 percent more complex this time, so 100 × 1.20 = 120 hours.

Similarly, if the product is 30 percent less complicated, then 100 × 0.7 = 70 hours. This is a simplistic yet easily understood process to estimate hours.

Costs are either accumulated by job order for the specific contract or at the end of the month if using mass production techniques.

4.6.1.4 Other Direct Costs Analysis Techniques

The cost analyst will look to ensure that proposed Other Direct Costs are not also included elsewhere, such as an overhead account, to avoid double charging. Special tooling and test equipment must be dedicated to this contract, or else an appropriate pro rata share of cost should be used (or the item should be expensed). Government-furnished equipment should not be available in this circumstance. Travel plans should be spelled out by trip and include airfare, car rental, per diem, and other incidentals (such as parking and tolls). Additional examples include computer shared time and royalty payments.

This section of the proposal may include rates for services transferred between divisions, subsidiaries, or affiliates of the contractor under a common control. They do not include profit for the transferring organization, but may include profit for the prime contractor. Any commercial services carry the established catalog or market rate per the established pricing practice of the transferring organization.

4.6.1.5 Overhead Analysis Techniques

Large defense contractors submit a proposal before the beginning of their accounting year to request a forward pricing rate agreement which would set forth both labor and indirect rates for negotiation on future contracts. DCAA reviews these proposed rates and renders recommendations for each. The auditor will see if each component of the rate calculations is reasonable, allocable and allowable (in terms of cost accounting principles and standards, as well as contract terms which forbid certain otherwise allowable practices, such as overtime labor). The proposed cost should also be necessary and prudent and allocated in reasonable proportion to the benefits received. The material allocation base will be total material dollars projected for the entire year. The labor allocation base will be total labor hours or dollars, or perhaps number of units produced or machine hours for manufacturing overhead components. The pool divided by the base yields a factor expressed as a percentage.

The auditor will begin analysis by identifying any unallowable costs and eliminate them from the base or pool. Then the estimated base and pool will be thoroughly reviewed for allocability and reasonableness. Once the legitimate cost components are identified, they will be converted to constant dollars. Finally, a historical comparison should be made with prior year bases and pools to see if the derived rate is consistent with history.

If the auditor concurs with the proposal, the rate is either incorporated into a formal agreement or at least recommended for acceptance by DCAA. If the auditor does not concur, the DCAA office will issue its own recommended rates. These may also be used as billing rates with contractor concurrence and finalized at a later date. Hence, DCAA does its overhead review work upfront rather than for each proposal throughout the year, and will use its recommended rates in its review of individual contract proposals.

4.6.1.6 G&A Analysis Techniques

Evaluation of G&A is similar to Overhead, in that rates are proposed by dividing the size of the pool by the total cost basis. Most firms will use a total cost base, though some may use a value-added base if such costs are segregable. However, the value-added base will be so much smaller that the G&A rate will be much higher than in a cost input environment.

4.6.2 Information to Support Analysis

The contracting officer may request that personnel with specialized experience, knowledge or skills in engineering, management or science perform a *technical analysis* of direct costs. Often, a cost analyst or procurement analyst performs this task. (S)he will review the proposal in detail to understand how each cost element was developed, and then determine how best to evaluate them. Complex proposals will include a description page for each work package to identify hours and any material cost, with a written explanation to justify these numbers.

The contracting officer requests field pricing assistance when the information available at the buying activity is inadequate to determine a fair and reasonable price. (S)he tailors the type of information and level of detail requested to the minimum necessary to help determine reasonableness. Such assistance normally includes:

- audit and technical reports on the cost elements of a proposal, including subcontracts;
- business, production or technical capabilities and practices of an offeror;
- identifying customarily granted or offered discounts;
- identifying general market conditions affecting determinations of commerciality and price reasonableness;
- information on related pricing practices and history;
- verifying sales history, including subcontracts;

- verifying historical data for an item not previously commercial that the offeror is now trying to qualify as a commercial item; and
- verifying the proposed catalog or price list.

Within DoD, the contracting officer may ask DCAA for rate information or, if the estimated price is large enough, for a full pricing report (this service is also available to civilian agencies, for a fee). The completed field pricing assistance need not reconcile the audit recommendations and technical recommendations. General access to the offeror's books and financial records is limited to the auditor; however the contracting officer may request the offeror provide or make available any data or records necessary to analyze the offeror's proposal.

The contracting officer considers whether a (sub)contractor has an approved purchasing system, has performed cost or price analysis of proposed subcontractor prices, or has negotiated the subcontract prices before negotiation of the prime contract. The prime contractor or subcontractor conducts appropriate cost or price analyses to establish the reasonableness of proposed subcontract prices, includes the results of these analyses in the price proposal, and submits any required subcontractor cost or pricing data with its own cost or pricing data. The contractor submits, or directs the subcontractor(s) to submit, cost or pricing data to the Government for subcontracts that are either $13.5 million in value or in excess of both the certified cost or pricing data threshold and 10 percent of the prime contractor's proposed price, unless the contracting officer believes such submission is unnecessary. The contracting officer may require subcontractor cost or pricing data below these thresholds if necessary to adequately price the prime contract. Subcontractor cost or pricing data is also certified as current, accurate and complete as of the date of price agreement. The contractor updates subcontractor data during source selection and negotiations. If there is more than one prospective subcontractor for any given work, the contractor need only submit to the Government cost or pricing data for the prospective subcontractor most likely to receive award.

After this initial review, a list of questions should be sent to the offeror's contracts representative. On major procurements, a fact-finding session will be held face-to-face to explore the proposal in more depth. Often, this is at the contractor's facility because the answers may not lie with the attendees, but rather with a person elsewhere in the facility who might not otherwise travel to the contracting office. The offeror is responsible for making available all facts which would contribute to the validity of both incurred costs and future costs. Fact-finding sessions should result in learning much more about the contractor's estimating assumptions and methodology, and identifying areas which need further clarification or revision. Upon return to the office, the cost analyst will review his/her notes to begin developing a prenegotiation position as to what a reasonable pricing structure should be.

Normally, for contractors other than educational institutions and nonprofit organizations, DCAA is the responsible Government audit agency to service both military and civilian agencies to provide recommendations to procurement and contract administration personnel after it reviews:[18]

- contractor estimating systems and procedures;
- cost proposals to ensure economy, effectiveness, and efficiency, and submit field pricing reports to document their findings;
- defective pricing proposals;
- review ongoing contracts for allocability, allowability and reasonableness;
- progress payments;
- reimbursement vouchers for cost-type contracts; and
- the financial and accounting aspects of the contractor's cost control systems and proposed and incurred costs.

The auditor may inspect the books under a cost-type contract at the plant or a subcontractor, with penalties for contractors who impede free access thereto. The auditor has the authority to decide what (s)he needs. In DoD, this requirement extends up to three years after final payment and includes the right to reproduce records.

FAR 42.707

Cost-sharing arrangements may call for indirect cost rates lower than the anticipated actual rates. In such cases, a negotiated indirect cost rate ceiling may be incorporated into the contract for prospective application. These cases include a new or recently reorganized company with no past or recent record of incurred indirect costs, a contractor with rapidly increasing indirect cost rates due to a declining volume of sales, or a contractor trying to enhance its competitive position by proposing indirect cost rates lower than those that may reasonably be expected to occur during contract performance (thereby causing a cost overrun). In such cases, an equitable ceiling covering the final indirect cost rates may be negotiated and specified in the contract. When ceiling provisions are utilized, the Government will not be obligated to pay any additional amount should the final rates exceed the negotiated ceiling rates, but any final rates below the negotiated ceiling rates will lead to rate reductions.

FAR 15.4

For contracts above the simplified acquisition threshold, the contracting officer will determine whether the price is based on competition, regulation or a commercial catalog or price list. If none of these apply, then the offeror will need to certify the cost or pricing data submitted with the proposal. The Head of the Contracting Activity may waive the requirement for certified cost or pricing data in exceptional cases, such as when the contractor previously furnished such data, and it was deemed adequate and remains current.

DFARS 215.407-5

All contractors should have acceptable estimating systems that consistently produce well-supported proposals that are acceptable as a basis for negotiation of fair and reasonable prices. A large business contractor must disclose, maintain, and review an estimating system if in its preceding fiscal year, the contractor received DoD (sub)contracts totaling $50 million or more for which certified cost or pricing were required. A firm with as little as $10 million in such (sub) contracts can also be directed to maintain an acceptable estimating system if the contracting officer, with concurrence of the ACO, determines this to be in the best interest of the Government (e.g., significant estimating problems are believed to exist or the contractor's sales are predominantly Government).

The cognizant contracting officer, in consultation with the auditor who conducts estimating system reviews, must determine the acceptability of the disclosure and approve or disapprove the system and pursue correction of any deficiencies. An acceptable system provides for using appropriate source data, utilizing sound estimating techniques and good judgment, maintains consistency, and adheres to established policies and procedures. The auditor documents findings and recommendations in a report to the contracting officer. If there are no significant deficiencies, the contractor's estimating system is acceptable and approved. If the contracting officer finds that there are one or more significant deficiencies due to the contractor's failure to meet one or more of the estimating system criteria, the contracting officer will make a written determination on any significant deficiencies and notify the contractor in writing of same, requesting the contractor to respond in writing within 30 days. (S)he will evaluate the contractor's responses to the initial determination and, in consultation with the auditor, make a final determination that the contractor's estimating system is acceptable and approved or else identify any remaining significant deficiencies. The contracting officer must then either request that the contractor either correct the deficiencies or submit an acceptable corrective action plan within 45 days showing milestones and actions to eliminate the deficiencies, or else disapprove the system and withhold payments.

PGI 215.407-5-70

If the contracting officer determines that there is a significant deficiency in the contractor's estimating system, (s)he sends copies of the determination and report to the contractor and requires a written response. Within 30 days of receiving the response, and after consultation with the auditor and evaluation of the contractor's response, the contracting officer makes a final determination. The auditor and contracting officer then monitor the contractor's progress in correcting deficiencies. If the contractor fails to make adequate progress, the contracting officer can take corrective action such as raising the issue to the attention of higher-level management, reducing or suspending progress payments, implementing or increasing the withholding, and recommending non-award of future contracts.

4.7 PROFIT

When price negotiations are not based on cost analysis, contracting officers need not analyze profit. When the price negotiation is based on cost analysis however, contracting officers in agencies that have a structured approach use it to analyze profit. If no such approval exists, then the guidelines discussed below are sufficient.

Elements of profit are subjective, but are intended to tie a greater profit opportunity to outstanding performance of more demanding tasks. They are based on contract type motivating the contractor to incur greater cost risk and input into performance. Hence, neither predetermined or historical rates nor unreasonably low rates are valid profit policies.

Contracting officers use the prenegotiation cost objective amounts as the basis to calculate the profit or fee prenegotiation objective. Before applying profit or fee factors, the contracting officer excludes any facilities capital cost of money included in the cost objective amounts, since the Government will not allow profit on top of the cost of money. If the prospective contractor does not propose facilities capital cost of money for a contract that will be subject to the cost principles, a contract clause will be necessary to make it an unallowable cost.

The contracting officer does not negotiate a profit or fee rate that exceeds the statutory limitations at 10 U.S.C. 2306(d) and 41 U.S.C. 254(b):

- for experimental, developmental, or research work performed under a cost-plus-fixed-fee contract, 15 percent of the estimated cost;
- for architect-engineer services for public works or utilities designs, plans, drawings, and specifications, six percent of the estimated cost of construction; and
- for other cost-plus-fixed-fee contracts, 10 percent of the contract's estimated cost.

The offeror need not submit breakdowns or supporting rationale for its profit or fee objective, but may do so voluntarily for the contracting officer to consider.

Three factors considered by the contracting officer in developing a profit or fee objective are contractor effort, contract cost risk, and management.

Contractor effort measures the complexity of the work and the resources required for contract performance. Greater profit opportunity is provided under contracts requiring a high degree of managerial and professional skill and to prospective contractors whose facilities, skills and technical assets indicate economical and efficient contract performance. Subfactors include:

- *Material acquisition*—purchased parts, raw material and subcontracted items. This includes the complexity of the items required, the number of purchase orders and subcontracts to be awarded and administered, whether established sources are available or new or alternate sources must be developed, and whether material will be obtained through routine purchase orders or complex subcontracts requiring detailed specifications.
- *Conversion direct labor*—the contribution of direct engineering, manufacturing, and other direct labor to convert data, raw materials, and subcontracted items into the contract. Considerations include the diversity of engineering, manufacturing and scientific labor skills required and the amount and quality of supervision and coordination.
- *Conversion-related indirect costs*—the labor elements in the allocable indirect costs receive the profit consideration they would earn if treated as direct labor. Other elements of indirect costs are evaluated to determine their level of merit based on either routine nature or significant contribution to the proposed contract.
- *General management*—G&A expense and how much they contribute to contract performance. Considerations include how overhead labor would be treated as if direct, whether elements within the pools are routine expenses or contribute significantly to the proposed contract, and whether the elements require routine or unusual managerial effort and attention.

The *Contract cost risk* factor measures the degree of cost responsibility and associated risk that the prospective contractor will assume as a result of the contract type contemplated. It considers the reliability of the cost estimate in relation to the complexity and duration of the contract task. This factor compensates contractors proportionately for assuming greater cost risks. The contractor assumes the greatest cost risk in a closely priced firm-fixed-price contract to perform a complex undertaking on time at a predetermined price. If the contract task is less complex or many of the contractor's costs are known at the time of price agreement, the risk factor is reduced accordingly. The contractor assumes the least cost risk in a cost-plus-fixed-fee level-of-effort contract because it is reimbursed for all costs determined to be allocable and allowable, plus the fixed fee. Time-and-materials, labor-hour, and firm-fixed-price level-of-effort term contracts are treated the same as cost-plus-fixed-fee contracts in this regard.

There are four different management factors used in setting a profit objective for the Government negotiator to achieve during negotiations. The *Federal socioeconomic programs* factor measures the degree of support given by the prospective contractor to such programs. Greater profit opportunity is provided to contractors that have displayed unusual initiative in these programs. The *Capital investments* factor considers the contribution of contractor investments to efficient and economical contract performance. A *Cost-control and other past accomplishments* factor recognizes a contractor's success in performing similar tasks effectively and economically, productivity improvements, and other cost-reduction accomplishments that will benefit the Government in follow-on contracts. Finally, an *Independent development* factor recognizes efforts for the contract end item without Government assistance, especially if the development cost was not recovered from Government sources.

Each agency may include additional factors in its structured approach or take them into account in the profit analysis of individual contract actions.

Excess profits are controversial because they are not subject to external evaluation in nongovernment industries. This concept developed during World War II out of fear that Federal dollars would be lost to excess profit. Under the Renegotiation Act of 1951, these fears were revived due to the noncompetitive nature of defense procurement.[19] The Renegotiation Board had authority to reset profits under Federal contracts but suffered from vague regulations and lack of resources, and lapsed in 1976. Efficient low-cost producers could have been penalized for excess profits. Fortunately, increased professionalism of government personnel and more stringent regulations led to better contract pricing and less risk of excess profits. This topic remains subject to lobbying on both sides of the issue.

DFARS 215.404

DoD uses a structured approach to develop a prenegotiation profit or fee objective on any negotiated contract action when certified cost or pricing data is obtained (except for cost-plus-award-fee contracts or contracts with Federally Funded Research and Development Centers, or when assessing cost realism in competitive acquisitions). Usually the contracting officer uses the weighted guidelines method; however a modified weighted guidelines method is available for nonprofit organizations other than FFRDCs. An alternate structured approach is also available for:

- a termination settlement;
- actions not exceeding the certified cost or pricing data threshold;
- architect-engineer or construction work;

- delivery of material from subcontractors; or
- if the weighted guidelines method does not produce a reasonable overall profit objective and the head of the contracting activity approves use of the alternate approach in writing.

The profit objective is calculated on DD Form 1547. Specific agreement on the applied weights or values for individual profit factors is not desired during negotiations; however the contracting officer may encourage the contractor to detail its proposed profit amounts in the weighted guidelines format or similar structured approach. The contracting officer must also verify that relevant variables have not materially changed (e.g., performance risk, interest rates, progress payment rates, distribution of facilities capital).

The weighted guidelines method focuses on four profit factors:

- performance risk,
- contract type risk,
- facilities capital employed, and
- cost efficiency.

The contracting officer assigns values to each profit factor. The value multiplied by the base results in the profit objective for that factor. Except for the cost efficiency special factor, each profit factor has a normal value and a designated range of values. The normal value is based on average conditions when compared to all goods and services acquired by DoD. The designated range provides values based on above normal or below normal conditions. In the price negotiation documentation, the contracting officer need not explain assignment of the normal value, but should address conditions that justify assignment of other than the normal value.

4.7.1 Performance Risk

DFARS 215.404-71-2

The first profit factor addresses the contractor's degree of risk in fulfilling the contract requirements. The factor consists of considering both the technical uncertainties of performance and the degree of management effort necessary to both ensure that contract requirements are met and reduce and control costs. It consists of three component considerations: Technical, Management and Cost Control.

Technical elements for the contracting officer to consider in the statement of work or specifications include:

- cost control and timely submission of definitization proposals for unpriced change orders and supplemental agreements:
- delivery schedule;
- performance specifications and tolerances;
- program maturity;
- technical complexity;
- technology applied or developed by the contractor; and
- warranty or guarantee extent.

The contracting officer selects a value for Technical effort between 3 and 7 percent, with the normal value at the midpoint of 5. An above-normal weight can be used where there is a substantial technical risk, such as where the contractor is:

- accepting an accelerated delivery schedule to meet DoD requirements;
- assuming additional risk through warranty provisions;
- manufacturing items using specifications with stringent tolerance limits;
- performing services and analytical efforts to exacting standards and of high importance to the Government;
- using highly skilled personnel or requiring the use of state-of-the-art machinery; or
- using independent development and investment that reduces the Government's risk or cost.

Hence, a value above normal is appropriate for more complex and vital effort to overcome difficult technical obstacles that require personnel with exceptional abilities, experience and professional credentials. Moreover, a maximum value may be appropriate for development or initial production of a new item (especially if concurrency is occurring) or if performance or quality specifications are tight.

On the other hand, a below-normal value may be appropriate where the technical risk is low, such as:

- follow-on or repetitive acquisition;
- less-skilled personnel;
- mature programs;
- routine data entry or integration of Government-furnished information;
- routine efforts; or
- simple requirements or technology.

For the most innovative contract efforts, DoD will replace the Technical range with a Technology range of 7 to 11 percent with a normal value of 9 percent. Such effort includes developing or applying new technology that changes the characteristics of an existing product or system and leads to improved technical performance or reliability, new products or systems that contain significant technological advances over their predecessors, or reduced costs. The contracting officer should consider the relative value of the proposed innovation to the acquisition as a whole, and use a higher value for a major positive impact on the product or program, and a below-normal value for modest benefits. This range does not apply to analyses or studies, or contracts primarily calling for a technical report.

The second component is for Management, where the contracting officer should evaluate the contractor's:

- adequacy of management approach to controlling cost and schedule;
- management and internal control systems by using information and reviews made by the contracting and field contract administration offices;
- management involvement expected on the contract; and
- support of Federal socioeconomic programs.

The standard range is again between 3 and 7 percent with a normal value of 5. The contracting officer may assign a higher-than-normal value when there is a high degree of management effort based on the contractor's:

- active participation in Federal socioeconomic programs;
- appropriate make-or-buy decisions;
- effort of integration or coordination;
- past performance; and
- value added in terms of difficulty and substance.

The contracting officer may use a maximum value when the effort has critical milestones, involves major international activities with significant management coordination, or requires complex and large scale integration. On the other hand, the contracting officer may assign a lower-than-normal value when the management effort is minimal, such as when the contractor:

- adds minimal value to an item;
- does not cooperate in proposal evaluation and negotiation;
- has a poor record of past performance;
- provides poor quality and untimely proposals;
- provides routine effort and requires minimal supervision; or
- runs a mature program and many end item deliveries have been made.

A value significantly below normal may be justified if the field contract administration offices disclose unsatisfactory management and internal control systems or the effort requires an unusually low degree of management involvement.

The third component is Cost Control, where the contracting officer should evaluate the contractor's:

- degree of cost mix in terms of the types of resources applied and value added by the contractor;
- expected reliability of the cost estimates and cost estimating system; and
- factors that affect the ability to meet the cost targets (e.g., foreign currency exchange rates and inflation rates).

The standard range is again between 3 and 7 percent with a normal value of 5. The contracting officer may assign a higher-than-normal value when there is a high degree of cost control effort based on the contractor's cost tracking and control, as well as fully documented and reliable cost estimates. On the other hand, the contracting officer may assign a lower-than-normal value when the management effort is minimal, such as when the contractor:

- fails to provide an adequate analysis of subcontractor costs;
- has a marginal cost estimating system;
- has a record of cost overruns or lack of cost control;
- has made minimal effort to initiate cost reduction programs;
- incurs costs prior to definitization;
- provides routine effort and requires minimal supervision; or
- runs a mature program and many end item deliveries have been made.

The analyst assigns a percentage weight to all three elements based on its relative input to the total performance risk. The total of the three weights equals 100 percent. Because DoD systems tend to be very complex, the Technical factor tends to have a higher weighting than the other two. For example, let's say the contracting officer selects a 60/15/25 split for Technical and Management/Cost, and assigns weights of 8, 7 and 6, respectively. Then,

$$(0.60 \times 0.08) + (0.15 \times 0.07) + (0.25 \times 0.06) = 0.048 + 0.0105 + 0.015 = 0.0735 \text{ or } 7.35\%.$$

The total Performance Risk is therefore 7.35 percent. The contracting officer will then multiply the total cost objective (excluding cost of money) by this percentage to derive a Profit Objective for this first component of profit.

4.7.2 Contract Type Risk

DFARS 215.404-71-3

The Contract Type risk factor addresses the degree of cost risk absorbed by the contractor for the given contract type. The working capital adjustment is added to the profit objective for contract type risk if the proposed contract is fixed-price that provides for progress payments. Though it uses a formula approach, it is intended to recognize the contractor's cost of working capital for different contract types, financing policies and the economic environment.

First, the contracting officer selects a value from the list of contract types (see table 4.4). Explanatory notes are necessary because this selection is not as easy as it seems. The firm-fixed-price contracts are actually distinguished by financing provisions. If the contract does not provide progress payments or performance-based payments (or perhaps does so only on a limited basis, such as financing of first articles), then the higher range is used. If performance-based payments are used however, a working capital adjustment is necessary in a future step and the factor range is reduced.

Second, a fixed-price incentive contract will receive a lower value than firm-fixed-price, and it will go lower if performance-based or progress payments are employed. If the contract has redetermination provisions, the factor will be on the lower end of the range. Third, cost-plus contracts do not receive

Table 4.4 Contract Type Risk Values

Contract Type	*Normal Value (percent)*	*Range (percent)*
Firm-fixed-price, no financing	5	4 to 6
Firm-fixed-price, with performance-based payments	4	2.5 to 5.5
Firm-fixed-price, with progress payments	3	2 to 4
Fixed-price incentive, no financing	3	2 to 4
Fixed-price incentive, with performance-based payments	2	0.5 to 3.5
Fixed-price with redetermination provision	1	0 to 1
Fixed-price incentive, with progress payments	1	0 to 2
Cost-plus-incentive-fee	1	0 to 2
Cost-plus-fixed-fee	0.5	0 to 1
Time-and-materials (including overhaul contracts priced on time-and-materials basis)	0.5	0 to 1
Labor-hour	0.5	0 to 1
Firm-fixed-price, level-of-effort	0.5	0 to 1

a working capital adjustment. Nor do contracts with performance-based payments receive a working capital adjustment.

The contracting officer should consider many elements that affect contract type risk such as:

- ceilings and incentive share lines;
- contract length;
- cost data adequacy and history for projections;
- economic environment;
- nature and extent of subcontracted activity;
- payment frequency for performance-based payments, risk of the payment schedule to the contractor and percentage of total amount of payments subject to such payments;
- product maturity;
- protective contract clauses (e.g., economic price adjustment clauses); and
- risks for foreign military sales not funded by U.S. appropriations.

If pre-contract costs have been authorized, the contracting officer assesses the extent to which costs have been incurred prior to definitization of the contract action. In such a case, contract type risk is in the low end of the designated range. If a substantial portion of the costs have been incurred prior to definitization, the contracting officer may assign a value as low as 0 percent, regardless of contract type. However, if the contractor demonstrates effective cost control, an additional point may be added to the range values in Table 4.4.

Once a value is selected, it is multiplied by total cost (excluding cost of money) to derive a second component of the profit objective.

4.7.3 Working Capital

The Working Capital Adjustment is based on three components: Costs Financed, Contract Length Factor and Interest Rate. Costs Financed equal total costs (excluding facilities capital cost of money) multiplied by the percentage portion of costs financed by the contractor. The portion that the contractor finances is generally what is not covered by progress payments. For example, if a contractor receives progress payments at 80 percent, the portion that the contractor finances is 20 percent. The progress payment rate for small businesses is not used for this calculation, only the customary progress payment rate for large businesses.

The Contract Length Factor is the period of time that the contractor has a working capital investment in the contract. This is the time necessary for the contractor to complete the substantive portion of the work, not necessarily the total period of contract performance, as it excludes periods of minimal effort,

Table 4.5 Contract Length Risk Values

Performance Period (in months)	Contract Length Factor
21 or less	.40
22 to 27	.65
28 to 33	.90
34 to 39	1.15
40 to 45	1.40
46 to 51	1.65
52 to 57	1.90
58 to 63	2.15
64 to 69	2.40
70 to 75	2.65
76 or more	2.90

option provisions and periods of performance on multiyear contracts beyond that required to complete the initial program year's requirements.

The contracting officer should use table 4.5 to select the contract length factor, should develop a weighted average contract length when the contract has multiple deliveries, and may use sampling techniques.

For example, a prospective contract has a performance period of 72 months with end items being delivered in the 36th, 48th, 60th, and 72nd months of the contract. The average period is 54 months and the contract length factor is 1.90.

The third component, Interest Rate, is established by the Secretary of the Treasury and is listed at https://treasurydirect.gov/government/interest-rates-and-prices/certified-interest-rates.

Now the contracting officer multiples the three factors to obtain the working capital adjustment. It may not exceed 4 percent of the contract costs (excluding cost of money).

4.7.4 Contractor Facilities Capital Employed

DFARS 215.404-71-4

This factor is designed to encourage and reward capital investment in facilities that benefit DoD. It recognizes the contractor who employs its own facilities capital in contract performance and its commitment to improve productivity. This exercise is necessary because interest expense is not allowable; however DoD wishes to recognize contractor investment, rather than reliance on Government-furnished equipment or inefficient rental costs. It does not matter if the capital is borrowed or furnished by owner equity. To be enticing, the rate of return on investment must be greater than the cost of capital; hence the opportunity is present for the contractor to recoup its capital investment expense.

The contractor proposes the facilities capital cost of money and capital employed by completing Form CASB-CMF. First, the contractor will list overhead pools and any direct-charging service centers. Next, (s)he will accumulate net book value of all facilities capital for the business unit. This amount must also include the value of capital-lease items and the allocated share of corporate or group facilities for the given accounting period. Note that this number will change each year, so contracts covering multiple years of performance may need multiple calculations.

Once the allocation base data is established, each base amount is multiplied by its corresponding cost of money factor. A different factor is calculated for each overhead base on Form CASB-CMF by calculating the net book value of all allocable facilities and equipment, then allocating them to each overhead pool. Joint facilities will need to be separately calculated and then distributed to the different cost pools by means of an approved accounting process. The total net book value of assets in a given pool is then multiplied by the cost of money rate set forth by the Secretary of the Treasury (which might be the same interest rate used in the Working Capital process) to derive a cost of money account for each pool. The firm will then divide the cost of money by the allocation base for each pool to derive a cost of money factor. Since the allocation base will be much the larger amount, the denominator will greatly exceed the numerator and the result will be a small fraction. The factor is customarily calculated to the fifth decimal place to reflect this circumstance.

The contracting officer will utilize the cost proposal and information from Form CASB-CMF to fill out DD Form 1861, Contract Facilities Capital Cost of Money. Then (s)he will extract contract overhead allocation base data by year from the evaluated cost breakdown or prenegotiation cost objective. This data will then be listed against each overhead pool and direct-charging service center. Generally, this means that each overhead pool as well as the G&A base will be listed. After adjusting each allocation base to match the prenegotiation position and verifying the cost of money factor, (s)he will multiply each allocation base by its corresponding cost of money factor to get the facilities capital cost of money estimated to be incurred each year. The sum of these products represents the estimated contract facilities capital cost of money for the year's effort.

Then the contracting officer will distribute the facilities capital employed across three categories of asset types (land, buildings, and equipment) in a manner similar to applying overhead rates to appropriate allocation bases to determine contract overhead costs. The relative percentages should equate to the percentage of total net book value invested in that type of facility. As with the Performance Risk calculation, all three percentages must add up to 100 percent. Total contract facilities cost of money is the sum of the yearly amounts.

The allocation percentages are critical because only the amount allocated to Equipment receives consideration on cost calculations. Over the course of time, DoD has moved in a direction that does not wish to recognize contractor investment in real estate. This means that neither Land nor Buildings capital is considered in Facilities Capital Employed calculations. This also means that the DD 1861 calculations are now more complicated than necessary, but unless and until DoD changes the methodology of calculation, it must be used.

If the value of intracompany transfers has been included in the cost objective before applying G&A expenses and profit, then the contracting officer will add (to the contractor's allocated facilities capital) the allocated facilities capital attributable to the equipment of those corporate divisions supplying the intracompany transfers.

The allowable range for the Equipment factor is between 10 and 25 percent of its allocated facilities capital. The norm is 17.5 percent.

When evaluating facilities capital employed, the contracting officer relates the usefulness of the facilities capital to the goods or services being acquired under the prospective contract. (S)he will then analyze the productivity improvements and other benefits to the industrial base enhancing benefits resulting from the facilities capital investment. Principally, this includes the economic value of the facilities capital (e.g., physical age, undepreciated value, idleness, and expected contribution to future defense needs). Then (s)he considers the contractor's level of investment in defense related facilities as compared with the portion of the contractor's total business that is derived from DoD. Finally, (s)he considers any contract clauses that reduce the contractor's risk of investment recovery, such as termination protection clauses and capital investment indemnification.

The contracting officer may assign a higher-than-normal value if the facilities capital investment has direct, identifiable, and exceptional benefits. This primarily occurs in case of investments in new equipment for research and development applications or state-of-the-art technology that reduce acquisition cost, improve product quality, or accelerate deliveries. The contracting officer may also assign a value significantly above normal when there are direct and measurable benefits in efficiency and significantly reduced acquisition costs on the effort being priced. Maximum values apply only to those cases where the benefits of the facilities capital investment are substantially above normal.

On the other hand, the contracting officer may assign a lower-than-normal value if the facilities capital investment has little benefit to DoD. Indicators are allocations of capital apply predominantly to commercial item lines, investments limited to office furniture and fixtures (or items well separated from contract performance, such as corporate aircraft and fitness centers), or old or idle facilities.

The contractor has the right to decline the cost of money as a recognized contract cost, and the Government has the right to decline its consideration based on auditor findings or other accounting shortcomings. A waiver clause must then be included in the contract to disallow the cost.

Contract Clauses

FAR 52.215-16, Facilities Capital Cost of Money, in solicitations with commercial organizations subject to cost principles. If so, the contract will replace this provision with the clause at FAR 52.215-17, Waiver of Facilities Capital Cost of Money.

FAR 52.215-17, Waiver of Facilities Capital Cost of Money, if not allowed in the contract.

4.7.5 Adjustments to Weighted Guidelines

DFARS 215.404-71-5

The cost efficiency special factor has no normal value; the contracting officer must exercise sound business judgment in selecting a value when this special factor is used. This final factor incentivizes contractors to reduce costs. If the contractor can demonstrate cost reduction efforts that benefit the pending contract, the contracting officer may increase the prenegotiation profit objective by an amount not to exceed four percent of total objective cost. The contracting officer may consider the following contractor activities:

- actual cost reductions achieved on prior contracts;
- adoption of process improvements to reduce costs;
- cost reduction initiatives (e.g., competition advocacy, technical insertion, obsolete parts control, spare parts pricing reform, value engineering, and outsourcing of ancillary functions). Metrics developed by the contractor such as fully loaded labor hours (i.e., cost per labor hour, including all direct and indirect costs) or other productivity measures may permit assessment of the effectiveness of the contractor's cost reduction initiatives over time;
- incorporation of commercial items and processes;
- investment in new facilities which contribute to better asset utilization or improved productivity;
- participation in Single Process Initiative improvements;
- reduction or elimination of excess or idle facilities; and
- subcontractor cost reduction efforts.

The contracting officer has maximum flexibility in determining how to evaluate the benefit the contractor's cost reduction efforts will have on the pending contract. Examples include quantity differences, learning, changes in scope, and economic factors such as inflation and deflation.

DFARS 215.404-72

For nonprofit organizations that receive sustaining support on a cost-plus-fixed-fee basis from a particular DoD department or agency, under the weighted guidelines method, two changes are authorized. If the standard designated range is used for Performance Risk, the fee objective is reduced by one percent of the costs and no value is used in the technology incentive designated range. Also, for Contract Type Risk, the designated range is –1 to 0 percent.

DFARS 215.404-73

The overall prenegotiation profit objective is reduced by the amount of facilities capital cost of money. The profit amount in the negotiation summary must be net of the offset. This offset is necessary because the profit values used in the weighted guidelines method were adjusted to recognize the shift in facilities capital cost of money from a profit element to a cost element and reductions were made directly to the profit factors for performance risk.

DFARS 215.404-74

In developing a fee objective for cost-plus-award-fee contracts, the contracting officer does not use the weighted guidelines method, but does apply the offset policy by reducing the base fee by the amount of facilities capital cost of money. No DD Form 1547 is completed.

DFARS 215.404-75

For nonprofit organizations that are FFRDCs, the contracting officer must first consider whether any fee is appropriate. Considerations shall include the FFRDC's:

- facilities capital acquisition plans;
- proportion of retained earnings (as established under generally accepted accounting methods) that relates to DoD contracted effort;
- provision for funding unreimbursed costs deemed ordinary and necessary to the FFRDC; and
- working capital funding as assessed on operating cycle cash needs.

When a fee is considered appropriate, (s)he must establish the fee objective in accordance with FFRDC fee policies in the DoD FFRDC Management Plan and not use the weighted guidelines method or an alternate structured approach.

Solicitation Provisions

DFARS 252.215-7003, Requirement for Submission of Data Other Than Certified Cost or Pricing Data—Canadian Commercial Corporation, when contracting with the Canadian Commercial Corporation. Do not use DFARS 252.215-7010, Requirements for Certified Cost or Pricing Data and Data Other Than Certified Cost or Pricing Data, in a sole-source solicitation to the Canadian Commercial Corporation that is cost-reimbursement if the contract value is expected to exceed $700,000, fixed-price if the contract value is expected to exceed $500 million, or a sole-source acquisition that does not meet the thresholds. Do not use this clause in lieu of DFARS 252.215-7010 in competitive acquisitions.

DFARS 252.215-7004, Requirement for Submission of Data Other Than Certified Cost or Pricing Data—Modifications—Canadian Commercial Corporation—in a sole-source solicitation to the Canadian Commercial Corporation and the resultant contract is either cost-reimbursement over $700,000 or fixed-price over $500 million in value.

DFARS 252.215-7008, Only One Offer, in competitive solicitations, unless below the simplified acquisition threshold, for disaster assistance, small business or socioeconomic set-asides, a broad agency announcement for basic or applied research or development, or architect-engineer services. Include FAR 52.215-20, Requirements for Certified Cost or Pricing Data and Data Other Than Certified Cost or Pricing Data, with any appropriate alternate if requesting submission of data other than certified cost or pricing data with the offer. In such a case, include DFARS 252.215-7009, Proposal Adequacy Checklist, in the solicitation.

DFARS 252.215-7010, Requirements for Certified Cost or Pricing Data and Data Other Than Certified Cost or Pricing Data, instead of FAR 52.215-20 (same title), when submission of certified cost or pricing data or other cost or pricing data will probably be required. Use the basic provision when submission of certified cost or pricing data is required to be in the FAR Table 15-2 format, or if it is anticipated, at the time of solicitation, that the submission of certified cost or pricing data may not be required. Use Alternate I to specify a format for certified cost or pricing data other than the format required by FAR Table 15-2.

DFARS 252.215-7011, Requirements for Submission of Proposals to the Administrative Contracting officer and Contract Auditor, when using DFARS

252.215-7010 and copies of the proposal are to be sent to the ACO and contract auditor.

DFARS 252.215-7012, Requirements for Submission of Proposals via Electronic Media, when using DFARS 252.215-7010 and submission via electronic media is required.

DFARS 252.215-7013, Supplies and Services Provided by Nontraditional Defense Contractors.

Solicitation Provision and Contract Clause

DFARS 252.215-7002, Cost Estimating System Requirements, if awarded on the basis of certified cost or pricing data.

DFARS 252.215-7004, Exception from Certified Cost or Pricing Data Requirements for Foreign Military Sales Indirect Offsets.

4.8 DOCUMENTATION

FAR 15.406

The prenegotiation objectives establish the Government's initial negotiation position to assist in the contracting officer's determination of fair and reasonable price. They are based on the results of the contracting officer's analysis of the proposal, taking into consideration audit reports, fact-finding, field pricing assistance, independent Government cost estimates, price histories, and technical analysis. The scope and depth of the analysis supporting the objectives is directly related to the dollar value, importance and complexity of the pricing action.

The contracting officer and contractor are encouraged to reach a prior agreement on criteria for establishing closing or cutoff dates to minimize delays associated with proposal updates. Before agreement on price, the offeror updates data to the latest closing or cutoff dates for which the data are available.

The contracting officer documents in the contract file the principal elements of the negotiated agreement in a price negotiation memorandum, such as:

- purpose of the negotiation;
- description of the acquisition;
- name, position and organization of each person representing the contractor and the Government in the negotiation;
- current status of any contractor systems (e.g., accounting, compensation, estimating, and purchasing);

- if applicable, the exception used and the basis for not requiring cost or pricing data if above the data threshold;
- the extent to which the contracting officer relied on cost or pricing data in negotiations and any inaccuracy, incompleteness, or nonoccurrence (including actions taken for resolution and effect on negotiated price);
- summary of the contractor's proposal, any field pricing assistance recommendations, reasons for any pertinent variances from them, the Government's negotiation objective, and the final settlement. This includes discussing each major cost element (if using cost analysis) or source and type of data used to support price analysis;
- factors controlling the establishment of the prenegotiation objectives and the negotiated agreement, and an explanation of significant differences between the two positions;
- quantification of the impact of direction given by Congress, other agencies, and higher-level officials;
- basis for the profit or fee prenegotiation objective and the amount negotiated; and
- statement that price is fair and reasonable.

4.9 DEFECTIVE COST OR PRICING DATA

FAR 15.407-1

When a noncompetitive negotiation exceeds $750,000, the offeror will need to certify that to his best knowledge and belief, the cost and pricing data submitted is accurate, complete, and current as of the date when negotiations were completed. The certificate of current cost or pricing data is not a representation as to the accuracy of the contractor's judgment on the estimate of future costs or projections, but rather to data upon which the judgment or estimate was based. If the contractor had information reasonably available at the time of agreement showing the contrary, it is responsible for disclosure and is not limited by any lack of personal knowledge on the part of its negotiators.

If the contracting officer learns that any cost or pricing data submitted are inaccurate, incomplete, or noncurrent, (s)he immediately brings the matter to the attention of the prospective offeror, and considers the matter when negotiating the contract price. The price negotiation memorandum includes any adjustments made to the data used to negotiate the contract price.

If such a finding occurs after award and was in error on or before the date of final agreement, the Government is entitled to a price adjustment of any significant amount by which the price was increased because of the defective data, including subcontractor data. The contracting officer offsets, for any understated cost or pricing data submitted in support of price negotiations, the amount of the Government's claim for overstated pricing data arising out of the same pricing action. An offset is allowed only if the contractor certifies that, to the best of its knowledge and belief, it is entitled to the offset in the amount requested, and proves that the cost or pricing data were available before the "as of" date specified on the Certificate of Current Cost or Pricing Data but were not submitted. In addition to the price adjustment, the Government is entitled to recovery of any overpayment plus interest or penalty, provided that payment has been made for supplies or services accepted by the Government (overpayments do not result from contract financing, by definition).

The contracting officer may not reprice the contract solely because the profit was greater than forecast or because a contingency specified in the submission failed to materialize.

Solicitation Provisions and Contract Clauses

FAR 52.215-10, Price Reduction for Defective Cost or Pricing Data, when cost or pricing data will be required from the contractor or any subcontractor.

FAR 52.215-11, Price Reduction for Defective Cost or Pricing Data—Modifications, if cost or pricing data will be required from the contractor or any subcontractor to price contract modifications, and FAR 52.215-10 is not used.

FAR 52.215-12, Subcontractor Cost or Pricing Data, when FAR 52.215-10 is included.

FAR 52.215-13, Subcontractor Cost or Pricing Data—Modifications, when FAR 52.215-11 is included.

NOTES

1. This is an example of a *static budget*, which is prepared only for a specified level of activity and not adjusted due to volume changes.
2. EDGAR can be accessed at www.sec.gov/edgar/search-and-access.
3. OMB Uniform Guidance at 2 CFR Part 200, Appendix VIII, specifically exempts 33 types of organizations from the use of cost principles, principally nonprofit organizations which are not affiliated with educational institutions. Also exempted are state and local governments.
4. 29 U.S.C. 1001.
5. http://www.defenseinnovationmarketplace.mil.
6. These restrictions derive from the *Byrd Amendment*, 31 U.S.C.1352.
7. Defense Travel Management Office. The Per Diem, Travel and Transportation Allowance Committee, "Joint Travel Regulations," May 1, 2023.

8. *Boyle vs. United Technologies Corp.*, S. Ct. 487 US 500 (1988).

9. Pub. L. 103-160, section 841.

10. 41 U.S.C. 422 and 48 CFR Chapter 99. These standards are cross-referenced as FAR Chapter 99.

11. If the cost is a royalty exceeding $1,500, additional information is needed to assess each separate royalty or license fee.

12. Some large firms have procurement personnel dedicated to a large program. In such cases, the buyers may become direct labor charged to the program.

13. DoD has certain prescribed further exceptions to use of the -22 and -23 clauses.

14. An excellent source of information is the Contract Pricing Reference Guides from the Air Force Institute of Technology, now available from Defense Acquisition University at https://www.dau.mil/tools/p/cprg.

15. Consult your favorite project management textbook for sample templates.

16. The Program Management Institute has issued a similar work entitled "Practice Standard for Work Breakdown Structures."

17. In general, the harder-surface cutter will be more efficient in time but also be more expensive. The tradeoff here is labor cost versus purchase cost.

18. Cognizance of educational and nonprofit institutions is assigned to whichever service or agency has the most negotiated dollars awarded to the entity. With some medical institutions, this is the Department of Health and Human Services.

19. 50 U.S.C. App. 1211.

Chapter 5

Postaward

5.1 CONTRACT ADMINISTRATION SERVICES

5.1.1 Duties

FAR 42.0

Contract administration is the process whereby the parties ensure that the results or performance match the contract. Emphasis is placed on progress toward meeting delivery and schedule, invoicing and payment, and fulfilling contract conditions. On major contracts, this process often begins with a kickoff meeting to discuss the requirements and approach, and address administrative concerns. Subcontractor postaward conferences are also sometimes held.

The administrative team participates in the postaward conference, or kick-off meeting, which includes the awardee and all the stakeholders. This meeting is intended to reach a mutual understanding of contract requirements and resolve potential problems. During this conference, all the participating parties:

- discuss the roles and responsibilities of each team member;
- introduce and explain the incentive plan to ensure it is understood by everyone;
- review each individual requirement stated in the PWS, SOW and QASP;
- review the performance management process; and
- show how the Contractor Performance Assessment Reporting System will be used to document the contractor's performance.

Performance reviews may be conducted periodically to keep all stakeholders well informed of actual contract performance results. They provide documented performance trends and results to enable an open and honest discussion with the contractor concerning the results achieved. For most contracts, monthly or quarterly contractor performance reviews are appropriate. For contracts of extreme importance or contracts in performance trouble, more frequent meetings may be required. During this review, the acquisition team should be discerning whether the contractor's performance meets or exceeds the contract's performance standards and if any problems or issues can be addressed to mitigate risk.

FAR 42.0

Contracting officers may delegate contract administration or specific support services, either through interagency agreements or by direct request, to the cognizant *contract administration office* (CAO).[1] These offices are part of the Defense Contract Management Agency.[2] These offices have either geographic jurisdictions or corporation assignments, and accept contracts for administration based on these jurisdictional rules.

Assignment of a particular contract is based on the identity of the prime contractor's location. Since the prime contractor is responsible for managing its subcontracts, the CAO's review of subcontracts is normally limited to evaluating the prime contractor's oversight process and results. Therefore, supporting contract administration is not used for subcontracts unless the Government would either incur undue costs due to subcontract performance or else raise concern about successful completion of the prime contract.

The contracting officer normally delegates to the CAO the following contract administration functions, which are performed by *administrative contracting officers* (ACOs), individuals who are responsible for ensuring that contractors perform in accordance with contract specifications and clauses. ACOs have contract administrators on their staff to perform many of these functions (though only the ACO has a warrant to bind the Government to a position):

- administer the industrial security program;
- advise and assist contractors on priorities and allocations responsibilities;
- analyze quarterly limitation on payment statements and recover overpayments;
- approve final vouchers;
- assess compliance with cost, schedule and technical requirements for design, development, and production;

- assist contracting offices to obtain special assistance and priority ratings for privately owned capital equipment;
- cancel unilateral purchase orders when notified of nonacceptance by the contractor;
- close out contracts;
- conduct postaward orientation conferences for Government and contractor personnel to understand contract requirements and resolve potential problems;
- consent to the placement of subcontracts (but not if the prime contact is firm-fixed-price);
- coordinate the removal of urgently required material from a strikebound contractor's plant upon contracting officer authorization;
- deobligate excess funds after final price determination;
- determine that the contractor has a drug-free workplace and awareness program;
- determine the adequacy of the contractor's accounting system and disclosure statements and determine compliance with CAS and disclosure statements;
- determine the allowability of costs, and suspend or disapprove their payment;
- ensure contractor compliance with safety and quality assurance requirements;
- ensure contractor payment of rent;
- ensure processing and execution of duty-free entry certificates;
- ensure timely contractor notification of any anticipated cost overrun or underrun under cost-reimbursement contracts;
- ensure timely submission of reports;
- establish final indirect cost and billing rates;
- evaluate and monitor contractor procedures for restrictive markings on data;
- evaluate and recommend acceptance or rejection of waivers and deviations;
- evaluate contractor engineering efforts and management systems;
- evaluate contractor requests for Government property and changes to and use of existing property;
- issue and control Government bills of lading and other transportation documents;
- issue no-cost administrative changes;
- issue Notices of Intent to Disallow or not Recognize Costs;
- issue tax exemption forms;
- issue work requests under maintenance, modification, and overhaul contracts;
- maintain documentation of contractor performance under subcontracting plans and requirements;
- manage special bank accounts and make contractor payments;

- modify contracts to cover screening, redistribution, and disposal of excess Government property;
- monitor commercial financing provisions and contractor security to ensure adequacy to cover outstanding payments;
- monitor contractor environmental practices for adverse impact on contract performance or cost and compliance with environmental requirements;[3]
- monitor contractor ethics code;
- monitor contractor industrial labor relations and apprise the contracting officer and cognizant labor relations advisor of actual or potential labor disputes;
- monitor the contractor's financial condition and advise the contracting officer when it jeopardizes contract performance;
- monitor the contractor's value engineering program;
- negotiate and execute supplemental agreements to extend delivery schedules up to 90 days on contracts with an assigned Criticality Designator of C, with contracting office concurrence;
- negotiate forward pricing rate agreements and advance agreements regarding treatment of costs in future time periods;
- negotiate prices and execute supplemental agreements (e.g., for spare parts and provisioning);[4]
- perform engineering analyses of contractor cost proposals;
- perform preaward surveys to evaluate a prospective contractor's ability to perform a given contract;
- perform production surveillance and report delivery performance and slippages;
- perform property administration;
- process and execute novation and change-of-name agreements;
- provide appropriate recommendations to the contracting officer;
- release shipments from contractor's plants according to the shipping instructions, and review price adjustment proposals for amended shipping instructions;
- report items no longer needed for Government production;
- report to the contracting office any specification inadequacies;
- review all amended packaging and shipping instructions to ensure timely adjustments;
- review and (dis)approve contractor requests for payments under the progress payments or performance-based payments clauses;
- review and evaluate contractor logistics support, maintenance, and modification;
- review and evaluate contractors' proposals (including engineering and design studies) and furnish comments and recommendations to the contracting officer;

- review and evaluate preservation, packaging, and packing;
- review contractor compensation structure and insurance plans; and
- review contractor insurance plans and review earned value management system plans.

The ACO may negotiate and execute supplemental agreements to:

- adjust prices due to exercise of an economic price adjustment clause;
- amend shipping instructions;
- change interim billing prices;
- deobligate unexpended dollar balances exceeding known contract requirements;
- permit a change in place of inspection at origin specified in firm-fixed-price supply contracts awarded to nonmanufacturers;
- price out change orders;
- reduce line item quantities and deobligate excess funds on firm-fixed-price supply contracts due to delivery shortage (up to $250 or 5 percent of the contract price); and
- revise contract delivery schedules.

DFARS 242.2

DoD activities shall not retain any contract for administration that requires performance of any contract administration function at or near contractor facilities, except contracts for:

- airlift and sealift services;[5]
- architect-engineer services;
- ballistic missile sites (contract administration offices may perform supporting administration of these contracts at missile activation sites during the installation, test and checkout of the missiles and associated equipment);
- base, post, camp, and station purchases;
- communications services;
- construction and maintenance of military and civil public works, including docks, flood control, harbors, military housing, port facilities, public utilities, recreational facilities, and water resources;
- Defense Energy Support Center,
- Defense Logistics Agency;
- dependents Medicare program services;
- flight training;
- installation, operation and maintenance of space-track sensors and relays;
- management and professional support services;

- mapping, charting and geodesy services;
- National Security Agency;
- operation and maintenance of, or installation of equipment at, military test ranges, facilities and installations, or radar or communication network sites;
- research and development with universities;
- stevedoring contracts; and
- subsistence supplies.

PGI 242.302

For contracts assigned to DCMA for contract administration, the payment office is typically the cognizant Defense Finance and Accounting Service (DFAS) payment office as specified in the Federal Directory of Contract Administration Services Components (available at https://pubapp.dcma.mil/CASD/main.jsp), for contracts funded with DoD funds. The department or agency payment office can retain the payment function if authorized by defense financial management regulations or if the contract is funded with non-DoD funds. Multiple payment offices can be assigned if the contract is funded with both DoD and non-DoD funds.

FAR 37.6

There is sometimes a formal *contract management plan* to describe how the Government will administer oversee contract execution. It covers such topics as:

- acceptance criteria;
- changes in contractor personnel;
- communication process between parties;
- contract background, purpose and scope;
- contract changes and requests;
- contract closure;
- deliverables review and approval process;
- independent verification and validation;
- invoicing;
- performance metrics and milestones;
- program reviews;
- roles and responsibilities for each party; and
- status reporting and meetings.

FAR 42.6

Major Federal contractors with more than one operational location often have corporate-wide activities, policies and procedures requiring

Government review and approval that affect the work of multiple ACOs. To maintain consistent contract administration may require a corporate ACO to deal with corporate management and to perform selected contract administration functions on a corporate-wide basis. Typically, corporate ACOs administer CAS to corporate accounting practices, determine final indirect cost rates for flexibly priced contracts, and establish advance recommendations or agreements on corporate and home office expense allocations.

5.1.2 Business System and Cost Oversight

PGI 242.302(a)(S-75)

A formal program should be instituted to review contractor policies and procedures for cost monitoring and control at contractor locations where sales to the Government during the contractor's next fiscal year are expected to exceed $200 million in contracts based on incurred or projected costs. Contractors below this threshold may still be selected for monitoring if the contract administration office or the head of the contracting activity determines the cost benefits justify the enhanced monitoring or the head of the contracting activity decides that significant Government business exists with the contractor. Departments and agencies will discontinue the monitoring when the criteria are no longer met.

Contract administration offices (CAOs) designated as cost monitoring sites will select a cost monitoring specialist, usually the ACO or contract administrator. Working with the contract auditor, this person will:

- advise the ACO and CAO management of corrective action recommended to improve inefficient or uneconomical contractor conditions, policies, or practices, to include preparing a Notice of Intent to Disallow or Not Recognize Costs;
- consider review results in direct and indirect rate negotiations and contract negotiations;
- ensure the contractor implements corrective action recommended in the cost monitoring review reports;
- inform the auditor, contracting officer, program manager, and other responsible officials of issues affecting economical contract performance;
- maintain an inventory of planned and completed CAO, DCAA and other Government reviews and audits to mitigate duplication of efforts;
- maintain current organizational charts of the operations identifiable to the contractor's cost control functional centers;

- monitor direct and indirect rates and factors during the year, compare them to historical actual costs and to proposed or negotiated forward pricing rates and factors, and provide rate recommendations;
- perform approved functional reviews of contractor activities by obtaining access to pertinent contractor policies, procedures, and related data;
- prepare and maintain an annual written cost monitoring plan for reviewing contractor operations, and a final report summarizing all of the cost monitoring functions performed during the Government fiscal year;
- resolve disputes with the contractor regarding cost monitoring review findings or recommendations;
- review and approve the cost monitoring plan for the next fiscal year; and
- track the status of recommendations made to the contractor concerning cost performance stemming from all Government reports.

The annual cost monitoring plan is a strategy to negotiate, approve, and monitor contractor's direct and indirect rates, business systems, corrective actions to deficient processes, and cost controls. The idea is to coordinate the capabilities of the CAO, DCAA and other Government representatives to reduce erroneous, improper or unreasonable costs to Government contracts. The plan should provide coverage for each significant activity of the contractor over a period of 5 to 10 years, and for any forward pricing years the contractor proposes and the expected length of executed Government programs. The plan should be updated to reflect changed conditions as the year progresses. It should be consistent with the approved schedule, and any deviations should be explained in the final cost monitoring report. The plan must identify the organizations having the primary responsibility for performing the reviews during the coordination phase of the cost monitoring plan. The ACO is responsible for leading contractor purchasing system reviews and the DCAA auditor is responsible for leading estimating system reviews.

The CAO selects the activities for the cost monitoring plan. DCAA will complete its annual audit plan independently and communicate the approved audit plan to ensure the most effective monitoring approach. To ensure all Government interests are considered in the selection, the cost monitoring specialist should invite CAO, DCAA and other interested Government representatives to a meeting before the beginning of each Government fiscal year to identify and prioritize the areas to be reviewed during the coming year.

The selection team should consider the following data and assign primary responsibility in the selection process:

- contractor forecasts for future years supporting direct and indirect costs by functional centers of its cost control system and the results of the latest survey performed of such systems;
- contractor's accounting system showing the flow of costs by function;

- departures from established contractor productivity standards;
- determination of Government participation in the dollars attributable to the operations and cost accounts under consideration;
- financial variances from forecasts in prior years;
- idle or under-used capacity;
- organizational charts;
- recent reviews and audits performed by CAO, DCAA and other Government representatives and any outstanding weakness and deficiencies in the contractor's operations that will be considered for follow-up reviews or audits;
- under- or over-staffing; and
- visits or audit plans scheduled by other Government organizations.

The plan should reflect review and prioritization of contractor activity by considering:

- acquisition cycle stage;
- business and industry practices;
- contractor's operating methods;
- degree of technical and financial risk;
- extent of competition in awarded contracts;
- nature of the work;
- performance efficiencies previously demonstrated;
- previously reported findings and deficiencies;
- ratio of Government/commercial work;
- significant changes in the dollar level of the contractor's work and backlog; and
- types of contracts involved.

The annual cost monitoring report is a culmination of the Government activities performed during the fiscal year to conduct and maintain a formal monitoring program of contractor practices, policies and procedures to control costs charged to Government contracts. The report should also highlight both open and corrected deficiencies, and any newly reported deficiencies. It should also include the current status of all final, billing, and forward pricing rates.

The head of the local CAO or designee approves the annual cost monitoring report within 60 days of the end of the Government fiscal year. A copy of the approved report will be provided to the head of the local DCAA office within 15 days of approval.

DFARS 242.70

If the contracting officer makes a final determination to disapprove a contractor's business system, (s)he must identify one or more covered contracts subject to CAS and containing DFARS 252.242-7005, Contractor Business Systems, from which payments will be withheld. The total amount of payment withholding does not exceed 10 percent of progress payments, performance-based payments and interim payments under cost-reimbursement, labor-hour, and time-and-materials contracts billed under each of the identified covered contracts. The contracting officer has the sole discretion to identify the covered contracts from which to withhold payments.

The contracting officer, in consultation with the auditor or functional specialist, monitors the contractor's progress in correcting any deficiencies. The contracting officer will notify the contractor of any decision to decrease or increase the amount of payment withholding. If the contractor notifies the contracting officer that the contractor has corrected the significant deficiencies, the contracting officer will request the auditor or functional specialist to review the correction to verify that the deficiencies have been corrected. If the contracting officer concurs, (s)he discontinues the withholding of payments, releases any payments previously withheld, and approves the system. This should be resolved within 90 days of receipt of the contractor notification.

On the other hand, the contracting officer may determine after issuing this determination that the contractor has not corrected all significant deficiencies as directed by the contracting officer's final determination, or there is not a reasonable expectation that the corrective actions have been implemented. If so, (s)he can reduce withholding directly related to the significant deficiencies covered under the corrective action plan by at least 50 percent of the amount being withheld from progress payments and performance-based payments, and direct the contractor, in writing, to reduce the percentage withheld on interim cost vouchers by at least 50 percent.

If, at any time, the contracting officer determines that the contractor has failed to correct the significant deficiencies identified in the contractor's notification, (s)he will continue, reinstate, or increase withholding from progress payments and performance-based payments, and direct the contractor, in writing, to adjust interim cost vouchers accordingly. This will continue until (s)he determines that the contractor has corrected all significant deficiencies as directed by the final determination.

Solicitation Provision and Contract Clause

DFARS 252.242-7005, Contractor Business Systems, in solicitations and contracts (other than in contracts with educational institutions, Federally Funded Research and Development Centers, or University Associated Research Centers operated by educational institutions) when the solicitation or contract is subject to Cost Accounting Standards and includes any of the following clauses:

- DFARS 252.215-7002, Cost Estimating System Requirements.
- DFARS 252.234-7002, Earned Value Management System.
- DFARS 252.242-7004, Material Management and Accounting System.
- DFARS 252.242-7006, Accounting System Administration.
- DFARS 252.244-7001, Contractor Purchasing System Administration.
- DFARS 252.245-7003, Contractor Property Management System Administration.

5.1.3 Contracting Officer's Representative

The program office will assign a Contracting Officer's Representative (COR, or sometimes COTR for a technical representative) to provide program knowledge assistance to the contractor and contracting officer during contract performance.[6] As the eyes and ears of the contracting officer, the COR assists the contracting officer in technical monitoring or administration of the contract. The COR often serves as the onsite technical manager responsible for actual surveillance of the contractor's work and assessing actual contractor performance against contract performance standards. The COR monitors specific facets of the contract under the direction of the contracting officer, such as:

- inspect and accept deliverables;
- interpret technical requirements;
- monitor and evaluate contractor performance;
- monitor contractor use of Government-furnished property;
- recommend changes and corrective actions; and
- review invoices and contractor status reports.

The COR has no authority to commit the Government to a position, direct changes or authorize subcontract placement. The COR cannot authorize overtime (only the contracting officer may do so), but can examine time cards and authorized overtime, as well as any expenses.

The contracting officer will issue a designation letter to the representative immediately upon award. This letter manifests the duties of the representative and asserts that the contracting officer is qualified and trained to perform the duties. CORs might not be assigned for contracts that do not require frequent interaction with the contractor; a contract specialist or program management analyst may fulfill these duties in such cases. This certainly saves money and effort, but these individuals may not have in-depth program knowledge to address any programmatic issues that might arise.

PGI 201.602-2

A COR is required for all services contracts and any supply contract with a cost-reimbursable line item.[7] COR surveillance activities can be tailored to the dollar value and complexity of the contract. For geographically dispersed contracts with multiple task orders, contracting officers may appoint multiple CORs to provide local surveillance. A COR is not required for cost reimbursement supply contracts.

Contract Clause

DFARS 252.201-7000, Contracting Officer's Representative.

5.2 LABOR

5.2.1 Labor Laws

FAR Part 22

There are rules of behavior for both Government and contractor regarding organized labor. Collective bargaining and freedom of association for labor was ensured by the *National Labor Relations Act*,[8] which prohibits a firm from discriminating against employees regarding activities for or against a labor union, or who file charges or testify against the firm. The firm cannot interfere with labor union operations or refuse to bargain collectively with union representatives. Moreover, the firm cannot coerce or restrain employees from association, mutual aid or self-organization to bargain collectively for wages and better working conditions.

Agencies must remain impartial concerning any dispute between labor and contractor management without resort to conciliation, mediation, or arbitration. However, they will exchange information with other agencies to ensure a uniform Government approach concerning a labor-management dispute. The contracting officer may seek a voluntary agreement between management and labor to permit uninterrupted acquisition of supplies and services, but cannot become involved in the merits of the dispute. Normal plant inspection continues without regard to the existence of a labor dispute, strike, or picket line, unless personal safety is threatened. The head of the contracting activity may designate programs or requirements where contractors must notify the Government of actual or potential labor disputes that could delay timely contract performance.

Contractors are responsible for reasonably avoidable delays. They should try to use private boards or organizations to settle disputes but may file a charge with the National Labor Relations Board to seek injunctive relief in court. Beyond this however, contractors are not held responsible if their diligent efforts fail to end the dispute.

Contract labor normally uses a 40-hour workweek, or if outside the United States, the normal workweek for the area without a premium rate if for more than 40 hours per week. Contractors do not use overtime as a regular employment practice unless lower overall costs result or if necessary to meet urgent program needs. Therefore, solicitations normally do not specify delivery or performance schedules that require overtime at Government expense. During contract performance, the agency approving official must determine in writing that overtime is necessary to meet essential delivery or performance schedules, compensate for delays beyond the control and without the fault or negligence of the contractor, or eliminate extended production bottlenecks.

Contractor employees must record on their time cards all hours worked, including unbillable direct labor and any indirect labor. Managers with time-card approval authority review the accuracy of charge numbers and the hours charged at the end of the pay period. They should approve the time card only after the employee has done so, and are accountable for time card accuracy.

When an employee changes any recorded hours, the reason code becomes part of the time card's audit trail, providing an auditor with a comprehensive picture of the employee's labor charging during the pay period.

DFARS 222.101-4

When a contractor is unable to deliver urgent and critical items because of a work stoppage at its facility, the contracting officer must contact the labor advisor to obtain the opinion of the Federal Mediation and Conciliation Service or other mediation agency regarding the effect movement of the items would have on labor negotiations. Normally removals will not be made if they will adversely affect labor negotiations. Based on this input, (s)he requests in writing to remove the material to the contract administration office. The request should identify the items to be moved, mode of transportation and destination.

The contracting officer should then enlist the help of the agency's labor advisor or contract administration office to obtain agreement of both the management and the labor representatives to ship the material by normal means. If agreement cannot be reached, (s)he can ask the parties to permit movement of the material by military vehicles with military personnel. If all else fails, the labor advisor can get personally involved or else refer the matter to the agency head, who could order removal of the items from the facility.

DFARS 222.101-70

If a labor dispute delays performance of a contract for urgently needed stevedoring services, the contracting officer will attempt to have management and labor voluntarily agree to exempt military supplies from the labor dispute by continuing the movement of such material. If this fails, (s)he could consider contracting with reliable alternative sources of supply within the stevedoring industry and divert vessels to alternate ports able to provide necessary stevedoring services. Other options include utilizing civil service stevedores or military personnel to perform the work performed by contract stevedores.

PGI 222.101-3-70

For a dispute involving a product, project or service that is essential to meet schedules for urgently needed military programs or requirements, each contracting activity involved will develop data reflecting the impact of potential or actual labor disputes. The contracting activity then reports to the department labor advisor the (sub)contractor involved, impact, any alternate sources, and any action taken to reduce the impact. The labor advisor recommends to the head of the agency the impact on operations of a work stoppage for different lengths of time and any possible measures to minimize strike impact.

Solicitation Provisions and Contract Clauses

FAR 52.222-1, Notice to the Government of Labor Disputes, when designated by the agency head.

FAR 52.222-2, Payment for Overtime Premiums, if a cost-reimbursement contract is expected to exceed the simplified acquisition threshold. This does not apply to contracts to operate vessels or a cost-plus-incentive-fee contract that provides a target fee swing of at least plus or minus 3 percent and a contractor's share of at least 10 percent.

5.2.2 Convict Labor

FAR 22.2

The Federal Government encourages developing the occupational and educational skills of prison inmates.[9] A contractor may hire past or present Federal prisoners or parolees. State or local prisoners may also be hired if authorized to work for pay in the community in a voluntary approved work training program. However, to avoid unfair competition with salaried labor:

- employed workers cannot be displaced;
- local union representatives must be consulted (if applicable);
- no existing services contracts can be impaired;
- the pay rate must be that for similar work in the region; and
- the trade must have a surplus of available labor in the locality.

Solicitation Provision and Contract Clause

FAR 52.222-3, Convict Labor, if above the micro-purchase threshold for performance in the United States and outlying areas, unless subject to 41 U.S.C. 65, with Federal Prison Industries, Inc., or involving the purchase from a State prison of finished supplies that may be secured in the open market or from existing stocks.

5.2.3 Contract Work Hours and Safety Standards Act

FAR 22.3

The Contract Work Hours and Safety Standards Act[10] applies to contracts for laborers or mechanics (but not seamen). *Laborers* or *mechanics* include those who perform manual or physical duties, rather than mental or managerial.[11] Example labor types include apprentices, helpers and trainees, firefighters, guards, and watchmen. This definition also includes foremen who devote more than 20 percent of their time during a workweek performing duties of a laborer or mechanic.

No laborer or mechanic under the contract may work more than 40 hours in any workweek unless paid for all overtime hours at least 1.5 times the basic pay rate, regardless of whether the employer required or permitted the employee to do so.

When a computation discloses under-payments, the responsible (sub)contractor pays the affected employee any unpaid wages and then pays liquidated damages to the Government at the rate of $10 per affected employee per day worked. If the (sub)contractor fails or refuses to comply and the funds withheld do not cover the unpaid wages, the Government pays laborers the wages owed (or a prorated amount if sufficient funds are not available) plus liquidated damages. If the agency head finds that the violation was inadvertent, (s)he can waive liquidated damages if below $500. Any higher amount must go to the Secretary of Labor for final action. The contractor has 60 days to appeal the assessment via the contracting officer to the responsible agency official.

Per Executive Order 13706, Establishing Paid Sick Leave for Federal Contractors, Federal contract employees are subject to receiving sick leave from their employers at the rate of one hour of leave per 30 hours of work.

Solicitation Provisions and Contract Clauses

FAR 52.222-4, Contract Work Hours and Safety Standards Act—Overtime Compensation, if employing laborers or mechanics. Do not use if:

- exempt under Department of Labor regulations;
- for commercial items;

- for supplies with only incidental services that do not require substantial employment of laborers or mechanics;
- for transportation or transmission of intelligence;
- to be performed outside the United States or outlying areas; or
- valued at or below $150,000.

FAR 52.222-62, Paid Sick Leave Under Executive Order 13706.

5.2.4 Labor Standards for Construction

FAR 22.4

We have seen several statutes and executive orders prescribe labor requirements for contracts to construct, alter or repair public buildings and public works. A *construction, alteration or repair* contract addresses laborers and mechanics on a building or work site who alter, install, or remodel items that were fabricated off-site, or who finish them (e.g., decorate or paint). It also includes those workers who furnish or manufacture equipment, materials or supplies on the work site, or transport them between the work site and a facility dedicated to the construction project.

It must be noted, however, that these labor standards apply only to:

- construction work at a site where wage rates can be determined for the locality;
- dismantling, demolition, or removal of improvements;
- manufacture or fabrication at the worksite of construction materials and components by the (sub)contractor; and
- painting public buildings or works, either during original construction or as alteration or repair of an existing structure.

Recall that the Davis-Bacon Act requires wage determinations to be issued by the Department of Labor for such contracts over $2,000. Also, the *Copeland (Anti-Kickback) Act*[12] prohibits inducement, intimidation, surrender of compensation due, or threat of dismissal of any person employed under Federal construction contracts. This statute also requires each (sub)contractor to furnish a weekly statement of compliance for wages paid each employee during the preceding week.

DFARS 222.406-1

Upon contract award, the contracting officer provides a pre-construction letter to the prime contractor to state certain statutes and regulations which govern labor standards requirements contained in the contract. The contractor must send a copy of the letter to each subcontractor. A pre-construction meeting will be held if the prime contractor has not performed previous Government contracts or has had difficulty in complying with labor standards requirements on previous contracts, or to determine if the (sub)contractors intend to pay any required fringe benefits as specified in the wage determination or to elect a different method of payment.

Solicitation Provision

FAR 52.222-5, Construction Wage Rate Requirements-Secondary Site of the Work.

Contract Clauses

FAR 52.222-6, Construction Wage Rate Requirements.
FAR 52.222-7, Withholding of Funds.
FAR 52.222-8, Payrolls and Basic Records.
FAR 52.222-9, Apprentices and Trainees.
FAR 52.222-10, Compliance with Copeland Act Requirements.
FAR 52.222-11, Subcontracts (Labor Standards).
FAR 52.222-12, Contract Termination—Debarment.
FAR 52.222-13, Compliance with Construction Wage Rate Requirements and Related Regulations.
FAR 52.222-14, Disputes Concerning Labor Standards.
FAR 52.222-15, Certification of Eligibility.
FAR 52.222-16, Approval of Wage Rates.

5.2.5 Contracts for Materials, Supplies, Articles, and Equipment Exceeding $15,000

FAR 22.6

Replacing the Walsh-Healey Public Contracts Act, this long-titled legislation is perhaps better known by its legal citation of 41 U.S.C. 65. It addresses performance within the United States and certain possessions, in any amount exceeding $15,000, and includes or incorporates by reference provisions regarding child and convict labor, maximum hours, minimum wages, and safe and sanitary working conditions. Contracts to acquire the following supplies are exempt from the Act:

- agricultural or farm products processed for sale by the original producers;
- items where immediate delivery is required by the public exigency;

- newspapers, magazines or periodicals from sales agents or publisher representatives;
- perishables, including dairy, livestock, and nursery products;
- public utility services;
- purchases against a defaulting contractor if the contract was itself exempt; or
- supplies manufactured outside the United States, Puerto Rico, and Virgin Islands.

Upon the request of the agency head, the Secretary of Labor may exempt specific contracts or classes of contracts from application of one or more of the Act's stipulations when the conduct of Government business will be seriously impaired.

The $15,000 threshold applies to any subcontract and indefinite delivery contract or agreement (in terms of total orders placed thereunder), but ceases to apply if a contract is modified to an amount below the threshold.

Solicitation Provision and Contract Clause

FAR 52.222-20, Contracts for Materials, Supplies, Articles, and Equipment Exceeding $15,000.

5.2.6 Equal Employment Opportunity

FAR 22.8 through 22.9

Everyone has the right to be considered for employment without discrimination due to age, creed, color, gender identity, handicap (mental or physical), national origin, race, or sexual orientation. No contract or modification can be awarded to an entity found to be noncompliant with the requirements of Executive Orders 11246, Equal employment opportunity, and 13672, Prohibiting discrimination based on sexual orientation and gender identity. Each non-construction (sub)contractor with 50 or more employees and a (sub) contract of $50,000 or more (or totaling $50,000 or more or in any 12-month period) must develop a written affirmative action program for each of its establishments within 120 days from beginning its first such Government (sub)contract or bill of lading.

For construction contracting, each agency maintains a listing of geographical areas that are subject to affirmative action requirements, and specifies goals for minorities and women in covered trades. If a contracting officer anticipates an award over $10,000 in an area which is not covered, (s)he must request instructions from the Office of Federal

Contract Compliance Programs (OFCCP) regional office. Contracting officers give written notice to OFCCP within 10 working days of award of a construction contract. If the estimated amount of the (sub)contract is $10 million or more, the contracting officer requests clearance from the appropriate OFCCP regional office 30 days before the proposed award date or modification for new effort. If OFCCP does not respond within 15 days or a mutually agreed time frame, approval is assumed. The contracting officer need not request a preaward clearance if the specific proposed contractor is listed in OFCCP's National Preaward Registry[13] and the projected award date is within 24 months of its Notice of Compliance completion date in the Registry.

To demonstrate compliance, the contracting officer furnishes to the contractor multiple copies of the poster titled "Equal Employment Opportunity Is the Law." Many firms post this and similar notices on a bulletin board in the coffee mess, where it can be easily seen by all employees.

Using contract awards as a tool to enforce civil rights legislation may seem controversial and costly, but OFCCP has insufficient resources to enforce implementation in any other way. Moreover, the Supreme Court decided that contractors may be treated differently when Congress says so, and that a remedial program to place minorities on an equal footing for public contracting opportunities is valid.[14] Nonetheless, all or part of these requirements of Executive Order 11246 may be excluded for:

- contracts with religious entities or with state or local governments;
- effort for national security;
- facilities not connected with contracts;
- offering employment preference to Indians living on or near a reservation for work in that area;
- special circumstances of national interest; or
- work outside the United States by employees who were not recruited within the United States.

This Executive Order does not apply for transactions of $10,000 or less. This includes indefinite quantity contracts if the amount to be ordered in any year is not expected to exceed $10,000. The Equal Opportunity clause is applied once a single order exceeds $10,000, and continues in force for the contract's duration regardless of the amounts ordered, or expected to be ordered, in any future year. Note that Government bills of lading are not exempt, regardless of amount.

Per Executive Order 11141, Declaring a public policy against discrimination based on age, (sub)contractors may not discriminate against persons because of their age in terms of employment, promotion, or discharge. No additional contract clauses are required.

Solicitation Provisions

FAR 52.222-22, Previous Contracts and Compliance Reports, unless completely exempt from Executive Order 11246.

FAR 52.222-23, Notice of Requirement for Affirmative Action to Ensure Equal Employment Opportunity for Construction, if expected to exceed $10,000.

FAR 52.222-24, Preaward On-Site Equal Opportunity Compliance Evaluation, if non-construction (unless completely exempt from Executive Order 11246) and expected to be $10 million or more.

FAR 52.222-25, Affirmative Action Compliance, if non-construction (unless completely exempt from Executive Order 11246).

Solicitation Provisions and Contract Clauses

FAR 52.222-21, Prohibition of Segregated Facilities.

FAR 52.222-26, Equal Opportunity, unless exempt from Executive Order 11246. Use the clause with its Alternate I if the contract is exempt from one or more, but not all, of the requirements of Executive Order 11246.

FAR 52.222-27, Affirmative Action Compliance Requirements for Construction, if non-construction (unless completely exempt from Executive Order 11246) and expected to be in excess of $10,000.

Contract Clause

FAR 52.222-29, Notification of Visa Denial, if non-construction (unless completely exempt from Executive Order 11246) and performed in or on behalf of a foreign country.

5.2.7 Professional Employee Compensation

FAR 22.11

A *professional employee* is a person whose livelihood is based upon acquiring specialized knowledge through prolonged study. Professions include:

- accountants;
- actuaries;
- architects;

- dentists;
- engineers;
- lawyers;
- physicians;
- nurses;
- pharmacists; and
- scientists.

When the contract amount is expected to exceed $750,000 and the services will require numerous professional employees, offerors must submit for evaluation a total compensation plan of proposed salaries and fringe benefits for all professional employees working on the contract.

Solicitation Provision

FAR 52.222-46, Evaluation of Compensation for Professional Employees, when the negotiated contract amount is expected to exceed $750,000 and the services will require numerous professional employees.

5.2.8 Non-Displacement of Qualified Workers

FAR 22.12

When the Government awards a follow-on service contract to a firm who is not the incumbent contractor, the successor firm must offer all service employees currently working under the prior contract a right of first refusal for employment under the new contract in positions for which they are qualified. This requirement does not apply to (sub)contracts awarded:

- below the simplified acquisition threshold;
- for vending facilities;
- for service employees working under both a Federal and one or more non-federal service contracts;
- to SourceAmerica; or
- to sheltered workshops employing severely handicapped persons (this primarily occurs for custodians, elevator operators, messengers, or security guards).

At least 30 days before completion of the contract, the predecessor contractor must furnish to the contracting officer a certified list of the names of all service employees working under the contract and its subcontracts, along with anniversary dates of employment of each service employee. Any updated changes are due 10 days before contract completion. The contracting officer will furnish the final list to the successor contractor and, if requested, to the employees themselves or their authorized representatives. All current employees are notified of their rights in writing, either by personal letter or by posting a notice at the workplace, including their possible right to an offer of employment with the successor contractor. Failure to do so could result in suspension of payment by the contracting officer, as well as possible suspension or debarment.

Any job offer by the new contactor must give the employee 10 days to respond. An offer is not required when the employee will stay with the predecessor contractor on another assignment or has failed to show adequate work performance. Also, the successor contractor need not offer employment to all prior workers if it plans to reduce the workforce; however it must then wait 90 days to attract new talent (otherwise, it must first offer the position to displaced former employees).

The agency's senior procurement executive may waive this provision upon written determination that it would impair the ability of the Federal Government to economically or efficiently procure the services. The agency must provide the Department of Labor its waiver decision and analysis within five business days after the solicitation issuance date. Within the same time frame, the contracting officer must direct the contractor to notify affected workers and their collective bargaining representative in writing.

5.2.9 Veterans Affairs

FAR 22.13

In accordance with several statutes and an executive order,[15] (sub)contractors must list all employment openings for service labor lasting more than three days, unless filled from within the organization. They must take affirmative action to promote employment of qualified disabled veterans without discrimination to their disability or veteran's status. This requirement applies to all (sub)contracts for personal property and nonpersonal services (including construction) of $150,000 or more, unless waived by the Secretary of Labor. The (sub)contractor must submit a VETS-4212 Report, except for awards to state and local governments and foreign organizations where the workers are recruited outside of the United States. To verify if a proposed contractor has submitted a current VETS-4212 Report, the contracting officer either emails or consults the Department of Labor's database.[16]

The head of the agency may waive these requirements upon determination that the contract is essential to the national security, and that its award without complying with such requirements is necessary to the national security.

Possible sanctions for violation include withholding progress payments, contract suspension or termination, or debarment.

Solicitation Provision

FAR 52.222-38, Compliance with Veterans' Employment Reporting Requirements, if exceeding the simplified acquisition threshold and the contract is not for COTS.

Solicitation Provisions and Contract Clauses

FAR 52.222-35, Equal Opportunity for Special Disabled Veterans, Veterans of the Vietnam Era, and Other Eligible Veterans, if the expected value is $150,000 or more, unless the work is performed outside the United States by employees recruited outside the United States, or the Deputy Assistant Secretary of Labor has waived the clause. Use the basic clause with its Alternate I if only part of the clause is waived.

FAR 52.222-37, Employment Reports on Special Disabled Veterans, Veterans of the Vietnam Era, and Other Eligible Veterans, if containing FAR 52.222-35.

5.2.10 Employment of Disabled Workers

FAR 22.14

Per Section 503 of the Rehabilitation Act of 1973 and Executive Order 11758 (Delegating authority of the President under the Rehabilitation Act of 1973), Government contractors must take affirmative action to employ and advance qualified individuals with disabilities, without discriminating against their mental or physical disability. If notified by the appropriate agency official of violations, the contracting officer may withhold payments or institute sanctions, suspend, or terminate the contract, or begin debarment proceedings. The agency head, with the concurrence of the OFCCP, may waive any or all requirements if a waiver is deemed to be in the national interest.

Solicitation Provision and Contract Clause

FAR 52.222-36, Affirmative Action for Workers with Disabilities, if the expected value is $15,000 or more, unless the work is performed outside the United States by employees recruited outside the United States or OFCCP has waived the clause. Use the basic clause with its Alternate I if only part of the terms of the clause is waived.

5.2.11 Products Produced by Forced or Indentured Child Labor

FAR 22.15

When soliciting for supplies expected to exceed the micro-purchase threshold, the contracting officer must check the List of Products Requiring Contractor Certification as to Forced or Indentured Child Labor.[17] The List contains products which may have been mined, produced or manufactured by forced or indentured child labor under age 18 in a specified country. The offeror must certify in its offer that it will not supply any end product manufactured in a country identified on the List for that product, or that it is not aware of any such child labor in use. The Government may impose remedies if the contractor furnished an end product or component using forced or indentured child labor, or submitted a false certification regarding knowledge of the use of forced or indentured child labor. It may also impose remedies if the contractor failed to cooperate with an investigation of the use of forced or indentured labor by any Inspector General or the Department of Justice or Treasury.

Contract termination is the only available remedy for furnishing an end product or component using forced or indentured child labor. For the other situations, suspension or debarment for up to three years is authorized (as is contract termination).

Solicitation Provision:

FAR 52.222-18, Certification Regarding Knowledge of Child Labor for Listed End Products, if expected to exceed the micro-purchase threshold and are for the type of end products identified by country of origin on the List of Products Requiring Contractor Certification as to Forced or Indentured Child Labor. It is not used in solicitations for commercial items that include the provision at FAR 52.212-3, Offeror Representations and Certifications—Commercial Items. The contracting officer identifies whichever provision is used, the applicable end products and countries of origin from the List.

Solicitation Provision and Contract Clause

FAR 52.222-19, Child Labor—Cooperation with Authorities and Remedies, if expected to exceed the micro-purchase threshold.

5.2.12 Notification of Employee Rights Under the National Labor Relations Act

FAR 22.16

Executive Order 13496, Notification of Employee Right Under Federal Labor Laws, requires (sub)contractors that exceed the simplified acquisition threshold to post a notice informing employees of their rights to collective bargaining, and to include this requirement in subcontracts over $10,000 (unless performed solely outside the United States). The Department of Labor may investigate any (sub)contractor to determine violation of any of the requirements. If a violation is found, the Department of Labor may direct that the contract be cancelled, suspended or terminated (in whole or in part), and declare the contractor ineligible for further Government contracts. The Secretary of Labor may grant exemptions, including deleting or modifying the prescribed clause in contracts.

Solicitation Provision and Contract Clause

FAR 52.222-40, Notification of Employee Rights Under the National Labor Relations Act, unless below the simplified acquisition threshold, for work solely outside the United States, or exempted by the Secretary of Labor.

5.2.13 Combating Trafficking in Persons

FAR 22.17

(Sub)contractors and their employees cannot engage in the following activities during the period of performance of the contract:

- charge recruiting fees to employees;
- destroy immigration documents;
- fail to provide a written contract of employment where required by law;
- fail to provide transportation to departing employees from foreign countries;
- mislead job applicants about the terms of employment;
- procure commercial sex acts;
- provide unsafe housing;
- traffic persons involuntarily; and
- use forced labor in the performance of the contract.

The successful offeror must certify before award over $500,000 for non-COTS supplies or services to be performed outside the United States that has a compliance plan and is not in violation, or else has corrected any violation. The contractor must collect the same certification from any subcontractor meeting the same criteria. The contracting officer notifies the agency Inspector General of any violations.

Solicitation Provision

FAR 52.222-56, Certification Regarding Trafficking in Persons Compliance Plan, if over $550,000 and performed outside the United States, and not for commercial products.

Solicitation Provision and Contract Clause

FAR 52.222-50, Combating Trafficking in Persons. Use the basic clause with its Alternate I when the contract will be performed outside the United States.

5.2.14 Employment Eligibility Verification

FAR 22.18

Under the Department of Homeland Security (DHS), the United States Citizenship and Immigration Service's employment eligibility verification program (E-Verify) is the means to verify employment eligibility. Contractors may employ only individuals who are eligible to work in the United States. Contractors must enroll as Federal contractors in E-Verify, using it to verify employment eligibility of all new hires working in the United States. However, it can restrict such a review to Federal contract hires only if it is a Government agency (state, local or Indian), institution of higher education, or a surety performing under a takeover agreement entered into with a Federal agency pursuant to a performance bond.

The same requirement applies to subcontracts for services (unless part of a COTS item or service) and construction. The contractor need not verify employment eligibility of employees who hold an active security clearance, or for whom background investigations have been completed and credentials issued per Homeland Security Presidential Directive-12 (HSPD).

DHS and the Social Security Administration may terminate a contractor's memorandum of understanding and deny access to the E-Verify system. The terminating agency refers the matter to a designated agency official for possible suspension or debarment action.

Solicitation Provision and Contract Clause

FAR 52.222-54, Employment Eligibility Verification, if exceeding the simplified acquisition threshold, except for a period of performance less than 120 days, a COTS item or commercial services performed by the COTS provider, or work performed outside the United States.

5.2.15 Executive Compensation

FAR 4.14

Section 2 of the Federal Funding Accountability and Transparency Act of 2006, as amended by section 6202 of the Government Funding Transparency Act of 2008,[18] requires most contractors to report the total compensation of the five most highly compensated executives of itself and any first-tier subcontractor when the subcontract equals or exceeds $30,000 in value and is with a firm that does at least 80 percent of its total business (i.e., at least $20 million per annum) with the Federal Government. The first-tier subcontract award data is available at www.usaspending.gov, managed by the Department of Treasury. The compensation amount includes salaries and bonuses (both current and deferred) plus incentive payments, pension value changes and stock options. Any classified contracts and contracts with individuals are not included, nor are simplified acquisitions. Agencies review contractor reports on a quarterly basis to ensure that the information is consistent with contract information. The agency informs the contractor of any inconsistencies with the contract information and requires the contractor to correct the report, or else explain why it believes the information is correct. Agencies review the reports at www.fsrs.gov.[19] (Sub)contractors who had gross income in the previous tax year under $300,000 are exempt from the reporting requirement.

Solicitation Provision and Contract Clause

FAR 52.204-10, Reporting Executive Compensation and First-Tier Subcontract Awards, unless classified or a simplified acquisition.

5.2.16 Construction and Service Contracts in Noncontiguous States

DFARS 222.70

A restriction applies to construction and service contracts to be performed in whole or in part within a noncontiguous State and the unemployment rate in the noncontiguous State (i.e., Alaska or Hawaii) is in excess of the national average rate of unemployment as determined by the Secretary of Labor.[20]

A contractor awarded a contract performed in a noncontiguous state must employ individuals who are residents of that noncontiguous State and who, in the case of any craft or trade, possess or would be able to acquire promptly the necessary skills to perform the contract. The head of the agency may waive this requirement on a case-by-case basis in the interest of national security.

DFARS 222.73

Contracts for base operations support on Guam may be awarded as a result of a competition conducted under OMB Circular A-76. Any alien who is issued a visa or otherwise provided nonimmigrant status is prohibited from performing work under a contract for base operations support on Guam. Exceptions are legally admitted citizens the Republic of the Marshall Islands, the Federated States of Micronesia, or the Republic of Palau.

Solicitation Provision and Contract Clause

DFARS 252.222-7000, Restrictions on Employment of Personnel, when subject to this subpart. Insert the name of the appropriate noncontiguous State in paragraph (a) of the clause.

Contract clauses

DFARS 252.222-7002, Compliance with Local Labor Laws (Overseas).

DFARS 252.222-7003, Permit from Italian Inspectorate of Labor.

DFARS 252.222-7004, Compliance with Spanish Social Security Laws and Regulations.

DFARS 252.222-7005, Prohibition on Use of Nonimmigrant Aliens—Guam.

DFARS 252.222-7006, Restrictions on the Use of Mandatory Arbitration Agreements.

5.3 QUALITY

5.3.1 Quality Assurance

FAR 46.1 and .2

Quality assurance is a systematic process approach to provide confidence that supplies, services or data conform to requirements and achieve satisfactory performance. A successful quality assurance program specifies quality requirements, determines supplier capability, inspects deliveries, and motivates suppliers. When acquiring commercial items, the Government relies on contractor quality assurance systems before acceptance unless in-process inspection by the customer is customary in the market. For Government-specified items or services however, more active Government involvement is necessary in the quality assurance process. This process includes testing parts and material, both before ordering and during use to ensure that the required level of quality is met. This is typically completed before a contract or delivery order is issued, to ensure that the supplier has met the requirements.

Quality assurance differs from *quality control*, which is a quantitative approach to measure performance, compare it to a standard, and then act on the difference. It is an axiom of Federal procurement that the contractor is responsible for quality control, but the Government is responsible for quality assurance.

There is more to this concept than mere inspection of parts. Quality assurance looks at the contractor's systems and procedures to control quality and quantity in the plant, while *inspection* assures that products conform to specifications. The former intends to prevent quality problems while the latter looks only for nonconformities. A quality assurance program emphasizes feedback and corrective actions to correct process-driven failures. Quality control techniques include attribute sampling, random statistical sampling, and regression and correlation analysis. Statistical quality control is useful for prediction, testing output, detecting causes of variation, and analysis of same.

Acceptance sampling can be done based on either attributes or variables. Sampling by attributes is a statistical method based on sample size and aids a yes-or-no decision on acceptability. By contrast, acceptance sampling by variables records actual measurements, sets a range of tolerable limits, and then determines a percentage of defectives. It requires fewer samples and less inspection than the attribute method.

Material quality management is a joint function of engineering, production and purchasing departments. Engineering develops specifications and drawings, testing methods and procedures, and a range of acceptable qualities. Production considers cost constraints, inventory adequacy and manufacturing techniques. Purchasing handles order placement, performance monitoring, quality control, and sampling. These departments decide what level of detail should be used to assure vendor compliance. It can also help the Production department to lower costs and find suitable materials that are easy to work with.

The contracting officer will include specifications for inspection, testing and other quality requirements in the contract. Upon award, the contracting officer will issue instructions to the contract administration office and act on their recommendations or, if contract administration is retained, verify that the contractor fulfills the contract quality requirements. The contracting officer also ensures that nonconformances are identified and considered when determining the acceptability of supplies or services which do not meet contract requirements.

The Government may rely on the contractor to accomplish all inspection and testing at or below the simplified acquisition threshold to ensure conformance with contract quality requirements. The contractor's inspection system or program covers:

- drawings, specifications, and engineering changes;
- fabrication and delivery of products;
- manufacturing processes;
- preservation, packaging, packing, and marking;

- reliability and maintainability assessment;
- technical documentation (e.g., drawings, specifications, handbooks, manuals, and other technical publications); and
- testing and examination.

The extent of contract quality requirements and inspection for a given contract is based upon the technical description of the contract supply or service (i.e., commercial, Federal, or military), and its complexity and criticality. Complex items have quality characteristics requiring assembly, manufacturing, measurement, performance, and test operations. Noncomplex items require only simple measurement and testing the end item to determine conformance to contract requirements. The manufacturer may institute a process quality team or quality improvement team to maintain ongoing quality reviews and process improvements.[21]

Sometimes the nature of the supplies and services and their intended use requires the Government to test them before tender for acceptance, or perhaps pass judgment upon the adequacy of the contractor's internal work processes. This could also occur if a costly and detailed Government inspection is required, or costly correction or loss occurs due to defective deliverables.

The ACO maintains records of Government contract quality assurance actions, including the number of observations and defects, any decisions regarding the acceptability of the products, processes and requirements, and actions to correct defects. The ACO reports to the contracting office any defects observed in design or technical requirements (including quality), implements any written instructions from the contracting office, and recommends any changes necessary to the contract (as well as instructions or specifications) that will provide more effective operations or eliminate unnecessary costs.

Government quality assurance often requires performing inspection and related functions to see if a contractor has fulfilled the contract obligations regarding quality and quantity. It is conducted before acceptance by or under the direction of Government personnel. The Government can run a *physical configuration audit* to examine the item against its technical baseline (usually specifications or drawings) to verify that it conforms to the item's technical documentation. This is often done with items that are hard to manufacture, are being built by a new contractor, or come off a production line that had been shut down for some time.

Nonconforming supplies or services are classified as critical, major or minor. *Critical nonconformance* means a deficiency that is likely to result in hazardous or unsafe conditions for individuals using, maintaining, or relying upon the supplies or services, or is likely to prevent performance of a vital agency mission. *Major nonconformance* means a non-critical deficiency that is likely to result in failure of the supplies or services, or to materially reduce the usability of the supplies or services for their intended purpose. *Minor nonconformance* means a deficiency that is not likely to materially reduce their usability for their intended purpose, or is a departure from established standards with little impact on the effective use or operation of the supplies or services. Minor nonconformities are often accepted, perhaps with a price adjustment, but major or critical nonconformances are usually rejected.

When a contract is assigned for administration to a Government office located at a contractor's plant, the office verifies whether the supplies or services conform to contract quality requirements, and reports to the contracting office any defects observed in design, quality or technical requirements. The office will also recommend any changes to the contract, specifications, or instructions to improve effective operations or eliminate unnecessary costs.

Requiring compliance with higher-level quality standards is appropriate for complex or critical items when the technical requirements of the contract require control of work operations, in-process controls, and inspection. *Critical items* are components, material or subsystems that must be available at a specific time in production or else jeopardize cost, quality, or schedule. They could also be used to provide more attention to documentation, organization, planning, and work instructions. Examples of higher-level quality standards are:

- ANSI/ASQC E4—*Quality Management Systems for Environmental Information and Technology Programs—Requirements with Guidance for Use (2017)*;
- ANSI/ASQC/ISSO Q9001 (*Quality Management Systems—Requirements*, 2008), Q9002 (*Quality Systems—Model for Quality Assurance in Production, Installation, and Servicing*, 1997), or Q9003 (*Quality Systems—Model for Quality Assurance in Final Inspection and Test*, 1994).[22]

The ISO 9001 publication sets forth standards for a quality management system by stating principles and processes to design, develop and deliver a product or service. A firm can participate in a continuing certification process under ISO 9001 to show its compliance with the standard and its requirement for planned quality improvement.

FAR 46.402 and .403

Quality assurance may be performed either at *origin*, where the work is performed, or at *destination*, whether delivery will be made. The decision of where to perform quality assurance is based on a number of factors. It will be performed at source if Government inspection during contract performance is essential, such as concern that considerable loss would result from the manufacture and shipment of unacceptable supplies, or from the delay in making necessary corrections. Likewise, it should be performed at source if any other place would require uneconomical disassembly or destructive testing, or costly special packing and packaging if required test instruments or facilities are available only at source.

Quality assurance that can be performed at destination is normally limited to inspection of the supplies if they are purchased off-the-shelf and require no technical inspection, or if the necessary testing equipment is located only at destination. Any products which are processed under direct control of the National Institutes of Health or the Food and Drug Administration will be inspected at destination. Similarly, services performed at destination are inspected at the place of performance.

Brand-name products purchased for authorized resale through commissaries or similar facilities are normally inspected at destination. However, supplies destined for direct overseas shipment may be accepted by the contracting officer or an authorized representative by a tally sheet showing receipt of shipment signed by the port transportation officer or other designated official at the transshipment point. Overseas inspection of supplies shipped from the United States is only required in unusual circumstances if the contracting officer determines in advance that overseas inspection can be performed or makes necessary arrangements for its performance.

FAR 46.405

The contract administration office may determine the conformance of subcontracted supplies or services with contract requirements, but does not relieve the prime contractor of any responsibilities under the contract. The Government performs quality assurance at the subcontract level when required at source.

The program office may establish *critical success factors* to indicate the defect-free character of a product or service. More formally, the program office can conduct a *critical design review* to ensure the product meets the engineering and functional requirements, and that the specification ensures design compatibility between the item and such considerations as computer programs, equipment, facilities, and personnel. This review also assures that the design assesses producibility and risk areas, and reviews the preliminary product specification.

DFARS 246.2

Higher-level contract quality requirements are often used in addition to a standard inspection requirement. They are listed in the DoD Index of Specifications and Standards. They establish policies and procedures intended to ensure the safety and habitability of facilities, infrastructure and equipment acquired for use by DoD military or civilian personnel during military operations performed outside the United States, Guam, Puerto Rico, and the Virgin Islands.

Contracts (including task and delivery orders) for the construction, installation, repair, maintenance, or operation of facilities, infrastructure, and equipment configured for occupancy, including but not limited to, existing host nation facilities, new construction, and relocatable buildings acquired for use by DoD military or civilian personnel, shall require a pre-occupancy safety and habitability inspection.

To minimize safety and health risks, each contract covered by this policy shall require the contractor's compliance with DoD's Unified Facilities Criteria 1-200-01, High Performance and Sustainable Building Requirements, and its referenced standards for:[23]

- electrical systems;
- fire protection;
- plumbing;
- structural integrity;
- telecommunications networks;
- waste disposal; and
- water treatment.

Existing host nation facilities constructed to standards equivalent to or more stringent than the criteria are acceptable upon a written determination of the acceptability of the standards by the Discipline Working Group. Inspections to ensure compliance with the criteria shall be conducted in accordance with the inspection clause of the contract.

The combatant commander may waive compliance with the foregoing standards when it is impracticable to comply with such standards under prevailing operational conditions.

Program managers can also use advanced quality management systems such as MIL-STD-1916, DoD Preferred Methods for Acceptance of Product.

DFARS 246.4

The requirement for a QASP must be addressed and documented in the contract file for each contract except for those awarded using simplified acquisition procedures. For service contracts, the contracting officer should prepare a QASP to facilitate assessment of contractor performance. For supply contracts, the contracting officer should address the need for a quality assurance surveillance plan. Government contract quality assurance at source is not required for contracts or delivery orders valued below $300,000, unless:

- mandated by DoD regulation;
- required by a memorandum of agreement between the acquiring department or agency and the contract administration agency; or
- the contracting officer determines that:
  - contract technical requirements are significant (e.g., the technical requirements include drawings, test procedures, or performance requirements);
  - the product being acquired has critical characteristics, specific features identified that make Government contract quality assurance at source necessary, or specific acquisition concerns identified that make Government contract quality assurance at source necessary; and
  - the contract is being awarded to a manufacturer or producer, or else specific Government verifications have been identified as necessary and feasible to perform.

A CPARS report is filed on contracts over the simplified acquisition threshold. CPARS is an objective report of the contractor's performance against the contract cost, schedule and performance standards. The CPARS report goes into the Past Performance Information Retrieval System (PPIRS) database, which is used to communicate contractor strengths and weaknesses to source selection officials and contracting officers. These ratings are very important to a contractor because they can affect the contractor responsibility determination and therefore future business opportunities.

Solicitation Provision and Contract Clause

DFARS 252.246-7003, Notification of Potential Safety Issues, to acquire logistics support, maintenance, overhaul, or repair of (sub)systems, (sub) assemblies, and parts integral to a system; including repairable or consumable parts identified as critical safety items.

DFARS 252.246-7004, Safety of Facilities, Infrastructure, and Equipment for Military Operations, to construct, install, maintain, operate, or repair equipment, facilities or infrastructure configured for occupancy or use by DoD military or civilian personnel during military operations.

DFARS 252.246-7006, Wide Area WorkFlow Payment Instructions, to acquire commercial items and including DFARS 252.246-7003.

5.3.2 Inspection

FAR 46.4

Inspection involves testing and examining supplies or services to ensure they meet contract requirements. The Government has the right to make inspections and tests while work is in process and to require the contractor to maintain and provide records of its inspection work. Inspection can be performed online to avoid impacting the flow of items through the production line. The firm may also submit an item for examination and testing for Government test or witness before starting production to ensure that its methods can produce items that fulfill the contract's technical requirements.

Each contract designates the place(s) where the Government reserves the right to inspect, by or under the direction or supervision of Government personnel. Government inspection may also be done concurrently with contractor inspection. Government inspection is documented on an inspection or receiving report form, or commercial shipping document/packing list.

There are numerous methods of inspection that could be used by either the contractor or Government, each with its own uses and benefits. The Government usually inspects deliverables at or below the simplified acquisition threshold at destination by visual analysis for type and quantity, as well as damage, operability, preservation, packaging, packing, and marking. When repetitive purchases of the same item are made from the same manufacturer with a history of defect-free work, Government inspection may be reduced to a periodic check of occasional purchases.

Inspection at source allows use of contractor facilities to test and make corrections. Most complex hardware is inspected at source where Government in-plant inspectors are available. It is easier to hold contractors liable, although it could be a disadvantage if an inspector must be brought in from afar or is not familiar with the product. Inspection at destination means readily available Government personnel can ensure that the product works in less-than-ideal conditions and reveals damage in transit. However, this approach lacks the availability of contractor personnel and precludes inspection of packaging, preservation or shipping methods prior to shipment. If the contract provides for inspection at source, the place(s) of performance may not be changed without the authorization of the contracting officer.

The Government can physically inspect or test a product after contractor inspection, a process known as *product verification inspection.* Alternatively, *floor inspection* is done at the work station during assembly and fabrication. It minimizes material handling, storage and delay in process. However, it is not common because it is mostly informal in nature, slows piece work processing and creates too much idle time for the inspector.

Similarly, *flow* or *process inspection* easily identifies defective production, thereby preventing excessive accumulation of spoiled work. It also detects adverse quality trends promptly to introduce rapid corrective measures. On the other hand, flow inspection requires more people and equipment at more cost.

In contrast, *central inspection* has a location to take items for fine-tuned formal and impartial inspection that fully utilizes inspectors' time and improves supervision of them. But it does not eliminate gross errors or identify adverse trends or the responsible worker or equipment. Moreover, it requires rework on parts with minor defects, and increases material handling and cost.

Agencies prescribe procedures and instructions to use, prepare and distribute material inspection and receiving reports that validate Government receipt and inspection/acceptance. These procedures can also validate commercial shipping document/packing lists to show Government inspection and acceptance.

The contracting officer has several avenues of recourse if products or services fail inspection:

- address a dispute;
- consider latent defect, fraud or gross mistake;
- replace or correct at contractor's expense;
- require delivery and equitably adjust the process; or
- terminate for default.

Solicitation Provisions and Contract Clauses

FAR 52.246-1, Contractor Inspection Requirements, for supplies or services at or below the simplified acquisition threshold due to agency procedures, to ensure an explicit understanding of the contractor's inspection responsibilities, or the Government need to test the supplies or services in advance of acceptance or to pass judgment upon the adequacy of the contractor's internal work processes.

FAR 52.246-2, Inspection of Supplies—Fixed-Price, for supplies, or services that involve the furnishing of supplies, when a fixed-price contract is contemplated and the contract amount is expected to exceed the simplified acquisition threshold. Use the clause with Alternate I if a fixed-price incentive contract is contemplated. Use the clause with Alternate II if a fixed-ceiling-price contract with retroactive price redetermination is contemplated.

FAR 52.246-3, Inspection of Supplies—Cost-Reimbursement, for supplies, or services that involve the furnishing of supplies, when a cost-reimbursement contract is contemplated.

FAR 52.246-4, Inspection of Services—Fixed-Price, for services, or supplies that involve the furnishing of services, when a fixed-price contract is contemplated and the contract amount is expected to exceed the simplified acquisition threshold.

FAR 52.246-5, Inspection of Services—Cost Reimbursement, for services, or supplies that involve the furnishing of services, when a cost-reimbursement contract is contemplated.

FAR 52.246-6, Inspection—Time-and-Material and Labor-Hour, for a time-and-material contract or a labor-hour contract. Use the clause with its Alternate I if Government inspection and acceptance are to be performed at the contractor's plant.

FAR 52.246-7, Inspection of Research and Development—Fixed-Price, if fixed-price research and development exceeding the simplified acquisition threshold when the primary objective of the contract is the delivery of end items other than designs, drawings or reports.

FAR 52.246-8, Inspection of Research and Development—Cost-Reimbursement, if cost-reimbursement research and development when the primary objective of the contract is the delivery of end items other than designs, drawings, or reports. Use the clause with its Alternate I if the contract will be on a no-fee basis.

FAR 52.246-9, Inspection of Research and Development (Short Form), when neither FAR 52.246-7 nor FAR 52.246-8 is used.

FAR 52.246-11, Higher-Level Contract Quality Requirement, when the inclusion of a higher-level contract quality requirement is appropriate.

FAR 52.246-12, Inspection of Construction, if fixed-price for construction exceeding the simplified acquisition threshold.

FAR 52.246-13, Inspection—Dismantling, Demolition, or Removal of Improvements, for dismantling, demolition, or removal of improvements.

FAR 52.246-14, Inspection of Transportation, for freight transportation services (including local drayage) by rail, motor (including bus), domestic freight forwarder, and domestic water carriers (including inland, coastwise and intercoastal). Do not use the clause to acquire transportation services by air carriers or international ocean carriers. Do not use for freight services which are provided under bills of lading or negotiated for reduced rates.

5.3.3 Acceptance

FAR 46.5

Acceptance acknowledges that the supplies or services conform to applicable contract quality and quantity requirements. The Government assents to ownership of the supplies delivered, or consents to the services rendered. Acceptance may take place before, during or after delivery, depending on the contract terms and conditions. Supplies or services are ordinarily not accepted before completion of Government contract quality assurance actions. Acceptance is usually evidenced by a certification on an inspection/receiving report form or commercial shipping document or packing list.

Each contract specifies the place of acceptance, which is usually the same place where Government contract quality assurance occurs. Acceptance of supplies or services is the responsibility of the contracting officer, or ACO when this responsibility is assigned to a contract administration office.

A certificate of conformance may be used in certain instances instead of source inspection at the discretion of the contracting officer if in the Government's best interest, small losses would be incurred in the event of a defect, or the contractor's reputation or past performance makes it likely that the supplies or services furnished will be acceptable and any defective work would be corrected, repaired, or replaced without contest.

Solicitation Provision and Contract Clause

FAR 52.246-15, Certificate of Conformance.

5.3.4 Liquidated Damages

FAR 11.2

The contracting officer considers the potential impact on pricing, competition, and contract administration before using a liquidated damages clause. When delivery or timely performance is so important that the Government expects to suffer damage if the contractor is delinquent, and the damage would be difficult or impossible to estimate accurately or prove, then liquidated damages may be prudent. Liquidated damages are neither punitive nor negative performance incentives, but rather are compensation to the Government for probable damages. The liquidated damages rate reasonably forecasts compensation for these damages. The contracting officer may use more than one liquidated damages rate when the probable damage to the Government may change over the contract period of performance.

Construction contracts with liquidated damages provisions describe the rate(s) of liquidated damages assessed per day of delay, the estimated daily cost of Government inspection and superintendence, and an amount for other expected expenses associated with delayed completion, such as renting substitute property or paying for extended per diem expenses.

Solicitation Provisions and Contract Clauses

FAR 52.211-11, Liquidated Damages—Supplies, Services, or Research and Development, if fixed-price for supplies, services, or research and development when the contracting officer determines that liquidated damages are appropriate.

FAR 52.211-12, Liquidated Damages—Construction, for construction (other than cost-plus-fixed-fee) when the contracting officer determines that liquidated damages are appropriate. It can be modified to reflect multiple liquidation rates for multiple stages of work. Per DFARS 211.503, this clause is only required if the estimated value is at least $700,000 or where the contractor cannot control the pace of the work. Usage in smaller-value contracts is optional.

FAR 52.211-13, Time Extensions, for construction that uses the Liquidated Damages—Construction clause, when FAR 52.211-12 has been revised.

5.3.5 Variation in Quantity

FAR 11.3

A fixed-price supply contract may authorize Government acceptance of a variation in the quantity of items called for if caused by packing, loading, or shipping, or by allowances in manufacturing processes. Any permissible variation is stated as a percentage increase, decrease or both. It is based upon the normal commercial practices of a particular industry for a particular item. The permissible variation does not exceed plus or minus 10 percent unless a different limitation is established in agency regulations. Excess quantities of items totaling up to $250 in value may be retained without compensating the contractor, and excess quantities over $250 in value may, at the Government's option, be either returned at the contractor's expense or retained and paid for at the contract unit price.

Construction contracts may authorize a variation in estimated quantities of unit-priced items. If the variation between the estimated and actual quantity of a unit-priced item is more than plus or minus 15 percent, an equitable adjustment in the contract price is made if requested by either the Government or the contractor. The contractor may request an extension of time if the quantity variation requires it to complete performance. The contracting officer may extend this time limit before the date of final settlement of the contract.

Solicitation Provisions and Contract Clauses

FAR 52.211-16, Variation in Quantity, for fixed-price supplies or services.

FAR 52.211-17, Delivery of Excess Quantities, for fixed-price supplies.

FAR 52.211-18, Variation in Estimated Quantity, for fixed-price construction.

5.3.6 Transfer of Title and Risk of Loss

FAR 46.505

Regardless of when or where physical possession occurs, title for supplies passes to the Government upon formal acceptance. Unless the contract specifically provides otherwise, risk of loss of or damage to supplies remains with the contractor until delivery to a carrier if transportation is f.o.b. origin. Risk transfers upon acceptance by or delivery to the Government at the destination specified in the contract if transportation is f.o.b. destination.

The risk of loss or damage to nonconforming supplies remains with the contractor until cure or acceptance. The contractor is not liable for loss or damage to supplies caused by the negligence of Government agents, employees or officers acting within the scope of their employment.

Contract Clause

FAR 52.246-16, Responsibility for Supplies.

5.3.7 Nonconforming Supplies or Services

FAR 46.407

The contracting officer gives the contractor an opportunity to correct or replace nonconforming supplies or services within the required delivery schedule without additional cost to the Government. In fact, the Government may charge the contractor the cost of Government reinspection and retests because of prior rejection. The contracting officer ordinarily rejects supplies or services when the nonconformance is critical or major, or the supplies or services are otherwise incomplete. However, economy or urgency may require conditional acceptance of supplies or services to be in the best interest of the Government. If the nonconformance is minor, the contract administration office may accept or reject, except where this authority is withheld by the procuring contracting office.

When supplies or services are accepted with critical or major nonconformances, the contracting officer modifies the contract to provide for an equitable price reduction or other consideration. For conditional acceptance, amounts withheld from payments must be sufficient to cover the estimated cost and profit to correct deficiencies and complete unfinished work. For minor nonconformances, the contract need not be modified unless the savings to the contractor in fabrication or performance exceed the Government's cost of processing the modification.

Notices of rejection include the reasons therefore and are furnished to the contractor to avoid the possibility of acceptance being implied as a matter of law.

Government-wide responsibility for quality assurance support for acquisitions of biologics, drugs and other medical supplies is assigned to the Food and Drug Administration. Responsibility for food lies with the Department of Agriculture, except that seafood is assigned to the National Marine Fisheries Service of the Department of Commerce.

Any domestic contractor furnishing supplies is responsible for ensuring that they are not counterfeit. The contracting officer will access the Government-Industry Data Exchange Program to verify that its deliverables do not contain components or parts that are restricted.[24] If so, or if the contractor has reason to believe that it is counterfeit, it must notify the contracting officer within 60 days. Such a suspicion would likely come out of inspection or testing, or perhaps notification by an employee or outside party.

Solicitation Provision and Contract Clause

FAR 52.246-26, Reporting Nonconforming Items.

5.3.8 Defense Priorities and Allocations System

FAR 11.6

Title I of the Defense Production Act of 1950[25] requires preferential acceptance and performance of contracts and orders supporting certain national defense and energy programs. These include programs for military and energy production or construction, military assistance to any foreign nation, stockpiling, and space exploration and support. It also applies to emergency preparedness activities conducted pursuant to Title VI of the Robert T. Stafford Disaster Relief and Emergency Assistance Act.[26] The agency allocates facilities, materials, and services to promote these programs.

The Defense Priorities and Allocations System (DPAS) is a Department of Commerce process to address approved national defense, emergency preparedness, and energy programs. Two levels of priority for rated orders are established by the DPAS, identified by the rating symbols "DO" and "DX." All DX rated orders have equal priority with each other and take preference over DO rated and unrated orders. All DO rated orders take preference over unrated orders. Contracting officers follow agency procedural instructions concerning the use of rated orders. Contracting officers assign a criticality designator to each contract over the simplified acquisition threshold as follows:

- "A" for critical contracts and DX-rated contracts for unusual and compelling urgency, or for major systems;
- "B" for other items needed to maintain a production or repair line, preclude out-of-stock conditions, or meet user needs for nonstock items; and
- "C" for all contracts other than those designated "A" or "B."

Solicitation Provision

FAR 52.211-14, Notice of Priority Rating for National Defense, Emergency Preparedness, and Energy Program Use, when the award will be a rated order.

Contract Clause

FAR 52.211-15, Defense Priority and Allocation Requirements, in rated orders.

5.3.9 Production Surveillance and Reporting

FAR 42.11

Production surveillance is a function of contract administration to determine contractor progress and to identify any factors that may delay performance. Production surveillance involves Government review and analysis of contractor industrial processes and controls, performance, plans, and schedules. Simplified acquisitions should not normally require production surveillance. The contract administration office determines the extent of production surveillance based on:

- contractor financial capability;
- contractor performance history;
- criticality;
- performance schedule;
- prior experience with the supplies or services;
- production plan;
- reporting requirements for production progress and performance; and
- supplementary written instructions from the contracting office.

Contracting officers may require contractors to submit production progress reports from their own management systems.

DFARS 242.11

The ACO performs production surveillance on all contractors that have Criticality Designator A or B contracts, but not on Criticality Designator C contracts unless specifically requested by the contracting officer. Production surveillance requires that the ACO's staff conduct a periodic risk assessment of the contractor to determine the degree of production surveillance needed for all contracts awarded to that contractor. The risk assessment will:

- consider information provided by the contractor and the contracting officer;
- develop a production surveillance plan based on the risk level determined during a risk assessment;
- modify the production surveillance plan to incorporate any special surveillance requirements or contracts (including any requirements identified by the contracting officer) or potential contract delinquencies; and
- monitor contract progress.

Contracting officers assign criticality designator A to items with a priority 01, 02, 03, or 06 (if emergency supply of clothing) under DoD Manual 4140.01, Volume 5, DoD Supply Chain Materiel Management Procedures: Delivery of Materiel, criticality designator B to other formal contracts and criticality designator C to unilateral purchase orders.

Combined with these criticality designators, the Uniform Material Movement and Issue Priority System (UMMIPS) is part of the MILSTRIP system that ensure processing of material issue requests according to the military significance and urgency of the requiring activity. The significance of given activity dictates resource allocation for material, purchasing priority, storage, and transportation. There are 15 priority designators, numbered 1 through 15. Appropriate designators are assigned to each activity based on its relative military importance in different senses of urgency.

DoDI 5000.2, Operation of the Defense Acquisition System, identifies reporting requirements for defense technology projects and acquisition programs. Within four working days after receipt of the contractor's report, the CAO must provide the report and any required comments to the contracting officer and, unless otherwise specified in the contract, the inventory control manager. If the contractor's report indicates that the contract is on schedule and the CAO agrees, the CAO does not need to add further comments. In all other cases, the CAO must add comments and recommend a course of action.

The contracting officer specifies reporting instructions in the Schedule, such as:

- contract line items, exhibits, or exhibit line items requiring reports;
- frequency and timing of reporting (normally five working days after each reporting period);
- offices (with addressees/codes) where reports should be sent (the contracting office and contract administration office); and
- the following requirements for report content:
  - the problem, actual or potential, and its cause;
  - items and quantities affected;
  - when the delinquency started or will start;
  - actions taken to overcome the delinquency; and
  - estimated recovery date and/or proposed schedule revision.

Solicitation Provision and Contract Clause

FAR 52.242-2, Production Progress Reports, when production progress reporting is required, unless a construction contract or a Federal Supply Schedule contract is contemplated.

5.4 WARRANTY

FAR 46.7

A *warranty* provides a contractual right to correct defects based on a stated period of time or use, or the occurrence of a specified event. It is the seller's promise to the buyer regarding the condition, nature or usefulness of the supplies or services furnished under the contract. Generally, a warranty's purpose is to delineate the rights and obligations for defective items and services, and to foster quality performance. The benefits from a warranty must be commensurate with their cost to the Government. Factors to select the use of a warranty for a given contract include:

- complexity and function;
- contractor's charge to accept the deferred liability created by the warranty;
- degree of development;
- difficulty in detecting defects before acceptance;
- end use;
- Government administration and enforcement of the warranty;
- potential harm to the Government if the item is defective;
- reduced Government contract quality assurance requirements (if the warranty provides adequate assurance of a satisfactory product);
- state of the art; and
- trade practice (i.e., the cost of an item to the Government might be the same whether or not a warranty is included).

A warranty can be either express or implied in its nature. An *express warranty* includes specifications and descriptions which can be included in technical literature. An express warranty makes the seller responsible when the buyer relies on the warranty and always nullifies an implied warranty. By contrast, an *implied warranty* is conducted through discussion or observation as the buyer relies on the vendor's skill in selecting a specific product, such as merchantability and fitness for a particular purpose. For an implied warranty, knowledge of both parties is critical, and the seller is responsible only if the buyer could not determine the facts from the specifications.

The use of a warranty in an acquisition is approved in accordance with agency procedures. They are usually discouraged for use in cost-reimbursement contracts. Warranty clauses do not limit the Government's rights under an inspection clause regarding latent defects, fraud or gross mistakes that amount to fraud. Except for construction contracts, warranties apply notwithstanding inspection and acceptance clauses or other terms of the contract. Warranty clauses clearly state the nature of the item and its characteristics to be warranted, contractor obligations to the Government for breach of warranty, remedies available to the Government, and warranty scope and duration.

Contractor obligations under warranties extend to all defects discovered during the warranty period, but not to damage caused by the Government. A warranty may be required for any aspect that requires special protection (e.g., accessories, components, installation, packaging, packing, and preservation). If the Government specifies the end item's design, inspection requirements, materials, measurements or tolerances, or tests, the contractor's obligations for correction of defects are usually limited to defects in material and workmanship or failure to conform to specifications. If the Government does not specify the design, then the warranty extends also to the design's usefulness.

In case of defect, the Government normally may either obtain an equitable adjustment of the contract or direct the contractor to repair or replace the defective items at contractor expense. Alternate remedies include the Government retaining the defective item and reducing the contract price, or repair or replacement of the defective item by another source at contractor expense (and perhaps with contractor-furnished parts or instructions). Repair may be possible at the contractor's facility at contractor expense. In any event, the contractor is usually responsible for the cost of all labor and material to repair or replace, retransport, reinspect, retest, repack and remark any defective items.

The time period or duration of the warranty is clearly specified after consideration of estimated useful life, storage or shelf-life, and trade practice. This period does not extend the contractor's liability for patent defects beyond a reasonable time after acceptance by the Government. The warranty specifies a reasonable time for furnishing notice to the contractor regarding the discovery of defects.

Warranties help ensure that the product works correctly for a guaranteed period of time. They are used to enforce design and manufacturing requirements, combat defects in materials and workmanship, and achieve essential performance requirements. They may be tailored for the individual contract, but must be affordable. The Government has a self-insurance policy that applies after acceptance and warranty periods expire to any contract (other than firm-fixed-price), though the Government pays for the cost of correction.

Warranties should not be used if their costs exceed the value of protection to the Government, but should be used if the Government cost for corrections exceeds contractor cost. They should be used in cases of high logistics support costs or low administrative and enforcement cost.

Warranty cost should also be compared to risk. It should incentivize the contractor to produce higher quality products in light of its current quality assurance procedures. In this vein, reliability improvement or failure-free warranty of equipment motivates contractors to improve their equipment during the warranty period through no-cost engineering change proposals, and is usually used during an initial production run.

The packaging of the delivered supplies must clearly note the existence of a warranty, its substance and duration, and a point of contact if a defect is found.

DFARS 246.7

The chief of the contracting office must approve use of a warranty only when the benefits are expected to outweigh the cost, but need not approve its use in acquisitions for:

- commercial items;[27]
- supplies and services in construction contracts when using the warranties that are contained in Federal, military, or construction guide specifications;
- supplies and services in fixed-price type contracts containing quality assurance provisions that reference higher-level contract quality requirements; or
- technical data, unless the warranty provides for extended liability.

When deciding whether to use extended liability provisions, the contracting office should consider the likelihood that correction or replacement of the nonconforming data, or a price adjustment, will not give adequate protection to the Government; and the effectiveness of the additional remedy as a deterrent against furnishing nonconforming data.

PGI 246.710-70

Two attachments shall be included in solicitations and awards to specify the required data elements for warranties of serialized items.

First, the Warranty Tracking Information form specifies the data elements for electronic transmission of the list of warranty items. This provides the ability to trace a warranted item from delivery through completion of the effectivity of the warranty. Second, the Source of Repair Instructions specify the required warranty source of repair data elements for electronic transmission of the source of repair data for each warranty item. These attachments are completed electronically using the Product Data Reporting and Evaluation Program website.[28]

If the Government does not specify a warranty, the contracting officer may require offerors to provide warranty data by populating the "Warranty Tracking Information" attachment, as appropriate, and include the attachment as part of its offer.

The contractor is required to provide the unique item identifier for each warranted item and the warranty repair source information and instructions by the time of receipt and/or acceptance of warranted items.

Solicitation Provisions

DFARS 252.246-7005, Notice of Warranty Tracking of Serialized Items, if the Government does not specify a warranty and offerors will be required to enter data with the offer.

DFARS 252.246-7006, Warranty Tracking of Serialized Items if a warranty is involved. Include the Warranty Tracking Information and Source of Repair Instructions warranty attachments.

Solicitation Provisions and Contract Clauses

Because so many situations influence warranty conditions, the contracting officer may vary the terms and conditions of the clauses as needed.

FAR 52.246-17, Warranty of Supplies of a Noncomplex Nature, for noncomplex items when a fixed-price supply contract is contemplated and the use of a warranty clause has been approved under agency procedures. Use the clause with its Alternate II (there is no Alternate I) to specify that necessary transportation to correct or replace the item will be at Government expense.[29] Use the clause with its Alternate III if the supplies cannot be obtained from another source. Use the clause with its Alternate IV if a fixed-price incentive contract is contemplated. Use the clause with its Alternate V if recovery of the warranted items may involve considerable Government expense for disassembly and/or reassembly of larger items.

FAR 52.246-18, Warranty of Supplies of a Complex Nature, for deliverable complex items when a fixed-price supply or research and development contract is contemplated. The same conditions for Alternatives II through IV apply as in FAR 52.246-17.

FAR 52.246-19, Warranty of Systems and Equipment under Performance Specifications or Design Criteria, when performance specifications or design are of major importance, and a fixed-price supply, service, or research and development contract for systems and equipment is contemplated. The same conditions for Alternatives II and III apply as in FAR 52.246-17.

FAR 52.246-20, Warranty of Services, for services when a fixed-price contract for services is contemplated, unless FAR 52.246-19 is used.

FAR 52.246-21, Warranty of Construction, when a fixed-price construction contract is contemplated. Use the clause with its Alternate I if the Government specifies in the contract the use of any equipment by brand name and model.

DFARS 252.246-7001, Warranty of Data, in cost-reimbursement contracts along with DFARS 252.227-7013, Rights in Technical Data and Computer Software, when there is a need for greater protection or period of liability than provided by the inspection and warranty clauses. Use the basic clause when the contract is not firm-fixed-price or fixed-price incentive. Use Alternate I in fixed-price-incentive solicitations and contracts. Use Alternate II in firm-fixed-price solicitations and contracts.

DFARS 252.246-7002, Warranty of Construction (Germany), instead of FAR 52.246-21, Warranty of Construction, for construction when a fixed-price contract will be awarded and contract performance will be in Germany.

DFARS 252.211-7003, Item Unique Identification and Valuation, when obtaining commercial supplies and services and it is anticipated that the resulting contract will include a warranty for serialized items.

5.5 INDEMNIFICATION

FAR 46.8

Indemnification is an agreement by one party to compensate the other party for any loss suffered during contract performance. The loss can be caused by either party or by a third party. It is not appropriate for:

- architect-engineer services;
- commercial items;
- construction;
- information technology and telecommunications;
- maintenance and rehabilitation of real property; and
- simplified acquisitions.

The Government will generally act as a self-insurer by relieving contractors of liability for loss of or damage to Government property that occurs after acceptance of supplies delivered or services performed under a contract, and results from defects or deficiencies in the supplies or services.

However, the Government will not relieve the contractor of liability for loss of or damage to the contract end item itself, except for *high-value items*, which have a unit cost designated by the contracting officer (normally $100,000 per unit). Examples of such items include an aircraft or its engine, communication system, or computer system, missile, or ship.

In contracts requiring delivery of high-value items, the Government relieves contractors of contractual liability for loss of or damage to those items. However, the Government retains its rights to correct, repair or replace a defective item or component if discovered before the loss of or damage to a high-value item occurs. It also retains its right to equitable relief if discovered after loss or damage occurs, rather than repair or replacement. The Government will not provide any contractual relief when contractor liability is expressly provided under a contract clause or can be preserved without increasing the contract price. Moreover, this relief does not apply if any contractor insurance or self-insurance reserve covers liability for loss or damage suffered by the Government through purchase or use of the supplies or services. Finally it does not cover willful misconduct or lack of good faith by the contractor's management that in turn causes a defect or deficiency in the supplies or services, or Government's acceptance thereof.

DFARS 235.070

Per 10 U.S.C. 2354, and if authorized by the Secretary concerned, contracts for research and/or development may provide for indemnification of the (sub)contractors for claims by third persons (including employees) for death, bodily injury, or property loss or damage. It also covers loss of or damage to the contractor's property to the extent that it results from a risk defined by the contract as "unusually hazardous," or else arises from the direct performance of the contract and is not compensated by insurance or other means.

DFARS 246.870

All subcontractors must obtain electronic parts that are in production by the original manufacturer or an authorized aftermarket manufacturer with a contractual arrangement or express written authority with the original manufacturer, or a current design activity, to buy, repackage, stock, sell, or distribute the part. They can also obtain an electronic part currently available in stock from the original manufacturers, their authorized suppliers or original manufacturers or their authorized suppliers. Any electronic parts that are not in production or in stock by the original manufacturer or an authorized aftermarket manufacturer must be obtained from suppliers approved by the contractor, provided that the contractor uses established counterfeit prevention industry standards and processes (e.g., inspection, testing, and authentication), and assumes responsibility for the authenticity of parts provided by such suppliers. Further, its selection may be reviewed and approved by the contracting officer.

If the contractor obtains an electronic part or cannot confirm an electronic part is original, it must promptly notify the contracting officer in writing. If such notification is required for an electronic part to be used in a designated lot of assemblies to be acquired under a single contract, the contractor may submit one notification for the lot and provide identification of the assemblies containing the parts (e.g., serial numbers). The contractor is responsible for inspection, testing, and authentication, in accordance with existing applicable industry standards, and must provide documentation of same to the Government upon request. Moreover, the contractor must report if it obtains an electronic part from an unauthorized source or contractor (other than the original manufacturer) that refuses to accept flowdown of this clause, or cannot confirm that an electronic part is new or not previously used and that it has not been comingled in supplier new production or stock with used, refurbished, reclaimed, or returned parts. These precautions apply even if the (sub) contractor is purchasing electronic parts from the Federal Supply Schedule; suppliers accredited by the Defense Microelectronics Activity, or from Government inventory/stock. The cost of any required inspection, testing, and authentication of such parts may be charged as a direct cost.

The Government is responsible for the authenticity of the requisitioned electronic parts. If any such part is subsequently found to be counterfeit or suspect counterfeit, the Government will promptly replace such part at no charge and consider an adjustment in the contract schedule to the extent that replacement of the counterfeit or suspect counterfeit electronic parts caused a delay in performance.

Contractors that are subject to the cost accounting standards and that supply electronic parts or products that include electronic parts, and their subcontractors that supply same, are required to establish and maintain an acceptable counterfeit electronic part detection and avoidance system. Failure to do so may result in disapproval of the purchasing system by the contracting officer and/or withholding of payments.

A counterfeit electronic part detection and avoidance system will include risk-based policies and procedures that address processes for:

- control of obsolete electronic parts;
- design, operation, and maintenance of systems to detect and avoid counterfeit electronic parts and suspect counterfeit electronic parts;

- flow down of counterfeit detection and avoidance requirements;
- identifying and reporting suspect counterfeit electronic parts;
- inspection and testing of electronic parts, including criteria for acceptance and rejection;
- keeping continually informed of current counterfeiting information and trends;
- screening the Government-Industry Data Exchange Program (GIDEP) reports and other credible sources of counterfeiting information;
- maintaining electronic part traceability; and
- training personnel.

Contract Clauses

FAR 52.246-23, Limitation of Liability, for delivery of end items that are not high-value items.

FAR 52.246-24, Limitation of Liability—High Value Items, for delivery of high-value items.

FAR 52.246-25, Limitation of Liability—Services, for the performance of services. In contracts requiring both the performance of services and the delivery of end items, use all three Limitation of Liability clauses and identify in the contract schedule any high-value line items.

DFARS 252.235-7000, Indemnification Under 10 U.S.C. 2354—Fixed Price or DFARS 252.235-7001, Indemnification Under 10 U.S.C. 2354—Cost-Reimbursement, when the contractor is to be indemnified.

Solicitation Provisions and Contract Clauses

DFARS 252.235-7002, Animal Welfare, for research, development, test, and evaluation or training that use live vertebrate animals.

DFARS 252.235-7003, Frequency Authorization, for developing, producing, constructing, testing, or operating a device requiring a frequency authorization. Use the basic clause if agency procedures do not authorize the use of DD Form 1494, Application for Equipment Frequency Allocation, to obtain radio frequency authorization. Use Alternate I clause if agency procedures authorize the use of DD Form 1494, Application for Equipment Frequency Allocation, to obtain frequency authorization.

DFARS 252.235-7010, Acknowledgment of Support and Disclaimer, for research and development.

DFARS 252.235-7011, Final Scientific or Technical Report, for research and development.

DFARS 252.235-7004, Protection of Human Subjects, if performance includes research involving human subjects, but not for use of cadaver materials alone.

DFARS 252.246-7007, Contractor Counterfeit Electronic Part Detection and Avoidance System, when procuring electronic parts; end items, components, parts, or assemblies containing electronic parts; or services, if the contractor will supply electronic parts or components, parts, or assemblies containing electronic parts as part of the service. Do not use the clause in solicitations and contracts that are set aside for small business.

DFARS 252.246-7008, Sources of Electronic Parts, in solicitations and contracts, when using DFARS 252.246-7007.

5.6 FINANCIAL PROTECTIONS

The bonding process is designed to eliminate irresponsible contractors who may be unable to obtain financing and are therefore at risk of abandonment or nonperformance. A bond will compensate the government to some extent for the cost of substitute performance by a successor contractor. A surety is involved with the right to sue the contractor and any principals who may have guaranteed the bond, thereby providing another deterrent to nonperformance. Also, subcontractors benefit through assurance of payment, since mechanic's liens are not allowable under Government contracts.

5.6.1 Bonds

FAR 28.1

The *Miller Act*[30] requires bonds for any construction contract exceeding $150,000 and sometimes for supplies and services. *Bonds* are written instruments executed by a bidder or contractor (known as the *principal*), and a second party (the *surety*) to warrant fulfillment of the principal's obligations to a third party (the *obligee*, in this case the Government). If the principal's obligations are not met, the bond assures payment by the surety of the specified amount of loss incurred by the obligee. The bonding requirement can be waived by the contracting officer for work to be performed in a foreign country where it is impracticable for the contractor to furnish a bond. The Government determines the correct amount of the bond. There are six types of bonds:

- A *payment bond* assures contractor payments to all laborers and suppliers during contract performance. A payment bond is required only when a performance bond is required for this contract size, and only if its use is in the Government's interest. The bond amount is usually 100 percent of the contract amount.
- An *advance payment bond* secures fulfillment of contractor obligations under an advance payment clause of the contract. The contracting officer

determines the amount of the advance payment bond to protect the Government against liens.

- A *performance bond* secures performance and fulfillment of contractor obligations under a given contract. It usually equals the amount of the contract and replaces the advance payment bond.
- An *annual bid bond* secures all bids to be submitted during a specific fiscal year on contracts that would otherwise require their own bonds. Unlike the previously mentioned entries, this type of bond is not used in construction contracts.
- An *annual performance bond* also covers all bids to be submitted during a specific Government fiscal year, by securing fulfillment of contractor obligations on contracts that would otherwise require their own bonds. They provide a gross penal sum applicable to the total amount of all covered contracts. As with annual bid bonds, this type of bond is not used in construction contracts.
- A *patent infringement bond* secures fulfillment of contractor's obligations under a patent clause of the contract. No performance bond is furnished. The contractor's financial responsibility is often unknown or doubtful in these cases.

Though uncommon, performance bonds may be required for nonconstruction contracts exceeding the simplified purchase threshold to protect the Government's interest, such as:

- contractor asset sales or merger, and the Government desires assurance that the new entity is financially capable;
- contracts to dismantle, demolish or remove improvements;
- increase in contract price;
- providing Government property or funds to the contractor as partial compensation (e.g., retention of salvaged material); or
- substantial progress payments begun before delivery.

For construction contracts between $35,000 and $150,000, the contracting officer does not usually insist on performance bonds, but will instead select at least two of the following payment protections:

- a payment bond;
- a tripartite escrow agreement with a federally insured financial institution as escrow agent for all suppliers. The escrow agreement sets forth the terms of payment and resolution of disputes among the parties. The Government tenders payment to the escrow account rather than the contractor, and the escrow agent distributes the payments in accordance with the agreement;

- an irrevocable letter of credit from a financial institution (the preferred method);
- certificate of deposit from a federally insured financial institution;
- common payment method such as bank draft, certified or cashiers' check, currency, or money order; or
- U.S. bonds or notes.

A bond must include a *penal sum* or *penal amount* as a maximum amount (or a percentage of the bid price for a bid bond) for which the surety is obligated. If there is no individual surety, then this is the amount of security to be pledged to the Government.

The agent or underwriter authorized to bind the surety is an attorney-in-fact. An original, or a photocopy or facsimile of an original, power of attorney is included with the bid. The contracting officer treats the failure to provide a proper power of attorney at the time of bid opening as a matter of responsiveness, and addresses any concerns about the authenticity and enforceability of the power of attorney as a matter of contractor responsibility.

A *bid guarantee* provides assurance that the bidder will not withdraw a bid before acceptance, will execute a written contract, and will furnish required bonds and insurance agreements within the time specified in the bid. A bid guarantee must be accompanied by a performance bond (perhaps along with a payment bond), and is usually required whenever these bonds are required. The contracting officer inserts an amount for the bid guarantee which is adequate to protect the Government from loss should the successful bidder fail to execute bonds and contractual documents. This amount is normally at least 20 percent of the bid price, up to $3 million. Both a percentage and a maximum dollar limitation may be specified. This requirement can be waived by the chief of the contracting office (allowing submission of just the bond(s) without the guarantee) if in the best interest of the Government. These waivers are usually for overseas construction or emergency acquisitions, and are often sole-source contracts with proven contractors. Class waivers may be authorized by the agency head or designee.

In sealed bidding, noncompliance with a solicitation requirement for a bid guarantee requires rejection of the bid unless waived by the chief of the contracting office. For a negotiated procurement, noncompliance with a solicitation requirement for a bid guarantee will reject an initial proposal as unacceptable if award is based on initial proposals without discussion (unless waived). If discussions do occur, deficiencies in bid guarantees from offerors in the competitive range are addressed during discussions and the offeror has an opportunity to correct the deficiency.

The surety, upon its written request, may be furnished information on work progress, payments and the estimated percentage of completion, concerning the contract for which the bond was furnished. The same information may be furnished to persons who have provided labor or materials and have not been paid. The contracting officer shall, upon request, furnish the name and address of the surety(ies) of a payment bond to a subcontractor.

The head of the agency or designee will furnish a certified copy of the payment bond and the contract to any subcontractor who states by affidavit that it has supplied labor or materials for such work and either has not been paid or is being sued on the bond. The requestor may need to pay preparation costs.

During contract performance, the Government cannot withhold payments due to contractors or assignees merely because they have not been paid. However, after completion of the contract work, if the surety notifies in writing about the contractor's failure to meet its obligation to its subcontractors or suppliers, the contracting officer does withhold final payment. However, the surety must then agree to hold the Government harmless from any liability resulting from withholding the final payment. The contracting officer will authorize final payment upon agreement between the contractor and surety or upon a judicial determination of the rights of the parties.

DFARS 228.1

The requirement for performance and payment bonds is waived for cost-reimbursement contracts. However, for cost-type contracts with fixed-price construction subcontracts over $35,000, the prime contractor must obtain from each of its construction subcontractors performance and payment protections in favor of the prime contractor. For fixed-price construction subcontracts over $35,000, but not exceeding $150,000, payment protection must be sufficient to pay labor and material costs. For fixed-price construction subcontracts over $150,000, the prime contractor requires a payment bond sufficient to pay labor and material costs and a performance bond in an equal amount if available at no additional cost.

For Defense Environmental Restoration Program construction contracts, any rights of action under the performance bond shall only accrue to, and be for the exclusive use of, the obligee named in the bond. In the event of default, the surety's liability on the performance bond is limited to the cost of completing the contract work, less the balance of unexpended funds. Under no circumstances will the liability exceed the penal sum of the bond. The surety is not liable for indemnification or compensation of the obligee for loss or liability arising from personal injury or property damage, even if the injury or damage was caused by a breach of the bonded contract. Once it has taken action to meet its obligations under the bond, the surety is entitled to any indemnification and identical standard of liability to which the contractor was entitled.

Fidelity and forgery bonds generally are not required but are authorized for use when necessary for the protection of the Government or the contractor or the investigative and claims services of a surety company are desired.

Solicitation Provisions and Contract Clauses

FAR 52.228-1, Bid Guarantee.

FAR 52.228-2, Additional Bond Security.

FAR 52.228-12, Prospective Subcontractor Requests for Bonds, when a payment bond will be furnished, except for commercial items.

FAR 52.228-13, Alternative Payment Protections, if between $35,000 and $150,000. The contracting officer may establish a lower percentage for the bonds.

FAR 52.228-15, Performance and Payment Bonds—Construction, if over $150,000 and requires performance and payment bonds. The contracting officer may establish a lower percentage for the bonds. If no bid guarantee is involved, the contracting officer sets a period of time to return executed bonds.

FAR 52.228-16, Performance and Payment Bonds—Other than Construction. The contracting officer inserts the bond amount and a period of time (usually 10 days) to return executed bonds. Use Alternate I when only performance bonds are required.

5.6.2 Sureties and Bond Security

FAR 28.2

For a contract modification, the contracting officer must obtain *consent of surety*, an acknowledgment by a separate party that its bond given in connection with a contract continues to apply, unless an additional bond is obtained from another surety. Acknowledgment is not required if a contract modification is either beyond the scope of the contract or else changes the contract price more than either 25 percent or $50,000. A new surety may be necessary in these cases. Consent of surety is always required for a novation agreement.

Corporate sureties offered for contracts performed in the United States or its outlying areas must appear in the Department of the Treasury Circular 570, *Surety Companies Acceptable on Federal Bonds*.[31] This circular includes a maximum underwriting limit for each surety. The penal amount could exceed the underwriting limit only if the excess amount is coinsured or reinsured, and even then cannot exceed the underwriting limit of the coinsurer or reinsurer. For contracts performed in a foreign country, the contracting officer may accept a surety not appearing on Treasury Department Circular 570 if (s)he determines that it is impracticable for the contractor to use Treasury-listed sureties in the specific country.

Agencies always obtain adequate security for bonds, including coinsurance and reinsurance agreements when necessary. *Reinsurance* provides that a surety, for financial consideration, agrees to indemnify another surety against loss that could result from a bond it has issued. Acceptable forms of security include corporate or individual sureties, U.S. bonds or notes, and other negotiable instruments as previously listed for construction contracts. The contractor must execute and submit reinsurance agreements to the contracting officer within the time specified on the bid form, but no more than 45 calendar days after the bond execution.

The Government accepts from individual sureties only cash, readily marketable assets or irrevocable letters of credit from a federally insured financial institution to satisfy the underlying bond obligations. For a bond with a security interest in real property, the individual surety provides a mortgage title insurance policy equal to the amount of the lien, plus either a copy of the current real estate tax assessment or an appraisal dated within the past six months. The property is then valued at either its tax appraised value or 75 percent of its market value. The surety may request the contracting officer to accept a substitute asset for what is currently pledged.

An individual surety may be accepted only if a security interest is furnished with the bond. It may be provided by an escrow account with a federally insured financial institution in the name of the contracting agency, or by a lien on real property. The escrow account provides the contracting officer the sole and unrestricted right to draw upon all or part of the funds deposited in the account by written demand to the financial institution. This institution is in turn authorized to release to the surety all or part of the balance of the escrow account, including any accrued interest, upon written authorization by the contracting officer. The Government is not responsible for any costs to establish, maintain or administer the account. The terms of the escrow account cannot be amended without the consent of the contracting officer.

If an amendment to Circular 570 terminates a company's authority to qualify as a surety on Federal bonds, the contracting officer must review the outstanding contracts and take any action necessary to protect the Government. This could mean securing new bonds with other acceptable sureties.

The unencumbered value of the assets (excluding all outstanding pledges for other bond obligations) pledged by the individual surety equals or exceeds the penal amount (i.e., face value) of each bond. An offeror may submit up to three individual sureties for each bond, such that their combined value equals or exceeds the penal amount of the bond. The contracting officer will coordinate with the Department of the Treasury to confirm whether the assets are eligible to be pledged. Each individual surety accepts both joint and several liability up to the penal amount of the bond. Upon written request, the contracting officer may release the security interest on the surety's assets in support of a bid guarantee for an unsuccessful offer.

The contracting officer may grant a contractor a reasonable time to either add or substitute an acceptable surety if a current surety is determined to be unacceptable. However, if the contracting officer determines that no individual surety is acceptable to support a bid guarantee, the offeror is rejected as nonresponsible. If a small business, this decision is not referred to the SBA for a competency review, since the issue is strictly financial in nature.

The contracting officer releases the security interest on the individual surety's assets as soon as possible. The assets pledged in support of a payment bond may be released to a subcontractor upon receipt of either a Federal district court judgment or a sworn statement by the subcontractor (and notarized by the surety) that the claim is correct. The security interest is maintained for one year after final payment (90 days if the contract is not subject to the Miller Act), or for a longer period until all claims against the payment bond are resolved (or longer, if a performance bond has a longer warranty period).

Upon written request by the individual surety, the contracting officer may release a portion of their assets based upon substantial performance of the contractor's obligations under its performance bond. However, the unreleased portion of the lien must cover the remaining contract obligations, including payments to subcontractors and potential liabilities.

An individual may be excluded from acting as a surety by the agency head or designee for failure to fulfill or disclose obligations under a prior bond, or for misrepresenting either the value of available assets or outstanding liabilities. The surety is then listed in the SAM. Contracting officers cannot accept the bonds of unlisted sureties without written approval of the agency head or designee.

Any deposited U.S. bonds or notes include an executed power of attorney and agreement authorizing the collection or sale of these bonds or notes in case the bond's principal defaults. The contracting officer may either turn securities over to the authorized agency official, or else deposit them with a Federal Reserve Bank.

A separate irrevocable letter of credit may be furnished for each bond, requiring only a written demand and any letter of confirmation. If used as a bid guarantee, the irrevocable letter of credit expires at least 60 days after close of the bid acceptance period. If used as an alternative to corporate or individual sureties to secure a performance or payment bond, the letter's initial expiration date is at least one year from the date of issuance. The letter of credit automatically extends for one year until the period of required coverage ends and the contracting officer provides the financial institution with a written statement waiving the right to payment. However, the issuer may provide the beneficiary written notice of nonrenewal at least 60 days in advance of the current expiration date.

The irrevocable letter of credit must be issued or confirmed by a federally insured financial institution rated "investment grade" or higher. Letters of credit over $5 million must be confirmed by a second acceptable financial institution that had letter of credit business of at least $25 million in the past year, unless the issuer itself had that much business. The contracting officer must verify presence of federal insurance from the Federal Depositors Insurance Corporation and current credit rating from the Securities and Exchange Commission. If the contracting officer learns that a financial institution's rating has dropped below investment grade, (s)he will either give the contractor 30 days to substitute an acceptable irrevocable letter of credit, or else begin to draw on the line of credit.

Solicitation Provisions and Contract Clauses

FAR 52.228-11, Pledges of Assets.

FAR 52.228-14, Irrevocable Letter of Credit.

FAR 52.228-17, Individual Surety—Pledge of Assets (Bid Guarantee).

5.6.3 Insurance

FAR 28.3

Contractors provide insurance for workers' compensation, commingling property, or when directed by the Government due to contract terms or type of operation and ownership. The minimum amounts of insurance may be reduced when a contract is to be performed outside the United States and its outlying areas. Contractors for health care nonpersonal services must maintain medical liability insurance and indemnify the Government for liability-producing acts or omissions by the contractor, its agents and employees.

The policies contain an endorsement that preclude any cancellation or material change in the coverage adversely affecting the Government's interest, unless the insurer or the contractor so notifies the contracting officer in writing.

If the Government requires insurance to cover loss or damage to Government-furnished property, the contractor may either obtain a separate policy or include the risks in its existing policies. In either event, the policies must disclose the Government's interest in the property. Otherwise, the Government reserves the right to disapprove the purchase of any insurance coverage.

The Government considers several factors to set up an insurance program. Cost-type contracts impose insurance requirements on contractors such as injury and traffic accident liability; however fixed-price contractors only require insurance if performing on a Government installation. Fire, flood and theft liability coverage is common. Insurance costs and premiums are allowable, but not losses due to willful neglect.

By contrast, cost-reimbursement (sub)contracts usually require group insurance and liability protection. The contractor submits the group insurance plan for approval per agency regulations, including any change in benefits that could increase the cost to the Government. Aircraft and passenger liability insurance coverage in conjunction with contract performance should be at least $200,000 per person and $500,000 per occurrence for bodily injury (other than passenger liability), and $200,000 per occurrence for property damage. Coverage for passenger liability bodily injury must be at least $200,000 multiplied by the number of seats or passengers (whichever is greater). Bodily injury and property damage liability covering the operation of all automobiles used in contract performance should cover at least $200,000 per person, $500,000 per occurrence for bodily injury and $20,000 per occurrence for property damage. Employer's liability coverage should be at least $100,000, except in states with exclusive or monopolistic funds that prohibit workers' compensation written by private carriers.

This coverage should include property damage liability insurance for circumstances determined by the agency and any indemnity liability insurance (e.g., vessel collision liability and protection). The Government shares in any premium refunds or credits paid or allowed to the contractor. Note that occupational diseases are not compensated under Federal or state statutes, unless contract operations are too commingled with a contractor's commercial operations to make this practical.

Self-insurance is permitted. If at least half of the self-insurance costs at a contractor's business segment will be allocable to negotiated Government contracts (and equals at least $200,000 per year), the contractor submits information on its proposed self-insurance program or changes thereto for ACO approval. To qualify for a self-insurance program, a contractor demonstrates the ability to sustain the potential losses, such as:

- compliance with Federal and State laws and regulations;
- geographic dispersion of assets to avoid a single loss depleting them all;
- history of previous losses, including frequency of occurrence and the financial impact of each loss;
- sound financial condition, including available lines of credit; and
- type and magnitude of risk (e.g., minor coverage for a deductible, or major coverage for hazardous risks).

The ACO will not approve a program of self-insurance for catastrophic risks, but may agree to indemnify the contractor or recognize an appropriate share of premiums for purchased insurance. Self-insurance programs to protect a contractor against the costs of correcting its own defects in materials or workmanship also are not approved; however rework estimates and warranty costs are acceptable.

DFARS 228.304

DoD has established the National Defense Projects Rating Plan, also known as the Special Casualty Insurance Rating Plan, as a risk-pooling arrangement to minimize the cost to the Government of purchasing the liability insurance. The plan is to provide the necessary coverage more advantageously than commercially available coverage.

PGI 228.304

The plan is implemented by attaching an endorsement to the standard insurance policy forms for workers' compensation, automobile liability, employer's liability, comprehensive general. The endorsement states that the instant policy is subject to the National Defense Projects Rating Plan. The Plan applies to eligible defense contracts of one contractor with one or more departments/agencies.

A defense project is eligible when contracts represent, at the inception of the plan, at least 90 percent of the payroll for the total operations at project locations and the annual insurance premium is estimated to be at least $10,000. A contract is eligible when it is either domestic or foreign, cost-reimbursement type or fixed price with redetermination provisions.

Under construction contracts, subcontractors are included in the prime contractor's plan only when subcontractor operations are at the project site, and the subcontract provides that the prime contractor will furnish insurance.

DFARS 228.370

The contractor must comply with Service-unique instructions for the acquisition, development, production, modification, maintenance, repair, flight, or overhaul of aircraft. The Government acts as self-insurer. However, this policy does not apply to those contracts:

- awarded under FAR Part 12 procedures and are for the acquisition, development, production, modification, maintenance, repair, flight, or overhaul of aircraft;
- for commercial derivative aircraft that are to be maintained to Federal Aviation Administration airworthiness when the work will be performed at a licensed FAA repair station;

- for which a non-DoD customer (including a foreign military sales customer) has not agreed to assume the risk for loss or destruction of, or damages to, the aircraft; or
- strictly for activities incidental to the normal operations of the aircraft (e.g., refueling operations, minor non-structural actions not requiring towing such as replacing aircraft tires due to wear and tear).

Solicitation Provisions and Contract Clauses

DFARS 252.228-7000, Reimbursement for War-Hazard Losses, when FAR 52.228-4, Worker's Compensation and War-Hazard Insurance Overseas, is used and the head of the contracting activity decides not to allow the contractor to buy insurance for war-hazard losses.

DFARS 252.228-7001, Ground and Flight Risk
The clause may be modified only as follows:

- expressly define the "contractor's premises" where the aircraft will be located during and for contract performance. These locations may include contract premises which are owned or leased by the (sub)contractor, or premises where the (sub)contractor is a permittee or licensee or has a right to use, including Government airfields;
- include a modified definition of "aircraft" if the contract covers other than conventional types of winged aircraft, i.e., helicopters, vertical take-off or landing aircraft, lighter-than-air airships, unmanned aerial vehicles, or other nonconventional aircraft. The modified definition should describe a stage of manufacture comparable to the standard definition;
- modify "in the open" to include "hush houses," test hangars and comparable structures, and other designated areas; or
- revise paragraph (e)(3) of the clause to provide Government assumption of risk for transportation by conveyance on streets or highways when transportation is limited to the vicinity of contractor premises and incidental to work performed under the contract.

DFARS 252.228-7003, Capture and Detention, may be used when contractor employees are subject to capture and detention and may not be covered by the War Hazards Compensation Act (42 U.S.C. 1701 et seq.).

DFARS 252.228-7005, Accident Reporting and Investigation Involving Aircraft, Missiles, and Space Launch Vehicles, for the manufacture, modification, overhaul, or repair of these items.

DFARS 252.228-7006, Compliance with Spanish Laws and Insurance, for services or construction to be performed in Spain, unless the contractor is a Spanish concern.

5.6.4 Overseas Workers Compensation and War Hazard Insurance

FAR 28.305

The Defense Base Act extends the Longshoremen's and Harbor Workers' Compensation Act to employees working outside the United States on public works or contracts that are approved or financed under the Foreign Assistance Act of 1961.[32] A *public-works contract* is for a fixed improvement for the public use of the United States or its allies that involves onsite work such as:

- alteration;
- construction;
- dams;
- dredging;
- harbor improvements;
- housing;
- removal;
- repair; and
- roadways.

Similarly, the War Hazards Compensation Act protects employees against the risk of war hazards (injury, death, capture, or detention).[33] When a contractor's insurance policy or self-insurance program provides the workers' compensation coverage required by the Defense Base Act, the employees automatically receive war-hazard risk protection. If the Secretary of Labor waives applicability of the Defense Base Act to any (sub)contract, work location, or classification of employees, the benefits of the War Hazards Compensation Act are automatically waived for those employees, and the contractor provides workers' compensation coverage against the risk of work injury or death. The contractor then assumes liability toward the employees and their beneficiaries for war-hazard injury, death, capture, or detention. These liability or insurance costs are allowable. This is one instance where agencies may specify insurance requirements under fixed-price contracts.

Solicitation Provisions and Contract Clauses

FAR 52.228-3, Workers' Compensation Insurance (Defense Base Act), when the Defense Base Act applies and either the contract is for a public-work performed outside the United States, or will be approved or financed under the Foreign Assistance Act of 1961.

FAR 52.228-4, Worker's Compensation and War-Hazard Insurance Overseas, for a public work performed outside the United States and the Secretary of Labor waives use of the Defense Base Act.

FAR 52.228-5, Insurance—Work on a Government Installation, for fixed-price contracts exceeding the simplified acquisition threshold on a domestic Government installation (unless work is minimal). The contracting officer may require additional coverage and higher limits, or may reduce or eliminate coverage.

FAR 52.228-7, Insurance—Liability to Third Persons, if cost-reimbursement, other than construction and architect-engineer services.

FAR 52.228-8, Liability and Insurance—Leased Motor Vehicles.

FAR 52.228-9, Cargo Insurance, for transportation or related services, except when freight is shipped under rates subject to released or declared value.

FAR 52.228-10, Vehicular and General Public Liability Insurance, for transportation or related services if public vehicular liability insurance required by law is not sufficient.

5.7 VALUE ENGINEERING

FAR 48.1

Value engineering is a program designed to eliminate anything that increases costs (acquisition, operation, or support) without impairing essential functions or characteristics. There are two value engineering approaches. One is an incentive approach in which a contractor voluntarily uses its own resources to develop and submit value engineering change proposals (VECPs). The contract provides for sharing savings and paying the contractor's allowable development and implementation costs only if a VECP is accepted. This voluntary approach should not increase costs to the Government.

The second approach is a mandatory program in which the Government requires and pays for a specific value engineering program effort of a defined scope and level of effort as a separately priced contract line item. The contractor shares in savings on accepted VECPs, but at a lower rate than under the voluntary approach. This mandatory approach ensures that the contractor's value engineering effort is applied where opportunities may arise for considerable savings, consistent with the functional requirements of the end item. This approach is not permitted in architect-engineering contracts.

The contract under which the VECP is submitted is known as the *instant contract*. The VECP does not include quantity increases which could occur after acceptance due to additional orders, contract modification, exercise of options, or (if a multiyear contract) quantities funded after VECP acceptance. In a fixed-price contract with prospective price redetermination, the VECP refers to the period only for which firm prices are established.

The contracting officer must accept or reject the VECP within 45 days of receipt, or else notify the contractor promptly in writing with the reasons for delay and the anticipated decision date. The contractor may withdraw, in whole or in part, a VECP not accepted within the time period. Any VECP may be approved, in whole or in part, by a contract modification incorporating the VECP. Until the effective date of the contract modification however, the contractor performs in accordance with the existing contract. If the Government accepts the VECP but rejects subsequent deliveries (or the contractor fails to deliver), the contractor reimburses the Government for its proportionate share of payments. If the VECP is not accepted, the contracting officer notifies the contractor in writing of the reasons for rejection. Agencies establish guidelines for processing VECPs and may require incorporation of value engineering clauses in appropriate subcontracts.

Contracting officers must determine for each VECP the *sharing period*, during which the contractor and Government will share in the cost savings. The sharing period begins with acceptance of the first unit incorporating the VECP, and ends on a specific calendar date that is either set by the contracting officer (between 36 and 60 consecutive months) after the first unit affected by the VECP is accepted, or else the last scheduled delivery date of an item affected by the VECP. In establishing a sharing period, the contracting officer considers the:

- complexity and extent of the change;
- contractor's financial risk;
- development cost;
- number of units affected;
- performance and/or reliability impact; and
- remaining production period.

For contracts containing engineering development or low-rate-initial-production or early production units, the end of the sharing period is not based on a calendar date. Rather, the period is based on acceptance of the number of future contract units affected by the VECP and scheduled to be delivered during the time frame that spans the highest planned production rate. This time frame runs somewhere between 36 and 60 consecutive months, and is set by the contracting officer. Agencies may prescribe sharing future contract savings on all future deliverable units under any or all contracts awarded within the sharing period, even if the scheduled delivery date is outside the sharing period.

The Government may benefit from more savings than just a single contract. *Acquisition savings* result from applying a VECP to multiple contracts awarded by the same contracting office for the same unit. Acquisition savings include three components. Again we have *instant contract savings,* the net cost reductions on the contract under which the VECP is submitted and accepted. They equal the *instant unit cost reduction* of performance due to using the VECP on the instant unit, multiplied by the number of instant contract units affected by the VECP. This calculation is then reduced by the contractor's costs to develop, test, prepare, and submit the VECP and make the contractual changes required by Government acceptance. In service contracts, the instant unit cost reduction is the number of hours per line-item task saved by using the VECP on the instant contract, multiplied by the contract labor rate.

A second savings component is the *concurrent contract savings*, the net reductions in the prices of other contracts that are ongoing at the time the VECP is accepted. Third is the *future contract savings*, the product of the future unit cost reduction and the number of future contract units in the sharing base. For these savings calculations, *future unit cost reduction* is the instant unit cost reduction adjusted for projected learning or quantity changes during the sharing period. The *sharing base* is the number of affected end items on contracts of the contracting office accepting the VECP.

Net acquisition savings include instant, concurrent and future contract savings, less Government costs, shared between the parties as shown in table 5.1 (Government share is listed first). The contractor is entitled to a percentage share of any net acquisition savings which exceed the sum of Government costs and negative instant contract savings. *Government costs* address increases in logistics, maintenance, operations, and testing support, but exclude administrative costs to process the VECP and negative instant contract savings. *Negative instant contract savings* comprise the instant contract cost or price increases because development and implementation costs now exceed the instant contract savings.

Table 5.1 Government/Contractor Shares of Net Acquisition Savings (figures in percentages)

	Sharing Agreement	
Contract Type	*Incentive (Voluntary)*	*Program Requirement (Mandatory)*
Firm-Fixed-Price	50/50	75/25
Incentive	Per current contract arrangement; 50/50 on concurrent and future contracts	Per current contract arrangement; 75/25 on concurrent and future contracts
CPFF and CPAF	75/25	85/15

If the instant contract is not incentivized, the contractor's share of net acquisition savings is calculated and paid each time savings are realized. This could occur once or several times. When the instant contract is incentivized however, the contractor shares in instant contract savings through the contract's incentive structure. In either event, the contractor shares in the savings on all affected units scheduled for delivery during the sharing period. The contractor must maintain, for three years after final payment on the contract, records to identify the first delivered unit incorporating the applicable VECP.

Agencies establish procedures to fund and pay the contractor's share of both collateral savings and future contract savings. *Collateral savings* are measurable savings in the agency's overall projected collateral costs, excluding acquisition savings. Contractor shares of savings are paid through the contract under which the VECP was accepted. On incentive contracts, the contractor's share of all savings are paid as a separate firm-fixed-price contract line item on the instant contract within three months after concurrent contracts are modified to reflect price reductions due to use of the VECP. The parties agree whether the contractor's share of future contract savings is paid as subsequent contracts are awarded or in a lump-sum payment at the time the VECP is accepted. The lump-sum method is easier if a good estimate exists of how many items will be purchased for delivery during the sharing period, and if the funding is available.

Sharing on construction contracts applies only to savings on the instant contract and to collateral savings. The Government's share of savings is determined by subtracting Government costs from instant contract savings and then multiplying the result by either 45 percent for fixed-price contracts or 75 percent for cost-reimbursement contracts. Value engineering sharing does not apply to incentivized construction contracts. Contracts for architect-engineer services require a mandatory value engineering program to reduce total ownership cost, but no sharing of value engineering savings.

The Government shares collateral savings with the contractor, unless the head of the contracting activity has determined that the cost of calculating and tracking collateral savings will exceed the benefits to be derived. The contractor's share of collateral savings may range from 20 to 100 percent of the estimated savings to be realized during a typical year of use, up to $100,000, but may not exceed the contract's estimated target cost or firm-fixed-price at the time the VECP is accepted.

Profit or fee is excluded when calculating instant or future contract savings because incentive payments do not constitute profit or fee. Generally, profit or fee on the instant contract is not adjusted downward as a result of accepting a VECP.

A no-cost settlement may be used if reliance on other VECP approaches likely would not be more cost-effective. The contractor would keep all of the savings on the instant contract, and all savings on its concurrent contracts only. The Government would keep all savings resulting from concurrent contracts placed with other sources, savings from all future contracts, and all collateral savings. Use of this method must be by mutual agreement of both parties.

Incentivized performance or design-to-cost targets are not adjusted because of VECP acceptance. The only benefits of an accepted VECP which are rewarded under a value engineering clause are those not rewardable under other incentives.

The Government will unilaterally decide whether to accept or reject a VECP and to determine the duration of the sharing period. It also has full discretion to quantify collateral costs of Government-furnished property, logistic support, maintenance, and operations, as well as associated collateral savings.

Value Engineering is not used for:

- commercial products that do not involve special requirements or specifications;
- contracts exempted by the agency;
- engineering services from nonprofit organizations;
- personal services;
- product or component improvement; or
- research and development, other than full-scale development.

Solicitation Provisions and Contract Clauses

FAR 52.248-1, Value Engineering, in excess of the simplified acquisition threshold, except as provided above. Use the clause with its Alternate I if substantial savings to the Government may result from a sustained value engineering effort. Use the clause with its Alternate II if both a value engineering incentive and a mandatory program requirement are used. Use the clause with its Alternate III if the head of the contracting activity determines that the cost of computing and tracking collateral savings will exceed the benefits to be derived and a value engineering incentive is used. Use Alternates I and III if a value engineering program requirement is used, or Alternates II and III if both an incentive and a program requirement are used.

FAR 52.248-2, Value Engineering—Architect-Engineer, when the Government requires and pays for a specific value engineering effort in architect-engineer contracts.

FAR 52.248-3, Value Engineering—Construction, when the contract amount is estimated to exceed the simplified acquisition threshold, unless an incentive contract is contemplated. Do not include the clause in contracts of lesser value if the contracting officer sees a potential for significant savings. The contracting officer does not include the clause in incentive-type construction contracts. Use the clause with its Alternate I if the head of the contracting activity determines that the cost of computing and tracking collateral savings for a contract will exceed the benefits to be derived.

5.8 SUBCONTRACTING

5.8.1 Privity of Contract

The doctrine of *privity of contract* precludes granting any rights or obligations to a person or firm which is not a party to the contract. Only parties to contracts may enforce their rights or claim damages. Hence, the Government cannot impose itself into dealings between a prime and subcontractor; they must work out their disagreements themselves. For instance, if the prime contractor is in dispute with the subcontractor, the Government cannot (in most cases) get involved to mediate the dispute. Likewise, a subcontractor cannot bring suit against the Government; it must go through its prime contractor (or higher-tier subcontractor) for relief.

This relationship could become a concern when responsibility for a key area of performance flows down from prime to subcontractor. In such a case, requirements can be transferred and translated from a party to which the Government has recourse to another party whom the customer cannot legally touch. In this case, the contracting officer may withhold final payment if the surety agrees to hold the Government harmless from any resulting liability.

5.8.2 Make-or-Buy Program

FAR 15.407-2

When make-or-buy programs are required, the Government may reserve the right to review and agree on the contractor's make-or-buy program.[34] Contracting officers may require prospective contractors to submit make-or-buy program plans for negotiated acquisitions requiring cost or pricing data that are at least $11.5 million in value, except for research or development effort. Contracting officers may require prospective contractors to submit make-or-buy programs for lower-value negotiated acquisitions only upon written determination that the information is necessary. The solicitation includes a statement that the program and required supporting information must accompany the offer and describes evaluation factors for the proposed program, such as:

- availability of socioeconomic businesses for subcontracting;
- capability;
- capacity;
- control of technical and schedule interfaces;
- delivery or performance schedules;
- proprietary processes;
- technical risks; and
- technical superiority or exclusiveness.

The contractor's proposal discusses major items or work efforts that require company management review of the make-or-buy decision because they are complex, costly, needed in large quantities, or require additional equipment or real property to produce. Normally, make-or-buy programs should not include items or work efforts estimated to cost less than 1 percent of the total estimated contract price or any minimum dollar amount set by the agency.

The contracting officer may incorporate the make-or-buy program in negotiated contracts for major (sub)systems or their components, regardless of contract type. The program can also be used in a cost-type contract in which the contractor's share of the cost is less than 25 percent and technical or cost risks justify Government review and approval of changes or additions to the make-or-buy program.

Contracting officers normally do not agree to proposed "make items" when the products or services are not regularly manufactured or provided by the contractor, or are available from another firm at lower prices. However, the contracting officer may agree to these as "make items" if it is in the best interest of the Government. Possible reasons to do so include design secrecy, direct control over production and/or quality, integrating plant operations, overall lower Government-wide cost, unreliable suppliers, and using excess capacity to absorb fixed overhead.

By contrast, reasons to buy from vendors include:

- available vendor supplies and schedules;
- cost of specialty machinery;
- desire to maintain a stable workforce;
- desire to maintain multiple sources;
- labor and facilities specialization;
- limited in-house production facilities;
- lower cost;
- lower risk of quality or schedule problems;

- materials complexity;
- small volume requirements; and
- suppliers' research and knowledge.

PGI 215.407-2

The decision to request a make-or-buy plan should consider the prime contractor's:

- anticipated contract type and amount;
- assumption of risk;
- availability and experience of program office personnel to credibly analyze and evaluate a submission;
- complexity, configuration maturity or uniqueness associated with the end item or subsystems;
- critical path items;
- degree of vertical integration;
- impact on contract overhead rates with respect to maintaining work in-house;
- industrial base presence;
- integrated master schedule timelines and their tolerances for variation;
- internal resources;
- plant capacity;
- potential quality concerns associated with subcontracted items;
- proprietary data and/or trade secrets; and
- socioeconomic considerations.

Evaluation factors for the Government to use for a make-or-buy decision include the prime contractor's:

- component availability through existing sources (e.g. available inventory or other Government contracts);
- existing make-or-buy processes, including cost and technical risk considerations;
- justification for items it does not normally make;
- make-or-buy history;
- past performance, especially with respect to subcontract management;
- plant capacity; and
- technical, financial, and personnel capabilities.

Using a standard cost system to make this decision can identify inefficient suppliers or provide a critical look at the production process. This in turn provides both a negotiation tool and a quantitative basis for making a decision. The disadvantages of a standard cost-based decision process are calculation error, ignoring nonfinancial considerations, misinterpreting technical know-how and managerial expertise, and over-optimism.

Unlike contractors, the Government does not have a make-or-buy decision to make. Public policy requires it to buy unless industry cannot produce the item, production is limited, or the specification must remain under tight control.

5.8.3 Consent to Subcontract

FAR 44.2

If the contractor has an approved purchasing system, consent is required only for subcontracts specifically identified by the contracting officer in the contract. The contracting officer may require consent to subcontract if required to protect the Government due to subcontract complexity, type, value, or need for special surveillance. These subcontracts are usually for critical components, services or (sub)systems.

If the contractor does not have an approved purchasing system, consent to subcontract is required for cost-reimbursement, labor-hour and time-and-materials, and letter contracts. Consent is also required for unpriced modifications and delivery orders under fixed-price contracts that exceed either the simplified acquisition threshold or 5 percent of the total estimated contract cost, whichever is greater.

The ACO provides consent to subcontracts, except when the contracting officer retains the contract for administration or withholds the consent responsibility from delegation to the ACO. The following are considerations in this determination:

- adequate consideration obtained for any proposed subcontract that will involve the use of GFP and equipment;
- appropriate subcontract type for the risks involved;
- assessment of alternate subcontractor proposals;
- availability of property from Government sources;
- compliance with applicable cost accounting standards for awarding the subcontract;
- compliance with socioeconomic plans;
- consistency with the contractor's approved make-or-buy program;
- flowdown of required clauses and specifications;
- performing adequate cost or price analysis and obtaining accurate, complete and current cost or pricing data and certifications;
- presence of adequate price competition or sole-source justification;

- review of information in SAM; and
- translation of prime contract technical requirements into subcontract requirements.

Contracting officers do not consent to cost-reimbursement subcontracts in form if the fee exceeds statutory fee limitations or provides for cost-plus-a-percentage-of-cost payments. They will become wary if cost-reimbursement, labor-hour or time-and-materials subcontracts are used repetitively. They also will not consent to agreements that obligate the contracting officer to deal directly with the subcontractor, nor impose on the Government the results of arbitration, judicial decision or voluntary settlement between the prime contractor and subcontractor.

Subcontractors may insist on the right of indirect appeal to an agency board of contract appeals if affected by a dispute between the Government and the prime contractor. In such cases, the prime contractor and subcontractor are equally bound by the contracting officer's or board's decision. However, the contracting officer or the appeals board are not obligated to decide questions that do not arise between the Government and the prime contractor or are not cognizable under the Disputes clause.

Contractors may try to pass risk on to subcontractors due to market risk, production uncertainties from labor or material deficiencies, or social or personal hazards. Prudent contractors will minimize these issues by negotiating firm-fixed-price subcontracts before settling with the Government, and authorizing work only on a not-to-exceed basis. However, the contractor should pass along risk through correction-of-defects clauses and proper inspection techniques.

PGI 244.201

The requiring activity should determine if, based on the criticality of the component or system to be supplied and potential concerns about supply chain risk, written consent to subcontract by the contracting officer is necessary when subcontractors are selected or modified during the course of contract performance. Should the requiring activity conclude that a potential subcontractor is beyond the risk tolerance of the system and mission, the requiring activity must inform the contracting officer, who can exercise the authority granted in Section 806 of Pub. L. 111-383 to withhold consent for the contractor to subcontract with a particular source or exclude a source from consideration. Conversely, the contracting officer must first notify and obtain consent from the program manager before denying subcontract consent for any reason.

Solicitation Provisions and Contract Clauses

FAR 52.244-2, Subcontracts, when contemplating a definitive or letter contract that exceeds the simplified acquisition threshold. For a fixed-price contract however, unpriced contract actions (i.e., modifications or delivery orders) must be anticipated. Use of this clause is not required in fixed-price architect-engineer contracts, or contracts for mortuary, refuse or shipment and storage (of personal property) services when an agency-prescribed clause or approval of subcontractors' facilities is required.

FAR 52.244-4, Subcontracts and Outside Associates and Consultants (Architect-Engineer Services).

FAR 52.244-5, Competition in Subcontracting, if negotiated and the contract amount is expected to exceed the simplified acquisition threshold, except for an architect-engineer, firm-fixed-price (awarded competitively or whose prices are set by law or regulation), labor-hour, or time-and-materials contract.

DFARS 252.244-7000, Subcontracts for Commercial Items.

5.8.4 Contractor's Purchasing System Review

FAR 44.3

A *contractor purchasing system review* (CPSR) evaluates the efficiency and effectiveness of the contractor to subcontract and comply with Government policy. The review provides the ACO a basis to grant, withhold or withdraw approval of the contractor's purchasing system.

The ACO determines the need for a CPSR based on the past performance of the contractor and the complexity, dollar value, and volume of the subcontracts. If a contractor's Government sales (excluding competitively awarded firm-fixed-price and fixed-price with economic price adjustment prime contracts, and sales of commercial items) are expected to exceed $50 million during the next 12 months, a CPSR is usually needed (although the agency head for contract administration may adjust this figure up or down). A CPSR is not performed for a specific contract. This decision for a review must be revisited at least every three years.

Special attention during a CPSR is given to:

- compliance with Cost Accounting Standards in awarding subcontracts;
- degree of price competition obtained;
- management control systems and internal audit procedures for progress payments;
- market research;
- methods of evaluating subcontractor responsibility, including use of SAM;

- obtaining accurate, complete and current cost or pricing data and certification;
- planning, award and postaward management of major subcontract programs;
- pricing policies and techniques;
- quality standards invoked;
- socioeconomic subcontracting policies and procedures;
- treatment of affiliates and other concerns who work with the contractor; and
- use of appropriate contract types.

Surveillance is in accordance with a plan developed by the ACO with the assistance of audit, pricing, subcontracting, and technical specialists. The plan covers preaward, postaward, performance, and contract completion that affect the contractor's purchasing and subcontracting. The plan should also provide for reviewing the effectiveness of the contractor's corrective actions taken as a result of previous Government recommendations.

The ACO approves a purchasing system only after determining that the contractor's purchasing policies and practices are efficient and provide adequate protection of the Government's interests, and promptly notifies the contractor in writing of the granting, withholding or withdrawal of approval. The notification granting system approval will apply to all Federal Government contracts at that plant. It will waive the contractual requirements for advance notification in fixed-price contracts (but not for cost-reimbursement contracts) and consent to subcontracts unless selected for special surveillance. This approval is subject to withdrawal at any time at the ACO's discretion.

Consent to certain subcontracts or classes of subcontracts may still be required even though the contractor's purchasing system has been approved. This is usually because the CPSR or continuing surveillance has revealed sufficient weaknesses in a particular area of subcontracting to warrant special attention by the ACO.

The ACO withholds or withdraws approval of a contractor's purchasing system for major weaknesses when the contractor fails to provide sufficient information upon which to make an affirmative determination, or if contractor's purchasing system has so deteriorated as to threaten the Government's interest. Approval is withheld or withdrawn when there is a recurring noncompliance with requirements (e.g., advance notification, cost accounting standards, cost or pricing data, or small business subcontracts).

5.8.5 Subcontracts for Commercial Items and Components

FAR 44.4

Prime and subcontractors at all tiers incorporate commercial items or nondevelopmental items as components. They impose on these subcontractors only those clauses that implement law or executive orders applicable to subcontractors furnishing commercial items or commercial components, or else are consistent with customary commercial practice.

Contractors who purchase supply items from AbilityOne or SourceAmerica must go through the Defense Logistics Agency, GSA, and the Department of Veterans Affairs (if available through their distribution facilities) before placing an order with the central nonprofit agency.

The contracting officer may authorize purchases from Government supply sources of overhead supplies, but not production supplies. The contracting officer may restrict the authorization to certain facilities or specific contracts and is permitted to limit the authorization requirement for Government sources to a specific dollar amount, allowing the contractor to make smaller purchases from other sources. When appropriate, the contracting officer may specify if vesting of title will differ from other property acquired or furnished by the contractor for use under the contract.

The contracting officer may authorize cost-reimbursement contractors to obtain interagency fleet management system vehicles for short-term use and related services, such as:

- fuel and lubricants;
- inspection;
- maintenance;
- repair; and
- storage.

FAR 51.1 and 51.2

The contracting officer may authorize contractor use of Government sources of supply based on a written D&F due to lower cost, delivery, or suitability. Certain procedures are prescribed for obtaining an address activity code and GSA ordering. For vehicle rental, the contractor must furnish motor vehicle liability insurance covering bodily injury and property damage. This includes fuel from the Defense Logistics Agency Energy program funded by the Defense Working Capital Fund for use on cost-reimbursement contracts.[35]

DFARS 244.402

Any item less than $10,000 in value purchased by a DoD contractor for use in multiple contracts not identified to a particular contract is treated as a commercial item.

Solicitation Provisions and Contract Clauses

FAR 52.244-6, Subcontracts for Commercial Items and Commercial Components. Use the clause with its Alternate I when the head of the agency has waived the examination of records by the Comptroller General. Use the clause with its Alternate II if the acquisition will use fund appropriated or otherwise made available by the American Recovery and Reinvestment Act of 2009.

FAR 52.251-1, Government Supply Sources, when the contracting officer authorizes the contractor to acquire supplies or services from a Government supply source.

FAR 52.251-2, Interagency Fleet Management System (IFMS) Vehicles and Related Services, when a cost-reimbursement contract is contemplated, and the contracting officer may authorize the contractor to use IFMS vehicles and related services.

DFARS 252.251-7000, Ordering from Government Supply Sources, if including FAR 52.251-1.

DFARS 252.251-7001, Use of Interagency Fleet Management System (IFMS) Vehicles and Related Services.

5.9 PROPERTY

5.9.1 Capital Investment

Capital budgeting is the process used to decide how to pursue long-term investments such as new or replacement machinery or new plants. Several formal methods are used in capital budgeting:

- Net present value,
- Internal rate of return,
- Payback period, and
- Profitability index.

Net present value (NPV) estimates when and how much in future incremental cash flows will arise from the project, then discounts them to the current day to derive present value. NPV is the sum of all present values. All positive NPV projects are acceptable for investment, or perhaps only those with the highest NPV are funded. Management will look at the current discount rate (or *hurdle rate*) as the minimum acceptable return on an investment. NPV is the price to pay now for a future benefit.

The *internal rate of return* (IRR) is the discount rate that yields an NPV of zero, which equates NPV to initial cost outlay. The IRR method is used when a negative cash flow occurs at the start of the project, followed by future positive cash flows. Projects with an IRR higher than the hurdle rate are acceptable.

Executives generally prefer IRR over NPV because it is intuitively more appealing to use percentage rates of return than dollars of NPV. By graphing various pairs of production volume and associated costs, a break-even point can be derived to identify the point where cost equals revenue. The ratio of break-even point to total cost equals the marginal contribution per unit to fixed costs, which we will call MC. Then,

(MC × total quantity produced) – total fixed costs
= net earnings for the given level of output.

The *rate of return (or return on investment)* is the ratio of earnings or loss to the amount invested, expressed as a percentage. The numerator can be interest, profit or loss, while the denominator is the amount of capital, asset value or principal.

The third method used in capital budgeting is the *payback period*, or the length of time over which net cash savings must equal initial cash outlay. The firm would like to minimize this period to enjoy the benefits of investment as soon as possible.

The ratio of present value of net cash benefits to the present value of the initial outlay equals the *profitability index*, the fourth budgeting method. The index value for each option is then used to rank the attractiveness of each option. However, this approach has a serious shortcoming in that it ignores both the time value of money and the future beyond the payback period.

Of course, another option for a firm is to buy used capital equipment if it will lead to increased efficiency, productivity and/or quality. Used equipment may also be attractive if it reduces cash outlay or depreciation expenses, or otherwise leads to a higher return on investment. However, used equipment frequently needs repair, suffers from accelerated obsolescence and quality, and may have little or no warranty. Also, spare parts may not be available. So unlike the other options mentioned, this approach is based as much on facts as on derived metrics.

A final consideration in capital investment is *life-cycle cost or whole-life cost.* This is the total cost of an asset over its lifetime, sometimes colloquially referred to as "cradle-to-grave" cost. It is used to assess lease or buy options, and acquisition decisions by considering cost elements rather than mere price to derive the total cost of ownership. Such cost components include:

- acquisition,
- construction,
- depreciation,
- design,
- financing,
- maintenance,
- operations,
- planning,
- renewal or rehabilitation,
- replacement or disposal, and
- training.

5.9.2 Property Administration

FAR 45

Government-Furnished Property (GFP) is possessed or acquired by the Government and subsequently provided to the contractor for performance. GFP includes spares and property furnished for repair, maintenance, or modification. GFP also includes contractor-acquired property (often test or ground support equipment) which is deliverable under a cost contract to which the Government has title for continued use under the contract.

Contractors are ordinarily required to furnish all property necessary to perform Government contracts. The Government furnishes property to contractors only when the overall benefit to the contract outweighs the increased risk and cost of property administration, or if the Government requirements cannot otherwise be met. In this vein, agencies will encourage contractors to use voluntary consensus standards and industry best practices to manage Government property in their possession without requiring contractors to maintain a separate management system for GFP. They should ensure maximum reutilization of contractor inventory, such as property acquired by and in the possession of a (sub)contractor for which title is vested in the Government and is not needed to complete performance. This also means they will require contractors to declare as excess (or justify retaining) any Government property not needed for contract performance. Needless to say, they should minimize any competitive advantage a prospective contractor could have by using Government property.

Contractors are not liable for damage, loss or theft of GFP except under fixed-price contracts that are not subject to submission of cost or pricing data. However, the contracting officer may revoke the Government's assumption of risk when the property administrator determines that the contractor's property management practices are inadequate and/or present an undue risk to the

Government. Moreover, the Government may seek damages if it can show lack of good faith or willful misconduct, or improper consumption during contract performance.

All GFP is administered by tracking against a specific contract. A prime contractor that provides property to a subcontractor is still accountable to the Government for the GFP under the same contract. GFP is transferred from one contract to another only when firm requirements exist under the gaining contract. Such transfers are documented by modifications to both gaining and losing contracts.

If GFP is delivered late or defective, the contractor is entitled to an equitable adjustment in price or schedule. The contractor may also be instructed to sell or scrap the property after contract performance.

The Government may also furnish information or data to assist the contractor in performance. Since the Government is presumed to have *superior knowledge* in light of having custody of this information, it has a duty to disclose any information vital to cost proposal preparation or contract performance. This concept is similar to the ideas of good faith and fair dealing. However, this duty does not transfer between agencies, meaning that one agency is not held liable just because another agency had superior knowledge.

DFARS 245.1

When a contractor will be responsible for preparing requisitioning documentation to acquire Government-furnished property from Government supply sources, the contract requires that the documentation be prepared in accordance with Defense Logistics Management 4000.25-1, Military Standard Requisitioning and Issue Procedures (MILSTRIP).

DoD-furnished property will be marked based on DoD marking standards (MIL-STD-130N, "Identification Marking of U.S. Property") or other standards when the requiring activity determines that such items are subject to serialized item management. The list of GFP subject to serialized item management will be identified in the contract in attachments. The contractor will not be required to tag or mark items or property:

- determined by the head of the agency to be used to support a contingency operation or to facilitate defense against or recovery from nuclear, biological, chemical, or radiological attack;
- for which a D&F has been executed concluding that it is more cost-effective for the Government requiring activity to assign, mark and register the unique item identification after delivery from a small business concern or a commercial item. The D&F shall be executed by the Component

Acquisition Executive for an Acquisition Category (ACAT) I program or the head of the contracting activity for all other programs;
- previously marked as GFP;
- that are contractor-acquired property;
- to which the Government has acquired a lien or title solely because of partial, advance, progress, or performance-based payments;
- under any statutory leasing authority;
- which are intellectual property or software; or
- which are real property.

Contractors are not held liable for loss of Government property under negotiated fixed-price contracts awarded on a basis other than submission of certified cost or pricing data.

The cognizant contracting officer, in consultation with the property administrator, must determine the acceptability of the system, approve, or disapprove the system and pursue correction of any deficiencies. The property administrator will document findings and recommendations in a report to the contracting officer. The contracting officer then reviews findings and recommendations and, if there are no significant deficiencies, promptly notifies the contractor, in writing, that the contractor's property management system is acceptable and approved. If the contracting officer finds that there are one or more significant deficiencies, (s)he promptly makes an initial written determination on any significant deficiencies and notifies the contractor in writing, providing a description of each significant deficiency, and requests the contractor to respond, in writing, to the initial determination within 30 days. (S)he then evaluates the contractor's response to the initial determination, in consultation with the property administrator, makes a final determination and notifies the contractor, in writing, that either the contractor's property management system is acceptable and approved, and no significant deficiencies remain, or else identifies any remaining significant deficiencies and indicates the adequacy of any proposed or completed corrective action. The contracting officer requests that the contractor, within 45 days of receipt of the final determination, either correct the deficiencies or submit an acceptable corrective action plan showing milestones and actions to eliminate the deficiencies.

PGI 245.103-70

The requiring activity is the decision point as to whether or not to furnish property to contractors. The basis for any decision to provide Government property shall be documented by the requiring activity and provided to the contracting officer. Such documentation is not required when contractors are furnished property for repair, modification, or overhaul under a contract.

Prior to furnishing Government property to the contractor, the contracting officer must document four elements in the contract file. The first element is that the furnishing is in the Government's best interest. Discussion should address the following factors:

- contract type—Government property will enable the Government to obtain a more favorable contract type;
- economy—Furnishing Government property is the lowest cost or price alternative;
- industrial base—Government property is needed to ensure future capability to obtain a particular supply item or service;
- production schedule—Government property is crucial to achieving timely or accelerated delivery of a supply item or service;
- scarcity—The Government can obtain scarce items or is the only source of property necessary for successful execution of a contract;
- security—Government property is needed due to national security issues/concerns; and
- standardization—There is a critical need for precise replication.

The second element is that the overall benefit to the acquisition significantly outweighs the increased cost of administration, including property disposal. Property in the hands of contractors drives program costs. Therefore, in order to make the case that providing Government property to the contractor is worthwhile, the associated costs must be considered and the business decision justified. The costs of Government property removal and disposal, including demilitarization and disposal of environmentally regulated property, must be included. Costs must be either less than what the contractor might otherwise incur, or the demonstrated benefit to the Government must outweigh these additional contract costs.

The third element involves demonstrating that providing the property does not substantially increase the Government's risk. Risk must be discussed and documented with a formal risk analysis. For example, when furnishing Government property, the Government is ordinarily responsible for suitability of use, timely delivery, and replacement of defective Government property. Other risks may need to be considered, discussed, and documented.

The fourth element is when Government requirements cannot otherwise be met. Here the analysis must document why the furnishing of Government property is critical and significant to meet acquisition plan objectives.

PGI 245.103-73

Sustainment contracts, including those for performance-based logistics, life-cycle product, logistics, and weapon systems product support, may require the contractor to hold or manage Government inventory.[36] In such cases, regularly scheduled (typically, semiannually) inventory reporting from the contractor is required to ensure that inventory levels meet program requirements and Government inventory in excess of authorized amounts is identified. The requiring activity is responsible for providing the contracting officer with reporting requirements for Government inventory.

During acquisition planning, pricing contracts, exercising options, and assessing past performance, contracting officers should review the requiring activity's assessment of the information generated by the inventory reporting requirements.

PGI 245.105

Within 10 days of receiving the report, if the contracting officer makes a determination that there is a significant deficiency, the contracting officer should provide an initial determination of deficiencies and a copy of the report to the contractor and require the contractor to submit a written response. Within 30 days of receiving the contractor's response, the contracting officer, in consultation with the auditor or cognizant functional specialist, should evaluate the contractor's response and make a final determination.

The contracting officer and property administrator shall monitor the contractor's progress in correcting deficiencies. If the contractor fails to make adequate progress, the contracting officer takes whatever action is necessary to ensure that the contractor corrects the deficiencies. Examples of actions the contracting officer can take are withdraw or withhold approval of the system; bringing the issue to the attention of higher level management, implement or increase the withholding, and recommend nonaward of potential contracts.

When the contractor notifies the contracting officer that the contractor has corrected the significant deficiencies, the contracting officer requests the property administrator to review the correction to determine if the deficiencies have been resolved. The contracting officer will then determine if the contractor has corrected the deficiencies. If the contracting officer determines the contractor has corrected the deficiencies, the contracting officer's notification is sent to the auditor, payment office, property administrator, appropriate action officers responsible for reporting past performance at the requiring activities, and each contracting and contract administration office having substantial business with the contractor as applicable.

DFARS 245.107

Whenever the Contractor performs by using GFP, it must report physical receipt, any loss due to damage that occurs during work in process, transfer to another DoD contract, shipment to the Government or to a contractor, or when serially managed items are incorporated into a higher-level assembly, component, or end item. These events must be reported within seven business days of the date the change in status occurs, unless otherwise specified in the contract.

PGI 245.402-71

The accountability of Contractor-acquired property cannot be transferred between contracts, except as GFP. If the property was not anticipated at time of award, it can be transferred as a line item not separately priced. This is usually done for special tooling or test equipment, or for property destined for preservation and storage under a major acquisition program.

Solicitation Provisions and Contract Clauses

FAR 52.245-1, Government Property, when the Government will provide property and the procurement exceeds the simplified acquisition threshold. Use the clause with its Alternate I in contracts other than those identified in FAR 45.104(a), Responsibility and Liability for Government Property. Use the clause with its Alternate II to conduct basic or applied research at nonprofit institutions either of higher education or conducting scientific research.

FAR 52.245-2, Government Property (Installation Operation Services), in service contracts to be performed on a Government installation, GFP will be provided for initial provisioning only and the Government is not responsible for repair or replacement.

FAR 52.245-9, Use and Charges, when the Government Property clause is included.

DFARS 252.208-7000, Intent to Furnish Precious Metals as Government-Furnished Material.

DFARS 252.245-7000, Government-Furnished Mapping, Charting, and Geodesy Property, when mapping, charting, and geodesy property is to be furnished.

DFARS 252.245-7001, Tagging, Labeling, and Marking of Government-Furnished Property, when including FAR 52.245-1, Government Property.

DFARS 252.245-7002, Reporting Loss of Government Property, when including FAR 52.245-1, Government Property.

DFARS 252.245-7003, Contractor Property Management System Administration, when including FAR 52.245-1, Government Property.

DFARS 252.245-7004, Reporting, Reutilization, and Disposal, when including FAR 52.245-1, Government Property. For negotiated fixed-price contracts awarded on a basis other than submission of certified cost or pricing data for which Government property is provided, use the clause at FAR 52.245-1, Government Property, without its Alternate I.

DFARS 252.245-70XX, Management and Reporting of Government Property.

5.9.3 Solicitation and Evaluation Procedures

FAR 45.2

The contracting officer lists in the solicitation the GFP to be offered. In a competitive acquisition, the contractor is responsible for all installation, rehabilitation, or transportation costs to make the property available for use. The solicitation describes the evaluation procedures to be followed, including rental charges and other costs or savings to be evaluated. Offerors must list or describe all Government property that it or its subcontractors propose to use on a rent-free basis, along with the accountable contract under which the property is held and the contracting officer authorization for its use.

The contracting officer considers any potentially unfair competitive advantage that may result from the contractor possessing Government property by applying, for evaluation purposes only, a rental equivalent evaluation factor. The contracting officer ensures the offeror's property management plans or procedures for property accounting are consistent with the requirements of the solicitation.

5.9.4 Authorizing the Use and Rental of Government Property

FAR 45.3

Government property is normally provided on a rent-free basis. Any rental charges do not apply to Government property that is left in place or installed on contractor-owned property for mobilization or future Government production purposes. The contractor may request approval to use Government property under fixed-price contracts other than the contract to which it is accountable. If approved, the contracting officer obtains a fair rental or other adequate consideration.

DFARS 245.302

A contractor may use Government property on work for foreign governments and international organizations only when approved in writing by the contracting officer having cognizance of the property. The contracting officer may grant approval, provided the use will not interfere with foreseeable requirements of the United States, the work is undertaken as a DoD foreign military sale, or (for a direct commercial sale) the foreign country or international organization would be authorized to contract with the department concerned under the Arms Export Control Act.

When a particular foreign government or international organization has funded the acquisition of property, it cannot be assessed rental charges or nonrecurring recoupments for the use of such property.

DoD normally recovers a fair share of nonrecurring costs of special tooling and special test equipment by including these costs in its calculation of the nonrecurring cost recoupment charge when major defense equipment is sold by foreign military sales or direct commercial sales to foreign governments or international organizations. *Major defense equipment* is defined as any item of significant military equipment on the U.S. Munitions List having a nonrecurring research, development, test, and evaluation cost of more than $50 million or a total production cost of more than $200 million.[37] When the cost thresholds are not met, the contracting officer shall assess rental charges for use of special tooling and special test equipment pursuant to the Use and Charges clause if administratively practicable.

Rental charges for use of U.S. production and research property on commercial sales transactions to the Government of Canada are waived for all commercial contracts. This waiver is based on an understanding wherein the Government of Canada has agreed to waive its rental charges to the U.S. Government. Requests for waiver or reduction of charges for the use of Government property on work for other foreign governments or international organizations shall be submitted to the contracting officer, who is authorized to approve the requests in consultation with the appropriate functional specialist.

5.9.5 Title to Government Property

FAR 45.4

The Government retains title to all GFP until properly disposed. Under cost type and time and material contracts, the Government acquires title to all property for which the contractor is reimbursed. Under fixed-price contracts, the contractor retains title to all property acquired for use on the contract, unless identified as a deliverable end item. The Government acquires title to property acquired or fabricated by the contractor in accordance with the financing provisions or other contract requirements. If a deliverable item is retained by the contractor for use after inspection and acceptance by the Government, it is accountable to the contract through a contract modification listing the item as GFP.

5.9.6 Inventory Disposal Schedules

FAR 45.602-1

A contractor obtains the plant clearance officer's approval to remove Government property from an inventory disposal schedule when it:

- can return unused property to the supplier at fair market value and credit the contract (less any restocking fee);
- has requested continued use of Government property (and the plant clearance officer has consulted with program and technical personnel);
- is authorized to use the property on another Government contract; or
- wishes to purchase or produce an item at acquisition cost and credit the contract. *Acquisition cost* includes the purchase price of a capital asset and costs to position and prepare it for use.

Plant clearance officers initiate reutilization actions in the following order:

- reuse within the agency;
- (if educationally useful equipment and with GSA approval only) to other Federal agencies with a need for the property;
- transfer to schools and nonprofit organizations;
- reuse within the Federal Government; and
- donate as designated by GSA but only if it will not bear any costs incident to donation.

The screening period begins upon the plant clearance officer's acceptance of an inventory disposal schedule. The plant clearance officer determines whether standard or special screening is appropriate (the standard screening period is 46 days).

Upon approval at a higher level, plant clearance officers may abandon, destroy or donate to public bodies any surplus property that is not *sensitive property* (which is potentially dangerous to the public safety or security if stolen or lost, or subject to exceptional physical accountability, control, protection, and security). Examples of sensitive property include ammunition, controlled substances, explosives, hazardous materials or wastes, precious metals, radioactive materials, and weapons. The property also cannot require *demilitarization* which would render it unusable for, and not restorable to, the military purpose for which it was designed or is customarily used. Sensitive property not requiring demilitarization may be abandoned with contractor consent, but instructions are necessary for its proper care, handling, and disposal.

The contractor may dispose of scrap resulting from production or testing without Government approval. However, if the scrap requires demilitarization or is sensitive property, then the contractor must submit the scrap on an inventory disposal schedule.

DFARS 245.602

For termination inventory, plant clearance officers shall verify inventory schedules to determine allocability, condition and quantity. To assess allocability, they will review bills of material, contract requirements, delivery schedules, and other pertinent documents to determine whether schedules include property that are appropriate for use on the contract or exceed the quantity required for completion of the contract (but could be diverted to other commercial work or Government use). They also review the contractor's recent purchases of similar material, plans for current and scheduled production, stock record entries, and bills of material for similar items.

Next, they ensure that the physical condition of the property is reasonably consistent with the Federal Condition Code supplied by the contractor. Finally, they take measures to provide assurance that available inventory is in accordance with quantities listed on the inventory schedules. Quantities may be verified by actual item count, acceptance of labeled quantities in unopened/sealed packages, or scale counts.

Property will be screened DoD-wide, including the contracting and requiring agencies and, if appropriate, GSA. The requiring agency has priority for retention of listed items. All required screening must be completed before any sale of contractor inventory, including contractor inventory in overseas locations (foreign excess personal property) can take place. Upon request of the prospective donation, reutilization, transfer, or sales customer, the plant clearance officer will arrange for inspection of property at the contractor's plant in such a manner as to avoid interruption of the contractor's operations, and consistent with any security requirements.

DFARS 245.604-3

Plant clearance officers determine a best value sales approach (formal or informal sales) to include due consideration for costs, risks, and benefits, e.g., potential sales proceeds. The plant clearance officer may direct the contractor to issue informal invitations for bid (orally, telephonically, or by other informal media), provided that maximum practical competition is obtained, sources solicited are recorded, and informal bids are confirmed in writing.

Plant clearance officers will evaluate bids to establish that the sale price is fair and reasonable, taking into consideration:

- current published prices for the property;
- knowledge or tests of the market;
- nature, condition, location, and quantity of the property; and
- past sale history for like or similar items.

They will then approve award to the eligible and responsible bidder whose bid is most advantageous to the Government. Then they will notify the contractor of the bidder to whom an award will be made within five working days from receipt of bids.

Noncompetitive sales include purchases or retention at less than cost by the contractor. Noncompetitive sales may be made when the plant clearance officer determines that this method is essential to expeditious plant clearance, and the Government's interests are adequately protected. Noncompetitive sales must be at fair and reasonable prices, not less than those reasonably expected under competitive sales. Conditions justifying noncompetitive sales are:

- anticipated sales proceeds do not warrant competitive sale;
- no acceptable bids are received under competitive sale;
- removal of the property would reduce its value or result in disproportionate handling expenses;
- specialized nature of the property would not create bidder interest; or
- such action is essential to the Government's interests.

DAG CH 1–4.2.23

The program manager or contracting officer may appoint a property officer to maintain effective government property accountability and control. DoDI 4161.02, Accountability and Management of Government Contract Property provides instructions and guidance, assigns responsibilities, and prescribes procedures for the accountability and management of government contract property (but not intellectual property and software) in the custody of defense contractors. DoDI 5000.64, Accountability and Management of DoD Equipment and Other Accountable Property, outlines requirements for accountability of property management to support the life-cycle management and documentation of events, items and transactions.

5.9.7 Excess Property

DFARS 217.70

Exchange property is not excess but is eligible for replacement because of obsolescence or unserviceability. It is applied as whole or partial payment toward the acquisition of similar items designed and constructed for the same purpose. 40 U.S.C. 503 permits exchange of personal property and application of the exchange allowance to the acquisition of similar property, but does not authorize the sale of nonexcess personal property. DoD policy is to exchange, rather than replace, eligible excess and nonexcess property when economical and efficient. These exchanges are governed by the Federal Property Management Regulations issued by GSA and DoD Manual 4140.01, Volume 9, DoD Supply Chain Materiel Management Procedures: Materiel Programs.

The purchase request must include a certification that the property is eligible for exchange and complies with all conditions and limitations of the DoD Manual 4140.01. It also includes both a description of the property available for exchange and a written determination of economic advantage to the Government, that exchange allowances shall be applied toward or in payment of the items to be acquired and that the exchange property has been rendered safe or innocuous or demilitarized. Offerors are requested to furnish prices for the new items being acquired without any exchange and then with the exchange (trade-in allowance). If the lowest evaluated offer is an offer for the new items without any exchange, the contracting officer may award on that basis and forgo the exchange. If the successful offer includes an exchange, then one contract is awarded for both the acquisition of the new property and the trade-in of the exchange property. A separate contract for the exchange is only issued when the items must be acquired against a mandatory Federal supply schedule contract.

Solicitation Provision

DFARS 252.217-7002, Offering Property for Exchange, when offering nonexcess personal property for exchange. Allow a minimum of 14 calendar days for the inspection period in paragraph (b) of the clause if the exchange property is in the contiguous United States and at least 21 calendar days outside the contiguous United States.

5.10 INTERNATIONAL CONSIDERATIONS

5.10.1 Trade

FAR 25.4

Three major regulations govern the export of commercial and defense articles. *The International Traffic in Arms Regulations*, issued by the Department of

State, control the export of defense-related articles, services, and technical data, ensuring compliance with the Arms Export Control Act.[38] The U.S. Munitions List identifies these items. *The Export Administration Regulations* issued by the Department of Commerce control the export of dual-use commodities, software, and technology.[39] They are listed by Export Control Classification Number on the Commerce Control List. Finally, *National Security Decision Directive (NSDD) 189, National Policy on the Transfer of Scientific, Technical and Engineering Information*, directs that products of fundamental research be unrestricted as much as possible. Contracts for unclassified fundamental research generally do not involve any export-controlled items, information, or technology.

Trafficking persons for involuntary servitude and debt bondage is forbidden to DoD contractor employees, with penalties imposed by agency regulation. If the contracting officer receives information of such an event, (s)he must immediately notify the Combatant Commander responsible for the geographical area in which the incident has occurred.

DFARS 229.170-2

Bilateral agreements with foreign governments must include a provision that commodities acquired under contracts funded by U.S. assistance programs are exempt from taxation by the foreign government. If taxes or customs duties nevertheless are imposed, the foreign government must reimburse the amount of such taxes to the U.S. Government. The invoice should exclude these duties or taxes. This foreign tax exemption applies to any (sub)contract for commodities when the funds are appropriated by an annual foreign operations appropriations act and the value of the (sub)contract is $500 or more. This exemption does not apply to the acquisition of services, implemented through letters of offer and acceptance, other country-to-country agreements, or Federal interagency agreements. Moreover, reporting of noncompliance by the contractor is required.

PGI 229.101

The contracting officer may direct the contractor to litigate the applicability of a particular tax if the contract is a cost-reimbursement type or else a fixed-price type with a tax escalation clause such as FAR 52.229-4 and the direction is coordinated with the DoD Tax Policy and Advisory Group through the agency-designated legal counsel. Other international treaties may exempt the United States from the payment of specific taxes. The Department of State publishes a list of treaties on its website at www.state.gov.

Solicitation Provisions

DFARS 252.229-7012, Tax Exemptions (Italy)—Representation, if using DFARS 252.229-7003, Tax Exemptions (Italy). Do not use if the solicitation includes FAR 52.204-7.

Solicitation Provisions and Contract Clauses

DFARS 252.229-7001, Tax Relief, when a contract will be awarded to a foreign concern for performance in a foreign country. Use Alternate I clause when the contract will be performed in Germany.

DFARS 252.229-7002, Customs Exemptions (Germany), if requiring the import of U.S. manufactured products into Germany.

DFARS 252.229-7003, Tax Exemptions (Italy), when contract performance will be in Italy.

DFARS 252.229-7004, Status of Contractor as a Direct Contractor (Spain), if requiring the import into Spain of supplies for construction, development, maintenance, or operation of Spanish-American installations and facilities.

DFARS 252.229-7005, Tax Exemptions (Spain), when contract performance will be in Spain.

DFARS 252.229-7006, Value Added Tax Exclusion (United Kingdom), when contract performance will be in the United Kingdom.

DFARS 252.229-7007, Verification of United States Receipt of Goods, when contract performance will be in the United Kingdom.

DFARS 252.229-7008, Relief from Import Duty (United Kingdom), if solicited and awarded in the United Kingdom.

DFARS 252.229-7009, Relief from Customs Duty and Value Added Tax on Fuel (Passenger Vehicles) (United Kingdom), if solicited and awarded in the United Kingdom for fuels (gasoline or diesel) and lubricants used in passenger vehicles (excluding taxis).

DFARS 252.229-7010, Relief from Customs Duty on Fuel (United Kingdom), if solicited and awarded in the United Kingdom that require the use of fuels (gasoline or diesel) and lubricants in taxis or vehicles other than passenger vehicles.

DFARS 252.229-7011, Reporting of Foreign Taxes—U.S. Assistance Programs, if funded with U.S. assistance appropriations provided in the annual foreign operations appropriations act.

DFARS 252.229-7013, Tax Exemptions (Spain)—Representation, if including DFARS 252.229-7005, Tax Exemptions (Spain). Do not use if the solicitation includes FAR 52.204-7.

DFARS 252.229-7014, Full Exemption from Two-Percent Excise Tax on Certain Foreign Procurements. Include FAR 52.229-12, Tax on Certain Foreign Procurements, for an award to a foreign person exempt from Federal taxes per the IRS. Do not use the Governmentwide commercial purchase card for payment.

5.10.2 SAFETY Act

FAR 50.2

The Support Anti-terrorism by Fostering Effective Technologies Act of 2002 (SAFETY Act) has liability protections to promote development and use of anti-terrorism technologies to protect the nation, while providing risk and litigation management protections for (sub)contractors.[40]An *act of terrorism* means any unlawful act determined to use or attempt to use weapons or other methods intended to cause mass destruction, injury or other loss to citizens or institutions of the United States. It can also be an event which causes harm (including financial harm) to an entity, person or property in the United States, or in the case of a domestic U.S. air carrier or a United States-flag vessel, in or outside the United States. This includes a vessel based principally in the United States on which United States income tax is paid and whose insurance coverage is subject to regulation in the United States.

Agencies determine whether the technology to be procured is appropriate for SAFETY Act protections, send determinations to DHS to support contractor application(s) for SAFETY Act protections, and encourage offerors to seek SAFETY Act protections for their offered technologies (even in advance of a solicitation). The processing times vary for issuing determinations of applications, so this issue must be planned early in the acquisition cycle.

DHS will issue a *SAFETY Act certification* that a product has been approved for homeland security (i.e., that it conforms to the seller's specifications, will perform as intended, and is safe for use as intended). It will issue a *Qualified Anti-Terrorism Technology* (QATT) for any technology designed, developed, modified, procured, or sold for the purpose to detect, deter, identify, or prevent acts of terrorism or limiting the harm such acts might cause. A technology can include a:

- consulting service;
- design service;
- engineering service;
- equipment;
- information technology;
- product;
- service (including support services);
- software development or integration service;
- threat assessment; or
- vulnerability study.

DHS also issues a *block certification* for a technology class that it designates as approved for homeland security, and a *block designation* when the class is determined to be a QATT.

There is a preliminary step before obtaining either a SAFETY Act certification or QATT. A *pre-qualification designation notice* states that the technology to be procured either affirmatively or presumptively satisfies the technical criteria necessary to be deemed a QATT. The designation notice authorizes offeror(s) to submit streamlined applications for SAFETY Act designation and receive expedited processing of those applications.

Contracting officers may authorize contingent offers only if DHS issued a pre-qualification designation notice or a block designation or certification. The Government does not provide advance notice merely if potential offerors could obtain SAFETY Act designations or certifications for their offered technologies before release of a solicitation. Market research must show that there will be insufficient competition without SAFETY Act protections, or the subject technology would be sold to the Government only with SAFETY Act protections.

Contracting officers may award contracts presuming that DHS will issue a SAFETY Act designation and certification to the contractor, but only with approval of the chief of the contracting office. The contracting officer advises DHS of the timelines for potential award and consults DHS as to when it could complete evaluations of offerors' applications.

Solicitation Provisions

FAR 52.250-2, SAFETY Act Coverage Not Applicable, if the agency consulted with DHS on a questionable case of SAFETY Act applicability and then determined that SAFETY Act protection is not applicable for the acquisition; or DHS has denied approval of a pre-qualification designation notice.

FAR 52.250-3, SAFETY Act Block Designation/Certification, if DHS has issued a block designation/certification for the solicited technologies. Use the provision with Alternate I when contingent offers are authorized. Use the provision with Alternate II when offers are authorized to presume SAFETY Act designation or certification. The contracting officer may increase the number of days within which offerors must submit their SAFETY Act application.

FAR 52.250-4, SAFETY Act Pre-qualification Designation Notice, if DHS has issued a pre-qualification designation notice. Use the provision with its Alternate I when contingent offers are authorized. Use the provision with its Alternate II when offers presuming SAFETY Act designation or certification are authorized. The contracting officer may increase the number of days within which offerors must submit their SAFETY Act application.

FAR 52.250-5, SAFETY Act—Equitable Adjustment, in a solicitation, if either FAR 50.205-3 or 52.250-4 is used with its Alternate II; and in any resultant contract if DHS has not issued SAFETY Act designation or certification to the successful offeror before contract award.

5.11 ENVIRONMENTAL ISSUES

5.11.1 Energy and Water Efficiency

FAR 23.2

Federal Government procurement policy implements numerous environmental protections and initiatives. One such initiative is to purchase items which meet the Federal Energy Management Program (FEMP) standby power wattage recommendation, or else document the reason for not purchasing such items. This applies to products delivered for use by the Government, or by a contractor at a Federal facility, or incorporated into a building or public work during construction or maintenance. If FEMP has listed a product without a corresponding wattage recommendation, the contracting officer purchases items which use only one watt in their standby power consuming mode.

An agency is not required to procure an ENERGY STAR® or FEMP-designated product if the head of the agency determines in writing that no such product is reasonably available that meets the functional requirements of the agency, or is not cost-effective over the life of the product (taking energy cost savings into account).

Another initiative is an *energy-savings performance contract* which reduces energy use and cost in facilities and operations for up to 25 years. The energy service company finances the capital to implement energy conservation measures, and receives in return a negotiated share of cost savings. The contracting officer uses the selection method and terms and conditions in 10 CFR 436, Subpart B, and may use the "Qualified List" of energy service companies from the Department of Energy.[41]

Contract Clause

FAR 52.223-15, Energy Efficiency in Energy-Consuming Products.

5.11.2 Hazardous Material Identification

FAR 23.3

Another initiative addresses use of hazardous materials in deliverables or during performance per Federal Standard 313F (Material Safety Data Sheet, Preparation and Submission of). These Material Safety Data Sheets are submitted by the apparent successful offeror prior to contract award.

The contractor notifies the contracting officer prior to delivery of any radioactive materials, who then notifies receiving activities so that appropriate safeguards can be taken.

DFARS 223.3

The contracting officer provides any hazard warning labels received from apparent successful offerors to the cognizant safety officer.

Contractors must take reasonable safety precautions in handling ammunition and explosives to minimize the potential for mishaps.[42]

DFARS 223.71

10 U.S.C. 2692 prohibits disposal, storage or treatment on DoD installations of toxic or hazardous materials that are not owned either by DoD or by a member or a dependent of the armed forces assigned to or living on the installation. When storage of toxic or hazardous materials is authorized based on an imminent danger, the storage provided must be temporary and cease once the imminent danger no longer exists. Otherwise, the Secretary of Defense decides disposal or storage. The contract must specify the types and quantities of toxic or hazardous materials that may be temporarily stored, treated, or disposed of at a DoD facility or space launch facility in connection with the contract, as well as the conditions under which these activities are authorized.

The prohibition of 10 U.S.C. 2692 does not apply in many circumstances. It does not apply to the storage, treatment or disposal of materials that will be or have been used in connection with an activity of DoD or in connection with a service to be performed on a DoD installation for the benefit of DoD. Nor does it apply to the storage of strategic and critical materials in the National Defense Stockpile under an agreement for such storage with the Administrator of GSA.

Temporary storage or disposal of explosives is exempted when protecting the public or assisting agencies responsible for Federal, State or local law enforcement to store or dispose of explosives when no alternative solution is available. Such storage or disposal must be made in accordance with an agreement between the Secretary of Defense and the head of the Federal, State, or local agency concerned. The temporary storage or disposal of explosives is authorized to provide emergency life-saving assistance to civil authorities.

Excess explosives produced under a DoD contract can be disposed if the head of the military department determines that an alternative feasible means of disposal is not available to the contractor. This determination must take into consideration the available resources of the contractor, national defense production requirements and public safety.

Temporary storage of nuclear materials or nonnuclear classified materials is authorized in accordance with an agreement with the Secretary of Energy. Military resources intended to be used during peacetime civil emergencies in accordance with applicable DoD regulations may also be stored. So can materials of other Federal agencies in order to provide assistance and refuge for commercial carriers of such material during a transportation emergency. Any material that is not owned by DoD may be stored if the Secretary of the military department concerned determines that the material is required or generated in connection with the authorized and compatible use of a facility of DoD, including the use of such a facility for testing material or training personnel. If the materials are hazardous or toxic but not owned by DoD, they may be stored if the Secretary of the military department concerned determines that the material is required or generated in connection with the authorized and compatible use of a facility of that military department. The Secretary enters into a contract or agreement with the prospective user that is consistent with the best interest of national defense and environmental security, and provides for the prospective user's continued financial and environmental responsibility and liability with regard to the material. Non-DoD material may be stored if the Secretary of the military department concerned determines that the material is required or generated in connection with the use of a space launch facility located on a DoD installation or on other land controlled by the United States. Finally, the Secretary of Defense may grant an exception to the prohibition in 10 U.S.C. 2692 when essential to protect the health and safety of the public from imminent danger if the Secretary otherwise determines the exception is essential and if the storage or disposal authorized does not compete with private enterprise.

The Secretary of Defense may assess a charge for any storage or disposal, which will be identified in the contract with payment to the Government on a cost-reimbursable basis.

DFARS 223.7201

DoD 5100.76, Physical Security of Sensitive Conventional Arms, Ammunition, and Explosives, applies to contracts when such items will be provided to the (sub)contractor as Government-furnished property or are intended for DoD use. This policy does not apply when they are to be acquired under the (sub)contract is a commercial item or the (sub)contract will be performed in a Government-owned contractor-operated ammunition production facility.

DFARS 223.73

DoD policy is to minimize hexavalent chromium (an anti-corrosive) in items acquired by DoD as deliverables and construction material, due to the serious human health and environmental risks related to its use. This policy implements Executive Order 13423, Strengthening Federal Environmental, Energy, and Transportation Management and Executive Order 13693, Planning for Federal Sustainability in the Next Decade.

No contract may include a specification or standard that results in a deliverable or construction material containing more than 0.1 percent hexavalent chromium by weight in any homogeneous material in the deliverable or construction material where proven substitutes are available that provide acceptable performance for the application. An exception is for legacy systems that have passed Milestone A and their related subsystems, components and parts that already contain hexavalent chromium. However, alternatives to hexavalent chromium will be considered by the appropriate official during system modifications, follow-on procurements of legacy systems, or maintenance procedure updates. Additional sustainment related contracts (e.g., parts or services) for a system in which use of hexavalent chromium was previously approved are also exempted; so are critical defense applications if no substitute can meet performance requirements. A general or flag officer or a member of the Senior Executive Service from the Program Executive Office or equivalent level is authorized for granting such an exception.

Contract Clauses

FAR 52.223-3, Hazardous Material Identification and Material Safety Data. Use the clause with its Alternate I if the contract is awarded by an agency other than the Department of Defense.

FAR 52.223-7, Notice of Radioactive Materials.

DFARS 252.223-7001, Hazardous Warning Labels, when requiring submission of hazardous material data sheets.

DFARS 252.223-7002, Safety Precautions for Ammunition and Explosives, involving ammunition or explosives.

DFARS 252.223-7003, Change in Place of Performance—Ammunition and Explosives.

DFARS 252.223-7006, Prohibition on Storage, Treatment, and Disposal of Toxic or Hazardous Materials, to permit contractor access to a DoD installation. Use Alternate I when the Secretary of the military department issues a determination of exception.

DFARS 252.223-7007, Safeguarding Sensitive Conventional Arms, Ammunition, and Explosives, if DoD 5100.76-M applies. Complete paragraph (b) of the clause based on information provided by cognizant technical or requirements personnel.

DFARS 252.223-7008, Prohibition of Hexavalent Chromium, for supplies, maintenance and repair services, or construction.

5.11.3 Use of Recovered Materials

FAR 23.4

Both the Environmental Protection Agency and the Department of Agriculture have developed special rules to promote the use of recovered materials if either the item price or the aggregate amount paid in the prior fiscal year exceeds $10,000. An EPA-designated product is (or can be) made with recovered material listed in a procurement guideline and subject to EPA's purchasing recommendations.[43] These recommendations are set forth in a *Consolidated Recovered Materials Advisory Notice (RMAN) for the Comprehensive Procurement Guideline (CPG)*. Likewise, a USDA-designated item is part of a generic grouping of products that are (or can be) made with biobased materials and listed in a procurement guideline and subject to USDA purchasing recommendations.[44]

Agencies create their own programs to assure the use of products containing recovered materials and biobased products to the maximum extent without jeopardizing their intended use. Customarily, the agency will estimate, certify, and verify the amount of recovered material for EPA-designated products. Both the recovered material content and biobased programs require preaward certification that the products meet EPA or USDA recommendations. A second certification is required at contract completion for recovered material content. EPA and USDA may provide categorical exemptions for items they designate when procured for spacecraft system and launch support equipment, and military equipment for combat or related missions. The policy does not apply if the item cannot meet performance, delivery or cost requirements.

When both the USDA-designated item and the EPA-designated item could meet the agency's needs, the agency purchases the EPA-designated item.

Solicitation Provisions

FAR 52.223-1, Biobased Product Certification, to require the delivery or specify the use of USDA-designated items, unless including the clause at FAR 52.223-2.

FAR 52.223-4, Recovered Material Certification, if requiring the delivery or specifying the use of EPA-designated items, or include the clause at 52.223-17. The provision does not apply to COTS items.

Solicitation Provisions and Contract Clauses

FAR 52.223-2, Affirmative Procurement of Biobased Products Under Service and Construction Contracts, for services or construction unless the contract will not involve the use of USDA-designated items.

FAR 52.223-9, Estimate of Percentage of Recovered Material Content for EPA-Designated Items, if exceeding $150,000 or using EPA-designated products containing recovered materials. Use the clause with its Alternate I if technical personnel advise that estimates can be verified. The clause does not apply to COTS items.

FAR 52.223-17, Affirmative Procurement of EPA-Designated Items in Service and Construction Contracts, for services or construction unless not using EPA-designated items.

5.11.4 Drug-Free Workplace

FAR 23.5

The Drug-Free Workplace Act of 1988 (41 U.S.C. 8102) applies to all contracts and modifications above the simplified acquisition threshold performed entirely within the United States except for commercial items or when the agency head or designee determines that application would conflict with the agency's undercover operations. It does not occur where application would be inconsistent with either the international obligations of the United States or with the laws and regulations of a foreign country.

The offeror must agree to notify its employees that the unlawful manufacture, distribution, dispensing, possession, or use of a controlled substance is prohibited in the contractor's workplace, and to specify the actions that will be taken against employees for violations of such prohibition.

After determining in writing that adequate evidence exists to suspect noncompliance, the contracting officer may suspend contract payments, terminate a contract for default, or pursue suspension and debarment. Likewise, if contractor employees have been convicted of violations of criminal drug statutes occurring in the workplace, the contractor may be found to have failed to make a good faith effort to provide a drug-free workplace.

Solicitation Provision and Contract Clause

DFARS 252.223-7004, Drug-Free Work Force, if involving access to classified information or is necessary for national security or protecting the health or safety of those using the product or performance of the contract. Do not use the clause for commercial items, when performance will in whole or in part be outside the United States and its outlying areas (unless the contracting officer determines inclusion to be in the best interest of the Government), or if at or below the simplified acquisition threshold.

Contract Clause

FAR 52.223-6, Drug-Free Workplace.

5.11.5 Environmental Improvements

The term *green procurement* has come to mean purchasing products or services with minimal environmental impact. This includes eliminating risks to human health and the environment, such as preventing pollution. Green products consume less energy in their fabrication and usage, and contain fewer hazardous materials. They may be recycled, use less expendable packaging, and incur little or no disposal cost to the environment. Their usage requires fewer natural resources such as energy or water. ISO 14001:2015, Environmental management systems—Requirements with guidance for use, is the certification program for facilities to achieve green operating conditions.

However, green procurement faces some challenges:

- availability and delays in delivery;
- difficulty in implementing a program;
- lack of clear specifications;
- need for corporate commitment;
- purchasing habits; and
- sometimes higher prices, though this may be offset by less packaging, lower life-cycle cost, and recyclability.

FAR 23.7

To promote the use of green contracting, Federal acquisition environmental objectives are to:[45]

- eliminate or reduce the generation of hazardous waste and the need for special material processing (such as handling, storage, treatment, and disposal). This also includes creating plans, drawings, specifications, standards, and product descriptions to authorize material substitutions, extensions of shelf-life and process improvements;
- give preference to procuring chemicals, products and processes that minimize the depletion of ozone in the atmosphere;
- maximize the use of environmentally preferable products and services;
- promote energy efficiency and water conservation;
- promote the use of biobased products and nonhazardous and recovered materials;

- purchase only degradable plastic ring carriers; and
- realize life-cycle cost savings.

Agencies must meet at least 95 percent of their annual acquisitions for domestically used electronic products with Electronic Product Environmental Assessment Tool (EPEAT)–registered products. These products include computers, imaging equipment (such as copiers and fax machines) and televisions. The requirement does not apply only if there is no EPEAT standard for the specific product or the agency head determines that no such product meets agency requirements or is cost-effective.[46]

FAR 23.8

Federal agencies try to cost-effectively minimize procurement of materials and substances that contribute to the depletion of stratospheric ozone and/or result in the use, release, or emission of hydrofluorocarbons (which have the potential for high-altitude global warming).[47] They aspire to give preference to the procurement of acceptable alternative chemicals, products and processes. They will specify that contractors use an acceptable alternative to these hydrofluorocarbons in products and services where identified by EPA's Significant New Alternatives Policy (SNAP) program.[48] Examples of hydrofluorocarbon products include:

- aerosol lubricants;
- air conditioning equipment;
- bulk refrigerants and fire suppressants;
- clean agent fire suppression systems/equipment;
- preservative or sealing compounds such as aerosol mold release agents, corrosion prevention compounds and foam sealants;
- refrigeration equipment; and
- solvents, dusters, and freezing compounds.

In addition to transitioning to SNAP-approved alternatives, the contractor must maintain equipment to prevent and repair refrigerant leaks, recover and dispose of any equipment that emits or leaks hydrofluorocarbons (and reclaim same where possible). If the equipment contains at least 50 pounds of hydrofluorocarbons, the contractor must track annually this amount.

Additionally, SAM-registered contractors who receive at least $7.5 million in Federal contract awards in the prior Federal fiscal year must state if they publicly disclose greenhouse gas emissions and an emissions reduction goal, along with the website for any such disclosures.

FAR 36.2

Good environmental practices also apply to building (de)construction, as well as operation and maintenance. The Federal Government implements high-performance sustainable practices to ensure all new construction, major renovation, repair, and alteration of Federal buildings complies with the Guiding Principles for Federal Leadership in High-Performance and Sustainable Buildings.[49] This may include exploring alternatives to renovation that reduce existing assets' deferred maintenance costs. Any rehabilitation of Federally owned historic buildings must utilize best practices and technologies in retrofitting to promote long-term viability of the buildings. Cost-effective, innovative strategies (e.g., highly reflective or vegetated roofs) will be considered to minimize consumption of energy, water and other materials, as well as pollution prevention and waste elimination by diverting construction and demolition materials and debris.

Solicitation Provisions and Contract Clauses

FAR 52.223-10, Waste Reduction Program, for contractor operation and support services of Government-owned or -leased facilities.

FAR 52.223-11, Ozone-Depleting Substances, for supplies that may contain ozone-depleting substances, except for performance outside the United States and its outlying areas.

FAR 52.223-12, Refrigeration Equipment and Air Conditioners, for the maintenance, repair or disposal of any equipment using ozone-depleting substances as a refrigerant (e.g., air conditioners, refrigerators, chillers, or freezers), except for performance outside the United States and its outlying areas.

FAR 52.223-13, Acquisition of EPEAT®-Registered Imaging Equipment, for contractor operation and support services of Government-owned or -leased facilities.

FAR 52.223-14, Acquisition of EPEAT-Registered Televisions.

FAR 52.223-16, IEEE 1680 Standard for the Environmental Assessment of Personal Computer Products, for personal computer products, services that require furnishing or personal computer products for use by the Government, or contractor operation of Government-owned facilities. Use the clause with its Alternate I when sufficient EPEAT Silver registered products are available to meet agency needs.

FAR 52.223-20, Aerosols, for products containing hydrofluorocarbons or for maintenance or repair of electronic or mechanical devices.

FAR 52.223-21, Foams, for products containing hydrofluorocarbons or for insulation construction.

FAR 52.223-22, Public Disclosure of Greenhouse Gas Emissions and Reduction Goals-Representation, if the contractor is in SAM.

5.11.6 Pollution Prevention

FAR 23.9 and .10

Government policy is to purchase supplies and services in accordance with an environmental management system, and to specify how the contractor must comply. Every contract for performance on a Federal facility requires the contractor to provide information necessary to ensure Federal compliance with the emergency planning and toxic release reporting requirements.

Solicitation Provision

FAR 52.223-19, Compliance With Environmental Management Systems, if competitive and expected to exceed $100,000 and competitive 8(a) contracts of any value, except for acquisitions of commercial items or where impractical.

Solicitation Provisions and Contract Clauses

FAR 52.223-5, Pollution Prevention and Right-to-Know Information, for performance, in whole or in part, on a Federal facility. Use with Alternate I if for contractor operation or maintenance of a Federal facility which implemented or plans to implement an environmental management system. Use the clause with its Alternate II if the agency has determined that the contractor activities should be included within the facility compliance audit.

5.11.7 Text Messaging

(Sub)contractors must develop policies which ban text messaging while driving on Government business in a Federal, company or privately owned vehicle.

Solicitation Provision and Contract Clause

FAR 52.223-18, Encouraging Contractor Policies to Ban Text Messaging While Driving.

5.12 TRANSPORTATION

Transportation is critical to efficient distribution of supplies. The basic modes of transportation are:

- commercial air transport: air freight and forwarders;
- motor freight: contract carrier, private trucking, and small-shipment carriers;
- pipelines;
- railroads; and
- water transportation: overseas operations, intercoastal service or coastal trade.

Carriers can be distinguished by their terms of hire. *Common carriers* such as airlines, rail lines and truckers are regulated entities available for any firm and also provide their services to the general public. They usually follow preestablished delivery schedules, routes, and rate tables. In contrast, *contract carriers* work ad hoc by contract to a select clientele, such as a household moving company. A *private carrier* ships its own goods only, such as a furniture store. All these carriers interact through competition, and each has its own advantages in cost, reliability, and speed.

The traffic or transportation manager has numerous major concerns:

- carrier selection (including use of company-owned assets);
- equipment scheduling;
- expediting shipments;
- lease-or-buy analysis;
- most advantageous rate, including special charges or discounts;
- routing shipments; and
- tracing lost shipments.

5.12.1 Bill of Lading

FAR 47.001 through 47.1

A *bill of lading* is a transportation document used to evidence a contract of carriage, customs clearance, receipt, and title. The contracting officer authorizes domestic shipments on commercial bills of lading. Government bills of lading (executed by a Government official and bearing accounting data) may be used for international shipping, including for noncontiguous domestic trade shipments subject to regulation by the Surface Transportation Board involving traffic from or to Alaska, Hawaii or a territory or possession of the United States.

The preferred method of transporting supplies is by commercial carriers. However, Government-owned, leased or chartered vehicles, aircraft and vessels may be used if they are not otherwise fully utilized and result in substantial economies. In such cases, these modes of transit would most often be used for emergencies, local transportation between Government installations, or pickup and delivery for line-haul transportation that commercial carriers do not perform. Also, in these cases the Government generally acts as self-insurer without buying insurance and retains the risk of loss and/or damage to its property that is not the legal liability of commercial carriers.

Household goods are personal effects and property used in a dwelling. Transportation of such effects or property is usually arranged and paid for by the householder. It does not include property moving from a factory or store, or what the householder has purchased for use in the new dwelling and requested for transport. The contracting officer must specify in the contract all contractor liability for injury to people or damage to property, and how much insurance the contractor must maintain.

Solicitation Provisions and Contract Clauses

FAR 52.247-1, Commercial Bill of Lading Notations, when the contract will be either fixed-price f.o.b. origin greater than the simplified acquisition threshold, or a cost-reimbursement contract which may involve the movement of household goods.

FAR 52.247-67, Submission of Transportation Documents for Audit, if cost-reimbursement and the prime or first-tier cost-reimbursement subcontract will authorize reimbursement of transportation as a direct charge to the contract or subcontract.

5.12.2 Transportation and Related Services

FAR 47.2

It is generally more economical and efficient for most agencies to make use of term contracts and basic ordering agreements that have been executed by DoD and GSA to take advantage of personnel experienced in contracting for transportation and related services. If these instruments are not available, then agencies may obtain transportation or related services for which the cost does not exceed the simplified acquisition threshold.

A great deal of advance planning goes into transportation of deliverables. The solicitation must include a time schedule, origin points, destination points, freight description, exclusions (e.g., bulk or heavy or hazardous shipments), and quantity.

Storage and distribution points, depots and other receiving activities require advance notice of shipments en route from contractors' plants for movement control, such as certain hazardous materials and explosives, or classified or sensitive material. Advance notice may also be required for minimum carload or truckload shipments, regardless of the nature of the cargo.

This extensive process allows the destination to arrange for labor, materials handling equipment, space, and transportation control. This method also avoids incurring demurrage and vehicle detention charges.

The contracting officer specifies the contractor's liability for injury to persons or damage to property other than the freight being transported, and for loss of and/or damage to the freight being transported. The contracting officer also includes the amount of insurance the contractor is required to maintain.

DFARS 247.270

Specific procedures apply to stevedoring (loading cargo from a pier onto a vessel or vice versa) for vessels not owned or chartered by the Government. Because conditions vary at different ports, and sometimes within the same port, it is not practical to develop standard technical provisions covering all phases of stevedoring operations.

When including equipment loading and unloading at a dock and terminal, the offer must include tonnage or commodity rates that apply to the bulk of the cargo worked under normal conditions. These rates are quoted for handling a ton of a specified commodity and computed by dividing the hourly stevedoring gang cost by the estimated number of tons that can be handled in one hour. A *gang cost* is the total hourly wages paid to the workers in the gang, in accordance with the collective bargaining agreement between the maritime industry and the unions at a specific port, plus costs of workmen's compensation, social security and other taxes, unemployment insurance, liability and property damage insurance, general and administrative expenses, and profit. The contract must also include labor-hour rates that apply to services not covered by commodity rates, or to work performed under hardship conditions, plus rates for equipment rental.

DFARS 247.271

Normally, DoD will use requirements contracts to acquire services to prepare personal property for shipment or storage, and provide intra-area movement. DoD will try to award contracts on a calendar year basis, providing for option years, before November 1 of each year.

The contracting officer must define clearly in the solicitation each area of performance. (S)he will establish one or more areas, but hold the number to the minimum consistent with local conditions. Each schedule may provide for the same or different areas of performance. To determine the areas, (s)he will use political boundaries, streets or any other features as lines of demarcation. Considerations include total volume, size of overall area and need to serve isolated areas of high population density. (S)he will also specifically identify frequently used terminals and consider them as being included in each area of performance described in the solicitation.

The contracting officer must ensure that the Government's minimum acceptable daily capability will at least equal the maximum authorized individual weight allowance as prescribed by the Joint Federal Travel Regulations. (S)he will also encourage maximum participation of small business concerns as offerors.

Overseas commands, except those in Alaska and Hawaii, may modify these clauses to conform to local practices, laws, and regulations. In addition to designating each ordering activity, the contract must identify by name or position title the individuals authorized to place orders for each activity.

PGI 247.271

When two or more military installations or activities within the contiguous United States have personal property responsibilities in a given area, one activity must contract for the estimated requirements of all activities in the area.[50] The installation commanders concerned must designate the activity by mutual agreement. The Commander, Military Surface Deployment and Distribution Command (SDDC) must designate the contracting activity when local commanders are unable to reach agreement.

When requiring activities need unspecified additional services that exceed contractor capabilities available under contracts, contracting officers should use simplified acquisition procedures to satisfy those excess requirements. Additional services may include hoisting or lowering of articles, special packaging and (un)stuffing of sea van containers, including waiting time.

Contracting officers should consider contracting for local moves that do not require drayage by using hourly rate or constructive weight methods. The rate will include those services necessary for completion of the movement, including inventory, movement, removal of debris, and (un)packing.

Each personal property shipping activity must determine if local requirements exist for any additional services.

The contracting officer should identify additional services required that are incidental to an order before placing the order or, when applicable, during the pre-move survey. (S)he may obtain additional services by including them as items within the contract, provided they are not used in the evaluation of bids, or else using simplified acquisition procedures.

The contracting officer must either predetermine prices for additional services or negotiate them on a case-by-case basis. (S)he must authorize the contractor to perform any additional services, other than attempted pick up or delivery, regardless of the contracting method. The Defense Transportation

Regulation, Part IV, Chapter 404 provides procedures for preparing solicitations for personal property for shipment or storage, and intra-area or intra-city movement.

Of course, delays in shipping can and do occur. Carrier demurrage/detention is a charge made against a consignor (shipper) or consignee (receiver) for the extended use of carrier-furnished equipment when delays attributable to the consignor or consignee occur. Carrier demurrage/detention rules usually allow a period of free time for loading, unloading, or holding equipment. Carrier-published demurrage and detention rules and charges are not uniform from one carrier to another. Contracting officers should specifically address them in the contract. While demurrage/detention rules are published in individual carrier tariffs or agency tenders, contracting officers may negotiate contract-specific demurrage/detention rules and charges independent of any existing tariffs or tenders.

DFARS 247.301-71

For contracts that will include a significant requirement for transportation of items outside the contiguous United States, include an evaluation factor or subfactor that favors suppliers, third-party logistics providers, and integrated logistics managers that commit to using carriers that participate in one of the readiness programs (e.g., Civil Reserve Air Fleet and Voluntary Intermodal Sealift Agreement). These logistics managers or providers are firms that provide multiple logistics services. Some examples of logistics services are demand forecasting, distribution, information management, inventory maintenance, transportation management, and warehousing.

Solicitation Provisions

FAR 52.247-20, Estimated Quantities or Weights for Evaluation of Offers, when quantities or weights of shipments between each origin and destination are not known, but the provision states estimated quantity or weight for each origin/destination pair.

Solicitation Provisions and Contract Clauses

FAR 52.247-2, Permits, Authorities, or Franchises, when regulated transportation is involved.

FAR 52.247-3, Capability to Perform a Contract for the Relocation of a Federal Office. Use Alternate I to maintain a facility within the state and not require State authority to operate.

FAR 52.247-4, Inspection of Shipping and Receiving Facilities, when it is desired for offerors to inspect the shipping, receiving or other sites to ensure realistic bids.

FAR 52.247-5, Familiarization with Conditions, to ensure that offerors become familiar with conditions and location of services to be performed.

FAR 52.247-6, Financial Statement, to ensure that offerors are prepared to furnish financial statements.

FAR 52.247-7, Freight Excluded.

FAR 52.247-8, Estimated Weights or Quantities Not Guaranteed.

FAR 52.247-12, Supervision, Labor, or Materials.

FAR 52.247-13, Accessorial Services—Moving Contracts, for the transportation of household goods or office furniture.

FAR 52.247-14, Contractor Responsibility for Receipt of Shipment.

FAR 52.247-15, Contractor Responsibility for Loading and Unloading.

FAR 52.247-16, Contractor Responsibility for Returning Undelivered Freight.

FAR 52.247-17, Charges. The charges may not exceed the contractor's charges for the same service that is available to the general public or otherwise tendered to the Government. The contracting officer includes in the solicitation a tabulation listing each required service and the basis for the rate (e.g., "unit of weight" or "per work-hour," leaving space for offerors to insert the rates offered for each service).

FAR 52.247-21, Contractor Liability for Personal Injury and/or Property Damage.

FAR 52.247-22, Contractor Liability for Loss of and/or Damage to Freight other than Household Goods.

FAR 52.247-23, Contractor Liability for Loss of and/or Damage to Household Goods, including the appropriate rate per pound.

FAR 52.247-24, Advance Notification by the Government, when the Government is responsible for notifying the contractor in advance when hazardous materials are included in a shipment, and for specific service times or unusual shipments.

FAR 52.247-25, Government-Furnished Equipment With or Without Operators. Insert the kind of equipment and the locations where the equipment will be furnished.

FAR 52.247-26, Government Direction and Marking, when office relocations are involved.

FAR 52.247-27, Contract Not Affected by Oral Agreement.

FAR 52.247-28, Contractor's Invoices, in drayage or other term contracts. The contracting officer states the responsibilities of the contractor, contracting agency and consignee to annotate and distribute shipping and billing documents.

FAR 52.247-68, Report of Shipment (REPSHIP), when advance notice of shipment is required for safety or security reasons, or where carload or truckload shipments will be made to Government facilities.

DFARS 252.247-7000, Hardship Conditions.

DFARS 252.247-7002, Revision of Prices, when using negotiation.

DFARS 252.247-7003, Pass-Through of Motor Carrier Fuel Surcharge Adjustment to the Cost Bearer, for carriage in which a motor carrier, broker, or freight forwarder will provide or arrange truck transportation services that provide for a fuel-related adjustment.

DFARS 252.247-7007, Liability and Insurance.

DFARS 252.247-7014, Demurrage.

DFARS 252.247-7016, Contractor Liability for Loss and Damage.

DFARS 252.247-7028, Application for U.S. Government Shipping Documentation/Instructions, when shipping under Bills of Lading and Domestic Route Order under f.o.b. origin contracts, Export Traffic Release regardless of f.o.b. terms, or foreign military sales shipments.

Contract Clauses

FAR 52.247-9, Agreed Weight—General Freight, when the shipping activity determines the weight of shipments of freight other than office furniture.

FAR 52.247-10, Net Weight—General Freight, when the weight of shipments of freight other than household goods or office furniture is not known at the time of shipment and the contractor is responsible for determining the net weight of the shipments.

FAR 52.247-11, Net Weight—Household Goods or Office Furniture, when movements of Government employees' household goods or relocations of Government offices are involved.

FAR 52.247-18, Multiple Shipments, when multiple shipments are tendered at one time to the contractor for transportation from one origin to two or more consignees at the same destination.

FAR 52.247-19, Stopping in Transit for Partial Unloading, when multiple shipments are tendered at one time to the contractor for transportation from one origin to two or more consignees along the route between origin and last destination.

5.12.3 Standard Delivery Terms

There are a multitude of ways in which shipping charges are paid. Consequently, the Government has developed a multitude of clauses to cover each situation. These situations vary in terms of *f.o.b.* ("free on board") to indicate at what point the cost and risk of shipment passes from buyer to seller. Up to that point, delivery expense and risk is borne by the contractor.

FAR 47.303

F.o.b. origin covers up to delivery and placement on board the carrier (or its wharf or freight station) in the city from which the shipment will be made and from which line-haul transportation service (as distinguished from switching, local drayage, or other terminal service) will begin. This type of delivery would also allow for delivery to a U.S. Postal Service facility, or any Government-designated point located within the same city or commercial zone as the f.o.b. origin point specified in the contract.

Despite the early transfer of cost and risk to the Government, the contractor still has several responsibilities. It must pack and mark the shipment to comply with contract specifications or carrier requirements to protect the goods and minimize transportation charges. It must order carrier equipment requested by the Government or, if left to its own responsibility, of proper capacity. It must deliver the shipment undamaged to the carrier and secure it (i.e., block, brace, load, stow, and trim) on the carrier's vehicle. Finally, the contactor must complete the Government bill of lading prescribed by the contract administrator or the appropriate agency transportation office, or else a commercial bill of lading or other transportation receipt, and distribute as directed by the ordering agency.

There are several variations to f.o.b. origin regarding point of risk transfer, but contractor responsibilities remain the same unless otherwise indicated below.

F.o.b. origin, contractor's facility means the delivery is covered only until on board the conveyance of the contractor (or of the Government if specified) at the designated facility or address of shipment.

F.o.b. origin, freight allowed deducts from the contract price an allowance for freight, based on applicable published tariff rates (or Government rate tenders) between the points specified in the contract.

Under *F.o.b. origin, freight prepaid*, the cost of transportation is ultimately the Government's obligation but is prepaid by the contractor to the point specified in the contract. The contractor does not prepare commercial bills of lading under this method.

F.o.b. origin, with differentials adds to the contract price costs for place of delivery, transportation mode or vehicle type, as indicated in the contractor's offer.

F.o.b. destination is the opposite of f.o.b. origin. It means free of expense to the Government, with the contractor bearing cost and risk of delivery on board the carrier's conveyance to the consignee's facility. The Government is not liable for delivery, demurrage or storage charges involved before the actual delivery of the supplies to the destination, unless caused by an act or order of the Government. The Government is also not liable for *constructive placement* as defined in carrier tariffs, where the shipping container cannot be unloaded at the planned location but must unload elsewhere. The contractor must do the following:

- be responsible for loss or damage to the goods before receipt by the consignee;
- deliver the shipment in good condition to the point of delivery specified in the contract;
- furnish a delivery schedule and designate the mode of delivering carrier;
- pack and mark the shipment to comply with contract or carrier requirements;
- pay and bear all charges to the specified point of delivery; and
- prepare and distribute commercial bills of lading.

F.o.b. destination, within consignee's premises passes cost and risk to the Government upon delivery within the consignee's room. The contractor's responsibilities are the same as for f.o.b. destination.

Next, we have some intermediate methods of transport. Not quite the same as origin or destination, they require the contactor to bear cost and risk part way through the shipping process, then convert to Government responsibility the rest of the way.

F.a.s. vessel, port of shipment means "free alongside ship" and within reach of the vessel's loading tackle at the specified port. There is no expense to the Government until delivered alongside the ocean vessel. The contractor must:

- be responsible for any loss or damage occurring before delivery of the shipment to the point specified in the contract;
- pack and mark the shipment to comply with contract or carrier requirements to protect the goods and minimize transportation costs;
- pay and bear all transportation costs (including handling, heavy lifting and wharfage charges) up to this point;
- provide a clean dock or ship's receipt; and
- provide assistance at the Government's request and expense to obtain the documents required for export or import at destination.

Under *f.o.b. vessel, port shipment*, the only difference is that the contractor actually places the shipment onboard the vessel and need not provide clean bills of lading.

F.o.b. inland carrier, point of exportation differs only in that the conveyance is an inland carrier, not necessarily an ocean vessel.

F.o.b. inland point, country of importation is delivered to the specified inland point where the consignee's facility is located (again, this may not be an ocean vessel). Beginning with this method and for the rest of the methods below, the contractor does not provide documentation for export or import at destination.

Ex dock, pier, or warehouse, port of importation differs only in that the Government designates a dock or warehouse at the specified port.

C.&f. (cost & freight) destination means the contractor bears cost and risk on board the ocean vessel to the specified point of destination. The contractor also obtains and submits to the Government clean on-board ocean bills of lading to the specified point of destination. Further, at the Government's request and expense, the contractor provides certificates of origin and consular invoices issued in the country of origin or of shipment, or both, that may be required for importation into the country of destination.

C.i.f. (Cost, insurance, freight) destination adds to the c.&f. contractor duties the responsibility to pay for transportation and marine insurance. The contractor also obtains and submits to the Government an insurance policy or certificate providing the amount and extent of marine insurance coverage specified in the contract or agreed upon by the contracting officer.

F.o.b. designated air carrier's terminal, point of exportation is no different from f.o.b. inland point, except that the shipment is loaded aboard an aircraft, or delivered to the custody of the air carrier, at the air terminal specified in the contract. An air waybill may fulfill the need for a bill of lading.

F.o.b. designated air carrier's terminal, point of importation covers delivery only to the air carrier's terminal at the point of importation specified in the contract, and the Government bears the cost and risk of loading. The contractor does not normally obtain export paperwork under this method.

If it is advantageous to the Government, the contracting officer may authorize the contractor to ship supplies acquired f.o.b. origin to domestic destinations, including DoD air and water terminals, by common carriers on commercial bills of lading. Such shipments may not exceed 1,000 pounds (150 pounds by commercial air) and must be unclassified. No contract modification is necessary because the Government takes responsibility at time of loading on the carrier. The contractor is then reimbursed for transportation charges.

Contract Clauses

FAR 52.247-29, F.o.b. Origin.

FAR 52.247-30, F.o.b. Origin, Contractor's Facility.

FAR 52.247-31, F.o.b. Origin, Freight Allowed.

FAR 52.247-32, F.o.b. Origin, Freight Prepaid.

FAR 52.247-33, F.o.b. Origin, with Differentials, when it is likely that offerors may include in f.o.b. origin offers a contingency to compensate for unfavorable routing conditions by the Government at the time of shipment.

FAR 52.247-34, F.o.b. Destination.
FAR 52.247-35, F.o.b. Destination, within Consignee's Premises.
FAR 52.247-36, F.a.s. Vessel, Port of Shipment.
FAR 52.247-37, F.o.b. Vessel, Port of Shipment.
FAR 52.247-38, F.o.b. Inland Carrier, Point of Exportation.
FAR 52.247-39, F.o.b. Inland Point, Country of Importation.
FAR 52.247-40, Ex Dock, Pier, or Warehouse, Port of Importation.
FAR 52.247-41, C.&f. Destination.
FAR 52.247-42, C.i.f. Destination.
FAR 52.247-43, F.o.b. Designated Air Carrier's Terminal, Point of Exportation.
FAR 52.247-44, F.o.b. Designated Air Carrier's Terminal, Point of Importation.
FAR 52.247-65, F.o.b. Origin, Prepaid Freight-Small Package Shipments.

5.12.4 Determination of Delivery Terms

FAR 47.304 & 47.4

The contracting officer determines f.o.b. terms on the basis of overall costs. Solicitations state whether offerors must submit offers f.o.b. origin or destination, or both; or whether offerors may choose the basis on which they make an offer. The contracting officer considers the most advantageous delivery point. F.o.b. origin contracts present some desirable traffic management features:

- diversions to new destinations without price adjustment for transportation;
- flexibility when destinations are unknown or changeable:
- Government-controlled transportation;
- lower freight rates through Government rate tenders;
- premium cost transportation;
- small shipment consolidation stations;
- special routings or equipment (e.g., oversize shipments or circuitous routing); and
- use of transit privileges.

When destinations are tentative or unknown, the solicitation is f.o.b. origin only. When the size or quantity of supplies with security classification requires commercial transportation services, the solicitation is also likely to specify f.o.b. origin. Solicitations where acceptance must be at destination are normally on an f.o.b. destination only basis. Typically, forest products such as lumber and perishable or medical supplies subject to in-transit deterioration will be shipped on a destination basis. Also, when evaluation of f.o.b.

origin offers is anticipated to result in increased administrative lead time or cost that would outweigh the potential cost advantages, an f.o.b. destination arrangement may be preferred.

Solicitations for transportation within CONUS (Continental United States) may permit offers on the basis of either or both f.o.b. origin and f.o.b. destination, and are evaluated on the basis of the lowest overall cost to the Government.

When Government acquisitions involve shipments from CONUS to overseas destinations, delivery f.o.b. origin is used due to lower freight rates and flexibility to select both port of export and ocean transportation. However, bulk supplies (e.g., coal) that require other than Government-owned or operated handling, storage and loading facilities, and are destined for shipment outside CONUS, will be on a destination basis.

When supplies are acquired for known destinations outside CONUS but originate within CONUS, the contracting officer (for transportation evaluation purposes) notes in the solicitation the CONUS port of loading or point of exit and the water port of debarkation that serves the overseas destination. The contracting officer may also list in the solicitation other CONUS ports that meet the eligibility criteria so that offerors that are geographically remote from the regular port may be competitive for transportation costs. Unless logistics requirements limit the ports of loading to those listed in the solicitation, the solicitation permits offerors to nominate additional U.S. ports more favorably located to their shipping points that possess all requisite capabilities to be considered in the evaluation of offers.

The requiring activity considers the acquisition of carload or truckload quantities. Perhaps additional quantities of the supplies can be transported at lower unit costs or at a small increase in total transportation costs, without impairing the program schedule. In such a case, the contracting officer ascertains from the requiring activity if a known requirement for additional quantities could profitably be stored by the activity for future use, or to several using activities on the same transportation route or in the same geographical area. Because consolidation of small shipments into larger lots frequently results in lower transportation costs, the contracting officer, after consulting with the requiring activity and transportation office, may revise the delivery schedules to provide for consolidated deliveries.

Contracts include complete consignment and marking instructions at the time of award to ensure that supplies are delivered to proper destinations without delay. If supplies cannot be properly classified through reference to freight classification tariffs, the contracting officer obtains the applicable freight classification from the transportation office. If complete consignment information is not initially known, the contracting officer amends delivery instructions under the Changes clause once the information is known. Marking and consignment instructions for military shipments conform to

MIL-STD-129P (Military Standard Marking for Shipment and Storage), while shipments for civilian agencies are marked per Federal Standard 123H, Marking for Shipment (Civil Agencies).

When evaluating offers, contracting officers consider transportation and transportation-related costs, and the offerors' shipping and receiving facilities. The transportation officer provides the lowest available freight rates and related incidental charges that are or will be in effect on the expected date of the initial shipment, and on file or published on the date of bid opening. If rates or related charges become available after the bid opening or the due date of offers, they are not used in the evaluation unless they are brand new rates or access costs.

If a U.S.-flag air carrier cannot provide the international air transportation needed, or its use would not accomplish an agency's mission, foreign-flag air carrier service may be deemed necessary. Agencies disallow costs for U.S. Government-financed commercial international air transportation on foreign-flag air carriers unless the voucher contains a memorandum explaining why service by U.S.-flag air carriers was not available, or why it was necessary to use foreign-flag air carriers.

The contracting officer specifies the contractor's liability for injury to persons or damage to property other than the freight being transported, and for loss of and/or damage to the freight being transported. The contracting officer also includes the amount of insurance the contractor is required to maintain.

The contracting officer may wish to include transit arrangements in the solicitation so that a carload can be stopped at an intermediate point for storage or processing. A transit charge is added to the single through rate rather than citing multiple rates. The contractor may have earned commercial transit credits with the carriers, which can be used in f.o.b. origin offers to reduce transportation costs on a commercial bill of lading.

Federal employees and their dependents, consultants, contractors, and grantees must use U.S.-flag air carriers for U.S. Government-financed international air travel and transportation of their personal effects or property, if available. There is some flexibility if air travel is between two points outside the United States. Similarly, U.S.-flagged ocean vessels are required for use in ocean transportation for supplies owned by the Government or (sub)contractor, unless the rates are unreasonable.

Solicitation Provisions

FAR 52.247-46, Shipping Point(s) Used in Evaluation of F.o.b. Origin Offers.

FAR 52.247-47, Evaluation F.o.b. Origin.

FAR 52.247-49, Destination Unknown, when destinations are tentative and only for the purpose of evaluating offers.

FAR 52.247-50, No Evaluation of Transportation Costs.

FAR 52.247-51, Evaluation of Export Offers, when supplies are to be exported through CONUS ports and offers are solicited on an f.o.b. origin or f.o.b. destination basis. Use the clause with its Alternate I when the CONUS ports of export are DoD water terminals. Use the clause with its Alternate II when offers are solicited on an f.o.b. origin only basis. Use the clause with its Alternate III when offers are solicited on an f.o.b. destination only basis.

FAR 52.247-53, Freight Classification Description, when the supplies being acquired are new to the supply system, nonstandard or modifications of previously shipped items, and different freight classifications may apply.

DFARS 252.211-7004, Alternate Preservation, Packaging, and Packing, if it is feasible to evaluate and award using commercial or industrial preservation, packaging or packing.

Solicitation Provisions and Contract Clauses

FAR 52.247-45, F.o.b. Origin and/or F.o.b. Destination Evaluation, when offers are solicited on the basis of both f.o.b. origin and f.o.b. destination.

FAR 52.247-48, F.o.b. Destination—Evidence of Shipment, when supplies will or may be purchased f.o.b. destination but inspection and acceptance will be at origin.

FAR 52.247-52, Clearance and Documentation Requirements-Shipments to DoD Air or Water Terminal Transshipment Points.

FAR 52.247-55, F.o.b. Point for Delivery of Government-Furnished Property, when Government property is to be furnished under a contract and the Government will be responsible for transportation arrangements and costs.

FAR 52.247-56, Transit Arrangements.

FAR 52.247-57, Transportation Transit Privilege Credits.

FAR 52.247-58, Loading, Blocking, and Bracing of Freight Car Shipments.

FAR 52.247-59, F.o.b. Origin—Carload and Truckload Shipments, when it is contemplated that they may result in f.o.b. origin contracts with shipments in carloads or truckloads. This will facilitate realistic freight cost evaluations of offers and ensure that contractors produce economical shipments of agreed size.

FAR 52.247-60, Guaranteed Shipping Characteristics, when shipping and other characteristics are required to evaluate offers as to transportation costs for all contracts above the simplified acquisition threshold. The contracting officer deletes unrequired shipping characteristics from paragraph (a) of the clause. The award document shows the shipping characteristics used in the evaluation.

FAR 52.247-61, F.o.b. Origin—Minimum Size of Shipments, when volume rates may apply.

FAR 52.247-62, Specific Quantities Unknown.

FAR 52.247-63, Preference for U.S.-Flag Air Carriers, if greater than the simplified acquisition threshold (not for commercial items) when the U.S. Government-financed international air transportation of personnel (and their personal effects) or property might occur in the performance of the contract.

FAR 52.247-64, Preference for Privately Owned U.S.-Flag Commercial Vessels, if performance may involve ocean transportation of supplies subject to the Cargo Preference Act of 1954.[51] Use the clause with its Alternate I if the supplies are transported exclusively in privately owned U.S.-flag commercial vessels. Use the basic clause with its Alternate II for commercial items shipped for contingency operations (including UN or NATO humanitarian or peacekeeping operations), but not for ocean transportation services or construction.

FAR 52.247-66, Returnable Cylinders, whenever the contract involves the purchase of gas in contractor-furnished returnable cylinders and the contractor retains title to the cylinders.

5.12.5 Ocean Transport

DFARS 247.5

DoD implements the Cargo Preference Act of 1904, which applies to the ocean transportation of cargo owned or destined for use by DoD and several provisions in annual appropriations acts.[52] It does not address the Cargo Preference Act of 1954 because compliance with the 1904 Act historically has resulted in DoD exceeding the 1954 Act's requirements. Nor does it apply to ocean transportation of products obtained for contributions to foreign assistance programs or owned by agencies other than DoD unless the products are clearly identifiable for eventual use by DoD.

DoD contractors transport supplies exclusively on U.S.-flag vessels unless unavailable or the proposed charges to the Government are higher than charges to private persons for the transportation of like goods. Contracts must provide for the use of Government-owned vessels when security classifications prohibit the use of other than Government-owned vessels.

Any vessel used under a time charter contract for the transportation of supplies under this section has any reflagging or repair work performed in the United States or its outlying areas prior to acceptance of the vessel by the Government. The Secretary of Defense may waive this requirement upon determination that such waiver is critical to the national security of the United States.

When obtaining carriage requiring a covered vessel, the contracting officer must consider the extent to which offerors have had overhaul, repair, and maintenance work for covered vessels performed in shipyards located in the United States or Guam.

Authority to make determinations of nonavailability or excessive ocean liner rates and excessive charter rates is delegated to the Commander, U.S. Transportation Command (USTRANSCOM), for excessive ocean liner and intermodal rate determinations; and the Secretary of the Navy for excessive charter rate determinations. Reasonableness determinations can be based on published tariffs, industry publications or input from the Maritime Administration.

PGI 247.5

Contracting officers shall follow these procedures when ocean transportation is not the principal purpose of the contract, and the cargo to be transported is owned by DoD or is clearly identifiable for eventual use by DoD.

If the contractor notifies the contracting officer that the (sub)contractor considers that the freight charges proposed by U.S.-flag carriers are excessive or otherwise unreasonable, the contracting officer will prepare a report in determination and findings format. However, the 1904 Act is, in part, a subsidy of the U.S.-flag commercial shipping industry that recognizes that lower prices may be available from foreign-flag carriers. Therefore, a lower price for use of a foreign-flag vessel is not a sufficient basis, on its own, to determine that the freight rate proposed by the U.S.-flag carrier is excessive or otherwise unreasonable.

(S)he must also consider excessive profits to the carrier (to include vessel owner or operator) and the Government (i.e., costs beyond the economic penalty normally incurred by excluding foreign competition) resulting from the use of U.S.-flag vessels in extraordinarily inefficient circumstances. This requires an analysis of whether the cost is excessive, taking into account factors such as the differential between the freight charges proposed by the U.S.-flag carrier, an estimate of what foreign-flag carriers would charge based upon a price analysis, a comparison of U.S.-flag rates charged on comparable routes, and efficiency of operations regardless of rate differential. Efficiency considerations would include suitability of the vessel for the required transportation in terms of cargo requirements or vessel capacity, and the commercial reasonableness of vessel positioning required.

The contracting officer forwards the report to either Military Sealift Command or USTRANSCOM, depending on the mode of transport. Upon receipt of a determination by the Secretary of the Navy or the Commander, USTRANSCOM, respectively, that U.S. flag rates are excessive or unreasonable, the contracting officer provides the contractor with written approval to use a non-U.S. flag carrier, in accordance with that determination.

Alternatively, direct purchase of ocean transportation may include time or voyage charters or related services, ocean bills of lading, subcontracts under Government contracts or agreements for ocean transportation services, and ocean liner contracts (including contracts where ocean liner transportation is part of an intermodal movement).

Solicitations for direct purchase of ocean transportation provide a preference for U.S.-flag vessels, an evaluation criterion for offeror participation in the Voluntary Intermodal Sealift Agreement, and an evaluation criterion considering the extent to which offerors have had overhaul, repair, and maintenance work for all covered vessels in an offeror's fleet performed in shipyards located in the United States or Guam. Work performed in foreign shipyards is not considered if performed as emergency repairs due to accident, emergency, act of God, or an infirmity to the vessel, and safety considerations warranted taking the vessel to a foreign shipyard. Nor is foreign shipyard work considered if paid for or reimbursed by the U.S. Government. Nonavailability of U.S.-flagged vessels determinations must be made by either Military Sealift Command or the Army's Military Surface Deployment and Distribution Command in lieu of USTRANSCOM.[53]

If the contracting officer concludes that the freight charges proposed by U.S.-flag carriers may be excessive or otherwise unreasonable, (s)he prepares a D&F that includes analysis of the carrier's costs and profit, efforts taken to negotiate a reasonable price (including referral to a level above the contracting officer) and analysis of whether the costs are excessive (i.e., costs beyond the economic penalty normally incurred by excluding foreign competition). This D&F is then forwarded to Military Sealift Command or Military Surface Deployment and Distribution Command for review and forwarding to Secretary of the Navy or USTRANSCOM for final approval. Upon receipt of their determination that U.S. flag rates are excessive or unreasonable, the contracting officer shall provide the contractor with written approval to use a non-U.S. flag carrier, in accordance with that determination.

Solicitation Provisions

DFARS 252.247-7022, Representation of Extent of Transportation by Sea, unless a direct purchase of ocean transportation services or with an anticipated value at or below the simplified acquisition threshold. Do not use if the solicitation includes FAR 52.204-7.

DFARS 252.247-7026, Evaluation Preference for Use of Domestic Shipyards—Applicable to Acquisition of Carriage by Vessel for DoD Cargo in the Coastwise or Noncontiguous Trade, for a covered vessel for carriage of cargo for DoD.

Solicitation Provisions and Contract Clauses

DFARS 252.247-7023, Transportation of Supplies by Sea, except for direct purchase of ocean transportation services. Use Alternate I if any of the supplies to be transported are commercial items that are shipped in direct support of U.S. military contingency operations, exercises, or forces deployed in humanitarian or peacekeeping operations when the contract is not a construction contract. Use Alternate II if any of the supplies to be transported are commercial items that are commissary or exchange cargoes transported outside of the Defense Transportation System for a construction contract.

DFARS 252.247-7025, Reflagging or Repair Work, for time charter of a vessel for the transportation of supplies, unless a waiver has been granted in accordance with 247.572(c)(2).

DFARS 252.247-7027, Riding Gang Member Requirements, for the charter of, or contract for carriage of cargo by, a U.S.-flag vessel. Security background checks are processed by the Military Sealift Command.

Contract Clause

DFARS 252.247-7024, Notification of Transportation of Supplies by Sea, if the offeror made a negative response to the inquiry in DFARS 252.247-7022, Representation of Extent of Transportation by Sea.

5.13 COST MANAGEMENT

5.13.1 Earned Value Management

FAR 34.2

OMB Circular A-11 (Preparation, Submission and Execution of the Budget), requires an *Earned Value Management System* (EVMS) for major acquisitions. EVMS strives to integrate cost, schedule, and technical performance (including personnel, facilities and equipment) with risk management to objectively measure program progress and make program management more efficient. This approach provides an early warning of performance deficiencies and helps to prevent unwarranted expansion in scope of work (colloquially known as *scope creep*). The contractor develops or chooses a system to provide accurate and timely data, but must eventually comply with the ANSI/EIA Standard 748, Earned Value Management Systems. Contractors submit EVMS monthly reports (including subcontractors). The Government will conduct an Integrated Baseline Review (IBR) to verify the technical content and realism of the related performance budgets, resources, and schedules.[54]

Measuring actual values against these objective baselines will determine the earned value of performance. This review provides a mutual understanding of the inherent risks in contractor performance plans and underlying management control systems, and should lead to developing a risk management plan.

DFARS 234.2

For cost or incentive contracts and subcontracts valued at less than $20 million, the application of earned value management is optional and is a risk-based decision. For firm-fixed-price contracts and subcontracts of any dollar value, the application of earned value management is discouraged. The cognizant contracting officer determines the acceptability of the contractor's earned value management system and approve or disapprove the system and pursue correction of any deficiencies.

DAG CH 1–4.2.16

Production contractors must use internal performance management processes that plan and assign all work scope to the applicable areas in the product-oriented WBS. These processes must also objectively assess work accomplishments and variances, implement corrective actions, and provide forecasts of cost and schedule for decision-making and situational awareness. Using this approach, contractors can (in order):

- plan and assign all work scope;
- integrate scope, schedule, and cost to measure performance;
- record actual costs incurred;
- assess work accomplishment and variances;
- implement corrective actions; and
- use performance information for forecasts and decision-making.

Another advantage of EVM is that the program manager receives accurate and timely performance information that is the same as what the contractor uses, measures progress objectively and relates time-phased budget to scope of work. This information enables independent government predictions of future cost and schedule conditions.[55]

EVMS is required for cost- and/or incentive-type contracts and subcontracts valued at or above $20 million and at least 18 months performance, unless waived by the Component Acquisition Executive. For (sub)contracts over $100 million, the contracting officer must approve the contractor's EVMS. The program manager can impose EVMS on lower-priced (sub) contracts based on risk analysis after considering type of work and level of reporting and schedule criticality to a program's mission. The basic tenet of EVM is that the value of a piece of work is equal to the amount of funds budgeted to complete.

The Integrated Program Management Report (IPMR) contains the instructions for a contractor to provide cost and schedule performance on DoD acquisition contracts, even when EVM is not required on contract. This report provides performance data to identify problems early in the contract and forecast future contract performance. It is required monthly for contracts and orders of $20 million or more. For subcontracts, flow-down is determined by the prime contractor. Per PGI 234.201, the contracting officer must respond to a deficiency report within 10 days of receipt, allowing the contractor 30 days to respond. Final determination must be shared with the cognizant auditor or functional specialist to initiate monitoring of contractor corrective action.

The Contract Funds Status Report supplies funding data about defense contracts to program managers to update and forecast contract funding requirements. It is used to plan contract funding changes and develop funding requirements and budget estimates. This funding data also helps to determine funds in excess of contract needs and available for de-obligation. The report is required for contracts over six months in duration and usually (but not necessarily) of at least $1 million in value. This report includes fee or profit dollars in its data, whereas the Integrated Program Management Report covers just costs. These two reports are consistent with each other, but not identical.

Before contract award, an integrated baseline is developed with time-phased resources to fulfill the scope of work. As work is performed, completion is measured against the baseline; in this way, the corresponding budget value is "earned." Cost and schedule variances from this value can be determined and analyzed. The program manager can identify significant drivers, forecast future cost and schedule performance, and develop corrective action plans. If the deviation is significant, then updated risk assessment activities may be necessary because deviations are often indications of a technical problem. EVM can thus be used to measure both performance and management and to forecast future conditions.

An Integrated Baseline Review by the program manager and contractor is performed continuously, not just once, especially as the baseline changes. Now the program manager can assess the risk in the contractor's plan for completing the contractual scope of work. The scope of these reviews can be tailored to the nature of the work effort. The review is performed at least six months after contract or option execution or modification, although they can be performed any time at the discretion of the program manager. Other triggers for a review could be completion of the Preliminary or Critical Design Review, significant shift in the content or timing of the Baseline, or at the start of the production option. A preaward review is permitted if included in the Statement of Work.

If performance measurement against budgets or contractual milestones becomes unrealistic, the contractor may want to request an Over-Target Baseline or Over-Target Schedule. The request includes a top-level projection of cost and/or schedule growth, stating whether a single point adjustment to remove performance variances occurs, and a schedule of implementation for the process. The program manager must formally approve the results and can direct initiation of this process.

Program management uses the following information to assess schedule and cost performance.

- **Contract Work Breakdown Structure (WBS)**—breaks down the scope of work into a hierarchical decomposition of effort into accounts which are further broken into discrete work packages.
- **Budgeted Cost for Work Scheduled (BCWS)**—after resources are time-phased against the work packages to create a planned value, the values add up to their control account level and all control accounts add up to the baseline against which performance is measured. Upon the close of each reporting period, the contractor reports the BCWS planned during each reporting period and the cumulative total to date.
- **Performance Measurement Baseline (PMB)**—the sum of all control accounts, creating the time-phased budget plan against which performance is measured. Usually, a PMB forms an "S" type curve, and the slope of that curve where there is a significant change is of special interest.
- **Budget at Completion (BAC)**—the sum of all BCWS at completion. Its value can be stated at the work package, control account or higher level, though the cumulative BCWS at completion is most important.
- **Management Reserve**—monetized work set-aside for unplanned but in-scope work that usually arises in contract execution. There should be a relationship between the amount set aside for reserve and the relative risk of the program. High rates of reserve burn typically indicate a lack of discipline in program planning. However, management reserve is owned and managed by the contractor and is not a government-controlled item.
- **Budgeted Cost for Work Performed (BCWP)**—the budgeted dollar value of work completed during each reporting period and the cumulative total of work completed. This is another translation of work into a monetized figure. The BCWP can be based on an objective assessment of work actually performed. The rate at which BCWP is credited significantly impacts an evaluation of program performance and possible forecasted end states.
- **Actual Cost of Work Performed (ACWP)**—all contract direct and indirect costs, recorded in the financial accounting records during each reporting period. Some actuals may be estimated due to various timing issues with materials or subcontractors.

- **Schedule Variance (SV)**—the monetary difference between the BCWP and BCWS shows if the contractor is ahead of or behind schedule. Significant variances are analyzed for cause and budgetary impact, but may not have a bearing on schedule if the work package has enough slack to complete within the plan.
- **Cost Variance (CV)**—the difference between the BCWP and ACWP. Again, significant variances are analyzed to determine the cause and impact. Negative cost variance usually appears in the months following a recovery in schedule variance.
- **Estimate at Completion (EAC)**—EACs are generated at the lowest level of integrated management control and then integrated upwards into a program-level EAC. To verify that a contractor EAC reasonably reflects known and anticipated risks and opportunities, it should derive realistic both best- and worst-case EACs that reasonably reflect the nature of risk on the contract. Since all programs contain known and unknown risks, there is always some variation between work scope budgeted and downstream estimate of cost at completion. Moreover, the government program management office EAC may use different assumptions than the contractor and may therefore derive a different result.
- **Variance at Completion (VAC)**—the difference between the BAC and EAC. This is the projected amount of overrun or underrun against a contractual scope of work. Significant variances are analyzed to determine the cause and impact to develop corrective action. The Government decides the significant variance thresholds for reporting.
- **Cost Performance Index (CPI)**—a measurement of cost efficiency in the management of the program. While a CPI of at least 1.0 is desirable, trends in the measurements are important. Trouble areas in the program will be canceled out by the areas with exceptionally positive performance.
- **Schedule Performance Index (SPI)**—a measurement of work accomplishment efficiency. While an SPI of at least 1.0 is favorable, a program manager can review the trend of SPI and be able to forecast future performance. SPI is reviewed in conjunction with the IMS to assess actual schedule performance. As with CPI, a summarized top-level WBS SPI measurement can mask trouble areas in lower level WBS elements.
- **To-Complete Performance Index (TCPI)**—a value of the CPI required from a given point forward to reach the contractor's reported BAC or EAC. It is best used as a comparative index to CPI. If for any given reporting period the TCPI is 5 percent greater than the cumulative CPI, it should be investigated, and if 10 percent or greater, then the reported EAC is probably not achievable.
- **Integrated Master Plan (IMP)**—a depiction of leadership decision-making approaches, it offers key insights into true EVM performance and serves as the foundation of the IMS. It defines all the events, accomplishments,

and completion criteria necessary to successfully execute the program and is traceable to the WBS and Statement of Work. It consists of program events or decision points/reviews, significant accomplishments and accomplishment criteria.

- **Integrated Master Schedule (IMS)**—an integrated schedule developed by networking detailed program activities to list activities and events by time. It defines all program activities and their relationships to one another in terms of realistic constraints of time, funding, and people. It supports time and cost estimates, opens communications among program personnel and establishes their commitment to program activities.

An underrun to the budget does not automatically mean excess funds have become available. Situations occur where contractors are asked to move budget from control accounts that have cost underruns and apply the remaining budget to new work—an activity sometimes known as "harvesting underruns." However, underrunning budget in the baseline should not be used to develop new baseline activities. The budget amount comprises the resources estimated to be required to complete the contracted scope of work, whereas the funded amount comprises the actual government dollars obligated on the contract and available for payment for work being accomplished on the contract. The contract budget base need not equal either the amount of obligated funding or the contract price.

The IPMR's primary value to the government is its utility in reflecting current contract status and projecting future contract performance. Program managers should require EVM data to a level that matches the risks on the program. EVM data can be reported at different levels on different WBSs based on the risk and management needs. EVM data are for management of project execution, not cost estimating for which the government has other dedicated means to obtain data.

Solicitation Provisions

DFARS 252.234-7001, Notice of Earned Value Management System, instead of the provisions at FAR 52.234-2, Notice of Earned Value Management System—Preaward IBR, for cost or incentive contracts valued at $20,000,000 or more, and for other contracts for which EVMS will be applied.

Solicitation Provision and Contract Clause

FAR 52.234-2, Notice of Earned Value Management System—Preaward IBR, to require the contractor to use an EVMS and for which the Government requires an IBR prior to award.

DFARS 252.234-7002, Earned Value Management System.

FAR 52.234-3, Notice of Earned Value Management System—Post Award IBR, to require the contractor to use an EVMS and for which the Government requires an IBR after contract award.

FAR 52.234-4, Earned Value Management System, to require a contractor to use an EVMS.

5.13.2 Should-Cost Review

Should-Cost is a technique to seek out and eliminate low-value-added or unnecessary elements of program cost, motivate better cost performance and reward contractors that succeed in achieving these goals. Should-Cost analysis can be used during contract negotiations (particularly for sole-source procurements), and throughout program execution. This could free up funds for other pressing needs or enhanced capability.

DFARS 215.407

The following Should-Cost management aspects can be used to identify potential cost reductions, develop cost targets, and manage investment costs throughout the acquisition life cycle:

- benchmark against similar programs and other programs performed by the same contractor or in the same facilities;
- challenge the basis for indirect costs in contractor proposals;
- consider value engineering change proposals;
- eliminate unnecessary pass-through costs;
- identify any alternative technology or material that can potentially reduce development or life-cycle costs;
- identify opportunities to break out components as Government-furnished items;
- integrate modeling and simulation into the testing process;
- investigate integrated developmental or operational testing;
- justify each ingredient of program cost in terms of need and reduction ability;
- review supply chain management to encourage subcontractor competition and cost performance;
- review system specifications, design and build strategy for schedule reduction, facility and production enhancements, reductions of scrap rates and rework, and lower cost material options; and
- track recent program cost, schedule and performance trends and identify ways to reverse negative trend(s).

FAR 15.407-4

Should-cost reviews do not assume that a contractor's historical costs reflect efficient and economical operation, but rather evaluate the economy and efficiency of the contractor's existing equipment, management, materials, methods operating systems, real property, and workforce. These reviews are accomplished by a multifunctional team of Government contracting, contract administration, audit, engineering, and pricing representatives. The reviews promote both short- and long-range economies and efficiencies to reduce the cost of performance, either by program or company-wide.

A *program should-cost review* evaluates direct cost elements such as labor and material, and associated indirect costs, usually associated with the production of major systems, when the:

- contract will be a sole-source award;
- future year production requirements are expected for large quantities of like items;
- initial production has already taken place;
- items have a history of increasing costs;
- personnel with the required skills are available for the duration of the review;
- time is available to plan and adequately conduct the should-cost review; and
- work is so defined to permit an effective analysis and major changes are unlikely.

Accounting, management, manufacturing, and subcontract management are normally reviewed in a should-cost review. The contracting officer considers the findings and recommendations in the review team report when negotiating contract price, and establishes a follow-up plan to monitor the correction of uneconomical or inefficient practices. These reviews are usually mentioned in the program's acquisition plan.

An *overhead should-cost review* evaluates indirect costs (e.g., depreciation, fringe benefits, G&A, plant maintenance and security, real property and equipment, shipping and receiving, and taxes). A separate audit report is required. The following factors are considered when selecting contractor sites for overhead should-cost reviews:

- changes in accounting systems, management, or business activity;
- corporate reorganizations, mergers, acquisitions, or takeovers;
- dollar amount of Government business;
- importance of system or program;

- level of Government participation;
- level of noncompetitive Government contracts; and
- volume of proposal activity.

The objective of the overhead should-cost review is to evaluate significant indirect cost elements in depth and identify and recommend corrective actions regarding inefficient and uneconomical practices. The ACO should use this information to form the basis for the Government position in negotiating a forward pricing rate agreement with the contractor.

PGI 215.407-4

DCMA (or the Navy on behalf of SUPSHIP) may perform an overhead should-cost review of a contractor business unit when the projected annual sales to DoD exceed $1 billion and more than 30 percent of total business, production or development of a major weapon system or program is anticipated (usually on a sole-source basis), significant volume of proposal activity is anticipated, and contractor cost control/reduction initiatives appear inadequate. These overhead should-cost reviews are labor intensive, involving participation by the contracting, contract administration and audit offices. These reviews are usually at least three years apart.

DoDI 5000.02T ENCLOSURE 2: 6.e

For MDAPs and MAIS programs, it is DoD policy to budget to the Independent Cost Estimate unless an alternative estimate is specifically approved by the MDA. However, program managers will develop a Should-Cost estimate as a management tool to control and reduce cost. Program managers should not allow the independent cost estimate to become a self-fulfilling prophecy. Should-Cost is a management tool designed to proactively target cost reduction and drive productivity improvement into programs. The Should-Cost approach challenges managers to identify and achieve savings below budgeted most-likely costs. Should-Cost analysis can be used during contract negotiations (particularly for sole-source procurements), and throughout program execution, including sustainment. Program managers proactively seek out and eliminate low-value-added or unnecessary elements of program cost, to motivate better cost performance wherever possible, and to reward those that succeed in achieving those goals.

Should-Cost estimates used in contract negotiations will be based on the Government's reasonable expectation of successful contractor performance, consistent with the contractor's previous experience and other relevant data. Realized Should-Cost savings will be retained at the lowest organizational level possible and applied to priority needs. Should-Cost applies to programs in all ACATs, in all phases of the product's life cycle, and to all elements of program cost.

Program managers will develop, own, track, and report against Should-Cost targets. Estimates and results will be provided at milestone reviews and at specified decision points. For MDAPs and MAIS programs, program managers will report progress against Should-Cost goals at Defense Acquisition Executive Summary reviews.

DAG CH 6–3.6.6.1

By contrast, *Will-Cost* estimates are directed at ACAT I programs or an Acquisition Decision Memorandum. Managers scrutinize each cost element under their control and assess how it can be reduced without unacceptable reductions in value received. Program managers determine specific and measurable items or initiatives that can achieve savings against the Will-Cost estimate or long-term returns in production or sustainment efficiency. These items are tracked and managed as part of Should-Cost estimate progress reporting. However, they are primarily for Government use only for budgeting and reporting, are based on historical data, and do not represent baseline savings opportunities.

The following Should-Cost management aspects can be used to identify potential cost reductions, develop cost targets, and manage investment costs throughout the acquisition life cycle:

- benchmark against similar DoD programs and other programs performed by the same contractor or in the same facilities;
- challenge the basis for indirect costs in contractor proposals;
- consider value engineering change proposals;
- eliminate unnecessary pass-through costs;
- identify any alternative technology or material that can potentially reduce development or life-cycle costs;
- identify items contracted through a second- or third-party contract;
- identify opportunities to break out components as Government-furnished items;
- integrate modeling and simulation into the testing process;
- investigate integrated developmental or operational testing;
- justify each ingredient of program cost in terms of need and reduction ability;
- review supply chain management to encourage subcontractor competition and cost performance;
- review system specifications, design and build strategy for schedule reduction, facility and production enhancements, reductions of scrap rates and rework, and lower cost material options; and
- track recent program cost, schedule and performance trends and identify ways to reverse negative trend(s).

Solicitation Provision and Contract Clause

DFARS 252.215-7015, Program Should-Cost Review.

5.13.3 Billing Rates

FAR 42.704

A *billing rate* is an indirect cost rate established temporarily for interim reimbursement of incurred indirect costs and adjusted as necessary pending establishment of final indirect cost rates.

The contracting officer or auditor ensures that the billing rates are as close as possible to the final indirect cost rates anticipated for the contractor's fiscal period, adjusted for unallowable costs. When the contracting officer or auditor determines that the dollar value of contracts does not warrant submission of a detailed billing rate proposal, the rates may be set by adjusting the prior year's indirect cost experience to eliminate nonrecurring and unallowable costs and reflect new or changed conditions.

Once established, billing rates may be prospectively or retroactively revised by mutual agreement of the parties to prevent substantial overpayment or underpayment. When agreement cannot be reached, the billing rates may be unilaterally determined by the contracting officer.

When the contractor provides the contracting officer with the certified final indirect cost rate proposal, the parties may mutually agree to revise billing rates to reflect the proposed indirect cost rates, reflecting historically disallowed amounts from prior years' audits, until the proposal has been audited and settled. The historical decrement is determined by either the contracting officer or the auditor.

Similarly, final indirect cost rates are established by either the contracting officer or auditor. Within 120 days (or longer, if approved in writing by the contracting officer) after settlement of the final annual indirect cost rates for all years of a physically complete contract, the contractor submits a completion invoice or voucher reflecting the settled amounts and rates. If the contractor fails to do so on time, the contracting officer may determine the amounts due to the contractor and issue a unilateral contract modification as a final decision. In simple cases for contractors without an ACO, DCAA can establish final billing rates.

Under cost-reimbursement research and development contracts with universities or other educational institutions, payment for reimbursable indirect costs may be made using predetermined final indirect cost rates. Unless their use is approved at a level higher than the contracting officer, such rates are not used when there has been no recent audit of the indirect costs, frequent or wide fluctuations in the indirect cost rates and their bases over a period of years, or the estimated reimbursable costs for any given contract are expected to exceed $1 million annually.

OMB Circular A-87, Cost Principles for State, Local, and Tribal Governments, concerns cost principles for contracting with state and local governments. It establishes procedures for a cognizant agency to approve indirect costs associated with federally funded programs and activities. The indirect cost rates negotiated by the agency are used by all Federal agencies. Other nonprofit organizations are covered by OMB Circular A-122, Cost Principles for Nonprofit Organizations.

5.13.4 Final Indirect Cost Rates

FAR 42.7

Establishing final indirect cost rates provides a uniform approach with a contractor supporting multiple contracts or agencies, and timely settlement of cost-reimbursement contracts. Billing rates provide a method for interim reimbursement of indirect costs at estimated rates, subject to adjustment during contract performance and at the time the final indirect cost rates are established.

A single agency is responsible for establishing final indirect cost rates for each business unit. These rates are binding on all agencies and contracting offices, unless otherwise prohibited by law or the contracting officer determines that an audit conducted by another agency is acceptable.

Established final indirect cost rates are used to negotiate the final price of fixed-price incentive and fixed-price redeterminable contracts, and cost-reimbursement contracts, unless the quick-closeout procedure is used. In accordance with 10 U.S.C. 2324(h) and 41 U.S.C. 256(h), a proposal is not accepted, and no agreement is made to establish final indirect cost rates, unless the costs have been certified by the contractor. The agency head may waive the certification requirement when determined to be in the interest of the United States if the contract is with a foreign government or international organization, state or local government, educational institution, or nonprofit organization.

If the contractor has not certified its proposal for final indirect cost rates and a waiver is not appropriate, the contracting officer may unilaterally establish the rates. Such rates are based on audited historical data and set low enough to ensure that unallowable costs will not be reimbursed.

FAR 42.707

Cost-sharing arrangements may call for indirect cost rates lower than the anticipated actual rates. In such cases, a negotiated indirect cost rate ceiling may be incorporated into the contract for prospective application. These cases include a new or recently reorganized company with no past or recent record of incurred indirect costs, a contractor with rapidly increasing indirect cost rates due to a declining volume of sales, or a contractor trying to enhance its competitive position by proposing indirect cost rates lower than those that may reasonably be expected to occur during contract performance (thereby causing a cost overrun). In such cases, an equitable ceiling covering the final indirect cost rates may be negotiated and specified in the contract. When ceiling provisions are utilized, the Government will not be obligated to pay any additional amount should the final indirect cost rates exceed the negotiated ceiling rates, and any final indirect cost rates below the negotiated ceiling rates will lead to rate reductions.

Solicitation Provision and Contract Clause

FAR 52.242-4, Certification of Indirect Costs, for establishment of final indirect cost rates.

5.13.5 Disallowance of Costs

FAR 42.8

At any time during the performance of a contract other than firm-fixed-price contract (with or without an economic price adjustment clause), the ACO may issue the contractor a written notice of intent to disallow specified costs incurred or planned. A notice of intent to disallow such costs usually results from monitoring contractor costs. In the event of disagreement, the contractor may submit to the contracting officer a written response. The ACO then either withdraws the notice or makes a written decision within 60 days.

FAR 42.803

When contracting officers receive vouchers directly from the contractor and approve or disapprove them, the process follows agency procedures. If the examination of a voucher raises a question regarding the allowability of a cost under the contract terms, the auditor may issue a notice of contract costs suspended and/or disapproved simultaneously to the contractor and the disbursing officer, with a copy to the cognizant contracting officer, requesting deduction from current payments of all costs claimed but not considered reimbursable. If the contractor disagrees with the deduction from current payments, it may request the contracting officer to pay the unreimbursed costs and to discuss the findings and/or file a claim under the Disputes clause.

DFARS 242.8

The contract auditor is the authorized representative of the contracting officer for receiving vouchers from contractors electronically or by other delivery methods as directed by the terms of the contract and approving interim vouchers that were selected using sampling methodologies for provisional payment and sending them to the disbursing office after a pre-payment review. Interim vouchers not selected for a pre-payment review will be considered to be provisionally approved and will be sent directly to the disbursing office. All provisionally approved interim vouchers are subject to a later audit of actual costs incurred. Auditors will also review completion/final vouchers and send them to the administrative contracting officer, and issue DCAA Forms 1, Notice of Contract Costs Suspended and/or Disapproved, to deduct costs where allowability is questionable. The administrative contracting officer approves all completion/final vouchers and sends them to the disbursing officer and may issue or direct the issuance of DCAA Form 1 on any cost when there is reason to believe it should be suspended or disallowed.

Solicitation Provision and Contract Clause

FAR 52.242-1, Notice of Intent to Disallow Costs, unless firm-fixed-price or fixed-price with an economic price adjustment clause.

5.13.6 Resolving Cost Impacts

FAR 30.606

If a contract or modification represents at least $100,000 in total impact to other contracts, the contracting officer will coordinate with other affected contracting officers before negotiating and resolving the cost impact, and prepare a negotiation memorandum to send to the auditor and the other contracting officers. Adjustments reflect a *pro rata* share of the cost impact. For unilateral changes and noncompliances, the contracting officer does not adjust the price for fixed-price contracts, and does not increase the aggregate price of all contracts, but must individually adjust cost-type contracts.

For noncompliances that involve estimating costs, the contractor corrects the noncompliance and adjusts any paid invoices to reflect the adjusted contract prices. The contractor also corrects noncompliant contract cost accumulations for any affected contracts and adjusts interim payment requests and final vouchers to reflect the costs that should have been paid using the compliant practice.

For a CAS price adjustment or determination of noncompliance of a subcontractor, the chief financial officer for the subcontractor furnishes a copy of the negotiation memorandum or determination to the counterpart for the next higher-tier subcontractor.

FAR 42.708

Under the quick closeout procedure, the contracting officer negotiates the settlement of indirect costs for a specific contract, in advance of determining final rates. In this case, the contract must be physically complete, and agreement must be reached on a reasonable estimate of allocable dollars. The amount of unsettled indirect cost to be allocated to the contract must not exceed $1 million or 10 percent of the estimated total value of the contract or order. The contracting officer must assess the risk of settlement based upon the contractor's accounting, estimating, and purchasing systems.

Determining final indirect costs under the quick-closeout procedure does not affect any other contracts for over- or under-recoveries of costs allocated or allocable to the subject contract. Indirect cost rates used in quick closeout are not considered a binding precedent when establishing final indirect rates for other contracts.

Penalties are assessed against contractors which include unallowable indirect costs in either final indirect cost rate proposals or the final statement of costs incurred or to be incurred under a fixed-price incentive contract. This provision applies to all contracts in excess of $800,000, except fixed-price contracts without cost incentives.

If the indirect cost is unallowable under a cost principle, the penalty equals the disallowed costs plus interest on any paid portion of the disallowance. If the indirect cost was determined to be unallowable before proposal submission, the penalty is doubled. These penalties are in addition to any other administrative, civil, and criminal penalties. It is not necessary for unallowable costs to have been paid to the contractor in order to assess a penalty. The contracting officer may also need to refer the matter to a criminal investigative organization for further review and remedy.

The contracting officer waives penalties when the contractor withdraws the proposal before the Government formally initiates an audit, then submits a revised proposal, and the amount of the unallowable costs is $10,000 or less. The contractor must provide its established policies, evidence of personnel training, and an internal control and review system that assures precluding unallowable costs from being included in final indirect rate proposals. An acceptable self-governance program will outline specific accounting controls and compliance tests for indirect costs. Finally, any unallowable costs subject to the penalty must have been erroneously incorporated into the proposal.

Solicitation Provisions and Contract Clauses

FAR 52.242-3, Penalties for Unallowable Costs, if over $750,000, except fixed-price contracts without cost incentives or any firm-fixed-price contract for the purchase of commercial items.

5.13.7 Bankruptcy

FAR 42.9

When notified of bankruptcy proceedings, agencies must strive to protect the Government's financial interests and property. The contracting officer will furnish the notice of bankruptcy and pertinent contract information to contracting, financial, legal, and property offices. With their advice and input, the contracting officer will then determine the amount of the Government's potential claim against the contractor for unclosed contracts.

Solicitation Provision and Contract Clause

FAR 52.242-13, Bankruptcy, if exceeding the simplified acquisition threshold.

5.13.8 Cost As an Independent Variable

Cost As an Independent Variable (CAIV) is a DoD strategy that entails setting aggressive yet realistic cost objectives when defining and managing operational requirements to acquire defense systems. Cost objectives must balance mission needs with projected out-year resources, taking into account existing technology, maturation of new technologies and anticipated process improvements in both DoD and industry. As system performance and cost objectives are decided based on cost-performance trade-offs, cost becomes more of a constraint and less of a variable. CAIV principles apply throughout a system's life cycle. The key principles of CAIV are:

- early and continuous customer participation in setting and adjusting program goals throughout the program;
- realistic but aggressive cost objectives are set early and updated for each phase of an acquisition program;
- requirements stated in terms of capabilities and may be exchanged, substituted or adjusted (capabilities are established at the system level only); and
- trade space (i.e., cost with respect to performance) around the cost objective.

5.14 CONTRACT FINANCING

5.14.1 Invoicing

FAR 32.905

A contractor requests payment by submitting an *invoice*. Authorized payments are processed for interim payments under a cost-reimbursement contract for services and partial deliveries accepted by the Government. Invoices are also prepared for lease and rental charges, and of course for final cost or fee payments.

Payment is based on receipt of a proper invoice and satisfactory contract performance. A proper invoice must include the following items:

- contract number (including order number) and contract line item number;
- contractor name and address;
- description, quantity, unit of measure, unit price, and extended price;
- discount for prompt payment terms;
- electronic funds transfer banking information, if required by the agency;
- invoice date and number;
- name and address of contractor official to whom payment is to be sent;
- point of contact (name, title, mailing address, and phone number) to notify in case of a defective invoice;
- shipping and payment terms (e.g., shipment number and date, bill of lading number and weight of shipment on Government bills of lading); and
- Taxpayer Identification Number (TIN), if required by agency procedures.

If the invoice does not comply with these requirements, the designated billing office returns it within seven days after receipt with the reasons for rejection. However, a defective invoice must be returned within three days on contracts for fish, meat or meat food products; and within five days on contracts for perishable agricultural or dairy products, and food products prepared from edible fats or oils.

Other than cost-reimbursement contracts for services (which do not require such a report), the invoice must match up with a receiving report which cites:

- contract or order number;
- date supplies were delivered or services performed;
- date the designated Government official accepted the supplies or services or approved the progress payment request;
- description of supplies delivered or services performed;

- quantities of supplies received and accepted or services performed; and
- signature, printed name, title, mailing address, and telephone number of the designated Government official responsible for acceptance or approval functions.

The Government will not make invoice payment more than seven days prior to the due date unless the agency head determines otherwise. Payment is made via electronic funds transfer.

If so permitted by contract clause, the contractor is entitled to payment for accepted partial deliveries of supplies or partial performance of services that comply with all applicable contract requirements, provided that prices can be calculated from the contract items.

If determined necessary to withhold payment to protect the Government's interests, the contracting officer may unilaterally modify the contract to require the contractor to withhold up to 5 percent of the amount due, up to a maximum of $50,000. This happens in shipbuilding contracts, and sometimes in contracts with major corporations to facilitate final cost and rate settlement.

5.14.2 Financing Methods

FAR 32.1

Contract financing payment is an authorized Government disbursement of monies to a contractor prior to acceptance of noncommercial supplies or services. They are not the same as invoice payments because they address other purposes used in flexible payment processes. These would include advance or performance-based payments, interim payments under a cost reimbursement contract or progress payments.

These methods are expected to be self-liquidating through contract performance. The intent is to finance contractor working capital, not facility expansion. The contract price should show a commensurate reduction to reflect the more favorable payment terms.

There is a prescribed order of preference of contract financing methods:

- private financing without Government guarantee. The contractor arranges through a private lender, such as a bank, to obtain necessary working capital without asking the Government for assistance;
- *customary contract financing* without specific reviews or approvals by higher management. This method includes both customary progress payments and performance-based payments.[56] *Performance-based payments* rely on either objective quantifiable methods or accomplishment of defined

events. Both versions of contract financing payments may be used if the contractor cannot bill for the first delivery until well after work begins (normally at least four months for small businesses and at least six months for large firms). These payments cover expenditures during the predelivery period that would severely impact the contractor's working capital. The payment rate is 80 percent for large businesses and 85 percent for small businesses;

- *loan guarantees* made by a Federal Reserve bank on behalf of a designated guaranteeing agency to enable contractors to obtain financing from private sources;
- *unusual contract financing* require specific reviews or approvals by the head of the agency or as provided for in agency regulations; and
- *advance payments* which are *liquidated* (set-off) from future payments due to the contractor. Advance payments are generally used only in the following circumstances:
  - acquiring property for the Government;
  - financially weak contractors (or those who cannot receive finances);
  - Government-Owned-Contractor-Operated facilities;
  - national security;
  - nonprofit firms;
  - payments to subcontractors; or
  - small businesses.

The value of contract financing to the contractor is reflected in a reduced bid or negotiated price, or else contract terms and conditions that are more beneficial to the Government than usual. However, adequate new consideration is required for changes or additions to contract financing after award. This consideration could be a price adjustment reflecting the value of the anticipated amount and duration of contract financing at the imputed financial costs of equivalent working capital. Or it could be the estimated profit rate to be earned during the contract.

The contracting officer may reduce or suspend contractor payments when the agency head determines there is substantial evidence of a fraudulent request for advance, partial or progress payments for a contract or group of contracts. This authority does not apply to commercial interim payments or performance-based payments.

The due date for making contract financing payments is normally the 30th day (never less than the 7th day) after the billing office receives a proper contract financing request. The Government does not pay an interest penalty to the contractor due to delayed contract financing payments.

The contracting officer provides Government financing only to the extent needed for prompt and efficient performance. To determine this, (s)he considers the availability of private financing, predelivery expenditures, impact of production lead times on working capital, and the contractor's financial status. Because these financing methods are intended to be self-liquidating through contract performance, they are not intended for expanding contractor-owned facilities or acquiring fixed assets.

The contractor's need for contract financing is not a responsibility factor or evaluation criterion for contract award. Likewise, a certificate of competency from the SBA has no bearing on the contractor's need for or entitlement to contract financing.

If the contracting officer confirms a subcontractor claim that it has not been paid in accordance with the payment terms of the subcontract, (s)he may reduce or suspend progress payments.

Upon receipt of accelerated payments from the Government, prime contractors must pay small business subcontractors on an accelerated timetable to the maximum extent practicable, and upon receipt of accelerated payments from the Government. They must notify the contracting officer if they have missed or delayed a payment to a small business.

FAR 22.009

The Government provides accelerated payments as a matter of course to all small business (sub)contractors when permitted by law within 15 days of receipt of a proper invoice. This process may include using a Government-wide commercial credit card to make payments.

DFARS 232.102

Progress payments based on percentage or stage of completion are authorized only for contracts for construction, shipbuilding, and ship conversion, alteration, or repair. However, percentage or stage of completion methods of measuring contractor performance may be used for performance-based payments.

For undefinitized actions, the contracting officer may establish provisional delivery payments to pay contractors for the costs of supplies and services delivered to and accepted by the Government under the following contract actions:

- letter contracts contemplating a fixed-price contract;
- orders under basic ordering agreements or indefinite-delivery contracts;
- spares provisioning documents annexed to contracts; and
- unpriced equitable adjustments on fixed-price contracts.

Provisional delivery payments are not preferred and should be used sparingly, priced conservatively and reduced by liquidating previous progress payments in accordance with the Progress Payments clause. These payments cannot include profit, exceed obligated funds or influence the definitized contract price.

Solicitation Provision and Contract Clause

FAR 52.232-40, Providing Accelerated Payments to Small Business Subcontractors.

Contract Clauses

FAR 52.232-1, Payments, for fixed-price supplies or services, or nonregulated communication services.

FAR 52.232-2, Payment under Fixed-Price Research and Development Contracts.

FAR 52.232-3, Payments under Personal Services Contracts.

FAR 52.232-4, Payments under Transportation Contracts and Transportation-Related Services Contracts.

FAR 52.232-5, Payments under Fixed-Price Construction Contracts.

FAR 52.232-6, Payments under Communication Service Contracts with Common Carriers.

FAR 52.232-7, Payments under Time-and-Materials and Labor-Hour Contracts. The contracting officer can require the contractor to withhold 5 percent of amounts due, up to a maximum of $50,000.

FAR 52.232-8, Discounts for Prompt Payment, for a fixed-price supply or service contract.

FAR 52.232-9, Limitation on Withholding of Payments, if two or more terms authorize temporary withholding of amounts payable to the contractor.

FAR 52.232-10, Payments under Fixed-Price Architect-Engineer Contracts.

FAR 52.232-11, Extras, for fixed-price supplies, services, or transportation.

FAR 52.242-5, Payments to Small Business Subcontractors.

DFARS 252.232-7017, Accelerating Payments to Small Business Subcontractors-Prohibition on Fees and Consideration, when acquiring commercial items using accelerated payments to small businesses.

5.14.3 Commercial Item Purchase Financing

FAR 32.2

For purchases of commercial items, contract financing is normally a contractor's responsibility. However, in some markets financing by the buyer is a commercial practice, so the contracting officer may include financing terms in such contracts when, in the best interest of the Government, the:

- contract is awarded competitively or, if sole source, adequate consideration is obtained based on the time value of the additional financing, because it could be more advantageous to the offeror than its normal method of customer financing;
- contract price exceeds the simplified acquisition threshold;
- Government's best interest is served;
- need for adequate security is met;
- payment office concurs with using liquidation provisions; and
- sum of commercial advance payments before performance begins does not exceed 15 percent of the contract price.

The solicitation should specify what type of security is acceptable for Government financing. If the Government is willing to accept other forms of security, the offeror specifies the form it will provide, and the resulting contract will so specify. Contractor net worth and liquidity may be sufficient by itself to match the maximum unliquidated amount of contract financing payments. If not, then a lien against the plant, inventory or work-in-process is possible. The Government has the right to verify the existence and value of contractor assets, and whether they are already covered by a lien.

Subject to agency regulations, the contracting officer may determine the offeror's financial net worth and liquidity to be adequate security. Nonetheless, the value of the security equals or exceeds the maximum unliquidated amount of contract financing payments due to the contractor. The value of security may be adjusted periodically during contract performance. Other acceptable forms of security include a(n):

- guarantee of repayment from a person or corporation of proven liquid net worth;
- irrevocable letter of credit from a federally insured financial institution;
- surety bond that guarantees repayment of the unliquidated contract financing; or
- title to identified contractor assets of adequate worth.

The Government's lien takes priority to all other liens and is effective immediately upon the first payment, without any filing or notice by the United States. The contract specifies what the lien is upon (e.g., inventory, plant or work in process). The Government has the right to verify the existence and value of the assets. The contractor certifies that the assets subject to the lien are free from any prior encumbrances (e.g., capital equipment loans, installment purchases, lines of credit, revolving credit arrangements, or working capital loans).

The contracting officer may either specify the financing terms in the solicitation or permit each offeror to propose its own customary financing terms. If specified in the solicitation, contract financing cannot be an evaluation factor of proposals, and proposals of alternative financing terms are not accepted. However, an offer may state that contract financing terms will not be used by the offeror. Unlike other financing methods, contract financing is not a basis for adjusting offerors' proposed prices because the effect of contract financing is already reflected in the pricing.

On the other hand, if an offeror proposes financing terms, the contracting officer must specify the invoice dates and interest rate, then adjust the proposed price for evaluation purposes to reflect the cost of providing the proposed financing. This is done by computing the imputed cost of financing payments and adding it to the proposed price. This adjustment is the product of payment amount, annual interest rate and number of years or fraction thereof.

Commercial financing payments are liquidated by deduction from these payments. Interest is calculated at the nominal discount rate specified in Appendix C of the Office of Management and Budget (OMB) Circular A-94, "Guidelines and Discount Rates for Benefit-Cost Analysis of Federal Programs" (2004). Financing payments computed on a whole contract basis are liquidated using a uniform percentage. Payment computed on a line item basis is liquidated only against that item.

DFARS 232.2

The standard prompt payment terms for commercial item contract advance payments financing is the contractor entitlement date specified in the contract, or 30 days after receipt by the designated billing office of a proper request for payment, whichever is later. For commercial interim payments, the second term is reduced to 14 days after receipt by the designated billing office of a proper request for payment, whichever is later.

Installment payment financing is not used for DoD contracts, unless market research has established that this form of contract financing is both appropriate and customary in the commercial marketplace. This approach includes a fixed number of equal interim financing payments (usually on a monthly basis) prior to delivery and acceptance of a contract item. When installment payment financing is used, the contracting officer uses the ceiling percentage of contract price that is customary in the particular marketplace (not to exceed 70 percent of the unit price for that item). The amount paid upon acceptance is reduced by the amount of installment payments made for the item.

Contract Clauses

FAR 52.212-4, Contract Terms and Conditions—Commercial Products and Commercial Services.

FAR 52.232-29, Terms for Financing of Purchases of Commercial Products and Commercial Services.

FAR 52.232-30, Installment Payments for Commercial Products and Commercial Services.

FAR 52.232-31, Invitation to Propose Financing Terms, if the offeror proposes commercial financing. The contracting officer inserts conditions of contractor entitlement, description of the computation method of payment amounts, frequency and form of payment, and security provided by the contractor.

5.14.4 Progress Payments Based on Costs

FAR 32.5

Progress payments are made based on costs incurred by the contractor as contract work progresses, to reflect the fair value of work performed. They do not include payments based on percentage or stage of completion accomplished, partial deliveries accepted by the Government, or submission of a contract termination proposal.

Progress payments may be customary or unusual. *Customary progress payments* use a rate of 80 percent of the total contract cost (90 percent for DoD small businesses). For undefinitized contract actions, the rate is always 80 percent regardless of size status. The contracting officer rejects as nonresponsive any bids conditioned on progress payments when the solicitation did not provide for them. Similarly, an invitation for bids may restrict the availability of progress payments to small business concerns only.

The contracting officer may provide *unusual progress payments* at higher rates only if the contractor will bear predelivery expenditures that are large in relation to contract price and the contractor's working capital and credit. The contractor's request must be approved by the head of the contracting activity or a designee. Per PGI 232.501-2, unusual progress payment arrangements require the advance approval of the Director of DPAP. Contracting officers must submit all unusual progress payment requests to the department or agency contract financing office for submission and approval to DPAP.

If the contract requires separate progress payment rates for separate portions of work, the contractor submits separate progress payment requests and separate invoices for the severable portions of work.

Progress payments are generally approved to a contractor that the ACO has found by previous experience or recent audit review (within the last 12 months) to be reliable and competent (and therefore capable of satisfactory performance). Also, the contractor must have an adequate accounting system and controls to properly administer progress payments, and be in sound financial condition. Otherwise, the ACO must first determine that the contractor will be capable of liquidating any progress payments or that the Government is otherwise protected against loss by additional protective provisions. The responsible audit agency or office is consulted as part of this process, thought the auditor may have sufficient information on hand so that a complete audit may not be necessary.

Postpayment reviews or audits are sometimes performed by the ACO to determine if the:

- contractor's accounting system, controls and certification are adequate and reliable;
- limitation on progress payments in the Progress Payments clause has been exceeded;
- unliquidated progress payments are supported by the value of the work accomplished on the undelivered portion of the contract; or
- unpaid balance of the contract price is adequate to cover the anticipated cost of completion, or if the contractor has adequate resources to complete the contract.

When satisfactory progress has not been achieved by a contractor during any period for which a progress payment is to be made, the contracting officer may retain up to 10 percent of the progress payment. Moreover, progress payments can be suspended by the contracting officer if the contractor is delinquent in payments to subcontractors, in a weakened financial condition, not maintaining a reliable accounting system and controls, or has been overpaid.

The contracting officer adjusts progress payments when necessary to ensure that the fair value of undelivered work equals or exceeds the amount of unliquidated progress payments. If the sum of the total costs incurred under a contract plus the estimated costs to complete the performance are likely to exceed the contract price, the contracting officer computes a loss ratio factor and adjusts future progress payments to exclude the element of loss. This sum of costs is the denominator in the ratio. The numerator is a revised contract price used in progress payment computations (the current ceiling price under fixed-price incentive contracts), plus the not-to-exceed amount for any pending change orders and unpriced orders. The contracting officer then divides the revised contract price by this sum of costs to derive the loss ratio factor.

If the contracting officer believes a loss is probable, future progress payment requests are modified by calculating the revised contract price and loss factor ratio as above, then determining the total costs eligible for progress payments. To find this number, (s)he multiplies the sum of paid costs eligible for progress payments by the loss ratio factor. The contracting officer must ensure that the costs applicable to items delivered, invoiced and accepted do not exceed the contract price.

Per DFARS 232.503-6, the contracting officer must prepare a supplementary analysis of the contractor's request for progress payments and calculate the loss ratio adjustment using the procedures in FAR 32.503-6(g). The contracting officer may request the contractor to prepare the supplementary analysis as an attachment to the progress payment request when the contracting officer determines that the contractor's methods of estimating the "Costs to Complete" are reliable, accurate, and not susceptible to improper influences. To maintain an audit trail and permit verification of calculations, the loss ratio adjustments should not result from altering or replacing data on the contractor's original request for progress payment.

If the contracting officer concludes that the contractor's figures in its progress payment request are not correct, (s)he shall prepare a supplementary analysis to be attached to the contractor's request, notify the contractor in writing of the differences and adjust all further progress payments with the revised figures until the difference is resolved.

The Government recoups progress payments by deducting liquidation amounts from payments for completed contract items. The contracting officer applies a liquidation rate (usually the same as the progress payment rate) to the contract price of contract items delivered and accepted. This is easily calculated by dividing the progress payments amount by the contract price, rounding the resultant percentage up to the next highest tenth. The contracting officer may adjust the estimated cost and the contract price to include the estimated value of any authorized work not yet priced and any projected economic adjustments. Here again, this total cost number cannot exceed either the Government's estimated price of all authorized work or the amount of funds obligated for the contract.

An alternate liquidation rate method is available for the contractor to retain the earned profit element of the contract prices for completed items. The alternate rate can be used if the:

- contract delivery schedule is at least 18 months long;
- contractor would not be paid for more than the costs of items delivered and accepted (less allocable progress payments) and the earned profit on those items;

- data on actual costs are available for the products delivered, or for a performance period of at least 12 months;
- rate has not been reduced in the preceding 12 months;
- the Government can recoup under each invoice the full extent of the applicable progress payments; and
- unliquidated progress payments would not exceed the limit prescribed in the Progress Payments clause.

The contractor must agree to certify annually, or more often if requested by the contracting officer, that the alternate rate continues to meet these conditions (with adequate supporting information).

The contracting officer may increase the liquidation rate for both previous and subsequent transactions, if the contractor experiences a lower profit rate than anticipated at the time the liquidation rate was established, for both items already delivered and subsequent progress payments. Moreover, the rate can be raised or lowered to be consistent with any successive changes to the contract price or target profit (under a fixed-price incentive contract with successive targets), or for a redetermined price under a contract with prospective price redetermination at stated intervals. Once the liquidation rate is changed, the contracting officer issues a contract modification to specify the new rate in the Progress Payments clause. No additional consideration for these contract modifications is necessary.

Excess unliquidated progress payments over the contract limit can be corrected by increasing the liquidation rate, decreasing the progress payment rate, or suspending progress payments. This would most likely happen in a cost overrun, poor contractor performance or high rejection or spoilage rate.

Once the title to materials or other inventories is vested in the Government under the Progress Payments clause, the contractor must obtain contracting officer approval to transfer the inventory items from the contract for either disposition or its own use. If the contracting officer grants this request, associated costs are eliminated from progress payments (thereby reducing progress payments outstanding), and billings are reduced to increase liquidation. The contractor cannot bill for the costs allocable to the transferred property, and must credit to or repay the Government the unliquidated progress payments allocable to the transferred property.

Except for normal spoilage, the contractor bears the risk for damage, destruction, loss, or theft of property, even though title is vested in the Government, unless the Government has expressly assumed this risk. If a loss occurs, the contractor must repay to the Government the amount of unliquidated progress payments based on costs allocable to the property. If Government title to materials, work-in-process, finished goods, and other property under the contract is compromised, the administrative contracting officer may suspend or reduce progress payments.

Subcontracts may include either performance-based payments or progress payments, but not both. Subcontracts for commercial purchases may include commercial item purchase financing terms. Contracting officer review or consent is not required merely because the subcontract includes financing payments, so long as the prime contractor has installed the necessary management control systems and audit procedures.

Once contract performance is complete and all contractor obligations under the contract are satisfied, including full liquidation of progress payments, any remaining excess property is outside the scope of the Progress Payments clause. Therefore, the contractor holds title to it.

DFARS 232.5

The contracting officer may approve progress payments when the contract price exceeds the funds obligated under the contract, provided the contract limits the Government's liability to the lowest of the:

- 100 percent of the funds obligated;
- liquidation rate;
- loss-ratio adjusted rate; or
- progress payment rate.

Prior to granting blanket approval of cost transfers between contracts, the ACO should determine that the contractor retains records of the transfer activity that took place in the prior month, prepares monthly a summary of the transfer activity that took place in the prior month and includes the total number and dollar value of transfers.

Solicitation Provisions

FAR 52.232-13, Notice of Progress Payments.

FAR 52.232-14, Notice of Availability of Progress Payments Exclusively for Small Business Concerns.

FAR 52.232-15, Progress Payments Not Included.

Solicitation Provision and Contract Clause

DFARS 252.232-7002, Progress Payments for Foreign Military Sales Acquisitions, where these conditions exist.

Contract Clauses

FAR 52.232-16, Progress Payments. The contracting officer inserts any unusual progress payment rate or liquidation rate that has been approved for the prime contractor or subcontractor. Use the clause with its Alternate I if the contractor is a small business concern. Use the clause with its Alternate II if the contract is a letter contract. Use the clause with its Alternate III if the contractor is not a small business firm and the award is an indefinite-delivery contract or basic ordering agreement.

DFARS 252.232-7004, DoD Progress Payment Rates, instead of Alternate I of FAR 52.232-16, if the contractor is a small business concern.

DFARS 252.232-7018, Progress Payments—Multiple Lots.

5.14.5 Payment Adjustments

FAR 32.503

Periodic postpayment reviews assess the validity of progress payments by determining that the:

- applicable limitation on progress payments has been met or exceeded;
- contractor has adequate resources to complete the contract;
- contractor provides no reason to doubt the adequacy and reliability of its accounting system, controls, and certification;
- unliquidated progress payments are fairly supported by the value of the work accomplished on the undelivered portion of the contract; and
- unpaid balance of the contract price will cover the anticipated cost of completion.

Under indefinite-delivery contracts, the contracting officer administers progress payments for each individual order as if each were a separate contract, unless agency procedures provide otherwise.

The Government has the right to reduce or suspend progress payments, or to increase the liquidation rate. Such actions are taken only after notifying the contractor of the intended action and providing an opportunity to discuss and evaluate the effect on the contractor's credit arrangements, financial condition, operations, or projected cash requirements. Even after full liquidation of progress payments, if the contracting officer finds that contract performance is endangered by the contractor's financial condition or failure to make progress, (s)he can direct the contractor to make additional operating or financial arrangements without loss to the Government.

Except for normal spoilage, the contractor bears the risk for property damage, destruction, loss, or theft, even though title is vested in the Government, unless the Government has expressly assumed this risk. If a loss occurs, the contractor must repay to the Government the amount of unliquidated progress payments based on costs allocable to the property. If Government title to property (including finished goods, materials, and work-in-process) under the contract is compromised, the ACO may suspend or reduce progress payments. The contractor is not obligated to pay for the loss of property for which the Government has assumed the risk of loss.

Subcontracts may include either performance-based payments or progress payments, but not both. Subcontracts for commercial purchases may include commercial item purchase financing terms. Contracting officer review or consent is not required merely because the subcontract includes financing payments, so long as the prime contractor has installed the necessary management control systems and audit procedures.

If the contracting officer finds the contractor to be delinquent in paying the costs of contract performance but the contractor's financial condition is satisfactory, the contracting officer may continue progress payments if the contractor agrees to cure the payment delinquencies, avoid further delinquencies and arrange to complete the contract without loss to the Government.

If the contractor has, in good faith, disputed amounts claimed by subcontractors, the contracting officer cannot consider the payments delinquent until these amounts are established through arbitration or litigation. However, the amounts are excluded from costs eligible for progress payments so long as they are in dispute.

5.14.6 Performance-Based Payments

FAR 32.10

Performance-based payments are contract financing payments and therefore not subject to the interest-penalty provisions of prompt payment. They are made in lieu of progress payments, but not for architect-engineer services or construction contracts (including shipbuilding or ship conversion, alteration, or repair) that provide for progress payments based upon a percentage or stage of completion. This type of payment is not used for cost-reimbursement line items or contracts awarded through sealed bidding.

Unless agency procedures prescribe the bases for establishing performance-based payment amounts, the contracting officer may establish them on any rational basis, usually based either on objective, quantifiable methods or accomplishing defined events. Common examples of estimates include stages of completion, hours needed to achieve an event or criterion, or projected cost of performance of particular events. The payments may be made either on a whole contract or by deliverable item, but not due merely to the passage of time. Events or criteria may be either cumulative or severable, but not until a dependent event or criterion has occurred.

If a contract action significantly affects the price, event or performance criterion, the contracting officer adjusts the performance-based payment schedule appropriately. Total performance-based payments may not exceed 90 percent of the contract price or item price. The contract specifies the amount of each performance-based payment as a dollar amount or percentage of the contract price or item unit price.

Performance-based amounts are liquidated by deducting a percentage or a designated dollar amount from the delivery payments, ensuring complete liquidation by the time of final payment.

The contracting officer ensures that the Government title is not compromised by other encumbrances. Ordinarily, (s)he may rely upon the contractor's certification contained in the payment request. The existence of any such encumbrance violates the contractor's obligations under the contract, and (s)he may suspend or reduce payments under the Performance-Based Payments clause. Also, the contractor must repay any performance-based payments related to damaged or lost property. Finally, any accelerated payments due to a small business subcontractor must be paid promptly.

DFARS 232.10

Performance-based payments are designed to assist the contractor in costs incurred during the performance of the contract based on achieving performance outcomes. Therefore, performance-based payments should never exceed total cost incurred at any point during the contract. The standard payment terms for performance-based payments is either the contractor entitlement date specified in the contract, or 14 days after the billing office receives a proper invoice, whichever is later.

Prior to using performance-based payments, the contracting officer must first agree with the offeror on price using customary progress payments before negotiation begins on the use of performance-based payments, then analyze the performance-based payment schedule using the performance-based payments (PBP) analysis tool.[57]

The offeror/contractor submits a proposed performance-based payments schedule that includes all performance-based payments events, completion criteria and event values along with the projected expenditure profile in order to negotiate the value of the performance events. Note that these payments are not based on costs incurred, but rather on performance outcomes. For modifications to contracts that already use performance-based payments financing, the basis for negotiation must include performance-based payments. The PBP analysis tool will be used in the same manner to help determine the price for the modification. The only difference is that the baseline assuming customary progress payments will reflect an objective profit rate instead of a negotiated profit rate. The parties must also negotiate the consideration to be received by the Government if the performance-based payments payment schedule will be more favorable to the contractor than customary progress payments.

Since these nontraditional firms probably do not comply with cost accounting principles or standards, they need only comply with GAAP. Moreover, DCAA has no authority to audit them.

Solicitation Provisions

FAR 52.232-28, Invitation to Propose Performance-Based Payments, if inviting offerors to propose performance-based payments. Use the provision with its Alternate I in competitive negotiated solicitations if the Government intends to adjust proposed prices for evaluation purposes.

FAR 52.232-32, Performance-Based Payments.

DFARS 252.232-7012, Performance-Based Payments—Whole-Contract Basis, or DFARS 252.232-7013, Performance-Based Payments-Deliverable-Item Basis, depending on how the contract financing is arranged.

DFARS 252.232-7015, Performance-Based Payments-Representation.

DFARS 252.232-7016, Notice of Progress Payments or Performance-Based Payments, if one or the other will be used in the resultant contract.

5.14.7 Loan Guarantees for Defense Production

FAR 32.3

Section 301 of the Defense Production Act authorizes loan guarantees for contract performance related to national defense.[58] Unlike conventional loans from private institutions, Federal Reserve Banks serve on behalf of DoD as the guaranteeing agency to purchase a stated percentage of the loan and share any losses up to the guaranteed percentage. The guarantee is less than 100 percent of the loan, unless the agency determines that contractor performance is vital to the national defense and no other means of financing is available. The financial institution collects and disburses funds and administers the loan. A (sub)contractor that needs operating funds to perform a contract may always apply to a financial institution for a loan, which may then apply to its district Federal Reserve Bank for a guarantee before it extends credit. This means the Government will back the full value of the loan.

The contracting officer prepares a certificate of eligibility for a contract deemed to be of material consequence, when requested by the contract financing office or other interested agency, or if the application for a loan guarantee relates to a (sub)contract within his/her cognizance. This certificate and associated data on the contractor's financial status and performance is reviewed to determine whether authorization of a loan guarantee would be in the Government's interest. If the contractor has several major national defense contracts, then relatively minor contracts need not be reviewed. However, if the contracting officer determines that a certificate of eligibility is not justified, (s)he must document the facts and reasons supporting that conclusion and furnish them to the agency contract finance office.

Any certificate of eligibility must discuss the contractor's past performance and the relationship to performance schedules. The certificate must then determine that the supplies or services to be acquired are essential to the national defense, and that the contractor has the facilities and the technical and management ability required for performance.

If the contractor is not a small business, the certificate must also determine that there is no practicable alternate source for the acquisition without prejudice to the national defense. This analysis must discuss the following factors:

- comparative prices available from other sources;
- disruption of established subcontracting arrangements;
- extent to which other sources would need contract financing to perform;
- prejudice to the national defense if a contract with another source conflict with a major defense acquisition policy (e.g., mobilization base);
- technical ability and facilities of other potential sources;
- time and expense involved in repurchasing for contracts or parts thereof, such as potential claims under a termination for convenience or delays incident to any future default;
- urgency of performance schedules; and
- willingness of other sources to enter into contracts.

The guaranteeing agency evaluates the contractor's financial status and performance to determine if a loan guarantee is in the Government's interest. If this evaluation is favorable, it then sets both the maximum dollar amount and maturity date of the loan, then completes a standard form of authorization as prescribed by the Federal Reserve Board. The agency then transmits the authorization through the Federal Reserve Board to the nearest Federal Reserve Bank. The Bank then executes and delivers to the financing institution a guarantee agreement, with the terms and conditions approved for the particular case. The financing institution will then make the loan.

Note that the agency does not consider the percentage of guarantee requested by the financing institution in determining the contractor's eligibility. The agency usually employs an asset formula to limit the guarantee to 90 percent (or less if the contractor has inadequate working capital or credit) of the contractor's investment (e.g., payrolls and inventories). The formula excludes:

- amounts for which the contractor has not done any work or made any expenditure;
- amounts that would become due as the result of later performance under the contracts;
- cash collateral or bank deposit balances; and
- progress payments.

The agency usually requires a contractor under a guaranteed loan to execute an assignment of claims under defense production contracts. This includes any contracts entered into during the term of the guaranteed loan that are eligible for financing. This approach is not required (but still permitted) if the assignment of claims would create an undue administrative burden, such as when the contractor has many smaller dollar-value contracts, the contractor's financial condition is strong enough that an assignment of claims is unnecessary to protect the Government, or the agency does not consider increased protection of such a loan to be necessary.

A subcontract or purchase order subject to notice of assignment is problematic. It is not eligible for financing under guaranteed loans if the prime contractor reserves the right to pay the assignor directly (or jointly to the assignee). Nor is the contractor eligible if it reduces or sets off assigned proceeds under defense production contracts due to claims against the borrower.

If a substantial share of the contractor's defense contracts are covered by surety bonds, or the bond amount is substantial related to contractor net worth, the agency will not authorize a loan guarantee unless the surety subordinates its rights and claims to the loan to the financing institution. However, the loan guarantee agreement gives the financing institution the benefit of contract payments proportionate to its loans before any notice of default. Borrowings outside the guaranteed loan are discouraged but not prohibited by the Government.

The use of guaranteed loans as a contract financing mechanism requires the availability of congressional authority. DoD has not requested such authority in recent years, and none is now available. Nevertheless, the mechanism is in place as discussed above.

5.14.8 Advance Payments for Non-Commercial Items

FAR 32.4

A Government agency is the least preferred method of contract financing, and used only when the agency head or designee determines in writing that the advance payment is necessary either to the public interest or to facilitate the national defense. Advance payments cannot exceed the contractor's interim cash needs based on its own working capital and cash flow analysis required for contract performance or reimbursements. Nonetheless, advance payments may be appropriate for:

- acquisition at cost of property for Government ownership;
- classified actions where the agency does not desire assignment of claims;
- experimental, research or development work with nonprofit educational or research institutions;
- financially weak contractors whose technical ability is essential to the agency, and whose performance and financial controls are closely monitored;
- management and operation of Government-owned plants;
- small business concerns; or
- when a loan by a private financial institution is not practicable even with a loan guarantee, often due to remote geographic performance.

Sealed bidders may request advance payments before or after award, even if the invitation for bids does not contain an advance payment provision. However, any bid that requires advance payments as a basis for acceptance is rejected.

The agency will submit a letter of credit for a 12-month or longer contract totaling at least $120,000; otherwise a check directly from the Treasury is in order. Interest is computed at the end of each month on the daily unliquidated balance of advance payments. The interest is computed at the higher of two rates: either the published prime rate of the financial institution holding the special bank account, or the rate established semiannually by the Secretary of the Treasury.

Interest-free advance payments may be authorized by the agency head or delegate for contracts with nonprofit education or research institutions (such as demographic surveys or research studies), to operate Government-owned facilities, or with state or local government (on a cost-reimbursement basis). If a contract provides interest-free advance payments, the contracting officer may require the contractor to charge interest on advances or down-payments to subcontractors and then credit the Government for the amount. Interest is also allowed on advance payments to acquire property for Government ownership, if in combination with supply (sub)contracts. Interest charges are not allowed for cost-reimbursement contracts.

If advance payments are approved, the contracting officer provides for a paramount lien in favor of the Government to cover deliverable supplies, any credit balance for advance payments, and property that the contractor acquires for contract performance to which the Government has valid title. The agency may waive the need to deposit the advances in a special account and the countersignature requirement due to the contractor's financial strength, good performance record and minimal history of cost disallowances.

DFARS 232.404

These requirements do not apply to advertisements in high school and college publications for military recruitment efforts when the contract cost does not exceed the micro-purchase threshold.

DFARS 232.470

An advance payment pool agreement is a means of financing the performance of more than one contract held by a single contractor. It is especially convenient for the financing of cost-type contracts with nonprofit educational or research institutions for experimental or research and development work when several contracts require financing by advance payments. When appropriate, pooled advance payments may also be used to finance other types of contracts held by a single contractor. They may be established without regard to the number of appropriations involved, to finance contracts for one or more department(s) or contracting activity(ies) or in addition to any other advance payment pool agreement at a single contractor location when it is more convenient or otherwise preferable to have more than one agreement.

Contract Clauses

FAR 52.232-12, Advance Payments. Use the clause with its Alternate I to waive the countersignature requirement. Use the clause with its Alternate II for a cost-reimbursement contract. Use the clause with its Alternate III to use a more rapid liquidation. Use the clause with its Alternate IV for advance payments at no interest. Use the clause with its Alternate V if the requirement for a special account is eliminated.

DFARS 252.232-7000, Advance Payment Pool, if subject to the terms of an advance payment pool agreement with a nonprofit organization or educational institution. Normally, use the clause in all cost reimbursement type contracts with the organization or institution.

DFARS 252.232-7005, Reimbursement of Subcontractor Advance Payments—DoD Pilot Mentor-Protégé Program, when advance payments will be provided by the contractor to a subcontractor pursuant to an approved mentor-protégé agreement.

5.14.9 Contract Debts

FAR 32.6

Contract debts are amounts paid to or due from a contractor who is not entitled to them under the terms and conditions of the contract. They include:

- billing and price reductions due to price redetermination or defective cost or pricing data;
- breach of contract obligations for contract financing or GFP;
- damages or excess costs related to defaults;
- deficiencies in quality;
- delinquency in contractor payments for deferred or postponed collections;
- duplicate or erroneous payments;
- errors in quantity or billing;
- financing payments determined to be in excess of the contract limitation;
- Government expense of correcting defects;
- increased financing payment liquidation rates;
- overpayments disclosed by quarterly statements under price redetermination or incentive contracts;
- price adjustments due to CAS noncompliances or changes in cost accounting practices;
- reimbursing Government protest costs; and
- reinspection costs for nonconforming supplies or services.

The contracting officer demands repayment of any contractor debts (unless due to payment office error) because (s)he is not allowed to offset the debt amount against future payments. The payment office collects any contract debts, plus any duplicate and erroneous payments, and authorizes debt liquidation per agency procedures.

For debts resulting from specific contract clause provisions, the contracting officer notifies the contractor that payment should be made promptly, and that interest is due in accordance with the terms of the contract. Interest is computed from the date specified in the applicable contract clause until repayment by the contractor. The interest rate is specified in the applicable contract clause. However, for a debt arising from a price reduction for defective pricing or specified in a CAS clause in the contract, interest is computed from the date of overpayment by the Government until repayment by the contractor at the underpayment rate established by the Secretary of the Treasury, for the periods affected.

Additional interest charges usually apply to any debt unpaid after 30 days from the issuance of a demand. If the debt remains unpaid, the contracting officer issues a final decision by certified mail, return receipt requested, and a copy to the payment office. The payment office will then begin to withhold payments. If the debt continues beyond 180 days, it is referred to the Department of the Treasury for collection.

Each agency has an official authorized to grant deferment or installation payments; the contracting officer does not have this authority. Such a request might be granted if the contractor cannot pay in full at once or is deemed essential to the national defense. If the request is granted, a payment schedule is required, including interest, along with periodic financial reviews. For debts under $100,000 (excluding interest), the designated agency official may compromise the debt, though most agencies do not authorize contracting officers to do so.

In contrast, an equitable interest credit is applied when the:

- amount of debt initially determined is subsequently reduced through appeal;
- amount collected by the Government exceeds that assessed on appeal under the Disputes Clause;
- collection procedures result in over-collection of the debt due; or
- Government unduly delayed payments to the contractor during the period to which the interest charge applied (unless an interest penalty was paid for late payment).

DFARS 232.611

OUSD(AT&L) may exempt contracts (in exceptional circumstances) from administrative interest charges. Other exceptions are contracts for instructions of military or ROTC personnel at civilian schools and colleges, basic agreements with telephone companies for communications services and facilities, and transportation contracts with common carriers.

DFARS 232.71

The Internal Revenue Service is authorized to levy up to 100 percent of all payments made under a DoD contract, up to the amount of the tax debt. The contractor must promptly notify the contracting officer when a levy may result in an inability to perform the contract and advise the contracting officer whether the inability to perform may adversely affect national security. The contracting officer promptly notifies the DPAP when the contractor's inability to perform will adversely affect national security or will result in significant additional costs to the Government.

Solicitation Provisions and Contract Clauses

FAR 52.232-17, Interest, if:

- at or below the simplified acquisition threshold;
- for paid advertisements;
- with a foreign government or instrumentality;
- with a State or local government or instrumentality;
- with Government agencies; or
- without any provision for profit or fee with a nonprofit organization.

DFARS 252.232-7010, Levies on Contract Payments.

5.14.10 Contract Funding

FAR 32.7

Per the Anti-Deficiency Act, no Government employee may create or authorize an obligation in excess of the funds available, or in advance of appropriations.[59] Before signing a contract, the contracting officer obtains written assurance that adequate funds are available, or else conditions the contract upon availability of funds. This assurance is in the form of a financial accounting data sheet which specifies the budgeted allocation and other financial details, including amount obligated, and is attached as the last page of the contract or modification.

Similarly, a financial accounting data addendum sheet is attached to the procurement request. It includes the budgetary data, but of course lacks any obligated amount. Note that when *bulk funding* is used, the contracting officer receives a block of funds to assign against several awards for a specified purpose and period of time, but must still track all awards to ensure that the total amount of obligations does not exceed the total amount funded.

The contracting officer may initiate a contract action to be funded in the new fiscal year (before funds are available) for operation and maintenance or for continuing services (e.g., rentals, utilities, and supply items not financed by stock funds) necessary for normal operations and consistently covered in the past by appropriated funds. However, the Government may not accept supplies or services under a contract conditioned upon the availability of funds until the funds are actually available.

A one-year indefinite-quantity or requirements contract for services funded by annual appropriations may extend into the next fiscal year if any specified minimum quantities will be ordered in the current fiscal year. Likewise, a contract funded by annual appropriations may not cross fiscal years except under statutory authorization or when the contract calls for an end product that cannot be subdivided for separate performance in each fiscal year (e.g., expert or consultant services). An agency may contract, exercise an option or place an order for severable services that begin in one fiscal year and end in the next fiscal year if the period of the award does not exceed 12 months. In this case, funds for the initial fiscal year may cover the total amount.

If the contract is limited in funds and the contractor approaches the funding limit (normally if 75 percent of the ceiling will be reached within the next 60 days), the contracting officer must notify the contractor in writing that the contract is terminated or will not be further funded, or else the specific amount of additional funds allotted or the estimated increased cost. If the Government is still considering a funding increase, it must so notify the contractor, in which case the contractor is free to stop work when funding ends or work further only at his own risk.

Funding instability is a serious problem for major systems acquisition professionals. Three ways a contracting officer can mitigate funding instability are by using Cost As an Independent Variable, multiyear procurement authority and priced options.

Some supplies or services must be acquired subject to supplier license agreements, such as computer software and services. Many of these agreements contain indemnification clauses that conflict with Federal law and could violate the Anti-Deficiency Act. FAR 52.232-22 is intended to avoid this problem by expressly voiding such an agreement.

DFARS 232.7

A fixed-price contract may be incrementally funded only if the contract or any exercised option is for severable services, does not exceed one year in length and is incrementally funded using funds available (unexpired) as of the date the funds are obligated. If the contract uses funds available from multiple (two or more) fiscal years, it may be incrementally funded if using research and development appropriations or Congress has otherwise authorized incremental funding. An incrementally funded fixed-price contract will be fully funded as soon as funds are available.

Per 10 U.S.C. 2410a, the contracting officer may enter into a contract, exercise an option or place an order for severable services for a period that begins in one fiscal year and ends in the next fiscal year if the period of performance does not exceed one year.

Upon receipt of the contractor's notice, the contracting officer promptly provides written notice to the contractor that the Government will (or is considering to) allot additional funds for continued performance (while increasing the Government's limitation of obligation in a specified amount), or else terminate the contract. If additional funds are allotted, the contracting officer must also indicate whether the contractor is entitled by the contract terms to stop work when the Government's limitation of obligation is reached and that any costs expended beyond the Government's limitation of obligation are at the contractor's risk.

Upon learning that the contract will receive no further funds, the contracting officer promptly gives the contractor written notice of the Government's decision and terminate for the convenience of the Government. Therefore, sufficient funds must be allotted to the contract to cover the total amount payable to the contractor in the event of termination for the convenience.

Solicitation Provisions and Contract Clauses

FAR 52.232.39, Unenforceability of Unauthorized Obligations, in all solicitations and contracts.

DFARS 252.232-7007, Limitation of Government's Obligation, in solicitations and resultant incrementally funded fixed-price contracts. The contracting officer may reduce the contractor's notification period in paragraph (c) of the clause from its default value of 90 days.

Contract Clauses

FAR 52.232-18, Availability of Funds, if the contract will be chargeable to next fiscal year's funds and contract action will initiate before availability.

FAR 52.232-19, Availability of Funds for the Next Fiscal Year, if a one-year indefinite-quantity or requirements contract for services is contemplated and the contract is funded annually and will extend beyond the initial fiscal year.

FAR 52.232-20, Limitation of Cost, for a fully funded cost-reimbursement contract.

FAR 52.232-22, Limitation of Funds, for an incrementally funded cost-reimbursement contract.

5.14.11 Assignment of Claims

FAR 32.8

Under the Assignment of Claims Act, a contractor may assign funds due under a contract[60] if the:

- assignee sends a written notice of assignment to the contracting officer, bond surety and disbursing officer;
- assignment covers all unpaid amounts due under the contract;
- assignment is made only to one bank or other financing institution (if multiple parties finance the contract, only one party may be their agent or trustee) without further assignment;
- contract does not prohibit the assignment; or
- contract specifies payments aggregating $1,000 or more.

No payments to the assignee may be recovered due to contractor liability to the Government. Assignments can be reassigned unless prohibited if it is not in the Government's best interest. The Government may apply any liability against payments due, especially if the assignee has not made a loan or commitment to do so, or if the amount due on the contract exceeds the loan amount made or expected. Nonetheless, a no-setoff provision can be placed in the contract (which requires a determination by the head of the agency due to national defense or emergency and publication in the Federal Register). A no-setoff provision applies for any contractor liability to the Government, such as fines or penalties, payroll withholds or taxes payable. Once these obligations are satisfied, any balance due under the contract may be paid if the assignment is released by the assignee.

DFARS 232.8

Only contracts for personal services may prohibit the assignment of claims. DDP has determined that a need exists for DoD to agree not to reduce or set off any money due or to become due under the contract when the proceeds have been assigned in accordance with the Assignment of Claims provision of the contract. Nevertheless, if departments/agencies decide it is in the Government's interest, or if the contracting officer determines that an offeror is significantly indebted, they may exclude the no-setoff commitment.

The assignee sends a true copy of the instrument of assignment and an original and three copies of the notice of assignment to each of the ACO, sureties, if any, and disbursing officer of the payment office (who only needs one copy of the notice of assignment).

Contract Clauses

FAR 52.232-23, Assignment of Claims, if expected to exceed the micro-purchase threshold, unless the contract will prohibit the assignment of claims. Use the clause with its Alternate I if no-setoff commitment has been authorized.

FAR 52.232-24, Prohibition of Assignment of Claims, where in the Government's interest.

Solicitation Provision and Contract Clause

DFARS 252.232-7008, Assignment of Claims (Overseas), instead of FAR 52.232-23, Assignment of Claims, when contract performance will be in a foreign country. Use Alternate I if using FAR 52.232-23.

5.14.12 Prompt Payment

FAR 32.9

The *due date* to pay an invoice payment is the 30th day after either the billing office receives a proper invoice from the contractor or Government acceptance of supplies or services, whichever is later. For a final invoice after contract settlement, the time for acceptance begins on the effective date of the settlement. The due date for cost-reimbursement contracts for services is 30 days after receipt of a proper invoice, provided that some work has been done. For food products, payment must be made not later than the seventh day after delivery for meat or fish, and the tenth day for perishable agricultural commodities or dairy products.

To compute an interest penalty due to the contractor, Government acceptancc is deemed to occur on the 7th day after the contractor delivers supplies or performs services, unless there is a disagreement over quality, quantity or contractor compliance. If actual acceptance occurs within this timeframe, the Government bases the determination of an interest penalty on the actual date of acceptance. The contracting officer may specify in the contract a longer period to inspect and test the supplies furnished or to evaluate the services performed (except for commercial items).

For construction contracts, the due date for making progress payments is 14 days after the designated billing office receives a proper payment request. The due date for payment of Government reserves is 30 days after approval by the contracting officer for release (or else as specified in the contract) based on satisfactory progress in contractor performance.

If the contractor owes interest on unearned amounts, the Government recovers this interest from subsequent payments to the contractor, which reverts to the United States Treasury.

When a discount for prompt payment is taken, the designated payment office will pay the contractor as close as possible to, but not later than, the end of the discount period. The payment office pays an interest penalty automatically, without request from the contractor, when all of the following conditions have been met:

- billing officer received a proper invoice;
- designated payment office paid the contractor after the due date;
- Government processed a receiving report authorizing payment, and there was no disagreement over quantity, quality, or contractor compliance;
- Government takes a discount for prompt payment improperly;
- interim payment on a cost-reimbursement contracts for services is made more than 30 days after the designated billing office receives a proper invoice; and

- payment amount for a final invoice is not subject to further contract settlement action.

DFARS 232.9

Prompt payments do not apply in emergency or contingency operations, nor when hazardous substance release has occurred or is threatened and the head of the contracting activity has determined that conditions exist that limit normal business operations and payments will be made upon receiving documentation (i.e., contract, invoice, and receiving report) from the operational area. These limitations could include:

- documents received in support of payment requests and shipments require language translations that cannot be performed and documented within normal business processing times.
- foreign vendors are not familiar with or do not understand DoD contract requirements (i.e., proper invoice, receiving documentation, and contracting terms);
- military mission priorities override the availability of appropriately skilled personnel in support of back-office operations;
- mobility impairments and security concerns restrict free movement of personnel and documents necessary for timely processing;
- support infrastructure, hardware, communications capabilities, and bandwidth are not consistently available such that normal business operations can be carried out; and
- support resources, facilities, and banking needs are not consistently available for use as necessary in carrying out normal business operations.

If the head of the contracting activity determines that the operational area has stabilized, (s)he will issue a contract modification to each contractor performing in the operational area under review. The modification deletes DFARS 252.232-7011 and activates the applicable FAR Prompt Payment clause in the contract. If the head of the contracting activity subsequently determines that the operational area has destabilized, (s)he must determine that conditions exist that limit normal business operations. The contracting officer will then issue a contract modification to reactivate the clause.

Usually, Government acceptance or approval can occur within the seven-day constructive acceptance period specified in the Prompt Payment clauses. Construction progress payments can, in most cases, be made within the 14-day period allowed by FAR 52.232-37, Prompt Payment for Construction Contracts. While the contracting officer may specify a longer period, such change should be coordinated with the Government offices responsible for acceptance or approval and for payment. Reasons for specifying a longer period include but are not limited to inspection or testing requirements, nature of the work or supplies or services, resources available at the acceptance activity, and shipping and acceptance terms. A constructive acceptance period of less than 14 days is not authorized. Generally, the contracting officer inserts the standard due date of 14 days for interim payments on cost-reimbursement contracts for services in the clause at FAR 52.232-25, Prompt Payment, when using the clause with its Alternate I.

The restrictions on early payment do not apply to invoice payments made to small business concerns. However, contractors shall not be entitled to interest penalties if the Government fails to make early payment.

Solicitation Provision and Contract Clause

DFARS 252.232-7011, Payments in Support of Emergencies and Contingency Operations. Use with either the approved Payment clause or FAR 52.212-4, Contract Terms and Conditions—Commercial Items.

Contract Clauses

FAR 52.232-25, Prompt Payment, for commercial items or when payment terms and late payment penalties are established by another governmental authority (e.g., tariffs). Use the clause with its Alternate I if the contract is a cost-reimbursement contract for services.

FAR 52.232-26, Prompt Payment for Fixed-Price Architect-Engineer Contracts.

FAR 52.232-27, Prompt Payment for Construction Contracts.

5.14.13 Electronic Funds Transfer (EFT)

FAR 32.11

The Government provides all contract payments through EFT unless:

- a contract is paid in foreign currency;
- for contingency or emergency operations;
- it would compromise classified information;
- the agency does not expect to make multiple payments to the recipient within a year;
- the payment is to a location outside the United States or Puerto Rico;
- the payment office loses the ability to release payment by EFT;

- there is only one source of supply or service and the Government would be seriously injured without using another payment method; or
- urgency dictates another payment method.

A Government-wide commercial purchase card charge authorizes a third-party financial institution that issued the purchase card to immediately pay the contractor. The Government reimburses the third party at a later date. The contract identifies the third party and the particular purchase card to be used but does not cite the purchase card account number, which is provided separately to the contractor to ensure privacy. If the payment exceeds the micro-purchase threshold, the contracting officer must first consult SAM for any delinquent contractor debt subject to collection.

DFARS 232.70

Contractors submit payment requests and receiving reports in electronic form via Wide Area WorkFlow, except for:

- classified contracts or purchases when electronic submission and processing of payment requests could compromise the safeguarding of classified information or national security;
- contracts awarded by deployed contracting officers in the course of military operations such as, contingency, humanitarian, or peacekeeping operations or responses to natural disasters or national or civil emergencies, when access to the Wide Area WorkFlow by those contractors is not feasible;
- purchases to support unusual or compelling needs of the type described in FAR 6.302-2, when access to Wide Area WorkFlow by those contractors is not feasible;
- when DoD is unable to receive payment requests or provide acceptance in electronic form; and
- when the ACO has determined, in writing, that electronic submission would be unduly burdensome to the contractor and furnishes a copy of the determination to their Senior Procurement Executive.

When the Government-wide commercial purchase card is used as the method of payment, only submission of the receiving report in electronic form is required.

DoD officials receiving payment requests in electronic form shall process the payment requests in electronic form. When payment requests and receiving reports will not be submitted in electronic form, they should be submitted by facsimile or conventional mail.

For payment of commercial transportation services provided under a Government rate tender or a contract for transportation services, the use of a

DoD-approved electronic third-party payment system or other exempted vendor payment/invoicing system (e.g., PowerTrack, Transportation Financial Management System, and Cargo and Billing System) is permitted.

For submitting and processing payment requests and receiving reports for rendered health care services, use of TRICARE Encounter Data System as the electronic format is permitted.

Solicitation Provisions and Contract Clauses

DFARS 252.232-7003, Electronic Submission of Payment Requests and Receiving Reports.

DFARS 252.232-7006, Wide Area WorkFlow Payment Instructions, when the WorkFlow process is used for payment requests.

DFARS 252.232-7009, Mandatory Payment by Government-wide Commercial Purchase Card, when placing orders or calls valued at or below the micro-purchase threshold is anticipated and payment by Government-wide commercial purchase card is required for these orders or calls.

Contract Clauses

FAR 52.232-33, Payment by Electronic Funds Transfer—Central Contractor Registration, unless payment is made through a third-party arrangement.

FAR 52.232-34, Payment by Electronic Funds Transfer—Other than Central Contractor Registration, if a nondomestic EFT mechanism is used and identified in the contract, or if the contractor is not required to be enrolled in SAM.

FAR 52.232-35, Designation of Office for Government Receipt of Electronic Funds Transfer Information, if EFT information is to be submitted to other than the payment office in accordance with agency procedures.

FAR 52.232-36, Payment by Third Party, if payment is made by a charge to a Government account with a third party such as a Government-wide commercial purchase card.

FAR 52.232-37, Multiple Payment Arrangements, if the contract or agreement includes delivery orders and the ordering office will designate the method of payment for individual orders.

FAR 52.232-38, Submission of Electronic Funds Transfer Information with Offer, if FAR 52.232-34 is included, a nondomestic EFT is used and an offeror is required to submit EFT information prior to award.

5.15 PAST PERFORMANCE INFORMATION

FAR 42.15

Past performance information for future source selection purposes regards a contractor's actions under previously awarded contracts. It includes the contractor's record of:

- accurate billings;
- adherence to contract schedules, including the administrative aspects of performance;
- commitment to customer satisfaction;
- conforming to contract requirements and to standards of good workmanship;
- forecasting and controlling costs;
- integrity and business ethics;
- performance to achieve small business subcontracting goals (excluding awards to NIB or SourceAmerica);
- personnel knowledge and experience;
- quality of service;
- reasonable and cooperative behavior;
- reliability;
- responsiveness to customer direction;
- subcontract management; and
- timely submission of reports.

Upon contract completion, the COR and contracting officer complete a Past Performance survey for use on future proposal evaluations. Past performance evaluations are also prepared for each construction contract of $750,000 or more (or less if desired). Evaluations are also done for each construction contract terminated for default, regardless of contract value. The same principles apply to architect-engineer services contracts of $35,000 or more.

Past performance evaluations are prepared once the work under the contract or order is completed. Interim evaluations are prepared annually (or more often if specified by the agency) to provide current information for contracts or orders whose period of performance (including options) exceeds one year. The content of the evaluations is tailored to contract complexity, complexity, and size. Agencies evaluate contractor performance for each contract or order exceeding the simplified acquisition threshold, (but not for firm-fixed-price or fixed-price with economic price adjustment arrangements). Agencies will assess cost control, management, quality of product or service, schedule and timeliness, and small business subcontracting. They may also consider any negative findings (e.g., defective cost or pricing data, failure to meet contractual reporting requirements, late payments to subcontractors, suspension and debarments, tax delinquency, terminations, trafficking violations, etc.).

Each factor is rated on a five-point scale (exceptional, very good, satisfactory, marginal, and unsatisfactory). Incentive and award fee data must be entered into CPARS, which will transmit the data to PPIRS. The contractor receives a draft copy of the evaluation and has 14 days to review and rebut the data. Any disagreements must be resolved at a level above the contracting officer. Agencies use the PPIRS information for any contract completed within the past three years (six for construction and architect-engineer contracts).

5.16 CONTRACT CHANGES/MODIFICATIONS

5.16.1 Modifications

FAR 43.1

Only contracting officers acting within the scope of their authority may execute contract modifications on behalf of the Government. No other Government personnel may direct or encourage the contractor to perform additional work, or create the impression that they have authority to bind the Government.

Contract modifications are normally priced before their execution unless this would adversely affect the interest of the Government. Otherwise, a ceiling price is negotiated.

Contract modifications may be unilateral or bilateral. A *unilateral* modification is signed only by the contracting officer. It covers administrative changes that do not affect the substantive rights of the parties (e.g., a change in the paying office or appropriation data), change orders and termination notices.

A *bilateral* modification, also known as a *supplemental agreement*, is signed by both the contractor and the contracting officer. It covers negotiated equitable adjustments due to the issuance of a change order, definitizes letter contracts, and reflects agreements of the parties that modify the terms of contracts. These instruments may include a not-to-exceed price that caps contractor expenditures while price negotiations are underway. A not-to-exceed clause can also be used in a cost-reimbursement contract to limit a particular cost element, such as material or travel.

The *effective date* is when the modification or amendment goes into force. For a solicitation amendment, change order or administrative change, the effective date is the issue date of the document. For a supplemental agreement, the effective date is the date agreed upon by the contracting parties. For a modification that confirms a termination for the convenience of the Government, the effective date of the confirming notice is the same as the effective date of the initial notice. For a modification converting a termination for default to a termination for the convenience, the effective date is the same as that for the termination for default. The same dating logic applies to a letter determination of the amount due in settlement of a contract termination for convenience.

Contract Clause

FAR 52.243-7, Notification of Changes, in negotiated research and development or supply contracts to acquire major weapon systems or subsystems. If the contract amount is expected to be less than $1 million, the clause is used only if the contracting officer anticipates that the contractor may allege that the Government has effected changes not identified in writing and signed by the contracting officer.

5.16.2 Change Orders

FAR 43.2

Government contracts contain a Changes clause that permits the contracting officer to make unilateral changes within the general scope of the contract by issuing a Standard Form 30 to modify the contract. Subject matter for changes includes:

- contract period;
- delivery point or rate;
- price;
- provision of an existing contract;
- quantity; or
- specifications.

The contractor continues performance of the contract as changed, except that in cost-reimbursement or incrementally funded contracts the contractor is not obligated to continue performance or incur costs beyond the limits established in the Limitation of Cost or Limitation of Funds clause. This allows the parties to plan a course of action in case additional funds are not forthcoming. The contractor files a claim for any price adjustment within 30 days, and can also claim in writing that the change is out-of-scope for the contract.

Although contractor accounting systems are seldom designed to segregate the costs of performing changed work, the contractor must still be prepared to revise their accounting procedures to comply with the Change Order Accounting clause. These include nonrecurring costs (e.g., engineering labor and obsolete or reperformed work), distinct new work caused by the change order (e.g., prototypes or backfit or retrofit kits), and recurring work (e.g., labor and material).

Price changes need not be increases. Price decreases do occur as a result of relaxing specifications, level of effort or delivery time. These are known as *deductive changes*.

When change orders are not forward priced, they require a supplemental agreement reflecting the equitable adjustment. If an equitable adjustment in the contract price and/or delivery terms can be agreed upon in advance, only a supplemental agreement need be issued. Changes issued pursuant to a clause giving the Government a unilateral right to make a change (e.g., an option clause) require only one document, as do administrative changes.

A change is *in-scope* if it affects drawings, packing, shipment, specifications, or time/place of delivery or performance. It must be reasonable to conclude that the subject matter was within the contemplation of the parties when the contract was executed. Otherwise, it is out-of-scope and requires a negotiated settlement with the contractor, which could result in a price increase. The contractor should always verify direction that represents potential change with the contracting officer. Such a change can include a direction by the contracting officer to accelerate performance (known as *constructive acceleration*) when a schedule slip is due to an excusable delay.

Changes are priced out using specific costs to be incurred in performance, rather than after-the-fact costs or total cost of performance. Although interest is generally unallowable for ongoing business operations, a contractor may recover interest cost to a third party on borrowing when necessary to process a change order. This includes an imputed interest expense for an unfunded unilateral change or wrongful withholding of progress payments.

Constructive changes occur where the Government impacts the contract by an oral or written act without following procedures. This could occur if the contracting officer omitted an action or an authorized official issued a directive. An informal requirement to perform produces a formal requirement.

The *cardinal change* doctrine has therefore been created to provide a remedy when contractors are directed by the Government to perform work which is outside the general scope of the contract. A cardinal change is not covered by the Changes clause because it fundamentally alters the work from that bargained for when the contract was awarded. Deciding if a change is within the general scope of the contract is affected by the character and magnitude of the change, and its cumulative effect upon the project (known as the Wunderlich rule *after the court case which gave rise to this judicial ruling*).[61] For example, a change incorporating extensive redesign effort due to defective specifications is beyond the scope of the contract and therefore constitutes a cardinal change.

DFARS 243.204

Unpriced change orders with an estimated value exceeding $5 million have special rules. Unpriced change orders for foreign military sales and special access programs are not subject to this subsection, but the contracting officer will apply the policy and procedures to them to the maximum extent practicable. If not, the contracting officer shall provide prior notice, through agency channels, to the Deputy Director, DPAP (Contract Policy and International Contracting).

Most unpriced change orders include a not-to-exceed price. Unpriced change orders contain definitization schedules within the earlier of 180 days after issuance of the change order (this date may be extended but may not exceed the date that is 180 days after the contractor submits a qualifying proposal) or the date on which the amount of funds obligated under the change order is equal to more than 50 percent of the not-to-exceed price. If the contractor does not submit a timely qualifying proposal, the contracting officer may suspend or reduce progress payments. These restrictions do not apply to unpriced change orders for the purchase of initial spares.

The Government shall not obligate more than 50 percent of the not-to-exceed price before definitization. However, if a contractor submits a qualifying proposal before 50 percent of the not-to-exceed price has been obligated by the Government, the limitation on obligations before definitization may be increased to no more than 75 percent. These limitations do not apply to unpriced change orders for ship construction and ship repair or purchase of initial spares. The head of the agency may waive the above limitations if deemed necessary to support a contingency operation or a humanitarian or peacekeeping operation.

When the final price of an unpriced change order is negotiated after a substantial portion of the required performance has been completed, the head of the contracting activity ensures the allowed profit reflects any incurred costs and reduced cost risk to the contractor for costs incurred during contract performance before final price negotiation and of the remainder of the contract.

A request for equitable adjustment to contract terms that exceeds the simplified acquisition threshold may not be paid unless the contractor certifies the request.

Solicitation Provisions and Contract Clauses

FAR 52.243-1, Changes—Fixed-Price, when a fixed-price contract for supplies is contemplated. Use the clause with its Alternate I if the requirement is for services, other than architect-engineer or other professional services, and no supplies will be furnished. Use the clause with its Alternate II if the requirement is for services (other than architect-engineer services, research and development, or transportation) and supplies are to be furnished. Use the clause with its Alternate III if the requirement is for architect-engineer or other professional services. Use the clause with its Alternate IV if the requirement is for transportation services. Use the clause with its Alternate V if it is desired to include the clause in solicitations and contracts when a research and development contract is contemplated.

FAR 52.243-2, Changes—Cost-Reimbursement, when a cost-reimbursement contract for supplies is contemplated. Use the clause with its Alternate I for services and no supplies will be furnished. Use the clause with its Alternate II for services and supplies are to be furnished. Use the clause with its Alternate III for construction. Use the clause with its Alternate V for research and development. Note that Alternate IV is not in use.

FAR 52.243-3, Changes—Time-and-Materials or Labor-Hours, when a time-and-materials or labor-hour contract is contemplated.

FAR 52.243-4, Changes, to dismantle, demolish or remove improvements; and fixed-price construction contracts in excess of the simplified acquisition threshold.

FAR 52.243-5, Changes and Changed Conditions, for construction below the simplified acquisition threshold.

FAR 52.243-6, Change Order Accounting, for supply and research and development contracts of significant technical complexity, if numerous changes are anticipated. The clause may be used in construction contracts, too.

DFARS 252.243-7001, Pricing of Contract Modifications, when anticipating and using a fixed-price type contract.

DFARS 252.243-7002, Requests for Equitable Adjustment, when estimated to exceed the simplified acquisition threshold.

5.16.3 Delays and Suspensions

FAR 42.13

If performance is late, the contracting officer assesses actual need and the reason for lateness, such as:

- contractor's past performance;
- contractor's potential to deliver to a revised schedule;
- cost;
- excusability;
- impact on other Government programs;
- need for additional testing or material; or
- party of cause—Government or contractor.

Based on the concept of *force majeure*, delay is excusable if due to acts of God or nature, external labor strikes or Government action. The contractor is protected from default, excess reprocurement costs or liquidated damages.

If corrective action is necessary however, the Government has several avenues available. A *suspension of work* under an architect-engineer or construction contract may be ordered by the contracting officer for a reasonable period of time. Otherwise, the contractor may submit a written claim for increased cost of performance, excluding profit.

Stop-work orders may be used in negotiated contracts if work stoppage may be required for reasons such as advancement in the state-of-the-art, production or engineering breakthroughs, or realignment of programs. Generally, a stop-work order will be issued only if advisable to suspend work pending a Government decision and a supplemental agreement is not feasible. Issuance of a stop-work order is approved at a level above the contracting officer. Stop-work orders are not used if a termination decision is made. As soon as feasible after a stop-work order is issued, the contracting officer should discuss the matter with the contractor and before its expiration, either cancel the stop-work order (subject to the same approvals as for its issuance), extend the period of the stop-work order if both parties agree by supplemental agreement, or terminate the contract.

Government Delay of Work provides for administrative settlement of contractor claims that arise from delays and interruptions in the contract work caused by the acts, or failures to act, of the contracting officer or authorized Government official. Settlement includes any cost impact (excluding profit) but not more than 20 days before notification, and any resultant delivery date adjustment.

Solicitation Provisions and Contract Clauses

FAR 52-242-14, Suspension of Work for fixed-price construction or architect-engineer services.

FAR 52.242-15, Stop-Work Order, for supplies, services or research and development. Use the clause with its Alternate I if a cost-reimbursement contract is contemplated.

FAR 52.242-17, Government Delay of Work, for supplies other than commercial or modified-commercial items. Use is optional for services or for commercial or modified-commercial items. This clause does not apply if another contract clause provides for an equitable adjustment because of the delay or interruption (e.g., the Changes clause).

5.16.4 Novation and Change-of-Name

FAR 42.12

A *novation agreement* is a three-way agreement between a contractor, successor in interest and the Government. The contractor guarantees contract performance, the successor is a transferee to assume all contractual obligations, and the Government is the buyer recognizing the roles of the other parties.

A contractor must request the contracting officer in writing to recognize a successor in interest to its contracts or a name change. The responsible contracting officer then notifies each contract administration office and contracting office affected by such a proposed agreement (with a list of all affected contracts) and requests submission of any comments or objections to the proposed transfer within 30 days after notification.

The request must include the:

- balance sheets of both parties, as evidence that security requirements have been met;
- certified copy of decision by board of directors and/or stockholders concurrence;
- consent of sureties;
- evidence of transferee's capability to perform;
- list of all affected contracts between transferor and Government (along with contract numbers and types, contracting office identity, dollar amounts, and remaining unpaid balances);
- purchase or sale agreement or memorandum of understanding; and
- transferee's certificate and articles of incorporation.

Upon receipt of the necessary information, the contracting officer determines whether it is in the Government's interest to recognize the proposed successor in interest on the basis of comments received and the proposed successor's responsibility and performance on prior Government contracts.

The novation agreement references any agreement between the transferor and transferee regarding the assumption of liabilities and obligations (e.g., CAS noncompliances, environmental cleanup costs, final overhead costs, or long-term incentive compensation plans). The guarantor may obtain a performance bond or else guarantees performance. Cost allocability provisions apply, except that a cutoff provision segregates government obligations before novation from those after. The Government does not pay cost increases due to the transfer.

Because 41 U.S.C. 15 prohibits transfer of Government contracts from the contractor to a third party, it may recognize a third party as the successor in interest to a Government contract due to transfer of all contractor assets or those assets involved in performing the contract. This would include incorporation of a proprietorship or partnership, sale of assets with assumption of liabilities, or transfer of assets due to a merger or corporate consolidation. A novation agreement is unnecessary when there is a change in the ownership due to a stock purchase without legal change in the contracting party or control of the assets.

If the contracting officer concurs with the successor, (s)he executes a novation agreement with the transferor and the transferee. It ordinarily provides that the transferee assumes all the transferor's obligations under the contract and waives all rights under the contract against the Government. The agreement also guarantees performance by the transferee (a performance bond may suffice).

If only a name change is involved and the Government's and contractor's rights and obligations remain unaffected, the parties merely execute an agreement to reflect the name change.

When it is in the Government's interest not to concur in the transfer of a contract from one company to another, the original contractor remains under contractual obligation to the Government, and the contract may be terminated for default if the original contractor cannot perform.

5.17 EXTRAORDINARY CONTRACT ACTIONS

FAR 50.1

Public Law 85-804 empowers the President to authorize agencies operating in connection with the national defense to enter into, amend and modify contracts, without regard to other provisions of law, whenever such action would facilitate the national defense. Requirements to implement Public Law 85-804's authority include that the action cannot obligate the Government to more than $35 million without notifying the Senate and House Committees on Armed Services in writing of the proposed obligation, and 60 days of continuous session of Congress have passed since the transmittal of such notification. The approving authority must find that the action will facilitate the national defense. The authority is vested within the Secretary of the Department but can be delegated to another official for actions up to $75,000. The contractor submits a written request for payment within six months after furnishing, or arranging to furnish, supplies or services in reliance upon an informal commitment, and the approving authority finds that, at the time the commitment was made, it was impracticable to use normal contracting procedures (a process known as *ratification*). The cost must be within the limits of the amounts appropriated and the statutory contract authorization. Other legal authority within the agency must be lacking or inadequate. The resultant contract must cite the law or executive order, the circumstances justifying the action, and states that the action will facilitate the national defense.

Indemnification agreements authorized by an agency head are not limited by appropriated amounts and do not require Congressional notification.

Public Law 85-804 is not authority for:

- awarding a cost-plus-a-percentage-of-cost contract;
- making a contract that violates existing law limiting profit or fees;

- providing for other than full and open competition; or
- waiving any bid bond, payment bond or performance bond required by law.

Indemnification is not normally available for any supply or service that has been, or could be, designated by DHS as a QATT. An exception occurs if the Secretary of Defense has determined that the exercise of authority under Executive Order 10789 is necessary for the timely and effective conduct of the U.S. military or intelligence activities.[62] Another exception would be if DHS has advised whether the use of the authority under the SAFETY Act would be appropriate and the Director of OMB has approved the exercise of authority under the Executive Order.

FAR 1-602.3 and 50.103-2

Under rare circumstances, the Government can amend a contract without consideration to ensure fairness and the national interest, such as when a loss under the contract will impair the contractor's ability to perform on an essential contract, or the contractor's continued operation as a source of supply is found to be essential to the national defense. The loss must be more than just lost profit—it must go to the heart of the contractor's ability to produce. When the Government action, while not creating any liability on the Government's part, increases performance cost and results in distress or a loss to the contractor, fairness may dictate the need to make some adjustment appropriate.

A contract may be amended or modified to correct or mitigate the effect of a mistake or ambiguity. This occurs when the contract does not clearly express the agreement as both parties understood it, the contractor made a mistake that should have been apparent to the contracting officer, or the parties made a mutual mistake as to a material fact.

Unauthorized (or *informal*) *commitments* occur when a firm responds to a Government official's written or oral instructions and delivers supplies or services in anticipation of compensation without a formal contract. The official must have the apparent authority to issue the instruction, but lack real authority (which should be a rare occurrence, since somebody has overstepped their authority). Again, fairness would dictate that the firm be paid a reasonable amount for expended effort. Only the head of the contracting activity can ratify an unauthorized commitment. The resulting contract must fulfill all requirements for properness as any other contract, including a fair and reasonable price and available funding at the time of the occurrence.

The contracting officer or other agency official will request the contractor to support any request to definitize an informal commitment with any of the following information:

- amounts withheld by the Government;
- analysis of the request's monetary elements, including how the actual or estimated dollar amount was determined and the effect of approval or denial on contractor profits before Federal income taxes;
- any obligations of the Government yet to be performed;
- contemporaneous affidavits, correspondence and memorandums;
- description of the contracts involved, dates of execution and amendments, items being acquired, price or prices, delivery schedules, and any relevant contract provisions;
- financial statements or cost analyses, preferably certified by a certified public accountant, to support the request's monetary elements;
- payments received, due and to become due, including advance and progress payments;
- persons connected with the contracts who have factual knowledge of the subject matter, including their names, offices or titles, addresses, and telephone numbers;
- steps taken to reduce losses and claims to a minimum;
- when work under the contracts or commitments began, progress made to date and the contractor's remaining obligations and expectations for completion; and
- why the subject matter cannot now, and could not at the time it arose, be addressed under the contract.

If the request involves possible amendment without consideration, and essentiality to the national defense is a factor, additional contractor information may be requested:

- any claims known or contemplated by the contractor against the Government involving the contracts;
- any tax refunds to date, and an estimate of those anticipated, for the period from the date of the first contract involved to the estimated completion date of the last contract involved;
- balance sheets, preferably certified by a certified public accountant, as of the request date for the contractor's fiscal year immediately preceding the date of the first contract, each subsequent fiscal year, and projected as of the completion date of all the contracts involved;
- course of events anticipated if the request is denied;
- efforts made to obtain funds from commercial sources to enable contract completion;
- estimate of the final price of the contracts, including changes, escalation and extras;

- estimated time required to complete each contract if the request is granted;
- estimated total profit or loss from other Government business and all other sources, from the date of the first contract involved to the estimated completion date of the last contract involved;
- estimated total profit or loss under the contracts at the estimated final contract price, broken down between profit or loss (both to date and at completion);
- factors causing the loss under the contracts involved;
- minimum amount the contractor needs as an amendment without consideration to enable contract completion, and the detailed basis for that amount;
- original breakdown of estimated costs (including contingency allowances) and profit;
- present estimate of total costs under the contracts involved, broken down between costs accrued to date and completion costs, and between costs paid and those owed; and
- salaries, bonuses, and other compensation paid or furnished to the principal officers or partners, and of all dividends and payments to stockholders in any form since the date of the first contract involved.

If the request involves possible amendment without consideration because of Government action, and essentiality to the national defense is not a factor, the Government may request, instead of the above, the precise Government action that the contractor considers to have caused a loss under the contract, with supporting evidence. The contractor will also be requested to furnish its original breakdown of estimated costs (including contingency allowances) and profit, and its estimated total loss under the contract, including that resulting specifically from the Government action.

The contractor must also include income statements for annual periods subsequent to the date of the first balance sheet. All statements must be consolidated and then broken down by affiliates. They show all transactions between the contractor and its affiliates, partners and stockholders, including loans to the contractor guaranteed by any stockholder or partner.

Contract Clauses

FAR 52.250-1, Indemnification Under Public Law 85-804, whenever the approving official determines that the contractor shall be indemnified against unusually hazardous or nuclear risks. Use the clause with its Alternate I in cost-reimbursement contracts.

5.18 DISPUTES

FAR 33.202

The Contract Disputes Act of 1978, as amended, establishes procedures and requirements to assert and resolve claims.[63] It does not apply to a foreign agency or government, or an international organization, if the agency head determines that application of the Act to the contract would not be in the public interest.

5.18.1 Claims

FAR 33.206

A contractor's allegation that it is entitled to rescission or reformation of its contract in order to correct or mitigate the effect of a mistake is treated as a claim under the Act. A contract may be reformed or rescinded by the contracting officer if the contractor would be entitled to such remedy or relief under the law of Federal contracts. The claim must be certified if it exceeds $50,000 ($150,000 for small businesses).

All issues are initially handled by the contracting officer until his/her final written decision is rendered. After that, the contractor can file suit in the Court of Claims. Defense contractors could also go to the Armed Services Board of Contract Appeals after the contracting officer's decision, and then go to the U.S. Claims Court if the Board does not concur with its claim. The parties may agree to an accelerated procedure which requires a hearing within six months of filing the claim. The contracting officer will compile a file of the contract and all relevant correspondence, affidavits, and final decision.[64]

Contractor claims are submitted in writing to the contracting officer for a decision within six years after accrual of a claim, unless the contracting parties agreed to a shorter time period.

When submitting any claim exceeding $100,000, contractors must certify to the following:

> I certify that the claim is made in good faith; that the supporting data are accurate and complete to the best of my knowledge and belief; that the amount requested accurately reflects the contract adjustment for which the contractor believes the Government is liable; and that I am duly authorized to certify the claim on behalf of the contractor.

This discourages submission of frivolous claims and encourages settlement. Certification is not required if the contracting officer renders a final decision without it—otherwise, a failure to certify precludes contractor recovery and judicial review. The Government pays interest at the rate fixed by the Treasury on a contractor's claim for the amount due from the date that the contracting officer receives the claim or payment otherwise would be due, whichever is later, until the date of payment.

The contracting officer issues the decision within 60 days after receiving a certified claim (if over $100,000) or written request for a decision (if not over $100,000). Any failure of the contracting officer to issue a decision within the required time periods is deemed a denial of the claim, and the contractor may appeal or file suit.

The contracting officer must respond to any claim with a final decision. An appeal must be submitted within 90 days from the date of receipt to the agency board of contract appeals, with a copy to the Contracting officer. The offeror may also bring action directly in the U.S. Court of Federal Claims within 12 months after date of receipt.

Any amount determined payable under the decision, less any portion already paid, is paid without awaiting contractor action as to appeal, without prejudice to the rights of either party.

Agencies may require a contractor to continue contract performance in accordance with the contracting officer's decision pending a final resolution of any claim arising under (or relating to) a contract clause, other than the Disputes clause.

Claims over $50,000 in value are entitled to interest payments from the Government. Similarly, fraudulent claims or those based on misrepresenting facts are subject to civil penalties.

Solicitation Provisions and Contract Clauses

FAR 52.233-1, Disputes, unless with a foreign government or international organization. Use the clause with its Alternate I if continued performance is necessary pending resolution of any claim arising under or relating to the contract. Use Alternate I of the clause when acquiring:

- aircraft;
- missile systems;
- naval vessels;
- related electronic systems;
- spacecraft and launch vehicles; or
- tracked combat vehicles.

Alternate I is also used when the contracting officer determines that continued performance is vital to the national security or public health and welfare, or when the head of the contracting activity determines that continued performance is necessary pending resolution of any claim that might arise under or be related to the contract.

FAR 52.233-4, Applicable Law for Breach of Contract Claim.

DFARS 252.233-7001, Choice of Law (Overseas), when contract performance will be outside the United States and its outlying areas, unless otherwise provided for in a government-to-government agreement.

5.18.2 Alternative Dispute Resolution

FAR 33.214

Alternative dispute resolution (ADR) is a procedure voluntarily used to resolve controversies by mutual consent (e.g., arbitration, conciliation, facilitation, fact-finding, mediation, mini-trials, and ombudsmen). This increases the opportunity for inexpensive and expeditious resolution. The parties must voluntarily agree to participate in the ADR process in lieu of formal litigation. Obviously, participation by officials of both parties with the authority to resolve the issue is necessary.

If either party rejects a request for ADR proceedings, it provides to the other party a written explanation citing specific reasons that ADR procedures are inappropriate for the resolution of the dispute. ADR procedures may be used whenever the contracting officer has authority to resolve the issue. If a claim has been submitted, ADR procedures may be applied to all or a portion of the claim. The claim must be certified if it exceeds $100,000. The contracting officer's decision is required within 60 days; however if above that dollar threshold the contracting officer can take longer upon notifying the contractor of the anticipated decision date. When ADR procedures are used after the contracting officer's final decision, the time limitations or procedural requirements to file an appeal of the contracting officer's final decision continue in effect and do not result in a reconsideration of the final decision.

Several possible procedures can be utilized to resolve disputes. A third party may become involved to facilitate a negotiated settlement. A mediator could be used to go one step farther and recommend a solution without imposing it. Attorneys could represent each party to derive a collaborative law settlement. Finally, voluntary arbitration can be invoked for a third party to impose a solution.

Unless required by law and specified in agency guidelines, a solicitation does not require arbitration as a condition of award. Contracting officers have flexibility to select the appropriate ADR procedure to resolve the issues in controversy as they arise. Any written agreement to use arbitration specifies a maximum award that may be issued by the arbitrator.

5.19 CONTRACT TERMINATION

5.19.1 Notification and Response

FAR 49.1

The contracting officer terminates contracts for default or convenience only in the Government's interest. The Government cannot terminate a contract merely to avoid anticipatory profits without a change in circumstances after award.[65] The contracting officer issues a no-cost settlement instead of a termination notice when the contractor will accept it, no GFP was furnished and no outstanding payments or debts are due to the Government. When the price of the undelivered balance of the contract is less than $5,000, the contract is not normally terminated for convenience, but rather allowed to run to completion.

The contracting officer issues a notice of termination by a written notice to the contractor via certified mail and return receipt, which cites the effective date and extent of termination, along with steps the contractor must take to minimize the impact on personnel. The Government will assign a termination contracting officer (TCO) to negotiate any settlement with the contractor, including a no-cost settlement if appropriate. The TCO may be the procuring or administrative contracting officer, or may be a specially designated individual. The procuring contracting officer will release of excess funds resulting from the termination unless this responsibility is specifically delegated to the TCO.

If the same item is under contract with both large and small business concerns and a partial termination for convenience is necessary with the balance of the effort still required, preference is given to the continuing performance of small business contracts over large business contracts, unless the chief of the contracting office determines that this is not in the Government's interest.

If in the best interest of the Government, and with the contractor's written consent, the contracting office may reinstate the terminated portion of a contract in whole or in part by amending the termination notice. Sometimes, in lieu of a termination, the Government will issue a stop work order to direct the contractor to suspend work on the affected portion of the contract and take steps to mitigate risk and liability of the parties. Such an order may cover all or only part of the work, which may be reinstated only by mutual agreement of the parties. It is good for 90 days unless the parties agree to a different time frame. The contractor must stop the designated work to minimize cost incurrence, and could negotiate an equitable adjustment to address any cost or schedule impact.

The notice and Termination for Convenience clause generally require that the contractor:

- advise the TCO of any special circumstances precluding the stoppage of work; otherwise stop work immediately on the terminated portion of the contract;
- continue performing any continued portion of the contract;
- dispose of termination inventory per TCO direction;
- notify the TCO in writing of any legal proceedings growing out of any subcontract or other commitment;
- protect and deliver property in which the Government has or may acquire an interest;
- settle outstanding liabilities and proposals;
- submit a complete settlement proposal and any request for an equitable adjustment for the continued portion, supported by evidence of any cost increase; and
- terminate all subcontracts thereunder.

The TCO will hold a conference with the contractor and plan to examine the settlement proposal of the prime contractor and subcontractors, referring each subcontractor settlement proposal of at least $100,000 to the audit agency for review and recommendations. The TCO will negotiate settlement with the contractor, and determine any elements that cannot be agreed on.

Within 30 days, the TCO shall recommend release of excess funds to the contracting officer (generally, no action is taken if this amount is below $1,000). When the contracting officer terminates a contract for commercial items for the Government's convenience, the contractor is paid a settlement calculated by either the percentage of the contract price reflecting the percentage of the work already performed, or else by multiplying the number of direct labor hours expended before the effective date of termination by the hourly rates(s). Such a contractor is not required to comply with the cost accounting standards or contract cost principles, nor is the Government allowed to audit the contractor's records solely because of the termination.

FAR does not prescribe a clause to cancel or terminate orders under communication service contracts with common carriers because special agency requirements apply to these services. An appropriate clause, however, may be prescribed at the agency level.

Solicitation Provisions and Contract Clauses

FAR 52.249-1, Termination for Convenience of the Government (Fixed-Price) (Short Form), if fixed-price and not expected to exceed the simplified acquisition threshold, except for architect-engineer services or research and development work with an educational or nonprofit institution on a nonprofit basis. Do not use this clause if the contract contains FAR 52.249-4, -12 or -14. Use the clause with its Alternate I if the contract is for demolition, dismantling or removal of improvements,

FAR 52.249-2, Termination for Convenience of the Government (Fixed-Price), if fixed-price and expected to exceed the simplified acquisition threshold. Do not use for dismantling and demolition contracts, or any exception cited under FAR 52.249-1. Use the clause with its Alternate I if the contract is for construction. Use the clause with its Alternate II if the contract is with a Government agency, foreign or domestic, and it is inappropriate to pay interest on excess partial payments. Use the clause with its Alternate III in contracts for construction, if desired.

FAR 52.249-3, Termination for Convenience of the Government (Dismantling, Demolition, or Removal of Improvements) if fixed-price to dismantle, demolish or remove improvements, and exceeding the simplified acquisition threshold. Use the clause with its Alternate I to contract with a Government agency, foreign or domestic, and it is not appropriate to pay interest on excess partial payments.

FAR 52.249-4, Termination for Convenience of the Government (Services) (Short Form), in fixed-price contracts for services where the successful offeror will not incur substantial charges to prepare for and execute the contract, without additional termination settlement charges.

FAR 52.249-5, Termination for the Convenience of the Government (Educational and Other Nonprofit Institutions), for research and development work with an educational or nonprofit institution without a fee or profit payment.

FAR 52.249-6, Termination (Cost Reimbursement), if cost-reimbursement, except for research and development with an educational or nonprofit institution on a no-fee basis. Use the clause with its Alternate I in construction contracts. Use the clause with its Alternates II and V in a contract with a Government agency, foreign or domestic, and the requirement to pay interest on excess partial payments is inappropriate, and then add Alternate III if the contact is for construction. Use the clause with its Alternate IV for a time-and-material or labor-hour contract.

FAR 52.249-7, Termination (Fixed-Price Architect-Engineer), for fixed-price architect-engineer services.

FAR 52.249-8, Default (Fixed-Price Supply and Service), if fixed-price and exceeding the simplified acquisition threshold. Use the clause with its Alternate I for transportation or related services.

FAR 52.249-9, Default (Fixed-Price Research and Development), for fixed-price research and development exceeding the simplified acquisition threshold, except those with educational or nonprofit institutions on a nonprofit basis.

FAR 52.249-10, Default (Fixed-Price Construction), if fixed-price exceeding the simplified acquisition threshold. Use the clause with its Alternate I if the contract is for demolition, dismantling or removal of improvements.

Use the clause with its Alternate II for a fixed-price contract for construction if the contract is to be awarded during a period of national emergency. Use the clause with its Alternate III for demolition, dismantling or removal of improvements during a period of national emergency.

FAR 52.249-12, Termination (Personal Services).

FAR 52.249-14, Excusable Delays, if cost-reimbursable for supplies, services, construction, and research and development, and in time-and-material and labor-hour contracts.

Contract Clause

DFARS 252.249-7000, Special Termination Costs, may be used in an incrementally funded contract when its use is approved by the agency head, the contract term is two years or more, the contract is estimated to exceed $25 million in RDT&E funding or total production investment in excess of $100 million, and adequate funds are available to cover the contingent reserve liability for special termination costs.

Insert in paragraph (c) a negotiated amount that represents their best estimate of the total special termination costs to which the contractor would be entitled. Consider substituting an alternate paragraph (c) when the contract covers an unusually long performance period or the contractor's cost risk associated with contingent special termination costs is expected to fluctuate extensively over the period of the contract. The alternate paragraph (c) should provide for periodic negotiation and adjustment of the amount reserved for special termination costs. Occasions for periodic adjustment may include the Government's incremental assignment of funds to the contract, the time when certain performance milestones are accomplished by the contractor, or other specific time periods agreed upon by the contracting officer and the contractor.

5.19.2 Settlement of Subcontracts

DFARS 249.7003

A prime contractor will need to notify any first-tier subcontractor over $700,000 that its prime contract has been terminated. In turn, the first-tier subcontractor must notify any lower-tier subcontractor over $150,000, which in turn must notify all its subcontracts over $150,000, and so on.

FAR 49.108

A subcontractor has no rights against the Government upon the termination of a prime contract, but may have rights against the prime contractor or its customer subcontractor. The prime contractor and each subcontractor must submit a *settlement proposal* to determine final pricing of their subcontract. A settlement proposal is considered a claim under the False Claims Act and is deducted from the gross settlement amounts payable for completed articles or work at the contract price. Deductions are not made to retain or dispose of termination inventory, nor for advance or partial payments. *Partial payments* are authorized to be made upon completion of a specified unit(s) being delivered and accepted under the contract. The term partial payment also applies to an approved termination claim prior to final settlement of the total termination claim.

Contractors settle with subcontractors following the same policies and principles as settling prime contracts. However, the basis and form of the subcontractor's settlement proposal need only be acceptable to the prime contractor or the next higher tier subcontractor. Each settlement requires accounting and other data sufficient for adequate review by the Government. Absent a court order, the Government will not pay the prime contractor for loss of anticipatory profits or consequential damages due to termination of a subcontract.

The TCO examines each subcontract settlement to determine its good faith, need and reasonableness, as well as allocability to the terminated portion of the contract. The TCO may, upon written request, give written authorization to the prime contractor to settle subcontracts in whole or in part without approval when the amount of settlement is $100,000 or less, if satisfied with the adequacy of the procedures used by the contractor to settle settlement proposals. Any termination inventory included in the settlement is disposed of as directed by the prime contractor, without TCO review or screening requirements. The TCO does not authorize subcontractors to settle with lower tier subcontractors, but may authorize a prime contractor to approve such a request.

The TCO treats any subcontractor judgment against a prime contractor as a cost of settling with the prime contractor, provided the subcontract contained a termination clause excluding payment of anticipatory profits or consequential damages. The prime contractor must have made reasonable efforts to settle with the subcontractor, and cooperated with the Government in defense of the court action.

The TCO may direct the prime contractor to assign to the Government all interests, rights and titles under any subcontract terminated because the prime contract was terminated. The Government also has the option to settle and pay any settlement proposal arising out of the termination of subcontracts when it is in the Government's interest. This could occur if a sole-source subcontractor faces a delay by the prime contractor in settlement or payment of the subcontractor's proposal that will jeopardize its financial position.

Contract Clause

DFARS 252.249-7002, Notification of Anticipated Contract Termination or Reduction.

5.19.3 Settlement Agreements

FAR 49.109 and .112

A *settlement agreement* is a contract modification settling all or a severable portion of a settlement proposal. The TCO executes a no-cost settlement agreement if the contractor has not incurred (or agrees to waive) costs for the terminated portion of the contract and no amounts are due the Government.

The TCO attempts to settle in one agreement all rights and liabilities of the parties under the contract or its terminated portion, rather than partial settlements for particular items of the prime contractor's settlement proposal. A partial settlement may be executed if the issues are clearly severable from other issues and partial settlement will not prejudice either party's interests in disposing of the unsettled part of the settlement proposal.

The TCO may negotiate jointly two or more termination settlement proposals of the same contractor under different contracts, even if with different contracting offices or agencies. The resulting settlement may lead to one agreement covering all contracts involved, or a separate agreement for each contract involved.

If the contractor and TCO cannot agree on a termination settlement, or if a settlement proposal is not submitted within the period required by the termination clause, the TCO gives the contractor at least 15 days' notice by certified mail to submit written evidence substantiating the amount previously proposed. The contractor has the burden of establishing proof satisfactory to the TCO of the amount proposed (e.g., affidavits, audit reports, vouchers, verified transcripts of books of account). The TCO may request the contractor to submit additional documents and data. After reviewing the information available, the TCO determines the amount due and transmits a copy by certified mail (return receipt requested) to the contractor. The contractor may appeal, under the Disputes clause, any settlement by determination, except if it failed to both submit the settlement proposal in the required time frame and failed to request an extension of time.

Before approving any partial payment, the TCO obtains accounting or engineering reviews of the data submitted in the settlement proposal. If review of the data indicates that the requested partial payment is proper, reasonable payments may be authorized in the discretion of the TCO up to:

- 100 percent of the contract price, adjusted for undelivered acceptable items completed before the termination date, or later completed with the approval of the TCO;
- 100 percent of the amount of any subcontract settlement paid by the prime contractor if the settlement was approved or ratified by the TCO;
- 90 percent of the direct cost of termination inventory, including costs of direct labor, purchased parts, raw materials, and supplies;
- 90 percent of other allowable costs (including indirect costs and settlement expense) allocable to the terminated portion of the contract; and
- 100 percent of partial payments made to subcontractors.

When an assignment of claims has been made under the contract, the Government shall not make partial payments to other than the assignee unless the parties to the assignment consent in writing.

If any partial payment is made for completed end items or for costs of termination inventory, the TCO must protect the Government's interest in the inventory. This is done by either obtaining title to the completed end items or termination inventory, or else creating a lien in favor of the Government, paramount to all other liens, on the completed end items or termination inventory.

The TCO deducts from the gross amount of a partial payment all unliquidated balances of progress and advance payments (including interest) allocable to the terminated portion of the contract. (S)he also deduct all credits arising from the purchase, retention or sale of property included in the payment request.

The total amount of all partial payments should not exceed the amount that will become due to the contractor because of the termination. If the total of partial payments exceeds the final settlement amount, the contractor must repay the excess to the Government on demand, together with interest computed at the rate established by the Secretary of the Treasury from the date the excess payment was received by the contractor to the date of repayment. However, interest will not be charged for any excess payment caused by a reduction in the settlement proposal due to disposition or retention of termination inventory, as determined by the TCO. Nor is interest charged on overpayment under cost-reimbursement research and development contracts without profit or fee if the overpayments are repaid to the Government within 30 days of demand.

If the contract authorizes partial payments on settlement proposals before final settlement, a prime contractor may request them after submission of interim or final settlement proposals. A subcontractor submits its application through the prime contractor, which attaches its own invoice and recommendations to the subcontractor's application. Partial payments to a subcontractor are made only through the prime contractor after it submits its settlement proposal.

5.19.4 Additional Principles for Fixed-Price Contracts Terminated for Convenience

FAR 49.2

The TCO allows profit on preparations made and work done on the terminated portion of the contract, but not on the settlement expenses. Anticipatory profits and consequential damages are not allowed. The contractor's efforts in settling subcontractor proposals are considered in determining the final profit rate. Profit is not allowed for subcontracted material or services that, as of the effective date of termination, have not been delivered. Nor is profit allowed if the contractor would have incurred a loss had the entire contract been completed. For a construction contract, profit is allowed on the prime contractor's settlements with subcontractors for actual work in place at the job site, but not on settlements for materials on hand or for preparations made to complete the work.

From the settlement amount, the TCO deducts the agreed price for any part of the termination inventory purchased or retained by the contractor for the terminated contract, and the proceeds from any materials sold but not paid or credited to the Government. The TCO also deducts the fair value of any of the termination inventory that (before transfer of title to the Government or buyer) is undeliverable due to damage, destruction, loss, or theft. Normal spoilage and inventory for which the Government assumed the risk of loss are not deducted.

Promptly after the effective date of termination, the TCO arranges for all completed but undelivered end items to be inspected and accepted, and determines which ones should be delivered under the contract. The contractor invoices any accepted and delivered end items at the contract price and excludes them from the settlement proposal. However, accepted end items which are not to be delivered under the contract are included in the settlement proposal at the contract price, adjusted for any saving of freight charges and any purchase, retention or sale credits. For construction contracts, work in place accepted by the Government is not considered a completed item even though the work may have been paid for.

5.19.5 Settlement Proposals

FAR 49.206

The final settlement proposal must be submitted within one year from the effective date of the termination, unless the period is extended by the TCO.

With the consent of the TCO, proposals may be filed in successive steps covering separate portions of the contractor's costs. The contractor prices out its proposal using either the inventory or total cost basis.

Use of the *inventory basis* for settlement proposals is preferred. The contractor may propose only costs allocable to the terminated portion of the contract, and must itemize:

- components, dies, fixtures, jigs, and tooling;
- engineering costs;
- general and administrative costs;
- initial costs;
- metals, purchased parts and raw materials at purchase cost;
- other proper charges;
- profit or adjustment for loss, less unliquidated advance and progress payments and other credits;
- settlement costs with subcontractors;
- settlement expenses; and
- work in process and finished parts at manufacturing cost.

The inventory basis is also appropriate for partial termination of a construction or related professional services contract, partial or complete termination of supply orders under any terminated construction contract, and complete termination of a unit-price professional services contract.

When use of the inventory basis is not practicable or will unduly delay settlement, the *total-cost basis* may be used if approved in advance by the TCO and if:

- production has not begun, and accumulated costs represent planning and preproduction expenses only;
- termination is complete and involves a letter contract;
- the contract does not specify unit prices; or
- unit costs for work in process and finished products cannot readily be established.

A total-cost proposal is priced at the difference between original contract price and actual cost of performing the contract as changed.

For a complete termination, the contractor itemizes costs incurred under the contract up to the effective date of termination, including the costs of settlements with subcontractors and an allowance for profit or adjustment for loss. The settlement price includes deductions for all end items delivered (or to be delivered) and accepted, and all unliquidated advance and progress payments and disposal and other credits. Consideration for allowable profit includes avoiding anticipatory profits or consequential damages, and calculating loss.

When the total-cost basis is used under a partial termination, the settlement proposal is not submitted until the continued portion of the contract is completed. The same pricing rules apply, but include all costs incurred to the date of completing the rest of the contract. Within 120 days from the effective date of termination, the contractor submits to the TCO complete disposal schedules reflecting inventory allocable to the terminated portion of the contract.

The total amount payable to the contractor for a settlement, before deducting disposal or other credits and exclusive of settlement costs, must not exceed the contract price less payments otherwise made or due under the contract.

After partial termination, a contractor may request an equitable adjustment in the price(s) of the continued portion of a fixed-price contract. The TCO forwards the proposal to the contracting officer, except when negotiation authority is delegated to the TCO.

The TCO determines any adjusted fee based on a percentage of contract completion or terminated portion thereof. This amount is a function of the extent and difficulty of the contractor's:

- effort to stop performance;
- planning and scheduling;
- production;
- settlement of terminated subcontracts;
- supervision;
- technical and engineering effort; and
- termination inventory disposal.

The completed effort is compared with the total work required by the contract. The ratio of costs incurred to the total estimated cost of performance or the terminated portion is only one factor in computing the percentage of completion. The contractor's adjusted fee excludes any fee for subcontract effort included in subcontractors' settlement proposals.

5.19.6 Termination for Default

FAR 49.4

Termination for default occurs because of the contractor's actual or anticipated failure to perform its contractual obligations. This means that the contractor has failed to deliver the supplies or perform the services within the time specified in the contract, or failed to make progress to the point of endangering contract performance. It also could entail failure to comply with a contract provision, or perhaps the contractor has notified the Government that it does not intend to perform (known as *anticipatory repudiation*). However, if the contractor can establish that it was not in default or that the failure to perform is excusable (i.e., arose out of causes beyond the control and without the fault or negligence of the contractor), a termination for default will convert into a termination for the convenience of the Government.

The contracting officer considers several factors to determine whether to terminate a contract for default:

- applicable laws and regulations;
- availability of the supplies or services from other sources;
- best interest of the Government;
- contract terms;
- cost of reprocurement;
- effect of a termination for default on the ability of the contractor to liquidate guaranteed loans, progress payments or advance payments;
- essentiality of the contractor and the effect of a termination for default upon the contractor's capability as a supplier under other contracts;
- impact of default on other contractor obligations;
- the specific failure and reasons for it; and
- urgency of the need and the time period required to obtain them from other sources, compared with the time delivery could be obtained from the delinquent contractor.

The Government's rights after a termination for cause include all the remedies available to any buyer in the marketplace. The Government's preferred remedy is to acquire similar items from another contractor and to charge the defaulted contractor with any excess reprocurement costs, along with any incidental or consequential damages incurred due to termination.

The Government is not liable for the defaulted contractor's costs on undelivered work and is entitled to repayment of advance and progress payments. The Government may elect to require the contractor to transfer title and deliver to the Government any completed supplies and manufacturing materials. However, the Government may not acquire any completed supplies or manufacturing materials unless it does not already have title under another provision of the contract. The contracting officer may acquire manufacturing materials to furnish to another contractor only after considering any difficulties that the other contractor may have in using the materials. The

Government pays the contract price for any completed supplies and manufacturing materials.

After the Government has paid the contractor, it protects itself from overpayment due to potential liability to laborers and material suppliers for lien rights against the completed supplies or materials. Hence, before paying for supplies or materials, the contracting officer must:

- ascertain whether the payment bonds are adequate to satisfy all claims, or if similar bonds should be obtained;
- obtain agreement from the contractor and lienors to ensure release of the Government from any potential liability to the contractor or lienors;
- require the contractor to furnish appropriate statements from laborers and material suppliers disclaiming any lien rights they may have to the materials and supplies; and
- withhold from the amount due for the materials or supplies any amount the contracting officer determines necessary to protect the Government's interest.

The contractor is liable to the Government for any damages or excess costs to acquire supplies and services similar to those terminated for default.

If the contractor has failed to perform or deliver, no notice of failure or possibility of termination for default need be sent to the contractor before the actual notice of termination. However, if the Government has taken any action that might be construed as a waiver of the contract delivery or performance date, the contracting officer sends a notice to the contractor setting a new date to make delivery or complete performance, and reserving the Government's rights under the Default clause.

If the contractor merely fails to perform some other contract provision (e.g., not furnishing a required performance bond), or so fails to make progress as to endanger performance of the contract, the contracting officer gives the contractor a written *cure notice* specifying the failure and providing 10 days (or longer period as necessary) to cure the failure. Upon expiration of this time period, the contracting officer may issue a notice of termination for default unless the failure to perform has been cured.

If termination for default appears appropriate, the contracting officer may issue a *show cause notice* to notify the contractor in writing of the possibility of the termination, repeats the contractual liabilities if the contract is so terminated, and requests the contractor to show cause as to why the contract should not be terminated for default. The notice may state that failure of the contractor to present an explanation may be taken as an admission that no valid explanation exists.

Any such notice or termination document is copied to the surety. If requested by the surety and agreed to by the contractor and any assignees, future checks may be mailed to the contractor in care of the surety. The contractor forwards a written request to the disbursing officer to direct the change in address.

If the contractor is a small business, the contracting officer provides a copy of any cure notice or show cause notice to the contracting office's small business specialist and the contractor's SBA Regional Office.

If the contracting officer determines before issuing the termination notice that the failure to perform is excusable, the contract is not terminated for default, but may be terminated for convenience. In lieu of termination for default, the contracting officer may permit the contractor, surety or guarantor to continue performance of the contract under a revised delivery schedule, or permit the contractor to continue performance by means of a subcontract or other business arrangement with an acceptable third party. If the requirement for the supplies and services no longer exists, and the contractor is not liable to the Government for damages, then the parties may execute a no-cost termination settlement.

The termination for default notice must state:

- contract number and date;
- acts or omissions constituting the default;
- the contractor's right to proceed further under the contract (or a specified portion of the contract) is terminated;
- the supplies or services terminated may be purchased against the contractor's account, and that the contractor will be held liable for any excess costs;
- if the contracting officer has determined that the failure to perform is not excusable, that the notice of termination constitutes such decision;
- the Government reserves all rights and remedies provided by law or under the contract, in addition to charging excess costs; and
- the notice constitutes a decision that the contractor is in default as specified and that the contractor has the right to appeal under the Disputes clause.

When the supplies or services are still required after termination, the contracting officer repurchases them against the contractor's account as soon as possible. The contracting officer may repurchase a quantity in excess of the undelivered quantity terminated for default if necessary, but cannot charge excess costs against the defaulting contractor for more than the undelivered quantity terminated for default (including variations in quantity permitted by the terminated contract). Generally, the contracting officer decides whether or not to repurchase before issuing the termination notice. If repurchase is made at a higher price than in the terminated contract, the contracting officer makes written demand on the contractor for the total amount of the excess. In addition to excess repurchase costs, the contracting officer promptly assesses and demands any liquidated damages to which the Government is entitled under the contract.

FAR 49.403

Settlement principles for a cost-reimbursement default are the same as when a contract is terminated for convenience, with a few differences. A 10-day notice to the contractor before termination for default is required. The contractor is reimbursed all allowable costs, and an appropriate reduction is made in the total fee. However, the costs of preparing the contractor's settlement proposal are not allowable and excess repurchase costs cannot be recovered.

5.19.7 Surety-Takeover Agreements

FAR 49.404

Because the surety is liable for damages resulting from contractor default, the surety has rights and interests to complete the contract work and apply any undisbursed funds. Therefore, the contracting officer must consider any surety proposals for completing the contract. Hence, the contracting officer permits surety offers to complete the contract, unless the contracting officer believes that the firms or persons proposed by the surety to complete the work are not competent and qualified, or the proposal is not in the best interest of the Government.

The surety may include a takeover agreement in its proposal, fixing its rights to payment from retained percentages and unpaid progress estimates. After the effective date of termination, the contracting officer may enter into a written agreement with the surety (or a tripartite agreement including the defaulting contractor) to resolve the contractor's residual rights and assertions to unpaid prior earnings.

Any takeover agreement requires the surety to complete the contract and the Government to pay the surety's cost and expenses up to the balance of the contract price unpaid at the time of default. The contracting officer does not pay the surety more than the amount spent to complete the work and discharge its liabilities under the defaulting contractor's payment bond. Such payments must be only on authority of a tripartite agreement, GAO or court. If contract proceeds have been assigned to a financing institution, the surety is not paid from unpaid earnings without the institution's written consent.

The defaulting contractor's unpaid earnings, retained percentages and progress estimates for work accomplished before termination, are subject to debts due the Government. However, these earnings can be used to pay the surety its actual costs and expenses incurred in the completion of the work, but excluding its payments and obligations under the payment bond. The surety is bound by contract terms governing liquidated damages for unexcused delays in completion of the work. If the surety does not arrange for completion of the contract, the contracting officer awards a new contract based on the same plans and specifications.

5.20 SOME FINAL THOUGHTS

The Government cannot be run like a business. It is managed by national priorities and objectives established by Congress and interpreted by the courts. By contrast, industry operates under a profit/loss concept because they have different goals, needs and objectives. Industry is more responsive to a competitive marketplace and internal goal pressures. Government organizations must also comply with legal and administrative restrictions not imposed on the private sector. It requires its contractors to comply with legal and ethical precedents not always found in industry, and tends to reduce emphasis on the importance of traditional success barometers like profitability, producibility, and productivity.

Many factors preclude some companies from entering Federal contracting and thereby constrict the industrial base. Over the past 50 years, risk in Government contracting has shifted considerably through changes in Government policy. Contract type for research and development has shifted away from firm-fixed-price to more flexible forms of contracting. Repeated cost overruns on design issues have led to a "fly-before-you-buy" approach. Market instability has fallen due to greater spending and longer lead times. Some firms are dismayed by the exculpatory clauses that excuse the Government from responsibility for inadequate performance. And so forth.

To maintain and expand the industrial base, contractors must address a number of issues that bear on Federal sales and national security:

- accounting practices;
- complexity and paperwork due to legislation and regulation;
- computer-aided design and manufacturing;
- contract disputes and remedies;
- cost of environmental compliance;
- critical material sources;
- facilities and processes;
- foreign competition and sources of supply;
- idle capacity;
- intellectual property rights;

- lead times for critical parts and components;
- limited potential growth;
- make-or-buy;
- manpower skills;
- need for new manufacturing technologies;
- need to increase competition;
- productivity;
- profit policy;
- socioeconomic concerns;
- source selection procedures;
- stability of requirements and funding;
- strategic resource base planning;
- subcontractors;
- surge capacity and surge planning;
- technology transfer; and
- vertical integration to ensure resource base.

Additional trends that impact DoD contracting today include increases in:

- contract consolidation;
- expanding the contractor and industrial bases;
- modernizing information technology equipment and methods;
- rapid prototyping and cutting-edge technology;
- shared services by different agencies (financial, grants, human, information management) will emphasize contracts that feature best-in-class performance; and
- simplified acquisitions.

Nonetheless, the Government can take many steps to improve industrial effectiveness. It can advocate design of systems and components which minimize the need for critical materials (including reclaiming materials) and scarce skilled labor. Management can review program design, manufacturing management and production capability, and production readiness. Programs also address these conditions in acquisition plans and solicitations.

Targeted procurements for specific items in specific geographic regions can improve the local economy, such as the recovery from Hurricane Katrina on the Gulf Coast. Defense spending during World War II and Vietnam helped to reduce unemployment and increase disposable income. The Federal Government can finance fiscal policy through borrowing, printing money and legislation. Procurements can be directly controlled by the Government and Congress.

The Government also faces societal challenges in today's market. Contract spending is squeezed due to contemporary budget woes. Less flexible contract types are advocated to curb cost overruns. A number of contactor positions are being brought back in-house to civil service positions, although the slow Federal hiring process challenges the success of this initiative. Also, Federal managers have seen reforms proposed many times in the past, usually with little or no effect. Proper management and implementation of such issues will impact the future of federal contract management.

NOTES

1. These offices are listed in the Federal Directory of Contract Administration Services Components, available at https://piee.eb.mil/pcm/xhtml/unauth/index.xhtml.

2. The exceptions are the Superintendents of Shipbuilding, which are located with the Department of the Navy, which administer ship construction contracts.

3. This includes delivery or use of products that are biobased, environmentally preferable, energy-efficient, or possess recovered materials.

4. *Provisioning* is a process to determine the items required to maintain and support equipment for a set time period. Firm requirements for quantity or type are not known at time of award, so a generic line item is used to order items later after requisition. Provisioning is best known to procure spare and repair parts, but can also be used for data, engineering support, equipment, and GFP repair.

5. Air Mobility Command and Military Sealift Command may perform contract administration services at contractor locations solely in these contracts.

6. DoD Instruction 5000.72, DoD Standard for Contracting Officer's Representative (COR) Certification, November 6, 2020.

7. Guidance on COR appointment and duties is provided in the DoD COR Handbook, March 22, 2012.

8. 29 U.S.C. 151.

9. See Executive Order 11755, Relating to prison labor, December 29, 1973, as amended by Executive Order 12943, Further amendment to Executive Order No. 11755, December 13, 1994.

10. 40 U.S.C. 3701.

11. This definition specifically excludes executives, supervisors, administrators, and clerks.

12. 18 U.S.C. 874 and 40 U.S.C. 3145..

13. https://www.dol.gov/agencies/ofccp/pre-award.

14. *Fulilove v Klutznick*, 448 U.S. 448 (1980).

15. These include the Vietnam Era Veterans' Readjustment Assistance Act of 1972 (38 U.S.C. 4212), Executive Order 11701, Employment of veterans by Federal agencies and Government contractors and subcontractors (January 24, 1973), and the Veterans Employment Opportunities Act of 1998 (5 U.S.C. 2108).

16. https://www.dol.gov/vets/vets4212.htm.

17. https://www.dol.gov/ilab/reports/child-labor/list-of-goods.

18. 31 U.S.C. 6101..

19. Federal Funding Accountability and Transparency Act Subaward Reporting System is managed by GSA. See Federal Funding Accountability and Transparency Act Subaward Reporting System at https://www.fsrs.gov.

20. A "noncontiguous state" means Alaska, Hawaii, Puerto Rico, the Northern Mariana Islands, American Samoa, Guam, the U.S. Virgin Islands, Baker Island, Howland Island, Jarvis Island, Johnston Atoll, Kingman Reef, Midway Islands, Navassa Island, Palmyra Atoll, and Wake Island.

21. *Kaizen* is a well-known example of a manufacturer's quality program. Designed to humanize the workplace and eliminate unnecessary hard work and waste in processes, kaizen requires people at all levels of the firm to participate, including external stakeholders. The format for kaizen can be individual, suggestion system or a working group chaired by a line supervisor. Kaizen's approach focuses on making small changes and monitoring results, then adjusting the process for continual improvement. At Toyota, where kaizen got its impetus, the culture of continual small improvements and standardization tended to compound productivity improvement.

22. For those who enjoy demystifying acronyms: ANSI—American National Standards Institute, ASME—American Society of Mechanical Engineers, ISO—International Organization for Standardization. These are standards-issuing bodies accepted by various industries.

23. The criteria can be found at https://www.wbdg.org/ffc/dod/unified-facilities-criteria-ufc/ufc-1-200-01.

24. www.gidep.org.

25. 50 U.S.C. App. 2061 et seq.

26. 42 U.S.C. 5195 et seq.

27. For non-commercial items, use MIL-STD-129, Marking for Shipments and Storage, and MIL-STD-130, Identification Marking of U.S. Military Property, when marking warranty items.

28. https://www.pdrep.csd.disa.mil/pdrep_files/other/wsr.htm.

29. Alternate I was deleted and is no longer in use.

30. 40 U.S.C. 3131.

31. Department of the Treasury, Bureau of the Fiscal Service. "Department of the Treasury's Listing of Approved Sureties (Department Circular 570)."

32. 42 U.S.C. 1651, 33 U.S.C. 901 and 22 U.S.C. 2151, respectively.

33. 42 U.S.C. 1701.

34. Lease-or-buy decisions are made in a similar manner, except the option is to possess the item or equipment for a short term rather than permanently. The evaluation methods and constraints are identical.

35. DFARS 251.101.

36. 10 U.S.C. 2337(c).

37. DoD Directive 2140.02, Recoupment of Nonrecurring Costs on Sales of U.S. Items, May 22, 2013.

38. 22 CFR 120-130.

39. 15 CFR 730-774.

40. 6 U.S.C. 441.

41. https://www.energy.gov/eere/femp/federal-energy-management-program.

42. These precautions are spelled out in DoD 4145.26-M, DoD Contractors' Safety Manual for Ammunition and Explosives. When work is to be performed on a Government-owned installation, an alternative regulation of the DoD component or installation may be used as a substitute for or supplement to DoD 4145.26-M.

43. 40 CFR Part 247.

44. 7 CFR Part 2902, Subpart B, available at https://www.biopreferred.gov/BioPreferred.

45. This policy is reflected in Executive Order 12873, Federal Acquisition, Recycling, and Waste Prevention, October 20, 1993.

46. A list of EPEAT-registered products that meet IEEE 1680 can be found at http://greenelectronicscouncil.org/epeat/epeat-overview. For further information, see https://www.epa.gov/greenerproducts/recommendations-specifications-standards-and-ecolabels-federal-purchasing.

47. This policy is encapsulated in Executive Order 12843, Procurement Requirements and Policies for Federal Agencies for Ozone Depleting Substances, April 21, 1993.

48. www.epa.gov/snap.

49. www.wbdg.org/FFC/FED/hpsb_guidance.pdf.

50. For general cargo provisions, see DTR 4500.9-R, Defense Transportation Regulation (DTR), Part II, Chapter 201, paragraphs L, M, N, and S (available at http://www.ustranscom.mil/dtr/dtrp2.cfm).

51. 46 U.S.C. 1241.

52. 10 U.S.C. 2631.

53. The Secretary of the Navy will decide for voyage and time charters.

54. Office of the Assistant Secretary of Defense (Acquisition, Technology and Logistics). "Department of Defense Earned Value Management System Interpretation Guide," March 14, 2019.

55. DoD's official guidance on EVMS is Department of Defense Earned Value Management System Interpretation Guide, available at https://www.acq.osd.mil/evm/docs/DoD%20EVMSIG.pdf.

56. Progress payments will be discussed in detail later.

57. http://www.acq.osd.mil/asda/dpc/pcf/pricing-topics.html#pdp.

58. 50 U.S.C. 4558.

59. 31 U.S.C. 1341.

60. 31 U.S.C. 3727.

61. *United States v. Wunderlich*, 342 U.S. 98 (1951).

62. The very lengthy title of E.O. 10789 is "Authorizing agencies of the Government to exercise certain contracting authority in connection with national-defense functions and prescribing regulations governing the exercise of such authority" and is dated November 14, 1958.

63. 41 U.S.C. 601-613.

64. This is known as a *Rule 4 File*, named after the applicable administrative law procedure.

65. This is known as the Torncello Rule, after the case where it was raised by the court (*Torncello vs. United States*, 231 Ct.Cl. 20, 1982).

Bibliography

RECURRING REFERENCES

American Law Institute and the National Conference of Commissioners on Uniform State Laws. (2014). *Uniform Commercial Code.* Eagan, MN: Thomson West. This is the code that governs commercial transactions and provides a baseline for understanding the concepts of contract law. A readily available location to access the UCC was retrieved March 6, 2023, from https://www.law.cornell.edu/ucc.

Defense Acquisition University. *PGI Procedures, Guidance, and Information.* Available online at https://www.acq.osd.mil/dpap/dars/dfarspgi/current/index.html. This is a critical and comprehensive resource for acquisition, cost estimating, and program management within the Defense community.

Federal Acquisition Regulatory Council. (2020). *Federal Acquisition Regulation.* Washington, DC: Government Printing Office. FAR is also printed in the Code of Federal Regulations, Title 48, Chapter 1, and available online at www.acquisition.gov/browsefar. This is the bible of Federal contracting and a necessary reference book for all practitioners.

Government Printing Office. (2016). *United States Reports*. Washington, DC: Government Printing Office. This is where Supreme Court decisions are published.

National Archives and Records Administration. (2007). *Code of Federal Regulations*. Washington, DC: National Archives and Records Administration. This is the repository for all Federal regulations. See also Federal Register. *Code of Federal Regulations*. Washington, DC: Government Printing Office.

Office of the Law Revision Council, House of Representatives. (2012). *United States Code*. Washington, DC: Government Printing Office. This is the official record of all Federal statutes.

USDA(AT&L). *Defense Acquisition Guidebook*. Retrieved July 15, 2018, from https://aaf.dau.edu/guidebooks. This is very useful guidance for implementing official DoD doctrine. Note that DAG is in the process of being retired in favor of thematic booklets which are preceded by "DAG" in this book. Note also that these booklets do not use any numeric citations like other Government sources; hence page numbers must be cited.

———. *Defense Federal Acquisition Regulation Supplement* (2006). Washington, DC: Government Printing Office. FAR is also printed in the Code of Federal Regulations, Title 48, Chapter 2, and available online at https://www.acq.osd.mil/dpap/dars/dfarspgi/current/index.html. This publication supplements FAR with regulations that are just as mandatory to DoD, and is another essential reference book for practitioners in the Defense community.

DOD DOCUMENTS

DoD has issued many directives and instructions which bear upon some aspect of contracting. The most pertinent ones for DoD acquisition are cited here. All are published in Washington, DC, by the Department of Defense, unless otherwise noted. DoD Directives and DoD Instructions are available from https://www.esd.whs.mil/DD.

Air Force Institute of Technology. *Contract Pricing Reference Guide*. It is now maintained by Defense Acquisition University. Retrieved July 14, 2018, from https://www.dau.mil/tools/p/cprg.

Defense Acquisition University. Quality Assurance Surveillance Plan." Retrieved May 13, 2023, from https://www.dau.edu/cop/ace/_layouts/15/WopiFrame.aspx?sourcedoc=/cop/ace/DAU%20Sponsored%20Documents/SAM_QASP%20Template.docx&action=default&DefaultItemOpen=1.

———. "Service Acquisition Mall: Acquisition Requirements Roadmap Tool (ARRT)." Retrieved May 13, 2023, from https://www.dau.edu/tools/Documents/SAM/home.html.

Defense Contract Management Agency. Acquisition Program Transition Workshops, Fort Belvoir, VA, October 2011. Retrieved March 8, 2023, from https://apps.dtic.mil/sti/pdfs/ADA606209.pdf.

———. "Federal Directory of Contract Administration Services Components." Retrieved May 15, 2023, from https://pubapp.dcma.mil/CASD/main.jsp (accessible from DoD websites only).

Defense Information Security Agency. "DoD Cloud Computing Security." Retrieved May 14, 2023, from https://public.cyber.mil/dccs.

Defense Logistics Management Standards Office. "Military Standard Requisitioning and Issue Procedures." DLM 4000.25-1, dated April 2, 2019.

Defense Procurement Acquisition Policy. "Contractor Performance Assessment Reporting System." Retrieved May 14, 2023, from www.cpars.gov.

———. "DoD Independent Government Cost Estimate (IGCE) Handbook for Services Acquisition." February 2018.

———. "Guidebook for the Acquisition of Services." Retrieved May 14, 2023, from https://www.acq.osd.mil/asda/dpc/cp/cc/docs/corhb/ref/Guidebook_for_Acquisition_of_Services_24March2012.pdf.

———. "Market Research/Market Intelligence." Retrieved on May 14, 2023 from https://www.acq.osd.mil/asda/dpc/cp/policy/docs/sa/2017_Market_Research_Guide_(Final).pdf.

Defense Travel Management Office. "The Per Diem, Travel and Transportation Allowance Committee: Joint Travel Regulations." May 1, 2023.

Department of Defense. "DIBNet Portal." Retrieved May 14, 2023, from https://dibnet.dod.mil.

———. The DoD Cloud Computing Security Requirements Guide, Version 1 Release 4, January 14, 2022.

———. DoD Directive 2140.02, "Recoupment of Nonrecurring Costs on Sales of US Items." May 22, 2018.

———. DoD Directive 5000.01, "The Defense Acquisition System." July 28, 2022.

———. DoD Directive 5230.11, "Disclosure of Classified Military Information to Foreign Governments and International Organizations." June 16, 1992.

———. DoD Directive 8140.01, "Cyberspace Workforce Management." October 5, 2020.

———. DoD Directive 8500.01, "Information Assurance." Revised October 7, 2019.

———. "DoD Index of Specifications and Standards." 41 CFR 101-29.216.

———. DoD Instruction 1100.22, "Policy and Procedures for Determining Workforce Mix." April 12, 2010.

———. DoD Instruction 2000.16 "DoD Antiterrorism Standards." November 17, 2016. This instruction is not available to the general public—only to authorized DoD users.

———. DoD Instruction 4161.02, "Accountability and Management of Government Contract Property." DoD Manufacturing Technology Program. Retrieved May 14, 2023, from www.dodmantech.com.

———. DoD Instruction 5000.02T, "Operation of the Adaptive Acquisition Framework." June 8, 2022.

———. DoD Instruction 5000.64, "Accountability and Management of Government Contract Property." April 27, 2017.

———. DoD Instruction 5000.72, DoD Standard for Contracting Officer's Representative (COR) Certification. November 6, 2020.

———. DoD Instruction 5000.74, "Defense Acquisition of Services." June 24, 2021.

———. DoD Instruction 5000.75, "Business Systems Requirements and Acquisition," dated January 24, 2020.

———. DoD Instruction 5000.80, "Operation of the Middle Tier of Acquisition." December 30, 2019.

———. DoD Instruction 5000.81, "Urgent Capability Acquisition." December 31, 2019.

———. DoD Instruction 5000.85, "Major Capability Acquisition." November 4, 2021.

———. DoD Instruction 5000.87, "Operation of the Software Acquisition Pathway." October 2, 2020.

———. DoD Instruction 5000.88, "Engineering of Defence Systems." November 18, 2020.

———. DoD Instruction 5000.91, "Product Support Management for the Adaptive Acquisition Framework." November 4, 2021.

———. DoD Instruction 5010.44, "Intellectual Property (IP) Acquisition and Licensing." October 16, 2019.

———. DoD Instruction 5100.76, "Physical Security of Sensitive Conventional Arms, Ammunition, and Explosives." April 17, 2012.

———. DoD Instruction 8500.01, "Cybersecurity." October 7, 2019.

———. DoD Instruction 8500.2, "Information Assurance Implementation." October 7, 2019.

———. DoD Manual 4140.01, Volume 5, "DoD Supply Chain Materiel Management Procedures: Delivery of Materiel," February 7, 2023.

———. DoD 4145.26-M, "DoD Contractors' Safety Manual for Ammunition and Explosives," March 13, 2008.

———. DoD Manual 8570.01-M, "Information Assurance Workforce Improvement Program." November 10, 2015. This document will eventually be replaced with DoD 8140.01 Manual.

———. DoD Memorandum, "Updated Guidance on the Acquisition and Use of Commercial Cloud Computing Services." December 15, 2014.

———. DTR 4500.9-R, "Defense Transportation Regulation." Retrieved May 14, 2023, from http://www.ustranscom.mil/dtr.

———. MIL-HDBK-245D. "Department of Defense Handbook: Preparation of a Statement of Work (SOW)." April 3, 1996.

———. MIL-STD-129P, "Military Standard Marking for Shipment and Storage." October 29, 2004.

———. MIL-STD-130N, "Identification Marking of US Property." August 26, 2019.

———. MIL-STD-881C, "DoD Work Breakdown Structure Standard." October 3, 2011.

———. MIL-STD-1916, "DoD Preferred Methods for Acceptance of Product." Revised June 2014.

Joint Chiefs of Staff. JCS 3170.01I, "Joint Capabilities Integration and Development System and Manual." August 31, 2018. Retrieved March 9, 2023, from https://www.acq.osd.mil/asda/jrac/docs/2018-JCIDS.pdf.

———. "Joint Publication 1, Doctrine for the Armed Forces of the United States." June 19, 2020. Retrieved May 14, 2023, from https://www.jcs.mil/Portals/36/Documents/Doctrine/pubs/jp1_0.pdf.

Office of the Assistant Secretary of Defense (Acquisition, Technology and Logistics). "Department of Defense Earned Value Management System Interpretation Guide." March 14, 2019.

Office of the Assistant Secretary of Defense, Readiness and Force Management, "Private Sector Notification Requirements in Support of In-sourcing Actions." January 29, 2013. Retrieved May 15, 2023, from https://www.acq.osd.mil/

dpap/dars/pgi/docs/Private_Sector_Notificaton_Requirements_in_Support_of_In-sourcing_Actions.pdf.

Under Secretary of Defense (Acquisition Technology & Logistics), "DoD Business Rules for the Synchronized Predeployment and Operational Tracker (SPOT)." May 10, 2018. Retrieved May 15, 2023, from https://www.acq.osd.mil/dpap/policy/policyvault/USA001528-15-DPAP.

———. "Other Transactions Guide for Prototype Projects." January 2017.

Under Secretary of Defense (Comptroller). DoD FMR 7000.14-R. "Department of Defense Financial Management Regulation (DoD FMR)." Retrieved May 15, 2023, from https://comptroller.defense.gov/fmr.

ADDITIONAL GOVERNMENT SOURCES

Unless otherwise noted, all other sources were published in Washington, DC, by the identified department or agency. Note that capitalization practices vary over time and with different departments.

Air Force Institute of Technology. "Interpretive Guide to the Evaluation/Demonstration Review Checklist for C/SCSC (Appendix E, Joint Information Guide)." Wright-Patterson Air Force Base, OH: Air Force Institute of Technology, September 1991. This document is commonly known as "the Bowman Guide." Retrieved May 15, 2023, from https://www.secnav.navy.mil/rda/OneSource/Documents/CEVM/Tools%20and%20Examples/DOD%20Guides/BowmanInterpretiveGuide1.pdf.

Committee on National Security Systems. "National Security Telecommunications and Information Systems Security Policy No. 11." Washington, DC: Committee on National Security Systems, July 2003.

Department of Agriculture. "BioPreferred." Retrieved May 15, 2023, from https://www.biopreferred.gov/BioPreferred.

Department of Commerce, "Commerce Control List," Retrieved May 15, 2023, from www.bis.doc.gov/index.php/regulations/commerce-control-list-ccl.

———. "The Export Administration Regulations." 15 CFR 730-774. 2016. Retrieved May 15, 2023, from www.bis.doc.gov/index.php/regulations/export-administration-regulations-ear.

———. "National Technical Information Service." Retrieved May 15, 2023, from https://www.ntis.gov.

———. "North American Industry Classification System." Retrieved May 15, 2023, from www.census.gov/naics.

Department of Energy. "Architectural and Transportation Barriers Compliance Board Electronic and Information Technology (EIT) Accessibility Standards." (36 CFR 1194). June 2002.

———. Office of Energy Efficiency and Renewable Energy. Homepage retrieved May 15, 2023, from https://www.energy.gov/eere/femp/federal-energy-management-program.

Department of Homeland Security. "National Response Framework." Retrieved May 15, 2023, from https://www.fema.gov/emergency-managers/national-preparedness/frameworks/response.

———. Homeland Security Presidential Directive (HSPD)-12, August 5, 2005. Retrieved May 15, 2023, from https://www.dhs.gov/homeland-security-presidential-directive-12.

Department of the Interior. Bureau of Land Management. "Federal Helium Suppliers." Retrieved May 15, 2023, from https://www.blm.gov/programs/energy-and-minerals/helium/federal-helium-program.

Department of Justice, Federal Prison Industries. "UNICOR." Homepage retrieved May 15, 2023, from www.unicor.gov.

Department of Labor. "List of Products Requiring Contractor Certification as to Forced or Indentured Child Labor." Retrieved May 15, 2023, from https://www.dol.gov/agencies/ilab/reports/child-labor/list-of-products.

———. "VETS-4212 Veterans Contract Reporting." Retrieved May 15, 2023, from https://www.dol.gov/agencies/vets/programs/vets4212.html.

———. Wage Determinations Online. Retrieved May 15, 2023, from https://sam.gov/content/home.

Department of the Treasury, Bureau of the Fiscal Service. "Department of the Treasury's Listing of Approved Sureties (Department Circular 570)." Retrieved May 15, 2023, from https://www.fiscal.treasury.gov/surety-bonds//list-certified-companies.html. This site lists companies holding certificates of authority as acceptable sureties on Federal bonds, and acceptable reinsuring companies.

———. "USASpending.gov." Retrieved May 15, 2023, from www.usaspending.gov.

Environmental Protection Agency, Office of Solid Waste. "Consolidated Recovered Materials Advisory Notice (RMAN) for the Comprehensive Procurement Guideline (CPG)." September 14, 2007. Retrieved May 15, 2023, from Consolidated Recovered Materials Advisory Notice (RMAN) for the Comprehensive Procurement Guideline (CPG) (epa.gov).

———. "Significant New Alternatives Policy (SNAP) program." Retrieved May 15, 2023, from www.epa.gov/snap.

Federal Acquisition Institute. www.fai.gov. Retrieved May 15, 2023. The Institute develops acquisition workforce standards through training, education, and research. It identifies education needs, evaluates agency procurement education programs, monitors career development programs, and maintains a reference library.

Federal Emergency Management Agency. Federal Continuity Directive 1, "Federal Executive Branch National Continuity Program and Requirements." January 7, 2017.

———. "Federal Continuity Directive 2, Federal Executive Branch Mission Essential Functions and Candidate Primary Mission Essential Functions Identification and Submission Process." June 13, 2017.

———. Federal Preparedness Circular 65, Federal Executive Branch Continuity of Operations. July 26, 1999.

———. "Homeland Security Presidential Directive 20, National Continuity Policy." May 4, 2007.

———. "National Response Framework." Retrieved May 15, 2023, from www.fema .gov/emergency-managers/national-preparedness/frameworks/response.

General Services Administration. "Acquisition.gov." Retrieved May 15, 2023, at https://www.acquisition.gov.

———. "Contractor Performance Assessment Reporting System." Retrieved May 15, 2023, from www.cpars.gov.

———. "eBuy." Retrieved May 15, 2023, from www.ebuy.gsa.gov/ebuy.

———. "Electronic Subcontracting Reporting System (eSRS)." Retrieved May 15, 2023, from www.esrs.gov.

———. "The System for Award Management." Retrieved May 15, 2023, at https:// SAM.gov.

———. "FEDRamp." Retrieved May 15, 2023, from www.fedramp.gov.

———. "Federal Funding Accountability and Transparency Act Subaward Reporting System." Retrieved May 15, 2023 from https://www.fsrs.gov/.

———. "Federal Standard 123H, Marking for Shipment (Civil Agencies)." August 8, 2007.

———. "Federal Standard No. 313F, Material Safety Data Sheet, Preparation and Submission of." July 2014.

———. "Index of Federal Specifications, Standards and Commercial Item Descriptions." Accessed May 15, 2023, at https://www.gsa.gov/buy-through-us/purchasing-programs/requisition-programs/gsa-global-supply/supply-standards/index-of-federal-specifications-standards-and-commercial-item-descriptions.

———. "GSA Board of Contract Appeals." Retrieved July 15, 2018, from www.cbca .gov. Rules of Procedure and Cases: Appeals, Travel Cases, Rate Cases, Relocation Cases, 2007 to present.

National Archives. "Executive Orders." National Archives stores all Executive Orders dating back to 1994 at https://www.federalregister.gov/presidential-documents/executive-orders. For older orders, see www.archives.gov/federal-register/executive-orders. Specific Executive Orders consulted and referenced herein are:

———. "Executive Order 10582, "Implementing the Buy American Act." Amended September 9, 1987.

———. "Executive Order 10789, Authorizing agencies of the Government to exercise certain contracting authority in connection with national-defense functions and prescribing regulations governing the exercise of such authority." Amended February 28, 2003.

———. "Executive Order 11141, Declaring a public policy against discrimination based on age." February 12, 1964

———. "Executive Orders 11246, Equal employment opportunity." Amended July 21, 2014.

———. "Executive Order 11701, Employment of veterans by Federal agencies and Government contractors and subcontractors." January 24, 1973.

———. "Executive Order 11755, Relating to prison labor." December 13, 1994.

———. "Executive Order 12073, Federal Procurement in Labor Surplus Areas." August 16, 1978.

———. "Executive Order 12549, Debarment and Suspension." February 18, 1986.

———. "Executive Order 12674, Principles of ethical conduct for Government officers and employees." April 12, 1989, as modified by Executive Order 12731 (same title). October 17, 1990.

———. "Executive Order 12731, "Principles of ethical conduct for Government officers and employees." October 17, 1990.

———. "Executive Order 12873, Federal Acquisition, Recycling, and Waste Prevention." October 20, 1993.

———. "Executive Order 12843, Procurement Requirements and Policies for Federal Agencies for Ozone Depleting Substances." April 21, 1993.

———. "Executive Order 12889, "Implementation of the North American Free Trade Act." December 27, 1993.

———. "Executive Order 12928, "Promoting Procurement With Small Businesses Owned and Controlled by Socially and Economically Disadvantaged Individuals, Historically Black Colleges and Universities, and Minority Institutions." September 16, 1994.

———. "Executive Order 12943, Further amendment to Executive Order No. 11755." December 13, 1994.

———. "Executive Order 13101, Greening the Government through Waste Prevention, Recycling, and Federal Acquisition." September 1998.

———. "Executive Order 13423, Strengthening Federal Environmental, Energy, and Transportation Management." January 24, 2007.

———. "Executive Order 13496, Notification of Employee Right Under Federal Labor Laws." January 30, 2009.

———. "Executive Order 13502, Use of Project Labor Agreements for Federal Construction Projects." February 6, 2009.

———. "Executive Order 13658, Establishing a minimum wage for contractors." February 12, 2014.

———. "Executive Order 13672, Prohibiting discrimination based on sexual orientation and gender identity." July 21, 2014.

———. "Executive Order 13706, Establishing Paid Sick Leave for Federal Contractors." September 9, 2015.

———. "Executive Order 13834, Efficient Federal Operations." May 17, 2018.

National Conference of Commissioners on Uniform State Laws. "Uniform Computer Information Transactions Act." Retrieved May 15, 2023, from www.ucitaonline.com.

National Industries for the Blind. Homepage retrieved May 15, 2023, from https://nib.org.

National Institute of Building Sciences. "Guiding Principles for Federal Leadership in High-Performance and Sustainable Buildings." December 1, 2018. Retrieved May 15, 2023, from https://www.acquisition.gov/gsam/570.117-2.

National Institute of Standards and Technology. Federal Information Processing Standards Publication Number 201-3, "Personal Identity Verification of Federal Employees and Contractors." Gaithersburg, MD: National Institute of Standards and Technology, January 2022.

———. Special Publication 800-145: "The NIST Definition of Cloud Computing." September 2011.

———. "Special Publication 500-267B Revision 1:USGv6 Profile." 2022.

National Science Foundation. "Master Government List of Federally Funded R&D Centers," February 2023. Retrieved May 15, 2023, from www.nsf.gov/statistics/ffrdclist.

National Security Council. "National Security Decision Directive (NSDD) 189, National Policy on the Transfer of Scientific, Technical and Engineering Information." September 21, 1985. Retrieved May 15, 2023, from https://irp.fas.org/offdocs/nsdd/nsdd-189.htm.

Office of Federal Procurement Policy. "Improving the Management and Use of Interagency Acquisitions." June 6, 2008. Retrieved May 15, 2023, from https://www.gsa.gov/cdnstatic/Integrated_Technology_Services/OMB%20Memo%2020080608%20iac_revised.pdf.

Office of Management and Budget. The OMB maintains the instructions and circulars it issues at www.whitehouse.gov/omb/information-for-agencies/circulars.

———. "OMB Circular A-11, Preparation, Submission and Execution of the Budget." Revised August 15, 2022.

———. "OMB Circular No. A-21, Cost Principles for Educational Institutions." Revised May 10, 2004.

———. "OMB Circular A-76, Performance of Commercial Activities." Revised October 31, 2006.

———. "OMB Circular No. A-87, Cost Principles for State and Local Governments." Revised May 10, 2004.

———. "OMB Circular A-94, Guidelines and Discount Rates for Benefit-Cost Analysis of Federal Programs." Revised February 17, 2023.

———. "OMB Circular A-119, Federal Participation in the Development and Use of Voluntary Consensus Standards and in Conformity Assessment Activities." January 27, 2016.

———. "OMB Circular No. A-122, Cost Principles for Nonprofit Organizations." May 10, 2004.

———. "OMB Circular A-123 Appendix D, Compliance with the Federal Financial Management Improvement Act." Revised December 23, 2022.

———. "OMB Circular A-130, Managing Information as a Strategic Resource." Revised July 28, 2016.

Office of Personnel Management. "Status of Telework in the Federal Government: Report to Congress, Fiscal Year 2021." December 2022. This is an annual report, but there is always a serious time lag until the data is analyzed and reported; this is the most recent copy available at time of writing.

Securities and Exchange Commission. *EDGAR*. Retrieved May 16, 2023, from www.sec.gov/edgar/search-and-access.

Small Business Administration. "Table of Size Standards." Washington, DC: Small Business Administration. Retrieved May 16, 2023, from www.sba.gov/document/support--table-size-standards.

Small Business Administration, Office of Advocacy. "Frequently Asked Questions About Small Businesses." March 2023. Retrieved May 16, 2023, from https://advocacy.sba.gov/wp-content/uploads/2023/03/Frequently-Asked-Questions-About-Small-Business-March-2023-508c.pdf.

———. Pro-Net. Retrieved May 16, 2023, from www.pro-net.sba.gov/textonly/pro-net/search.html.

———. Small Business Innovative Research. Retrieved May 16, 2023, from www.sbir.gov.

U.S. AbilityOne Commission. "AbilityOne." Retrieved July 15, 2018, from www.abilityone.gov. This is the Javits-Wagner-O'Day Government site.

U.S. International Trade Commission. "Harmonized Tariff Schedule of the United States." Retrieved May 16, 2023, from https://hts.usitc.gov/current.

OTHER SOURCES

American National Standards Institute. "E4—Quality management systems for environmental information and technology programs." Washington, DC: American National Standards Institute, 2017.

———. Standard 748D—"Earned Value Management Systems." Revised 2018.

American National Standards Institute/American Society of Mechanical Engineers. "National Quality Assurance—1." Washington, DC: American National Standards Institute. Revised 2022.

Association for Supply Chain Management, "Supply Chain Operations Reference Model: SCOR 12.0 Quick Reference Guide." Chicago, IL, 2017. Retrieved May 16, 2023, from http://www.apics.org/ docs/default-source/scor-p-toolkits/apics-scc-scor-quick-reference-guide.pdf.

Beck, Kent, et al. "Manifesto for Agile Software Development." Retrieved May 16, 2023, from http://agilemanifesto.org.

Global Electronics Council. "epeat." Retrieved May 16, 2023, from https://epeat.net/.

Government Industry Data Exchange Program. www.gidep.org. Retrieved May 16, 2023. This organization promotes sharing of technical data between Government and industry to save resources.

International Standards Organization. ISO 9001, "Quality Management Systems." Geneva, Switzerland: International Standards Organization. Revised 2015.

———. ISO 9002, "Quality Systems—Model for Quality Assurance in Production, Installation, and Servicing." Geneva, Switzerland: International Standards Organization, 1994.

———. ISO 9003, "Quality Systems—Model for Quality Assurance in Final Inspection and Test." Geneva, Switzerland: International Standards Organization, 1994.

———. ISO 31000, "Risk Management—Principles and Guidelines on Implementation." Geneva, Switzerland: International Standards Organization. Revised 2018.

———. ISO 14001, "Environmental Management Systems—Requirements with Guidance for Use." Geneva, Switzerland: International Standards Organization, 2015.

Lindner, Dan. *An Insider's Guide to Working for the Federal Government.* Lanham, MD: Bernan Press, 2020.

Martinson, Otto B. et al. "Profit '76" Washington, DC: Logistics Management Institute, 1976. Available at Defense Technical Information Center. Retrieved March 2, 2021, from https://apps.dtic.mil/sti/pdfs/ADA038334.pdf.

Mill, John Stuart. *Principles of Political Economy.* London, UK: John W. Parker, 1859. Mill was a political economist in 19th-century Great Britain who argued that individual nations can benefit based on competitive trade advantages.

National Conference of Commissioners on Uniform State Laws. "*UCITA Online—A Commercial Code for the Information Age?*" (Uniform Computer Information Transactions Act). Retrieved May 16, 2023, from http://www.ucitaonline.com.

National Institute of Building Sciences. "High-Performance and Sustainable Buildings Guidance." December 01, 2018. Retrieved May 16, 2023, from www.wbdg.org/FFC/FED/hpsb_guidance.pdf.

Parliament, House of Commons (1677). *Statute of Frauds.* Retrieved May 16, 2023, from Institute of Historical Research, London, UK at http://www.british history.ac.uk/statutes-realm/vol5/pp.839-842. See also Raithby (1819).

Polydys, Mary Linda, and Stan Wisseman. "Software Assurance in Acquisition: Mitigating Risks to the Enterprise." Washington, DC: National Defense University Press, February 2009. This document is now managed by U.S. Computer Emergency Readiness Team, Department of Homeland Security.

Project Management Institute. *Practice Standard for Work Breakdown Structures.* Newton, PA: Project Management Institute, 2006. Third Edition, 2019.

Raithby, John, ed. (1819). *Statutes of the Realm.* Vol. 5, 1628–80. South London, UK: Great Britain Record Commission Institute of Historical Research. See also Parliament (1677).

Ricardo, David. *On the Principles of Political Economy and Taxation* (1817). Mineola, NY: Dover Publication, 2004. Ricardo was a political economist in 19th-century Great Britain who strongly advocated for free trade.

SAE International, Inc., "EIA Standard-748-D, Earned Value Management Systems." Warrendale, PA: SAE International, Inc., January 8, 2019.

Smith, Adam. *An Inquiry into the Nature and Causes of the Wealth of Nations* (1776). Chicago: University of Chicago Press, 1976. Smith was a political economist in 18th-century Great Britain who argued that a specific party could produce a good or service more efficiently than others.

Index

About the Author

Dan Lindner possesses 40 years of experience in Federal acquisition and program management for the Departments of Defense and Homeland Security. He was a longtime contracting officer for the Navy and is well versed in federal acquisition policy and procurement regulations. He has chaired review panels and study teams, negotiated contracts for major weapons system components, worked daily with administrative contracting officers, established a remote buying office, and served as a Small and Disadvantaged Business Utilization Specialist. As a staff aide to the Assistant Secretary of the Navy, he conducted personal briefings on pending Congressional issues affecting defense acquisition and coauthored the Procurement Reform Act of 1986. Dan also established and chaired the Environmental Committee for Defense Acquisition Regulatory Council, and was a member of the Cost Principles Committee, gaining expertise with Cost Accounting Standards.

Dan also has a lengthy career in the private sector, working closely with technical and acquisition clients to define business needs and product requirements, counseling program managers and contracting officers to develop effective strategies, and helping to develop winning proposals. He also served as Vice President for Mindcorp, Inc., a small business which furnished program management support to both Federal and commercial clients. He developed and reviewed information system accreditation packages and provided expertise to Federal offices on securing information systems. He also chaired interagency e-commerce and information systems working groups and managed deployment of a new software application.

In academia, Dan was an instructor for both the Navy Office of Human Services and Fairfax County (Virginia) Adult and Community Education to develop and teach newly hired employees and acquisition professionals about procurement basics. He has developed and delivered presentations in national conventions and corporate meetings on Portfolio Management, Network Security, and Contract Administration. Dan wrote *A Guide to Federal Contracting: Principles and Practices* to cover Federal contracting across all departments and agencies, both defense and civilian. He has written numerous monographs on Defense acquisition, baseball, information technology, and travel.

Dan has been cited over 10 times by Marquis *Who's Who in America* and in the *Who's Who* editions for information technology, science and engineering, and the world. He earned five Navy Performance Awards and the Director of Defense Procurement Award for Innovation in Procurement. He has earned several professional designations over time, including Certified Professional Contracts Manager, Project Management Professional, Level III Certification under the Defense Acquisition Workforce Improvement Act, Certified Information Systems Manager, and Certified in Risk and Information Systems Control.

Dan earned his bachelor of arts degree in both government and economics from Lehigh University, and an MBA from the George Washington University. He was cited as an honors graduate from both schools. He also graduated from the Supervisory Excellence Program for the Department of the Navy. He resides with his family in Virginia.